Tax on Property

Tax on Property

145 London Road
Kingston upon Thames
Surrey
KT2 6SR
Tel: 144(0) 870 241 5719
Fax: 144(0) 870 247 1184
E-mail: customerservices@cch.co.uk

© 2004 Wolters Kluwer (UK) Ltd

ISBN 1 84140 549 3

British Library Cataloguing-in-Publication Data

A catalogue record for this book is available from the British Library.

Typeset in the United Kingdom by J&L Composition, Filey, North Yorkshire
Printed in Great Britain by Page Bros (Norwich) Ltd

About the authors

About the general editor

Colin Davis MA FCA FTII was formerly an Inspector of Taxes and a Partner in Spicer and Peglar which later merged with Deloitte. Colin became a Technical Officer at the Chartered Institute of Taxation in 1997, with responsibility for corporate and international tax matters. Colin writes extensively on tax matters.

About the contributors

Gill Carter is a chartered accountant and a chartered tax adviser. She is a Director of Carter & Co (Editorial Services) Ltd, specialising in writing and editing taxation training and reference material. She also engages in public practice as a Partner of Carter & Co.

Ian Fleming is the Group Indirect Tax Specialist for Armstrong Watson, Chartered Accountants. The firm covers the whole of the North of England as well as Southern Scotland. Before joining Armstrong Watson in 1989, Ian served in Customs & Excise for 26 years – mainly on fraud investigation. He is a Director of the Institute of Indirect Taxation and Chairman of the North East Chapter of the VAT Practitioners Group. He can be contacted on 01228 591000 or by e-mail at indirecttax@shoelina.co.uk.

Shelagh Pearce LLB (Hons) and **Stephen Taylor** CTA (Fellow), ATT are Partners in Pearce Taylor Taxation that provides VAT advice and consultancy services to accountants, lawyers and private clients. Stephen worked for Customs & Excise dealing with VAT for many years before helping found Pearce Taylor Taxation. He is currently Chairman of the South West branch of the Chartered Institute of Taxation. Both Stephen and Shelagh lecture on VAT and contribute to a number of publications, amongst which are the *CCH British VAT Reporter* and *Allen's VAT News*.

Preface

Anyone who has ever had to deal with the taxation of property will know from experience that this is an extremely complex area, and finding your way through the maze of tax laws whilst avoiding the many pitfalls is a daunting task.

Recent years have seen major changes in property taxation law, including the replacement of stamp duty by stamp duty land tax, the amendments to the VAT option for taxation and the introduction of aggregates levy.

Previously, *Kluwer's Tax on Property* (on which the present book is based) kept readers abreast with changes in the area. This was a loose-leaf publication that was updated 5 times a year for nearly 30 years, a testament to the growing complexity of the subject matter. This new publication, *Tax on Property*, aims to deal more comprehensively with the taxation of transactions involving property by including residential property and inheritance tax as well as industrial and commercial property. It states the law as at 1 August 2004.

Please note that the male gender has been used for simplicity and without discrimination to denote both genders throughout this publication.

Colin Davis
November 2004

Contents

Table of cases

(References are to paragraph numbers)

Abbreviations

AC	Law Report – Appeal Cases
All ER	All England Law Reports
BTC	British Tax Cases
BVC	British VAT Cases
Ch	Law Reports, Chancery Division
EG	Estates Gazette
EWCA Civ	Court of Appeal (Civil Division) for the jurisdiction of England and Wales
IR	Inland Revenue
KBD or KB	Law Report – King's Bench Division
LON	VAT Tribunal Office reference
MAN	VAT Tribunal Office reference
QB or QBD	Law Report – Queen's Bench Division
SAL	South Africa Law Report
SpC	Special Commissioners
TC	Tax Cases
VATTR	VAT Tribunal Report
WLR	Weekly Law Report

Table of statutes

(References are to paragraph numbers)

Table of statutory instruments

(References are to paragraph numbers)

1 Occupation of business premises

1.1 Status of property owners

1.1.1 General

The status of a property owner may well affect the tax treatment of a particular transaction in respect of his property. In very general terms, property owners may be divided into two main classes:

- traders, who occupy their own premises for the purposes of their trade, whether on a freehold or leasehold basis; and
- other property owners, who may be subdivided into property investors or property dealers.

In addition, special tax treatment may be given for specific classes of taxpayer.

1.1.2 Owner-occupier traders

Such persons are concerned with the occupation of their premises for trading purposes, rather than deriving any income or capital profit from the property itself. For the most part, where such profits arise, they are treated as investment profits rather than dealing profits. The following points might also be noted as specifically relating to owner-occupier traders.

1. Brief mention is made of the allowable revenue expenses in respect of trade premises, for deduction in computing trading profits, at **2.1**.

2. The treatment of casual rental income is also explained at **2.1**.

3. Such traders will be interested in the provisions relating to capital allowances for plant and equipment installed in their building, and as to whether or not the building itself qualifies for industrial buildings allowances, as noted in **Chapter 5**, together with the additional points relating to interest payments dealt with in **Chapter 8**.

4. Relief may be available to an owner-occupier trader in respect of a premium paid on a lease of less than 50 years, in so far as that premium is taxable in the landlord's hands, as noted at **2.2.3**.

5. As far as the general tax position of a trader is concerned, the taxation of trading profits is outside the scope of this book, which is concerned with property alone. Nevertheless the notes relating to the tax position of

property dealers (see **Chapter 3**) may perhaps be helpful, but are in no way comprehensive since they are aimed at traders in one particular commodity, ie land.

6. Again the special rules relating to premiums received and sale and lease-back transactions may apply to a trader sub-letting part of his premises for a premium, or carrying out a sale and leaseback transaction, as appropriate.

7. Otherwise any profit from the disposal of a property falls to be taxed under the normal capital gains tax rules. A number of particular reliefs may be available to an owner-occupier trader in respect of profits derived from the disposal of his trading premises, for these purposes.

8. Finally some transitional allowance may be available to a trader on the disposal of his trading premises, if he had occupied those premises since before 5 April 1963, as noted in **Chapter 2**.

1.1.3   Property investors and dealers

The distinction between a property investor and a property dealer is not always clear-cut. In general terms a property investor is one who acquires or develops his property with a view to its retention for rental income. On the other hand a property dealer is one who acquires or develops the property with a view to selling it on at a profit. The problem therefore chiefly relates to the intentions of the taxpayer at the time he acquired or developed the property in question, rather than his motives at the time of sale. There may be however occasions where a property investor changes his intentions in respect of a particular property, so that it is deemed to be appropriated to dealing stock, or vice versa.

Each transaction really needs to be looked at in the light of its own circumstances. Thus for example a property investor may still carry out an isolated dealing transaction, or one that is treated as such, and in the same way a property dealer may acquire a property for long-term investment purposes. In the latter case it may be better for the investment property to be held in a separate company in order to limit the possibility of tainting the investment transaction and avoid the potential argument that it is part of the dealing activity.

The general distinction between these two types of taxpayer, and the factors affecting the issue, are discussed in **Chapter 3**. Note particularly that, where an investment property is acquired or developed with a view to its sale at a profit, the resultant profit may nonetheless be assessed as income.

The distinction between dealers and investors is important. Thus receipts from property transactions may well be treated in a different manner, depending on the status of the taxpayer. Property dealers are dealt with in **Chapter 3**. Investors are dealt with, as regards income, in **Chapter 2** and capital gains in **Chapter 8**.

1.1.4 Property developers

As far as a property developer is concerned, the position depends upon his motives in carrying out the development: ie as to whether he intends to retain the property after development as an investment for its rental income or for his own occupation, or whether he intends to sell the property at a profit. References to property speculators are for the most part confined to those persons who buy and sell land or property on a dealing basis, but without carrying out any development. Property dealers and developers are dealt with in **Chapter 3**.

1.2 Owner-occupation by traders, etc.

1.2.1 Rent payable

Rent payable in respect of premises occupied for the purposes of a trade or profession are deductible in computing the profits, normally on the accruals basis.

1.2.2 Interest payable

The position of interest is particularly complex; it can be treated as either a distribution or an expense depending upon the circumstances – see **Chapter 6**.

1.2.3 Proprietor's living accommodation

Expenditure on the upkeep of a flat above his business premises, used by the proprietor to allow him to work outside normal business hours, is not deductible, since it is not incurred 'wholly and exclusively' for business purposes (*Mason v Tyson (HMIT)* (1980) 53 TC 333).

1.2.4 Sale and leaseback situations

As in the case of Schedule A, the allowance of rent payable under such an arrangement may be restricted, if the commercial rental value of the property is less than the rent payable under the lease taken back. Again an owner-occupier trader who effects such an arrangement may also be in a situation where part of the proceeds of sale are treated as taxable income, included in his trading profits – see below.

1.2.5 Capital expenditure and improvements

The position relating to expenditure incurred on premises, where part of the cost relates to necessary repairs and maintenance work and part has the effect of improving the premises, does require separate consideration. Such expenditure is allowed in the trader's Schedule D Case I computation to the extent that it the cost of repair, etc. work. Thus the improvement element only is disallowed. Part of the disallowed amount may qualify for capital allowances – see below and **Chapter 5**.

Pre-acquisition dilapidations

Different treatment may however apply in the case of expenditure to put right dilapidations arising before the property concerned is acquired. There is no statutory provision to prevent the deduction of such costs. It is a matter of general tax law as to whether the expense is incurred as a capital expense or as a revenue expense. Normally such expenditure is disallowed as being the capital cost of putting the property right and making it fit for the purposes for which it is acquired (see *Law Shipping Co Ltd v IR Commrs* (1923) 12 TC 621 and *Jackson v Laskers Home Furnishers Ltd* (1956) 37 TC 69). On the other hand, where the property is capable of use, so that the repairs are not essential to make it fit for use as a profit-making asset, and the purchase price would be no higher if the repairs were carried out by the vendor, and where the costs are written off to the revenue account under established principles of sound commercial accounting, the expenditure incurred in such repair work is allowed (*Odeon Associated Theatres Ltd v Jones (HMIT)* (1971) 48 TC 257).

If however the work involves the complete replacement of the main part of the property, it is likely to be regarded as capital expenditure rather than repairs (*Wynne-Jones(HMIT) v Bedale Auctions Ltd* (1976) 51 TC 426).

Capital allowances

A trader may also be able to claim depreciation allowances in respect of expenditure incurred in the acquisition or construction of industrial buildings or hotels, or for the time being of commercial buildings in an enterprise zone, or in the provision of plant and equipment for use in his trade – as explained in **Chapter 5**.

Premiums, etc. paid

Where a trader leases trading premises for a period not exceeding 50 years and pays a premium under the lease, if the landlord is assessed on a part of that premium as if it were rental income, the tenant trader is allowed an additional deduction in computing the profits of his trade. The proportion of premium that is assessed on the landlord is spread equally over the whole of the period of the lease and, so long as the tenant trader continues to use the property in connection with his trade, he may deduct the appropriate amount each year as if it were additional rent paid by him in that year – see **Chapter 2**.

A payment to amend the terms of a lease so that tobacco duty would be excluded from the tenant's turnover, which formed the basis for calculating part of the rent, was held to be a capital payment and therefore is not deductible in computing the tenant's trading profits even though paid out to reduce a revenue commitment (*Tucker(HMIT) v Granada Motorway Services Ltd* (1979) 53 TC 92).

Sea walls

Unfortunately the special provisions relating to expenditure on sea walls are only available under Schedule A, and so are not available to an owner-occupier trader. If therefore he can claim no other relief under general capital allowances provisions, he may have a problem. Where he occupies the premises as a tenant, he might seek some agreement with the landlord whereby the landlord carries out the relevant work and charges him an increased rent. Where the property is occupied as a freehold, the position is more difficult. In severe cases, a sale and leaseback arrangement might be contemplated, but should be tackled extremely cautiously – bearing in mind all the other implications and tax situations that might be involved in such a transaction (see practically every other chapter in this publication!).

A payment made by the tenant to vary any of the terms of a lease is likely to be treated as a premium (ICTA 1988, s. 34(5)) and tax relief would be available over the remaining period of the lease as noted above (ICTA 1988, s. 87) – see **Chapter 2**.

1.2.6 Transitional

Where a trader has occupied premises since before 5 April 1963, he may be entitled to some additional transitional relief in respect of the annual value of that property when he comes to sell it or otherwise permanently ceases to use it for his trade – see **Chapter 2**.

1.3 Sub-letting of surplus accommodation

1.3.1 Deduction for rental deficits

Where premises that have been occupied for the purposes of a trade or profession become surplus to requirements, the rents payable on those premises do not thereby cease to be deductible in computing the profits of the trade (*Falkirk Iron Co Ltd v IR Commrs* (1933) 17 TC 625). If the premises are sub-let, then any rents receivable are deducted from the rents payable, and the net rental loss is deductible in computing profits (*Hyett (HMIT) v Lennard* (1940) 23 TC 346).

1.3.2 Provision for future deficits

In some cases, it may be appropriate to provide for the liability to pay rents in the future, subject to a reduction for anticipated sub-letting rents. In the case of *Herbert Smith v Honour (HMIT)* [1999] BTC 44, the High Court held that the taxpayer firm was entitled to a deduction for a provision for future rents, calculated in accordance with generally accepted accounting practice. Following that decision, the Revenue issued a press release on 20 July 1999 accepting that there is no longer a tax rule that denies provisions for anticipated losses or expenses. This was followed by an article in *Tax Bulletin* Issue 44 (December 1999), which stated that a provision made in accounts will be allowable for tax purposes if (and only if):

- it is in respect of allowable revenue expenditure (and not, for example, in respect of capital expenditure;
- it is required by UK generally accepted accounting practice (GAAP);
- it does not conflict with any specific tax rule governing the time at which expenditure is allowed, and
- it is estimated with sufficient accuracy.

1.3.3 Treatment of rent as trading receipts

Generally, where a trader lets part of his trading premises (but not property held as trading stock by a property dealer), it is Inland Revenue practice to treat the rent as forming part of his trading receipts (subject to conditions – see IR *Tax Bulletin*, February 1994), rather than a separate source under Schedule A, unless the property is only occupied in connection with a trade of providing services to tenants of the property. This simplifies the whole question of the allowance of expenditure for traders. Presumably an appropriate proportion of any expenditure incurred in the provision of sea walls is allowable against such rental income (see Inland Revenue Booklet IR 150: *Taxation of Rents*, paragraphs 501–506).

1.4 Sale and leaseback

1.4.1 Rent exceeding commercial rent

Disallowance of excess rent

In the case of a sale and leaseback, if the rent payable under the leaseback exceeds a commercial rent, the excess is disallowed in computing business profits (ICTA 1988, s. 779).

The legislation actually refers to a transfer of an interest in land, which includes not just a sale, but also:

- the grant of a lease, or any other transaction involving the creation of a new estate or interest in the land concerned;
- the surrender or forfeiture of an existing lease, and
- any transaction or series of transactions affecting land, or an estate or interest in land, such that some person is the owner, or one of the owners, before and after the carrying out of the transaction or transactions, but another person becomes or ceases to become one of the owners,

(s. 779(3)).

The legislation also catches the situation where:

(a) land, or any estate or interest in land, is transferred from one person to another,

(b) as a result of any transaction of series of transactions affecting the land or any estate or interest in the land, the transferor, or any person associated with him, becomes liable to make any payment other than rent under a lease, being either a rentcharge or some other payment connected with the land,

(s. 779(2)).

The rules disallow the excess of any payment at (b) over a commercial amount.

Commercial rent

'Commercial rent' means the rent that might be expected to be paid under a lease of the land negotiated in the open market at the time when the actual lease was created. It is to be assumed that the open market lease:

- is of the same duration as the actual lease;
- is subject to the same terms and conditions as the actual lease as regards liability for maintenance and repairs, and

- provides for rent payable at uniform intervals at a uniform rate or at rates that progress in line with the actual lease,

(s. 779(8)).

1.4.2 Short leases

The additional provisions described below apply whenever a lessee of land who is entitled to tax relief in respect of the rent payable:

- assigns the lease or surrenders it in consideration for a capital sum not otherwise taxable as income;
- at a time when the lease has no more than 50 years to run, and
- takes (or his associate takes) a new lease of the whole or any part of the same land for a term not longer than 15 years.

The provisions only apply to actual sales – and not to indirect disposals, notional disposals, or disposals by way of gift, etc. (ICTA 1988, s. 780(1)).

Increases in rent

If, instead of surrendering the lease:

- the lessee simply agrees with the landlord to vary its terms by increasing the rent payable in consideration for a capital sum, and
- the additional rent only covers a period of not more than 15 years starting with the receipt of the capital sum (or if that sum is paid in instalments, the last such instalment),

the lessee is treated as if he had surrendered his original lease and had been granted a new lease of not more than 15 years – but otherwise on the same terms as the original lease for this purpose (ICTA 1988, s. 780(6)).

Basic charge

The provisions operate to charge to tax a proportion of the amount received for the sale or surrender of the original lease as if it were an income receipt (ICTA 1988, s. 780(1)).

The proportion so taxable is calculated under a formula $(16 - n)/15$,

where n is the term of the new lease expressed in years. If the term is less than one year, n is taken as one. Otherwise odd months and days are not mentioned. They should therefore be claimed as a part of a year, and it is believed that the Inland Revenue accepts computations on this basis (ITCA 1988, s. 780(3)).

Example 1.1

Wilfred Squires is treated as surrendering his 41-year lease in exchange for £35,000 and a leaseback for only ten years. His assessment under these provisions is calculated as follows:

£35,000 × (16 − 10)/15 = £14,000

The proportion of the capital sum thus treated as income is chargeable in one of two ways. If the rents payable under the original lease were deductible in a computation of trading profits, the amount is treated as a trading receipt. In any other case, it is chargeable under Schedule D Case VI for the year or period in which the capital sum is received (ICTA 1988, s. 780(3)).

Term of leaseback

The rules for ascertaining the term of the leaseback for this purpose generally rely on the provisions of the lease itself, but in some cases the lease may be treated as ending at an earlier date. Thus where the aggregate rent payable for any period beginning with the grant of the lease and ending at some time within 15 years thereafter is greater than the aggregate rent payable in the period of corresponding length immediately following that period, the leaseback is treated as having a term of length equal to that first period only. This is to overcome the problem of 'front-end loading', where the purchaser/lessor seeks to recover his capital outlay out of higher rents charged during the earlier years of a longer lease.

Example 1.2

Wilfred Squires surrenders his 41-year lease in exchange for the sum of £35,000 and a leaseback for 40 years, under which the rent payable during the first ten years is at £10,000 per annum and thereafter at £5,000 per annum. The rents payable during the early part of the leaseback and the subsequent period of corresponding length are ascertained as follows:

Years 1 to 10 – £10,000 per annum × 10   £100,000

Years 11 to 20 – £5,000 per annum × 10   £ 50,000

Since the aggregate rents in the first decade exceed those payable in the second decade, the new lease is treated as being for a ten-year term only.

If either the landlord or tenant can determine the lease before the end of its term, or if the tenant can reduce the amount of rent he must pay under the lease, the lease is treated as having a term ending on the first occasion on which such determination or reduction can take place (ICTA 1988, s. 780(2)).

Deductions

No expenditure may be deducted from the proceeds of disposal for the above purposes – not even expenses incurred in arranging or carrying out the transactions. The provisions apply to the gross sum received itself. However, any part already taxed as income as a premium or trading receipt is not a 'capital' sum for this purpose, as noted below, and only the balance is considered here(s. 780(1)(*a*)).

Partial leaseback

If the land leased back only represents a part of the leasehold land sold, these provisions apply only to so much of the consideration received for the sale as may reasonably be apportioned to the property leased back (s. 780(4)).

Property dealers

Where the property is held as dealing stock, the proceeds of sale are already brought into tax as income in computing the property dealer's taxable trading profits. Again, therefore, the proceeds are not regarded as a 'capital' sum and the provisions of this chapter do not apply.

Subsequent rental payments

Relief for the rents payable under the new lease may still be restricted if the rent exceeds a commercial rent, giving a double disadvantage.

Exemptions and reliefs

As seen, the tax charge arising under these provisions falls to be assessed under Schule D Cases I, II, V or VI – and the normal exemptions and reliefs available in respect of income assessed thereunder are available here also.

Losses

No loss can arise under these provisions, since no expenditure may be deducted from the proceeds of sale – and indeed the provisions may still apply even if the lessee makes an overall loss on the sale. Any such loss suffered on the sale is therefore dealt with under the relevant capital gains tax legislation. In fact the loss arising for capital gains tax, etc. purposes is increased by the amount assessed under the provisions of this chapter – since that part of the proceeds taxed as income is left out of account in computing the allowable loss for those purposes.

1.4.3 Relief for rent

The provisions discussed above only apply if tax relief was available in respect of rent payable under the original lease, by way of a deduction under one of the following specified heads:

- as an expense in computing the profits of a Schedule A business;
- as an expense in computing the profits of a trade, profession or vocation – ie if paid in respect of the trader's premises;
- as a deduction from profits chargeable under Schedule D Case VI;
- in a management expenses claim of an investment company – ie if paid in respect of the investment company's own premises;
- as a deduction against employment income,
- as an allowable expense in computing taxable profits arising from woodlands,

(ICTA 1988, ss. 779(13) and 780(1)).

1.4.4 Associates

As mentioned, if the leaseback is taken by an associate instead of the original lessee himself, the provisions may still apply. The following are treated as associated for this purpose:

- an individual and his relative – brother, sister, ancestor or lineal descendant – and the husband or wife of such relative;
- an individual and his spouse or such spouse's relative – as before, including the spouse's in-laws;
- a trustee and the settlor of the trust or anyone associated with the settlor;
- a person and any company or partnership controlled by that person and/or that person's associates,
- any two or more companies or partnerships are associated if they are under common control by any person and/or that person's associates;
- joint owners are associated with any person associated with any one of them, in relation to the jointly owned property (ICTA 1988, ss. 780(7) and 783(10), and see ICTA 1988, s. 840, for definition of 'control' and ICTA 1988, s. 670(2) for definition of 'settlor').

1.4.5 Overseas property

Whilst the charge to tax under these provisions is not restricted to property situated in the UK, it does only apply as and when tax relief was given for the rents payable under the original lease under one of the specified heads. If therefore the property is occupied for the purposes of a trade, etc. assessable to tax under Schedule D, Cases I, II or V, or if it is occupied in connection with an investment business carried on by a company so that rents are deductible in a management expenses claim, or similar situations, the provisions might well apply. On the other hand, if the overseas property is sub-let and the profit rental falls to be taxed as income from a foreign possession under Schedule D, Case V, the legislation does not apply. It is therefore necessary to have close regard to the way in which tax relief for rental payments is granted.

1.5 Remediation of contaminated land

1.5.1 Introduction

As from 11 May 2001, certain expenditure incurred in cleaning up contaminated land in the UK will qualify for a 150 per cent deduction in computing profits (FA 2001, Sch. 22). The relief will be reviewed after five years of operation.

The land must be acquired by a company for the purposes of a *trade* carried on by that company. It must be in a contaminated state at the time of acquisition and the company must incur capital expenditure which is 'qualifying land remediation expenditure' in respect of the land (FA 2001, Sch. 22, Para. 1).

Revenue expenditure on cleaning up contaminated land qualifies for a deduction under general principles, but it too will qualify for the 150 per cent deduction, if it is qualifying land remediation expenditure, as from 11 May 2001. This applies where the expenditure is incurred for the purposes of a *trade or a Schedule A business* (FA 2001, Sch. 22, Paras 12, 13).

1.5.2 Qualifying land remediation expenditure

The expenditure must be on land all or part of which is in a contaminated state. It must be on 'relevant land remediation' directly undertaken by the company. The expenditure must be expenditure which would not have been incurred if the land had not been contaminated, and it must not be subsidised.

Three categories of expenditure qualify:

- expenditure on employee costs;
- expenditure on materials, and
- qualifying expenditure on sub-contracted land remediation,

(FA 2001, Sch. 22, Para. 2).

Nuclear sites are excluded from the new relief (FA 2001, Sch. 22, Para. 3(2)).

Relevant land remediation is work done for the purpose of preventing or minimising any harm, or pollution of controlled waters, caused by the contaminated state of the land, or work done to restore the land or waters to their former state. The work must be done on the land itself, adjoining land or any controlled waters affected by the land. Activities which are preparatory to the above work also qualify (FA 2001, Sch. 22. Para. 4).

'Land' includes any building standing on the land (Interpretation Act 1978, Sch. 1). Therefore, it is understood that expenditure on the removal of harmful asbestos from a building, where the building is not demolished, qualifies for the relief.

Employee costs include secondary Class I NICs on the directors' or employees' remuneration, plus pension contributions. The directors or employees must be directly and actively engaged on the land remediation. Where an individual is only partly so engaged, an apportionment of the costs has to be made. However, if the qualifying proportion would be more than 80 per cent, then the whole of the costs qualifies, and if it would be less than 20 per cent, then none of the costs qualifies (FA 2001, Sch. 22, Para. 5).

Any materials must be employed directly in the relevant land remediation (FA 2001, Sch. 22, Para. 6).

A company incurs sub-contracted land remediation expenditure if it pays a sub-contractor to carry out the work (FA 2001, Sch. 22, Para. 9). If the company and the sub-contractor are connected persons, relief is restricted to the sub-contractor's expenditure (FA 2001, Sch. 22, Para. 10). Otherwise, the whole of the payment to the sub-contractor qualifies (FA 2001, Sch. 22, Para. 11).

1.5.3 Land remediation tax credit

If the 150 per cent deduction creates or augments a trading loss or Schedule A loss, then the company may claim a repayable tax credit of 16 per cent of the lesser of:

- 150 per cent of the qualifying expenditure, and
- the unrelieved loss;

(FA 2001, Sch. 22, Paras. 14, 15).

In arriving at the unrelieved loss, it is assumed that relief will be claimed against total profits for the same accounting period under ICTA 1988,

s. 392A or 393A. Further, to the extent that the loss is carried back under s. 393A(1)(b) or surrendered under the group relief provisions, it will not qualify for credit (FA 2001, Sch. 22, (14)). However, no account is taken of losses brought forward from earlier periods or losses carried back from a later period.

Payment of the tax credit has to be claimed, and the Revenue may set off any corporation tax due to it. Further, the Revenue is not obliged to pay any tax credit until the PAYE tax and NICs relating to the employment costs have been paid (FA 2001, Sch. 22, Para. 16). The tax credit paid to any company is not income for tax purposes (FA 2001, Sch. 22, Para. 18). To the extent that tax credit is claimed, the amount of any loss will be reduced (FA 2001, Sch. 22, Para. 17).

Claims for tax credit should be included in the company's CT 600 return or amended return (FA 1998, Sch. 18, Paras. 83H–83I). The time limit is two years from the end of the accounting period in which the expenditure is incurred (Para. 83K). There are penalties for fraudulent or negligent claims (Para. 83L).

2 Property letting

2.1 Introduction

2.1.1 The charge to tax under Schedule A

Tax is charged under Schedule A on the annual profits arising from a business carried on:

- for the exploitation, as a source of rents or receipts
- of any estate, interest or rights in or over land in the UK.

To the extent that any transaction is entered into for such exploitation, it is deemed to be entered into in the course of such a business (ICTA 1988, s. 15(1)).

It is well established in the case law that the letting of property on a commercial basis amounts to a business. Most recent cases have related to VAT, but the principles apply for direct taxation purposes also (see, eg *DA Walker* [1976] VATTR 10; *J Prescott*, MAN/77/239; *JW Wilcox* [1978] VATTR 79, etc.).

The receipts which are to be included in the Schedule A computation include:

- payments in respect of a licence to occupy or use land;
- payments for the exercise of rights over land;
- rent charges, ground annuals and feu duties,
- other annual payments reserved in respect of, or charged on, or issuing out of, land.

2.1.2 Interaction of Schedule A and Schedule D Case I

It is well established that income which falls under Schedule A is excluded from Schedule D. The leading case on this point is *Salisbury House Estate Ltd v Fry(HMIT)* (1930) 15 TC 266. Although that case related to the pre-1963 Schedule A, which was based on an 'annual value', it has been accepted as establishing the principle of the exclusivity of the Schedules.

Schedule A imposes a charge to tax on income from the exploitation of any estate, interest or rights in or over land in the UK (ICTA 1988, s. 15). However, where additional services are provided, the income from the provision of those services may fall within Schedule D.

The Revenue recognises that there are three basic possibilities:

- the whole activity, ie the letting plus the services, amounts to a trade;
- the whole activity is part of the Schedule A business,
- the provision of services amounts to a trade separate from the Schedule A letting business;

(Booklet IR 150, paragraph 512).

It is unlikely that the whole activity will amount to a trade unless the landlord remains in occupation of the property. This may be true in the case of a hotel, guest house or bed and breakfast business, for example. However, the letting of property by itself is not a trade (per Lord MacMillan in the *Salisbury House* case).

The whole activity is part of the Schedule A business unless the services provided go further than the normal services provided by a landlord. Such normal services include:

- the cleaning of stairs and passages in multi-unit premises;
- the provision of hot water and heating;
- rent collection and the arrangement of new lettings,
- arrangements for the repair of the property.

Services which are considered to go further than the normal services of a landlord include:

- the regular cleaning of rooms when they are let and not just between lettings;
- the regular supply of clean linen,
- the regular provision of meals;

(Booklet IR 150, paragraph 516).

Some income which technically falls within Schedule A is taxed under Schedule D Case I, and some rents from land are explicitly excluded from Schedule A. These items are considered below.

2.1.3 Tied premises

Rents received in respect of tied premises are brought into the lessor's computation of profits derived from his trade under Schedule D Case I – rather than under Schedule A (whether under the rules for income tax or corporation tax). The lessor is similarly allowed to deduct any rent paid by him in respect of the premises in calculating the profits of his trade – but not to deduct lump sum payments to induce tenants to terminate their leases so that the trade can be carried on through managers (*Watney Combe Reid & Co Ltd v Pike*

(HMIT) [1982] BTC 288). Where only part of the premises are tied premises, the normal Schedule A computation is made in respect of the letting as a whole, and then an appropriate proportion, on a fair and just apportionment, is attributed to the tied premises themselves and dealt with on this basis (ICTA 1988, s. 98).

2.1.4 Mines and quarries

Profits from land are charged to tax under Schedule D Case I where they arise to any of the following concerns:

- mines and quarries (including gravel pits, sand pits and brickfields);
- ironworks, gasworks, salt springs or works, alum mines or works and water works with streams of water;
- canals, inland navigation, docks and drains or levels;
- fishings;
- rights of markets and fairs, tolls, bridges and ferries;
- railways and other ways,
- other similar concerns (ICTA 1988, s. 55).

Rents and royalties arising from land used in connection with any of the above concerns are charged to tax under Schedule D (ICTA 1988, s. 119).

2.1.5 Farming and market gardening

Farming and market gardening is treated as a trade or part of a trade. The profits therefrom are chargeable to tax under Schedule D Case I (ICTA 1988, s. 53). However, farmers and market gardeners may also derive income falling under Schedule A from their land in addition to their trading profits.

2.1.6 Electric line wayleaves, etc.

Rents, royalties, etc. receivable from easements relating to electric, telegraphic or telephonic wires or cables are chargeable to tax under Schedule D. However, if the chargeable person also has Schedule A income from the same land, the receipts from the wayleaves are included in the Schedule A computation (ICTA 1988, s. 120).

2.1.7 Exclusion of certain items falling within Schedule D Case I

The following are excluded from the charge under Schedule A:

- profits from farming or market gardening, and the associated averaging provisions;
- profits from mines, quarries and other concerns within ICTA 1988, s. 55;
- receipts and expenses relating to tied premises, and the associated provisions of ICTA 1988, s. 98, and
- mining and other rents within ICTA 1988, ss. 119 and 120.

2.1.8 Caravans and houseboats

A right to use a fixed caravan or houseboat in the UK is treated as a right deriving from land in the UK. Accordingly, rents and receipts from the letting of such assets are within Schedule A.

2.2 Computation of Schedule A profits

2.2.1 Application of Schedule D Case I principles

The profits are to be computed in accordance with the principles applicable to the computation of trading profits (ICTA 1988, s. 21A). They are to be based on accounts that show a true and fair view of the profits or losses concerned (FA 1998, s. 42). This means that:

- the profits are to be ascertained from accounts drawn up on a commercial basis in accordance with generally accepted accounting practice;
- the accruals basis applies, whereas the arising/paid basis applied under the old rules;
- the 'wholly and exclusively' principle applies, with the result that expenditure which is not incurred wholly and exclusively for the purposes of the Schedule A business is not allowable as a deduction in computing the profits;
- the distinction between capital and revenue applies, but this is subject to specific provisions which bring certain capital receipts into charge as income,
- capital allowances are given as a deduction in computing the profits (CAA 2001, ss. 248–250).

Certain provisions which apply for Case I purposes are specifically applied for Schedule A purposes:

- apportionment of profits in accounts between chargeable periods (ICTA 1988, s. 72);
- disallowance of business entertainment expenditure (ICTA 1988, s. 577);
- deduction for redundancy payments (ICTA 1988, ss. 579, 580);
- expenses of training courses for employees (ICTA 1988, ss. 588, 589);
- expenses of counselling services for employees (ICTA 1988, ss. 589A, 589B);
- payments for restrictive covenants (FA 1988, s.73);
- rules determining the accounting period in which remuneration is deductible (FA 1989, s.43);
- disallowance of certain expenses in connection with non-approved retirement benefits schemes (FA 1989, s. 76);
- expenditure in connection with security assets (FA 1989, ss. 112, 113),
- disallowance of provisions for future repairs.

The provisions of ICTA 1988, s. 82, which disallow interest payable to non-residents in certain circumstances, are not to apply for the purposes of computing the Schedule A profits (ICTA 1988, s. 21A(3)). However, as far as corporation tax is concerned, interest payable continues to be dealt with under the loan relationships provisions (see **Chapter 6**).

The provisions of ICTA 1988, s. 87, which give a deduction in computing trading profits for part of a lease premium which is taxed as income in the hands of the lessor, are not to apply for the purposes of computing the Schedule A profits (ICTA 1988, s. 21A(3)). This does not, however, stop the deduction which the lessor can obtain for any premium which he pays against the premium which he receives (as to which, see ICTA 1988, s. 37).

Certain detailed rules applicable to Case I are applied for the purposes of computing Schedule A profits (ICTA 1988, s.21B). They are as follows:

- the rules relating to post-cessation receipts and expenses (ICTA 1988, ss. 103–106, 108, 109A and 110);
- the rules relating to partnership changes (ICTA 1988, s.113),
- the rules granting relief for pre-trading expenditure (ICTA 1988, s.401(1)).

2.2.2 Expenditure

The kind of expenses which will be encountered in connection with Schedule A businesses will be expenses of maintenance, repairs, insurance and management of the properties concerned. They will be brought into account in accordance with generally accepted accounting practice.

The following expenditure may be deducted when paid from rental receivable in computing taxable profits:

1. any rent, rent charge, ground annual, feu duty, or other payment made by the landlord in respect of the property;

2. the cost of repairing and redecorating the property – both internally and externally, and including painting;

3. expenditure on maintenance, including the maintenance of common parts of a block of offices or flats;

4. the cost of such services as the landlord is obliged to provide under the terms of the lease, including for example the upkeep of gardens for a block of flats;

5. expenditure incurred for the benefit of tenants on such items as private roads, drains, ditches, walls, fences, gutters, etc.;

6. the upkeep of estate offices, and salaries and wages of employees engaged on full-time estate management or the provision of services to tenants;

7. any premiums on a comprehensive policy of insurance in respect of the fabric of the property (but not insurance against loss of rent) and the cost of insurance valuations;

8. the cost of rent collection, including agent's commissions, etc.;

9. professional fees in preparing accounts and computations relating to the property;

10. pensions to retired employees, or their widows, in proportion to the amount of their services formerly allowed as a deduction under the above;

11. the cost of advertising properties for letting,

12. it is understood that the Revenue's practice is to allow the cost of legal and professional fees on the grant or renewal of a lease only where:

    (a) a new lease is granted for a period not exceeding 21 years, or
    (b) a lease is renewed for a period not exceeding 50 years.

It is believed that advertising costs (see **(11)** above) may be allowed on a similar basis.

As regards the distinction between capital and revenue, the Court of Appeal has held that a lump sum received by a property holding company for the assignment of rental income arising on certain properties over a five-year period was of a capital nature (*John Lewis Properties plc v IR Commrs* [2003] BTC 127, following *C & E Commrs v Paget* [1989] BTC 5,146). The properties were occupied by John Lewis for the purposes of its trade. It followed that there was a part disposal of the right to receive rents for capital gains purposes but rollover relief was available.

2.2.3 Repairs to let property

In the June 2002 edition of *Tax Bulletin* (Issue 59), the Revenue published the following guidance on repairs to let property.

'Schedule A: Computation of profits: Repairs to let property

Following the withdrawal, from April 2001, of extra statutory concession ESC B4 (maintenance and repairs of property obviated by alterations, etc.: Schedule A assessments) we have been asked for more guidance on what constitutes an allowable repair for Schedule A purposes.

Background: Computation of Schedule A profits

New rules for computing the profits of a Schedule A business were introduced by Finance Act 1995 for individuals and by Finance Act 1998 for companies. Broadly speaking, the profits of a Schedule A business are now computed in the same way as the profits of a trade. This means that the starting point for the computation is a set of accounts drawn up in accordance with generally accepted accounting practice. The profit or loss shown by the accounts is then subject to any adjustments required or authorised by law.

In certain small cases the "cash basis" can be used as an alternative to the "earnings basis". The circumstances are set out in paragraphs 90–92 of the Inland Revenue booklet IR 150 *Taxation of rents: A guide to property income.*

Whatever basis is used the accounts have to be examined to see whether or not any expenditure falls to be excluded by specific tax legislation as explained in the relevant case law. Broadly speaking expenses are allowable provided they are incurred wholly and exclusively for the purposes of a Schedule A business and are not capital expenditure.

This article clarifies what type of expenditure on building work undertaken on a let property is allowable and what is not.

Capital expenditure

The cost of the house or block of flats that is being let is capital expenditure and so is the cost of any additions or improvements. So if you add to the premises something that was not there before, for example if you build an extension or a new porch, this is capital expenditure. It does not matter how small the addition is. If you add an extractor fan or fit an additional cabinet in the bathroom or kitchen, this is also capital expenditure.

A landlord is most likely to incur capital expenditure before a property is let for the first time or between lettings. For example the landlord may decide to improve the property by creating ensuite facilities where there were none before. This is capital expenditure.

Repairs to let property

To decide whether expenditure incurred on "repairs" to property is allowable, the first step is to identify the "entirety" that is being repaired. The doctrine of the "entirety" has been well summarised by Buckley, LJ in *Lurcott v Wakeley* (1911) AER 41 as follows:

> "Repair is restoration by renewal or replacement of subsidiary parts of the whole. Renewal, as distinguished from repair, is reconstruction of the entirety, meaning by the entirety not necessarily the whole, but substantially the whole subject matter under discussion . . . it follows that the question of repair is in every case one of degree, and the test is whether the act to be done is one which in substance is the renewal or replacement of defective parts or the renewal or replacement of substantially the whole."

In the case of residential accommodation we accept that the "entirety" will normally be the house or the block of flats that is let. So if your roof is damaged and you replace the damaged area, your expenditure is allowable.

Even if the repairs are substantial, that does not of itself make them capital for tax purposes, provided the character of the asset remains unchanged. For example, if a fitted kitchen is refurbished the type of work carried out might include the stripping out and replacement of base units, wall units, sink etc., re-tiling, work top replacement, repairs to floor coverings and associated re-plastering and re-wiring. Provided the kitchen is replaced with a similar standard kitchen then this is a repair and the expenditure is allowable. If at the same time additional cabinets are fitted increasing the storage space, or extra equipment is installed, then this element is a capital addition and not allowable (applying whatever apportionment basis is reasonable on the facts). But if the whole kitchen is substantially upgraded, for example if standard units are replaced by expensive customised items using high quality materials, the whole expenditure will be capital. There is no longer any relief for "notional repairs", that is the notional cost of the repairs that would otherwise have had to be carried out.

What we regard as a repair will necessarily change with the passage of time to reflect technological improvements. This issue was considered in the tax case *Conn (HMIT) v Robins Brothers Ltd* (1966) 43 TC 266. As a result we accept that the replacement of a part of the "entirety" with the nearest modern equivalent is allowable as a repair for tax purposes and not disallowable as improvement expenditure.

An example is double-glazing. In the past we took the view that replacing single-glazed windows with double-glazed windows was an improvement and therefore capital expenditure. But times have changed. Building standards have improved and the types of replacement windows available from retailers have changed. We now accept that replacing single-glazed windows by double-glazed equivalents counts as allowable expenditure on repairs.

Generally, if the replacement of a part of the "entirety" is like for like or the nearest modern equivalent, we accept the expenditure is allowable revenue expenditure.'

2.2.4 Provisions for future repairs

It is provided specifically that no deduction is to be allowed for expenditure on the repair of premises held for the purposes of a Schedule A business beyond the 'sum actually expended' on such repairs (ICTA 1988, s. 21A(3) applying s. 77(1)(d)). Historically, the Revenue interpreted this as meaning that the deduction is limited to the expenditure disbursed or paid in the period concerned, ie that the cash basis applies. This interpretation was challenged before the Special Commissioners in the case of *Jenners Princes Street Edinburgh Ltd v IR Commrs* (1988) SpC 166.

In that case, the company had a feasibility study carried out into the repair of a listed building. In its accounting period ended 31 January 1995, it resolved to carry out the repairs in accordance with the feasibility study. It made a provision for the estimated costs of the repairs. The repairs were carried out, and payment was made for them, in the following two accounting periods. The Special Commissioners allowed the provision.

The expenditure was actually incurred, albeit in the two subsequent accounting periods. Further, the provision was ascertained with sufficient accuracy to satisfy the requirements of *Southern Railway of Peru v Owen (HMIT)* [1957] 36 TC 602, *Johnston v Britannia Airways Ltd* [1994] BTC 298, etc. The Commissioners held that 'expended' meant expended in the accountancy sense, rather than being paid out in cash, and that the accruals basis applied. It is clear, however, that the above decision does not cover the case where a landlord makes provisions (rather than accruals) for future expenditure to be incurred in respect of accrued dilapidations. Such provisions are essentially sinking fund provisions.

Where a landlord receives contributions from commercial tenants in respect of accrued dilapidations, he is chargeable on the contributions receivable, on the normal accruals basis. It would seem that the case of *Weeks v Symons (HMIT)* ([1983] BTC 18) will not help a landlord to get a deduction for sinking fund provisions.

2.2.5 Flat management companies: residential service charges

Under the new rules, residential service charges received by occupier-controlled flat management companies will ordinarily be outside the scope of Schedule A since they will be viewed as being received by trustees under the Landlord and Tenant Act 1987, s. 42. However, rents receivable by such companies, such as ground rents, are within the charge to tax under Schedule A since they fall outside the scope of s. 42. Investment income arising on such sums held in a designated bank account are chargeable to income tax at the rate applicable to trusts (see *Tax Bulletin,* Issue 37, October 1998).

2.2.6 Change of accounting basis

Where there is a change of accounting basis, the opening balances at the beginning of the period of account starting with the change will not be the same as the closing balances at the end of the preceding period. The difference is a prior year adjustment. This has to be brought into account as a Schedule A profit or loss in the period of account starting with the change. This ensures that all receipts and expenses are taxed and allowed once and once only (FA 1998, Sch. 6).

2.3 The Schedule A rules: Income tax

2.3.1 Persons chargeable and basis of assessment

Income tax under Schedule A is chargeable on the person receiving or entitled to the income within Schedule A.

The amount chargeable for any tax year is the full amount of the profits arising in that year (ICTA 1988, s. 21).

2.3.2 Computation of Schedule A profit

The rules set out at **2.2** above apply. It is important to note that, for income tax purposes, interest payable for the purposes of the Schedule A business is allowable as a deduction in computing the Schedule A profit or loss. This contrasts with the corporation tax rules, under which interest payable continues to be dealt with under the loan relationships legislation.

2.3.3 Interest payable: application of Case I principles

The normal rules of Schedule D Case I apply. This means that the interest is allowable as a deduction in computing the profits of the Schedule A business if it satisfies the 'wholly and exclusively' rule (ICTA 1988, s. 74).

The purchaser of a property may finance the purchase by using his own funds, by borrowing, or by a combination of both. If the purchase is financed wholly or partly by the purchaser's own funds, the purchaser may, at some future date, decide effectively to withdraw part of his own capital from the Schedule A business and replace it with borrowings. In this case, interest on the additional borrowings is not automatically excluded from relief, no matter how he uses the capital that he withdraws.

In the kind of refinancing considered in the preceding paragraph, the amount of capital withdrawn should not exceed the amount of capital introduced. Further, if the resultant gearing is so high that the letting is unlikely to show profit, the Revenue may seek a disallowance of interest under the 'wholly and exclusively' rule.

2.3.4 Co-ownership of property

The joint ownership of property does not, of itself, amount to a partnership. Therefore, where property is let otherwise than as an activity ancillary to the activities of a partnership, each co-owner is responsible for declaring his share of the joint income in his tax return. This income will not feature in a partnership statement. In the case of a company co-owner, the company's share will be included in its accounts.

Where one co-owner is responsible for managing the property and producing the rental income statements, the Revenue will usually address any queries to this person. If, as a result of their enquiries, the Revenue considers it necessary to amend the self-assessment returns of other co-owners, or to raise assessments, it will issue separate notices under TMA 1970, s. 28A or s. 29 to each co-owner (*Tax Bulletin*, Issue 25).

2.3.5 Married couples

Income arising from property held in the names of a husband and his wife is deemed, for tax purposes, to be held in equal shares unless the contrary be established (ICTA 1988, s. 282A). Where, in fact, the property is held in unequal shares, the couple may make a declaration to that effect (ICTA 1988, s. 282A(3) and 282B). Where a declaration is made, the income is taxed on the basis of the actual beneficial shares.

The declaration has effect in relation to income arising after the date on which it is made, but it does not have effect unless notice is given to the Revenue within 60 days of that date (ICTA 1988, s. 282B(3)).

Form 17 is used by married couples to elect to have income from property held jointly taxed on a basis other than 50/50. The election is under ICTA 1988, s. 282B. The couple can make an election only where the property is held in unequal shares, and they are entitled to the income arising in proportion to those shares.

The new form 17 may be found on the Internet at www.inlandrevenue.gov.uk/menus/otherforms.htm.

2.3.6 Partnerships

Where a partnership has rental income from land in the UK, that is deemed to be a separate Schedule A business carried on by the partnership (ICTA 1988, s. 15(1), Para. 1(3)). This business is separate and distinct from any Schedule A business which may be carried on by any particular partner.

If any of the partners is an individual, the profits and losses from the partnership's Schedule A business are computed as though the partnership were an individual (ICTA 1988, s. 111(2) as applied by s. 21A(1)). In other words, the computation will be made for the partnership as a whole. Computations will be made for each accounting period of the partnership.

The Schedule A profits of the partnership are then apportioned between the partners for each of the accounting periods concerned. Each partner must then apportion his share of partnership Schedule A profits to tax years in accordance with ICTA 1988, s. 72 as applied by s. 21A(2). The amount apportioned to any year must be included in each partner's self-assessment for that year. The accounts basis applies where the partnership's rental business is ancillary to a trade or profession, together with the special rules for commencements and cessations (ICTA 1988, s. 111(4)).

The same principles apply in respect of a partnership overseas letting business within Schedule D Case V, as to which, see ICTA 1988, s. 65A(4).

Further information on partnerships will be found in Inland Revenue Booklet IR 150: *Taxation of Rents* at paragraphs 26–43 and Appendix 3.

2.3.7 Partnerships involving companies

If any partner in a partnership is a company, a Schedule A computation for the partnership must be prepared on the basis that the partnership is a company (ICTA 1988, s. 114(1)). Each company partner's share is then apportioned to that company's accounting periods and included in its corporation tax returns for the periods concerned (once again applying ICTA 1988, s. 72). Its share of any loan relationship deficit, foreign exchange gains and losses, and gains and losses on financial instruments will also have to be apportioned.

The same principles apply in respect of a partnership overseas letting business within Schedule D Case V (ICTA 1988, s. 65A(4)).

It will be appreciated that if a partnership has both individual partners and company partners, two computations will be required for each accounting period concerned, one on an income tax basis and one on a corporation tax basis.

2.3.8 Partnership changes

Where there is a change in the composition of a partnership (eg where a partner joins or leaves the partnership) the Schedule A computations for the partnership are prepared on the basis of a continuing business. However, if there is a complete change of ownership (ie no partner before the change continues after the change) then the business is deemed to have ceased and a new business commenced on the occasion of the change (ICTA 1988, s. 113).

2.3.9 Farmers

The 'averaging' rules of ICTA 1988, s. 96 do not apply for Schedule A purposes (ICTA 1988, s. 21A(4)).

2.4 The Schedule A rules: Corporation tax

2.4.1 Basis of computation

The letting of all property situated in the UK by the same company is treated as a single business.

Schedule A profits are to be computed in accordance with the principles applicable to the computation of trading profits, except that the following are excluded from the computation:

- interest payable, and other items which come within the 'loan relation-ships' legislation – as to which, see **Chapter 6**: such items will continue to be dealt with under that legislation;
- foreign exchange gains and losses which come within the provisions of FA 1993, ss. 125–170 – such gains and losses will continue to be dealt with under that legislation,
- profits and losses on financial instruments which come within the provisions of FA 2002, Sch. 26: such gains and losses will continue to be dealt with under that legislation,

(ICTA 1988, s. 15(1), Para. 2(3)).

Contributions payable by tenants to a flat management company under Landlord and Tenant Act 1987, s. 42 in respect of variable service charges and sinking funds will ordinarily be outside the scope of the new Schedule A provisions. Such contributions will not normally give rise to a profit in the hands of the flat management company. Under s. 42 such contributions are required to be paid into a trust fund. The company is not beneficially entitled. Interest arising on such a fund is chargeable to income tax at the rate applicable to trusts. However, any rents receivable by flat management companies, such as ground rents, are outside the scope of s. 42 and are thus within Schedule A (*Tax Bulletin*, Issue 37, October 1998).

In the case of a non-resident company, a Schedule A business which is within the charge to corporation tax is treated as a separate business from any Schedule A business chargeable to income tax (ICTA 1988, s. 15(1A)). A non-resident company is within the charge to corporation tax if it carries on a trade in the UK through a branch or agency, but otherwise it is chargeable to income tax on income arising in the UK (ICTA 1988, s. 11). Therefore, it appears that this rule applies where a non-resident company commences or ceases to carry on a trade in the UK through a branch or agency.

2.4.2   Property situated abroad

Profits from the letting of property situated outside the UK continue to be chargeable to corporation tax under Schedule D Case V (ICTA 1988, s. 70A).

2.5   The Schedule A rules: Furnished lettings

Income from furnished lettings is treated as part of the Schedule A business profits (ICTA 1988, s. 15(1), Para. 4).

The rules relating to the rent a room scheme and to furnished holiday lettings are not affected by the changes to the Schedule A basis of computation.

In the case of residential property, no capital allowances are normally given for plant and equipment except in the case of installations in the common parts of a block of flats. However, some allowance is usually made to cover depreciation and replacement of free-standing furnishings and equipment against income received from furnished lettings. The Inland Revenue's current practice (as confirmed and clarified in Extra-Statutory Concession B47) is to allow the taxpayer to claim either:

- a replacement allowance, where no relief is given for the cost of the original item, but expenditure on any replacements is deductible in full, or
- a 10 per cent deduction from rental receipts – the deduction being calculated after first excluding any additional rental receipts in respect of council tax and water rates and/or services, etc.

Example 2.1

Terry Bridgewater acquires a flat, which he furnishes at a cost of £1,500 and leases out at £500 per annum net of council tax. In year 2 he spends £80 on renewing furnishings. He can claim an allowance calculated under one of the following bases:

		Year 1	Year 2
(a)	Cost of replacement (actual)	£ –	£ 80
(b)	Percentage of rents (10%)	£ 50	£ 50

He would probably claim on the basis of (b).

Where the 10 per cent deduction is allowed, no further deduction is given for the cost of renewing furniture or furnishings. Whether or not the 10 per cent allowance is claimed on the free-standing items, the landlord can also claim the cost of renewing fixtures which are an integral part of the buildings and which are revenue repairs to the fabric (eg baths, washbasins, toilets, etc.). In existing cases, where some other basis for calculating the allowance for furnishing had already been agreed before 1975/76, the established basis may continue so long as the let properties remain in the same ownership.

In some cases, a premium may be payable on the grant of the lease or tenancy. Part of this premium will be deemed to be rent under ICTA 1988, s. 34(1). It is understood that the Revenue accepts that the 10 per cent deduction applies to this deemed rent as well as to the actual rent.

This point, unfortunately, is not dealt with in the Revenue's *Property Income Manual*.

The old 10 per cent wear and tear allowance for furnished residential property continues to be available in respect of items not qualifying for capital allowances under the machinery and plant rules (Extra-Statutory Concession B47 and Inland Revenue Booklet IR 150, paragraphs 347–362). This is intended to cover depreciation of items such as:

- beds, suites and other moveable furniture
- TVs
- fridges and freezers
- carpets and wall coverings
- curtains
- linen
- crockery or cutlery
- cookers, washing machines, dishwashers, etc.

The 10 per cent applies to the net rent from the property concerned. This is the gross rent less any council tax, water and sewage rates, and other charges normally payable by the landlord.

For items qualifying for capital allowances but on which capital allowances are not claimed, a 'renewals basis' deduction may be claimed. This means that the cost of replacing the items concerned may be claimed, but not the cost of providing them or the cost of additions. The capital allowance basis is normally more beneficial, since allowances are obtained for the initial provision of the items concerned. The renewals basis may also be applied to items for which the 10 per cent deduction could be claimed but is not actually claimed (Inland Revenue Booklet IR 150, paragraphs 363–367).

2.6 Premiums, etc.

2.6.1 General comments

Introduction

The provisions explained in this section apply to assess income tax or corporation tax at normal rates on a proportion of certain sums received in respect of the use of property as being the equivalent of rental income – the proportion depending upon the length of the lease, etc. involved: the shorter the lease, the greater the taxable amount.

The income element is treated as a receipt of the Schedule A business. The only significant change is that these rules have been extended to premiums received in respect of properties outside the UK. Whether there is a premium at all will, in relation to non-UK property, be determined by reference to the law applicable to the property concerned.

The legislation applies primarily to any sum received by way of premiu... respect of the grant of a lease of land in the UK for a term not exceeding 50 years. 'Premium' in this context includes any sum paid by a tenant to his landlord, in his capacity as landlord, in consideration for the grant of a lease (*Clarke (HMIT) v United Real (Moorgate) Ltd* [1988] BTC 49). In addition, other similar sums received may be treated as a premium for this purpose, including sums received for the variation or waiver of the terms of a lease, or in lieu of rent, or for the forfeiture or surrender of a lease, or finally if the tenant is obliged to carry out any work on the property that has the effect of improving the landlord's reversionary interest – when the enhancement in value is also treated as a deemed premium.

An analogous situation arises where, instead of letting the property, a person sells it with a right to take it back on advantageous terms at some later date – by way of either repurchase or leaseback. The difference between the two considerations is treated as if it were a premium paid by the purchaser for the right to use the property during the intervening period.

Furthermore, if a landlord could charge a premium but does not do so (eg where he charges less than a rack rent, but with no premium), and the tenant subsequently realises the premium value of the property by assigning his lease for a consideration, the tenant may then be liable to tax on the sum he receives for his assignment in place of the landlord. Generally such leases will not have been granted at arm's length. Watch also the position of the assignee.

The provisions do not normally apply to a 'premium' received by a lessee for the assignment of an existing lease (as opposed to the grant of a new lease), unless it represents the assignment of a lease originally granted at an under-value or there is some arrangement for repurchase or leaseback at a later date, as above.

No provision is made for the deduction of expenses, except where the recipient of the sum has himself paid a premium to a superior landlord who has been taxed thereon. Where the premium is itself received in instalments, the taxpayer may elect to pay the tax in instalments also (ICTA 1988, s. 34(8)).

Part disposal

The receipt of a sum by way of premium is, in general, regarded as a part disposal of the property. The following points should also be noted.

Any balance of premium, etc. not taxed under this chapter, then falls to be considered in terms of other taxes: including whether it represents a trading receipt in respect of the part disposal of dealing stock; whether it falls within the legislation covering sale and leaseback arrangements; or finally as a part disposal under the capital gains tax legislation.

Value Added Tax

The scope of VAT is framed so as to be extremely wide and the term 'supply of services' includes anything done for a consideration including, if so done, the granting, assignment or surrender of any right (VATA 1994, s. 5(2)(b)). Customs & Excise considers that the payment of a premium from the landlord to the tenant to induce the tenant to enter into the lease is consideration for the supply of a service; the premium is standard-rated. Where the payment is from the tenant to the landlord (to induce the landlord to accept the surrender of the lease where, for example, it has become onerous) Customs & Excise contends that the landlord is making a supply that is exempt unless the landlord has exercised the taxation option.

Tax implications for tenants

Where a landlord is assessed to tax under these provisions, and the tenant paying the premium himself sub-lets the property, or occupies it for the purposes of his trade, he is given some tax relief in respect of that part of the premium taxable in the landlord's hands.

Where a premium is forgone by the landlord, and the tenant subsequently 'cashes in' on this benefit by assigning his lease for a sum of money, he may well find himself taxable on the same basis that the landlord would have been, had he actually charged the premium forgone – and possibly also a third-party assignee of the lease, on a subsequent sale of the lease.

Finally, where a person is liable to pay a premium direct to a non-resident, he may be obliged to deduct income tax therefrom and account for it to the Inland Revenue.

2.6.2   Taxable situations

Grant of leases

The provisions apply to a premium that is required to be paid under the terms of a lease granted for a term not exceeding 50 years in respect of an interest in property in the UK, where any rental income arising is assessable to taxation under the provisions of Schedule A (ICTA 1988, s. 34(1) – and see also ICTA 1988, s. 15).

The provisions also apply to any like sum, whether required under the terms of the lease or under the terms subject to which it is granted, and whether or not described as a premium, and whether paid to the landlord himself or to a person connected with him (see below). They would thus apply to 'key money' or any other sum paid on entry to a leased property, such as any excess over a reasonable amount paid for fixtures and fittings. They also apply to a *grassum* in Scotland. For this purpose a lease includes an agreement for a lease and tenancy, but not a mortgage of property (ICTA 1988, s. 24(1) and (5)).

Surrenders, waivers or variations of leases

Other sums received in respect of a lease of not more than 50 years may be accorded similar treatment.

Thus where, under the terms of his lease, a tenant pays a sum in lieu of rent (or part thereof) for any period, or as a consideration for the surrender of a lease, the amount so paid is treated in the same way as a premium for these purposes (ICTA 1988, s. 34(4)).

Again an amount paid by a tenant in consideration for the variation or waiver of the terms of his lease, otherwise than a payment by way of rent, is treated as a premium for these purposes (ICTA 1988, s. 34(5)). A general payment to avoid proceedings for breach of the terms of a lease and its forfeiture is regarded as a payment for the variation of a lease (*Banning v Wright* (1972) 48 TC 421).

Tenant's improvements

A charge also arises if the tenant is obliged to carry out any work on the premises under the terms of the lease granted. The landlord is deemed to have received a premium equivalent to the increase in the current value of his reversionary interest in the property attributable to such work. The increase is ascertained by comparing the value of the landlord's interest with the value if no such terms had been included in the lease – both being ascertained at a time immediately after the commencement of the lease.

Where the landlord is an intermediate landlord and his reversionary interest only lasts for a short period before the property reverts to his superior landlord, no problem should arise. Nor should there be any problem with regard to specialised improvements, such as fittings, etc. of no general value other than specifically to the tenant.

> ## Example 2.2
>
> Andy Wood grants a lease of land for a term of 25 years. His tenant agrees that, in consideration for the lease (ie as part of the terms under which it is granted), he will put up a building on the land. The tenant negotiates a lower rent – understandably, since he will never obtain full benefit from the building, which will revert back to Andy Wood at the end of the lease.
>
> Andy Wood's reversionary interest in the property (including the right to rental income) is valued at £150,000 immediately after the lease is granted – but would only be worth £125,000 if his tenant had not undertaken to carry out the building work but was still liable to pay the same reduced rent. Andy Wood is then taxable as if he had received a premium of £25,000 (£150,000 − £125,000).

Expenditure incurred by the tenant on repairs, etc. which, if borne by the landlord, would be allowable for deduction against rental income, is not however treated as a taxable sum or a premium under these provisions (ICTA 1988, s. 34(3)).

A landlord who is assessed on a deemed premium in respect of tenant's improvements is entitled to treat the amount assessed as an expense in computing the capital gains tax liability on a subsequent disposal of the property (TCGA 1992, Sch. 8, Para. 7).

However no similar relief is given to a property dealer in respect of tenant's improvements to trading stock (ICTA 1988, s. 99).

Sales with right to repurchase

In the absence of special provisions, it would be possible to get around the provisions discussed above by assigning the grantor's interest subject to a right to have it assigned back to him at some future time instead of granting a lease. This is counteracted by ICTA 1988, s. 36 which provides that such an arrangement is to be treated in the same way as the grant of a lease for a premium where:

- the length of the lease is the time between the assignment and repurchase, and
- the notional premium is the difference between the consideration for the assignment and the consideration for the repurchase.

If the date of the repurchase is not fixed, then the earliest possible date is taken (ICTA 1988, s. 36(1)).

If the consideration for the repurchase varies with the repurchase date, the lowest possible consideration is taken. The assessment may then be revised on the basis of the actual figures if the taxpayer so claims. The claim must be made within six years after the date of repurchase (ICTA 1988, s. 36(2)).

The provisions apply where a person connected with the assignor has the right of repurchase.

Example 2.3

Oliver Mills owns waste land ripe for development. Thomas Bridges, a contractor, is willing to pay £5,000 for dumping waste material thereon. They arrange that, instead of charging a rental royalty for dumping rights, Oliver Mills sells the land for £6,000, but has an option to repurchase it three years later at a price of £1,000. Thus he receives his fee of £5,000 and recovers the land thereafter. The difference between the two considerations is treated as a premium received by Oliver Mills in consideration for the grant of a three-year lease.

The amount taxed as income is treated as part of the Schedule A profit (ICTA 1988, s. 36(4A)).

Sales with right to leaseback

Similar provisions apply where an interest in land is sold under terms that provide for the grant of a lease out of that interest back to the vendor or to a person connected with him (see below) – as if the grant of the lease were a reconveyance. The vendor/lessee is treated as paying a consideration for the reconveyance equal to any premium actually payable under the leaseback, together with the value of the purchaser's reversionary interest immediately after the lease had started to run as ascertained at the date of sale (s. 36(3) to (5), ICTA 1988).

Example 2.4

If in **Example 2.3**, instead of retaining an option to repurchase his land, Oliver Mills arranges to lease it back for a period of 99 years at a rent of £100 per annum, he is still taxable under these provisions. If, for example, Thomas Bridges' subsequent reversionary interest in the land (the right to receive £100 per annum for the next 99 years, and the prospect of vacant possession thereafter) is worth say £1,000, the deemed premium amounts to £5,000 (proceeds £6,000, less value retained by purchaser £1,000).

These provisions do not apply when the leaseback is granted and begins to run within one month of sale – since it is hardly likely that any benefit to the vendor/lessee could be regarded as a rental benefit for such a short period. Thus the provisions would not apply in the case of an ordinary sale and leaseback arrangement carried out as a finance-raising transaction. However special provisions may otherwise apply to the proceeds of such an arrangement if the interest in property disposed of consists of a leasehold interest with not more than 50 years to run and the leaseback is for not more than 15 years. Further provisions may apply to restrict the tax allowance in respect of any rental payments made under such arrangements if they exceed the rack rent of the property.

Premiums forgone

Whilst the provisions do not apply to notional disposals by way of gift, etc., unless a premium is actually received, a situation can arise where a landlord forgoes a premium and the tenant realises the amount forgone by selling the benefit of his lease.

Where, therefore, a landlord grants a lease for a term not exceeding 50 years and the rent payable under that lease is not at a rack rent, or if otherwise having regard to the terms of the lease the landlord could require the payment of a premium or an additional premium if the lease were at arm's length, then if the tenant subsequently assigns the lease for some consideration, that consideration may be taxed in the tenant's hands as if he receives a premium. The assessment is limited to the amount of the premium forgone by the landlord. This deemed premium is treated as if it were received by the tenant in respect of a lease for the original term of the lease, not just the remaining term. Moreover, if the consideration for the assignment is less than the amount of premium forgone by the landlord, and the assignee subsequently sells on the lease himself, he may also be taxed on the consideration he receives up to the balance of that excess. The provisions can apply through any number of assignees.

Example 2.5

James Moore leases a property to his sister Janet for a term of 20 years at a rent of £1,000 and, since the rack rent value is much higher, he would be able to ask a premium of £20,000 in an arm's length transaction but in fact charged none. Janet Moore subsequently sells her lease to Brian Wall (an independent third party) for £15,000. She is assessed to tax as if she herself had received a premium of that amount, but in respect of the original 20-year period.

Subsequently Brian Wall re-assigns the lease for the sum of £25,000. He is also taxable as if part of that sum is a premium – even though both his transactions are at arm's length. The amount treated as a premium is £5,000 – being the difference between the premium forgone by James Moore and the deemed premium taxed in Janet Moore's hands (but restricted to the difference between the price paid and that received by him, if necessary) – again attributable to the whole 20-year period.

In case of difficulty, those concerned can seek protection by arranging for a statement to be submitted to the Inspector of Taxes, showing whether or not a charge arises under these provisions, with a request that the Inspector certifies the accuracy of the statement if he is so satisfied (ICTA 1988, s. 35(1) to (3)).

Such transactions may well of course involve other tax situations. In particular the original grant of a lease at an undervalue between connected persons gives rise to a part disposal for capital gains tax purposes on a notional basis in the hands of the lessor. Thus for capital gains tax purposes the lessor is taxed on the notional premium, whereas for these purposes the lessee is assessed.

Receipts by other persons

It may be that the premium, or deemed premium, is paid to some other person, other than the landlord himself. If it falls to be taxed under the provisions explained above, such other person receiving the payment is charged to tax, rather than the landlord – except in the case of a cash premium required under the original lease, where the recipient is not connected with the landlord (ICTA 1988, s. 34(6) and (7)).

2.6.3 Term of the lease

The term of a lease for the above purposes is generally ascertained under the provisions of that lease, but subject to the following rules:

- if the terms of a lease, for example in respect of forfeiture, or other circumstances render it unlikely that the lease will run beyond a date before the expiry of the term provided in the lease, and the premium is not greater than the amount that would be required for such a shorter lease, the term is taken as ending not later than on that date;
- if the term of the lease can be extended by the tenant, one may take account of circumstances whereby it is likely that he would extend the lease,
- if the tenant, or any person connected with him, is or may become entitled to the grant of a further lease of the same premises or part of them, the lease may be treated as continuing until the expiry of that further lease.

These rules are applied by reference to the facts either known or ascertainable at the time of the grant of the lease, or its waiver or variation. It is assumed that the landlord and tenant are acting at arm's length, and anti-avoidance provisions are included if any benefits, etc. are given to secure a tax advantage here. The rules apply to leases granted, varied or waived after 12 June 1969. Somewhat different rules may apply to the determination of the term of a lease granted before that date (ICTA 1988, s. 38(1) to (4) and (7), and Sch. 30, Paras. 2, 3).

Where a sum is received in lieu of rent, or for the variation or waiver of the terms of a lease, the duration of that lease for these purposes is taken as being the period in respect of which the sum is paid. Thus a payment under a 60-year lease to reduce the rents payable over the next 20 years is treated as a premium under a 20-year lease (ICTA 1988, s. 34(4)(*a*) and (5)(*a*)).

Where the terms of a lease provide that the tenant may terminate the lease at a specified time on payment of a specified sum, the term of the lease as respects that sum ends at that specified time if in fact the tenant exercises his right of termination (Inland Revenue Assessment Procedures Manual, paragraph AP 1492).

Similarly, in the case of a sale with a right to reconveyance or leaseback, the term of the deemed lease is taken as the period between the date of sale and the earliest date allowed for the vendor to re-acquire the property under the terms of that sale (ICTA 1988, s. 36(1)).

2.6.4   Connected persons

For the above purposes one person is connected with another as follows:

- an individual is connected with his relatives (brother, sister, ancestor or lineal descendant), and the individual's husband or wife and their relatives;
- a trustee is connected with the settlor of the trust, and any person connected with the settlor, and with a company connected with the settlement;
- a partner is connected with his partners, and their husbands, wives and relatives (but not in-laws), except in relation to partnership assets under bona fide commercial arrangements;
- companies are connected with each other if they fall under certain common control provisions;
- a company is connected with another person if that person, together with any persons connected with him , has control of the company,
- finally, any two or more persons acting together to control a company are treated as connected with one another in relation to that company (see ICTA 1988, s. 839).

2.6.5 Time at which charge arises

The general rule is that the deemed rent arises at the time when the lease is granted (ICTA 1988, s. 34(1)).

However, where a premium is payable under the terms of a lease in lieu of rent or for the surrender of the lease, the deemed rent arises when the premium becomes payable (s. 34(4)(*b*)).

Where a premium is payable for the variation or waiver of the terms of a lease, the deemed rent arises when the contract providing for the variation or waiver is entered into (s. 34(5)(*b*)).

2.7 Computations

2.7.1 Basic charge

The proportion of premium taxed in this way is equivalent to the whole amount of the premium, less a reduction of 2 per cent or 1/50th for each year of the term of the lease other than the first year. Only whole years are taken into account. Thus a lease granted for five and a half years gives rise to an 8 per cent deduction (2 per cent for each of four years), so that 92 per cent of the premium is taxed as if it were rental income. In the same way a lease granted for one year 11 months is taxable in full (ICTA 1988, s. 34(1)).

Example 2.6

Harry Cliffe grants a lease for a term of eight years at a premium of £10,000. He is liable to tax on a proportion thereof, assessable as if it were rental income under Schedule A, calculated as follows:

		£
Premium received		10,000
Less: Deductions		
Term of lease	8 years	
Less one	1	
Net	7	
$7 \times 2\% = 14\%$		1,400
Taxable as rental income		£8,600

Under the Schedule A rules, the principles applicable to the calculation of trading profits apply, so bad debt relief could be claimed for any unpaid amount.

In the case of a sale with a right to reconveyance, if the date of reconveyance is not fixed but the price for reconveyance is, the price is taken as equal to the lowest amount possible under the terms of the sale. The vendor may then, within six years after reconveyance, reclaim any tax overpaid by adjusting the original assessment to an assessment based on the actual date and consideration for the reconveyance (ICTA 1988, s. 36(2)).

Example 2.7

Looking again at the deal between Oliver Mills and Thomas Bridges, assume that they agree another variation – whereby Thomas Bridges buys the land for £10,000 and agrees to sell it back for £8,000, reduced by £1,000 for each year that he retains the land with a minimum of £2,000.

Oliver Mills is initially assessed as follows:

		£
Sale price		10,000
Minimum repurchase price		2,000
Deemed premium		8,000
Less: Deduction		
Deemed term of 'lease'	6 years*	
Less one	1	
Net	5	
5 × 2% = 10%		800
Initially taxable as rental income		£7,200

(*The earliest date the land can be repurchased at the minimum price.)

Three years later Oliver Mills buys the land back for £5,000, under the terms of his agreement. He claims that the original assessment be recomputed as follows:

	£
Sale price	10,000
Repurchase price	5,000
Deemed premium	5,000
Less: Deduction	
Deemed term of 'lease' 3 years*	
Less one 1	
Net 2	
2 × 2% = 4%	200
Taxable as rental income	£4,800

He thus claims tax repayment on £2,400 (£7,200 − £4,800) initially overcharged.

2.7.2   Deductions

Expenses are, in principle, capable of being deducted for income tax purposes under the normal business tax rules. They are however likely to be capital rather than revenue and therefore will not be deductible.

Premiums paid

In the same way no deduction is normally allowed in respect of the cost of the property – not even a premium paid to a superior landlord. However some deduction may be allowed from premiums taxable in this way, in respect of any premium paid by a sub-landlord to his superior landlord on which the superior landlord himself has suffered tax under these provisions (or would be assessed but for some tax exemption). But if the superior landlord is taxed on a deemed premium in respect of tenant's improvements, and the sub-landlord can already claim capital allowances in respect of the expenditure under the provisions explained in **Chapter 5**, no further relief is given here.

Relief

The deduction is calculated by taking a fraction of that part of the premium that is assessed as income in the hands of the superior landlord, equal to A/B where A is the period for which the premium is received by the sub-landlord, and B is the period for which the premium is paid to the superior landlord – the term in both cases being ascertained under the rules set out at **2.2** above. The deduction is given against the taxable proportion of the premium received by the sub-landlord, rather than the gross premium before calculating the taxable amount (ICTA 1988, s. 37).

Example 2.8

In **Example 2.6** above, Harry Cliffe is taxed on £8,600 out of £10,000 received as a premium. Suppose that his tenant, Alfred Mason, sub-lets the property for a period of five years at a premium of £6,000. The proportion taxable as rental income in Alfred Mason's hands is calculated as follows:

		£
Premium received		6,000
Less: Deduction		
Term of sub-lease	5 years	
Less one	1	
	4	
4 × 2% = 8%		480
Taxable as rental income		£5,520
Less: Relief for premium taxed		
in landlord's hands –		
Premium × A/B		
£8,600 × 5/8 =		5,375
Reduced taxable amount		£4,145

Sale and repurchase

As noted above, the sale of land with a right to repurchase may be treated as if the difference between the sale consideration and the repurchase price was a premium on the grant of a lease taxable on the original vendor. However, the original purchaser is not entitled to any tax deduction in respect of the vendor's tax charge – neither against any premium the original purchaser himself receives as above, nor against subsequent rental income or trading profits as below (ICTA 1988, s. 37(1)).

Rental deductions: sub-landlords and traders

Where a sub-landlord does not himself receive a premium but only a rental income under his sub-letting, or if the premium received is insufficient to allow full offset of the relief available as above, he is allowed an additional deduction in computing rental profits under Schedule A as if the appropriate fraction of that part of the premium assessed on the superior landlord was paid by him as rent – spread equally over the actual period of his lease. Apportionment on a time basis to accounting periods is required where the lease is assured, or ends, part way through an accounting period. No relief is available, however, for expenditure on tenant's improvements carried out by the intermediate landlord if they qualify for capital allowances – see **Chapter 5** (ICTA 1988, s. 37).

Example 2.9

If, in **Example 2.8**, Alfred Mason sub-lets the property but does not charge any premium, he can deduct £1,075 (1/8 × £8,600, taxable in his landlord's hands) from his rental receipts each year for the whole eight-year period.

If he charges a premium as above, he uses up this relief for the first five years against his own taxable premium – so that a rental deduction of £1,075 is only available against rents from a subsequent letting in years 6 to 8.

If he only charges a premium of £3,000 (taxable £2,760), he does not require the whole of the relief available in years 1 to 5 against the taxable premium and can spread the balance, £2,615, as if he paid rent of £523 per annum in those years – reverting to £1,075 per annum again in years 6 to 8.

Somewhat similarly, where a lessee pays a premium in respect of property used in connection with a trade carried on by him, other than a deemed premium in respect of tenant's improvements where the trader can claim capital allowances – see **Chapter 5** – and part of that premium is assessed on the landlord under these provisions (or would be assessed but for some tax exemption) the tenant trader is allowed an additional deduction in computing the profits of his trade. The proportion of the premium assessed on the landlord is spread equally over the whole of the relevant period and, so long as the tenant trader continues to use the property in connection with his trade, he may deduct the appropriate proportion each year as if it were additional rent paid by him in that year. If the tenant has already been allowed some deduction against, for example, a taxable premium received by him under a partial sub-letting of his property, no further relief is available for that amount – only any unrelieved balance (ICTA 1988, s. 87).

Where the lease is assigned, the balance of any relief is available to the assignee (ICTA 1988, s. 87(2)). If the lease is surrendered to the landlord there is no mechanism for clawing back the allowance given nor for allowing the balance of the relief that would have been available.

Whilst the computation of Schedule A profits for income tax proceeds by applying business computation rules, relief is not available under s. 87 to a tenant liable under Schedule A.

Surplus trading premises sub-let at a loss

Where premises which have been occupied for the purposes of a trade have become surplus to requirements, and have been sub-let at a loss, the net rental deficit is allowed as an expense in computing the profits of the trade (*Hyett(HMIT) v Lennard* (1940) 23 TC 346). If the trader subsequently pays a premium to the landlord to vary the terms of the lease (eg to reduce the outstanding term), it is doubtful whether he can obtain relief under ICTA 1988, s. 87 for the taxable part of the premium. The premises are not occupied for the purposes of the trade during the relevant period and are not regarded as dealt with as 'property employed for the purposes of a trade' for the purposes of s. 87(4). A possible solution for a corporate trader is to extract the property from the computations for the trade and deal with the sub-letting as a Schedule A source, with any loss being set off against total income, etc. under s. 392A. For an individual or partnership, however, this would simply generate a Schedule A loss which could only be carried forward against future Schedule A profits under s. 379A.

Information and notification

An assessment to taxation under these provisions may not necessarily just affect the person being assessed to tax. In particular it may affect the relief obtained by a tenant paying the premium, if the tenant himself sub-lets the property, or if he occupies the premises in the course of the trade. Accordingly, where it appears to an Inspector of Taxes that a determination of any liability under these provisions may also affect other persons, he is obliged to give them due notice of his proposal to make a determination and to advise them of their rights. Such other persons may then object to the proposed determination within 30 days of that notice. Failing any such objection, the Inspector can then carry on and settle the matter without further regard to the rights of other persons. If an objection is raised, it is treated as an appeal and the determination of the appeal is binding on all concerned. The Inspector is given powers to acquire information to enable him to give such notice as may be appropriate (ICTA 1988, s. 42).

2.7.3 Exemptions and reliefs

Exemptions

Since the amount chargeable under these provisions is assessed as rental income under Schedule A, it follows that any general tax exemptions and reliefs available in respect of tax charged under those heads also apply in respect of the charge to tax here.

Payment of tax by instalments

In addition, special relief is granted to allow the tax to be paid in instalments where the premium is itself received in instalments.

Payment may be made by instalments if the landlord can satisfy the Inland Revenue that he would otherwise suffer undue hardship. The number and amount of the instalments is at the discretion of the Inland Revenue (subject to a maximum period of eight years ending no later than the time at which the final instalment is due) (ICTA 1988, s. 34(8)).

The Inland Revenue's policy regarding payment by instalments is as follows:

'In considering whether undue hardship would arise, the Revenue would look primarily to the question whether the vendor or disponer could reasonably be expected to pay the tax on the full amount immediately, in the light of the resources made available by the particular transaction involved. Regard would not normally be paid to the other resources of the taxpayer if it could be shown that the instalment arrangement was in the circumstances, and apart from any tax considerations, a normal commercial arrangement and reflected a genuine deferment of the enjoyment of the consideration. The Revenue practice would, of coures, be kept under review, in the light of its effect on actual cases arising.

[Parliamentary Debates, House of Commons, 22 June 1972, Official Report, Standing Committee E, Cols. 1358–1359.]'

Where payment of tax by instalments is agreed, interest is only payable on the instalments of tax if such instalments are paid late.

2.7.4 Losses

Where a landlord is also a tenant then the amount treated as rent paid may be deducted from any amounts treated as rent received of a Schedule A business (ICTA 1988, s. 37).

Similarly the allowance to a trader in respect of a premium taxable in the hands of his landlord may give rise to, or increase, a Schedule D Case I loss in respect of his trade.

2.7.5 Non-residents

Where a premium is paid direct to a person whose usual place of abode is outside the UK, the person making the payment may be required to deduct income tax at the basic rate from that proportion of the premium that is chargeable to tax under these provisions (as if it were a payment falling within ICTA 1988, ss. 349 and 350) – leaving it to the non-resident (strictly, a landlord whose usual place of abode is outside the UK) to recover any over-deduction of tax thus suffered.

Detailed regulations provide for a comprehensive tax deduction and accounting mechanism. The regulations permit agents to register branches with the Inland Revenue. Agents and, where applicable, tenants will be required to account for tax quarterly (calendar quarters) in much the same way as companies account for tax on distributions (ICTA 1988, s. 42A). Payments may be made gross where the Revenue has approved an application by the landlord and issued a notice to the tenant or agent.

2.7.6 Overseas property

The basis of computation of the Schedule D Case V profit is essentially the same as the Schedule A rules (ICTA 1988, ss. 65A, 70A).

This means that part of any premium received for the grant of a lease or sub-lease of property situated abroad of less than 50 years can be brought within the Case V computation on the same basis as applies for Schedule A purposes.

Whether a receipt is a premium will need to be determined by reference to the property law applicable in the country where the property is located.

The provisions relating to artificial transactions in land will not need to be considered because, by implication, those provisions only apply where any part of the land is situated in the UK (ICTA 1988, s. 776(14)).

2.8 Reverse premiums

2.8.1 The charge to tax as income

A reverse premium receivable on the *grant* of a lease or other estate or interest in land is taxed as income. Where the lease is entered into for the purposes of a trade, the reverse premium is a trading receipt. In other cases, it is a Schedule A receipt (FA 1999, Sch. 6). A reverse premium payable on the *assignment* of a lease is not caught by these rules unless the assignor is connected with the landlord or acting as nominee or at the direction of the landlord, or of a person connected with the landlord (*Tax Bulletin*, Issue 44, December 1999).

In general, the premium is brought into account in the chargeable period in which it is receivable, on normal accounting principles. Where the parties are connected persons and the arrangements are non-arm's length arrangements, the whole amount or value of the premium is brought into account in the period in which the grant occurred. However, if the grantee enters into the lease, etc. for the purposes of a trade, profession or vocation that had not commenced at the time of the grant, the reverse premium is brought into account in the first period of account of trading (FA 1999, Sch, Para. 3).

There is no corresponding statutory deduction for the payment of the premium, but where it is paid in the course of a trade (eg by a property developer) it will be deductible as an expense in computing trading profits under general principles. In other cases, it would have to be argued that the premium was enhancement expenditure, in that the grant of the lease enhanced the value of the landlord's interest in the property concerned.

The rules catch reverse premiums payable to the tenant or to a person connected with him, and whether or not paid by the person granting the interest or by a person connected with him (FA 1999, Sch.6, Para. 1).

2.8.2 Commencement date

The rules apply to any reverse premium received on or after 9 March 1999, unless it was a payment or benefit to which the recipient was entitled immediately before that date (FA 1999, Sch.6, Para. 1). In determining whether he was so entitled before 9 March 1999, no account is taken of any arrangements made on or after that date. The Revenue has given the following examples to illustrate this:

- If an agreement for a lease was made on or before 8 March 1999 without provision for a reverse premium, but the arrangements were varied on or after 9 March 1999 to incorporate a reverse premium, then the reverse premium is taxable.
- If an agreement for a lease was made on or before 8 March 1999 incorporating a provision for a reverse premium of say £1 million, and the arrangements were varied on or after 9 March 1999 to incorporate an increased reverse premium of say £1.5 million then the increase of £0.5 million in the reverse premium is taxable.

2.8.3 Meaning of 'reverse premium'

A reverse premium is a payment or other benefit received by way of inducement in connection with the grant. Clearly, the most common form of inducement is a cash payment from the landlord to the tenant. However, a payment to a connected third party is also caught. Other forms of inducement include:

- rent-free periods
- a contribution to tenant's costs, such as start-up, fitting out or re-location, and
- the assumption by the landlord of the tenant's liabilities, such as any continuing obligation to pay rent under an existing lease, or the payment of a capital sum to terminate an existing lease.

Not all of the above examples give rise to a tax liability under the lease premium rules. *Tax Bulletin*, Issue 44 gives the following examples.

Taxable

- Contributions towards specified tenant's costs, such as fitting out, start-up or relocation;
- sums paid to third parties to meet obligations of the tenant, such as rent to a landlord under an old lease, or a capital sum to terminate such a lease,
- the effective payment of cash by other means, for example, the landlord's writing off of a sum which the tenant owes.

Not taxable

- The grant of a rent-free period of occupation;
- replacement by agreement of an existing lease at a rent which a change in market conditions has made onerous by a new lease at a lower rent,
- replacement by agreement of an existing lease containing some other provision the tenant has found onerous by a new lease without the onerous condition.

Fitting out costs

Fitting out costs are usually the responsibility of the tenant. The key issue here is whether the expenditure relates to landlord's fixtures or to tenant's fixtures or chattels.

If the tenant incurs expenditure on landlord's fixtures, and the landlord reimburses the cost, that reimbursement is not a taxable reverse premium. This would cover expenditure on the fabric of the building itself.

However, if the landlord reimburses the costs of tenant's fixtures or chattels, that is a taxable reverse premium. The main exception is where the tenant's expenditure qualifies for capital allowances. In this case, the amount reimbursed is set off against the expenditure, and capital allowances may be claimed on the excess only (FA 1999, Sch. 6, Para. 5).

There is likely to be a mismatch only where the landlord reimburses tenant's expenditure which does not qualify for capital allowances, such as expenditure on partitions which are not required to be moved, for example.

2.8.4 Exclusions from the charge

Where the tenant occupies the property concerned as his only or main residence, the reverse premium is not taxable under the reverse premium rules.

Any reverse premium received for the grant or assignment of an interest in land as the first leg of a sale and leaseback transaction is not taxed under these rules. The provisions of ICTA 1988, ss. 779, 780 apply (as to which, see **Chapter 1**).

2.8.5 Connected persons and relevant arrangements

The definition of connected persons in ICTA 1988, s. 839 applies. Relevant arrangement means the grant of the interest and any arrangements entered into in connection with it.

2.8.6 Capital gains tax and VAT

The capital gains tax treatment of reverse premiums is dealt with in **Chapter 8**.

The VAT treatment of reverse premiums is dealt with in **Chapter 11**.

2.9 Rent factoring

2.9.1 Introduction

The legislation described below applies to companies that participate in rent factoring schemes. It applies in relation to transactions entered into on or after 21 March 2000 that are 'finance agreements'. It provides for amounts received under such agreements to be charged to tax as income under

Schedule A, rather than under the capital gains tax rules (see now ICTA 1988, ss. 43A–43G). Typically, the schemes involve a company giving up the right to future rental income in respect of land in the UK by transferring the rights to receive rents or by granting a lease at a premium.

2.9.2 Finance agreements

A transaction is a finance agreement if a company's accounts, drawn up in accordance with normal accounting practice, record a financial obligation in relation to the money 'received' in the transaction (ICTA 1988, s. 43A(1)).

Broadly speaking, 'normal accounting practice' means UK GAAP. References to a company's accounts include references to the consolidated accounts of the group of which it is a member. The 'recipient' of money is the company that takes it into account for corporation tax purposes or would if it were resident in the UK.

2.9.3 The charge to tax

When a person receives a 'finance amount', the full amount received is treated as rent taxable as profit of a Schedule A business in the chargeable period in which the finance agreement is made (ICTA 1988, s. 43B). A 'finance amount' is the amount advanced under a rent factoring transaction.

2.9.4 Exceptions from the charge

The charge under ICTA 1988, s. 43B does not apply in the following circumstances:

(a) where the financial obligation in respect of the finance amount is to be reduced over a term exceeding 15 years;

(b) where the arrangements for the reduction of the financial obligation depend substantially on the entitlement to capital allowances of a person who is not connected to the person transferring the right to receive rent;

(c) where the finance agreement is for the sale of land with a right to reconveyance – in which case, ICTA 1988, s. 36 applies;

(d) where the sale and leaseback provisions of ICTA 1988, s. 780 apply, or

(e) where the finance amount is taxed in computing the profits of a trade.

As regards (c), the exception applies if ICTA 1988, s. 36(1) would apply if the reconveyance price was less than the sale proceeds of the land. However, s. 36

is disapplied, so that the new provisions do apply, in relation to a second charge to a rent factoring transaction which takes the form of a sale of an interest in land followed by the grant of a lease back to the vendor.

The exception in (d) does not apply where the computation relates to life assurance business, where special rules apply (ICTA 1988, s. 43F).

2.9.5　Interposed lease

Where the finance amount takes the form of a premium for a lease of land in the UK, the premium is taxed as rental income business in the chargeable period in which the finance agreement is made (ICTA 1988, s. 43D). In a transaction involving a chain of two or more leases the section applies only in relation to the premium reflected by the financial obligation recorded in the accounts.

There are exceptions where:

- the financial obligation is to be reduced over a term exceeding 15 years; or
- the lease has a term not exceeding 15 years, or
- the term of the lease is not significantly different from the term over which the liability is to be reduced.

The existing rules of Schedule A apply in measuring the life of a lease.

There are also exceptions where:

- the arrangements for the reduction of the financial obligation depend substantially on the entitlement to capital allowances of a person who is not connected to the person granting the lease, or
- all or part of the premiums are taxed in computing the profits of a trade (subject to a similar proviso for life insurance companies).

2.9.6　Exclusion of double charge

For leases with terms of more than 15 years but not more than 50 years, where premiums are taxed under the rent factoring legislation, there will not also be a charge under the existing Schedule A provisions.

2.10　Transitional

Whilst the provisions generally only apply to leases granted on or after 4 April 1963, they also apply to a variation or waiver after that date of a lease granted beforehand (ICTA 1988, s. 39(1) and (2)).

Correspondingly no relief is available to a sub-landlord or trading tenant where the premium was paid to a superior landlord before 4 April 1963, even though it might otherwise have been taxed in the hands of the superior landlord if paid after that date (ICTA 1988, s. 37).

The rules for the ascertainment of the term of a lease were altered in June 1969. The rules relating to leases granted before 12 June 1969, except in relation to a subsequent variation or waiver of such a lease or in calculating any trading losses or Schedule A losses carried forward against future profits arising in a later period, are preserved in ICTA 1988, s. 38(7) and Sch. 30.

2.11 Exemptions and reliefs

2.11.1 Charities

Charities are exempt from income tax in respect of income arising under Schedule A or Schedule D from rents or other receipts from an estate, interest or right in or over any land, whether situated in the UK or elsewhere to the extent that the income is actually applied for charitable purposes (ICTA 1988, s. 505).

2.11.2 Approved pension funds

Approved pension funds are exempt from income tax in respect of income arising from investments held for the purposes of the approved scheme (ICTA 1988, s. 592(2)). This covers Schedule A income, and corresponding Schedule D Case V income, from property investments held for the purposes of the scheme. However, if the scheme becomes over-funded, part of the income may become taxable in accordance with the provisions of ICTA 1988, Sch. 22 Para. 7.

However, the exemption for investment income of pension funds does not extend to a pension fund's share of income from a Property Investment LLP of which it is a member (ICTA 1988, s. 659D). A property investment LLP is an LLP whose business consists wholly or mainly in the making of investments in land and the principal part of whose income is derived therefrom (ICTA 1988, s. 842B).

2.11.3 Rent a Room scheme

This scheme provides for exemption from income tax on profits from letting furnished accommodation in the taxpayer's only or main residence, provided that the gross receipts are £4,250 or less in the relevant tax year. If receipts exceed the £4,250 exemption, the excess is treated as the taxable rental income, with no deduction for expenses, instead of the actual profit (F(No2)A 1992, Sch. 10).

Gross receipts include not only rents but also payments for the provision of any other goods or services, such as meals, cleaning, laundry, etc. in connection with the letting.

The scheme does not apply to rooms let as an office or for other business purposes.

The limit of £4,250 is halved if during the relevant tax year someone else received income from letting accommodation in the same property. This may happen where the property is owned jointly.

The exemption need not be claimed. In some circumstances, it might be better to compute the actual profit or loss for the year. An obvious example is where there is a loss.

Further information is available in the Revenue's booklet IR 150.

2.11.4   Furnished holiday lettings

Profits and losses from qualifying furnished holiday lettings are treated as trading profits or losses, rather than as Schedule A profits or losses. The main benefit of this provision is the more generous relief for losses, since Schedule A profits and losses are computed in the same way as trading profits and losses (ICTA 1988, ss. 503, 504). A further benefit is the availability of capital gains tax reliefs such as rollover relief.

For the letting to qualify, the property must be:

- available for holiday letting to the public on a commercial basis for 140 days or more; and
- let commercially for 70 days or more, and
- not occupied for more than 31 days by the same person in any period of seven months,

for the period mentioned below.

The period is:

- in a continuing period of holiday letting, the relevant tax year; or
- in the first year of letting, the 12 months starting with the date of the first letting,

- in the final year of letting, the 12 months ending with the date of the last letting.

Where more than one unit of accommodation is let, it is sufficient that each unit satisfies the 140-day and seven-month rules. The taxpayer may then claim averaging treatment in order to satisfy the 70-day rule (ICTA 1988, s. 504(6)).

An averaging claim must be made within the usual 'two-year' time limit.

Further information is available in the Revenue's booklet IR 150.

2.12   Losses

2.12.1   Schedule A business losses: income tax

General

Where a Schedule A loss arises, it is carried forward to the following year and set off against Schedule A profits of that year. Any unrelieved loss is carried forward to the next year and so on (ICTA 1988, s. 379A(1)).

Overseas property

There is a similar carry forward relief for losses of an overseas property business. The carry forward is, of course, against future profits of that business (ICTA 1988, s. 379B).

Excess capital allowances

To the extent that a Schedule A loss is attributable to the deduction for capital allowances, it may be set off against general income for the year in which it arises. However, if there is a balancing charge, the capital allowances have first to be set against that balancing charge, so that only the net amount is available for relief against total income. There is a corresponding reduction in the amount of loss carried forward (ICTA 1988, s. 379A(2)(a), (3)).

Relief against total income must be claimed by the first anniversary of 31 January following the end of the tax year concerned. This is also the deadline for filing an amended return. The claim should be included in the return or amended return (ICTA 1988, s. 379A(3)).

Agricultural property

To the extent that a Schedule A loss is attributable to allowable agricultural expenses of an agricultural estate, it may be set off against total income of the year of loss (ICTA 1988, s. 379A(2)(b)).

An agricultural estate is any land which is managed as one estate and which consists of or includes agricultural land. For this purpose land includes any houses or other buildings.

Agricultural land means land, houses or buildings in the UK which are occupied for the purposes of husbandry (ICTA 1988, s. 379A(10)).

Allowable agricultural expenses means expenses of maintenance, repairs, insurance or management of the agricultural estate, other than interest on loans. There is an apportionment of expenses where part of an estate is occupied partly for husbandry and partly for other purposes (ICTA 1988, s. 379A(8), (9)).

Furnished holiday lettings

Losses from furnished holiday lettings are dealt with as trading losses (see ICTA 1988, s. 503).

2.12.2   Schedule A business losses: corporation tax

Relief against total profits

Where a Schedule A loss arises in any accounting period, it may be set off against the company's total profits for that accounting period (ICTA 1988, s. 392A(1)).

Any unrelieved loss may be carried forward to the next accounting period if the company carries on the Schedule A business in that period. It may then be treated as a Schedule A loss of that next period, which means that it is available against total profits of that next period, and so on (ICTA 1988, s. 392A(2)).

If the company has an investment business, and its Schedule A business ceases, any unrelieved Schedule A loss can be treated as excess management expenses and relieved under the provisions of ICTA 1988, s. 75.

The reliefs set out above are available where the Schedule A business is carried on, on a commercial basis or in the exercise of statutory functions (ICTA 1988, s. 392A(5)).

Overseas property

Any loss from an overseas property letting business may be carried forward and set off against Schedule D Case V profits from the same business in the next and subsequent accounting periods (ICTA 1988, s. 392B).

This relief is available where the business is carried on on a commercial basis or in the exercise of statutory functions (ICTA 1988, s. 392B(2)).

Group relief

A Schedule A loss may be surrendered under the group relief provisions. However, it is assumed that the loss is first set against the company's total profits for the same accounting period. Only the excess loss is available for group relief.

If the company also has excess charges and management expenses, the excess charges are surrendered first, then the excess Schedule A loss, then the excess management expenses. This order is, in fact, beneficial to the company (ICTA 1988, s. 403(3)).

However, Schedule A losses brought forward from earlier periods are not available for surrender in the current period (ICTA 1988, s. 403ZD(3)(a)).

Group relief is available only where the business is carried on on a commercial basis (ICTA 1988, s. 403ZD(3)(b)), and there is a restriction for dual resident companies (FA 1998, Sch. 4, Para. 37).

Change of ownership

The restrictions on the carry forward of trading losses (ICTA 1988, s. 768) and excess management expenses (ICTA 1988, ss. 768B and 768C) are to apply in relation to Schedule A losses where there is a change of ownership of the company concerned (ICTA 1988, s. 768D).

2.12.3   Furnished holiday lettings

Losses from furnished holiday lettings are dealt with as trading losses (ICTA 1988, s. 503).

2.12.4   Limited partnerships

The restrictions on relief for trading losses which apply in relation to limited partners (ICTA 1988, s. 118, I) are to apply in relation to Schedule A losses (FA 1998, Sch. 5, Para. 35).

2.12.5 Transitional

Any unrelieved excess of old Schedule A expenses for accounting periods ending before 1 April 1998 may be carried forward as a Schedule A loss. Similarly, Case VI losses arising in such accounting periods from furnished lettings may be carried forward as a Schedule A loss (Sch. 5, Para. 71, FA 1998).

2.13 International aspects

2.13.1 Foreign taxes and double taxation agreements

Income from immovable property normally remains taxable in the country in which the property is situated (see, for example, Article 6 of the OECD Model Convention). This includes income that, in the UK, is taxed under Schedule A.

Where the owner or landlord is resident abroad, he may claim relief for any UK tax against the tax payable in his country of residence. The owner or landlord's UK liability is dealt with under the non-resident landlords' scheme, which is discussed below.

Where the owner is resident in the UK but the property is situated abroad, the charge to UK tax is under Schedule D Case V, as explained below. Credit for any foreign tax may be claimed under the UK's unilateral relief provisions (ICTA 1988, ss. 790–797).

In the event that relief for foreign tax is not fully available in this way, any unrelieved tax is treated as an expense.

In the case of a non-domiciled UK resident, double tax relief is given by grossing-up his remittances of foreign income to take account of the tax suffered abroad. UK taxation is then calculated on this grossed up amount, and the tax thus ascertained is offset by the amount of the foreign tax addition (ICTA 1988, ss. 788–806).

2.13.2 Non-residents: the non-resident landlords' scheme

The scheme

ICTA 1988, s. 42A gives the Board power to make regulations for the deduction of tax at source from certain payments of rent and other sums taxable under Schedule A which are made to non-resident landlords, and for the payment of that tax on a quarterly basis.

The regulations are the Taxation of Income from Land (Non-Residents) Regulations 1995 (SI 1995/2902). The scheme is administered by the Centre for Non-Residents, from whom detailed guidance may be obtained in the form of booklet IR 140: *Non-resident Landlords, their Agents and Tenants.* Guidance notes on the operation of the scheme may be accessed from the Revenue's website at www.inlandrevenue.gov.uk/cnr/nr.landlords.htm. The Centre for Non-Residents may be contacted at St John's House, Merton Road, Bootle L69 9BB; tel: 0151 472 6208; fax: 0151 472 6067.

Persons liable to account for tax

Any tenant of property in the UK is required to deduct income tax at the basic rate from any rent or other sums chargeable under Schedule A payable directly to a non-resident landlord if:

- the rent and other sums are in aggregate at the rate of £5200 per annum or more; or
- the Board gives the landlord written notice requiring him to deduct tax.

This applies whether the rent, etc. is payable in the UK or abroad (ICTA 1988, s. 42A(2)(a) and SI 1995/2902, reg. 3).

Any agent in the UK who acts on behalf of a non-resident landlord (a letting agent) and who has power to receive rents, etc. from property in the UK must deduct tax at the basic rate from the net amount remaining after deducting any allowable expenses paid out of the rents, etc. (ICTA 1988, s. 42A(2)(b) and SI 1995/2902 regs. 3 and 9).

Persons who are required to account for tax under these rules are called 'prescribed persons'.

The Revenue has given the following guidance on the sums from which tax is deductible.

'*Examples of rental income*

Rental income includes a wide variety of receipts arising from land and property. In particular, rental income includes:

- income from letting furnished, unfurnished, commercial and domestic premises, and from any land;
- where property is let furnished, any separate sums from the tenant for the use of the furniture;
- rent charges, ground rents and feu duties;
- premiums and other similar lump sums received on the grant of certain leases;
- income arising from the grant of sporting rights, such as fishing and shooting permits;

- income arising from allowing waste to be buried or stored on land;
- income from letting others use land – for example, where a film crew pays to film inside a person's house or on their land;
- grants received from local authorities or others contributing to expenditure which is an allowable expense such as repairs to a let property;
- rental income received through enterprise investment schemes;
- income from caravans or houseboats where these are not moved around various locations;
- service charges received from tenants in respect of services ancillary to the occupation of property, and
- insurance recoveries under policies providing cover against non-payment of rent.'

Premiums

Lump sums received up front for the grant of a lease of 50 years or less are liable to income tax. Such receipts are generally called 'premiums'. They are treated wholly or partly as rental income.

The amount treated as rental income is calculated on a sliding scale which depends on the length of the lease. The rule is that the amount treated as rental income is the premium reduced by 2 per cent of the premium for each complete year of the lease after the first. Thus:

- the full amount of the premium is treated as rental income where the lease is for less than two years;
- 98 per cent of the premium is treated as rental income if the lease is for two years or more but for less than three years;
- 96 per cent of the premium is treated as rental income if the lease is for three years or more but for less than four years;
- and so on until none of the premium is treated as rental income if the lease is for more than 50 years.

More information is provided about premiums in leaflet IR150.

Income which is not rental income

There are certain receipts which arise out of the use of land which are not rental income. These include:

- income from woodlands managed on a commercial basis;
- income from the types of concerns listed below:
  - mines and quarries (including gravel pits, sand pits and brickfields),
  - ironworks, gasworks, salt springs or works, alum mines or works and water works and streams of water,
  - canals, inland navigations, docks, and drains or levels,
  - rights of markets and fairs, tolls, bridges and ferries,
  - railways and other ways,
  - lettings of tied premises by traders, and

- income which arises in the course of carrying on a trade such as running a hotel.

A non-resident landlord is a landlord whose usual place of abode is outside the UK (reg. 1). The landlord may be an individual, a company, the trustees of a settlement, etc. If the landlord is a partnership, each partner is treated as a separate landlord in respect of his share of the Schedule A income. The same applies in relation to joint ownership of property.

The Revenue has given the following guidance on the meaning of 'usual place of abode'.

'Individuals have a usual place of abode outside the UK if they usually live outside the UK. But individuals are not regarded as having a usual place of abode outside the UK if they are temporarily living outside the UK for, say, six months or less.

Companies that have their main office or other place of business outside the UK, and companies incorporated outside the UK, normally have a usual place of abode outside the UK. However, companies which are treated as resident in the UK for tax purposes do not have a usual place of abode outside the UK for the purposes of the NRL scheme even if they are incorporated outside the UK.

Non-resident companies with a UK branch which is chargeable to Corporation Tax do not have a usual place of abode outside the UK for the purposes of the NRL scheme.

Trustees have a usual place of abode outside the UK if all the trustees have a usual place of abode outside the UK (following the rules for individuals and companies, as appropriate). If one or more of the trustees do not have a usual place of abode outside the UK, the trustees are not a non-resident landlord for the purposes of the NRL scheme.'

An agent whose activity on behalf of the non-resident landlord is confined to the provision of legal advice or legal services is not liable to account for tax under the above rules.

Registration with CNRL

A 'prescribed person' is required to notify the Centre for Non-resident Landlords (CNRL) within 30 days of the date on which he became a prescribed person. That date will be the first occasion on or after 6 April 1996 on which he receives rent, etc. as agent for, or pays rent, etc. directly to, a non-resident landlord (SI 1995/2902, reg. 7).

Where the tenant or agent is a partnership, the partnership is treated as a prescribed person (reg. 5).

A letting agency with more than one branch may apply to have each branch treated as a separate 'prescribed person' if the average number of non-resident landlords for each branch is at least five (reg. 6).

Quarterly returns and payment of tax

Each prescribed person must make quarterly returns to CNRL of the amounts for which he is liable to account under the regulations. The procedure is similar to the CT61 procedure by which companies account for tax deducted at source from annual payments. Quarters end on 30 June, 30 September, 31 December and 31 March. Each return must be submitted within 30 days after the end of the quarter to which it relates (SI 1995/2902, reg. 10). Returns are made on Forms NRLQ.

The tax payable for any quarter is due 30 days after the end of the quarter. Interest runs from the due date on tax paid late (reg. 10(5), (6)).

In the case of a tenant, the return for any quarter must show the rents and other sums payable from which tax is deductible and the amount deductible therefrom (reg. 8). Tax is not deductible from rents, etc. payable to a company where that rent, etc. is attributable to a UK branch of the company and is liable to corporation tax (reg. 8(3)). It is up to the tenant to make enquiries regarding the status of the landlord. In certain cases, the landlord may obtain permission from CNRL to receive rents, etc. gross (see below). Where this happens, CNRL will authorise the tenant to pay the rent gross.

In the case of a letting agent, the return will show the rents, etc. receivable on behalf of the non-resident landlord and the expenses payable out of those rents. The agent must account for tax on the excess of rents, etc. receivable over allowable expenses. Where tax is paid for any quarter, and in a subsequent quarter the allowable expenses exceed the income, the excess of expenses may be carried back against rents, etc. received in previous quarters in the same financial year for the same landlord. In this case, there will be a refund of tax for the previous quarter in which the expenses are set off. Failing this, the excess expenses may be carried forward to the next quarter, within the same financial year and in respect of the same landlord. Separate computations are required for each landlord. The Revenue has given the following guidance on allowable expenditure.

'Broadly, in calculating the profits of a rental business expenses are allowable where:

- they are incurred wholly and exclusively for the purposes of the rental business, and
- they are not of a capital nature.

The cost of land and buildings and the cost of improvements and alterations is expenditure of a capital nature.

Subject to [the above points], the following expenses paid by letting agents and tenants will normally be deductible expenses:

- accountancy expenses (incurred in preparing rental business accounts but not for preparing personal tax returns);
- advertising costs of attracting new tenants;
- charges for inventories;
- cleaning;
- costs of rent collection;
- Council Tax while the property is vacant but available for letting;
- gardening;
- ground rent;
- insurance against loss of rents;
- insurance claim fees;
- insurance on buildings and contents;
- interest paid on loans to buy land or property [unless MIRAS relief is claimed];
- interest paid on loans to build or improve premises [unless MIRAS relief is claimed];
- legal and professional fees;
- letting agents' fees;
- maintenance charges made by freeholders, or superior leaseholders, of leasehold property;
- maintenance contracts (for example, gas servicing);
- provision of services (for example, gas, electricity, hot water);
- rates;
- rental warranty and legal expenses insurance;
- repairs which are not significant improvements to the property, including:

  - damp and rot treatment,
  - mending broken windows, doors, furniture, cookers, lifts, etc.,
  - painting and decorating,
  - replacing roof slates, flashing and gutters,
  - repointing, and
  - stone cleaning;

- water rates.

If any expenses which are deductible in computing the profits of the rental business have borne Value Added Tax (VAT) and that VAT cannot be relieved as 'input tax' because, for example, the landlord is not registered for VAT, the deductible expense is the amount inclusive of VAT.

Letting agents and tenants can deduct those expenses which they pay or which are paid on their direction. This means:

- they cannot deduct expenses which the landlord pays, even if they have details of the expenses;
- they cannot deduct expenses which have accrued in a quarter but which have not been paid in the quarter;
- they cannot deduct capital allowances; and
- they cannot deduct any personal allowances due to the landlord.'

Annual return

An annual return is required for each financial year (year to 31 March). This is a summary of the quarterly returns, showing the amount for which the tenant or agent has to account for the financial year. This return is due by 5 July immediately after the end of the year (SI 1995/2902, reg. 11). This return is made on Form NRLA.

Certification, etc.

Any person required to account to the Inland Revenue for tax under this scheme is entitled to deduct and retain that tax from the rents, etc. which he is liable to pay to the non-resident landlord and to be indemnified by the non-resident landlord for all such tax (ICTA 1988, s. 42A(3)). The person must, however, provide the landlord with a certificate for the financial year concerned showing the amount of tax for which he has accounted to the Revenue for that year. This certificate must be provided by 5 July immediately after the end of the year (SI 1995/2902, reg. 12).

Application for payment of rent, etc. gross

A non-resident landlord who can satisfy the Board that he will comply with the tax law as it applies to him may apply to have his rents, etc. paid without deduction of tax (SI 1995/2902, reg. 17). Application is made on Form NRL1 (individuals), NRL2 (companies) or NRL3 (trustees). These forms are obtainable from CNRL. If the Board approves the application, it will notify the tenant or agent accordingly.

If the Board refuses the application, the applicant may appeal to the General Commissioners with the right to opt for the Special Commissioners. Notice of appeal must be given to the Board within 90 days of the date of the notice of refusal (SI 1995/2902, reg. 17(7)–(9)).

Power to raise assessments

The Board may raise an assessment on any prescribed person if it is dissatisfied with any return that he has made or if he has failed to make a return in circumstances where the Board believes that a return should have been made.

Any assessment may be made to the best of the Board's judgement (SI 1995/2902, reg. 10(9)).

Tax charged under an assessment is due 14 days after the date of issue of the notice of assessment unless it is due on an earlier date under the rules set out above (ie 30 days after the end of the quarter to which it relates). There is the usual right of appeal to the Special Commissioners within 30 days (SI 1995/2902, reg. 10(10) and TMA 1970, s. 31(1)(c), (3)).

Penalties

The penalty for a late return is an amount not exceeding £300. If the failure to submit the return continues after this penalty is imposed, there is a further penalty not exceeding £60 per day for each day on which the failure continues.

The penalty for fraudulently or negligently submitting an incorrect return is an amount not exceeding £3,000 (TMA 1970, s. 98, Tables 1 and 2: references to regulations made under ICTA 1988, s. 42A).

Information powers

A prescribed person must maintain sufficient records to show that he has complied with the regulations (SI 1995/2902, reg. 15). These records may be inspected by a Revenue officer (reg. 14). The Board may require any prescribed person to supply it with such information as may reasonably be required to establish that he has complied with the regulations (reg. 13).

More than one letting agent

Where there is more than one letting agent for the same source of income, it is the 'last agent' who must operate the tax deduction scheme. He is the agent who pays the income directly to the landlord (SI 1995/2902, regs. 3(4), 4). However, the agents may jointly elect that one of them (not necessarily the last agent) be responsible. He is referred to as the 'elected agent' (reg. 4(1)).

2.13.3   Transfer of assets abroad

In the absence of special provisions, it would be possible for UK resident persons to avoid tax on rental income, etc. arising from properties situated in the UK by arranging for their interest in the properties to be acquired or held by companies or trusts resident abroad. This is counteracted in a number of ways:

- Income tax at the basic rate on rents payable to non-residents is recoverable from the tenant or agent, who is required to deduct the tax at source from rental payments, as explained above. This limits any avoidance to the difference between the basic rate of income tax and either the higher rate of income tax or the standard rate of corporation tax.

- If the UK person is a company and the interest is held by a subsidiary in a low tax country, the Controlled Foreign Companies legislation will apply.
- If the UK person is an individual who is ordinarily resident in the UK, the provisions described below may have the effect that the rental income arising to the overseas company or trust is deemed to be his income for tax purposes. These provisions are to be found in ICTA 1988, ss. 739–746.

The purpose of s. 739, ICTA 1988 is to counteract the avoidance of income tax, capital gains tax or inheritance tax by individuals who are ordinarily resident in the UK by means of a transfer of assets abroad. The section applies where, as a result of such a transfer, or as a result of the transfer and any associated operations, income becomes payable to persons resident or domiciled outside the UK. If such an individual has power to enjoy the income, whether immediately or at some future time, then the income is deemed to be his income. It is chargeable to tax under Schedule D Case VI. Credit is given for any tax deducted at source.

Further, if such an individual receives a capital sum that is connected with the transfer or the associated operations, then the income of the non-resident person is deemed to be his income. A capital sum includes a loan or the repayment of a loan.

'Associated operations' and 'power to enjoy' are defined in ICTA 1988, s. 742. Simple situations are where:

- the overseas person is a company and the individuals control the company;
- the overseas person is a settlement and the individuals are beneficiaries, even if only discretionary beneficiaries,
- the overseas person is a company or settlement and the individuals are loan creditors.

The above provisions are supplemented by provisions which apply where an individual who is ordinarily resident in the UK receives a benefit which is not otherwise chargeable to income tax, by virtue or in consequence of the transfer of assets or associated operations (ICTA 1988, s. 740). The individual is chargeable on the greater of the value of the benefit and the accumulated income of the non-resident person, unless that income is caught by ICTA 1988, s. 739.

The above legislation does not apply if the transfer and associated operations were bona fide commercial transactions not designed to avoid tax, or if none of the purposes of the transactions was the avoidance of tax.

The legislation applies irrespective of whether the individuals were ordinarily resident or not at the time when the transfer took place (ICTA 1988, s. 739(1A)).

2.13.4 Transfer pricing

The transfer pricing provisions of ICTA 1988, Sch. 28AA apply to the letting of land and buildings between companies under common control. Such companies could be parent and subsidiary, fellow subsidiaries or parallel companies controlled by the same persons.

If the rent payable exceeds a market rent, then the excess is disallowed in computing the lessee's profits.

In the absence of such provisions, profits could be stripped out of the UK by excessive rental charges. Although such rents are subject to deduction of tax under the non-resident landlords' scheme, nevertheless if the tenant's profits are otherwise chargeable to income tax at the higher rate or to corporation tax at the standard rate, tax could be avoided.

The transfer pricing provisions apply automatically under the corporation tax self-assessment regime. Companies are required to create and keep records to substantiate their transfer pricing policies and any adjustments made in their self-assessment returns. The Revenue has issued the following guidance on record-keeping.

> 'Taxpayers should prepare and retain such documentation as is reasonable given the complexity or otherwise of the relevant transations (or series of transactions) and which identifies:
>
> - relevant commercial or financial relations falling within the scope of the new legislation;
> - the nature and terms (including prices) of relevant transactions (including transactions which form a series, and any relevant offsetting transactions);
> - the method or methods by which the nature and terms of relevant transactions were arrived at, including any study of comparables and any functional analysis undertaken;
> - how that method has resulted in arm's lengths terms, etc. or, where it has not, what computational adjustment is required and how it has been calculated. This will usually include an analysis of market data or other information on third party comparables;

- the terms of relevant commercial arrangements with both third party and group customers. These will include contemporaneous commercial agreements (eg service or distribution contracts, loan agreements), and any budgets, forecasts or other papers containing information relied on in arriving at arm's length terms, etc. or in calculating any adjustment made in order to satisfy the requirements of the new transfer pricing legislation.

The documentation should exist at the latest by the time the Return is made.

Documents should be kept for:

- Six years from the end of the chargeable period to which they refer or for which there could be a related tax effect; or
- until enquiries to which the documents are relevant are complete;

whichever is the longer.'

(*Tax Bulletin*, Issue 37, October 1998)

2.13.5   Overseas property

Income from the letting of overseas property is chargeable under Schedule D Case V. The letting of such property is treated as a separate business, the profits of which are to be computed in accordance with the new Schedule A rules.

The Schedule A business computation rules are to be applied to overseas properties as if they were a single business separate from the Schedule A business comprising UK properties. The profits and losses of all overseas properties will therefore be pooled, though not with those of UK properties (ICTA 1988, s. 65A(1)). During the transitional period, however, there is no pooling of overseas properties (see below).

Relief is not available for expenses of foreign travel, etc. under ICTA 1988, ss. 80 and 81 (ICTA 1988, s. 65A(2)).

The provisions relating to the commercial letting of furnished holiday accommodation are to be disregarded (ICTA 1988, s. 65A(3)).

Capital allowances are extended to overseas property lettings (CAA 2001, s. 15(1)(d)).

2.13.6   Individuals domiciled abroad

Where an individual is resident in the UK but domiciled elsewhere, his assessments to UK income tax are limited to so much of the overseas income as he actually remits here. The assessments are therefore raised on the above basis, but by reference to the amount remitted in each year of assessment, rather than the amount of profits actually arising in that year. The usual rules relating to constructive remittance of income (by back-to-back loans, etc.) apply (ICTA 1988, s. 65(4) and (5)).

2.13.7 Unremittable income

Where income proves to be unremittable to the UK, by the laws of the overseas territory or the executive action of its government or the impossibility of obtaining foreign currency in that territory, and the landlord cannot otherwise receive the money in the UK, he may claim to defer the tax liability arising thereon until such time as it can be remitted (ICTA 1988, ss. 584 and 585).

2.13.8 Indirect ownership

In the absence of special provisions, it would be possible for UK resident persons to avoid tax on rental income, etc. arising from properties situated abroad by arranging for their interest in the properties to be acquired or held by companies or trusts resident abroad. This is counteracted in a number of ways:

- If the UK person is a company and the interest is held by a subsidiary in a low tax country, the Controlled Foreign Companies legislation will apply.
- If the UK person is an individual who is ordinarily resident in the UK, the provisions described below may have the effect that the rental income arising to the overseas company or trust is deemed to be his income for tax purposes. These provisions are to be found in ICTA 1988, ss. 739–746.

The purpose of ICTA 1988, s. 739 is to counteract the avoidance of income tax, capital gains tax or inheritance tax by individuals who are ordinarily resident in the UK by means of a transfer of assets abroad. The section applies where, as a result of such a transfer, or as a result of the transfer and any associated operations, income becomes payable to persons resident or domiciled outside the UK. If such an individual has power to enjoy the income, whether immediately or at some future time, then the income is deemed to be his income. It is chargeable to tax under Schedule D Case VI. Credit is given for any tax deducted at source.

Further, if such an individual receives a capital sum which is connected with the transfer or the associated operations, then the income of the non-resident person is deemed to be his income. A capital sum includes a loan or the repayment of a loan.

'Associated operations' and 'power to enjoy' are defined in ICTA 1988, s. 742. Simple situations are where:

- the overseas person is a company and the individuals control the company;
- the overseas person is a settlement and the individuals are beneficiaries, even if only discretionary beneficiaries,
- the overseas person is a company or settlement and the individuals are loan creditors.

The above provisions are supplemented by provisions which apply where an individual who is ordinarily resident in the UK receives a benefit which is not otherwise chargeable to income tax, by virtue or in consequence of the transfer of assets or associated operations (ICTA 1988, s. 740). The individual is chargeable on the greater of the value of the benefit and the accumulated income of the non-resident person, unless that income is caught by ICTA 1988, s. 739.

The above legislation does not apply if the transfer and associated operations were bona fide commercial transactions not designed to avoid tax, or if none of the purposes of the transactions was the avoidance of tax.

The legislation applies irrespective of whether the individuals were ordinarily resident in the UK when the transfer of assets took place (ICTA 1988, s. 739(1A)).

2.14 Transitional – historic (pre-1963) Schedule A

2.14.1 Premises occupied for the purposes of a trade before 5 April 1963

Where a trader occupied premises for the purposes of his trade up until 5 April 1963, he was assessed to income tax under the rules of the old 'Schedule A' on the annual value of those premises. He was then allowed to deduct this annual value from his trading profits, in computing his tax liability under Schedule D Case I. The deduction related to the annual value of the premises as charged to tax during the basis period. These provisions applied equally to individuals and to companies, since the latter were also assessed to income tax on a similar basis, rather than corporation tax as at present.

When the old 'Schedule A' was phased out at 5 April 1963, no further assessments on the annual value of property were made. However, at the same time, no further relief was granted in respect of the annual value already assessed to taxation under 'Schedule A' from profits computed and assessable under Schedule D Case I from 1963/64 onwards. Where therefore the Schedule D Case I assessments were based on the profits arising in a preceding period, there might well be an assessment under 'Schedule A' for which there was no subsequent deduction under Schedule D Case I.

As a transitional measure, it was therefore provided that relief should be given in respect of such otherwise unrelieved assessments – not at the time, but only on a subsequent occasion, as and when the trading premises permanently cease to be used by the trader, as such, whether as a result of a sale, or a lease of the premises, or even if he merely ceases to use them altogether or uses them for some other purpose. The unrelieved amount of annual value assessed under 'Schedule A' is allowed as a deduction in computing the profits of the trade in the year in which the premises cease to be used (see ICTA 1988, Sch. 30).

Example 2.10

Jimmy Hills carries on a manufacturing business, commenced in 1956. He occupies the same factory throughout, which had an annual value of £1,000 for the purposes of the old 'Schedule A'.

He makes up his accounts to 31 December each year. His assessment to income tax for 1962/63 in respect of his trade was therefore based on the accounts to 31 December 1961, and contained a deduction for the annual value on which Schedule A tax was suffered in 1961 (ie 95/365ths of the Schedule A assessment for 1960/61 and 270/365ths of the assessment for 1961/62). He was allowed no further deduction for Schedule A assessments in computing his Schedule D Case I liabilities for 1963/64 or 1964/65. He thus suffered tax under Schedule A without any tax relief under Schedule D in respect of 95/365ths of the 1961/62 Schedule A assessment and the whole of the 1962/63 assessment.

He then sells the premises in 1992. He will be allowed a further deduction in computing the tax liability for 1993/94 (based on his 1992 profits) of 460/365ths of the annual value of £1,000 – ie £1,260 – as if it was a trading expense in that year. Thus the relief for tax paid in 1961/62 and 1962/63 would eventually be given in 1993/94!

If the same facts applied to a limited company, as opposed to an individual, similar treatment would be given and the deduction of £1,260 would be set off against the trading profits accruing in the accounting period ended 31 December 1992 – but relief would be given at corporation tax rates, rather than income tax.

3 Property dealing and development

3.1 General comments

The provisions explained in this chapter seek to charge as income, at normal income tax or corporation tax rates, the whole of any profit derived from the disposal of a property in the course of a trade or other similar ventures.

The provisions apply to the disposal of property or an interest in property by a property dealer (including someone who develops property for resale in the course of a trade) or a disposal by way of an adventure in the nature of a trade. It is not always clear whether the taxpayer is in fact carrying on a property dealing activity, or merely realising an investment. Whilst little statutory guidance is available as to what constitutes a trade for this purpose, some help can be obtained from a review of those points that have affected the outcome in previous tax cases – as discussed below.

There is however one particular anti-avoidance provision under which any profit derived from a non-trading transaction may be taxed as an income profit (ICTA 1988, s. 776). This provision applies to a property investment that is acquired or developed with a view to the realisation of a profit; to the indirect disposal of property held as trading stock, for example by the sale of shares in a property dealing company; and more particularly to other indirect disposals of property. Further details are given below.

As to whether profits from property transactions are chargeable on a capital gains tax basis, rather than as dealing profits, much depends on the intentions of the owner – particularly at the time of acquisition or development. It may therefore be helpful to record the underlying intentions of such transactions at the time (in minutes, correspondence, etc.) by way of supplementary 'evidence'. If the taxpayer is already a property dealer or developer, or wishes to avoid investment properties being dealt with as trading stock, he should consider arranging trading and investment transactions through separate 'vehicles', such as separate property dealing and investment companies or partnerships. In the case of individuals or close companies particularly, if the transaction would otherwise fall within the provisions of s. 776, it may be better to accept liability under Schedule D Case 1.

It is necessary to consider whether any proceeds from a property transaction are chargeable as rental income, under the provisions explained in **Chapter 2**, particularly if the proceeds represent a part disposal by way of the grant of a lease at a premium for a period not exceeding 50 years.

The legislation relating to sale and leaseback transactions and capital gains tax does not apply to proceeds taxed under the provisions explained in this chapter, since those other chapters do not apply to amounts already taxable on an income basis.

Finally rental receipts, and premiums taxed as such, are excluded from the computation of trading profits and charged separately under Schedule A.

3.2 Taxable situations

3.2.1 Trading transactions

The purchase and sale of property may be undertaken in the course of a trade of dealing in land, or may itself constitute a trading adventure. In either case, any profit or loss on sale will fall within Schedule D Case I. Whether or not any particular transaction in property is a trading transaction is discussed in detail below.

3.2.2 Property development

The purchase, development and sale of property is a trading activity. If a property is acquired otherwise than by purchase, or is acquired otherwise than for development, but is then developed and sold, the development and sale is still a trading activity. The property will have been 'appropriated' to the trading venture at or before the start of the development, as discussed below. However, if a property held as an investment is refurbished prior to sale, and the refurbishment relates to dilapidations occurring during the investor's period of ownership, that is not a trading activity.

Many property developments are undertaken as joint ventures. This is dealt with below.

3.2.3 Appropriations to and from trading stock

A property is deemed to be sold and reacquired at market value in the following circumstances:

(a) where it is held as trading stock and is taken out of the trade – eg for occupation as the private residence of the individual proprietor, a partner of the partnership proprietor, or a director of the corporate proprietor;

(b) where it is held as trading stock but a decision is made not to sell it but to keep it as an investment and let it out for rent;

(c) where it is held as trading stock but a decision is made not to sell it but to keep it and occupy it as a fixed asset for the purposes of the business,

(d) where it is held as an investment or fixed asset but a decision is made to develop it for sale or to transfer it to a trade of property dealing or development.

In the case of a group of companies, the decision at (b)–(d) above may involve the transfer of the property to another member of the group.

The subject of appropriations is dealt with in detail below.

3.2.4   Capital gains taxed as income

In certain circumstances, where a person realises a gain of a capital nature (whether directly or indirectly) from property situated in the UK, that gain is taxed as income under Schedule D Case VI (ICTA 1988, s. 776). The circumstances are that:

- land, or property deriving its value from land (eg shares in a company which owns land) is acquired with the sole or main object of realising a gain from disposing of the land; or
- land is held as trading stock, or
- land is developed with the sole or main object of realising a gain from disposing of the land when developed.

This is discussed in detail below.

3.3   What is a trade?

3.3.1   General approach

Unfortunately there is no detailed statutory definition of what exactly constitutes a trade, except that it 'includes every trade, manufacture, adventure or concern in the nature of trade' (ICTA 1988, s. 832(1)). The question has been looked at by the courts on numerous occasions and some help is therefore available from a wealth of case law on the subject. The case law has established a number of 'badges' of trading, which assist in narrowing the distinction between the realisation of a trading profit and the realisation of a capital gain. There is a full discussion of this subject in the Inland Revenue's *Business Income Manual* at paragraphs BIM 20000ff.

As will be seen, the main factor is the underlying motive of the taxpayer in carrying out the transaction. If however this does not, of itself, provide any definite conclusion, a number of other corroborative factors may be looked at for further assistance, as follows:

1. Is there a history of similar transactions (although a single transaction may be an 'adventure in the nature of a trade')?

2. Is the transaction related to a trade which the taxpayer carries on?

3. Is the transaction in an asset which is normally the subject matter of a trade? (Land may either be held as an investment or traded, and when land is sold this factor is likely to be neutral.)

4. Is the transaction carried out in a way typical of a trade in that asset?

5. How is the transaction financed? Short term or excessive borrowings may indicate an intention of a quick sale, pointing to a trade.

6. Was the asset resold as it stood or was work carried out on it prior to resale? If work was carried out, that is an indication of trade.

7. Was the asset sold in one lot or sold piecemeal?

8. What were the purchaser's intentions at the time of purchase? An intention to resell in the short-term may indicate a trade, whereas an intention to hold indefinitely may indicate an investment transaction.

9. Did the item purchased provide enjoyment for the purchaser or pride of possession or produce income pending a resale? If so this may indicate an investment transaction. (However, the fact that land purchased does not produce income does not necessarily indicate a trade. An intention to hold and subsequently realise a capital profit does not necessarily indicate that the transaction is a trading transaction.) This list is a summary of factors listed in *Marson (HMIT) v Morton* [1986] BTC 377. These and other aspects, together with some notes relating to part disposals, are considered in greater detail below.

3.3.2 Underlying intentions

Primarily it is a matter of establishing the underlying objectives and intentions of the taxpayer in carrying out the transaction – particularly his intentions at the time of his acquisition of the property concerned. If there is a clear intention to resell the property at a profit at the time of its acquisition, the transaction constitutes an adventure in the nature of a trade (see for example *Clark v Follet (HMIT)* (1973) 48 TC 677). On the other hand, if there is no trading intention in the first instance, then a subsequent intention to sell does not of itself constitute an adventure in the nature of a trade (*Taylor v Good (HMIT)* (1974) 49 TC 277).

This theme runs thoughout the whole series of tax cases on the subject. For example, where the taxpayer contracts to sell the property before he even acquires it, whether or not it is an isolated transaction, the intention to resell the property is clearly established and it is therefore treated as an adventure in the nature of a trade (*Johnston (HMIT) v Heath* (1970) 46 TC 463). Similarly, where property is bought and sold, and the object is to make a profit out of the transaction rather than to hold the property permanently, it is again regarded as an adventure in the nature of a trade (*Burrell, Webber, Magness, Austin & Austin v Davis (HMIT)* (1958) 38 TC 307). In the same way, where property is acquired as trading stock, and included in the purchase is additional land not required as trading stock, a sale of the surplus land is also regarded as a trading transaction, if there is no intention of retaining such surplus land (*Snell(HMIT) v Rosser, Thomas & Co* (1968) 44 TC 343). However, it should be emphasised that the absence of the profit-making motive does not necessarily deprive the transaction of its trading character (*Smith v Incorporated Council for Law Reporting for England and Wales* (1914) 6 TC 477). In *Kirkham v Williams (HMIT)* [1991] BTC 196, the acquisition of land with the intention of developing part of it for resale was held to be a trading venture although the taxpayer argued that he had acquired the land as a capital asset for his business and had used part of it for storage and office space. The profit realised on disposal of the whole property was taxable under Schedule D Case I.

Change of intentions

Difficulties may arise in a case where the taxpayer, having acquired a property with one intention, changes his intention and then disposes of the property. This is particularly relevant in the case of an investment property, which the owner decides to sell but, before sale, increases the value by some development, or obtaining planning permission, etc. Does the development represent a trading activity, so that the property is deemed to be appropriated from investment to trading activities; or has he merely done what any prudent owner would do to improve the price he can realise from his investment?

The Revenue's approach to a change of intention is set out in the *Inspector's Manual*, paragraphs 2613–2315. Inspectors are instructed to pursue cases where there is a *clear change of intention*. This will normally be evidenced by some physical change. For example, premises previously occupied for the purposes of the business as a fixed asset may be demolished and a new building may be constructed for sale. The greater the physical change, the stronger the evidence of a change of intention. However, development of infrastructure, such as the partitioning of land into plots, the construction of an access road or the laying in of mains services may not be conclusive evidence of a trading intention. Similarly, the obtaining of planning consent is not, by itself, conclusive evidence of trading.

The position falls to be established on the basis of general intentions, coupled with ancillary evidence in respect of the additional pointers discussed below. Normally, however, unless a material operation is carried out on the property, it is regarded as the sale of the original asset without any appropriation.

Development implications

Even where the property remains a capital asset, its development may still have other tax implications. It may represent a development for the purposes of ICTA 1988, s. 776 and, if carried out with the intent of realising a profit from the disposal of the property, that profit may be taxable on an income basis – see **6.2.3** below.

Appropriations to dealing activities

A taxpayer may wish to establish a change of intention through an appropriating of this nature – for example, there may be benefits in a loss situation involving an investment property. Particularly in the case of a company, it may be helpful if the property can, at the time of its appropriation, be transferred to another 'person' – who could thus more easily demonstrate a different intention with respect to the property from the outset of ownership.

Thus a property investment company could transfer the property to a dealing company, already existing within a 75%+ group of companies or specifically set up as a subsidiary for that purpose. This would also help to avoid the investment status of the original company being prejudiced in any way. For this latter reason, ie to retain his status as an investor, an individual might perhaps transfer the property to a dealing company, or to a partnership dealing in property in which others have an interest (see *Bowie (HMIT) v Reg Dunn (Builders)* (1974) 49 TC 469 – where the subsequent realisation of property by a company was held to be a trading transaction, even though it would have been merely the realisation of an investment, had the individual retained it).

No intentions whatsoever

In certain cases the taxpayer may have no intention whatsoever at the time he acquired the property. Thus, for example, where property is settled by way of *inter vivos* trust, or on the death of a previous owner, and it does not form part of a property-dealing trade transferred at the same time, the transferee may hardly be said to have deliberately acquired the property with a view to realising a profit from its resale. Normally therefore a subsequent realisation of the property concerned is not treated as an adventure in the nature of a trade. However, particular circumstances may arise where the transferee is treated as having started a trade of dealing in land (see *Balgownie Land Trust v IR Commrs* (1929) 14 TC 684 and also *Pilkington v Randall* (1966) 42 TC 662).

Intentions of others

The position becomes very much more difficult where a person deliberately sets out to effect a series of transactions through the use of trusts, etc., although the person may not actually carry out any of the transactions involved himself. In one such case, the person concerned was held not to be assessable on profits derived by others (although whether the Inland Revenue could have succeeded if it had chosen to attack one of the parties who did actually benefit from the transaction is a matter of conjecture – see *Ransom v Higgs* (1974) 50 TC 1). It seems likely however that a similar transaction carried out at the present time would fall within the wide-ranging provisions of ICTA 1988, s. 776 (enacted after that case), particularly those provisions relating to a series of transactions and indirect disposals.

3.3.3 Previous history of similar transactions

Where a purchase and sale transaction follows a series of similar transactions, it may be regarded as *prima facie* evidence of an intention to resell, and so treated as a dealing transaction (see *Pickford v Quirke (HMIT)* (1927) 13 TC 251, and also *Mitchell Bros v Tomlinson (HMIT)* (1957) 37 TC 224).

Indeed, where there is a precedent of previous trading, a transaction of a similar nature may be regarded as a trading operation itself – even though the taxpayer actually resides in the property himself at times (*MacMahon and MacMahon v IR Commrs* (1951) 32 TC 311). A similar case involved a taxpayer who, encouraged by having previously built a bungalow for his own occupation and subsequently sold it, went on to build a second bungalow, to occupy it for a while and then sell that also. The second transaction was regarded as a trading transaction (*Page v Pogson (HMIT)* (1954) 35 TC 545). Such a decision in relation to subsequent transactions ought not to affect the treatment of any profit derived from the first sale of a series of disposals, unless the later transactions were contemplated from the beginning.

Difficulty may arise in the case of a taxpayer owning a large number of investment properties which he decides to sell as and when possible – and the decision is followed by a series of sales covering a number of years. The subsequent sales then perhaps give the appearance of disposals in the course of a trade, whereas the properties were acquired as an investment. Has there therefore been any change in intention giving rise to an appropriation from capital assets to trading stock?

Some regard may have to be had to the subsequent conduct of the business and the application of the proceeds. But, provided that the original investment intention can be clearly demonstrated, and no further development or enhancement takes place in respect of the properties, they should be regarded as disposals of capital assets (see *West v Phillips (HMIT)* (1958) 38 TC 203 and also *Bradshaw v Blunden (HMIT) (No. 2)* (1960) 39 TC 73).

3.3.4 Taxpayer's general background

The position also needs to be reviewed in the light of the taxpayer's general activities. Two cases may be distinguished here. In the first, a company acquired a wide concession of mining rights, lands, railways, etc. and set out to exploit these assets for profit. As a result, the profits derived from a disposal of land were taxed as trading receipts *(Thew (HMIT) v South West Africa Co* (1924) 9 TC 141). In the other case, a company that had been established by charter surrendered its charter in consideration for land. Parcels of the land were then sold from time to time, in fact as quickly as the company could dispose of them. It was held in this case that the company was not trading and was simply disposing of its surplus assets *(Hudson Bay Co v Stevens* (1909) 5 TC 424).

Other motives for the transactions may however be ignored, if they are not inconsistent with a finding that the transaction represented an adventure in the nature of a trade *(Tempest Estates v Walmsley (HMIT)* (1976) 51 TC 305).

3.3.5 Taxpayer's expertise

Where a taxpayer is closely connected with property by virtue of his trade, profession or other expertise, this often sways the issue.

A particularly damning occupation seems to be that of a builder. An extreme example may be taken in the case of a builder who built most of his houses for letting, and very rarely ever sold the properties. One house was built in 1929 and was not sold until 1953. However the Commissioners found as a fact that the sale was part of his trading activities, and the Courts could not upset this finding *(Oliver v Farnsworth (HMIT)* (1956) 37 TC 51). On the other hand, if the builder is able to clearly show his intentions and to distinguish between property held as trading stock and property held as an investment outside his trade, the fact that he was a builder should not set a precedent for all his property transactions *(Harvey v Caulcott (HMIT)* (1952) 33 TC 159). Estate agents and the like also seem to be at risk here. But the fact that a property company is run by an estate agent is not necessarily of itself damning and the company may still be regarded as operating on its own behalf independently (see *Emro Investments v Aller (HMIT)* (1954) 35 TC 305 – although in this case the property investment company was found to be trading, mainly because of the large number of transactions taking place over a period of years).

A lack of expertise may also be a contributory factor in deciding that a person's transaction in a particular case was only carried out with the object of resale and so was an adventure in the nature of a trade. (See *IR Commrs v Fraser* (1942) 24 TC 498, a case involving the purchase and sale of whisky, where the taxpayer had no expertise in this particular commodity and was unlikely to require the amount involved for his own consumption. Perhaps the moral of this case is to consume the whisky regardless, beat the taxman, and die happy if young.)

3.3.6 Finance

If the acquisition of property is only financed on a short-term basis, it may well be regarded as *prima facie* evidence of an intention to resell the property at an early date, and thus treated as a trading transaction. This is not always the case, especially where the taxpayer can show an intention of re financing the acquisition on a long-term basis. Indeed, particularly in the case of a developer for investment, the provision of long-term finance is usually delayed until after development has been completed and perhaps the property let. One would expect the developer however to enter into negotiations for long-term finance at an early stage. The sale of surplus land to finance property trans-actions also requires consideration, and two cases must again be distinguished here. If the taxpayer acquires land surplus to requirements, and sells off the surplus land as an essential part of the overall plan to finance the retained land, particularly if the taxpayer has insufficient resources to otherwise pay for the purchase, etc., it is regarded as an adventure in the nature of the trade (*Iswera v Ceylon CIR* (1965) 1 WLR 663). On the other hand, where a taxpayer seeks to acquire a property as his own home but is compelled to purchase additional land as well, and he is able to show that he has ample resources available to have carried out the transaction without necessarily having to sell off the surplus land, a subsequent disposal of the surplus land has been regarded as capital sale rather than a trading transaction (*IR Commrs v Paul* (1956) 3 SALR 335).

3.3.7 Period of ownership

A sale of property soon after its acquisition certainly has the appearance of a trading transaction. But again the period over which the property is owned is not necessarily conclusive evidence as to the nature of the transaction. If the property is acquired and subsequently disposed of within a relatively short period, a contention that the disposal represents the realisation of an investment needs to be supported by strong corroborative evidence as to the original motive to invest at the time it was acquired, perhaps with further evidence to show investment reasons for the change in original intention and the decision to sell – for example, because of a change in the investment climate or some other factor not originally anticipated at the time of acquisition.

On the other hand, the length of ownership of the property may not necessarily be conclusive proof that it was held throughout as an investment either. For example, where land is acquired as trading stock and held for any number of years, even if it is continuously let and never built upon, its disposal may still be regarded as a trading venture and not the sale of an investment (*Orchard Parks v Pogson (HMIT)* (1964) 42 TC 442).

3.3.8 Continuing or recurring benefit

Normally, when considering a capital asset as opposed to trading stock, one would expect it to form the source of some continuing annual income, or that it would be used by the taxpayer himself on a continuing basis, or otherwise that it would give rise to some recurring annual benefit (see, for example, *Cooksey & Bibby v Rednall (HMIT)* (1949) 30 TC 514). If however it appears that the only benefit that could be obtained from the transaction is a profit from the resale of the asset concerned, it may well be regarded as an adventure in the nature of a trade (*Wisdom v Chamberlain (HMIT)* (1968) 45 TC 92). Where there is some duality of purpose, so that the taxpayer acquires a property with the possibility of using it or receiving income from it and also of realising a profit from its resale, one has to consider which is the more important aspect of the transaction. If the main intention is to derive some use or income from the property, and the possibility of an ultimate profit is only an additional incentive in the original acquisition, then it is dealt with on the basis of a capital asset. If however the property is acquired with a view to resale at an early opportunity, and the receipt of income in the meantime is only a contributory element, then it is likely to be treated as a trading transaction.

The remarks of Cross J are particularly relevant here:

> 'Of course, the mere fact that when you buy a property, as well as intending to use and enjoy it, you have also in your mind the possibility that it will appreciate in value, and that a time may come when you may want to sell it and make a profit on it, does not of itself make you a trader; but if the position is that you intend to sell it as soon as you can to recover the cost of the purchase, the position is obviously very different.' (See *Turner v Last (HMIT)* (1965) 42 TC 517.)

3.3.9 Objects and other formal powers

In general one would expect a company whose objects were to invest in property only to carry out investment transactions – and in the same way a dealing company, only to carry out trading transactions. Again however such evidence is not regarded as conclusive. Nevertheless, a dealing company is almost always treated as a trader in this way, unless there is particularly strong evidence to suggest that a transaction should be treated on another basis (see, for example, *IR Commrs v Toll Property Co* (1952) 34 TC 13 and *Forest Side Properties (Chingford) v Pearce (HMIT)* (1961) 39 TC 665).

3.3.10   Accounting treatment

The accounting treatment of a transaction often gives a good indication of the taxpayer's intentions. Thus, for example, where property is treated as trading stock in the taxpayer's accounts, even if the taxpayer claims that the property is held as an investment and passes a resolution to that effect, it is still treated as a trading transaction (*Granville Building Co v Oxby (HMIT)* (1954) 35 TC 245).

Again however the accounting treatment is not regarded as an overriding factor. Take for example the case of a company that acquires land and sells it undeveloped shortly thereafter. Even though the company has never traded before and the land is treated as a fixed asset in its accounts, it may nevertheless be regarded as a trading transaction (*Shadford (HMIT) v H Fairweather & Co* (1966) 43 TC 291).

3.3.11   Development or improvement

It may be found that the taxpayer has, by some action, altered the value of the property before its sale. Again it is necessary to review his intentions – this time not only on acquiring the property, but also in effecting the enhancement. For example, many property investment companies run their business on the basis of acquiring a property, developing it, and then letting it for its rental income. On the other hand, a property dealer may similarly acquire land and develop it, but subsequently sell it. Thus a property developer may have either investment or dealing intentions. In the simple case of an acquisition of land, where planning permission is obtained and then the land sold, it is likely to be treated as a trading transaction (*Cooke v Haddock(HMIT)* (1960) 39 TC 64). Similarly, where an asset is acquired and expenditure is incurred in doing it up, and then it is immediately resold at a profit, the transaction is probably an adventure in the nature of a trade (see *IR Commrs v Livingston and Others* (1926) 11 TC 538 – a case dealing with a ship, but nevertheless with similar implications).

A typical case is that of a developer, who acquires and develops property but waits until the development is completed and fully let before deciding whether to retain it as an investment or sell it on. Where no clear investment intention can be discerned, an early sale of the property might well be treated as a trading transaction. If however the property is retained for a conclusive period on an investment basis, it should then be regarded as a capital asset. The Inland Revenue normally adopts a 'wait and see' attitude in such cases. But if the property owner can clearly demonstrate his original investment intentions, he should not be deterred from an early sale for investment reasons, simply because the Inspector of Taxes has adopted this attitude. As an example, a group of companies was gradually built up with the intention of developing properties to create investments for retention, where possible, or for otherwise turning to account. The sale of properties in the course of liquidation was held to be a realisation of capital and not a trading receipt – the decision being based on the primary investment intention, with no evidence of trading intention in the group's history (*Lionel Simmons Properties Ltd v IR Commrs* (1980) 53 TC 461).

3.3.12   Part disposals

Again difficulty may arise in connection with a part disposal of property, where the part disposed was acquired with a trading intention, but the part retained was acquired as a capital asset. In most cases it should be possible to distinguish between the land acquired as a capital asset and that acquired for trading purposes, and to produce separate computations for the trading activities. The disposal of land surplus to requirements out of a larger piece of land has already been discussed above.

It may be however that the original acquisition was, say, of freehold land, followed by a subsequent disposal on a leasehold basis, perhaps after development, where the taxpayer lets the property for a premium but retains the freehold reversion. It is then necessary to establish whether the development, etc. of the land was carried out with the object of improving the rental value of the freehold reversionary interest, or alternatively to realise a profit from the proceeds of granting leases on the land.

The absence of an overall cash profit from the transaction – ie where the premium received on the grant of lease is no greater than the cost of acquiring and developing the property – is not of itself conclusive evidence. If however the premium received is no greater than the development costs, and the rental value of the retained freehold reversion has in fact been improved over and above its undeveloped rental value, this should go a long way towards demonstrating the investment intention in carrying out the development. But where there is already a history or background of trading, and the sales proceeds not only recover the development costs but a part (if not all) of the original cost of the land, then the whole transaction may become taxable on a trading basis – including the market value of the retained freehold reversionary interest as a taxable receipt on its appropriation as an investment. Where the freehold reversion is only retained pending a sale as and when the development is completed and fully let, the whole transaction is treated as a dealing transaction – with the freehold reversion being treated as trading stock until sold.

3.3.13   Tenant's purchase and sale of superior interest

It is not uncommon for the holder of a leasehold interest to acquire the freehold reversion or headlease of the same property and to merge the two interests. The unencumbered freehold or headlease may then be sold, and the vendor may or may not take a leaseback. If the premises are occupied for the purposes of a trade carried on by the vendor, so that the original interest was held as a fixed asset, or if the original interest was held as an investment with subleases being granted to produce rental income, then the taxpayer may argue that any gain on disposal of the freehold or headlease is a capital gain.

The Revenue may not accept this argument. It may argue that, although the original leasehold interest was held as a capital asset, the freehold reversion or headlease was acquired for resale and never formed part of the taxpayer's capital structure. Therefore, any gain on disposal of that interest is a trading profit. This would include the 'marriage value' of merging the two interests (see *Inspector's Manual*, paragraphs IM 2620–2626).

If the premises were occupied for the purposes of the taxpayer's trade, and the taxpayer takes a leaseback so that the premises continue to be occupied for the purposes of that trade, then the Revenue will not normally argue for a trading profit. Similarly, if the property was held as an investment and the taxpayer takes a leaseback subject to the existing subleases, so that he continues to hold his interest as an investment, the Revenue will not normally contend for a trading profit. This is, or course, subject to the sale and leaseback provisions discussed in **Chapter 1**. If there is no leaseback, the Revenue will argue that the original leasehold interest was appropriated to a trading adventure at the time of acquisition of the superior interest. The effect is that the marriage value is taxed as a trading profit rather than a capital gain. Although the rate of tax may be the same, there is no possibility of rollover relief in respect of a trading profit.

3.3.14   Shares in property companies

It is extremely difficult for an individual to establish that any loss sustained on transactions in shares is a trading loss. A speculator in shares is not regarded as a trader in shares (*Salt v Chamberlain (HMIT)* (1979) 53 TC 143). It is therefore unlikely that an individual would be allowed a loss on a share transaction as an income deduction. However, where a gain arises in respect of shares in a company that owns land, part or all of that gain may be taxable as income under Schedule D Case VI in accordance with ICTA 1988, s. 776. In particular subsection (4) provides that land is disposed of if, by any one or more transactions concerning property deriving its value from the land, control over the land is effectually disposed of. Section 776 is discussed further in **Chapter 4**.

3.4 Joint ventures

3.4.1 Sharing of risk and reward

In any property development project, the following persons are usually involved:

(a) a landowner or landowners;

(b) the developer;

(c) a financier (eg a bank);

(d) an investor (eg an insurance company or gross fund);

(e) a builder, and

(f) tenants of the completed development.

Very often, because of the risks and rewards, a property development may be carried out as a joint venture by any combination of (a)–(d) above. The spreading of risk and reward between developer and investor is often achieved under forward funding arrangements.

The spreading of risk and reward between developer and landowner may result in the landowner sharing in the proceeds on sale of the completed development and being taxed under ICTA 1988, s. 776 as discussed in **Chapter 4** ('slice of action' schemes) if he is not taxed under Case I.

A financier may agree to receive a share of profits from the development in lieu of interest at normal commercial rates.

3.4.2 The financier's share of profit

If the financier is not a party to the joint venture, but is merely a creditor, then his share of profit represents consideration for the use of money. As such, it will be taxed as income under Schedule D Case III, unless it is treated as a distribution under ICTA 1988, s. 209 as to which, see **Chapter 6**.

In the case of a corporate lender, the loan relationship provisions will apply unless the distribution rules apply. It is considered that the accruals basis should be adopted. However, the interest does not accrue evenly on a time basis, but arises on the disposal of the property for the purposes of FA 1996, s. 85(3). The mark to market basis is considered to be inappropriate since it would result in profits being anticipated in the case of a profitable development. If the financier is a party to the joint venture, then his share of the profit may be taxed under Schedule D Case I.

3.4.3   The structure of the joint venture

A single development joint venture will usually be conducted either:

- as a contractual joint venture; or
- through the medium of a joint venture company.

Contractual joint venture

A joint venture contract will usually provide that:

- any landowner will make his land available for development at an agreed initial value and will grant the developer a licence to enter on the land and carry out the development;
- any financier will provide loans on terms which may provide for interest to be payable (usually rolled up until the development is sold) or may provide for the financier to receive a share of the profits in lieu of interest;
- where two or more developers are involved, any property acquisition will be made by them as tenants in common under a trust for sale;
- the developer will carry out the development, and
- any disposal consideration will be applied in paying the landlord his initial value, repaying the financier his loans plus interest, and reimbursing the developer for any costs he has incurred plus possibly a management fee, with any surplus consideration (ie profit) being divided in agreed proportions (eg in proportion to the land value plus costs incurred or finance provided).

No profit arises until there is a disposal or part disposal of the site or finished development. Small part disposals of land surplus to the requirements of the development may simply be treated as reducing the cost of work in progress unless, on the facts, there is a profit element in the part disposal. Other part disposals (eg after planning consent has been obtained and some infrastructure work has been carried out) may well give rise to a profit. The allocation of costs incurred and any part of the initial land value to the part disposed of is done on an actual basis as far as possible with general costs apportioned (not necessarily on a straight acreage basis).

It will be apparent that the landowner has not made any disposal at the start of the development under the type of agreement envisaged above, but has merely appropriated his land to the development This may give rise to a deemed disposal and reacquisition under TCGA 1992, s. 161(1), but the gain or loss can be rolled over in accordance with s. 161(3). The important points are that no tax liability need arise until there is an actual disposal in pursuance of the joint venture and that indexation relief is available up to the time of the appropriation of the land to the joint venture. Each party to the joint venture is chargeable to income tax or corporation tax under Schedule D Case I on his or its share of the profits. Similarly, any loss arising is a Case I loss. Whether a deficiency of sale proceeds is dealt with in the same way as a surplus is a matter for agreement between the parties. The allocation of the deficiency between the parties will be followed for tax purposes.

Partnership

A joint venture may constitute a partnership, especially where more than one project is carried out. The direct taxation consequences are no longer significant now that each partner is taxed separately on his share of partnership profits. However, a partnership must be registered separately for VAT purposes (VATA 1994, s. 45) and each partner is jointly liable for the partnership's debts (eg liabilities to contractors, banks, etc.). Thus there are important commercial aspects of being a partnership. The VAT position is considered in more detail in **Chapter 11**.

In the case of a partnership, it may be appropriate for an intending party to a joint venture to set up a limited liability company to be the actual joint venture party. Its share of profits will be chargeable to corporation tax. They may then be distributed by way of dividend or by distribution in a winding up of the company.

Joint venture company

In view of the commercial risks attaching to any property development, many joint ventures are carried out by limited liability companies set up and owned by the persons who would otherwise be direct parties to the joint venture. The joint venture company will carry out a trading venture. Profits will be distributed by way of dividend, or distribution in a winding up, after the completion of the project. Losses will be borne first by equity shareholders, then preference shareholders, then loan creditors in accordance with company law and the rights attaching to the various classes of capital in the company.

A number of specific tax issues arise in connection with joint venture companies:

- whether any loss sustained by the joint venture company is available for surrender under the group relief and consortium relief provisions;
- whether any interest payable by the joint venture company falls to be treated as a distribution under ICTA 1988, s. 209;
- whether any annual interest payable by the joint venture company to joint venture parties can be paid without deduction of tax at source;
- what relief is available to an investor who suffers a loss on his investment in the joint venture company.

These issues are considered below.

Relief for loss on investment

Unfortunately, the relief against total profits or total income given by ICTA 1988, ss. 573 and 574, for losses on unlisted shares in trading companies is not available in relation to property development companies (s. 576(5)). Therefore any relief for a loss on shares or securities in, or other loans to, a property development company is available only under the capital gains tax rules. This serves to emphasise the importance of setting up the company so that effective relief is obtained for its trading losses. A capital gains tax loss may arise on an actual disposal of the shares or securities or on liquidation of the company following the sale of the development. A loss may also arise on a negligible value claim or, in the case of a loan, on a claim under TCGA 1992, s. 253 or 254.

3.5 Private Finance Initiative projects

Reproduced below is the text of an article that appeared in *Tax Bulletin* Issue 40 (April 1999). This article deals with typical situations that arise where a public authority (the purchaser) which has surplus land enters into a contract with a PFI operator for the provision of services and where the land is either sold or developed.

3.5.1 Private Finance Initiative (PFI) projects: treatment of surplus land

'*Introduction*

One of the ways in which the public sector can arrange for such things as schools, hospitals or prisons to be built or refurbished and serviced, is by entering into a PFI project. These projects often involve a private sector company (or companies) agreeing to design, build or renovate and operate a property in order to provide accommodation and related services to agreed standards, in return for annual service charges (the unitary charges). The contracts are for quite lengthy periods, typically 25–30 years.

The legal contracts which underlie such projects are invariably complex, involve large amounts and are often commercially sensitive. The projects frequently give rise to novel and difficult tax issues which have to be resolved within very tight time constraints. In recognition of these difficulties and the importance of the Private Finance Initiative, a working group has been set up to consider the tax aspects of PFI, consisting of representatives from the various parties advising the private sector, a Treasury official and Inland Revenue Head Office technical specialists. The intention of the group is to identify points and issues specific to PFI which have caused particular difficulty, with the aim, where possible, of publishing articles which clarify the position.

This article, the first arising from those discussions, considers the correct treatment for tax purposes where surplus land (or cash) is introduced by the public sector body.

Background – accounting treatment

The following three paragraphs contain a brief review of the relevant accounting treatment, which it is hoped readers will find of use as an overview, before looking at the issues in detail.

The Accounting Standards Board issued Amendment to FRS5 "Reporting the substance of transactions: Private Finance Initiative and similar contracts" in September 1998, which gives guidance on the accounting treatment to be used when dealing with PFI contracts. The amendment, which inserts Application Note F into FRS5, refers to the entity which acquires the services (eg an NHS trust) as the "purchaser", and the entity which supplies the service under the PFI contract to, for example the NHS trust, as the "operator"; the same terminology is used in this article.

The accounting by the operator is governed by Application Note F to FRS5 and the application of FRS5 involves those that prepare and audit financial statements taking a view on the substance of transactions, so that their commercial effects are properly reflected therein. In general, this involves taking a view on whether the property used in providing PFI contracted services is on or off balance sheet. In general, the operator has an interest in the property (eg a lease) and in most PFI schemes, significant risk rests with, or is transferred to, the operator. In such circumstances, the property is shown under FRS5 as the physical asset of the operator. However, if the degree of risk transfer is low, the property may be on the balance sheet of the public sector purchaser. In such circumstances, the transaction is often termed "off balance sheet to the operator", but more accurately, what this means is that the operator is viewed for accounting purposes as having a financial asset, reflected in its accounts as a debt due from the purchaser (similar to a finance lease receivable), rather than a physical asset of the property.

In simple terms, if the property is off balance sheet to the operator, it is likely to be on the balance sheet of the purchaser. However, the accounting analysis by the public sector is carried out under Treasury Guidance rather than FRS5 and so it is possible that there will be other outcomes – the physical asset could be on either both or neither balance sheets. This article considers only the position regarding the financial statements of the operator.

Treatment of land introduced into the PFI contracts

Public sector organisations will often wish to minimise the annual service charge (the unitary charge) to be paid for the supply of services procured under a PFI contract, and where the purchaser has land surplus to its own requirements, it may decide to introduce that land into the PFI contract, in order to reduce the unitary charge.

The purchaser and the operator will generally determine the price of the unitary charge on the basis of a discounted cash flow model, which is produced by using a set of assumptions negotiated by the parties. The introduction of land as a contribution towards the project costs (in order to reduce the unitary charge), and the timing of the realisation of the value of the land, will have an impact on the cash flow of the operator and, therefore, on the price to be charged to the purchaser. The value of the land for tax purposes will be the price agreed between the parties which is specified in the documentation, being in accordance with the facts and intentions of the parties.

As has been previously stated, PFI transactions are by their very nature complex. When considering the correct tax treatment where surplus land of the purchaser is introduced into a particular contract, the terms of the relevant documentation, *providing this accords with the facts,* will be an important indicator. Another important indicator will also be the purpose of the payment from the point of view of the purchaser (as opposed to the purpose of the receipt from the operator's perspective) as evidenced by the documentation itself. Typically, we have found that land is introduced into a PFI project by the purchaser, in one of the following ways:

1. the purchaser has land surplus to its requirements and introduces that land as a payment (in money's worth) on account of future unitary receipts;
2. the purchaser has previously identified land which is surplus to its requirements, has entered into an agreement for the disposal of that land to a developer and arranges for all or part of the proceeds to be paid direct by the developer to the operator as a payment on account of future unitary receipts;
3. land is introduced by the purchaser as a payment in money's worth in order to reduce the capital cost of the project to the operator;
4. the proceeds arising from the disposal of land are introduced by the purchaser in order to reduce the capital cost of the project to the operator.'

The following examples consider the accounting and tax treatments to be applied in straightforward circumstances.

'*Example 1*

An NHS trust (the purchaser) enters into a PFI contract with an operator and has identified surplus land with a current market value of £10 million – assumed to be the fair value for accounting purposes – which it wishes to be introduced as a payment on account of future unitary receipts, and the documentation makes this clear.

Accounting treatment: Under FRS5, the accounting treatment will follow the substance of the transaction and (assuming initially that the physical asset – the hospital – is on the balance sheet of the operator) the total capital cost of the project will be debited to fixed assets in the operator's balance sheet and depreciated in the normal way. The contribution of land is, therefore, recorded by the operator as an asset at its fair value of £10m (as part of project assets or separately from them according to whether the land is used in the project). The credit entry is to 'deferred income'. (The contribution has to be recorded as 'deferred income' rather than being used to reduced the project cost because of certain accounting rules in the Companies Act 1985.) The 'deferred income' is released to profit and loss account over the period to which the contribution relates. In general this would be the whole of the contract period.

Alternatively, where the hospital is off the operator's balance sheet – the operator, therefore, has a financial asset – the Companies Act rules referred to above do not apply. The operator will set up a financial asset equal to the total amount of its investment. The operator would treat receipts from the purchaser as being partly interest and finance charges earned and partly collection of principal and the fair value of a contribution (ie the £10 million) would be treated in much the same way – credited to the financial asset – and would, therefore, affect the pattern in which interest is earned on the amount of the principal that is outstanding from time to time.

Tax treatment: Although the accounting treatment under FRS5 is an important consideration for tax purposes, particularly when determining the time at which receipts are to be taxed, it cannot determine whether the relevant item falls to be treated as income or capital. Here, the documentation (being in accordance with the facts and the intentions of both parties) shows that the introduction of the land is to reduce the future payments made by the purchaser to the operator and is, in effect, a prepayment of the unitary charge. The release of the contribution to the operator's profit and loss account will be chargeable to tax as income of the operator's trade and it is likely that the timing of the income for taxation purposes will follow the accounts treatment. Where the land is not immediately sold then its market value at the date of signing the PFI contract will be taken as the value of the prepayment of the unitary charge for tax purposes. If the land is subsequently appropriated to capital account (as an investment or for some other purpose), the market value of the land at the date of approriation will be taken to establish whether any further adjustment is required for tax purposes of the operator (see Example 6, Tax Treatment, (a)) to reflect any profit or loss arising whilst in the operator's ownership to the date of appropriation.

Example 2

An NHS trust introduces land valued at £ 10m into a PFI contract, to be used as a contribution to the construction costs and the documentation makes this clear. Accounting treatment: The accounting treatment is no different to that in Example 1 above, irrespective of how the land or cash proceeds are to be utilised. Taxation treatment: As previously stated, whilst the accounting treatment is useful, it cannot determine the correct tax treatment. As with Example 1, providing the documentation reflects the facts and intentions of both parties, the tax treatment will accord with it and the contribution will fall to be treated as a contribution towards the capital costs of construction. Once that has been so established:

(a) the operator is treated as having received a capital contribution resulting in a reduction in the base cost of the asset, eg the hospital for capital gains tax purposes, in accordance with Taxation of Chargeable Gains Act 1992 (TCGA 1992, s. 50). The Revenue considers that where exceptionally the grant is not from a body listed in TCGA 1992, s. 50 a reduction in the base cost of the asset is still required for tax purposes, since it is considered that the operator has not incurred the expenditure for the purposes of TCGA 1992, s. 38.

(b) if the agreement specifies the costs to be met by the contribution, this will be followed when deciding whether any reduction in expenditure qualifying for capital allowances is required under the Capital Allowances Act 2001, s. 532 unless, exceptionally, the facts require a different approach.

(c) if there is a partial contribution – for example, towards the cost of a building with many different elements – then the grant will be apportioned across the various categories of expenditure (eg buildings, plant etc) unless the parties have agreed how the contribution is to be allocated in which case that allocation will be followed unless the facts dictate otherwise.

Any allocation of the contribution must, as has been previously emphasised, be consistent with the facts and, for example, no contribution can exceed the amount of the capital expenditure to which it is allocated. If there is an excess, then the excess has to be reallocated over other categories and in these circumstances, the Revenue will pay particular attention to the facts to see whether the excess should correctly be treated as a prepayment of the unitary charge. However, an excess of contributions over related costs would only occur if the expenditure incurred was less than the amount of the contribution taken over the project life. For example, consider a project where a contribution of £5 million was to be made towards assets which did not qualify for capital allowances. If in the first year only £1 million was spent but by the end of the construction, £6 million had been spent on non-qualifying assets, there would be no need for a reallocation. If, however, by the time the construction was completed only £3 million had been spent on non-qualifying assets, then the remaining £2 million would be allocated over the remaining categories of expenditure.

Example 3

An NHS trust has previously realised proceeds from the disposal of surplus land and wishes to contribute all or part of those proceeds to the PFI operator, as a payment on account of future unitary receipts and the documentation makes this clear.

Accounting and tax treatments: The accounting and tax treatments will be exactly the same as in Example 1, reflecting the reality of the situation that cash has effectively passed from the purchaser to the operator on day 1 of the contract in order to be spread over the period of the contract reducing the purchaser's future annual unitary charge payments.

Example 4

An NHS trust has previously realised proceeds from the disposal of surplus land and wishes to contribute all or part of those proceeds to the PFI operator, as a contribution to the construction costs of the project and the documentation makes this clear. Accounting and tax treatments: The accounting and tax treatments will be exactly the same as in Example 2.

Example 5

An NHS trust enters into a PFI contract with an operator and has identified surplus land with a current market value of £10 million – assumed to be the fair value for accounting purposes – (or previously realised proceeds of £10 million from the disposal of surplus land) and wishes to contribute all or part of those proceeds to the PFI operator. The documentation is silent on how the land (or proceeds) are to be used. Accounting and tax treatments: In such cases, particular care needs to be taken to ensure both the tax and accounting treatments reflect the facts of the case. However, if the documentation is silent then the taxation treatment would normally follow the accounting treatment, producing the same result as in Example 1.

Example 6

A purchaser wishes to contribute land to a PFI project involving the construction of a property on a new site (site A), agreeing that once the building on the new site can be occupied, the old site (site B) will be vacated with title passing to the operator. The operator takes title to site B at the end of the construction phase and sells it at some later point. The calculation of the unitary charge assumes a sale of site B for £10 million with the value to be used either:

(i) as a reduction in the unitary charge, or
(ii) to fund the construction costs.

Accounting treatment: The accounting treatment is identical to the previous example irrespective of how the proceeds from the sale of site B are to be utilised, ie when site B is contributed, it is recorded as Dr land, Cr deferred income, which is released into income over a period in accordance with the principles set out above.

The operator would subsequently also have to monitor the carrying value of site B for possible impairment, if classified as trading stock, under SSAP9 'Stocks and long-term contracts', and if as a fixed asset, under FRS11 'Impairment of Fixed Assets'. In accordance with those accounting standards, any loss on an asset is required to be recognized when the loss is known, with recoveries of value also being recorded, and hence the carrying value of the site may fluctuate until disposal when its value can be determined. (Assets classified as 'investment properties', however, are treated differently, in accordance with SSAP 19.)

If the operator's accounts showed it carrying a financial asset rather than a physical asset, as in the first example, the value attributed to site B would be taken to reduce the carrying value of the financial asset, ie Dr land, Cr financial asset.

Tax treatment: It is particularly important in this type of situation to establish precisely what has happened and especially the purpose of the payment (from the purchaser's point of view), since this will be an important indication in determining the tax treatment, which is likely to follow that in Examples 1 and 2, subject to the following. Additional consideration may be needed where the land is retained for a period of time, which may result in eventual disposal proceeds which are different from the value (of the land) introduced into the PFI contract. For example, it may not be possible for the land to be sold immediately, or there could be delays in gaining vacant possession or the land may only become available at a much later date for other reasons. In such circumstances:

(a) where the land is (eventually) sold, say at a profit, it will be necessary to establish whether that profit is to be returned to the purchaser (with no additional tax consequences) or whether the operator can retain all or part of that profit. In these circumstances, it will normally be the case that the profit will be taxed under Schedule D Case I. In calculating the 'excess profit' the land would be deemed to have a cost equal to its agreed value (£10 million in this case) and the timing of the taxation of these profits will depend upon the particular facts of the case:

(b) where the land is sold shortly after the construction works have been completed with the proceeds required to be used to pay for the construction works the taxation treatment will be similar to those set out in Example 2 dealing with an up front capital contribution.'

3.5.2 Miscellaneous matters

It should be recognised that the above article is based on the most straightforward of situations and is intended to give only general advice – at the end of the day, the treatment of a particular transaction will always depend upon its own particular facts. It should also be noted that this article does not consider, nor address, any stamp duty or VAT implications.

3.5.3 PFI operators: schedule of charge

Reproduced below is an article which appeared in *Tax Bulletin*, Issue 43 (October 1999) dealing with the appropriate head of charge for profits arising from a lease of fully serviced accommodation.

'This article addresses the appropriate schedule of charge of income arising from a PFI deal involving a lease of fully serviced accommodation. It reflects the Revenue's view of how such income should be assessed, and the consequential effects on loss relief available.

Schedule A or Schedule D Case I?

General principles

1. Many PFI schemes will be structured in the form of a lease granted by the body commissioning the work – "the purchaser" – to the service provider – "the operator" – followed by a leaseback from the operator to the purchaser. Where this happens – or similar arrangements are entered into under which the operator acquires an interest in or rights over exploiting that interest – it will be necessary to consider whether all or any part of the payments made to the operator are chargeable under Schedule A. A similar problem was addressed in the previous article in relation to stamp duty. As foreshadowed there, the application of the legislation in Part I I.C.T.A. 1988 will not necessarily give the same result as stamp duty law and practice.

2. If the operator itself has an interest in land, and grants rights of occupation to the purchaser (normally by way of a sublease or licence to occupy), some part of the unitary charge will necessarily be attributable to the right of occupation, and hence assessable under Schedule A. This will be so even where the lease prescribes in terms a rent of a peppercorn, and even though payment of the unitary charge is contingent on performance by the operator of other services to specified standards. The Revenue would expect the part of the unitary charge payable for the right to occupy land to be calculated on a just and reasonable basis.

3. It will be a question of fact whether the 'other services' referred to in the previous paragraph are sufficient to constitute a trade on first principles. If the operator is carrying on a trade, the Revenue will accept that it is a "trading company" for the purposes of consortium relief (ICTA 1988, s. 413(3)(c)) provided that trade is its sole or main activity. The test is what the company does. The mere fact that the Schedule A element of a unitary charge constitutes a significant proportion – or even exceeds 50% – of the total gross income will not **of** itself mean the company is not a trading company for the purposes of s. 413(3)(c). The test is whether, as a matter of fact, the **main** activity of the company is trading.

4. If the operator retains the right to grant leases or licences to third parties in respect of part of the land or property in question, any sums received under such agreements will ordinarily be within Schedule A.

5. References above to payments made to or sums received by the operator do not include payments of interest for late settlement, payments under normal commercial indemnities or other non-recurring commercial payments. The tax treatment of such amounts will depend on their commercial character.

Group relief

6. In many P6I schemes the operator will be a consortium company (that is (a) a directly held company owned by the consortium members or (b) a company owned 90% by a consortium holding company as defined by s. 413(3)(b)). Where losses arise in a consortium company, group relief will be available where the consortium company is a "trading company" – that is "*a company the business of which consists wholly or mainly in the carrying on of a trade*".

7. If a consortium company is a "trading company", any Schedule A losses (as from 1 April 1998) will be capable of being surrendered as consortium relief assuming that all the other relevant conditions are met.

8. In determining whether a consortium company is a "trading company", it will be necessary to establish what the company mainly does. If its main activity is the provision of services – and the provision of accommodation (and the generation of rental income) is ancillary to that – then the company will ordinarily be a trading company as defined by s. 413(3)(c).

9. As discussed in paragraph 3, it will be a question of fact what a company's main activity is. It will be necessary to look not merely at the level of income generated by each activity but to consider, for example, how the company's resources (e.g. management time, capital employed, etc.) have been used.

10. There are PFI cases where a Revenue view on the schedule of charge has already been sought in accordance with the terms of Code of Practice 10, and where agreement has been given that the whole of the unitary charge is assessable as trading income. The Revenue will not seek to revisit the treatment of any such case.'

3.5.4 Scope of trade

In *Tax Bulletin*, Issue 60 (August 2002), the Revenue provided the following further guidance.

'PFI projects can be structured in a variety of ways and the trade of a PFI operator can cover a wide range of activities. At one end of the spectrum is the operator who builds a facility as the setting in which to carry on the trade. An example is the operator whose trade is running a prison and who constructs a prison on land acquired for that purpose. There is the operator who builds a facility in order to rent it out, with related support services. For example an operator acquires land to build a hospital, leases it to an NHS Trust and also provides non-clinical support services to the lessee by way of trade. In both of these examples the construction costs are capital expenditure for tax purposes and relief is only available against Schedule A or Case I income to the extent that it qualifies for capital allowances.

At the other end of the spectrum is the PFI operator who does not acquire a major interest in land, such as a freehold or leasehold, and whose trade is the provision of design, construction and maintenance services. An example is the operator who contracts to build and maintain a road or hospital on land that belongs to the purchaser. In such circumstances the design and construction costs, together with the costs of any other services provided, are revenue expenditure for tax purposes. None of this expenditure will qualify for capital allowances.

Scope of trade

The question of whether or not a PFI operator is carrying on a trade of providing services is, generally, not in dispute. The scope of such a trade is a separate question.

As noted above, this is essentially a question of fact. Each case will depend upon its own particular facts and it is not, therefore, possible to provide a definitive checklist of all the factors to consider. However, the intention of the operator, the terms of the PFI agreement, as well as what the operator actually does, are all relevant factors.

The operator's stated intention does not, by itself, resolve the question of the scope of the trade. As Lord Justice Atkin noted, in *Collins v The Firth Brearley Stainless Steel Syndicate* 9 TC 520 at p. 573, "in order to examine the facts you must look at what the company purported to do, and also at what it in fact did". Where the facts point to a different conclusion, as for example in the case of *The Alianza Company v Bell* 5 TC 60, the stated intention cannot prevail over what it is that the operator in fact does. The question is what trade is actually carried on, not what trade the operator claims to carry on. However, where the facts are equivocal, the intention of the operator may well be a relevant factor in reaching a conclusion.'

3.6   Computations

3.6.1   General approach

The general principles applicable to Schedule D Case 1 apply. Profits are ascertained from accounts drawn up in accordance with UK GAAP, subject to any adjustments required or authorised by law (FA 1998, s. 42).

Timing of recognition of trading receipts

The date of disposal of property, for Schedule D Case I purposes, is not governed by any statutory provisions, but usually follows the accounting treatment under UK GAAP. In practice, the Revenue will accept an accounting basis which recognises disposals either on a contracts basis or on a completions basis, provided that the basis is applied consistently from year to year. It is common practice for house builders to recognise disposals on a completions basis, for example.

Where the completions basis is adopted, but in a particular case the purchaser takes possession or pays a substantial part of the purchase consideration before completion, the Revenue may insist on taking the date of that earlier event as the date of disposal. This would not normally apply in the case of a customary 10 per cent deposit payable on exchange of contracts in a house purchase. Similarly, where the purchase price is payable in instalments and the formal completion and conveyance is deferred until all instalments are paid, the profit or loss on sale is spread over the instalment period.

The disposal consideration includes the value of any property taken in part exchange. It became common practice in the recession of the early 1990s for house builders to take existing properties in part exchange from purchasers of new homes. The value of any house taken in part exchange is the amount of sale consideration discharged by the transfer of that property. Where the total sale price is not stated as such, the value of any property taken in part exchange is the market value of that property. The disposal consideration also includes the value of any mortgage taken by the vendor in respect of any part of the sale price. Where a sale is completed, the property is disposed of for the full sale consideration and the vendor then has a debt due from the purchaser for any unpaid amount, subject to a provision for doubtful debts where the mortgage does not give the vendor full security and there is doubt as to whether the purchaser can pay the outstanding debt in full.

3.6.2 Valuation of closing stock and work in progress

Cost

Stock is usually valued at the lower of its cost or net realisable value. For this purpose cost includes all direct costs of acquisition and enhancement, including incidental costs. For a property dealer (including someone who develops property in the course of a trade), it would be unusual to include any addition in respect of overheads (except perhaps in a one company/one property situation) – unless the dealer was also a builder, in which case one would expect building costs to include an element of overheads.

Interest on money borrowed to acquire and develop the property may normally be added to the cost of closing work in progress.

For accounting periods ending on or after 1 April 1996 relief is governed by the loan relationships provisions of FA 1996. In relation to property development, this means that relief is obtained as and when the interest is charged to the profit and loss account – see **Chapter 6**.

Sometimes an expense which has been included in stock or work in progress in the accounts needs to be excluded for tax purposes (eg entertainment expenditure).

Net realisable value

The net realisable value of a property is taken as the amount at which it is expected that it can be sold without creating any further profit or loss in the year of sale, ie the estimated proceeds of sale less due allowance for all further costs to completion and less all costs to be incurred in marketing and selling the property – including, for example, advertising the property for sale, agent's commission and legal costs.

Whilst a provision for an anticipated loss is not normally allowed for tax purposes, it may reduce the estimated market value of the property at the end of the chargeable period and so may be taken into account in this way. Losses under long-term contracts may be allowed to be spread over the period of the contract, provided that the taxpayer also brings in profits on such contracts over the contract period in the same way – but this would affect developers rather than dealers.

Change in basis

Normally the value included at the end of one period of account is also taken as the value to be used at the beginning of the next period. Similarly the same basis of valuation should be used consistently from one year to another. If however there has been some change in the method of valuing stock, as between the opening stock figure in any year and the closing stock, some modification may be required to the resultant profits for tax purposes.

As regards periods of account ending on or after 1 August 2001, the adjustments are specified by FA 2002, Sch. 22. Their effect is to ensure that all profits are taxed once and once only and all losses are allowed once and once only. This means that and profit or loss on re-statement of opening stock or WIP is brought into account for tax purposes.

This treatment applies to changes in the basis of valuing long-term contracts as well as short-term ones.

3.6.3   Part disposals

Where there has been a part disposal of property during the accounting period, and part remains undisposed of at the end of that period, some apportionment of the costs incurred in respect of that property is required – in order to compute the cost applicable to the part retained, for the purposes of bringing in the closing stock figure. Again no statutory basis is provided, but normal accounting principles are applied as appropriate in the circumstances.

For example, in the case of land being disposed of in separate plots, the apportionment might be on the basis of the area involved. Other costs, such as the cost of laying out roads and services, would again be apportioned between those plots to which they relate. There may be other factors, however, which would lead one to suppose that a greater proportion of cost should be attributed to one area rather than another – and each case needs to be looked at on its own merits.

In the absence of any reasonable basis for the allocation of costs in this way, and in particular in the case of a freehold reversion where a lease has been granted at a premium, the Inland Revenue normally accepts an apportionment of cost in proportion to the value of the retained interest and the proceeds of disposal of that part sold.

Again where the freehold reversion, etc. is to be retained permanently, it is treated as the appropriation of trading stock as a capital asset – and its value is included in trading profits as if it had been sold at its market value.

Example 3.1

Arthur Colley acquires 3 acres of land at a cost of £300,000 – its full value as housing land. He builds 24 houses on the land at a cost of £90,000 each and sells each house for £170,000. At the end of the first year he has completed and sold 9 houses. Assuming the plots are of equal size and value, his trading profit for the year is calculated as follows:

	£	£
Proceeds of sale (9 × £170,000)		1,530,000
Building costs (9 × £90,000)	810,000	
Land costs –		

$$\frac{\text{No. of houses sold}}{\text{Total no. of house plots}} \times \text{Total cost}$$

$\frac{9}{24} \times £300,000 =$	112,500	
		922,500
Trading profit for year		£607,500

If however the development consisted of a mixture of houses, the allocation of cost of land may not be so straightforward. Suppose that the development consisted of only 10 houses selling for £170,000 (still costing £90,000 each to build) and a further 10 houses selling for £200,000 (costing £108000 each to build). The more expensive houses are sited on the better part of the estate. Again 9 houses are sold during the first year, 4 of the more expensive variety and 5 of the cheaper type.

An allocation of the cost of land on an area basis may give an inequitable result, not taking into account the additional value attributable to the better part of the estate. Perhaps one could first allocate the total cost of land between the various parts of the estate on a valuation basis – and then subdivide the cost allocated to that part according to the area occupied by each house.

Alternatively a reasonable allocation might be achieved by reference to the actual and anticipated net proceeds of sale, after deducting building costs, as follows:

	£
Total anticipated net proceeds –	
Total proceeds (10 × £200,000 + 10 × £170,000)	3,170,000
Building costs (10 × £108,000 + 10 × £90,000)	1,980,000
Total net proceeds	£1,190,000
Proceeds of actual sales (4 × £200,000 + 5 × £170,000)	1,650,000
Building costs (4 × £108,000 + 5 × £90,000)	882,000
Net proceeds	768,000
Land costs –	
Net proceeds × Cost	
Total anticipated net proceeds	
$= \dfrac{£768,000}{£1,190,000} \times £300,000$	= 193,613
Trading profit for year	£574,387

3.7 Appropriations to and from stock

Where there is no disposal of a property, but the trader appropriates it from his stock in trade (for his personal use or enjoyment, for retention as an investment asset, or for disposal otherwise than by sale in the course of his trade) such an appropriation is treated as a notional disposal and the current market value of the asset is brought into the computation as if it were a trading receipt (*Sharkey (HMIT) v Wernher* (1955) 36 TC 275 – and see also *Bradshaw v Blunden* (No. 2) (1960) 39 TC 73). This treatment is not considered to apply to expenditure incurred on the construction of a fixed asset for use in the trade (Inland Revenue Statement of Practice A32) so that a builder who constructed his own workshop or office could transfer it from his stock in trade at cost.

Similar treatment is given in respect of property previously held as a capital asset but appropriated by the taxpayer to his trade as trading stock. Again the appropriation is treated as the acquisition of dealing stock at its current market value in computing the profits from his trade.

A corresponding treatment is given to the appropriated item for the purposes of capital gains tax. Thus where trading stock is appropriated for other purposes, it is treated as if the asset was acquired, for capital gains tax purposes, for a consideration equal to the amount brought into the accounts of the trade in respect of the appropriation, ie its market value. Similarly where property held as a capital asset is appropriated to trading stock, it is treated as having been sold at its market value for the purposes of capital gains tax on that occasion (TCGA 1992, s. 161(1) and (2)). Where a capital asset is appropriated to trading stock, and a chargeable gain or allowable loss arises, the taxpayer can elect that the gain or loss is deducted from, or added to, the cost of trading stock thus acquired. The implications involved and possible occasions when such an election would be of benefit are discussed more fully in **Chapter 8** (s. 161(3)).

Intra-group transfers

The above rules are reinforced by similar rules which deal with the situation where an asset is transferred intra-group and either:

(a) the transferor held it as trading stock but the transferee acquires it otherwise than as trading stock (eg as an investment or fixed asset); or

(b) the transferor held it otherwise than as trading stock but the transferee acquires it as trading stock.

In (a), the transfer is effectively deemed to take place at market value, so that a trading profit or loss arises to the transferor based on that value and the transferee acquires it at that value (TCGA 1992, s. 173(2)).

In (b), the transferee company is deemed to acquire the asset otherwise than as trading stock (so that the intra-group provisions apply), but is then deemed immediately to appropriate it to trading stock. This means that the deemed disposal and reacquisition rule applies, together with the right of election to roll over any gain or loss under s. 161(3).

Whether or not the transferee acquires the asset as trading stock is a question of fact. In *Coates (HMIT) v Arndale Properties* [1984] BTC 438, an attempt was made to roll over a loss, effectively converting a CGT loss into a trading loss. However, the House of Lords held that the company had not acquired the asset as trading stock.

The above decision has been reinforced by TCGA 1992, Sch. 7A, Para 10, which prevents the rollover of a pre-entry loss under s. 161(3).

3.8 Disposal of stock to another trader

3.8.1 General rule

Where property is transferred from the trading stock of one trader to the trading stock of another trader, the transfer normally takes place on an arm's length basis and is treated as a sale in the first trade and a purchase in the second at the transfer price.

3.8.2 Non-arm's length transfers: transfer-pricing adjustments

If the transfer is not at arm's length, and one of the parties is not trading, or is not within the charge to UK tax in respect of such trade, the sale price is adjusted to the price that the property would have fetched if the transaction had been between independent persons dealing at arm's length (ICTA 1988, Sch. 28AA). In principle, the transfer pricing rules apply to transactions within the UK as from 1 April 2004, subject to the exemptions for small and medium-sized enterprises (FA 2004, ss. 30–32).

If both transferor and transferee are trading in the UK in respect of the property, there was no statutory basis for an adjustment to the transfer price prior to 1 April 2004. Nevertheless the question has been considered by the courts in the past and on occasions a suitable adjustment has been made. Where there is a material discrepancy between the transfer price and the market value of the property, and the property is sold by the transferee shortly afterwards at a large profit, the market value may be substituted for the transfer price (*Skinner (HMIT) v Berry Head Lands* (1971) 46 TC 377). On the other hand, if the transferor is not himself a trader, and he transfers a property at substantially below its market value, it is more difficult for the transferee property dealer to contend that the acquisition should be taken at the market value of the property. In such circumstances the assessment may well be confirmed on the basis of the profit derived by the property dealer computed by reference to the actual transfer price (*Jacgilden (Weston Hall) v Castle (HMIT)* (1969) 45 TC 685).

Thus whilst the Inland Revenue often accepted a transfer from one trader to another at other than market value without adjustment to the transfer price, provided both are trading in the UK, this treatment was not mandatory.

3.8.3 Transfers on cessation or death

Exceptionally, where the transfer of stock takes place at the discontinuance of a trade, the valuation of stock at the close of trading does have a statutory basis (ICTA 1988, s. 100). As from 1 April 2004, however, s. 100 does not apply where the transfer pricing rules apply (s. 100(1ZA)).

First of all, if the stock is sold for valuable consideration to an independent trader in the UK, and the cost may be deducted by the purchaser as an expense in computing his trading profits, the closing stock is brought in at an amount equal to the proceeds of sale (s. 100 (1A)(a)).

But where the trade is discontinued and the parties are connected, the consideration is instead deemed to be what the price would have been if the sale or transfer had been a transaction between independent persons dealing at arm's length (s. 100(1A)(b)).

Connected parties may, however make a joint election to use the greater of:

* the *acquisition value* of the stock, and
* the consideration received for it,

where each of these comes to less than the arm's length price. Acquisition value is, in effect, what would have been the value of the stock adopted in accounts if they had been drawn up to a point just before the discontinuance. In other words, it is normally the actual cost less any potential write-down to net realisable value that would fall to be made just before the discontinuance (s. 100(1C)).

The rationale of permitting such an election is to deal with the circumstances when the arm's length rule would impose tax on unrealised profits even though no tax advantage was sought. If an election is made, it must be signed by both parties and sent to the Inspector no later than two years after the end of the chargeable period in which the trade is discontinued. In all other circumstances the closing stock is valued at the price that it would fetch, if sold on the open market at the time of cessation (ICTA 1988, s. 100 (1)(b)).

3.9 Rental income

Rental income derived from property held as trading stock is separately assessed under Schedule A, and excluded from trading profits assessable under Schedule D Case I. The expenses incurred during the chargeable period that would normally be allowable under Schedule A are offset against income assessable under that Schedule as far as possible – see **Chapter 2** for the general rules applicable.

Expenditure may only be taken into account in computing trading profits in so far as the income assessable under Schedule A is insufficient to give full allowance. Any unrelieved expenditure under either basis is carried forward as a trading loss, rather than a Schedule A loss. Where expenditure is disallowed in computing rental profits under Schedule A as being 'capital' expenditure, it may nonetheless be deductible in computing trading profits if it relates to property held as dealing stock.

Example 3.2

Frank Westfield carries on a property dealing business. His accounts include the following revenue items on two properties held as trading stock:

	Property 1 (£)	Property 2 (£)	Total (£)
Rental income	4,000	6,000	10,000
Less: Outgoings	6,500	3,500	10,000
Net rental receipts	£(2,500)	£2,500	£ –
	(Loss)		

If both properties are let on landlord's repairing leases, the whole of these items are left out of account in computing trading profits under Schedule D, and are dealt with under Schedule A – the loss on the first property being offset against the net profit on the second under the normal Schedule A 'pooling' basis.

If, however, the second property is let on a tenant's repairing lease, it is assessable separately under Schedule A, with no relief for the loss on the first property. Since no relief is available for the loss under Schedule A, it is brought back into the Schedule D computation. Thus if there is no other trading income or expenditure in the period, it gives rise to a trading loss (available then to set against the Schedule A assessment or any other income in that period – see **6.5** below). If other trading profits are available, the loss restricts those profits, leaving the Schedule A assessment still standing.

Where rental income is credited against the cost of work in progress on a property development, it will not usually be taxable until released to the profit and loss account through cost of sales. This is subject to the proviso that the accounting treatment must comply with generally accepted accounting practice.

3.10 Premiums received and paid

The receipt of a premium under a lease of less than 50 years (or an amount treated as such) may give rise to a tax assessment as if part of that amount were rental income – under the special rules explained in **Chapter 2**. As with rental income, the amount of premium thus taxed excluded from trading profits, with only the net amount included as a trading receipt (ICTA 1988, s. 99(2) and (3)).

However, tenant's improvements assessed as rental income in the hands of a landlord who is a property dealer are not deductible in this way – so that the proceeds of a subsequent sale may still be taxed in full.

Where the dealer's reversionary interest in the property is not disposed of during the same accounting period, it is necessary to apportion the cost of acquisition of the property between the partial realisation and the part retained.

Premiums paid are regarded as a trading expense in acquiring the leasehold interest in the property concerned. If rental income is then derived from that interest, and the premium is taxed in the hands of the landlord recipient, the dealer may claim a deduction in respect of the deemed rental payment under the ordinary Schedule A rules. Otherwise of course the premium is allowed in his trading computations, when he subsequently disposes of the property. There can be no double allowance – so that any part of the premium allowed under Schedule. A is no longer available in computing trading profits.

3.11   Abortive and deferred expenditure

3.11.1   Abortive projects

Where expenditure is incurred on an abortive project, such as the investigation of a possible property acquisition which falls through, or in an unsuccessful attempt to obtain planning permission, the expenditure is normally allowed in computing trading profits, provided that it is incurred wholly and exclusively for the purposes of that trade. In other words, it is necessary to show that the project would have been dealt with as a trading project, if it had been carried out.

No difficulty should arise, except perhaps where the taxpayer both invests and deals in property. It is then necessary to establish that the project would have formed part of his trading activities, and not have been retained as an investment, had it been successful.

3.11.2   Deferred expenditure

In some instances a project may be under consideration for a period extending beyond the end of the accounting period in which the expenditure was incurred. Should the expenditure be allowed in that period, or carried forward to a future period?

In some cases, no actual asset may yet exist at the accounting date to be valued as closing stock, but normal accounting principles apply. If it is likely that the project will prove successful and the expenditure recovered, it may be carried forward to the following period, as deferred revenue expenditure, etc. If on the other hand it seems unlikely that the expenditure will be recovered, it should be written off in the current accounting period. Each case needs to be dealt with on its own merits. The case of *Gallagher v Jones (HMIT)*, *Threlfall v Jones (HMIT)* [1993] BTC 92 is authority for the proposition that the starting point for the determination of profits is the need to apply the principles of commercial accounting.

3.11.3   Anticipated losses

There is no provision for anticipating future losses by the creation of a provision out of taxable profits. The only way this can be achieved, in the case of property held as dealing stock, is to reduce the closing stock valuation to its market value in its present state – which presumably would take into account any future expenditure necessary to put the property into a fully marketable state.

3.12   Waste disposal

Tax relief may be obtained for expenditure incurred by traders on both preparing and making good landfill sites for waste disposal (ICTA 1988, s. 91A and 91B). It is available only to persons holding a 'relevant licence' which is either:

- a disposal licence under Part I, Control of Pollution Act 1974 or Part II, Pollution Control and Local Government (Northern Ireland) Order 1978, *or*
- a waste management licence under Part II, Environmental Protection Act 1990 or similar provision in force in Northern Ireland.

A deduction is available against trading profits when a person holding a relevant licence makes a *site restoration* payment after 5 April 1989 in the course of carrying on a trade. The deduction is allowed in the period of account in which the payment is made (s. 91A(1), (2)). A site restoration payment is a payment made in connection with the restoration of a site, or part of a site, which ceased to be used for carrying out waste disposal activities prior to the payment being made, and was made in order to comply with the conditions of the licence or the grant of planning permission to use the site for waste disposal (s. 91 A(4)).

For these purposes, waste disposal activities consist of the collection, treatment, conversion and final depositing of waste materials (s. 91A (5)).

The Revenue's interpretation of restoration expenditure is set out at some length in *Tax Bulletin*, Issue 34 (April 1998) as follows:

'**What is restoration expenditure?**

The legislation defines a "restoration payment" as a payment made in connection with the restoration of a site or part of a site and in order to comply with the condition of a relevant licence or a relevant agreement. "Restoration" is not defined and it therefore takes its usual dictionary meaning of replacing, reconstructing or returning something to its original state.

We do not regard the legislation as applying to sites other than those where waste disposal activities within s. 91A(5) have taken place. For example, the legislation does not apply to sites where contamination has occurred as a result of the "on site" disposal of industrial, etc. waste unless the disposal was under a relevant licence as defined in s. 91 A(6) or there is a relevant agreement within s. 91A(7). Similarly, a local authority may require that contaminated land on a former industrial site be restored as a condition of their giving planning permission for development. However, that requirement is unlikely to be under s. 106 of the Town and Country Planning Act 1990 or the other statute listed in s. 91A (7). Unless it is under the specific statute, s. 91A will not be in point.

There are a number of different elements of expenditure, all of which are generally incurred after waste disposal has ceased and capable of being described as restoration expenditure.

One is the cost of covering the site with an impermeable layer, subsoil and topsoil, contouring, drainage, seeding, tree planting and other similar activities directed to returning the site to a condition where it is suitable for alternative use. These activities can readily be identified as restoration. They are generally, but not necessarily, incurred after waste deposition at the site has ceased, are normally made "once and for all" and have the effect of changing the physical appearance of the site. This expenditure has all the marks of capital expenditure and relief is available in accordance with s. 91A in so far as it cannot be relieved by way of capital allowances [s. 91A(3)(b)].

Another type of expenditure is on the continuation of work which is first required while the site is being used for waste disposal. As soon as waste is deposited, unless it is totally inert, it begins to decompose, producing noxious liquids and potentially hazardous or flammable gases. Many sites will have pipes, pumps, and possibly treatment plant, etc. installed to sample and deal with these potentially polluting substances. Waste disposal licences will generally require the site operator to undertake a programme of sampling and analysis to establish that no problems exist or arise. As a result, during the active life of the site when waste deposition is taking place, a programme of sampling, analysis and treatment, etc. will begin. This will continue seamlessly into the period after waste disposal has ceased and might then be described as "aftercare".

We see no distinction between the costs of the routine monitoring and treatment, etc. described above during the active life of the site and subsequently after waste deposition has ceased. Therefore, we accept that the costs of routine monitoring, analysis and treatment is revenue expenditure, whenever incurred and, as such, is outside s. 91A. Such expenditure should be dealt with as ordinary revenue expenditure.

Provisions for restoration expenditure

We acknowledge that generally accepted accounting practice requires a provision be made for future restoration expenditure. The costs of restoration can only be matched against the income generated from waste disposal and are a charge against that income. Since the decomposition of waste and the resulting potential environmental problems can occur over many tens of years the waste site operator will have a long-term commitment to carry out "restoration" work.'

However, s. 91A only permits a deduction for a site restoration payment in the period of accounts in which the payment is made. It has been suggested that the wording of s. 91 A(3)(a) implies that provisions are allowable but that is not the case given the clear statement of the position in s. 91A(1). In order to explain the wording of s. 91A(3)(a) it is necessary to outline the background to the legislation. Until the decision in the tax case of *Rolfe (HMIT) v Wimpey Waste Management* [1989] BTC 191 restoration expenditure was in practice treated as a revenue deduction. However, the *Wimpey* decision established that both preparation and restoration expenditure (such as recovering the site and planting trees, etc.) were capital and, therefore, no revenue deduction could be allowed. Subsequently, what is now s. 91A was enacted to give relief for restoration expenditure.

Since the new legislation gives relief on an 'as paid' basis, without s. 91 A(3)(a) it would have been possible to claim a deduction for expenditure when paid 'post Wimpey' which had previously been allowed as a provision 'pre Wimpey'. Thus s. 91A(3)(a) does not allow a provision but denies a double deduction in the circumstances described.

In so far as a provision for restoration is for capital expenditure that provision is not allowable in computing Case I profits. It would not be allowable under the normal rules that prohibit a provision for expenditure, such as capital expenditure, which would be disallowable when incurred, nor under s. 91A which only permits a deduction when the (capital) expenditure is incurred. However, where a provision for restoration costs is for revenue expenditure, the question of s. 91A does not arise. Such a provision would be allowable as a Case I deduction, subject to the usual rules. In the context of provisions for expenditure that will be incurred scores of years in the future the questions of accuracy and appropriate discounting may be in point. Subject to those questions a provision for the future revenue costs of routine monitoring and treatment of gases and leachate are likely to be allowable.

Tax Bulletin, Issue 51 (February 2001) deals with the distinction between the capital costs of engineering a site to receive waste and the revenue costs of creating internal cells.

'Preparation expenditure

Engineering a modern waste disposal site to the point where waste can be deposited often includes constructing an impermeable clay layer, or laying an artificial lining, across the base and sides of the site. When the site has eventually been filled these elements, together with the final capping, create a containment structure for the whole site that is likely to fulfil that function for decades. We view the costs of creating such a containment structure as capital expenditure.

Internal earthworks

For practical and financial reasons, the base and sides of the containment structures are often built in sections, with internal barriers, or "bunds", on the open sides to create the first level of internal cells. Provided these internal cells are filled and sealed within two years, we accept that the costs of the internal earthworks, ie the bunds and any internal caps, are revenue expenditure. However, the cost of the base and sides, which form part of the site containment structure, remain capital expenditure.'

Relief is also available to a person holding a relevant licence who incurs *site preparation* expenditure for the deposit of waste materials in relation to a waste disposal site and who submits a claim, in prescribed form, to the Inland Revenue. The deduction is available against trading profits for a period of account ending after 5 April 1989 (ICTA 1988, s. 91B). The amount available for relief is calculated in accordance with the following formula:

$$(A - B) \times \frac{C}{(C + D)}$$

where:

- A is the cumulative site preparation expenditure incurred by the person at any time before or during the period in question but excluding expenditure for which a trading deduction has been obtained in earlier periods under *other* sections or which would qualify for capital allowances in the normal way;
- B is the cumulative total of expenditure previously allowed as a deduction under *this* section;
- C is the volume of waste materials deposited on the site during the period,
- D is the unused capacity of the site at the end of the period.

Where any of the above expenditure was incurred prior to 6 April 1989, the figure in A above is reduced by the sum produced by the following formula:

$$(E) \times \frac{F}{(F + G)}$$

where:

- E is the expenditure incurred before 6 April 1989;
- F is the volume of waste materials deposited before 6 April 1989,
- G is the unused capacity at 5 April 1989.

Note the 'cut off' difference between expenditure *paid* for the purpose of making good and expenditure *incurred* for the purpose of preparation. Where the relevant invoice is raised in one period and paid in the next one, preparation expenditure will be related to the first period and restoration expenditure to the second.

Any expenditure incurred for the purposes of a trade to be commenced after 31 March 1993 will be treated as incurred on the first day on which the trade is carried on (ICTA 1988, s. 91B (10A)).

3.13 Miscellaneous points

3.13.1 Costs of raising finance

The incidental costs of obtaining a qualifying loan may also be claimed as a trading expense.

Such incidental expenses include fees, commissions, advertising, printing, etc. incurred wholly and exclusively for the purposes of obtaining finance (even if abortive), of providing security or of repaying it. But no relief is given for stamp duty, exchange losses or the cost of protection therefrom, or any premium on repayment or discount on issue.

Loans qualify for this purpose if the interest thereon is deductible in computing profits or gains for tax purposes. But loans which are converted into shares or other non-qualifying securities within three years of issue are excluded (ICTA 1988, s. 77).

For corporation tax purposes, s. 77 does not apply. Instead, relief is given under the 'loan relationships' rules discussed in **Chapter 6**. The accounts basis will apply.

3.13.2 Pre-trading expenses

Pre-trading expenditure incurred in the seven years before trading commences is treated as having been incurred on the first day of trading for companies and in the first tax year for individuals (ICTA 1988, s. 401). The day on which a trade commences will depend on the nature of the activity being undertaken. In principle, the trade commences when the 'raw material' has been acquired and the enterprise commences to turn the material into the 'product' that is to be disposed of *(Birmingham and District Cattle By-Product Co v IR Commrs* (1919) 12 TC 92). In the case of a trade of property dealing or development, the trade would normally start on the purchase of the property with an intention to use it in the trade, even if further activity is held up by the need for finance, planning consent, etc. Relief is not available under s. 401, for expenditure which qualifies for relief under the 'loan relationships' provisions.

As far as companies are concerned, the above rule does not apply to loan relationship deficits (as to which, see **Chapter 6**).

3.13.3   Valuation costs

Any costs incurred by a company in making a valuation to comply with Companies Act 1985, Sch. 7 is allowed as a deduction in computing trading profits (Inland Revenue Press Release dated 10 September 1971).

3.14   Timeshare schemes

3.14.1   Nature of a timeshare scheme

A timeshare is a right to the exclusive occupation of certain furnished accommodation for a particular week or weeks each year for a specified number of years. The vendor is usually a property developer and the consideration for the grant or sale of the right is usually a lump sum payable by the purchaser to the developer. Usually, the agreement for the sale or grant of the time share requires the purchaser to pay an annual service charge to a management company.

Technically, the timeshare is a licence to occupy. It is not an interest in land. However, since the sale of timeshares reduces the value of the vendor's interest, the Revenue considers that the sale of a timeshare may be viewed as a transaction in land.

3.14.2   Tax treatment

Where a builder or developer constructs a block of timeshare apartments and sells timeshares, this is regarded as part of the trading activities.

If a landowner constructs such a block and sells timeshares, this is regarded as an adventure in the nature of trade. The land on which the block is built will have been appropriated to the trading adventure. If a landowner refurbishes an existing building and sells timeshares, this may amount to a trading adventure, and probably will do so if the refurbishment involves a change of use or extensive alterations. The existing building will have been appropriated to the trading adventure. Each case is considered on its facts, but the extent of the refurbishment, the number of timeshare units sold and the nature of the management services to be provided are all relevant factors.

In any Case I computation, the value of 'closing stock' will be the value of the land and building subject to the existing timeshares sold. Unsold units are valued at the lower of cost and net realisable value.

If a sale of timeshare units falls to be dealt with under the capital gains tax legislation, then clearly each sale will be regarded as a part disposal of the vendor's interest in accordance with TCGA 1992, s. 21(1) and s. 22(1) – as to which see **Chapter 8**.

3.15 Forward funding of property development

A key problem for any property developer is the financing of the development. In many cases, the developer will seek a purchaser for the proposed development in advance of actually carrying it out. Such a purchaser may be an insurance company, a gross fund or some other investment institution. The tax implications of any such arrangement will depend on how it is structured.

One possibility is that the developer sells the property to the investor before any development takes place and the investor then engages the developer under a contract whereby the developer arranges for the development to be carried out. Effectively, the developer becomes a main contractor who, in turn, enters into contracts with architects, construction companies, engineering companies, etc. for the carrying out of the works. In this case, there may be an immediate profit or loss on disposal of the undeveloped site, and there will be a further profit or loss on the development contract.

In any substantial development or redevelopment, the development contract will be a 'long-term contract' as defined in SSAP 9. Any profit will be recognised for tax purposes as and when it is properly recognised in accordance with SSAP 9. A loss will be recognised for tax purposes at any time if, and to the extent that, a profit would have been recognised at that time. It will be appreciated that, for accounting purposes, a loss may be recognised at an earlier stage than a profit (SSAP 9, paragraphs 10, 11). For tax purposes, however, neither profits nor losses may be anticipated (see *BSC Footwear v Ridgway (HMIT)* (1971) 47 TC 495 and *Gallagher v Jones (HMIT), Threlfall v Jones (HMIT)* [1993] BTC 92).

In determining the amount of any profit or loss at any given time, it is necessary to ascertain:

(a) the costs incurred up to that time, and

(b) the estimated future costs to complete the contract, including any rectification work.

The sum of (a) and (b) is then compared with the contract price. In some cases, there may be difficulty in ascertaining the contract price due to alterations in the specification leading to disputes as to whether certain items are extras. SSAP 9, paragraph 26 requires that a conservative estimate be made of the amount likely to be received. This is included in the contract price.

As regards (b), future cost estimates will include provisions for disputed claims. Where the developer refuses to admit liability, the provision may be disallowed to the extent that it has the effect of augmenting a loss on a contract in progress or of deferring recognition of a profit on a completed contract. The leading case on this point is *James Spencer & Co v IR Commrs* (1950) 32 TC 111, which established the principle that a provision for a disputed liability is not allowable until liability is admitted or until it is determined by a competent court. At that point, a provision may be allowed if the amount of the liability can be estimated with reasonable accuracy *(IR Commrs v Titaghur Jute Factory* (1978) 53 TC 675). The contract price may comprise, or include, the grant to the developer of a headlease where the rent payable is a percentage of the rents receivable under sub-leases to be granted by the developer to occupiers of the building. The value of this lease will need to be brought into account when profits or losses fall to be recognised in the developer's accounts. It will usually be the developer's intention to sell the headlease once all of the sub-leases are in place. The sale consideration will then be a trading receipt in the normal way.

In some cases, the headlease may be granted at the commencement of the development so that the developer carries out the development as holder of that headlease. The principles of stock valuation will then apply, as discussed above. Whether or not an initial profit arises on the disposal of the developer's original interest to the investor in consideration for the leaseback can only be determined on a case by case basis. Clearly, the value of the headlease will be the appropriate multiple of the expected rental profit (based on current market rates of return on comparable properties) less the cost of carrying out the development and the developer's profit margin.

Another possibility is that the investor agrees to fund the development by loans, and takes an option to acquire the completed development. In this case, there is no disposal by the developer until the option is exercised. In valuing the work in progress on the development, the net realisable value will be the option price less costs to complete the development. The option contract may also give the developer the right to take a headlease back from the investor as described above. This will be part of the disposal consideration.

3.16 Exemptions and reliefs

3.16.1 Charities

Charities are exempt from tax on income arising from rents and 'other receipts' in respect of land situated in the UK or elsewhere (ICTA 1988, s. 505). The exemption is, however, subject to two conditions:

- the interest in land must be held for charitable purposes, and
- the income must actually be applied for charitable purposes only.

The exemption does not extend to trading profits such as profits from property development.

3.16.2 Friendly societies

A registered friendly society is exempt from tax on income from its life and endowment business, subject to certain conditions (ICTA 1988, s. 460). This covers in particular income falling under Schedule D Case I or Case VI. The exemption must be claimed.

An unregistered friendly society may claim exemption only if its income does not exceed £160 per annum (ICTA 1988, s. 459).

3.16.3 Local authorities and Health Service bodies

A local authority in the UK is exempt from income tax and corporation tax on all of its income (ICTA 1988, ss. 519, 519A).

3.16.4 Approved pension funds

Exemption from income tax may be claimed in respect of income from investments held for the purposes of an exempt-approved scheme (ICTA 1988, s. 592). Clearly, this exemption does not cover trading transactions. Further, it is not clear whether an asset which is subject to a transaction giving rise to a Case VI profit under s. 776 can be said to be an investment held for the purposes of the scheme.

3.16.5 Trade unions and employers' associations

Certain trade unions and employers' associations may claim exemption from income tax and corporation tax in respect of non-trading income which is applicable and applied for the purposes of provident benefits (ICTA 1988, s. 467). This appears to cover profits arising under s. 776. They must, however, be precluded either by Act of Parliament or by their rules from assuring any person for:

- a lump sum exceeding £4,000, or
- an annuity exceeding £825 per annum.

3.17   Non-residents

3.17.1   Trade carried on in the UK

A non-resident person is chargeable to UK tax on the profits of any trade exercised within, or carried on in, the UK (ICTA 1988, s. 18(1), (2)). In relation to transactions in land situated in the UK, if those transactions amount to a trade (which includes an adventure or concern in the nature of trade), then the trade will almost certainly be regarded as carried on in the UK. This follows from the test formulated by Lord Atkin in *Smidth v Greenwood* (1922) 8 TC 193:

> 'I think the question is, where do the operations take place from which the profits in substance arise.'

In the case of land situated outside the UK, if the contracts involved are made in the UK, that is (non-conclusive) evidence that the trade is exercised in the UK (see, for example, *Firestone Tyre and Rubber v Lewellin* (1957) 37 TC 111). Contracts are usually made at the place where the acceptance of the offer is received. If the acceptance is posted, it is treated as received at the place of posting. Therefore, it is not difficult to ensure that contracts relating to property situated outside the UK are made outside the UK.

Where the taxable transactions are carried out through a branch or agency in the UK, the non-resident principal is chargeable in the name of the branch or agent (see now FA 1995, s. 126(2) and Sch. 23 (1)).

If the non-resident person is an individual, or a company that does not carry on a trade through a branch or agency in the UK, the charge is to income tax. In the case of a company that does carry on a trade through a branch or agency in the UK, the charge is to corporation tax (ICTA 1988, s. 11(2)).

Although the provisions of FA 1995, ss. 128 and 129 exclude certain income from the charge to income tax and corporation tax, trading profits are not within the excluded income. Such profits are, therefore, within the charge to UK tax whether or not the non-resident person has a branch or agency in the UK. In practice, it may be difficult for the Inland Revenue to collect the tax in the absence of such a branch or agency.

3.17.2   Branches, agencies and UK representatives

A non-resident who carries on a trade in the UK may be charged to tax in the name of any UK representative of his (FA 1995, Sch. 23, Para. 1).

A branch or agency in the UK is the non-resident's UK representative in relation to any income from the trade which arises directly or indirectly through or from that branch or agency (FA 1995, s. 126(2)). If the branch or agency is carried on by persons in partnership, then the partnership as such is treated as the UK representative (s. 126(5)).

A branch or agency means any factorship, agency, receivership, branch or management (FA 1995, s. 126(8) and TMA 1970, s. 118). However, an agent is not a UK representative for a non-resident unless he carries on a regular agency for that non-resident. Similarly, a broker is not a UK representative for the non-resident merely by reason of acting as such on a normal commission basis (FA 1995, s. 127).

Therefore, an estate agent in the UK is not chargeable as a UK representative in respect of property trading transactions carried out through him as such, provided that he does no more than is customary in his business. Similarly, a firm of solicitors in the UK is not a UK representative merely because it has been engaged to deal with the conveyancing work. However, if the estate agent or solicitor has, and habitually exercises, an authority to conclude contracts on behalf of the non-resident, then he is a UK representative of the non-resident.

3.17.3   Double tax agreements

The tax position of a non-resident may be governed by a double tax agreement between the country of his residence and the UK. In particular such an agreement may define the circumstances in which he becomes liable to UK taxation on commercial profits arising in the UK – usually confining liability to the case where he has a permanent establishment in the UK. The term 'permanent establishment' is usually defined to include:

- a place of management;
- a branch;
- an office;
- a factory;
- a workshop,
- a mine, an oil or gas well, a quarry or any other place of extraction of natural resources.

Further, a building site or construction or installation project is usually a permanent establishment if it lasts for more than 12 months. An agent who has, and habitually exercises, in the UK an authority to conclude contracts in the name of a non-resident person is a permanent establishment in respect of such contracts. This ties in with the definition of UK representative in FA 1995, ss. 126 and 127.

3.17.4 Dual resident companies which are non-resident under a double taxation treaty

Where a company is dually resident, under domestic legislation, in the UK and another country, the company's residence for certain purposes is determined by a 'tiebreaker' clause in the double taxation treaty between the UK and the other country. Where the company is regarded for treaty purposes as non-resident then it will generally be regarded as non-resident, after 29 November 1993, for all UK tax purposes (FA 1994, s. 249 to 251).

3.17.5 Partnerships

Partnerships managed and controlled abroad that undertake business in the UK will not be treated as entities separate and distinct from the partners (ICTA 1988, s. 111). Each non-resident partner is changeable to UK tax on his share of the profits arising through the trade carried on in the UK (s. 112).

Where a UK resident company is a partner in such a partnership, that company's share of profits is established by computing the profits as if the partnership were a UK resident company itself, although other partners are dealt with on the above basis (ss. 112 and 114).

3.17.6 Self-assessment, etc.

Where a non-resident individual is chargeable to income tax on trading profits arising in the UK, he is required to give notice of liability to the Inspector of Taxes within six months of the end of the tax year in which the profits arise. He must then complete a self-assessment return including Pages NR1 and 2.

Where a non-resident person has a UK representative, that representative is also responsible for giving notice of liability, whether under TMA 1970, s. 7, in the case of an individual, or FA 1998, Sch 18, Para. 2, in the case of a company liable to corporation tax. Further, the representative is responsible for completing any self-assessment in the case of a non-resident individual.

3.17.7 ICTA 1988, s. 776 (artificial transactions in land)

Section 776, extends to non-residents where the land in question is situated within the UK, but not when it is situated abroad – as noted in **Chapter 4**. Moreover, if a non-resident is entitled to any consideration that becomes taxable under that section, the Inland Revenue may direct that the payment of that sum to him should be made under deduction of tax (ss. 776(13) and 777(9)).

Alternatively, if the Revenue can show that the opportunity of realising the gain or any part of it was provided directly or indirectly by some other person, then it can assess that other person on the gain or part thereof (s. 776(8)). This procedure may well be followed if the other person is resident in the UK. The same rule applies where the gain is attributable partly or wholly to value provided by the other person.

3.18 Overseas property

3.18.1 Schedule D Case I or Case V?

Firstly it is necessary to determine whether the profits derived from the sale of property fall to be assessed under Schedule D Case I or Schedule D Case V. As will be seen, this question has some importance – particularly as concerns the relief of losses against other income (restricted under Case V) and the special basis of assessment under Case V for an individual who is not domiciled in the UK, or else not ordinarily resident here. Schedule D Case I covers a trade carried on in the UK or elsewhere, and Schedule D Case V deals with income arising from foreign possessions (including the possession of a trading activity outside the UK). Whilst these are not mutually exclusive, a pattern has emerged over the years. Where the overseas property forms part of a general trade carried on both in the UK and abroad, the assessment clearly falls to be made under Case I of Schedule D – even when the overseas activities are carried on through a separate branch. In order for the assessment to arise under Case V, the trade must be carried on wholly abroad (ICTA 1988, s. 18(3) – and see *Colquhoun v Brooks* (1889) 2 TC 490). Moreover the exercise of management and control in the UK, or indeed mere tacit oversight, can be sufficient to bring the charge under Case I (*San Paulo (Brazilian) Railway Co v Carter* (1896) 3 TC 344 and *Egyptian Hotels v Mitchell* (1914) 6 TC 152). Where therefore an individual wishes to seek benefit from an assessment under Schedule D Case V, he may need to consider setting up his foreign trade as a separate partnership wholly managed and controlled abroad – being careful to ensure that he only exercises his own powers under the partnership whilst being personally abroad (eg at partnership meetings held in the foreign country concerned). Alternatively he might consider setting up the venture as a foreign company (again managed and controlled abroad), and take his share of profits as remuneration for an employment where the duties are wholly performed abroad – where the assessment under Schedule E follows similar lines to an assessment under Schedule D Case V.

Apart from the main points mentioned above, there are only minor differences between Case I and Case V – chiefly relating to the basis of assessment of profits in the case of an individual.

3.18.2 Computation of profits

For a company, income from a foreign trade assessable under Case V is computed in accordance with the same rules as Schedule D Case I (ICTA 1988, s. 70(2)).

In the case of an individual, again profits are computed as under Schedule D Case I – but see below for the position of a non-domiciled person. Special rules under Schedule D Case V relate to income that proves unremittable to the UK, by reason of the laws of an overseas territory, or the executive action of its government, or the impossibility of obtaining foreign currency in that territory. Where the taxpayer cannot otherwise receive the money in the UK, he may claim to defer the tax liability arising thereon until such time as it can be remitted (see ICTA 1988, ss. 584 and 585). Also premiums on a policy of insurance against war risks or in respect of injury to employees cannot be deducted (ICTA 1988, s. 586 and 587).

3.18.3 Losses

In the case of a company deficiencies of income from lettings of overseas properties may be carried forward for set off against future income of the same property (ICTA 1988, s. 392B). In the case of an individual, the rules allow a Case V loss to be set off against other such foreign trading profits arising in the same or the next following year of assessment (ICTA 1988, s. 379B), or for it to be carried forward against future profits from the same overseas trade or in the case of a terminal loss carried back against earlier profits of the same trade (ICTA 1988, s. 391).

3.18.4 Persons domiciled or ordinarily resident outside the UK

Where a person is domiciled outside the UK or, being a British subject or a citizen of the Republic of Ireland, is not ordinarily resident in the UK, he is only assessed to UK tax on the basis of any foreign profits actually remitted and received in the UK, rather than profits arising, during the basis period. The usual rules relating to constructive remittances of income apply. Thus the assessment is based on amounts received during the basis period (as opposed to the year of assessment) ascertained on the above basis. Correspondingly losses are not available as allowable losses under Schedule D Case V on this basis, since one cannot remit monies that have been lost. On the other hand, if profits are retained abroad to cover those losses, such profits are not assessable here (ICTA 1988, s. 65 to 67 – and see also *Newstead (HMIT) v Frost* (1980) 53 TC 525).

In computing any double tax relief available to a person assessable on a remittance basis in this way, the amount remitted to the UK is grossed up to take account of the foreign tax paid thereon – and the assessment is then computed by reference to that gross amount. Double tax relief is then given in respect of the foreign tax by deduction from the UK liability. The relief is confined to the amount of tax suffered on the income actually remitted here on this basis, and is not available in respect of foreign tax on other unremitted income.

Example 3.3

If in the previous example Edwin Banks is domiciled abroad, and he remits £2,000 of his net profit to the UK. his tax liability is calculated as follows:

	£
Amount remitted	2,000
Foreign tax credit (at 40% of total)	1,333
Assessable total	£3,333
Income tax at 60%	2,000
Less: Double tax relief	1,333
Net UK tax	£ 667

If he were domiciled here, his UK tax liability on the whole of the profit would be £2,400 as noted in the previous example.

If he were domiciled abroad and remitted the whole of his net profit after foreign taxes he would also pay UK tax of £2,400. and his total tax burden would be equal to that payable on profits arising from a UK source.

3.18.5 ICTA 1988, s. 776 (artificial transactions in land)

It is not clear whether ICTA 1988, s. 776 may apply to land situated outside the UK where the taxpayer is himself resident in the UK. The author's view is that it does not. This follows from the wording of subsection (14) which reads as follows:

'This section shall apply to all persons, whether resident in the United Kingdom or not, if all or any part of the land in question is situated in the United Kingdom.'

The implication is that if no part of the land is situated in the UK, then the section does not apply.

In the absence of special provisions, it would be possible for UK resident persons to avoid tax on profits arising from transactions in properties situated abroad by arranging for the transaction to be carried out by companies or trusts resident abroad. This is counteracted in a number of ways.

- If the UK person is a company and the interest is held by a subsidiary in a low tax country, the Controlled Foreign Companies legislation may apply.
- If the UK person is an individual who is ordinarily resident in the UK, the provisions described below may have the effect that the profits arising to the overseas company or trust are deemed to be his income for tax purposes. These provisions are to be found in ICTA 1988, ss. 739–746.

The purpose of s. 739 is to counteract the avoidance of income tax, capital gains tax or inheritance tax by individuals who are ordinarily resident in the UK by means of a transfer of assets abroad. The section applies where, as a result of such a transfer, or as a result of the transfer and any associated operations, income becomes payable to persons resident or domiciled outside the UK. If such an individual has power to enjoy the income, whether immediately or at some future time, then the income is deemed to be his income. It is chargeable to tax under Schedule D Case VI. Credit is given for any tax deducted at source.

Further, if such an individual receives a capital sum which is connected with the transfer or the associated operations, then the income of the non-resident person is deemed to be his income. A capital sum includes a loan or the repayment of a loan.

'Associated operations' and 'power to enjoy' are defined in s. 742. Simple situations are where:

- the overseas person is a company and the individuals control the company;
- the overseas person is a settlement and the individuals are beneficiaries, even if only discretionary beneficiaries;
- the overseas person is a company or settlement and the individuals are loan creditors.

The above provisions are supplemented by provisions which apply where an individual who is ordinarily resident in the UK receives a benefit which is not otherwise chargeable to income tax, by virtue or in consequence of the transfer of assets or associated operations (s. 740). The individual is chargeable on the greater of the value of the benefit and the accumulated income of the non-resident person, unless that income is caught by s. 739.

The above legislation does not apply if the transfer and associated operations were bona fide commercial transactions not designed to avoid tax, or if none of the purposes of the transactions was the avoidance of tax. The legislation applies irrespective of whether the individuals were ordinarily resident in the UK when the transfer of assets took place (s. 739(1A)).

4 'Artificial' transactions in land

4.1 Introduction

The legislation brings certain gains of a capital nature within the charge to income tax or corporation tax under Schedule D Case VI. It is not regarded as an alternative to Case I. Therefore, if a transaction is within Case I then it is not within ICTA 1988, s. 776. On the other hand, to the extent that a transaction falls within s. 776, it is outside the scope of capital gains tax (TCGA 1992. s. 37).

There are two common situations where this legislation applies:

- 'slice of action' schemes, and
- 'diversion' schemes.

A slice of action scheme is a scheme where a landowner who is not a developer sells land to a developer for a consideration that includes a share of any profit or proceeds from the subsequent development of the land. The consideration may also include a fixed sum payable at the time of the disposal. The Revenue accepts that the fixed sum is not within s. 776, but argues that the subsequent participation in the profits or sale proceeds is caught (see *Page (HMIT) v Lowther* [1983] BTC 394 mentioned below). A diversion scheme usually attempts to dress up a trading transaction in such a way that the gain is realised by a person who is outside the charge to UK tax. An example is the purchase of land for resale, with an intermediate sale to a non-resident company or trust (see *Sugarwhite v Budd (HMIT)* [1988] BTC 189 mentioned below).

The section applies whenever land, or an asset deriving its value from land (see below), is acquired or developed with the sole or main object of realising a profit from the disposal of the land; or where land is held as trading stock, and a capital profit is realised by means of an indirect disposal of an interest in that land. The provisions are therefore primarily concerned with the intention of the taxpayer at the time of his acquisition of an interest in the land, or its development, regardless of any subsequent change in motive on his part (ICTA 1988, s. 776(2)).

In ascertaining the intentions of the taxpayer, the objects or powers of any company, partnership or trust, as set out in its memorandum and articles of association or other document, are not taken as conclusive evidence as to the intention of that taxpayer (s. 777(4)).

4.2   Scope of provisions

The provisions not only attack the person acquiring, developing or holding the land in question, but also any persons connected with him or anyone else, who by virtue of some arrangement or scheme may also derive a capital sum from the disposal – and whether such person realises the gain himself or obtains it for some other person. In addition there are very far reaching provisions covering all manner of arrangements, series of transactions, and indirect disposals (ICTA 1988, s. 776(2), (4), (5) and (6) and s. 777(2) and (3)).

The scope of the provisions might well be illustrated by reference to a case involving the sale of property by a UK resident group of companies (controlled by the taxpayer and family trusts) to two companies resident in Guernsey (held by trustees in Guernsey for the benefit of the taxpayer's family), followed by its subsequent repurchase later by the same UK group at an enhanced price. The taxpayer was assessed on the profit realised by the overseas companies, although he derived no gain himself, only indirectly for his family, and even though both transactions took place at full market values (*Yuill v Wilson* (1980) 52 TC 674).

Another example is that of trustees granting a long lease of land to a developer for a premium reflecting a proportion of the value of the underleases which were granted by the developer on completion of the development. Here it was the developer who developed the land with the sole or main object of realising a gain from disposing of it and the trustees who obtained the capital profit through the arrangement for the premium to reflect the value created by the development. The trustees were accordingly chargeable despite the fact that they had sold a fixed asset which they had acquired without a trading motive, and that they had not developed it themselves (*Page (HMIT) v Lowther* [1983] BTC 394).

Again, where an individual sold land at an undervalue to a Bahamian company which subsequently sold it at a profit, that company was found to be party to the arrangement by which the individual indirectly disposed of the land, so that its profit was to be treated as income (s. 776(2) and (3)). Since however the opportunity to realise that profit was provided by the individual, it was instead to be taxed as his income under s. 776(8) (*Sugarwhite v Budd (HMIT)* [1988] BTC 189).

The Revenue has indicated that it will apply s. 776 where a land dealer makes a gift of property to a connected individual prior to its sale, so that a profit arises to that individual. On the other hand, where shareholders sold all their shares in a land dealing company immediately after the company had sold its land, it was held that the sale of the shares was not part of an arrangement or scheme whereby the land was sold indirectly, so that there was no gain of a capital nature on the sale of the shares – and that even if there was such a scheme or arrangement the exemption under s. 776(10), which is described below where the company sells the land in the normal course of its trade, would apply (*Chilcott v IR Commrs* (1982) 55 TC 446).

Unlike under certain other anti-avoidance provisions there is no exemption for bona fide commercial transactions. The statement in s. 776(1) that 'the section is enacted to prevent the avoidance of tax by persons concerned with land or the development of land' is not sufficient to prevent the section from being applied to transactions that are clearly within its ambit, even though the transactions may not be carried out with intent to avoid tax (*Page (HMIT) v Lowther* [1983] BTC 394).

The Inland Revenue is given wide powers to obtain information for the purposes of these provisions,including information regarding unidentified transactions and arrangements (s. 778 and *Essex and Others v CIR and Another* (1980) 53 TC 720).

4.3   Chargeable property

For this purpose land includes not only an estate or interest in land or buildings but also other assets deriving their value from land. The latter also includes a shareholding in a company, or an interest in a trust or partnership, which derives its value directly or indirectly from land – as well as an option or right of consent or embargo affecting land. The Inland Revenue is given powers to look through any series of such interests – so that the provisions can apply, for example, to the disposal of an interest in a trust which holds a share in a partnership, which itself owns shares in a property company (ICTA 1988, ss. 776(13) and 777(5)).

A letter granting the taxpayer a share in two property development schemes was held to constitute a trust giving an equitable interest in the properties and so fell within s. 776 (*Winterton v Edwards (HMIT)* (1980) 52 TC 655 and *Byfield v Edwards (HMIT)* (1979) 52 TC 655).

4.4   Timing

The gain is chargeable as income in the chargeable period in which the gain is realised (ICTA 1988, s. 776(3)(*a*)). A sequel to the case of *Yuill v Wilson* (1980) 52 TC 674 was that of *Yuill v Fletcher* [1984] BTC 164, where most of the consideration was subject to a contingency, and was eventually paid to the taxpayer in instalments when the contingency had expired. It was held that the gain was taxable in the periods in which the consideration was received, rather than in the period in which the disposal took place when the value of the contingent rights was smaller.

4.5 Development

The development of a property with the view to the realisation of a profit also falls within the section. No statutory definition of 'development' is given for this purpose, nor has its meaning yet been amplified by the courts. The Revenue's view is that 'development' means any physical adaptation or preparation for a new use.

However, merely obtaining planning permission on land is not regarded as development in the ordinary sense of the word. Nor does a change in the use of a property of itself give rise to a development. Nevertheless, if such a change of use involved some material alterations, etc. it may be treated as development for this purpose. Similarly the demolition of an existing building, or other site clearance work, should only be regarded as work preparatory to development and not development itself. However, once foundation work is started on a new building, this must surely be regarded as a development for these purposes.

4.6 Appropriation of dealing stock

The section can create difficulties in certain situations. For example, where property has been appropriated from dealing stock as an investment asset, there is a deemed disposal of the property in computing the profits of the trade. But this may not be the end of the story. Technically the property was originally acquired with a view to the realisation of a profit on its resale. Therefore the question arises as to whether any capital profit derived from a subsequent sale of the property, now held as an investment, is chargeable under this section. The question can only be answered in the light of all the relevant facts of a particular case. It may be appropriate to take advantage of the clearance procedure outlined below.

4.7 Shares in property dealing companies

The provisions do not apply to a profit derived from the sale of shares in a property dealing company, or its holding company, even if those shares are acquired with a view to the realisation of a profit, provided that all the land held as dealing stock is subsequently disposed of by the company in the normal course of its trade so as to procure that all opportunity of profit from that land arises to that company. It would therefore be appropriate for the vendor of such shares to obtain some suitable warranty from the purchaser that, so far as he is able, he will procure that the trading stock is disposed of on this basis. Otherwise difficulties might arise if, for example, the purchaser subsequently arranges that the dealing stock is appropriated as an investment – which will not be regarded as a disposal in the ordinary course of trading (ICTA 1988, s. 776(10)).

4.8   Asset strippers

Difficulties can arise where shares giving control of a company are acquired with a view to procuring the realisation of a profit from selling property held by that company as a capital asset. The overall transaction may fall within the section due to the purchaser's intention at the time he buys the shares, being assets deriving their value from property. The section seeks to assess the *whole* of the gain realised from the disposal of the property, not necessarily just the profit arising from the transaction. It thus seems that any increase in the value of the property since its original acquisition by the company, including an increase in value accruing before the shares in that company changed hands, may be vulnerable under the section. An application for clearance in such circumstances might also be considered here.

4.9   Acquisition of other interests

As noted, the provisions apply to charge tax on the *whole* of the gain arising from the disposal of the property. Further difficulties can arise when other interests are acquired in the property. For example, a person wishing to dispose of his freehold reversionary interest in a property may wish to improve the sale price by buying out the tenant's leasehold interest to obtain vacant possession. Has the taxpayer acquired the leasehold interest with a view to realising the profit from disposing of his freehold interest, and does the whole of the gain thus realised by him on the sale of the freehold with vacant possession then become taxable under ICTA 1988, s. 776 as a result?

Under the section, one interest in land is treated as separate from another interest in the same land, so that it should be possible to split the proceeds of sale received as between that part applicable to the original reversionary interest and that part applicable to the purchased leasehold interest. Hence at most only the latter proceeds fall within the section. At least therefore that part of the gain attributable to the freehold reversion escapes the provisions of this section – including a proportion of any uplift in values resulting from the merger of the two interests. Nevertheless it may be advisable to take advantage of the clearance procedure.

4.10   Intra-group transfers

Consider also the case of a 75%+ group of companies, where a property investment is transferred from one company within the group to another company, prior to its ultimate sale outside the group, perhaps in order to match chargeable gains with allowable losses for capital gains tax purposes. The second company acquires the property with a view to its resale at a profit – at least at a profit to the group if not to itself, depending on whether or not the inter-company transfer price equals the expected proceeds of sale – thus technically bringing the transaction within ICTA 1988, s. 776. Where the inter-company transfer is made purely to match gains with losses, the Inland Revenue has, in the past, gone on record as saying that it would not seek to operate the section in such circumstances alone. As from 1 April 2000, it may not be necessary to make an intra-group transfer, because an election under TCGA 1992, s. 171A may be made in order to match gains and losses (see **Chapter 8**).

4.11   Private residences

The provisions do not apply to a private owner-occupied residence, if the capital gain is exempt from capital gains tax under the principal private residence provisions (see **Chapter 8**), or would be exempt but for the fact that it was acquired wholly or partly with a view to resale at a profit (ICTA 1988, s. 776(9)).

4.12   Non-residents and property situated abroad

The section is extended to non-residents, where the land in question is situated within the UK. Although there is no similar restriction to land in the UK only, in the case of a UK resident there is perhaps an implied restriction to this effect (ICTA 1988, s. 776(13)). If a non-resident is entitled to any consideration that becomes taxable under these provisions, the Inland Revenue may direct that the payment of that sum should be made under deduction of tax (s. 777(9)).

The issue of a direction is rare as the direction may only be made where a person is presently entitled to a payment, but before the payment is made.

A present entitlement only arises when a contract comes into existence. Therefore, there is only a narrow window of opportunity for the Revenue to issue a direction – between contract and completion (*Pardoe (HMIT) v Entergy Power Development Corp.* [2000] BTC 87).

4.13   Clearance procedure

A procedure is available whereby, if full details of a transaction or proposed transaction are submitted to the Inspector of Taxes, the Inspector is required to give a ruling as to whether or not he is satisfied that the resultant profit will not be chargeable under this section. The wording however does call for some criticism. Thus the applicant may be disappointed to receive a reply to the effect that the Inspector is not satisfied that the gain would not be chargeable – which may not necessarily indicate that the Inspector believes the gain to be in fact taxable under ICTA 1988, s. 776, but merely that he is not satisfied either way. The author believes that this is an all too easy answer if the position is not clear cut or the transaction is very involved – precisely the type of situation where, under this very difficult legislation, a definitive reply by way of clearance or otherwise is required (s. 776(11)).

It may be that the Inspector considers that a particular transaction for which clearance is sought falls within Schedule D Case I. In this case the Inspector will normally state in any clearance letter that the provision of a clearance under s. 776 does not prevent the Revenue from seeking to charge tax under Case I (*Inspector's Manual,* paragraph IM 4751). Finally, any clearance is valid only in relation to the particular applicant (IM 4752).

4.14   Computation of chargeable profit

4.14.1   General principles

There is scant statutory guidance as to how the profit is computed for an assessment under ICTA 1988, s. 776. The section itself gets over this problem by simply requiring that the gain is to be computed 'as is just and reasonable in the circumstances'! In addition, the value of anything obtained from the disposal of the property is brought into account – so that, for example, where property is exchanged for shares in a company, the shares are valued and included as the proceeds of disposal.

The Revenue follows the principles of Schedule D Case I. Indeed this treatment is specifically required in certain circumstances, such as where a leasehold interest is disposed of and a freehold reversion retained. Similarly, where a premium is received, and a proportion thereof is taxable as rental income under Schedule A, it is also treated in the same way as in a Schedule D Case I computation (s. 776(6)(*a*) and (*b*)).

Relief for outgoings is confined to expenditure attributable to the property disposed of itself (ss. 776(6) and 777(6)).

It has never been clear whether this restriction on allowable expenditure operated to exclude relief for interest payable. In most cases, if interest is payable on a loan to fund the acquisition, then the transaction is likely to be dealt with as a trading transaction. As regards corporation tax, relief under the 'loan relationships' legislation is available (FA 1996, s. 83).

4.14.2   Developments

Where the charge to tax arises as a result of a development of property with an intention to sell at a profit, and there was no such intention to sell at the time the property was acquired, the taxpayer may eliminate any part of the gain attributable to the period before he decided to develop the property – noting particularly the reference to the decision to develop here, rather than the decision to sell.

This is achieved by treating the property as if it had been appropriated to dealing stock at the time the decision to develop was made – by bringing it into the computations at its full market value at that time. This same market value is also treated as the proceeds of disposal for the purposes of computing any chargeable gain arising from the subsequent disposal as a result of the appropriation (s. 776(7) and (11)).

Example 4.1

Douglas Rhodes purchases a factory for use in his business at a cost of £200,000. Several years later he no longer requires the premises and tries unsuccessfully to sell them at their value of £250,000. He is subsequently advised that, by carrying out substantial modernisation, he will improve the chances of a sale and increase the sale value. By this time the premises are worth £270,000. The modernisation costs £90,000 and is substantial enough to represent a 'development' for s. 776 purposes. He then sells the property for the sum of £400,000. Douglas Rhodes is assessed to tax as follows:

(a) Capital gains tax

Deemed proceeds (= value at time of decision to develop)	£270,000
Less: Cost	200,000
Chargeable gain subject to indexation relief	£ 70,000

(b) s. 776

Proceeds		£400,000
Less: Value as above	£270,000	
Modernisation costs	90,000	360,000
Profit assessable		£40,000

In a case where an individual was assessed on gains he had procured for others, and where a major proportion of the proceeds of disposal were retained by the purchaser against certain contingencies, it was decided that the computation of the gain chargeable for a particular year could only include the proceeds of disposal actually received during the year, excluding any amounts retained against contingencies. The full costs were deducted against the initial receipts, with no allocation to future contingent receipts (although perhaps the Inland Revenue could have sought to bring the value of these future receipts into the computation). But, where this basis of calculation produced a loss for one of the persons for whom the gain had been procured, such loss could not be deducted from other profits derived for other persons. Presumably the door is still open for further assessments upon the release of the balance of sale proceeds (*Yuill v Wilson* (1980) 52 TC 674).

5 Capital allowances

5.1 Introduction

Under UK tax legislation, there is no general provision for the allowance of depreciation of property, whether commercially justifiable or not – so that any depreciation provided in accounts is added back to taxable profits, but subject to a claim for certain specific allowances granted on a statutory basis, called capital allowances, as set out below.

5.1.1 Land and buildings

No allowance is granted in respect of expenditure incurred in acquiring land, whether freehold or leasehold (unless it represents a premium paid to a superior landlord who is taxed on a part thereof as if it were rental income – see **Chapter 2**). Nor for the most part is any allowance given for the depreciation of buildings, particularly none in respect of residential property, offices, shops or similar commercial properties unless situated in an enterprise zone. But an allowance is granted in respect of industrial buildings and hotels, as set out in this chapter.

5.1.2 Plant and machinery

An allowance is also granted in respect of expenditure incurred on plant and machinery installed in an industrial or commercial building (whether that building itself qualifies as an industrial building or an hotel or not) – and also in common parts of a block of flats (but not equipment, etc. installed in individual flats or houses). Such items would include heating, ventilation, lifts, lighting in certain circumstances, and other ancillary items. Relief for expenditure on such items therefore extends to most buildings.

5.2 Industrial buildings

5.2.1 Introduction

The allowances described in this part, called industrial buildings allowances, are granted in respect of *capital* expenditure incurred on the acquisition, construction or alteration of a building that is occupied for a qualifying purpose.

A company generally must make a claim for the amount of allowances required (FA 1998, Sch. 18 Paras. 78–83), whereas an individual may effectively of disclaim what is not required (CAA 2001, s. 56(4)), in the return or amended return submitted to the Inland Revenue.

5.2.2   Owner occupiers and landlords

The allowances are available to both a landlord, who incurs expenditure on the provision of a qualifying building for letting, and also to a trader who incurs expenditure in providing him with a qualifying building for the purpose of his trade.

5.2.3   Plant and equipment in buildings

Where a building includes the installation of plant or equipment, it may be possible to claim a greater write off of the expenditure under the allowances available in respect of such items, so that such expenditure should be claimed separately. It is therefore important for an analysis of the expenditure to be obtained at an early stage in the construction process or in negotiating an allocation of the purchase price. Similar allowances can be claimed for expenditure on fire safety, thermal insulation and safety at sports grounds.

5.2.4   Giving effect to Industrial Buildings Allowances

Where the building is occupied for the purposes of a trade, the allowances are given as a deduction in computing the profits of the trade, and any balancing charge is treated as a trading receipt (CAA 2001, s. 352). Where the building is let, the allowances are given as a deduction in computing the profits of the rental business, and any balancing charge is treated as a receipt of that business (CAA 2001, s. 353).

5.2.5   The qualifying conditions

The right to claim allowances in respect of industrial buildings depends on three main aspects:

- whether the building qualifies as an industrial building, which in turn depends on the purposes for which it is occupied;
- whether qualifying expenditure has been incurred on the provision of such a building, and
- whether the person concerned has a qualifying interest in the building, called 'the relevant interest'.

5.2.6   What is an industrial building?

A building or other structure qualifies as an industrial building if it is occupied for the purposes of one of the following trades or undertakings (CAA 2001, ss. 271–281) shown in Tables 5.1 and 5.2.

Table 5.1 Trades which are 'qualifying trades'	
1. *Manufacturing*	A trade consisting of manufacturing goods or materials.
2. *Processing*	A trade consisting of subjecting goods or materials to a process. This includes (subject to s. 276(3)) maintaining or repairing goods or materials.
3. *Storage*	A trade consisting of storing goods or materials: (a) which are to be used in the manufacture of other goods or materials, (b) which are to be subjected, in the course of a trade, to a process, (c) which, having been manufactured or produced or subjected, in the course of a trade, to a process, have not yet been delivered to any purchaser, or (d) on their arrival in the UK from a place outside the UK.
4. *Agricultural contracting*	A trade consisting of: (a) ploughing or cultivating land occupied by another, (b) carrying out any other agricultural operation on land occupied by another, or (c) threshing another's crops. For this purpose 'crops' includes vegetable produce.

Table 5.1 cont.	
5. *Working foreign plantations*	A trade consisting of working land outside the UK used for: (a) growing and harvesting crops, (b) husbandry, or (c) forestry. For this purpose 'crops' includes vegetable produce and 'harvesting crops' includes the collection of vegetable produce (however effected).
6. *Fishing*	A trade consisting of catching or taking fish or shellfish.
7. *Mineral extraction*	A trade consisting of working a source of: Mineral deposits. 'Mineral deposits' includes any natural deposits capable of being lifted or extracted from the earth, and for this purpose geothermal energy is to be treated as a natural deposit. 'Source of mineral deposits' includes a mine, an oil well and a source of geothermal energy.

Table 5.2 Undertakings which are 'qualifying trades' if carried on by way of trade	
1. *Electricity*	An undertaking for the generation, transformation, conversion, transmission or distribution of electrical energy.
2. *Water*	An undertaking for the supply of water for public consumption.
3. *Hydraulic power*	An undertaking for the supply of hydraulic power.
4. *Sewerage*	An undertaking for the provision of sewerage services within the meaning of the Water Industry Act 1991.
5. *Transport*	A transport undertaking.

Table 5.2 cont.	
6. *Highway undertakings*	A highway undertaking, that is, so much of any undertaking relating to the design, building, financing and operation of roads as is carried on: (a) for the purposes of, or (b) in connection with, the exploitation of highway concessions.
7. *Tunnels*	A tunnel undertaking.
8. *Bridges*	A bridge undertaking.
9. *Inland navigation*	An inland navigation undertaking.
10. *Docks*	A dock undertaking. A dock includes: (a) any harbour, and (b) any wharf, pier, jetty or other works in or at which vessels can ship or unship merchandise or passengers, other than a pier or jetty primarily used for recreation.
Expenditure on the construction of a qualifying hotel or sports pavilion also qualifies (CAA 2001, s. 271(1)(b)).	

Subjecting goods or materials to a process

The subjection of goods or materials to a process includes packaging and sorting *(Kilmarnock Equitable Co-operative Society v IR Commrs* (1966) 42 TC 675 – see below), but not a crematorium *(Bourne (HMIT) v Norwich Crematorium* (1967) 44 TC 164 – where the learned judge commented: 'I can only say that, having given the matter the best attention that I can, I conclude that the consumption by fire of the mortal remains of *homo sapiens* is not the subjection of goods or materials to a process within the definition of industrial buildings'. Money in the form of coins and notes has been held not to be 'goods and materials' for this purpose. Consequently a part of a building used by a security company for packeting wages, storing money and for communications purposes did not qualify as an industrial building *(Buckingham (HMIT) v Securitas Properties* (1980) 53 TC 292).

The *Securitas* case was followed in the later case of *Girobank plc v Clarke (HMIT)* [1998] BTC 24. Girobank incurred capital expenditure on the construction of a building that was used as a processing centre for processing cheques and other documents. These documents were received from customers. Information from the documents was fed into the company's computer situated in another location. The documents were then sorted and batched before onward transmission to the clearing banks. The court upheld the decision of the Special Commissioner that the documents were received not as goods, but as documents carrying information. They were not acquired as trading stock. Therefore they were not 'goods or materials' within the meaning of CAA 1990, s. 18(1)(e). The court did, however, accept that the building was not an office within the meaning of s. 18(4). Further, it approved the wide interpretation of 'subjection to a process' offered by Lindsay J in the High Court ([1996] BTC 241 at 259), who found nothing in the authorities that limits the very broad width of 'any process' to processes only of an industrial character.

It is not necessarily required of a process that it alters the goods or materials subjected to it in any way. It may suffice that the process should clean, sort or package the goods or materials fed into it. Further, it is not necessary that the process be carried out with a view to the sale or disposition of the goods or materials processed. However, a process does connote a substantial measure of uniformity of treatment or system of treatment.

The meaning of 'subjection to a process' was considered again in the case of *Bestway (Holdings) v Luff (HMIT)* [1998] BTC 69. The Bestway group of companies operated a number of wholesale cash and carry warehouses. Its customers were mainly retailers and caterers. The goods sold were groceries, tobacco, confectionery, wines, beers, spirits and household goods. At one of the warehouses, there was a rice mill for cleaning rice and pulses. At other warehouses there were freezer compartments. The operations carried on at these warehouses were the checking and sorting of goods, repackaging of goods on arrival, labelling, unpacking, and reading product codes. The Revenue accepted that the rice mill and the freezer units qualified for capital allowances, but refused the company's claims on the warehouses generally. The court upheld the finding of the Special Commissioner that the operations described above were mere preliminaries to the sale of the goods. They were of no substantial significance and did not amount to the subjection of goods to a process. Further, the trade was not one of storage, since the storage of the goods was not an end of the trade in itself.

Following the decision in the *Bestway* case, the Revenue published the following material in *Tax Bulletin*, Issue 44 (December 1999).

'Part of a trade

To qualify for IBA the building or structure must be in use for the purposes of a qualifying trade. The qualifying trade does not need to be the whole of the trade carried on, it can be a part of the trade (CAA 2001, s. 276).

We previously took the view that anything done in the course of a trade is a part of the trade for this purpose.

Bestway shows that this view was too wide. The court held that although the activities in question do not need to be self-contained, they must be a significant, separate and identifiable part of the trade carried on.

A trade which consists in the storage of goods or materials

The decision in *Bestway* clarifies the meaning of the phrase "trade which consists of the storage of goods or materials". The court held that the determining factor in deciding whether the goods are stored is the purpose for which they are kept or held. A building is only used for storage if the purpose of keeping goods there is their storage as an end in itself. There is no such use for storage if the goods are kept there for some other purpose. Storage which is merely a necessary and transitory incident of the conduct of the business is not sufficient. The decision in *Crusabridge Investments v Casings International* 54 TC 246 was distinguished as the collection and storage of tyres was an essential part of the business in that case.

Consequences of the decision in *Bestway*

The main impact is likely to be on those wholesale trades where we have previously accepted, in the particular circumstances of the case, that there was a qualifying part trade of storage of goods or materials which would be used in the manufacture of other goods or materials or subjected in the course of a trade to a process. In order for the building or structure to continue to qualify for IBA, the storage must form a significant, separate and identifiable part of the trade and be conducted as a purpose and end in itself, not just a necessary and transitory incident of the conduct of the wholesale business. Each case will have to be considered on its own facts. The sort of business which may be affected by the *Bestway* decision is a builders' merchant where it has previously been accepted that a building or structure in use for the purposes of the trade which consists in the storage of building materials that are to be used in the manufacture of other goods or materials would qualify. Depending on the facts, such storage may no longer qualify the building or structure for IBA.

Where claims to IBA have been accepted for previous periods in accordance with our previous prevailing practice and IBA ceases to be due as a result of the revised view of the meaning of "part of a trade" and a "trade which consists in the storage of goods or materials", the revised view should be applied to claims of that taxpayer for chargeable periods ending after 31 December 1999. Claims for periods ending on or before 31 December 1999 in respect of the expenditure that has been agreed as qualifying for IBA under our previous prevailing practice will be allowed subject to any other changes in the nature and conduct of the trade that may affect entitlement to IBA for those periods, such as the admission of retail customers or the outsourcing of supplies.'

The subjection of goods or materials to a process does include the maintaining or repairing of any goods or materials. The building does not however qualify where the maintenance and repair is carried out on items used in the person's own trade unless use in that trade will itself qualify for the allowance. For example, work carried out by the maintenance department of a department store would not qualify. A plant hire operator's depot does not qualify as an industrial building where nothing is actually made there – but any building or structure provided for the welfare of workers employed in such a trade, including in particular a sports pavilion, also qualifies as an industrial building (CAA 2001, s. 275).

Toll roads and highways

Qualifying expenditure comprises expenditure both on the road and on superstructures such as toll booths and gates used for the purpose of the toll road undertaking. Such an undertaking is regarded as a trade, and the person carrying on the undertaking is treated as occupying the toll road for that purpose. It is a precondition of obtaining a writing-down allowance that the person incurring the expenditure should have an interest in the land at the end of the period, and that the interest should be the relevant interest in relation to the expenditure. A person entitled to charge tolls is regarded as having the relevant interest provided he has incurred expenditure on the construction of the road, even if he does not have an interest in the road, since the right to charge tolls is regarded as a qualifying interest in the road. A highway undertaking is defined as so much of an undertaking relating to the design, building, financing and operation of any roads as is carried on for the purpose of exploiting highway concessions. Highway concessions are in turn defined, in relation to any road, as any right to receive sums from the Department of the Environment for the use of the road by the general public or the right to charge tolls in respect of the road (CAA 2001, s. 341(4)).

Offices, retail shops, etc.

Specifically excluded are any buildings or structures which are used as a private residence, office, retail shop, showroom, or for any ancillary purposes (CAA 2001, s. 277). However the drawing office of a company that carried on business as structural steel engineers has been held to be an industrial building, rather than an office, for this purpose. The drawing office was situated in a separate building altogether, close to the works, but not otherwise qualifying as an industrial building. Nevertheless the taxpayer was able to claim allowances in respect of that part of the building that was used by the drawing office (*IR Commrs v Lambhill Ironworks* (1950) 31 TC 393).

In the case of *Sarsfield (HMIT) v Dixons Group plc* [1998] BTC 288, it was held that a company within a group may carry on a qualifying trade of storage even if the goods stored in its warehouses are transferred to a retail company in the same group. In that case, the trade of storage was held to be an independent undertaking in its own right. The retail trades carried on by other companies in the group were likewise independent undertakings. The conduct of a separate undertaking is the antithesis of an ancillary activity and the existence of the group relationship was irrelevant. The trade of storage was not ancillary to the trade of the retail company. There are special allowances for commercial buildings in enterprise zones, and for hotels.

Warehouses

The reference in Table 5.1 to a trade which consists in storage might seem to imply that the storage must be of goods belonging to a third party for a specific fee. This appeared to be consistent with the ruling in *Dale (HMIT) v Johnson Bros* (1951) 32 TC 487 where the building used for storage did not qualify for the allowance, because the company was largely storing its own goods, not those of a third party. This finding could be criticised on the grounds that it overlooked the fact that under what is now CAA 2001, s. 276 a reference to a trade includes a reference to part of a trade. Recognition was given to this principle in the case of *Kilmarnock Equitable Co-operative Society v IR Commrs* (1966) 42 TC 675, where the company acted as general retailers and sellers of coal in bulk. An allowance was granted in respect of a building for housing machinery for the screening, weighing and packing of coal belonging to the company before its sale. It was held that the screening, etc. was an identifiable part of the trade – though in this case it was a trade consisting in the subjection of goods or materials to a process, rather than a storage trade – even though no specific charge was made to the customer.

The Inland Revenue's view apparently is that an activity can constitute a part of a trade if it is capable of being sub-contracted on its own, but there appears to be no statutory backing for this test.

The decision in *Crusabridge Investments v Casings International* (1980) 54 TC 246 departed further from the *Dale (HMIT) v Johnson Bros* (1951) 32 TC 487 principle noted above. Here a qualifying trade of storage was established where the company both stored used tyres which it had purchased for storing and sale to remoulders (viz goods which are subject to further processing) and stored remoulded tyres for sale on commission (viz goods which, having been processed, have not yet been delivered to any purchaser). Following this the Inland Revenue stated that a building will qualify where it is used for warehousing and storage by traders and wholesalers, and where the goods involved are to be used for industrial process, though not where the premises are used for storage for retailing purposes.

Despite *Dale (HMIT) v Johnson Bros* (1951) 32 TC 487, therefore, the implication of these decisions and of the Inland Revenue statement is that warehousing and storage will qualify as an industrial purpose, even where this activity is part of a wider activity such as buying and selling and where no fee is specifically charged for the warehousing and storage. Where some of the goods stored in a warehouse are manufactured by the occupier, and some have been bought in for retail sale, and the two types of stock are mixed together, it may still be regarded as an industrial building for this purpose (*IR Commrs v Saxone Lilley & Skinner (Holdings)* (1967) 44 TC 122).

An inland warehouse at which goods were stored after being transported from an inland container depot or collected from an airport did not qualify as an industrial building, since it was not used for the storage of goods on their arrival by sea or air into the UK (*Copol Clothing v Hindmarch (HMIT)* [1984] BTC 35).

Kennels, albeit with special features, to house animals in quarantine were not considered to be used for the storage of goods (*Carr (HMIT) v Sayer & Anor* [1992] BTC 286).

Landlord and tenant

It is not stipulated who should be the party occupying the building, so expenditure by a landlord may qualify for the allowance where the building is occupied for a qualifying purpose by a tenant, or indeed by a subtenant or licensee (CAA 2001, ss. 271, 278).

The landlord should therefore consider the purposes for which a prospective tenant intends to occupy the premises, to see whether or not he will be able to benefit from the allowances. No doubt the prospective tenant will also be aware of the value of his intended occupation, if it thus enables the building to qualify for these allowances – so that both parties might perhaps share the tax benefit by negotiating a rent on appropriate terms, maybe including an appropriate clause restricting use of the premises to qualifying purposes so as to protect the landlord. In the same way a tenant wishing to lease office space for a drawing office ancillary to an industrial trade should be an attractive proposition to his intended landlord.

Part qualifying

Where only part of a trade qualifies as above, then only those buildings used for the qualifying part of that trade are treated as industrial buildings and no allowances are available in respect of non-qualifying buildings (CAA 2001, s. 276). Similarly, where only part of a building is used for a qualifying purpose, the allowances are only given in respect of that part – unless the capital expenditure incurred on the non-qualifying part of the building is no greater than 25 per cent of the expenditure incurred on the whole building, in which case the whole building may qualify (CAA 2001, s. 283).

There may therefore be some opportunities for effecting a tax saving when a new industrial building is being planned. Where for example a factory is planned to include office or showroom space, one might seek to limit the cost of the non-qualifying element to 25 per cent or less of the whole cost – so that allowances are available for the total. Any additional non- qualifying accommodation requirements could then perhaps be housed in a separate building altogether – or, where not immediately required, they might be dealt with by way of a (non-qualifying) extension to the factory at some subsequent date.

5.2.7 Qualifying expenditure

New buildings constructed

The allowances are available in respect of any capital expenditure incurred on the construction of an industrial building (CAA 2001, s. 271). If however any expenditure is recovered by way of a grant or subsidy, the allowances are restricted to the net expenditure (CAA 2001, s. 532). Expenditure on construction includes fees payable to architects, quantity surveyors, engineers, etc. in respect of the building. The cost of obtaining any necessary planning consent is not expenditure on construction and does not, therefore, qualify for IBAs. However, if a builder's quotation for the construction of a building includes the cost of obtaining planning consent, the Revenue does not seek to apportion the contract price between construction and planning application (*Inland Revenue Capital Allowances Manual*, CA1035–1037).

The following are not regarded as construction costs (CA1039):

(a) capitalised interest – following *Ben-Odeco v Powlson (HMIT)* (1978) 52 TC 459;

(b) the cost of a public enquiry;

(c) landscaping costs,

(d) legal expenses.

As regards (a), it is common practice to capitalise interest during the period of construction of a new building. If the building is to be retained as a fixed asset, that interest will not be written off in the accounts, but will be regarded as part of the cost of the asset for accounting purposes. For tax purposes, however, the interest will qualify for relief under the 'loan relationships' provisions discussed in **Chapter 6** (FA 1996, Sch. 9, Para. 14).

Land and preparation costs, etc.

Allowances are specifically confined to the cost of providing buildings, and no relief is available for the cost of land, or an interest therein. However expenditure incurred on preparing, cutting, tunnelling or levelling land, and the cost of ordinary work on the site preparatory to laying foundations may be included in qualifying costs. Similar costs preparatory to the installation of plant and machinery on a site if not otherwise eligible for relief will rank as expenditure on an industrial building (CAA 2001, s. 273).

Allowances may also be claimed by the owner of an industrial estate in respect of expenditure on the provision of private roads, provided that the tenants on the estate occupy the premises wholly or mainly as part of qualifying trades carried on by them (CAA 2001, s. 284).

New buildings purchased

Where the taxpayer purchases an existing industrial building, rather than having it constructed himself, he may still normally claim the allowances. The position of used buildings is dealt with separately below. Here we are talking about the acquisition of a new, unused building. It is the 'relevant interest' that must be purchased if the buyer is to qualify for allowances. This means for instance that if the seller owned the freehold when he constructed the building, one of two things must happen to enable the purchaser to claim the allowances:

- the seller must sell the freehold to him, *or*
- the seller must grant him a lease of more than 50 years for a premium and join in making an election under CAA 2001, s. 290 to the effect that the relevant interest is transferred to the buyer for a price equal to the premium. (The meaning of the relevant interest and the circumstances in which the election can be made are set out later in this section.)

Where the relevant interest is purchased from the builder who sold it in the course of his building trade, the allowances are granted on the price paid by the purchaser for the building – after eliminating the part of the price relating to the land. It is also necessary to eliminate any element attributable to arrangements having an artificial effect on the pricing (such as a rent guarantee) that goes beyond what would be included in the price of a similar building put on the market (CAA 2001, s. 357).

Where the purchase of the building when new is from someone other than the builder selling in the course of his trade, the allowances are granted on the lower of the original construction cost and the purchase price of the building. If however the previous owner (or a predecessor) had purchased from the builder selling in the course of his trade, the allowances available to the ultimate purchaser would be on the lower of his purchase price and the price originally paid to the builder. It is also necessary to eliminate any element attributable to artificial pricing, as above (CAA 2001, s. 357).

Example 5.1

Westhill Construction Ltd buys the freehold of a site and constructs industrial 'sheds' for selling in the course of its property development trade. Fairfax Mouldings Ltd is one of the intended occupiers, and pays £500,000 for the freehold of land with a shed. This sum is apportioned between land cost £150.000 and building £350,000. Consequently Fairfax will obtain allowances on £350,000, being the price attributable to the building.

If, instead, Westhill had sold the shed to a speculator for £500,000, and the speculator had sold it on to Fairfax for £600,000, the land value remaining unchanged, Fairfax could still claim allowances on only £350,000, being the original price for the building paid to the builder, not the £450,000 price paid by him.

Let us now go back to the original example and suppose that because Westhill wants to control the upkeep and appearance of the whole site it decides to sell the shed to Fairfax by way of the grant of a 55-year lease at a premium of £500,000 and a peppercorn rent. The position is now somewhat changed. As a property developer Westhill will have incurred revenue, not capital, expenditure on a construction of the building, and accordingly that expenditure will not enable Westhill to claim industrial buildings allowances. However, if the parties jointly elect for the premium to be treated as the price paid for the transfer of the relevant interest, Fairfax will be deemed to have incurred expenditure of £350,000 on the construction of the building. This follows from the provisions relating to the purchase of an unused building. Allowances will therefore arise to Fairfax in respect of the £350,000 on the basis that expenditure of that amount on construction was incurred by him on the date that sum became payable to Westhill.

Used buildings

A different position emerges where the building is purchased from a builder at a time when it has already been used. The purchaser is not regarded as incurring expenditure on the construction of the building. Instead it is to be assumed, so far as the purchaser is concerned, that the original expenditure incurred by the builder was capital expenditure and that appropriate writing-down allowances and a balancing allowance or charge had been made on its sale. Relief is then available for this residue spread over the remainder of the 25 years after the building was first brought into use. Where the vendor is not within the charge to UK tax, and so could not claim any allowances, the purchaser's allowances in those circumstances must be computed as if the vendor had been entitled to, and claimed, all the normal allowances (CAA 2001, s. 339).

In general, therefore, the purchaser of a used industrial building will now be entitled to allowances based on the lower of the vendor's original qualifying expenditure, or the price paid by the purchaser for the building. The information should preferably be obtained from the vendor at the time of purchase, since it is usually more difficult to obtain such information once the transaction has been completed. It may also be advisable to agree with the vendor the apportionment of the purchase price as between land and buildings – and indeed any plant and equipment therein which might qualify for separate allowances (CAA 2001, ss. 311, 339).

Alterations and improvements

Where capital expenditure incurred on the extension or substantial repair of an industrial building is disallowed as a deduction in computing trading or rental profits as a capital expense, the cost may qualify for allowances under these provisions. Where part of the expenditure is allowed as a revenue expense, only the balance qualifies for allowances here (CAA 2001, s. 272(3)). Larger allowances may be available in respect of expenditure on adding thermal insulation to an industrial building.

5.2.8   Who can claim?

Person incurring the expenditure

A claim for allowances is based upon *capital* expenditure incurred on the *construction or acquisition* of an industrial building, and is available to the person who incurs that expenditure. That person may not occupy the building himself but may instead have a tenant or licensee who uses the building as an industrial building. The tenant may in turn incur capital expenditure on further construction. The question of who may claim relief will then depend upon whether the person seeking to claim has the relevant interest in the building in relation to that expenditure.

Relevant interest

The 'relevant interest' in relation to an industrial building is the interest that the person who incurs the expenditure is entitled to in the building when he incurs that expenditure. Thus, where the owner of freehold land builds on that property, the relevant interest is the freehold. In the same way, where a leaseholder of property incurs expenditure thereon, his leasehold interest is the relevant interest in respect of that expenditure. If he has two or more interests in the same property, the superior reversionary interest is always taken as the relevant interest for this purpose. Thus, where the taxpayer owns both the freehold reversion and a sub-leasehold interest, the freehold is the relevant interest for this purpose. The taxpayer is regarded as retaining that relevant interest despite assignment of the sub-tenancy, but disposes of the relevant interest if he sells the reversionary interest, regardless as to whether he retains the sub-tenancy or not.

In the case of a building under construction, the relevant interest is taken as the interest that will be held, once the building is completed. For example, if the building is being constructed under a building agreement coupled with an agreement for a lease when the building is completed, the relevant interest is the leasehold interest as granted on completion of the building (CAA 2001, s. 286). The costs of acquiring a further interest in the building do not qualify for further allowances unless that interest qualifies as a relevant interest by virtue of some expenditure by the vendor.

Grant of leases

The grant of a lease out of the relevant interest is not normally treated as a disposal of that relevant interest. This is so whatever the term of the lease granted. Thus for example, where the relevant interest consists of a leasehold interest, and the person concerned grants a sub-lease out of the interest, he is still regarded as retaining the relevant interest, even where the sub-lease is for a term of only one day less than his own leasehold interest – and even if he charges a premium on that sub-lease, so that he recovers all his expenditure, and the rents he subsequently receives are equal to the rent he pays under his own lease. Thus to all intents and purposes the person has fully disposed of any effective interest in the property, but nonetheless retains the relevant interest for this purpose. The realisation of capital value attributable to an interest in land in an enterprise zone may give rise to a balancing charge or a reduction in the writing-down allowance in subsequent years. Provision is made for the relevant interest to pass from landlord to tenant in appropriate circumstances, if *both* parties so elect. As will be seen, such an election could be of considerable benefit where the landlord is a tax exempt body and the tenant is called upon to pay some premium under the lease.

The election is available in respect of the grant of a long lease (more than 50 years) out of the relevant interest, where the lease takes effect on or after 15 February 1978. The election must be signed by both landlord and tenant, and must be lodged within two years after the lease takes effect.

The effect of the election is that the tenant is treated as purchasing the relevant interest from the landlord at a price equal to any premium or other capital payment given in respect of the grant of the lease. If no premium, etc. is paid for the lease, the tenant obtains no allowance, and the landlord is entitled to a balancing allowance equal to any balance of unrelieved expenditure.

No election may be made, however, where the landlord and tenant are connected persons, except where the landlord is discharging statutory functions and the tenant is a company of which it has control. It also applies where the main benefit which may accrue to the landlord from the grant of the lease *and* the making of the election is the obtaining of a balancing allowance (CAA 2001, s. 291).

Relevant leasehold interests

Where the relevant interest consists of a leasehold interest, and the tenant disposes of his lease by way of surrender to his immediate landlord, the two interests merge and the landlord's interest then becomes the relevant interest. In the same way, if the tenant acquires his immediate landlord's interest in the property, the two interests also merge and the relevant interest becomes the new superior interest acquired by the leaseholder (CAA 2001, s. 289).

Termination of leases

The provisions go on to deal with the position at the termination of a lease, which may affect the relevant interest and the continuing right to any future allowances in respect of an industrial building. Where a tenant remains in possession of a building after the end of his lease, without actually renewing the lease but with the permission of his landlord, the lease is deemed to continue – so that if the leasehold interest is a relevant interest for the purposes of these provisions, the relevant interest remains in his possession. Similarly, where the lease gives the tenant an option to a new lease at the end of the first lease, the two leases are treated as one. But if the lease comes to an end and the landlord grants the same tenant a new lease, but the tenant had no option under the old lease, the relevant interest comes to an end.

If the landlord makes any payment to his tenant in respect of the building at the end of a lease, the relevant interest passes from the tenant to the landlord. In much the same way, where a lease comes to an end and a new lease is granted to another tenant, if the new tenant makes any payment to the outgoing tenant, the transaction is regarded as an assignment of one lease, rather than the termination of a lease and the grant of a new lease – so that the incoming tenant acquires the relevant interest from the old tenant (CAA 2001, s. 359). Thus where the relevant interest consists of a leasehold interest that terminates, and no payment is made to the tenant either by the landlord or by any new tenant, the relevant interest ends with the lease and does not pass to anyone else. In order for a successor to the property to qualify for future allowances, some payment must be involved – since his right to allowances depends on the amount paid by him for the industrial building in question.

If no sum is paid, or the relevant interest otherwise comes to an end, the tenant is entitled to a further balancing allowance, so as to write off any residue of expenditure not relieved so far.

Disposal of relevant interest

The position regarding the sale of the relevant interest before the building comes into use has already been discussed above, in relation to the amount of expenditure to be taken into account for the purposes of these allowances. As seen, the new owner of the relevant interest may claim allowances based on the lower of the original cost of construction (or the builder's selling price) and his own cost of acquiring the building concerned. Where the building has already been used, the amount of expenditure that may be claimed by the new owner is confined to the lower of the 'residue of expenditure' immediately after the sale by the previous owner and the price that he pays for the building himself. In general terms, however, where the building has always been used for qualifying purposes, this is equivalent to the lower of the vendor's original qualifying expenditure, or the price paid by the purchaser for the building.

Contributions by landlords or tenants

Where a trader, or the landlord of a tenant trader, contributes to capital expenditure on an industrial building whilst not actually owning the relevant interest in respect of that building, provided that the contributor and the owner are not 'connected persons' (ICTA 1988, s. 839), the contributor may be entitled to claim relief in respect of that expenditure (CAA 2001, s. 537).

Implications

Thus the right to claim allowances in respect of industrial buildings depends on the ownership of the relevant interest, as described above. In particular the relevant interest and the right to claim allowances may be retained, despite a disposal of virtually the whole of the owner's interest in the building – as for example where he retains a reversionary interest, however small.

Nominal disposals

In the same way, it would have been possible to dispose of the relevant interest in a property, whilst retaining virtually the whole of that interest – for example, by way of the grant of a 999-year lease to a related party for a premium and a peppercorn rent followed by the sale of the freehold reversion for a small sum. The vendor would thus dispose of his relevant interest, whilst retaining virtually full control of his property. In this way he would have been able to claim a tax allowance in respect of the balance of his qualifying expenditure, in so far as not already relieved. This was too tempting, and legislation was therefore introduced to deny the vendor the right to such balancing allowances in circumstances where he retains a subsidiary interest in the property (CAA 2001, s. 325).

5.2.9 Initial allowances

Since 1 April 1986 the availability of an initial allowance has generally been restricted to qualifying buildings in an enterprise zone. The rate of allowance in such a case is 100 per cent of the qualifying expenditure. The expenditure must be incurred, or a contract for the expenditure must be entered into, within ten years after the site was first included in the enterprise zone (CAA 2001, s. 298).

The provisions were extended, however, for expenditure incurred under a contract entered into in the year ended 31 October 1993 so as to provide a temporary entitlement to a 20 per cent allowance, as described below.

5.2.10 Writing-down allowances

New buildings

The only allowance now generally available for qualifying expenditure on industrial buildings outside enterprise zones is a writing-down allowance. This can be claimed each year in respect of capital expenditure incurred on the construction of an industrial building equal to 4 per cent of the original capital expenditure. The allowance is based on the original cost, rather than the reducing balance.

This writing-down allowance is only available where the person concerned owns the relevant interest at the end of the chargeable period in question, and the building is an industrial building (i.e. a building in use for a qualifying purpose) at the end of the period. Temporary disuse does not prevent the allowance from being claimed so long as the building remains an industrial building at the end of the period; nor does use for a non-qualifying purpose that does not bridge the end of a period. No allowance is available however if the relevant interest is disposed of before the end of the period, or if the building is in use for a non-qualifying purpose or is permanently disused at the end of the period.

Where the chargeable period is less than one year, the amount of the writing-down allowance is proportionately reduced.

These allowances continue until the whole of the original expenditure has been fully relieved or otherwise written off – including both the initial allowance (where expenditure was incurred before 1 April 1986 or the year ended 31 October 1993) and writing-down allowances (CAA 2001, s. 312).

Writing-down allowances are only given on the amount of qualifying expenditure on industrial buildings, not on the cost of acquiring land. For the purpose of writing-down allowances (and, where relevant, initial allowances) in respect of industrial buildings, the general rule is that expenditure is deemed to be incurred when the *obligation to pay the amount in question becomes unconditional* – even if it is actually payable at a later date.

Special provision is made where an obligation to pay an amount becomes unconditional as a result of the issue of a certificate (eg an architect's certificate) within a month after the end of a chargeable period and the asset in question becomes the payer's property prior to the end of that period. In such circumstances, the obligation is treated as having been incurred immediately prior to the year-end. Subject to the anti-avoidance provisions mentioned below, this will be the date on which the expenditure is deemed to have been incurred.

Anti-avoidance legislation prevents these provisions being used artificially to accelerate the time when allowances can be claimed. This applies where an agreement requiring expenditure to be paid more than four months after the obligation to pay becomes unconditional. In such a case, the expenditure is treated as having been incurred at the time when it actually becomes payable.

If the obligation to pay becomes unconditional earlier than under normal commercial usage and the only or main benefit of the acceleration of the obligation to pay is to enable allowances to be claimed in an earlier period, then the expenditure is treated as having been incurred when the amount actually becomes payable, whether or not this is within four months of the date when the obligation to pay becomes unconditional (CAA 2001, s. 5).

By way of exception to these rules, where a person purchases a new. unused industrial building, his expenditure is deemed to be incurred when the purchase price becomes payable – rather than on the date when the vendor is due to pay the builder for its construction.

Enterprise zones

The rate of annual writing-down allowance for expenditure on a building in an enterprise zone (see **3.3.7** below) is increased to 25 per cent (CAA 2001, s. 310(1)).

Notional allowances

Where the building is occupied for a non-qualifying purpose at the end of a chargeable period, so that no allowance is due for that period, the original expenditure must still be written down on a notional basis by the amount of allowance that would otherwise be given – so that it may restrict allowances available in the future (CAA 2001, s. 336).

Where a writing-down allowance is due but is not claimed, it is not given on a notional basis, so that the benefit can be recouped at a later stage if there is a sale within 25 years.

Used buildings

Writing-down allowances may also be available in respect of the acquisition of a relevant interest in a used industrial building, within certain limits. The amount on which allowances can be claimed and the way in which those allowances are calculated depends very much on the tax position previously enjoyed by the vendor of the relevant interest. In general, where the building has always qualified as an industrial building, it will be found that allowances may be claimed on the lower of the vendor's original qualifying expenditure and the price paid by the purchaser for the building (as opposed to any land, etc.). In fact the allowance is based on the 'residue of expenditure' immediately after the sale, which can more easily be explained after examining the vendor's situation on the disposal of his relevant interest. Unlike expenditure on new buildings, the writing-down allowance in the case of a second-hand building is calculated so as to allow the full write off of this residue of expenditure over the balance of a period of 25 years starting with the time when the building first came into use (or if the original expenditure on constructing, etc. the building was incurred before 6 November 1962, over the balance of a period of 50 years). The assumption therefore is that the building only has a useful life of 25 years (or 50 years) from the time when it was first used and that the residue of expenditure is written off evenly over the remaining part of that period (CAA 2001, s. 311).

Example 5.2

If a factory was constructed and first occupied in 1985 and the relevant interest therein is acquired in 1996, 11 years out of the 25-year period have already expired. Any residue of expenditure available to the purchaser of the relevant interest may therefore be written off evenly over the remaining 14 years. If this residue of expenditure amounts to £42,000, the purchaser is given a writing-down allowance of £3,000 in each of those years – subject to his retaining the relevant interest and the continued occupation of the building for qualifying purposes. (See also examples at **3.3.5** below.)

Where an adjustment arises under the VAT capital goods scheme (see **Chapter 11**) the VAT is added to or subtracted from the residue of expenditure, and the writing-down allowances for the remaining life of the building are based on the revised residue (CAA 2001, ss. 345–351).

5.2.11   Disposals and cessation of use

A balancing allowance or charge arises if any of the following events occurs within the 25-year writing-down period (50 years for expenditure incurred before 6 November 1962):

(a)   the relevant interest in the building or structure is sold;

(b)   the relevant interest depends on the duration of a foreign concession and comes to an end on the termination of that concession;

(c)   the relevant interest is a leasehold interest and it comes to an end otherwise than by reason of the acquisition of the immediate reversionary interest;

(d)   the building or structure is demolished or destroyed, or ceases altogether to be used;

(e)   the relevant interest is a highway concession and the concession comes to an end;

(f)   in the case of a building in an enterprise zone, capital value is realised within the meaning of CAA 2001, s. 328,

(g)   additional VAT is recovered in accordance with the capital goods scheme (SI 1995/2518, reg. 115).

As regards (d), the *Inland Revenue Capital Allowances Manual* gives the following examples of circumstances where inspectors will accept that a building has ceased altogether to be used:

- the building has become derelict;
- the building has become unfit for further use;
- the building is to be demolished because it is in the path of a new motorway,
- the site of the building is to be redeveloped (CA1262).

As regards (g), the VAT recovered is deducted from the residue of qualifying expenditure. A balancing charge arises only if the amount recovered exceeds that residue. No balancing allowance can arise under this heading (CAA 2001, s. 350(2)–(4)). Note that where the building includes fixtures that have qualified for machinery and plant allowances, any disposal consideration will have to be apportioned on a just and reasonable basis between the building and the fixtures in accordance with CAA 2001, s. 562. The amount apportioned to fixtures is then brought into the capital allowances computation for machinery and plant.

Disposals

The disposal and acquisition of a relevant interest in an industrial building chiefly arises from a sale of the relevant interest itself, although a deemed sale may also arise where a landlord makes any payment to an outgoing tenant at the end of his lease in respect of an industrial building, or where a new tenant makes a similar payment to the outgoing tenant. In these circumstances, the relevant interest passes from one person to another. The time of any sale is the time of the completion or when possession is given earlier (CAA 2001, s. 572(4)).

Cessation

In addition, the relevant interest may come to an end altogether, without passing to anyone else. This happens if the relevant interest is a leasehold interest which comes to an end, and no payment is made to the outgoing tenant by his landlord or any new tenant. Similarly the relevant interest comes to an end if the building ceases to be used altogether, or where it is demolished or destroyed.

Finally, a relevant interest ceases to have any meaning after 25 years from its original first use (or 50 years where the expenditure was incurred before 6 November 1962) – and no balancing adjustment arises.

Demolition or destruction

The demolition or destruction of an industrial building is the occasion of a balancing adjustment. The costs of demolition are added to the residue of expenditure and any insurance recoveries or compensation receipts are treated as disposal consideration (CAA 2001, s. 316).

Where a site is sold for redevelopment, it is often necessary to demolish existing buildings standing on the site. In the case of an industrial building, the question needs to be considered as to whether the demolition should be carried out by the vendor or the purchaser. This will affect eligibility for any balancing allowance and the consideration for the sale of the site. If the vendor can set off any balancing allowance against profits and can roll over any capital gain on the sale, it might be beneficial for him to carry out the demolition.

Temporary disuse

Where a building falls temporarily out of use, it is deemed to continue to be an industrial building during the period of temporary disuse if it qualified as an industrial building immediately before that period (CAA 2001, s. 354). Thus if it is subsequently used again for the purposes of the qualifying trade, there is no discontinuity in the industrial buildings allowances. Such allowances are deducted in computing the profits of the trade or against the income from the letting of the building. If in the case of such a building during the period of disuse, either:

- the trade for which it was in use ceases permanently, or
- a lease to which the relevant interest was subject comes to an end; industrial buildings allowances relating to periods after the above event continue to be available to the holder of the relevant interest. In the case of corporation tax, they are given by discharge or repayment of tax and are available primarily against Schedule A income. In the case of income tax, the allowances are given in computing the profits of a Schedule A business.

If there is a disposal of the relevant interest during the above period, any balancing charge is chargeable to corporation tax under Schedule D Case VI or to income tax under Schedule A, subject to the rules described below under *Balancing charge after cessation of trade.*

If there is no disposal, but the building begins to be used for a non-qualifying purpose, then writing-down allowances will cease.

Balancing adjustments

The day of reckoning then comes. It is necessary to see whether the owner of the relevant interest has received allowances in previous years on too generous or too small a scale – as compared with his own financial position arising from ownership.

Residue before sale

First one starts with the residue of expenditure *before* the sale, etc. – as opposed to the residue of expenditure *after* the sale in the hands of the purchaser. Broadly this consists of the original qualifying expenditure, less any initial and writing-down allowances actually given (CAA 2001, ss. 323, 324) plus or minus any final adjustment under the VAT capital goods scheme. Where a building is demolished, so that the relevant interest in that building comes to an end, the cost of the demolition is added to the tax written down value of the building in question, to arrive at the balancing adjustment (CAA 2001, s. 340).

Proceeds and adjustment

The residue before sale is then compared with the proceeds of sale, if the person concerned sells his relevant interest, or otherwise receives proceeds, insurance, salvage or compensation monies – remembering that one is only concerned with the building itself, so that total proceeds need to be apportioned between the building and any price received for land, etc. If the monies received exceed the residue before sale, the excess is recovered by way of a tax charge (a balancing charge) – although this balancing charge is restricted to the total allowances actually given to the vendor in the past. On the other hand, if the residue before sale exceeds the proceeds, the taxpayer is given an additional allowance equal to the excess (a balancing allowance). Where there are no proceeds whatsoever, a balancing allowance of this nature is given in respect of the whole of the residue before sale of the building (CAA 2001, ss. 318, 319).

Thus where the building has qualified as an industrial building throughout the period of his ownership of the relevant interest, even though there may have been temporary disuse, the taxpayer is given allowances equal to his original qualifying expenditure less any proceeds of disposal of his interest. This total comprises an original initial allowance, a series of writing-down allowances over the period of his ownership, and final balancing adjustment by way of allowance or charge to adjust the total to the required net figure (CAA 2001, ss. 318, 319).

Note that the Inland Revenue may adjust the split of any proceeds of disposal – taking together all items sold as part of one bargain, and including the value of any asset received in exchange – so as to arrive at a just apportionment. However, it is usually more difficult for it to reallocate an apportionment that has already been agreed between vendor and purchaser acting at arm's length – but see *Fitton v Gilders and Heaton (HMIT)* (1955) 36 TC 233 (CAA 2001, s. 562, 563).

Balancing charge after cessation of trade

If:

- a balancing charge arises in respect of a building which has fallen into temporary disuse, and
- immediately before the building fell into disuse it was used for the purposes of a qualifying trade carried on by the person on whom the balancing charge arises,

then the balancing charge may be treated as post cessation receipts under ICTA 1988, s. 103 or s. 104 so that any unrelieved trading losses, etc. may be set off in accordance with s. 105 (CAA 2001, s. 352, 354).

Disposals after 25 years

No balancing charge is to be made in respect of the disposal of an industrial building more than 25 years (50 years for pre-6 November 1962 expenditure) after it is first used. A balancing charge may arise on an earlier sale, even if all the allowable expenditure has been relieved by way of initial and annual allowances. Thus if the 25-year (50-year) period is nearly up, it may be preferable to delay a sale until after it has expired. But the Inland Revenue may seek to apply this provision to each separate addition to the building (CAA 2001, s. 314(4)).

Balancing adjustments: partially qualifying buildings

Original owner

If the building was not a qualifying industrial building throughout the period from first use to disposal – bearing in mind that use for a non-qualifying purpose prevents the building from being regarded as an industrial building for the duration of that use – then the balancing adjustment is made in one of two ways.

The first applies where the sale proceeds equal or exceed the original qualifying expenditure. Here the whole of the actual allowances previously given are recovered by a balancing charge (CAA 2001, s. 319, 320).

The second applies where the sale proceeds are less than the original qualifying expenditure or where there are no proceeds. Here the balancing adjustment is calculated by comparing the allowances actually given with the 'adjusted net cost' *not* the residue before sale. The adjusted net cost is taken as the original qualifying expenditure less any proceeds – reducing the net amount thus ascertained in the proportion that the period of qualifying use bears to the total period from first use to disposal. If the allowances given exceed the adjusted net cost, the difference is a balancing charge: whereas if the adjusted net cost exceeds the allowances given the difference is a balancing allowance (CAA 2001, s. 318–320).

Example 5.3

On 1 January 1986, Saunders & Co Ltd (having a 31 December year end) purchased from the builder an unused warehouse at a cost of £120,000. They immediately let it to a qualifying user for ten years. The warehouse was then let for a non-qualifying purpose for five years, before another qualifying user took up occupation. They sell the building to Bob Townley four and a quarter years later in 2005 for £100,000.

They received an initial allowance of 50 per cent, ie £60,000, and ten writing-down allowances of 4 per cent, ie £4,800 per annum. Note that the non-qualifying use did not bridge a year end, so that allowances were due in full. Their adjusted net cost is calculated as follows:

Original qualifying expenditure	£120,000
Proceeds of disposal	£100,000
Net cost	£ 20,000

$$\text{Net cost} \times \frac{\text{Qualifying period of use}}{\text{Total period}}$$

$$= £20,000 \times \frac{10 + 4\,\tfrac{1}{4}}{10 + 5 + 4\,\tfrac{1}{4}}$$

= £14,805

(Adjusted net cost)

Allowances actually given:	
Initial	£60,000
Writing-down (10 × £4,800)	£48,000
Total	£108,000
Difference = Balancing charge	£ 93,195

Note that no allowances were due in respect of the second period of qualifying use, since the residue of qualifying expenditure was zero at the commencement of that period (CAA 2001, s. 312). For further guidance on the calculation of 'adjusted net cost' see *Inland Revenue Capital Allowances Manual*, CA1268–1271.

Subsequent owner

The same principles apply when a subsequent owner sells the building, even if the relevant legislation has to be examined closely to determine how it works. Again, where the building was not an industrial building throughout his period of ownership, the allowances given to the subsequent owner are compared with his adjusted net cost. The adjusted net cost is the 'residue after sale' calculated when he purchased the building (see below) less any proceeds he receives on sale – reducing the net amount ascertained in the proportion that the period of qualifying use during his period of ownership bears to his total period of ownership. Non-qualifying use by a previous owner would not therefore affect his balancing adjustment on sale, which would be calculated in the normal way (CAA 2001, ss. 318–320).

Gifts and anti-avoidance provisions

A sale between connected parties otherwise than at an arm's length price is treated as a sale at market value (CAA 2001, s. 567).

If the sole or main benefit expected to accrue from a sale is the obtaining or increasing of a capital allowance, or is the avoidance or reduction of a balancing charge – even though the parties may not be connected – market value is applied (CAA 2001, s. 567). Exceptions to this treatment for industrial buildings allowances are, however, given in certain instances under the following heading.

Successions

A transfer of a trade from one company to another, where both companies are controlled as to at least three quarters by the same individuals or companies, is not regarded as a cessation of that trade and the occasion of a balancing adjustment for the transferee company, but is treated as if the trade is continued throughout by one single company.

Other successions give rise to a balancing adjustment, with the property being treated as disposed of by the predecessor to the successor at its full market value – including a partnership change where no 'continuation' election is made (ICTA 1988, s. 113(2)) and which therefore falls to be treated as a cessation (CAA 2001, ss. 557–559).

In the case of a husband and wife, if one spouse inherits a trade on the death of the other, capital allowances are calculated as if the assets had passed at open market value even if the profits are assessed on a continuation basis (see *Inland Revenue Capital Allowances Manual*, CA512).

Elections

Where the transferor and transferee are either a company or a partnership, and one controls the other or they are both under common control, they may jointly elect to substitute the residue of expenditure in place of the transfer price or market value – provided the transfer was not carried out just to obtain capital allowance benefits (CAA 2001, ss. 567, 568). In the case of a building transferred on or after 29 July 1988, any such election must be made within two years of the date of the transfer (CAA 2001, s. 570(5)).

For this purpose, control of a company is defined as the ability to secure that the affairs of the company are conducted in accordance with one's wishes – by means of holding shares, possessing voting rights, or any other powers conferred by the articles of association or other document. In the case of a partnership, control means the right to a share of more than one half of its assets or income (CAA 2001, s. 574(3)).

The election permitting the transfer to take place for tax purposes at residue of expenditure rather than market value or transfer price includes qualifying hotels and commercial buildings, and structures in enterprise zones. The election may be made only where both parties are entitled to capital allowances (CAA 2001, s. 570(2))

Retained interest in building

In the absence of anti-avoidance legislation, it would be possible to generate a balancing allowance by:

(a)   granting a lease or sub lease (a 'subordinate interest') out of the relevant interest to a connected person for a premium, and

(b)   selling the relevant interest subject to the subordinate interest.

Clearly, the premium at (a) does not generate a balancing adjustment unless the building is situated in an Enterprise Zone and the subordinate interest is granted within seven years of the incurring of the qualifying expenditure. Meanwhile, the relevant interest has become a reversionary interest, and the consideration for the disposal of that interest will reflect the value of that reversionary interest. Moreover, the value of the reversionary interest may be reduced further by arranging that the rent payable under the subordinate interest is less than the commercial rent that would be payable, given the amount of the actual premium payable on the grant of that interest.

Accordingly, the legislation provides that, in computing any balancing allowance on the disposal of a relevant interest which is subject to a subordinate interest, there must be added to the disposal consideration:

*   the premium payable on the grant of the subordinate interest, less any amount of that premium taxed as income under Schedule A, and
*   the additional disposal consideration which would have been obtained in a sale of the relevant interest on the open market if the rent payable under the subordinate interest was a commercial rent, bearing in mind the actual premium charged on the grant of the subordinate interest (CAA 2001, s. 325).

This adjustment is made only where:

*   the subordinate interest is granted to a connected person, or
*   the sole or main benefit which might be expected to accrue from the grant of the subordinate interest, the sale of the relevant interest, or transactions including that sale or grant was the obtaining of a balancing allowance.

The adjustment is reduced, in the case of a building in an Enterprise Zone, by any amount treated as capital value realised, in accordance with CAA 2001, s. 328(4).

The adjustment under the above rule can do no more than reduce any balancing allowance to nil. It cannot create a balancing charge (CAA 2001, s. 325(4), (5)).

5.2.12   Tax position of purchaser

Residue of expenditure

The allowances available to a purchaser depend on the tax position of the vendor. Thus the purchaser may claim allowances, based on the 'residue of expenditure' immediately after the sale. To arrive at this figure, first one takes the previous owner's residue before sale, which in a straightforward case consists of his original capital expenditure less the amount of the initial and writing-down allowances made to him. From the vendor's residue before sale one then deducts any balancing allowance made to him, or adds any balancing charge assessed on him. Since the balancing adjustments depend on the price paid for the relevant interest by the purchaser, and since a balancing charge may not exceed the allowances made to the vendor, the residue of expenditure immediately after the sale is normally equal to the lower of the vendor's original qualifying expenditure, or the price paid for the building by the purchaser.

Notional allowances

Where, however, there are any notional allowances, which could otherwise have been claimed by the vendor but for the building not being occupied for a qualifying purpose at the end of his chargeable period, etc., the notional allowances must also be deducted in arriving at the residue of expenditure, in the same way as they are deducted in arriving at the vendor's written down value. Moreover, the vendor's balancing adjustment will have been calculated by comparing the allowances given to him with his adjusted net cost (CAA 2001, ss. 332–334).

Example 5.4

Thus following Example **5.3**, the residue of expenditure qualifying for further industrial buildings allowances in Bob Townley's hands is calculated as follows:

	£	£
Saunders' original qualifying expenditure		120,000
Less: Allowances, etc. made to them:		
Initial allowance	60,000	
Writing-down allowances	48,000	
*Notional writing-down allowances	12,000	
		£120,000
		Nil
Plus: Balancing charge		£ 93,195
Residue after sale		£ 93,195

* CAA 2001, s. 336(1)–(4)

Writing-down allowances

As explained above, in the case of a purchased relevant interest, the annual allowances are calculated on the basis of the residue of expenditure, spread over the remaining part of a period of 25 years (or 50 years) from the date when the building was first occupied (CAA 2001, s. 311).

Example 5.5

Again continuing the above example, the residue of expenditure available to Bob Townley amounts to £93,195. The building was first occupied on 1 January 1976 and is purchased by him on 1 April 1995. Thus the residue of expenditure available to him is spread evenly over the remaining $5\frac{3}{4}$ years, ie at £16,208 per annum.

Miscellaneous

A number of other points must also be taken into consideration in calculating the residue of expenditure on which the purchaser may claim allowances in the future, as noted hereunder.

Interest retained by vendor

Where the balancing allowance otherwise available to the vendor on the disposal is restricted, because the vendor retains a subordinate interest in the property, the residue of expenditure is nevertheless calculated on the basis of the balancing adjustment that would have been made apart from the special rules referred to. Thus the allowances available to the purchaser may be restricted and to this extent the allowances are lost to both vendor and purchaser (CAA 2001, s. 325).

Partially qualifying buildings: initial allowances

It is not necessary to deduct notional initial allowances, as well as writing-down allowances, in arriving at the residue of expenditure where the expenditure was incurred at a time when initial allowances were available, ie up to 31 March 1986.

Example 5.6

Len Hands Ltd, having constructed a building in 1984, lets it for two years to a tenant who occupies it as offices, and then for four years to a tenant who occupies it for industrial purposes, before selling the building in 1990. In arriving at the residue of expenditure the company deducts notional writing-down allowances for two years and actual writing-down allowances for four years, but does not deduct notional initial allowances.

Acquisition after 25 years

Where the relevant interest is disposed of after the expiry of the period of 25 years (or 50 years) from the original occupation of the building, the whole of the vendor's expenditure will have been written off. No balancing charge is made whatever the proceeds of sale, so that no residue of expenditure is available for carry forward to the purchaser (CAA 2001, s. 314(4)).

No purchase price

Where no consideration is paid for a qualifying building, no residue of expenditure is then available to the successor to that interest. Similarly, if the relevant interest consists of a leasehold interest and that lease comes to an end, where neither the landlord nor the new incoming tenant make any payment to the previous tenant in respect of the building, the relevant interest does not pass to anyone else but simply lapses. Again the outgoing tenant is entitled to a balancing allowance equal to the residue of his unrelieved expenditure. If however the lease comes to an end simply because the tenant purchases the immediate reversionary interest in that lease, so that the two interests merge, his relevant interest continues into the merged interest and no disposal is deemed to take place at all (CAA 2001, s. 289).

5.2.13　Hotels

An allowance was introduced in respect of capital expenditure incurred in relation to qualifying hotels after 11 April 1978. The rules basically follow the provisions for industrial buildings allowances, subject to the modifications set out below (CAA 2001, ss. 271, 279).

Qualifying hotels

To qualify for relief, the hotel must be housed in a building of a permanent nature. In addition it must also comply with certain other requirements. These requirements have to be fulfilled during such parts of the 'season' – the period from April to October each year – as fall in a 12-month period and during which it is open. The 12-month period is normally the 12 months ended on the last day of the chargeable period or basis period for which relief is claimed – but if the hotel only came into use or attained sufficient letting rooms after the beginning of those 12 months, the 12-month period begins when the hotel first came into use or attained sufficient letting rooms. The following requirements must then be complied with:

- during this 12-month period, the hotel must be open for at least four months falling within the 'season';
- when open during the season, it must have at least ten private bedrooms available for letting to the public generally, not normally occupied by the same persons for more than one month – and the sleeping accommodation being offered by the hotel must consist mainly of such bedrooms,
- finally, again during this period, its services must normally include the provision of breakfast and an evening meal, the making of beds and the cleaning of rooms (CAA 2001, s. 279). Meals are treated as being provided when they are offered to guests as part of the hotel's normal facilities. The test would not be met if meals are available only on request (Inland Revenue Statement of Practice SP9/87).

Qualifying expenditure

The rules for identifying the expenditure qualifying for relief basically follow those applied for industrial buildings allowances, covering capital expenditure on the construction or acquisition of an hotel or its extension – including expenditure on extending the hotel so that it has ten or more letting rooms as a result – but not expenditure which is allowed as a revenue expense. It also includes any building provided and used for the welfare of workers employed in the hotel. In the case of an individual hotelier, or a person carrying on the hotel in partnership, any accommodation used by him or his family or household as a dwelling at a time when the hotel is open during the 'season' is excluded from relief (CAA 2001, ss. 279, 282 and 283).

Allowances given

The allowances are calculated in the same manner as industrial buildings allowances, with the rate of annual writing-down allowance at 4 per cent of the original cost.

The same rules regarding disposal or cessation of use also apply, including those relating to the calculation of the 'residue of expenditure' upon which the annual writing-down allowances due to the purchaser of an existing building are based. However, if an hotel ceases to qualify for allowances for a period of two years, it is treated as if it were sold for a price equal to its open market value, although this rule does not apply to a qualifying hotel within an enterprise zone. If the hotel ceases to be used temporarily, it may still continue to qualify for relief for a period of no more than two years after the end of the chargeable period or basis period in which it falls temporarily out of use (CAA 2001, s. 285, 317).

Where the hotel is situated in an enterprise zone, rates of allowances are increased.

Plant, equipment and fire safety

Note also the more valuable plant and machinery allowances available in respect of capital expenditure incurred on the provision of plant and equipment in the hotel and on fire safety. Such items would then be excluded from the claim for hotels allowances (CAA 2001, s. 7).

5.2.14 Enterprise zones

The Secretary of State is given powers to designate an area as an 'enterprise zone', and enhanced allowances are given for expenditure on the construction of qualifying buildings in such zones during the first ten years of the designation (CAA 2001, ss. 298, 305–308, 310(1)(a)).

However, where expenditure is deemed to have been incurred at a later date, because the owner had not commenced trading, or because he purchased an existing unused building, it is necessary that the cost of building work should be incurred after the designation of the enterprise zone also (CAA 2001, s. 298). Those areas which have been designated enterprise zones so far are as listed at the end of this section.

Qualifying buildings

For this purpose, a qualifying building includes a qualifying industrial building, a qualifying hotel, or a commercial building or structure. The latter includes any building or structure, not already qualifying as an industrial building or hotel, which is used for the purposes of a trade, profession or vocation, or which is used as an office – plus any non-qualifying part of the building if less than 25 per cent of the whole. But the definition specifically excludes any building in use as, or as part of, a dwelling house (CAA 2001, s. 281). Changes in use between one qualifying class of building and another do not trigger off a balancing charge or allowance (CAA 2001, s. 315).

Allowances given

The relevant provisions then apply the industrial buildings allowances. However, an initial allowance is given at the rate of 100 per cent for the period in which the expenditure is incurred. Moreover, if the owner only claims a part of the initial allowance (as an individual) or disclaims part of it (as a company), the rate of writing-down allowance is increased to 25 per cent (from 4 per cent). This allowance is given on a straight-line basis and is available if the building is in use for a qualifying purpose at the end of the relevant period. Thus these allowances are considerably more valuable than the normal industrial buildings allowances.

Example 5.7

Paul Williams buys from the builder a new office building in the Rotherham enterprise zone in March 2002 for £100,000. He lets it to Wray Enterprises Ltd. who occupy it for their bookmaking trade from May 2002.

Paul could claim a first-year allowance of £100,000 for the fiscal year 2001/02, but having insufficient taxable income he only claims £40,000. He can therefore claim writing-down allowances for subsequent years at 25 per cent of the cost until the whole of the cost has been allowed. Accordingly his allowances are:

	£
2001/02 initial	40,000
2002/03 writing-down (25%)	25,000
2003/04 writing-down (25%)	25,000
2004/05 writing-down (balance)	10,000
	100,000

It is necessary to eliminate any element attributable to artificial pricing (CAA 2001, s. 357). The purchaser of a second-hand building, however, does not qualify for accelerated allowances – being only entitled to the normal allowances. But at least such allowances can be claimed on a second-hand commercial building, as well as an industrial building or hotel, if the building were originally erected during the first ten years of the enterprise zone's designation.

Realisation of capital value

Prior to 1994, it was possible to avoid a balancing charge (or allowance) by disposing of a lesser interest whilst retaining the relevant interest, eg granting a 999-year lease out of a freehold. The ability to obtain a tax allowance for expenditure that is effectively borne by another person has been restricted where the expenditure relates to a building or structure in an enterprise zone. The realisation of capital value, capital sums and money equivalents, but excluding premiums chargeable as income, attributable to the subordinate interest is deducted from the tax written-down value and may give rise to a balancing charge or a restriction in the allowances available (CAA 2001, ss. 327–331). This provision applies where capital expenditure was incurred under a contract entered into after 12 January 1994 or under a conditional contract entered into before 13 January 1994 which becomes unconditional after 25 February 1994. The capital value must be realised within seven years of the original expenditure being incurred. The seven-year period does not apply if the arrangements for the acquisition of the relevant interest included provisions in respect of the realisation of capital value; in this case a balancing adjustment may arise whenever capital value is realised during the 25-year tax life of the building or structure (CAA 2001, s. 330).

Capital goods scheme

Under the capital goods scheme, a subsequent VAT liability or rebate may arise as outlined in **Chapter 11**. A VAT liability is treated as additional expenditure qualifying for the 100 per cent allowance where the liability is treated as being incurred during the ten-year period of designation as an enterprise zone. If the liability arises outside the ten-year period, relief will be given in the normal way in the case of an industrial building or hotel, but not in the case of other commercial buildings (CAA 2001, s. 346). Happily, there is no provision for capital allowances to be reduced where there is a VAT rebate.

Plant and machinery

By Inland Revenue concession, a taxpayer who is entitled to a 100 per cent allowance in respect of expenditure on a building in an enterprise zone can elect to have machinery or plant which becomes an integral part of the building treated as qualifying expenditure for the purposes of the 100 per cent allowance (Inland Revenue press release dated 6 January 1987).

Thermal insulation

The special provisions relating to expenditure on providing thermal insulation for a building do not apply to buildings qualifying for these accelerated enterprise zone allowances (CAA 2001, Sch. 3 (47) (6)).

Leased plant

Nor do the special rules relating to plant and equipment leased to persons not themselves qualifying for capital allowances apply, if the plant and equipment forms an integral part of a building qualifying for enterprise zone allowances (CAA 2001, Sch. 3, (47) (6)).

Enterprise zone unit trusts

So as to attract funds from those who could not otherwise afford to invest in enterprise zones, a number of unauthorised unit trusts have been developed which allow the 100 per cent allowances to pass directly to the unit holders for offset against their own income.

Following changes to the unauthorised unit trust tax rules in FA 1987, those allowances would have been available only to the trustees for offset against trust income. However, regulations have now been introduced to enable the previous treatment to continue (see SI 1988/267). This treatment applies only for capital allowance purposes. Thus, capital gains on the disposal of trust property are treated as gains of the trustees, not of the unit holders. A separate charge to tax is made on the unit holders in respect of gains arising on the disposal of their units (ICTA 1988, s. 469).

Designated enterprise zones

The Lower Swansea Valley	from 11 June 1981	
Corby	from 22 June 1981	
Dudley	from 10 July 1981	
Langthwaite Grange (Wakefield)	from 31 July 1981	
Clydebank	from 3 August 1981	
Salford Docks	from 12 August 1981	
Trafford Park	from 12 August 1981	
City of Glasgow	from 18 August 1981	
Speke (Liverpool)	from 25 August 1981	*now*
Gateshead	from 25 August 1981	*expired*
Newcastle	from 25 August 1981	
Belfast	from 21 October 1981	
Hartlepool	from 23 October 1981	
Isle of Dogs	from 26 April 1982	
Delyn	from 21 July 1983	
Wellingborough	from 26 July 1983	
Rotherham	from 16 August 1983	
Londonderry	from 13 September 1983	
Scunthorpe (Normanby Ridge & Queensway)	from 23 September 1983	
Dale Lane and Kinsley (Wakefield)	from 23 September 1983	
Workington (Allerdale)	from 4 October 1983	
Invergordon	from 7 October 1983	

North West Kent	from 31 October 1983
Middlesbrough (Britannia)	from 8 November 1983
North East Lancashire	from 7 December 1983
Tayside (Arbroath)	from 9 January 1984
Tayside (Dundee)	from 9 January 1984
Telford	from 13 January 1984
Glanford (Flixborough)	from 13 April 1984
Milford Haven Waterway (North Shore)	from 24 April 1984
Milford Haven Waterway (South Shore)	from 24 April 1984
Dudley (Round Oak)	from 3 October 1984
Lower Swansea Valley (No 2)	from 6 March 1985
North West Kent (extension)	from 10 October 1986
Inverclyde	from 3 March 1989
Sunderland (Castletown & Doxford Park)	from 27 April 1990
Sunderland (Hulton Riverside & Southwick)	from 27 April 1990
Monklands	from 24 September 1992
Motherwell	from 7 October 1992
Hamilton	from 13 October 1992
Dearne Valley Enterprise Zone No 2 (Highgate (Fields End) Business Park, Barnsley) Scheme	from 3 November 1995
Dearne Valley Enterprise Zone No 3 (Goldthorpe Industrial Estate, Barnsley) Scheme	from 3 November 1995
Dearne Valley Enterprise Zone No 6 (Wombwell Bypass (Waterside and Valley Business Parks) Barnsley) Scheme	from 3 November 1995
East Midlands Enterprise Zone No 1 (Holmwood) Scheme	from 3 November 1995
East Midlands Enterprise Zone No 2 (Holmwood) Scheme	from 3 November 1995
East Midlands Enterprise Zone No 3 (Holmwood) Scheme	from 3 November 1995

East Midlands Enterprise Zone No 4 (Manton Wood) Scheme	from 16 November 1995
East Midlands Enterprise Zone No 7 (Sherwood Business Park) Scheme	from 21 November 1995
East Durham Enterprise Zone No 1 (Bracken Hill) Scheme	from 29 November 1995
East Durham Enterprise Zone No 2 (Peterlee North West Industrial Estate) Scheme	from 29 November 1995
East Durham Enterprise Zone No 3 (Peterlee South West Industrial Estate) Scheme	from 29 November 1995
East Durham Enterprise Zone No 4 (Seaham Grange) Scheme	from 29 November 1995
East Durham Enterprise Zone No 5 (Fox Cover) Scheme	from 29 November 1995
East Durham Enterprise Zone No 6 (Dawdon) Scheme	from 29 November 1995
Tyne Riverside Enterprise Zone No 2 (Silverlink North) Scheme	from 26 August 1996
Tyne Riverside Enterprise Zone No 3 (Silverlink Business Park) Scheme	from 26 August 1996
Tyne Riverside Enterprise Zone No 4 (Middle Engine Lane) Scheme	from 26 August 1996
Tyne Riverside Enterprise Zone No 5 (New York Industrial Park) Scheme	from 26 August 1996
Tyne Riverside Enterprise Zone No 6 (Balliol Business Park West) Scheme	from 26 August 1996
Tyne Riverside Enterprise Zone No 7 (Balliol Business Park East) Scheme	from 26 August 1996

Tyne Riverside Enterprise   from 21 October 1996
Zone No 8 (Baltic
Enterprise Park) Scheme

Tyne Riverside Enterprise   from 21 October 1996
Zone No 9 (Viking
Industrial Park – Wagonway
West) Scheme

Tyne Riverside Enterprise   from 21 October 1996
Zone No 10 (Viking
Industrial Park – Blackett
Street) Scheme

Tyne Riverside Enterprise   from 21 October 1996
Zone No 11 (Viking
Industrial Park – Western
Road) Scheme

5.2.15 Transitional

First-year initial allowances

Where a person incurred qualifying capital expenditure on the construction of a new industrial building before 1 April 1986, which was occupied for the purposes of a trade, he was given an initial allowance in the first year. The rate of allowance depended upon the kind of building being constructed and the date on which the expenditure was incurred, as can be seen from the following table – which also encompasses buildings that qualified for other types of first-year allowance.

Building	Latest date	Initial allowance
Industrial building or qualifying dwelling house let on assured tenancy	13 March 1984	75%
	31 March 1985	50%
	31 March 1986	25%
Small industrial workshop	26 March 1985	100%
Qualifying hotel	31 March 1986	20%

It should be stressed that this initial allowance was only available in respect of expenditure incurred on the construction of new buildings, or on the price paid for a new, unused building. In no circumstances was it granted on the acquisition of a used building, even where the relevant interest was acquired.

Expenditure incurred

Normally initial allowances were granted in respect of industrial buildings as and when the expenditure was incurred. For this purpose the general rule was that expenditure was deemed to be incurred when the *obligation to pay the amount in question became unconditional* – even if it was actually payable at a later date. Special provision was made where an obligation to pay an amount became unconditional as a result of the issue of a certificate (eg an architect's certificate) within a month after the end of a chargeable period and the asset in question became the payer's property prior to the end of that period. In such circumstances the capital expenditure was treated as having been incurred immediately prior to the end of the period. Anti-avoidance legislation prevented these provisions being used artificially to accelerate the time when allowances could be claimed. This applied where an agreement required expenditure to be paid more than four months after the obligation to pay became unconditional. In such a case, the expenditure was treated as having been incurred at the time when it actually became payable.

If the obligation to pay became unconditional earlier than under normal commercial usage, and the only or main benefit of the acceleration of the obligation to pay was to enable allowances to be claimed in an earlier period, then the expenditure was treated as having been incurred when the amount actually became payable, whether or not this was within four months of the date when the obligation to pay became unconditional. The expenditure could in certain circumstances be allowed before the building was completed and occupied. It was however disallowed if the building was not subsequently occupied for a qualifying purpose – by way of an assessment to recover the allowance if necessary (CAA 1990, ss. 1 and s.159).

There were two exceptions. First, where a person purchased a new, unused industrial building, his expenditure was deemed to be incurred when the purchase price became payable rather than on the date when the vendor was due to pay the builder for its construction. Second, if the industrial building was being constructed for owner occupation by a trader who had not yet commenced to trade, any expenditure incurred before trading commenced was deemed to be deferred and was treated as being incurred on the first day of trading (CAA 1990, ss. 1 and 10(1)). These two exceptions fixed the date on which the expenditure was treated as having been incurred to arrive at the taxpayer's chargeable *period* for which the initial allowance was due. For the purpose of fixing the *rate* of allowance there were different rules. In the case of the purchase of a new, unused industrial building where the purchase price became payable after 13 March 1984, the rate of allowance was fixed by reference to the latest date on which any expenditure on the construction of the building was actually incurred (FA 1984, Sch. 12, Para. 1(3)(b) – now spent). In the case of an industrial building which was constructed for owner occupation by a trader who commenced trading after 13 March 1984, the rate of allowance was fixed by reference to the date on which the trader incurred the expenditure (Para. 1(3)(a) – now spent).

Example 5.8

Bury Manufacturing Ltd, whose accounting year end is 31 December, purchased a new, unused industrial building from Silverton Builders. Silverton incurred its last construction expenditure on 23 December 1983, and the contract stipulated that Bury was to pay the purchase price on 27 April 1984. Silverton qualified for an initial allowance in the year to 31 December 1984, but the rate of allowance was the 75 per cent rate applying before 14 March 1984, not the 50 per cent rate applying in April 1984.

As a transitional measure the 75 per cent initial allowance remained available for the following categories:

- expenditure incurred before 1 April 1987 due under a contract entered into before 14 March 1984 (FA 1984, Sch. 12 Para. 2(2) – now spent),
- certain expenditure qualifying for regional grants (CAA 1990, s. 2(2)–(4) and ss. 22(2), (3) and (10)).

Transitional spreading provisions

To prevent initial allowances being claimed at a higher rate on accelerated expenditure, certain expenditure had to be 'spread forward' to determine what allowances could be claimed. These spreading provisions applied if the main benefit of the early contract date was to secure higher allowances. Where this was the case, the provisions applied if capital expenditure was incurred by a person under a contract entered into after 13 March 1984 and before 1 April 1986, which either specified no date by which the contractual obligations should be fulfilled or specified a date after 31 March 1985 (Sch. 12, Paras. 5(1) and 8, FA 1984 – now spent). The total capital expenditure incurred under the contract had to be apportioned evenly over the period between the date the contract was entered into and the earlier of the completion date specified in the contract or 31 March 1987. If no completion date was specified in the contract, expenditure was treated as being spread over a period running to 31 March 1987 (Sch. 12, Paras. 5(2) and 9, FA 1984 – now spent). The initial allowance in either of the years ended 31 March 1985 or 1986 could not exceed the maximum allowable expenditure multiplied by the rate of initial allowance for that year. Any excess in either of those years was deemed to be incurred on 1 April in the following year (FA 1984, Para. 5(3) to (5), Sch. 12 – now spent).

Where these spreading rules were applied so that certain capital expenditure was deemed to have been incurred on 1 April 1985 or 1 April 1986 as the case may be, the balance of the expenditure incurred in the year which was not spread was apportioned on a time basis over the accounting periods of the taxpayer which overlapped these years (FA 1984, Para. 10, Sch.12 – now spent).

Example 5.9

Hotchkiss Ltd, which makes up its accounts to 31 March, contracted on 1 July 1984 for the construction of a factory extension costing £250,000 for completion on 1 August 1986. Payments were made on the dates provided for in the contract as follows:

1 July 1984	£100,000
1 July 1985	£100,000
1 August 1986	£50,000

It was accepted that the expenditure had been accelerated in order to obtain initial allowances at the higher rates.

Initial allowances could be claimed as follows:

Year to 31 March 1985

Expenditure incurred	£100,000
Maximum allowable expenditure	
£250,000 × 9/25	90,000
Excess, deemed to be incurred on 1 April 1985	£ 10,000
Allowance: 50% of £90,000	£ 45,000

Year to 31 March 1986

Expenditure incurred 1 July 1985	£100,000
Expenditure deemed to be incurred on 1 April 1985	10,000
	£110,000
Maximum allowable expenditure:	
£250,000 × 12/25	£120,000

Therefore no excess expenditure arises.

Allowance: 25% of £110,000	£ 27,500

Year to 31 March 1987

Expenditure incurred 1 August 1986	£ 50,000

No initial allowance due

Let us now suppose that Hotchkiss made up its accounts to 30 September instead of 31 March.

Accounting period to 30 September 1984

Proportion of maximum allowable expenditure incurred in year to 31 March 1985:

£90,000 × 6/12	£ 45,000
Initial allowance 50%	£ 22,500

No expenditure has been deemed to have been incurred on 1 April 1986, so no apportionment of expenditure incurred in the year to 31 March 1986 is required.

Accounting period to 30 September 1985

Proportion of maximum allowable expenditure incurred in year to 31 March 1985:

£90,000 × 6/12	£ 45,000
Expenditure incurred 1 July 1985	100,000
Expenditure deemed to be incurred on 1 April 1985	10,000
	£155,000

Initial allowances:	
50% of £ 45,000	£ 22,500
25% of £110,000	27,500
	£ 50,000

Accounting period to 30 September 1986

Expenditure incurred 1 August 1986	£ 50,000

No initial allowance due

Where expenditure was incurred before the commencement of a trade, the relevant date for the purposes of the spreading rules was the actual date that it was incurred and not the date the trade started (FA 1984, Sch. 12, Para. 5(6) – now spent).

Expenditure before 11 March 1981

An initial allowance of 75 per cent was given for expenditure incurred after 10 March 1981 and before 14 March 1984. Where the expenditure was incurred on or before 10 March 1981, the rate was 50 per cent if incurred after 12 November 1974, 40 per cent if incurred between 23 March 1972 and 12 November 1974, and 30 per cent if incurred between 6 April 1970 and 22 March 1972 – subject in each case to transitional provisions. Prior to 27 March 1980, where a landlord was building an industrial building for letting to a tenant trader, expenditure incurred before the tenancy started was deferred and treated as incurred in the chargeable period when the tenancy began.

Claims

An initial allowance was given automatically to a company subject to corporation tax. For expenditure incurred after 10 March 1981, all or any part of it could be disclaimed. For earlier expenditure the whole of the allowance had to be taken (FA 1981, s. 73(2) – now spent – and CAA 1990, ss. 144 and 145).

In other cases, such as an individual subject to income tax, the allowance, if wanted, had to be claimed. Where the expenditure was incurred after 10 March 1981 the claim need not be for the full allowance. For earlier expenditure either the full allowance had to be claimed or no claim made at all (FA 1981, s. 73(2) – now spent – and CAA 1990, ss. 140 and 141).

As an exception to the foregoing two paragraphs, where the expenditure was incurred prior to 11 March 1981, it was possible for any taxpayer, whether company or individual, to obtain less than the full 100 per cent initial allowance on small workshops – by disclaimer or by partial claim as the case may be.

In certain circumstances, it could be advantageous not to have the full initial allowance, as in the case of an individual who had insufficient income in the year in question to offset the whole of the allowance. Instead he could claim annual writing-down allowances for a longer period until the whole of the expenditure was written off.

Writing-down allowances

New buildings

Writing-down allowances could also be claimed at a rate of 4 per cent of the original cost of the capital expenditure.

Small workshops

Capital expenditure incurred on the construction of a qualifying industrial building (including any ancillary works) which was a 'small workshop' between 27 March 1980 and 26 March 1983 or which was a 'very small workshop' between 27 March 1983 and 26 March 1985 attracted increased rates of industrial buildings allowances – a 100 per cent initial allowance or, if disclaimed, a 25 per cent writing-down allowance (FA 1980, s. 75(1) and (4) – now spent). A 'small workshop' was any industrial building with a gross internal floor space not exceeding 2,500 square feet, and a 'very small workshop' one where the gross internal floor space did not exceed 1,250 square feet. If the workshop was part of a larger building, one could look at the part separately provided:

- that part was permanently separated by a brick or similar wall from the remainder of the building, other than as regards emergency exits or access to common parts, and
- it was intended and suitable for occupation separately from the remainder of the building apart from sharing common facilities.

Common facilities might include canteens, washrooms, fire escapes, loading bays or car parking – or such services as a central telephone switchboard, heating and ventilation. Where such facilities were available only to occupiers of small workshops, the cost of providing them would also qualify for the additional relief – and where shared with other non-qualifying occupiers, the capital expenditure was apportioned (FA 1980, s. 75(2) and (3) – now spent – and Inland Revenue Statement of Practice SP6/80).

The Inland Revenue were prepared to deal with an estate of small workshops on a global basis for industrial buildings allowances, without normally requiring full details of the occupancy of each unit (Inland Revenue Statement of Practice SP4/80, dated 26 March 1980). In the case of 'very small workshops' the 100 per cent first-year allowance was available for expenditure on the conversion of an existing previously used building into separate industrial units having an *average* size not exceeding 1,250 square feet – regardless of the fact that some of the individual units might have a larger area. The average size was to be measured at the time when all the units had come into use, or on 27 March 1986 if earlier (FA 1983, s. 31 – now spent).

Where the building qualified for increased allowances, the special provisions relating to expenditure on providing thermal insulation did not apply – nor did the rules relating to plant and equipment leased to persons not themselves qualifying for capital allowances, if such plant formed an integral part of the small workshop (FA 1980, s. 75(6) – now spent).

The accelerated rates of industrial buildings allowances are set out at the beginning of this chapter.

The purchaser of a second-hand small workshop could only claim the annual allowances available for industrial buildings generally, with no acceleration of relief.

Expenditure before 6th November 1962

In the case of a building where the expenditure was incurred prior to 6 November 1962, the annual allowance was only 2 per cent of the original cost (CAA 1990, s. 3(2)).

5.2.16   Transitional: hotels

Allowances given

An initial allowance was available for expenditure incurred before 1 April 1986 (or expenditure incurred before 1 April 1987 under a contract made before 14 March 1984), in which case the rate was 20 per cent. Where the expenditure was treated as having been incurred on the first day trading commenced and this was after 31 March 1986, initial allowances would be given so long as the expenditure was in fact incurred before 1 April 1986. When the hotel was bought unused an initial allowance would be available if the last day when actual construction expenditure was incurred was before 1 April 1986 (FA 1985, s. 66 – now spent).

5.3   Plant and machinery

5.3.1   Introduction

The provisions explained below deal with the capital allowances given in respect of the cost of providing plant and equipment for the purposes of a trade, a Schedule A business, a furnished holiday lettings business or an overseas property business (see CAA 2001, s. 15). The allowances are available for such plant contained in either industrial or commercial buildings, so that they also affect offices, shops, etc. as well as factories, warehouses and hotels – even though no allowance would be available for the cost of the building itself as in the case of an industrial building or hotel. They are not available in respect of plant and equipment incorporated in a single residential unit such as a house or flat, except in relation to a furnished holiday lettings business, although they may be claimed in respect of equipment, etc. provided for common use in a multiple residential property such as a block of flats (CAA 2001, s. 35).

The allowances for such plant and equipment are more generous than those available in respect of an industrial building or an hotel, and they should be claimed separately to take advantage of these higher rates. When constructing a new building or purchasing an existing building, the items of expenditure qualifying for allowances under these provisions should be isolated so that they may be claimed separately. In particular, in the case of a new construction, the builder or quantity surveyor, etc. should be asked to keep a separate note of the qualifying expenditure, since this may be more difficult to ascertain after the building has been completed. Similarly, when purchasing an existing building, agreement should be reached with the vendor as to the allocation of the purchase price between qualifying items of plant and equipment and the building, etc. itself.

5.3.2 Qualifying expenditure

The legislation on capital allowances contains no definition of 'machinery and plant'. In order to determine whether an asset is machinery or plant, so that expenditure on it qualifies for the relevant capital allowances, it has been necessary to look to case law. In relation to expenditure incurred after 29 November 1993 the Finance Act 1994 introduces a general rule that land, buildings and structures cannot be plant. The detailed rules are set out in Capital Allowances Act 2001, ss. 21–23.

Buildings

Expenditure on the provision of plant or machinery does not include expenditure on the provision of a building (which includes its construction or acquisition). A building includes an asset which:

- is incorporated in the building,
- although not incorporated in the building (whether because the asset is moveable or for any other reason), is in the building and is of a kind normally incorporated in a building, or
- is in, or connected with, the building and is in list A.

List A (CAA 2001, s. 21)

Assets treated as buildings

1. Walls, floors, ceilings, doors, gates, shutters, windows and stairs.

2. Mains services, and systems, for water, electricity and gas.

3. Waste disposal systems.

4. Sewerage and drainage systems.

5. Shafts or other structures in which lifts, hoists, escalators and moving walkways are installed.

6. Fire safety systems.

This is subject to the **exceptions** set out below.

Structures, assets and works
Expenditure on the provision of plant or machinery does not include expenditure on:

- the provision of a structure or other asset in list B (which includes its construction or acquisition), or
- any works involving the alteration of land.

List B (CAA 2001, s. 22)

Excluded structures and other assets

1. A tunnel, bridge, viaduct, aqueduct, embankment or cutting.

2. A way, hard standing (such as a pavement), road, railway, tramway, a park for vehicles or containers, or an airstrip or runway.

3. An inland navigation, including a canal or basin or a navigable river.

4. A dam, reservoir or barrage, including any sluices, gates, generators and other equipment associated with the dam, reservoir or barrage.

5. A dock, harbour, wharf, pier, marina or jetty or any other structure in or at which vessels may be kept, or merchandise or passengers may be shipped or unshipped.

6. A dike, sea wall, weir or drainage ditch.

7. Any structure not within items 1 to 6 other than:

   (a) a structure (but not a building) within Chapter 2 of Part 3 (meaning of 'industrial building'),
   (b) a structure in use for the purposes of an undertaking for the extraction, production, processing or distribution of gas, and
   (c) a structure in use for the purposes of a trade which consists in the provision of telecommunication, television or radio services.

'Structure' means a fixed structure of any kind, other than a building (as defined by s. 21(3)).

'Land' does not include buildings or other structures, but otherwise has the meaning given in Schedule 1 to the Interpretation Act 1978.

Exceptions

The following are not prevented from being plant or machinery by the above rules (CAA 2001, s. 23):

- thermal insulation of industrial buildings (s. 28);
- fire safety (s. 29);
- safety at designated sports grounds (s. 30);
- safety at regulated stands at sports grounds (s. 31);
- safety at other sports grounds (s. 32);
- personal security (s. 33);
- software and rights to software (s. 71),
- election relating to tax treatment of films expenditure (s. 40D, F(No.2)A 1992).

Items described in list C are not prevented from being plant or machinery by the above rules, but items 1 to 16 of list C do not include any asset whose principal purpose is to insulate or enclose the interior of a building or to provide an interior wall, floor or ceiling which (in each case) is intended to remain permanently in place.

List C

1. Machinery (including devices for providing motive power) not within any other item in this list.

2. Electrical systems (including lighting systems) and cold water, gas and sewerage systems provided mainly:

   (a)   to meet the particular requirements of the qualifying activity, or
   (b)   to serve particular plant or machinery used for the purposes of the qualifying activity.

3. Space or water heating systems; powered systems of ventilation, air cooling or air purification; and any floor or ceiling comprised in such systems.

4. Manufacturing or processing equipment; storage equipment (including cold rooms); display equipment; and counters, checkouts and similar equipment.

5. Cookers, washing machines, dishwashers, refrigerators and similar equipment; washbasins, sinks, baths, showers, sanitary ware and similar equipment; and furniture and furnishings.

6. Lifts, hoists, escalators and moving walkways.

7. Sound insulation provided mainly to meet the particular requirements of the qualifying activity.

8. Computer, telecommunication and surveillance systems (including their wiring or other links).

9. Refrigeration or cooling equipment.

10. Fire alarm systems; sprinkler and other equipment for extinguishing or containing fires.

11. Burglar alarm systems.

12. Strong rooms in bank or building society premises; safes.

13. Partition walls, where moveable and intended to be moved in the course of the qualifying activity.

14. Decorative assets provided for the enjoyment of the public in hotel, restaurant or similar trades.

15. Advertising hoardings; signs, displays and similar assets.

16. Swimming pools (including diving boards, slides and structures on which such boards or slides are mounted).

17. Any glasshouse constructed so that the required environment (namely, air, heat, light, irrigation and temperature) for the growing of plants is provided automatically by means of devices forming an integral part of its structure.

18. Cold stores.

19. Caravans (as defined) provided mainly for holiday lettings.

20. Buildings provided for testing aircraft engines run within the buildings.

21. Moveable buildings intended to be moved in the course of the qualifying activity.

22. The alteration of land for the purpose only of installing plant or machinery.

23. The provision of dry docks.

24. The provision of any jetty or similar structure provided mainly to carry plant or machinery.

25. The provision of pipelines or underground ducts or tunnels with a primary purpose of carrying utility conduits.

26. The provision of towers to support floodlights.

27. The provision of:

    (a) any reservoir incorporated into a water treatment works, or
    (b) any service reservoir of treated water for supply within any housing estate or other particular locality.

28. The provision of:

    (a) silos provided for temporary storage, or
    (b) storage tanks.

29. The provision of slurry pits or silage clamps.

30. The provision of fish tanks or fish ponds.

31. The provision of rails, sleepers and ballast for a railway or tramway.

32. The provision of structures and other assets for providing the setting for any ride at an amusement park or exhibition.

33. The provision of fixed zoo cages.

Interests in land

Expenditure on the provision of plant or machinery does not include expenditure on the acquisition of an interest in land (CAA 2001, s. 24). However, 'land' does not include:

- buildings or other structures, or
- any asset which is so installed or otherwise fixed to any description of land as to become, in law, part of the land.

Building alterations connected with installation of plant or machinery

Capital expenditure on alterations to an existing building incidental to the installation of plant or machinery is treated as expenditure on the provision of the plant or machinery (CAA 2001, s. 25).

Demolition costs

If:

- plant or machinery is demolished, and
- the last use of the plant or machinery was for the purposes of a qualifying activity,

then the net cost of the demolition to that person is treated as expenditure incurred on the provision of the other plant or machinery (CAA 2001, s. 26).

Case law

As noted above, the legislation contains no definition of what is plant and machinery although there are instances where it specifies that certain expenditure is to be treated as expenditure on the provision of plant and equipment for this purpose.

'Plant and machinery' falls to be interpreted in the natural meaning of the phrase to which the courts have added some guidance by their decisions in certain cases. The best known definition of plant was given in a case in the last century as follows:

> 'In its ordinary sense, it includes whatever apparatus is used by a businessman for carrying on his business – not his stock in trade, which he buys or makes for sale, but all goods and chattels, fixed or moveable, live or dead, which he keeps for permanent employment in his business (*Yarmouth v France* (1887) 19 QBD 647).'

Unlikely items

Other cases have decided that certain unlikely items may be regarded as plant for this purpose. Thus for example moveable partitions in an office block have been considered to be plant (*Jarrold (HMIT) v John Good & Sons* (1962) 40 TC 681) – although the Inland Revenue may seek to limit the application of this decision to such partitions as are actually moved from time to time in the course of an office re-organisation, so that the position is less clear where partitions are moveable but in fact are not actually moved. This should be contrasted with a case concerning prefabricated timber frame buildings which, although demountable and moveable, were nevertheless held to be buildings or premises and not plant (*St. John's School (Mountford and Anor) v Ward* (1975) 49 TC 524).

The construction of a new dry dock, including the excavation costs, was also regarded as an entire piece of apparatus and therefore plant for these purposes (*IR Commrs v Barclay, Curle & Co* (1969) 45 TC 221). This decision chiefly rested on the fact that the dry dock was one single integrated unit and that it performed a mechanical operation similar to that of a floating dock, contrasting with a case concerning a vessel that was converted into a floating restaurant club, which did not qualify as plant since it performed no mechanical function (*Benson (HMIT) v Yard Arm Club* (1979) 53 TC 67). On the other hand, the court has held that expenditure on the construction of an all weather race track did not qualify for plant and machinery allowances (*Shove (HMIT) v Lingfield Park* 1991 Ltd [2003] BTC 422).

Building or plant?

These definitions do not go very far however in establishing whether an item qualifies as plant, or is merely regarded as part of the building in which it is housed – and this aspect has been the subject of a number of judicial decisions.

One approach may be to establish whether the installation forms an integral part of a building, without which the building would be incomplete and unusable, or whether it is something added to an otherwise complete building for use in the occupier's trade. This approach was used in the case of a claim for allowances on the entire electrical installations in a department store. The special commissioners rejected the claim that the entire installation should be regarded as a single item of plant; rejected the claim that main switchboard or special light fittings were plant; but allowed the claim in respect of a transformer to reduce the electric current to a usable level. The House of Lords refused to disturb these findings of fact. The Inland Revenue accepted that the wiring to a number of specific items such as fire alarms, heating and ventilating systems and standby support systems qualified for allowances (*Cole Brothers v Phillips (HMIT)* [1982] BTC 208). Following an unreported decision by the Commissioners, the Inland Revenue has issued instructions to Inspectors of Taxes that a claim for allowances may be accepted if the expenditure comprises the cost of 'entire electrical installations' in new or existing buildings where there is a complete, purpose built system installed.

In another case, false ceilings were held not to be plant, since they merely provided covering and performed no mechanical function in carrying on the taxpayer's catering trade – despite arguments that the ceilings provided cover and support for various piping, wiring and other services and were decorative (*Hampton (HMIT) v Fortes Autogrill Ltd* (1979) 53 TC 691). By contrast, the Inland Revenue is known to have accepted as plant false ceilings which are part of a pressurised void integral to the functioning of the air conditioning.

A structure whose only purpose is to provide shelter, even if strictly not a building, is not plant (*Dixon (HMIT) v Fitch's Garage* (1975) 50 TC 509 – a canopy over petrol pumps, *Thomas (HMIT) v Reynolds* [1987] BTC 147 – an inflatable cover over a tennis court, and *Gray (HMIT) v Seymours Garden Centre (Horticulture)* [1995] BTC 320 – a glasshouse used to provide shelter for plants).

Two instances may also be referred to here, wherein the Inland Revenue accepted a claim for allowances in respect of plant contained in a building without contesting the matter. The claims included such items as:

- boilers;
- central heating equipment;
- lifts;
- air conditioning plant and ducts;
- fire sprinklers;
- partitions;
  storage heaters;
- incinerators;
  fluorescent light fittings;
- blinds;
  hanging rails;
- curtain rails,
- flag poles and a lightning conductor (literally to cap it all!).

Electrical and plumbing installations embedded in the fabric of a building, such as wiring and pipework, were excluded. In one case the allowances extended to sanitary fittings, such as baths, washbasins, showers, lavatories and cisterns – whereas in the other case such items were excluded (see *MacSaga Investment v Lupton (HMIT)* (1967) 44 TC 659 and *Lupton (HMIT) v Cadogan Gardens Developments* (1971) 47 TC 1).

In a reply by the Inland Revenue to an enquiry from the Consultative Committee of Accountancy Bodies (following the *St. John's School* case referred to above), they confirm that, whilst electrical wiring, cold water plumbing and gas piping is regarded as part of the cost of the building, expenditure on *apparatus* to provide electric light or power, hot water, central heating, ventilation or air conditioning, and expenditure on alarm and sprinkler systems, will qualify for capital allowances. Moreover relief will be given for the cost of baths, washbasins, etc. – and it is also understood that the Inland Revenue will extend this principle to the kitchen sink and a toilet as well (but not to soil and waste pipes).

In the case of a company running hotels and public houses, the provision of electric light fittings, decor and murals – including wall plaques, tapestries, murals, pictures and sculptures – whilst they formed part of the setting in which the trade was carried on, also served a 'functional' purpose in helping to create or enhance an atmosphere conducive to the comfort and well being of the customers, so that expenditure thereon qualified for capital allowances on plant and equipment (*IR Commrs v Scottish & Newcastle Breweries* [1982] BTC 187).

However, in *Wimpy International v Warland (HMIT)* [1987] BTC 591, a case involving the fitting out of 'fast food' outlets, it was held that if an item is, as a matter of general property law, incorporated as an integral part of the building or premises which house the trade, it cannot be plant no matter how purpose built the premises might be. Only if an item is not so incorporated, is it necessary to consider whether it performs some function in the trade. Accordingly, additions or improvements to the premises are excluded from being plant if they become part of the premises, irrespective of the function they may have in the carrying on of the business.

Installation costs

Most of the above items are included in the original construction of the building, so that it is essential to obtain a separate price from the builder in respect of such plant and equipment – perhaps starting from the bills of quantity. The claim should include not only the direct cost of providing the items concerned, but also any additional charges made by the builder in respect of works carried out by him on installation, and any architect's or other professional fees and handling charges added as a percentage on cost, etc. (although the Inland Revenue may challenge percentage fees, incorrectly in the author's opinion).

The cost of preparing, cutting, tunnelling or levelling land as a site for plant and machinery may qualify for industrial buildings allowances if no other relief is available.

Finance charges

Interest and commitment fees on monies borrowed specifically to finance the acquisition of plant and equipment, however, will not qualify for capital allowances, even if 'capitalised' in the taxpayer's accounts (*Ben-Odeco v Powlson (HMIT)* (1978) 52 TC 459).

Grants, etc.

Where the expenditure is recovered from other persons, and in particular where the cost is met directly or indirectly by the Crown or by any government or public or local authority, unless the recovery relates to a grant made under Part I of the Industry Act 1972, Part II of the Industrial Development Act 1982 or equivalent provisions for Northern Ireland (where allowances are still given on the full cost), the expenditure is treated as reduced by the amount recovered in computing the allowances given below (CAA 2001, ss. 532–536).

Fire safety

Where a person carrying on a trade incurs capital expenditure in connection with fire safety, which he cannot otherwise claim as a revenue expense in computing his trading profits, he may claim capital allowances in respect of the expenditure as if it had been incurred on plant and equipment. If the premises are subsequently disposed of, no disposal value is attributed to the expenditure, even if the purchaser makes some payment for it, so that there is no clawback of allowances given. This relief is however specifically confined to expenditure incurred in compliance with an order issued under the Fire Precautions Act 1971, s. 5(4), or in carrying out steps specified in a letter, etc. sent by the fire authority on an application for a fire certificate under that Act. Similar treatment is given to expenditure incurred in taking steps to enable premise to be used again, in consequence of an order prohibiting or restricting the use of those premises under the Fire Precautions Act 1971, s. 10. It seems a pity that the relief is only given after an application has caused some defect to be pointed out – and not when steps are taken voluntarily in advance (CAA 2001, s. 27). Relief is extended under the normal provisions of CAA 2001, s. 537 to a landlord who makes a contribution to a tenant's expenditure so qualifying. By Extra-Statutory Concession B16(b) the relief is further extended to a landlord incurring the expenditure if similar expenditure by the tenant would have qualified. There is doubt, however, whether this relief applies where the tenant is not carrying on a trade.

Under the Fire Precautions Act 1971, s. 2, the provisions of that Act originally only applied to hotels and boarding houses – and specifically excluded factories, offices, shops and other premises. However, the provisions were subsequently extended to include factories, shops, offices and railway buildings (but not covered markets) with effect from 1 January 1977 (Fire Precautions (Factories, Offices, Shops and Railway Premises) Order 1976/2009).

Whilst again the Fire Precautions Act 1971 only applies to Great Britain and not to Northern Ireland, relief is extended to similar expenditure in meeting the requirements of a fire authority under legislation applying in Northern

Ireland (see Inland Revenue Press Release dated 23 November 1978 and Extra-Statutory Concession B16(a)).

Thermal insulation in industrial buildings

Where a trader incurs capital expenditure in adding any insulation against the loss of heat to an industrial building or structure occupied by him for the purposes of his trade, he may claim capital allowances in respect of the cost as if it were expenditure on plant and equipment. Similar allowances are given for expenditure incurred by a landlord in respect of a tenanted industrial building. Perhaps therefore thermal insulation should be omitted from a new building and only 'added' at some later time (CAA 2001, ss. 27, 28).

However, this provision does not apply to an industrial building qualifying as a small workshop nor to a building qualifying for enterprise zone allowances.

Energy saving plant and machinery

Plant or machinery qualifies for first-year allowances under CAA 2001, s. 45A, as it falls within a technology class specified in the Energy Technology Criteria List and meets the energy saving criteria set out in that list. In the case of boilers, motors and drives, refrigeration and thermal screens it must be of a type that is included in the Energy Technology Criteria List or the Energy Technology Product List (SI 2001/2541). Plant or machinery falling within the technology class 'Combined Heat and Power' specified in the Energy Technology Criteria List must have a relevant certificate of energy efficiency.

Where one or more components of certain plant or machinery meet the required conditions, the amount qualifying for first-year allowances is the amount specified in the Energy Technology Product List in relation to that component.

The class of plant or machinery which becomes a fixture and which can be treated as owned by an energy services provider under CAA 2001, s. 180A(2) is the technology class 'Combined Heat and Power' specified in the Energy Technology Criteria List.

Further details may be found on the Enhanced Capital Allowances website at www.eca.gov.uk

Safety at sports grounds

Where a trader incurs capital expenditure in connection with a sports stadium used by him for the purposes of his trade, in order to obtain a safety certificate or as a result of any order under the Safety of Sports Grounds Act 1975, and the expense does not qualify as a revenue expense for set off against his trading profits, he may claim the cost as if it were expenditure on the provision of plant and equipment for the purposes of capital allowances under these provisions (CAA 2001, s. 30). This provision is extended to cover similar expenditure incurred before a designation order under that Act had come into operation, if it would have qualified for relief had such an order then been in operation and a safety certificate had then been issued or applied for (CAA 2001, s. 32,). With effect from 1 January 1988, similar relief is extended to relevant expenditure at any sports ground; this follows the broadening of the scope of the underlying safety legislation.

This relief is extended to expenditure incurred after 31 December 1988 for the purpose of complying with the extended local authority safety requirements under the Fire Safety and Safety of Places of Sport Act 1987: this introduced changes in the conditions which must be satisfied before safety certificates can be issued in respect of regulated stands at sports grounds (CAA 2001, s. 31).

It should, however, be noted that in a case relating to expenditure incurred before the above enactments, the replacement of a stand at a football stadium did not itself qualify as plant or machinery for capital allowances purposes (*Brown (HMIT) v Burnley Football and Athletic* (1980) 53 TC 357).

Personal security
Capital allowances are available where expenditure not otherwise qualifying for relief is incurred on the provision of security assets. The expenditure must be incurred by an individual or a partnership of individuals carrying on a trade, profession or vocation, in order to meet a special threat to the individual's personal physical security that arises wholly or mainly out of the particular activity.

A security asset is one which improves personal security and does not include a dwelling or its grounds, though it does include equipment attached to a building and also a structure such as a wall (CAA 2001, s. 33).

Business entertaining
Any asset used for providing business entertainment is treated as used otherwise than for the purposes of a trade, and no capital allowances may be claimed (ICTA 1988, s. 577).

Trading purpose
Expenditure will qualify for allowances if it is incurred on the provision of plant and equipment wholly and exclusively for the purposes of the trade and if the plant and equipment belongs to the taxpayer. Where the asset is acquired partly for non-trading purposes, capital allowances will be available in respect of a proportion of the expenditure incurred (CAA 2001, ss. 205–208).

The position of a landlord incurring expenditure on plant and equipment provided for use by a tenant is considered separately below.

Residential property – blocks of flats

The provision relating to capital allowances for plant and equipment are in general applicable to traders, using the plant, etc. in their trade, or to lessors, who lease the plant, etc. to traders, as is explained below. Landlords are not generally given these allowances if the plant, etc. is let for use in a dwelling house – noting the singular (CAA 2001, ss. 15(3) and 35).

The Inland Revenue is prepared to accept a literal interpretation of this proviso – particularly with regard to a block of flats. Thus where equipment is installed and in use in an individual flat, it is regarded as being in 'a dwelling house' and no allowances will be granted. On the other hand, plant and equipment installed in common parts of a block of flats will, in practice, be accepted as being available for allowances. Thus expenditure incurred on say the installation of a lift will be allowed, as will the cost of a boiler, etc. for a common central heating system – but not the cost of installing individual heating systems in each separate flat (such as night storage heaters).

It is understood that the Inland Revenue will accept, as an unpublished extra statutory concession, that where the cost of installing that part of a common central heating system that is actually contained in individual flats (eg the radiators and pipework) represents less than one quarter of the total installation (including the boiler, radiators in common parts of the building, etc.) the whole of the cost of the installation may be claimed. No separate rental for such equipment is required.

Example 5.10

Lester Coles installs central heating in the block of flats of which he is landlord. The boiler cost £7,000 (including builders' work to alter the basement to house it). Radiators and pipework cost a further £3,000.

If one fifth of the radiators, etc. are installed in common parts, he can claim capital allowances on the whole installation cost by concession – since less than one quarter of the total cost (£2,400 out of £10,000) relates to installations in the separate flats. If however only one eighth of the radiators etc. are installed in common parts of the block, the cost of installations in the flats exceeds one quarter of the whole (£2,625 out of the £10,000) and the claim for capital allowances is restricted to the balance (£7,375).

Proprietor's living accommodation

Furnishings in a flat above his business premises, used by the proprietor to allow him to work outside normal business hours, do not qualify for capital allowances since they are not used for the purposes of business (*Mason v Tyson (HMIT)* (1980) 53 TC 333).

5.3.3 Qualifying activities

Capital allowances are available to a *trader* who incurs capital expenditure on the provision of plant and equipment wholly and exclusively for the purposes of his trade (CAA 2001, s. 15). But note that costs incurred by a property dealer on his trading stock do not qualify as capital expenditure for this purpose. Where there is doubt as to the genuineness of the trade a tax avoidance motive could become relevant, even decisive (*Ensign Tankers (Leasing) v Stokes (HMIT)* [1992] BTC 110).

Alternatively, where a *landlord* acquires plant and equipment to lease out, he is deemed to incur the expenditure as if in a separate trade commencing on the first day of letting – so that the plant is treated as having been acquired wholly and exclusively for the purposes of a trade and the expenditure qualifies for capital allowances. The allowances are available whether or not the plant is used by the tenant for the purpose of a trade – unless the plant is let for use in a dwelling house. Thus the allowances are available to a landlord in respect of plant and equipment provided by him in a building let as a factory, office, shop, hotel, etc. – and also in a block of flats, but not in single dwelling units, such as a house or single flat. The allowances are given primarily against rental income and continue until the landlord permanently ceases to let the plant. There is no necessity for the plant to be leased separately – nor for a separate rent to be received (CAA 2001, ss. 15, 19).

In *Barclays Mercantile Industrial Finance Ltd v Melluish (HMIT)* [1990] BTC 209, it was held that FA 1980, s. 64 did not apply to the purchase by a finance leasing company of the master print of a film from the production company with all rights and lease back to a distribution company associated with the production company. The court held that the licences granted by the distribution company were not leases and that the master prints were used for commercial trading purposes within s. 64. It was also held that the object of the taxpayer was to make a profit from leasing. The sale and leaseback transactions were not artificial transactions entered into solely for the purpose of obtaining capital allowances within CAA 2001, s. 213.

5.3.4   Fixtures

Expenditure on fixtures

In the case of the *freeholder* incurring the expenditure, the plant and equipment will belong to him so that he is capable of making a claim for the allowances if he is a trader or a landlord. The position of a *leaseholder* or *licensee* is more complicated. When a person other than the freeholder incurs the expenditure and the plant and equipment becomes fixed to the building then it will at law belong to the freeholder – see *Stokes (HMIT) v Costain Property Investments* [1984] BTC 92. However, for capital allowances purposes it will be treated as belonging to the person who incurred the expenditure where he is the leaseholder or licensee of the land (or has an easement or servitude over it or has an agreement to acquire the freehold, or a lease, servitude or easement) (CAA 2001, s. 172).

Section 175(1)(e) refers to a licence to occupy land. The meaning of this is considered in a Revenue Interpretation in *Tax Bulletin*, Issue 47 (June 2000). The Revenue's view is that a licence to occupy arises only where a person has an exclusive licence to occupy the land in question. Its view is that a licence is a permission to enter and remain on land for such a purpose as enables the licensee to exert control over the land. The Revenue draws support for this view from rating law that says that there can be only one occupier of land. Therefore where a person can enter onto land for a subordinate purpose, such licence of entry would be something less than a licence to occupy. In the case of *Melluish (HMIT) v BMI (No 3)* [1995] BTC 381, a right of entry into a building for the purpose of repossessing equipment was held not to be a licence to occupy. In the case of *J.C. Decaux (UK) v Francis (HMIT)* (1996) Sp C 84, a right to enter land for the purpose of carrying out contractual obligations to repair and maintain equipment fell short of a licence to occupy. Customs & Excise has set out its views on this matter in more detail in relation to VAT (see **Chapter 11**).

Fixtures supplied under equipment leases

The rules outlined above can be overruled where plant and equipment fixed to a building is supplied under an equipment lease and a joint election is made by the lessor and the lessee. An equipment lease is one where the lessor leases the plant and equipment to a trader, or to a non-trading lessee, but does not lease it together with the building. Where the fixture would otherwise have been treated as belonging to the lessee if he had incurred the expenditure, the effect of the election is that it is treated as belonging to the lessor. No election can be made if the equipment lessor and the lessee are connected with one another (CAA 2001, s. 177).

These rules are tightened up, as from 24 July 1996, so as to exclude from relief:

- machinery and plant leased for use in a dwelling house, and
- machinery and plant leased to a lessee (eg a local authority) who is not within the charge to UK tax in respect of a trade for which the machinery or plant is used, or in respect of the leasing of that machinery or plant to another person (CAA 2001, s. 177). This partially reverses the decision of the House of Lords in the case of *Melluish (HMIT) v BMI (No 3)* [1995] BTC 381.

The equipment lessor is treated as selling the fixture for the capital sum he receives if he assigns the lease or the obligations of the lessee are discharged. On an assignment the assignee becomes the equipment lessor and the above rules continue to apply to him. If the lessee discharges his obligations by making a lump sum payment to the lessor, he is treated as acquiring the fixture for the capital sum he pays (CAA 2001, s. 195).

Fixtures on which a former owner had an allowance

A person incurring capital expenditure under any of the provisions which deem him to become the owner of fixtures is not entitled to capital allowances unless every previous owner who has claimed capital allowances on the fixtures has been required to bring a disposal value into his capital allowances computation on his disposal (CAA 2001, s. 185). If a claimant is not denied relief under the above rule, his qualifying expenditure is nevertheless restricted to:

- the disposal consideration brought into the vendor's or grantor's capital allowances computation, plus
- his own installation costs.

It will be appreciated that the vendor's disposal consideration is limited to his acquisition cost under CAA 2001, s. 62.

This chain of acquisitions and disposals is broken by any disposal of the machinery or plant at a time when it is not a fixture, provided that disposal is not to be a connected person. The purchaser under such a disposal may claim capital allowances on his acquisition cost plus installation cost. This then starts a new chain to which the above rules apply.

Note that this overriding restriction applies in relation to expenditure incurred by equipment lessors, expenditure incurred on the acquisition of a freehold or leasehold interest and expenditure incurred by an incoming lessee.

Acquisition of freehold or leasehold interest

The *freeholder* is entitled to the allowance as a trader or as a landlord by acquiring the freehold of land on which there is an existing building. The purchase price is apportioned, and he may claim allowances on the part relating to the plant and equipment installed in the building. The *leaseholder* will be entitled to allowances if he acquires a lease of an existing building that contains plant or equipment fixed to it. In the latter case, part of the sum paid by the leaseholder must have related to the fixture, and if capital allowances had previously been claimed in respect of it then the consideration paid must be brought into the seller's capital allowances computation. As mentioned earlier, the leaseholder can also claim allowances where he acquires the lease and pays a capital sum to an equipment lessor to discharge his predecessor's obligations under an equipment lease in respect of plant or machinery that has become a fixture (CAA 2001, s. 182). Where a fixture is deemed to belong to the purchaser of a freehold or leasehold interest in accordance with CAA 2001, s. 182, the expenditure on which the purchaser may claim capital allowances is restricted to the original cost of the fixture plus any installation costs incurred directly by the purchaser. Subject to this restriction, the vendor and purchaser may agree the purchase consideration. The same consideration is to be brought into the vendor's capital allowances computation as his disposal value. Any excess of actual expenditure is deemed to relate to the freehold or leasehold property itself.

If, instead of acquiring an existing lease, the leaseholder is granted a new lease and his landlord would have been entitled to capital allowances in respect of equipment fixed to the building in the period in which the lease is granted (or would have been if he was within the charge to tax), a joint election can be made to have the fixture treated as belonging to the leaseholder. In such circumstances, the leaseholder will be entitled to allowances on any capital sum paid by him in respect of the fixture, and the landlord will be treated as disposing of it for that amount. The election must be made within two years of the commencement of the lease. Anti-avoidance provisions exist to disallow the election if the lessor and lessee are connected or the main benefit of the transaction is to take advantage of the capital allowances position (CAA 2001, s. 183).

Where a fixture is deemed to belong to an incoming lessee in accordance with CAA 2001, s. 183 (eg on the grant of a lease for a premium), the expenditure on which the lessee may claim capital allowances is restricted to the original cost of the fixture at the time the premium was payable plus any installation costs incurred directly by the lessee. Subject to this restriction, the vendor and purchaser may agree the purchase consideration. The same consideration is to be brought into the vendor's capital allowances computation as his disposal value. Any excess of actual expenditure is deemed to relate to the premium for the lease of the premises. If the lessor was not entitled to capital allowances in respect of the fixture, the lessee may claim under CAA 2001, s. 184. Once again, however, the qualifying expenditure is restricted to the original cost of the fixture at the time the lease was granted. If a fixture is permanently separated from a building, it is treated as ceasing to belong to the leaseholder (or the holder of the qualifying interest) unless he owns it after it has been separated (CAA 2001, s. 191).

Election for alternative book value

In the case of an acquisition of a freehold or leasehold interest, or of expenditure incurred by an incoming lessee, the parties may jointly elect to compute capital allowances by reference to a specified amount not exceeding the smaller of the actual consideration and the vendor's or grantor's acquisition cost (CAA 2001, s. 198).

However, an election may not be made unless the vendor or lessor is required to bring the amount into his capital allowances computation as a disposal value. Further, the purchaser or lessee must acquire his interest in the land for the purposes of a trade, or of leasing otherwise than in the course of a trade, such that he is within the charge to UK tax in respect of that trade or leasing.

The election must be made by notice to the Inspector and may be delivered with the return for the relevant period, or may be delivered separately from the return. This election is irrevocable (CAA 2001, s. 200(3)).

Disposal value in avoidance cases

Where there is a deemed disposal of a fixture and the disposal value to be brought into the capital allowances computation would otherwise be less than the notional written-down value of the asset concerned, the disposal value is deemed to be that written-down value if the deemed disposal occurs in pursuance of tax avoidance arrangements (CAA 2001, s. 197).

Termination of lease

Where the interest in the land owned by the leaseholder or other person treated as owning the fixtures terminates (whether by sale, expiry of lease or otherwise), the fixture is treated as ceasing to belong to him and becoming the property of the landlord, with the result that a balancing charge or balancing allowance will be made. The allowances which can be claimed by a person who incurs expenditure on the provision of the fixture and is treated as acquiring it when it is treated as ceasing to belong to the leaseholder (eg on an assignment of the lease) are limited to the disposal proceeds which the leaseholder is required to bring into his capital allowance computation. The fixture continues to be treated as belonging to the leaseholder (or other holder of a qualifying interest) if his interest ceases as a result of his acquiring another interest in the land and the two interests merge (eg if a sub-leaseholder acquires the head lease). The same applies where a new lease is granted to the leaseholder on the termination of his prior lease, or he is allowed to continue in possession of the land after the termination of the lease, or where a new licence is granted to an existing licensee (CAA 2001, s. 189).

5.3.5 Contributions by landlords or tenants

Where a trader, or the landlord of a tenant trader, contributes to capital expenditure on plant and machinery that belongs to another person, and the contributor and that other person are not 'connected persons', the contributor may be entitled to claim relief in respect of that expenditure. The allowances are treated as though they derived from a trade separate from any existing trade carried on by the contributor, enabling the allowances to be given more quickly (CAA 2001, ss. 537, 538). The fact that the recipient of the contribution may be a gross fund or is otherwise unable to claim capital allowances does not prevent the contributor from claiming capital allowances in respect of his contribution.

The Inland Revenue allows a similar claim for relief in respect of expenditure incurred by landlords on fire safety (see above) or contributions to such costs (Inland Revenue Press Release dated 27 August 1976 and Extra-Statutory Concession B16).

5.3.6 When capital expenditure is incurred

As is the case with industrial buildings, the general rule is that expenditure is deemed to be incurred when the *obligation to pay the amount in question becomes unconditional* – even if it is actually payable at the later date.

Special provision is made when an obligation to pay an amount becomes unconditional as a result of the issue of a certficate (eg an architect's certificate) within a month after the end of a chargeable period and the asset in question became the payer's property prior to the end of that period. In such circumstances the capital expenditure is treated as having been incurred immediately prior to the end of the period. Anti-avoidance legislation prevents these provisions being used artificially to accelerate the time when allowances can be claimed. It will apply where an agreement requires expenditure to be paid more than four months after the obligation to pay becomes unconditional. In such a case, the expenditure is treated as having been incurred at the time when it actually becomes payable (CAA 2001 s. 5).

If the obligation to pay becomes unconditional on an earlier date than under normal commercial usage, and the only or main benefit of this acceleration of the obligation to pay is to enable allowances to be claimed in an earlier period, then the expenditure is treated as having been incurred when the amount actually becomes payable, whether or not this is within four months of the date when the obligation to pay became unconditional. Where, however, any expenditure is thus incurred for the purposes of a trade before that trade has actually commenced, the expenditure is treated as being incurred on the first day of trading and the allowances in respect of that expenditure are given on that day (CAA 2001, s. 12).

Hire purchase and other contracts

Where a person acquires plant and equipment for the purposes of his trade, etc. under a hire purchase agreement, the plant is deemed to be his own property as from the time when he entered into the contract for its acquisition. All instalments paid before the plant is first used are available for a claim for allowances at the normal time. Instalments paid after the plant comes into use in the trade are treated as incurred when the plant, etc. first came into use, so that capital allowances may be claimed in advance of payment.

Where a person fails to complete the contract, and thus never becomes the owner, but in the meantime has received allowances on the plant, he is treated as having disposed of the plant. For this purpose the disposal value is adjusted to take into account the excess allowances received as a result of his not having paid all the instalments, and any compensation or other payments which he may be entitled to – to the extent of the allowances given to him.

In the same way, where a person incurs expenditure in advance of the plant coming into use in his trade, for example by making stage payments to a manufacturer before delivery, he is nevertheless treated as the owner of that plant and equipment from the time he signs a contract for it, so that the stage payments are allowed as and when they become payable, provided that the person is actually carrying on a trade. Stage payments made before trading commences are deferred and the allowance only granted as and when trading commences, as seen above (CAA 2001, s. 67).

Example 5.11

Lester Coles spends £ 100,000 on the installation of central heating in the block of flats of which he is landlord. He signs the contract for the work in June 2003 and agrees to pay for it in ten quarterly payments (starting in June 2003) of £10,000 each. Work commences in July and is finished by October 2003. Assume the whole cost qualifies.

If one flat is already let, his deemed 'trade' has commenced – and he can claim allowances on the payments as they are paid, as follows:

	£
2003/04	40,000
2004/05	40,000
2005/06	20,000
	£100,000

If no flat is let until May 2004, so that his 'trade' does not begin until then, his claim for allowances on earlier stage payments is deferred as follows:

	£
2004/05	
Earlier payments	40,000
Current payments	40,000
	80,000
2005/06	20,000
	£100,000

Abortive expenditure

Capital expenditure incurred in anticipation of acquiring an asset may qualify for capital allowances (*Tax Bulletin*, February 1992). For relief to be available a contract will be necessary, 'providing that he shall or may become the owner of the machinery or plant on the performance of the contract' (CAA 2001, s. 67(1)(a)). The nil disposal value of the plant (CAA 2001, s. 61) will be brought into account when the taxpayer ceases to be entitled to the benefit of the contract without becoming the owner of the plant (CAA 2001, s. 68).

Partnerships

Where a partner provides plant or equipment for use in a trade carried on by the partnership, the firm can claim allowances in respect of that equipment, provided that no charge is made in the partnership accounts in consideration for the use thereof (CAA 2001, s. 264).

5.3.7 First-year allowances

First-year allowances are available for the following categories of qualifying expenditure:

- *Northern Ireland:* expenditure incurred by a small or medium sized enterprise (SME) in the period 12 May 1998 to 11 May 2002 qualifies for a 100 per cent FYA (CAA 2001, ss. 40, 52);
- *SMEs generally:* as from 2 July 1998 expenditure qualifies for a 40 per cent FYA (CAA 2001, ss. 44, 52), increased to 50 per cent for small enterprises for the year ending on 31 March 2005 (companies) or 6 April 2005 (individuals) (ss. 142 FA 2004);
- *small enterprises:* ICT expenditure qualifies for a 100 per cent FYA (CAA 2001, ss. 45, 52); and
- *energy saving plant and machinery:* expenditure incurred on or after 1 April 2001 qualifies for a 100 per cent FYA (CAA 2001, ss. 45A, 52) – see below.

The first-year allowance also applies to any additional VAT which is incurred on expenditure which itself qualifies (CAA 2001, ss. 235–237).

Timing of expenditure

The usual rules for establishing when expenditure is incurred contained in CAA 2001, s. 5 will apply (see above).

It is a requirement of the existing legislation that as the result of incurring the expenditure the claimant owns the asset at some time in the period for which the first-year allowance is being claimed (CAA 2001, s. 15). Special provisions exist to determine the ownership of fixtures, that is plant and equipment installed so as to become in law part of a building (CAA 2001, ss. 176–184).

There are also special provisions to deal with the situation where a person carrying on a trade incurs capital expenditure on the provision of plant and equipment for the purposes of the trade under a hire purchase or similar contract (CAA 2001, s. 67). In this situation it is provided that the plant and equipment is treated as belonging to the person at any time when he is entitled to the benefit of the contract (CAA 2001, s. 67(2)). This will be the date on which the contract is entered into. Further, all capital expenditure on the machinery or plant incurred after it has been brought into use is deemed to have been incurred at the time it is brought into use (CAA 2001, s. 67(3)).

Small and medium sized businesses

A company is an SME for any of its financial years if it qualifies as a small or medium sized company for that financial year under CA 1985, s. 247(3), and is not a member of a large group. This means that:

- its turnover must not exceed £11.2 million per annum;
- its assets must not exceed £5.6 million, and
- the number of its employees must not exceed 250.

If it is a member of a group, the group as a whole must satisfy the above criteria.

An unincorporated business is an SME if, on the assumption that the business was carried on by a company, that company would be an SME. The expenditure must be incurred for the purposes of a trade, profession or vocation. Expenditure incurred for the purposes of an investment business does not qualify for the new first-year allowances (CAA 2001, s. 48(3)).

Exclusions

Expenditure does not qualify for first-year allowances in any of the following circumstances:

- if the trade is discontinued in the chargeable period in which it is incurred;
- if it is expenditure on the provision of cars, ships, railway assets, etc. as set out in CAA 2001, s. 46(2);
- if it is expenditure falling within the transitional provisions relating to long-life assets under s. 38H;
- if the trade is one of leasing,
- if the provision of the machinery or plant is connected with a change in the conduct of a trade or business carried on by any person other than the person incurring the expenditure and the main purpose, or one of the main purposes, of the change is the obtaining of a first-year allowance (CAA 2001, s. 46(2)).

5.3.8 Writing-down allowances

An annual writing-down allowance may be claimed in respect of any 'pool' expenditure remaining unrelieved at the end of a chargeable period, at the rate of 25 per cent. This annual writing-down allowance is dependent on the length of the chargeable period, so that if the period is less than 12 months the writing-down allowance is restricted accordingly.

Where a trade has been undertaken by a company for only part of an accounting period then the writing-down allowance is restricted proportionately in much the same way as it would for an individual or partnership. This will be of concern where a property investor acquires a property and lets it out – including any fixtures. The fixtures are treated as having been provided in a separate trade, commencing at the time of the letting of the property, and subject therefore to a proportionate restriction.

Pool basis

The expenditure is dealt with as a single figure on a pool basis, rather than individually. This pool consists of the balance of unrelieved expenditure brought forward from the previous period, together with expenditure incurred during the period, less the value to be brought into account on the disposal of any item. Adjustment under the VAT capital goods scheme (see **Chapter 11**) will be added to or deducted from the pool as appropriate. The writing-down allowance is then calculated on this resulting figure.

Short-life assets

Assets which have a life expectancy of less than five years need not be brought into the pool where the expenditure is incurred after 31 March 1986. Instead, an election can be made for allowances to be calculated separately on each short-life asset (ie as if each formed a separate pool). Where actual depreciation outpaces capital allowances, this treatment enables a balancing allowance to be crystallised on sale instead of merely reducing the pool qualifying for future allowances.

If the asset is not disposed of within four years of the end of the chargeable period in which it was acquired, the balance of unrelieved expenditure is added to the main pool, so that the election will have had no effect. Certain assets cannot be treated as short-life assets (eg cars and ships). For the purposes of this publication, the most important exclusion relates to plant or equipment (whether fixed to a building or mobile) that is leased otherwise than in the course of a trade (CAA 2001, s. 84).

Long-life assets

Where a person incurs expenditure exceeding £100,000 in any chargeable period on 'long-life assets', the allowances for that expenditure are at the rate of 6 per cent per annum on the reducing-balance basis, rather than 25 per cent. The £100,000 limit is reduced proportionately for short accounting periods. Further, in the case of a company with associated companies, the £100,000 limit is shared equally between the company and its associates (CAA 2001, s. 99). In the case of a partnership, the limit applies to the partnership as a whole (CAA 2001, s. 98(2)). The expenditure that qualifies at the 6 per cent rate is dealt with as a separate pool in the capital allowances computation (CAA 2001, s. 101).

An asset is a long-life asset if its expected useful life is 25 years or more (CAA 2001, s. 91). Certain assets are excluded from the long-life assets rules and continue to qualify for writing-down allowances at the normal rates:

- assets which become fixtures in a dwelling house, retail shop, showroom, hotel or office, or in a building used for purposes ancillary thereto;
- motor cars,
- ships and railway assets where the expenditure is incurred before 1 January 2011 (CAA 2001, ss. 94, 95).

In the Revenue's view, each asset has to be considered as a whole: it is not permissible to treat parts of an asset separately from the asset itself, notwithstanding the provisions of CAA 2001, s. 571(1).

Where expenditure is incurred on improvements to an asset, the expected life of the improvements must be considered. In many cases, this will be the remaining expected life of the asset.

Where machinery and plant is installed in a building, the expected life of that machinery and plant will not necessarily be the same as that of the building. For example, lifts and airconditioning plant may need to be replaced long before the building is demolished (*Tax Bulletin*, Issue 30).

Claims

A company may disclaim all or part of the writing-down allowances due to it in respect of a chargeable period (CAA 2001, s. 56(2)), and an individual may claim a reduced amount if he so wishes.

Under CTSA, a company generally must make a claim for the amount of allowances required in the return or amended return submitted to the Inland Revenue (FA 1998, Sch. 18, Paras. 78–83).

5.3.9   Disposals and cessation of use

Where plant or equipment is disposed of (or is permanently lost or destroyed), or when the trade is permanently discontinued or the asset begins to be used wholly or partly for non-trading purposes, during the chargeable period, the disposal value is deducted from the pool residue of expenditure before calculating the writing-down allowance for that period. If the disposal value exceeds the balance of pool expenditure, an assessment (a balancing charge) is made equal to the excess. Thus, up to the residue in the pool, any over allowances are recovered by a restriction on current and future writing-down allowances, spread over a period, rather than an immediate clawback (CAA 2001, s. 55).

Disposal value

The disposal value in normal cases is taken as the net proceeds received, adjusted where appropriate under the VAT capital goods scheme (see **Chapter 11**), but restricted to the qualifying expenditure originally incurred in providing the plant or equipment. If the plant was acquired previously from a connected person, the restriction applies to the higher of the amounts incurred by the taxpayer or the connected person.

When the plant is lost, demolished or destroyed, the value is taken as any sum received by way of compensation, such as insurance monies, etc., again restricted to original cost. Where the plant is sold at less than market value, the disposal value is taken as the sum that it would fetch on the open market, also restricted as above – unless the purchaser claims allowances in respect of his cost or there is a charge to tax under Schedule E (CAA 2001, ss. 61–64).

The Inland Revenue may adjust the split of any proceeds of disposal – taking together all items sold as part of one bargain, and including the value of any asset in exchange – so as to arrive at a just apportionment. But it is usually more difficult for the Revenue to reallocate an apportionment that has already been agreed between vendor and purchaser acting at arm's length (CAA 2001, s. 562).

Where plant is disposed of before it is brought into use, if the full disposal value is less than the original expenditure, the shortfall is added to the pool, so that it qualifies for writing-down allowances in that and subsequent years. Any first-year allowance given in respect of the original cost is withdrawn, as noted above (CAA 2001, s. 58(6)).

Leases, licences, etc.

Where the interest in the land owned by the leaseholder or other person treated as owning a fixture terminates (whether by sale, expiry of lease or otherwise) the fixture is treated as ceasing to belong to him and becoming the property of the landlord, with the result that a balancing charge or balancing allowance will be made.

If the interest is sold, the disposal proceeds of the fixture to be included in the capital allowance computation are the part of the proceeds on which the purchaser can claim allowances (or would be able to claim allowances if he were entitled to do so) – but if the sale is at less than market value and the purchaser is unable to claim capital allowances, the open market price is substituted.

Where the occasion of the fixture being treated as ceasing to belong to the leaseholder etc. is the termination of the lease or other interest, the disposal proceeds are the amount received by way of compensation for the fixture or, failing this, nil.

Where the trade of the leaseholder ceases before the fixture is sold, destroyed or permanently lost, the disposal proceeds are taken as the appropriate proportion of the eventual sale price or compensation.

A balancing adjustment will also be required if a fixture begins to be used wholly or partly for non-trading purposes. The amount to be brought into account is the proportion of the sale proceeds which would be attributable to the fixture on a sale at market value (CAA 2001, s. 196).

Successions

Where a company transfers its trade to another company and both companies are controlled as to at least three quarters by the same individuals or companies, it is not regarded as the cessation of that trade and the occasion of the transferee company ceasing to use the plant and equipment – the trade being treated as if it was continued by one single company throughout.

In the case of an inherited business, provision is made for the successor to elect to take over plant and equipment at its residue of pool expenditure, without any revaluation (CAA 2001, s. 268).

Otherwise, however, successions do give rise to a deemed disposal of the plant and equipment concerned at its full market value, without any claim for first-year allowances in the hands of the successor – including a partnership change where no 'continuation' election is made (under ICTA 1988, s. 113 (2)) and which therefore falls to be treated as a cessation (CAA 2001, s. 265).

Where the successor and predecessor are connected with each other in terms of ICTA 1988, s. 839, they may jointly elect that the trade should not be treated as discontinued for the purposes of the capital allowances provisions – thus avoiding any deemed sale at full market value (CAA 2001, s. 266). However, the election is only available where, additionally, both parties are within the charge to UK tax on the profits of the trade transferred between them, and must be made within two years of the succession.

Moreover, the election is available not only where the predecessor and successor are connected with each other but also where:

- one is a partnership and the other is a member of that partnership; or
- one is a body corporate over which the other has control; or
- both are partnerships with at least one partner in common; or

- both are bodies corporate under common control, or
- one is a body corporate and the other is a partnership under common control.

Purchasers

There is no restriction in the allowances given to a purchaser of plant and equipment – as opposed to the case of an industrial building where the allowances may be restricted depending on the vendor's tax position – so that he may claim allowances on his own cost, even if the original cost of providing the plant or equipment as incurred by the vendor was much less.

5.3.10 Energy-saving plant and machinery, etc.

First-year allowances of 100 per cent are available for qualifying expenditure incurred on or after 1 April 2001 on energy saving plant or machinery which is unused and not second-hand (CAA 2001, s. 45A). The exclusions mentioned at **5.3.7** in relation to SMEs (long-life assets, assets for leasing, etc.) will also apply for this purpose.

The categories of plant or machinery which qualify and the energy-saving criteria which have to be met are set out in the Capital Allowances (Energy saving Plant and Machinery) Order 2001 (SI 2001/2541), which refers to lists of technologies or products issued by the Secretary of State for the Environment, Food and Rural Affairs. Details are available from DEFRA's website, at www.defra.gov.uk.

The specified technology classes are:

- boilers;
- motors and drives;
- refrigeration;
- thermal screens;
- heat pumps;
- radiant and warm air heaters;
- compressed air equipment;
- solar thermal systems,
- automatic monitoring and targeting equipment, (reg. 3(2)).

A certificate of energy efficiency signed by the Secretary of State may be required in support of a claim for first-year allowances in some cases (CAA 2001, s. 45B, and reg. 4).

Where some components of plant or machinery comply with the require-ments and some do not, the expenditure has to be apportioned. The Treasury will specify the amount apportioned to the qualifying components (CAA 2001, s. 45C and reg. 5).

Fixtures provided in connection with energy management services

The rules set out below enable an 'energy services provider' to claim capital allowances on capital expenditure incurred, in the course of providing the services, on plant or machinery which becomes a fixture. The provider and the client must jointly elect for these provisions to apply. The election must be made within two years after the end of the accounting period in which the expenditure is incurred (corporation tax) or within the normal time limit for an amended return (income tax). An election may not be made if the provider and the client are 'connected persons' (CAA 2001, s. 180A).

The provisions apply where the provider does not acquire any interest in the land concerned. They do not apply to plant or machinery provided for leasing or for use in a dwelling house.

An 'energy services provider' is a person who provides service under an 'energy services agreement'. This is an agreement for:

- the design of plant or machinery, or one or more systems incorporating plant or machinery;
- obtaining and installing the plant or machinery;
- the operation of the plant or machinery;
- the maintenance of the plant or machinery, and
- payments in respect of the operation of the plant or machinery to be linked to energy savings or increases in energy efficiency,

(CAA 2001, s. 175A).

Where a person acquires an interest in the land after the plant or machinery has become a fixture, and discharges the obligations of the client under the energy services agreement by means of a capital sum, he is treated as becoming the owner of the fixture with qualifying expenditure equal to that capital sum. However, this is subject to any prior right in relation to the fixture (CAA 2001, s. 182A). For example, the services provider may have a prior right as a result of making the election referred to above (CAA 2001, s. 181(3)).

If the services provider assigns his rights under the agreement, or the financial obligations of the client are discharged, he is treated as ceasing to be the owner of the plant and machinery (CAA 2001, s. 192A). In the case of an assignment, the assignee is treated as becoming the owner of the plant and machinery, with qualifying expenditure equal to the consideration given for the assignment (CAA 2001, s. 195A). In the case of a discharge of obligations, the client is treated as becoming the owner (s. 195B).

Expenditure on plant or machinery for gas refuelling station

First-year allowances of 100 per cent are available for capital expenditure incurred between 17 April 2002 and 31 March 2008 on new and unused plant or machinery for a 'gas refuelling station'. This is subject to the general exclusions in CAA 2001, s. 46 for leasing, etc.

A 'gas refuelling station' means premises, or part of premises, where vehicles are refuelled with natural gas or hydrogen fuel (CAA 2001, s. 45E).

The plant or machinery must be installed at the premises for use solely in refuelling vehicles with natural gas or hydrogen fuel (CAA 2001, s. 45E(2)). Such plant or machinery includes:

- any storage tank for natural gas or hydrogen fuel;
- any compressor, pump, control or meter used for or in connection with refuelling vehicles with natural gas or hydrogen fuel,
- any equipment for dispensing natural gas or hydrogen fuel to the fuel tank of a vehicle,

(CAA 2001, s. 45E(3)).

5.3.11 Transitional

First-year allowances

Before 1 April 1986, a first-year allowance was given in respect of expenditure incurred on plant and machinery.

Where capital expenditure was incurred after 21 March 1972 and before 1 April 1986, the person incurring that expenditure could claim a first-year allowance equal to a proportion of the cost incurred, as follows:

Expenditure incurred		Allowance
After	*Before*	
21 March 1972	14 March 1984	100%
13 March 1984	1 April 1985	75%
31 March 1985	1 April 1986	50%
31 March 1986		nil

The allowance was made in the chargeable period in which the expenditure was incurred – normally the date on which the obligation to pay became unconditional, unless incurred before trading commenced, in which case it was the day when the trade commenced. Such a first-year allowance was given whether or not the plant was brought into use during that chargeable period. The right to these allowances did not depend on an equivalent amount being written off in the taxpayer's account as depreciation.

Writing-down allowances

Pool basis

The pool of expenditure for annual writing-down allowances consisted of the balance of unrelieved expenditure brought forward from the previous period, together with any capital expenditure not qualifying for a first-year allowance (such as on a sale between connected persons), less the value to be brought into account on the disposal of any item. The writing-down allowance was then calculated on this resulting figure.

5.4 Other allowances

5.4.1 Research and development

Allowances are available for capital expenditure incurred by a trader on research and development related to that trade. Pre-trading expenditure on scientific research also qualifies. The allowance is at the rate of 100 per cent. It is given as a deduction in computing the profits of the trade for the period in which the expenditure is incurred. There are rules dealing with overlapping basis periods and gaps between basis periods. Allowances for pre trading expenditure are given in the period in which the trade commences (CAA 2001, ss. 437–451).

Expenditure on scientific research includes the provision of facilities for the conduct of scientific research (eg the provision of a laboratory building and the provision of machinery and plant in such a building). However, it does not include the acquisition of rights arising from scientific research, such as patent rights (CAA 2001, s. 438).

Scientific research means activities which are treated as such in accordance with normal accounting practice and which are not excluded by Regulations (ICTA 1988, s. 837A and SI 2000/2081). The Regulations refer to Guidance issued by the DTI on 28 July 2000. Activities are scientific research if they involve:

- the application of new scientific principles in an existing area of research, or
- the application of existing scientific principles in a new area of research.

However, the application of existing principles in an existing area is not regarded as scientific research, but technological development (see *Inland Revenue Capital Allowances Manual*, CA5002).

The information required by the Revenue for the purposes of dealing with a claim for scientific research allowances is set out at CA5004. Scientific research is related to a trade if, for example:

- it may lead to or facilitate an extension of that trade, or
- it is of a medical nature and has a special relationship to the welfare of workers employed in the trade (CAA 2001, s. 439(5)).

Expenditure on scientific research includes any related non-recoverable input VAT. Where there is an adjustment of that VAT under the capital goods scheme, any further non-recoverable tax is treated as additional qualifying expenditure and any rebate is taxed as a trading receipt (CAA 2001, ss. 446–449).

Expenditure on the acquisition of an interest in land does not qualify for the allowances, nor does expenditure on the provision of a dwelling. Therefore, where an existing building is acquired, there must be a just apportionment of the acquisition price between the land and the building (CAA 2001, ss. 438, 440).

A balancing charge may arise where an asset which has qualified for scientific research allowances ceases to belong to the person who claimed the allowances. This adjustment may arise on the disposal, destruction or demolition of the asset, for example. However, there is no balancing adjustment merely because the asset ceases to be used for scientific research (eg where a laboratory begins to be used for production or administration activities). The balancing charge is equal to the lesser of the 'disposal value' and the allowances given. There is no balancing allowance where the trader did not take the full allowance at the outset (CAA 2001, ss. 442, 443).

The disposal value is the sale consideration in the case of a sale at arm's length. In the case of a non-arm's length disposal, the value is the open market value of the asset. If the asset is destroyed, the value is the insurance or other compensation monies receivable (CAA 2001, s. 443).

5.4.2 Agricultural buildings and works

A person who has a freehold or leasehold interest in 'agricultural land' may claim capital allowances on capital expenditure incurred by him on the construction of:

- farmhouses;
- farm buildings;
- cottages;
- fences, or
- other works,

provided that the expenditure is incurred for the purposes of 'husbandry' on the agricultural land (CAA 2001, ss. 361–363). Note that the asset does not need to be situated on the agricultural land: provided that it is constructed for the purposes of husbandry on the land it qualifies for allowances (see *Inland Revenue Capital Allowances Manual*, CA4504). Similarly, if a landlord incurs expenditure on an asset used by the tenant for the purposes of husbandry on the agricultural land, his expenditure qualifies for allowances.

The capital allowances are given at the rate of 4 per cent per annum on a straight line basis, starting with the period in which the expenditure is incurred. 'Agricultural land' means land, houses or other buildings in the UK occupied wholly or mainly for the purposes of husbandry.

'Husbandry' includes any method of intensive rearing of livestock or fish on a commercial basis for the production of food for human consumption (CAA 2001, s. 362). Horticulture is also included, as is market gardening (*Inland Revenue Capital Allowances Manual*, CA4509).

A freehold interest includes an agreement to acquire such an interest. A lease includes an agreement for a lease where the term to be covered by the lease has already begun. It also includes a tenancy, but it does not include a mortgage (CAA 2001, s. 393). In Scotland, the estate or interest of the proprietor of the *dominum utile* is a major interest. This includes an agreement to acquire such an interest. In the case of property other than feudal property, the owner has a major interest.

The interest held by the person incurring any expenditure when he incurred it is the 'relevant interest' in relation to that expenditure. If the person has two or more major interests in the land, and one of them is reversionary on the others, that reversionary interest is the relevant interest. A major interest does not cease to be the relevant interest merely because a lease or sub lease is granted out of it (CAA 2001, ss. 364–368).

Farmhouses and cottages

Only one third of any expenditure on the construction of a farmhouse qualifies for relief. Indeed, the proportion may be smaller if the accommodation and amenities of the farmhouse are out of due relation to the nature and extent of the farm. In such a case, a just and reasonable proportion is taken (CAA 2001, s. 369(3) (4)).

A farmhouse is the building from which the farm business is run, which is not necessarily the same as the house in which the proprietor of the farm lives. However, in the case of *Lindsay v IR Commrs* (1953) 34 TC 287, it was held that a building occupied by a farm employee – which was the only dwelling house on the particular farm – was a farmhouse. A house which is the centre of operations for a market garden business is a farmhouse (*Inland Revenue Capital Allowances Manual*, CA4509).

There is no special definition of 'cottage'. The fact that a building is occupied by the proprietor of the farm does not prevent it from being a cottage. However, a cottage is not regarded as being used wholly for the purposes of husbandry if the person who occupies it is not working full time on the farm or market garden (*Inland Revenue Capital Allowances Manual*, CA4532). However, cottages occupied by retired farm workers, and buildings constructed to provide welfare facilities for employees qualify for allowances (*Inland Revenue Capital Allowances Manual*, CA4533).

Farm shops

As far as farm buildings are concerned, a farm shop qualifies for ABAs if and to the extent that it sells goods, etc. produced on the farm or market garden.

Other works

The *Inland Revenue Capital Allowances Manual* gives the following examples of 'other works':

- drainage and sewage works;
- water and electricity supply installations;
- walls;
- shelter belts of trees;
- silos;
- farm roads;
- the reclamation of former agricultural land, and
- the demolition of hedges.

Apportionment of expenditure

If an asset other than a farmhouse is used partly for husbandry on the agricultural land and partly for other purposes, then a proportionate part of the construction expenditure qualifies for allowances (CAA 2001, s. 369(5)).

Purchase of an unused building

Where an agricultural building, etc. is bought unused, the vendor is not entitled to ABAs on his construction costs, but the purchaser may claim allowances on the lower of the purchase price and the vendor's construction costs (CAA 2001, s. 370).

Transfer of relevant interest

Where the relevant interest in an agricultural building is transferred, the vendor ceases to be entitled to ABAs for any chargeable period after the period in which the transfer occurs. A proportionate allowance is given for that period. The purchaser is entitled to the allowances to which the vendor would have been entitled had he retained the relevant interest. There is, in general, no balancing adjustment on the transfer (CAA 2001, s. 375). However, the parties may elect to have a balancing adjustment computed. This means that the purchaser is then entitled to claim allowances on the lower of the purchase price and the vendor's construction costs (CAA 2001, ss. 380–382). The time limit for an election is:

- for income tax purposes, the first anniversary of 31 January following the end of the tax year in which ends the chargeable period in which the transfer occurs,
- for corporation tax purposes, two years after the end of the accounting period (presumably of the vendor) in which the transfer occurs.

Other balancing events

A balancing adjustment is computed where any agricultural building, etc is demolished or destroyed or otherwise ceases to exist (CAA 2001, s. 381(2)). The notional disposal consideration comprises any sale, insurance, salvage or compensation monies arising (CAA 2001, s. 383).

Manner of making allowances

In the case of a landlord who is within the charge to income tax, the allowances are given as a deduction in computing the Schedule A profits. In the case of a landlord within the charge to corporation tax, the allowances are given by discharge or repayment of tax and are available primarily against agricultural income and balancing charges (CAA 2001, s. 392).

In the case of a person carrying on a trade of husbandry on the agricultural land, the allowances are given as a deduction in computing the profits of the trade (CAA 2001, s. 391).

The manner of giving relief for capital allowances is considered further at **5.5** below.

Initial allowances

Expenditure incurred between 1 November 1992 and 31 October 1993 qualified for an initial allowance of 20 per cent (CAA 1990, s. 124A).

5.4.3 Flat conversion allowances

As from 11 May 2001, property owners and occupiers may claim 100 per cent initial capital allowances on *qualifying expenditure* on the renovation or conversion of vacant or underused space above shops and other commercial premises to provide flats for rent. The allowances work on a basis similar to Industrial Buildings Allowances for buildings in enterprise zones (CAA 2001, s. 393A–393W). They are given as a deduction in computing the profits of the Schedule A business of the person incurring the expenditure. Similarly, a balancing charge is treated as a Schedule A receipt (CAA 2001, s. 393T).

Qualifying expenditure

Qualifying expenditure means expenditure incurred on, or in connection with:

(a)   the conversion of part of a *qualifying building* into a *qualifying flat*;

(b)   the renovation of a flat in a qualifying building if the flat is, or will be, a qualifying flat, or

(c)   repairs to a qualifying building, to the extent that the repairs are incidental to expenditure within (a) or (b) above.

However, the part of the building which is converted must have been unused, or used only for storage, for a period of one year prior to the commencement of the conversion or renovation work. Expenditure on, or in connection with, the following does not qualify:

- the acquisition of land, or rights in or over land;
- the extension of a qualifying building, except for access to the flat(s);
- the development of land adjoining or adjacent to the qualifying building, or
- the provision of furnishings or chattels, (CAA 2001, s. 393B).

Qualifying buildings

The property must have been built before 1980. It must not have more than five floors in total, including accommodation in the roof, but excluding any basements. It must have been originally constructed so that the floors above the ground floor were primarily for residential use (CAA 2001, s. 393C).

The ground floor can have been originally either residential, or commercial, or mixed use. However, the whole or the greater part of the ground floor must, at the time the conversion work starts, be rated as follows for England and Wales:

- A1 – broadly speaking, retail shops
- A2 – financial and professional services
- A3 – food and drink
- B1 – offices not in A2, R&D and industrial processes which can be carried out in residential areas
- D1(a) – medical and health services, such as doctors' surgeries and dental practices.

The definition covers the same types of property in Scotland and Northern Ireland under their corresponding ratings legislation (CAA 2001, s. 393C(2)).

The upper floors must have been either unoccupied, or used only for storage, for at least one year before the conversion work starts. The qualifying expenditure will be apportioned if part of the upper floors satisfies this test, and part does not.

Qualifying flats

The conversion must take place within the existing boundaries of the building. Extensions will qualify if they are required only to provide access to the flat(s). But conversions, which form part of a larger scheme of development, do not qualify.

Each new flat must be self-contained, with external access separate from the ground floor premises. Each flat must have no more than four rooms, excluding kitchen and bathroom and small areas such as cloakrooms and hallways (CAA 2001, s. 393D).

High-value flats are excluded from the scheme. These are flats where the notional rent exceeds the following limits (CAA 2001, s. 393E):

No. of rooms in flat	Flats in Greater London	Flats elsewhere
1 or 2	£350 per week	£150 per week
3	£425 per week	£225 per week
4	£480 per week	£300 per week

The notional rent is based on a furnished letting between unconnected parties on a shorthold tenancy with no premium payable.

Initial allowances

The person who incurs the qualifying expenditure may claim a 100 per cent initial allowance for the chargeable period in which it is incurred. He may claim a reduced amount, in which case he will be entitled to writing-down allowances in later periods (CAA 2001, s. 393H,). However, the flat must be a qualifying flat at the time it is first suitable for letting as a dwelling (CAA 2001, s. 393I).

Writing-down allowances

The person claiming the allowances must have the relevant interest in the flat: that is the interest that the person who incurred the qualifying expenditure had when he incurred it (CAA 2001, s. 393F). The rules are the same as for IBAs (CAA 2001, s. 393F). The allowances are given at the rate of 25 per cent of the qualifying expenditure – ie on a straight line basis (CAA 2001, s. 393K). However, the allowance cannot exceed the residue of qualifying expenditure.

A reduced amount of writing-down allowances may be specified in the claim.

Note, however, that the purchaser of a qualifying flat cannot claim these allowances: they are available only to the person who incurred the qualifying expenditure. Also the person who incurred the expenditure cannot claim allowances if, before the end of the chargeable period, he has granted a lease of more than 50 years on the flat (CAA 2001, s. 393J).

Balancing adjustments

The balancing events and related disposal consideration are set out in a Table in CAA 2001, s. 393O. This is reproduced below.

Balancing event	*Proceeds from event*
1. The sale of the relevant interest	The net proceeds of the sale.
2. The grant of a long lease out of the relevant interest	If the capital sum paid in consideration of the grant is less than the commercial premium, the commercial premium. In any other case, the capital sum paid in consideration of the grant.
3. The coming to an end of a lease, where a person entitled to the lease and a person entitled to any superior interest are connected persons	The market value of the relevant interest in the flat at the time of the event.
4. The death of the person who incurred the qualifying expenditure	The residue of qualifying expenditure immediately before the death.
5. The demolition or destruction of the flat	The net amount received for the remains of the flat together with;
	(a) any insurance money received in respect of the demolition or destruction, and
	(b) any other compensation of any description so received, so far as it consists of capital sums.
6. The flat ceases to be a qualifying flat	The market value of the relevant interest in the flat at the time of the event.

However, there will be no recovery of allowances if a balancing event takes place more than seven years from the time the flat is completed and suitable for letting.

There is a balancing allowance if there are no proceeds from the event, or if the proceeds are less than the residue of qualifying expenditure (CAA 2001, s.393P).

As regards a sale, if the proceeds are attributable partly to the qualifying expenditure and partly to other expenditure, there is a just and reasonable apportionment (CAA 2001, s.393U).

On the termination of a lease, if the lessee remains in possession of the flat without a new lease being granted, the lease is treated as continuing as long as he remains in possession. If a new lease is granted to him on the exercise of an option, that is treated as the continuation of the first lease. If the landlord pays a sum to the lessee in respect of the flat, the lease is treated as surrendered in consideration for the payment. If a new lease is granted to another person and that person pays a sum to the first lessee, that is treated as the assignment of the first lease (CAA 2001, s. 393V). As regards demolition, the demolition costs may be added to the residue of qualifying expenditure for the purposes of computing the balancing adjustment (CAA 2001, s. 393S).

Meaning of 'lease'

A lease includes an agreement for a lease, and a tenancy, but not a mortgage.

5.4.4 Miscellaneous

Mineral extraction

Allowances may also be available in respect of expenditure in the working of a mine or oil well or other source of mineral deposits of a wasting nature, and for the capital cost incurred in the acquisition of mineral assets, but this is outside the scope of the present work (see CAA 2001, ss. 394–436).

Dredging

Where a person incurs capital expenditure on dredging in the course of a trade consisting of either maintaining or improving the navigation of a harbour, estuary or waterway, or in assisting vessels entering docks etc, the expenditure qualifies for an annual writing-down allowance of 4 per cent per annum, calculated on the original cost rather than the written-down value, until the expenditure has been written off. The general rules regarding the treatment of capital allowances apply to allowances in respect of dredging expenditure (CAA 2001, ss. 484–489).

Sea walls

A special relief is available in respect of capital expenditure incurred in the construction of a sea wall or other embankment required to protect a property from the sea or a tidal river. The relief is however only given to a landlord in respect of a leased property, and not to an owner-occupier trader. The relief is given by way of a deduction in computing rental profits under Schedule A, and does not therefore follow the normal treatment of allowances in respect of capital expenditure as noted below (ICTA 1988, s. 30).

5.5 Treatment of allowances

5.5.1 General

Having thus ascertained the amount of allowances that may be claimed in respect of capital expenditure, and who may claim them, consideration may now be given as to the way in which the allowances are treated. The treatment depends first and foremost on whether they are granted to a landlord in respect of the letting of a property, or to an owner-occupier trader. These two categories are therefore considered separately below. In each category different rules apply in considering the tax position of a company or individual, and the way in which allowances due to a partnership are made. Further notes are given on the position of a non-resident and property situated abroad.

5.5.2 Landlords

Generally

In general the allowances due to a landlord are given as a deduction in computing the Schedule A profits, furnished letting profits or overseas property business profits (CAA 2001 ss. 248–250 for machinery and plant and s. 353 for IBAs and s. 392 for ABAs).

Property investment companies

Allowances may be claimed by a property investment company in respect of plant and equipment used by the company in managing its own affairs (as opposed to managing its property investments, as dealt with above). These allowances are primarily set off against income generally, but any unrelieved allowances may be treated as a management expense and thus available against chargeable gains and for carry forward to succeeding accounting periods (ICTA 1988, s. 75(4)).

Non-residents

A non-resident letting property in the UK, and so within the charge to UK taxation in respect thereof, is entitled to the same capital allowances as a UK resident – computed and allowed in the same way. In the case of a company that carries on a trade in the UK through a branch or agency, the corporation tax rules apply. Otherwise the income tax rules apply.

5.5.3 Owner-occupier traders

Companies

In the case of companies, capital allowances are given by deduction in computing the trading profits arising during the accounting period. If the allowances exceed trading profits, they are treated as a trading loss.

Partnerships

Capital allowances are computed for the partnership as a whole and are given as a deduction in computing the Case I or Case II profits of the partnership. Similarly, any balancing charge is treated as a trading receipt (ICTA 1988, s. 111(2) and CAA 2001 s. 263). If the deduction of capital allowances creates or augments a loss, then each partner may claim relief for his share of the loss in accordance with ICTA 1988, ss. 380 or 381.

If the partnership includes a corporate partner, then the profits and capital allowances are computed for the partnership on a corporation tax basis, except that no deduction is given, at that stage, for the capital allowances in computing the profits. Each corporate partner is chargeable to corporation tax on its share of the trading profits less its share of the capital allowances applying corporation tax rules. This means giving the company's share of the capital allowances as a deduction in computing its share of partnership profits (ICTA 1988, s. 114). Any loss created or augmented by the deduction of capital allowances is relievable under ICTA 1988, ss. 393 or 393A.

Capital allowances are computed on an income tax basis for the partnership as a whole. The partnership Case I or Case II profits are computed giving the capital allowances as a business expense. The net profits are then apportioned between the partners and each individual partner must include his share of the net profits in his self-assessment (ICTA 1988, s. 111). If the deduction of capital allowances creates or augments a loss, then each partner may claim relief for his share of the loss in accordance with ICTA 1988, ss. 380 or 381.

Individuals

Capital allowances are deducted as an expense in computing the profits of the trade or profession. Similarly, any balancing charge is treated as a receipt of the trade or profession (CAA 2001, ss. 247, 251). Allowances and charges are given or imposed for periods of account, and there are special rules governing overlapping periods and gaps between periods (CAA 2001, s. 6(4), (5)).

Further guidance on Schedule D Cases I and II basis periods and periods of account will be found in the Inland Revenue Booklet SAT 1(1995). There are no special rules relating to the owner occupation of property for the purposes of a trade or profession.

Non-residents

A non-resident is allowed the same deductions as a UK resident trader in respect of expenditure incurred for the purposes of the trade carried on in the UK – so that he can claim the normal capital allowances in respect of expenditure on industrial buildings and plant and equipment acquired for use in his UK branch. The allowances are treated in the ordinary way as for a UK resident.

5.5.4   Claims for allowances

Corporation tax

Under CTSA, any claim for capital allowances must be made by being included in a return or amended return. A claim may be withdrawn by means of an amended return (FA 1998, Sch. 18, Para. 79).

The claim must be quantified at the time when it is made (Para. 80).

The general time limit for capital allowances claims is two years from the end of the accounting period concerned, which is the same as the normal time limit for filing an amended return under the forthcoming system of self-assessment of corporation tax (FA 1998, Sch. 18, Para. 82).

However, the time limit is extended to 30 days after the date on which any enquiry into the return for the accounting period concerned is completed, or the date on which any related appeal is determined (Para. 82).

The Board have discretionary power to accept a late claim (Para. 82(2)).

Income tax

Under self-assessment, any claim for capital allowances must be made by being included in a return or amended return (CAA 2001, s. 8). A claim may be amended by means of an amended return. The time limit is, therefore, the same as the time limit for submitting an amended return.

Under self-assessment, any claim for non-trade capital allowances must be made by being included in a return or amended return where possible (TMA 1970, s. 42(2), (5)). The claim must be quantified at the time when it is made (TMA 1970, s. 42(1 A)). A supplementary claim may be made by means of an amended return where an error or mistake is discovered in the original claim (TMA 1970, s. 42(9)). The time limit is the first anniversary of 31

January next following the end of the year of assessment, which is the same as the normal time limit for filing an amended return.

Partnerships

In the case of a partnership, a claim in respect of any trade, profession or business carried on by the partnership must be made in the partnership return (TMA 1970, s. 42(6)).

6 Relief for interest payable

6.1 The general rules

6.1.1 Trades

Interest payable wholly and exclusively for the purposes of a trade is allowed as a deduction in computing the profits of the trade, subject to certain constraints (FA 1996, s. 82(2)). The accruals basis applies, as with any other expense.

In the case of property development, interest is often included in the cost of work in progress whilst the development is being carried out. Relief is obtained as and when it is written off to the profit and loss account in accordance with GAAP.

6.1.2 Property letting businesses

Since the rules for trades apply in computing the profits of a property letting business under Schedule A or Schedule D Case V, it follows that interest payable wholly and exclusively for the purposes of that business qualifies for relief as for trade interest (see **Chapter 2**)).

6.1.3 Non-trade interest

Interest not falling within the above categories is dealt with:

- under the loan relationships legislation, as far as companies are concerned (see **6.6** below), and
- under the rather restrictive rules of ICTA 1988, s. 353, as far as individuals are concerned (see **6.4** below).

6.1.4 Non-allowable interest

Certain interest payable by companies is treated as a distribution under ICTA 1988, s. 209 (see **6.2** below), or as a disallowable expense under the thin capitalisation rules (see **6.3** below).

6.1.5   Annual interest payable under deduction of tax

In certain circumstances, annual interest payable by companies, or payable to non-residents, is subject to deduction of tax at source (ICTA 1988, s. 349(2)(a), (c) – see **6.4** below).

6.1.6   Interest payable to non-residents

Annual interest payable to non-residents is not allowable as a trading expense unless income tax is deducted from the payment or the following conditions are satisfied (ICTA 1988, s. 82):

- the trade must be carried on by a person residing in the UK;
- the liability to pay the interest must have been incurred wholly and exclusively for the purposes of the trade;
- either the activities for the purpose of which the interest was incurred were carried on outside the UK or the interest was payable in a foreign currency;
- the interest was payable outside the UK under the terms of the borrowing agreement, and
- the interest was actually paid outside the UK.

The above rule is, of course, subject to the provisions of any relevant double taxation agreement as regards the rate at which tax is to be deducted.

6.1.7   Interest on overdue tax

Generally, this interest is not allowable for tax purposes (TMA 1970, s. 90(1)). However, the general rule does not apply to interest on overdue corporation tax under CTSA (TMA 1970, s. 90(2)).

6.2   Interest treated as a distribution

6.2.1   Introduction

In the cases set out below, interest payable by a company is treated as a distribution. This means that it is not deductible in computing profits of any description. If such interest is received by a UK resident company, it is not chargeable to corporation tax (ICTA 1988, s. 208).

6.2.2 Securities

The rules are drafted in terms of interest payable on a security. However, they apply whether or not the security is backed by a charge on the company's assets and are extended to cover interest on money advanced without the issue of a security (ICTA 1988, s. 254(1)). In other words, they apply to interest on all company borrowings.

6.2.3 Interest in excess of a reasonable commercial return

Where the interest payable represents more than a reasonable commercial return on the principal, the excess is a distribution (ICTA 1988, s. 209(2)(d)).

6.2.4 75%+ subsidiaries: non-arm's length arrangements

For accounting periods ending on or before 31 March 2004, where the company paying the interest is a 75%+ subsidiary of the recipient, or both companies are 75%+ subsidiaries of a third company, the deduction for interest payable is limited to the amount that would have been payable in the absence of the relationship or arrangements between the companies (ICTA 1988, s. 209(2)(da)). However, this rule is disapplied where the recipient is within the charge to corporation tax (ICTA 1988, s. 212).

The rule operates where the rate of interest exceeds an arm's length rate, and also where the debt to equity ratio exceeds the maximum ratio that would be permitted on an arm's length basis.

As from 1 April 2004, the extended thin capitalisation rules apply (FA 2004, ss. 34, 37). These rules are discussed at **6.3** below. Where an accounting period straddles 1 April 2004, it is treated as two accounting periods for the purposes of these provisions, one ending on 31 March 2004 and the other beginning on 1 April 2004 (FA 2004, s. 37(3)).

6.2.5 Bonus issues of loan stock or debentures

Interest on any redeemable share capital or security that was the subject of a bonus issue is a distribution in its entirety (ICTA 1988, s. 209(2)(e)(i)). This rule does not apply in relation to bonus issues before 6 April 1965. This rule is also disapplied where the recipient is within the charge to corporation tax (ICTA 1988, s. 212).

6.2.6 Convertible securities

Interest payable on unlisted securities that are convertible directly or indirectly into shares is a distribution in its entirety (ICTA 1988, s. 209(2)(e)(ii)). This rule does not, however, apply where the terms of conversion are reasonably comparable with the terms of conversion of listed convertibles. This rule is also disapplied where the recipient is within the charge to corporation tax (ICTA 1988, s. 212).

6.2.7 Participating loans

Where the amount of interest depends on the results of the company's business, or any part of its business, the interest is a distribution in its entirety (ICTA 1988, s. 209(2)(e)(iii)). This rule is also disapplied where the recipient is within the charge to corporation tax (ICTA 1988, s. 212).

6.2.8 Securities connected with shares

Interest payable on securities that are connected with shares is a distribution in its entirety (ICTA 1988, s. 209(2)(e)(vi)). For this purpose, securities are connected with shares if, in consequence of the nature of the rights attaching to the securities or shares, it is necessary or advantageous for a person who has, or disposes of or acquires, any of the securities to have, or to dispose of or acquire, a proportionate holding of the shares. The rights attaching to the securities or shares include, in particular, any terms or conditions attaching to the right to transfer the shares or securities. This rule is also disapplied where the recipient is within the charge to corporation tax (ICTA 1988, s. 212).

6.2.9 Equity notes

Interest payable on equity notes is a distribution in its entirety (ICTA 1988, s. 209(2)(e)(vii)). An equity note is a security where, as regards the principal or any part of it:

- its terms contain no particular date by which it is to be redeemed;
- under its terms, the redemption date or latest such date, falls after the period of 50 years starting with the date of issue;
- under its terms, redemption is to occur after the end of that 50-year period if a particular event occurs and that event is certain or likely to occur, or
- the issuing company can secure that there is no particular redemption date, or that date falls after the end of the 50-year period,

(ICTA 1988, s. 209(9)).

This rule is also disapplied where the recipient is within the charge to corporation tax (ICTA 1988, s. 212).

6.2.10   The effect of double taxation agreements

The OECD Model Convention contains the following provisions relating to interest payable (Article 11).

> 'Where, by reason of a special relationship between the payer and the benefi- cial owner or between both of them and some other person, the amount of the interest, having regard to the debt claim for which it is paid, exceeds the amount which would have been agreed upon by the payer and the beneficial owner in the absence of such relationship, the provisions of this Article shall apply only to the last-mentioned amount. In such case, the excess part of the payments shall remain taxable according to the laws of each Contracting State, due regard being had to the other provisions of this Convention.'

Many of the UK's double taxation agreements contain a similar provision. This rule applies in particular where there is a 75%+ relationship as mentioned above. The text of the UK legislation was changed in 1995 to bring it into line with the Convention.

6.3   Thin capitalisation

6.3.1   The position up to 31 March 2004

The provisions of double taxation agreements are amplified in the UK by the provisions of ICTA 1988, s. 808A, which apply in interpreting a rule such as that quoted above from Article 11 of the OECD Model Convention. The special relationship provision is to be construed as requiring account to be taken of all relevant factors including whether, in the absence of the special relationship:

- a loan would have been made at all;
- the amount of the loan would have been less than the actual amount, and
- whether the rate of interest would have been lower than the actual rate.

The onus is on the taxpayer to show either that there is no special relation- ship or, if there is, the amount of interest that would have been payable in the absence of that relationship (ICTA 1988, s. 808A(2)). However, this does not apply where the special relationship provision expressly requires regard to be had to the debt on which the interest is paid in determining the excess interest and accordingly limits the factors to be taken into account (ICTA 1988, s. 808A(5)).

Extract from Tax Bulletin Issue 17 (June 1995)

'The arm's length approach

The legislation requires taxpayers and Inspectors to consider what would have happened in the absence of the intra-group relationship between the issuer and holder of the securities in question. As a result, the focus is on the facts and circumstances at the time the actual security was put in place or assigned.

It is worth stressing that the legislation is extremely broad in its scope. It is capable of applying where, even though a loan could have been obtained from a third party on identical terms, the transaction would not have taken place but for the group relationship. Such a case might arise where, for example, a company has a fixed-term third-party loan bearing interest at LIBOR + 1.00% which still has three years to run at the relevant time. This loan is repaid and replaced by a three-year intra-group loan carrying interest at LIBOR + 1.50%, but which otherwise has terms and conditions identical to the third-party loan it replaces. It is accepted that arm's length interest rates having increased since the original loan was obtained, LIBOR + 1.50% is an arm's length rate for a three year loan at the time the new loan is made. Nonetheless, given the lack of commercial logic in this change, we would contend that the arrangement would not have been entered into but for the group relationship and that the legislation applies with the result that all of the interest will be a distribution.

This is one reason why there can be no blanket 'let-out' for intra-group loans satisfying some crude formulaic test. Although we are aware of the importance to arm's length lenders of ratios of debt to equity or pre-tax and pre-interest profit to total interest payable ('income cover') they are insufficient, in themselves, to determine what would have happened at arm's length. Moreover, ratios such as these are far from being the only factors which potential lenders take into account.

Among the others probably the most important are:

- the business sector concerned;
- the nature of, and title to, any assets which might provide security;
- cash flow; and
- the general state of the economy.

Nonetheless, the legislation will most often be relevant in cases of thin capitalisation (a high ratio of debt to equity) or insufficient income cover. Consequently it may be helpful to explain our approach to these two aspects of the arm's length test. Commentators have suggested that the Revenue has been content to accept a 1:1 ratio of debt to equity and a 3:1 income cover ratio. Often the possibility of satisfying us that, in the circumstances of a specific case, arm's length ratios would have differed from these is also mentioned. While we understand why our approach has been construed in this way, it is to some extent misleading and certainly needs to be considered in context.

As with our approach to the legislation as a whole, when we consider such ratios, we focus on what would have been expected to happen at arm's length.

In our experience, third party lenders in the United Kingdom market almost always look at the consolidated debt to equity ratio of the group of companies to which the borrower belongs and the resources on which it could draw within that group to fund interest charges and capital repayments. Consequently, in the overwhelming majority of cases, we too look beyond the company issuing the security to the wider company grouping to which it belongs. Of course, the legislation is designed to protect the United Kingdom tax base. Accordingly, it limits the extent to which the wider group is taken into account by specifying that, for certain purposes, relationships with connected companies which are not part of the (defined) UK grouping as well as with the holder of the securities (except in respect of the securities in question) are to be disregarded.

It is also our experience that arm's length lenders in the United Kingdom revise their view of an acceptable level of gearing or income cover for particular groups at different times – although the variation has not been large in recent years. As a result, we may be able to say that a particular debt to equity ratio meets the arm's length standard today. We could not say that the same ratio would meet that standard even a year from now.

We are also aware that the relative importance of debt to equity ratios and other factors such as income cover or cash flow varies over time and between industries. In recent years, we have detected a trend away from simple debt to equity ratio criteria, perhaps reflecting the realisation that balance sheets can show flattering snapshots which are not representative of the position as a whole. This has been coupled with increased evidence of the continuing availability of loans being made subject to satisfying certain covenants – including meeting gearing and income cover targets at specified intervals. Our approach endeavours to reflect such trends.

As for the precise ratios themselves, arm's length lenders have always applied different standards when lending to different industries at any one time. So, for example, financial concerns and property holding groups have always been able to gear up to a greater extent than most other borrowers. Here too we follow the market pattern.

Despite the industry spread of acceptable ratios and the variation over time, we understand that the average debt to equity ratio of United Kingdom quoted companies has historically ranged around 0.6:1. It remains in that region at present. Similarly, we are aware of comment that lenders are currently concerned when the level of operating profit is less than four times the interest payable. Partly because an average is a point between the high and low positions and partly as a result of a desire to use our resources most effectively, we have in recent years tended to accept that, where a loan otherwise meets the arm's length test, if the United Kingdom grouping remains geared at something less than 1:1 and its income cover is at least 3:1, its financing should be regarded as satisfying the test as a whole. If not, further consideration would be appropriate. It must be stressed, however, that there are no hard and fast rules in this area and each case has to be considered on its own facts.'

Extract from Tax Bulletin 35 (June 1998)

'Is ICTA 1988 S. 808A now redundant?

Why does s. 209(8a) apply s. 808a for the purposes of s. 209(2)(da)?

Why is the list of matters outlined in s. 209(8b) similar to, but differently worded from, the equivalent list in s. 808a(2)?

ICTA 1988, s. 808A is an aid to interpreting certain "special relationship" provisions in the interest article of a number of our treaties. An aim of the 1995 domestic legislation was to broaden the range of cases to which the approach provided for in these treaties applied. Consequently where s. 209(2)(da) applies, it achieves the same result as a combination of the former domestic rules and treaty wording of the type dealt with in s. 808A(2) to (4). Nonetheless, s. 808A is not redundant since it continues to assist in construing the relevant treaty wording in cases where the 1995 distribution rules do not apply – ie, where the borrower is the ultimate group parent or where there is a special relationship between the parties which falls short of the 75% shareholder connection specified in that law.

To ensure that the approach of s. 808A was generalised in the 1995 domestic legislation, s. 209(8A) provided that, for the purposes of s. 209(2)(da), the s.808A rules are to apply in the same way as they apply for the purposes of a treaty special relationship provision. To make this effective it was necessary to do two things. First, the treaty term 'special relationship' to which s. 808A refers had to be aligned with the domestic law phrase 'relationship, arrangements or other connection' which appears in s. 209(2)(da). This is done in subparagraph (a) of subsection 209(8A). Secondly, it was necessary to ensure that the hypothetical special relationship provision introduced by subsection 209(8A) was one of the type to which subsections (2) to (4) of s. 808A would apply in determining what impact, if any, relationships involving borrower, lender and other parties might have had on the existence, quantum, interest rate or other terms of the loan. Subparagraph (b) of subsection 209(8A) together with subsection (8B) identify the hypothetical special relationship provision as being of the relevant type and so set the stage for subsections (2) to (4) of s. 808A to apply for the purposes of subsection 209(2)(da).

Although there appears to be a significant degree of overlap between (8B) and 808A(2), they are in practice doing different things. Subsection (8B) describes the subject matter of the hypothetical provision whereas subsection 808A(2) as amended indicates factors to be taken into account in applying that provision for the purposes of new subsection 209(2)(da).

What is the difference between the s. 209(2)(da) relationship referred to in subsection 209(8a)(a) and the relationship referred to in sub-paragraph (b) of the subsection?

Subparagraph (a) refers to the relationship, arrangements or other connection between the borrower and the lender. Subparagraph (b) is concerned with any relationship, arrangements or connection between the borrower and any other person.

Where the borrower's trade involves dealing with the lender or other non UK members of the group, does the legislation's emphasis on disregarding any relationship, arrangements or other connection (whether formal or informal) between the borrower and connected companies who are not part of the UK grouping mean that the borrower's trading income has to be disregarded for the purposes of the legislation?

We do not believe the legislation requires us to go so far. We are required to disregard the relationship, arrangements or connection with these other group companies, but not to disregard the fact that the borrower has a real source of income which an unrelated lender would take into account in considering whether, or how much, to lend. So, provided the intra-group trading is conducted on arm's length terms, we do not believe that the legislation requires us to assume that the borrower had no source of income whatsoever.

Will the revenue provide illustrations of how the 'UK grouping' rules in subsection 209(8d) work?

The 'UK grouping' may consist of:

- just the issuing company (or borrower) itself:
- the issuing company and its effective 51% subsidiaries (wherever resident);
- the top UK holding company in respect of which the issuing company is a 51% subsidiary [subject to subsection (8E)] together with all that holding company's 51% subsidiaries (wherever resident)

Figures 1 to 3 illustrate these cases in turn.

Figure I

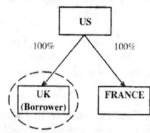

UK grouping for purposes of legislation

Figure II

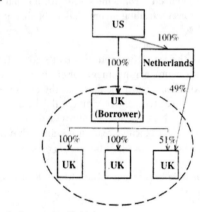

UK grouping for purposes of legislation

Figure III

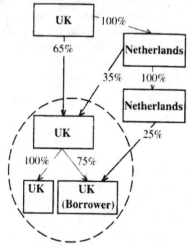

UK grouping for purposes of legislation

6.3.2 The position as from 1 April 2004

Application of the transfer pricing rules

As from 1 April 2004, the transfer pricing rules are applied in determining the extent to which interest payable by a company is allowable for tax purposes, and ICTA 1988, s. 209(2)(da), discussed at **6.2.3** above, is repealed, together with the corresponding exemption for the recipient under s. 212(1)(b) (FA 2004, s. 34 and Sch. 42 Part 2(2)). Where interest is disallowed under the transfer pricing provisions, it is treated as a disallowable expense, rather than as a distribution. The other provisions discussed at **6.2** continue to apply.

The transfer pricing rules apply to interest payable between UK companies as well as to interest payable by a UK company to an overseas company (FA 2004, s. 30(2) amending ICTA 1988, Sch. 28AA Para. 5). However, small enterprises are not subject to transfer pricing adjustments, and medium-sized enterprises are caught only if the Revenue so directs (ICTA 1988, Sch. 28AA, Para. 5B, 5C).

Whether excessive interest is payable

In determining whether excessive interest is payable by a company, it is necessary to take account of all factors, including:

- whether the loan to the company would have been made at all in the absence of a special relationship between the company and the lender;
- the amount that would have been advanced in the absence of that relationship, and
- the rate of interest, and any other terms that would have been imposed, in the absence of that relationship,

(ICTA 1988, Sch. 28AA, Para. 1A).

The existence of intra-group guarantees, or guarantees by joint venture parties of a joint venture company's indebtedness, is to be ignored in determining whether excessive interest has been charged. For this purpose, 'guarantee' includes 'any other relationship, arrangements, connection or understanding (whether formal or informal) such that the person making the loan. . .has a reasonable expectation that in the event of default . . . he will be paid by, or out of the assets of, one or more companies' (Para. 1A(7)). The borrowing company's own assets are not disregarded. Where these include shares in subsidiary companies, the effect is that the assets of the subsidiaries are taken into account as well.

The amount of interest to be disallowed is the excess of the actual amount charged over the amount that would have been charged if the loan had been restricted to an arm's length amount and if an arm's length rate of interest had been applied.

Guarantees

Intra-group guarantees are themselves subject to the transfer pricing provisions (ICTA 1988, Sch. 28AA, Para. 1B). The guarantor will, effectively, be treated as charging an arm's length fee based on amount not exceeding the amount that would have been guaranteed in the absence of the special relationship between the companies concerned. The same rule applies to guarantees by joint venture parties to a joint venture company.

Furthermore, a subsidiary company or joint venture company may be able to borrow more from a bank, or other unconnected third party, if there is a guarantee from the parent company or some other member of the group or joint venture consortium. In this case, some of the interest may be disallowed even though the lender is unconnected with the borrower.

Compensating adjustments

Where an adjustment is made to the computations of the paying company, there is a compensating adjustment to the computations of the recipient (ICTA 1988, Sch. 28AA, Para. 6, 6C, 6D).

Where an adjustment is made because of a guarantee, the guarantor is treated for all tax purposes as paying any interest that is disallowed on account of the existence of the guarantee (ICTA 1988, Sch. 28AA, Para. 6D). Where there are two or more guarantors, the total of compensating adjustments must not exceed the amount of interest disallowed (Para. 6D(3)). However, the basis of apportionment between them is not specified.

Compensating adjustments have to be claimed. The normal time limit is two years from the date on which the relevant CTSA return of the claimant company is made (Para. 6(5)).

Where the guarantor makes a payment to the borrower in respect of its compensation adjustment, that payment is neither allowable to the guarantor nor taxable in the hands of the borrower. However, the amount of the payment must not exceed the amount of the compensating adjustment (Para. 7C).

CTSA returns

Thin capitalisation adjustments have to be self-assessed. Further, the record-keeping requirements of FA 1998, Sch. 18, Para. 21 apply in respect of such adjustments.

6.4   Interest payable under deduction of tax

In the following circumstances income tax at the lower rate must be deducted from payments of yearly interest falling within Schedule D Case III and accounted for to the Inland Revenue (ICTA 1988, s. 4(1A)):

* when paid by a company (other than a bank) or local authority, unless the interest is payable in the UK on a loan from a bank carrying on a bona fide banking business in the UK (or in certain circumstances where the interest is payable to non-residents on quoted Eurobonds);
* when paid by or on behalf of a partnership, where at least one of the partners is a company, again unless the interest is paid to or by a bank as above;
* when paid by any person to another person whose usual address is outside the UK (ICTA 1988, s. 349(2)). This issue has to be decided at the time of payment of the interest (*Appletree Group & Anor v Flood* (2002) Sp C 351).

As regards the first point above, with effect from 1 April 2001, payment may be made gross where the person beneficially entitled to the interest is a UK resident company or a partnership of companies each of which is resident in the UK (ICTA 1988, s. 349A, 349B).

Interest falls within Schedule D Case III if its source is within the UK (ICTA 1988, s. 18(3)). The most important factors determining the location of the source are:

* the residence of the debtor, ie the place in which the debt will be enforced;
* the source from which the interest is paid;
* where the interest is paid, and
* the nature and location of the security for the debt,

(*Tax Bulletin*, Issue 9, November 1993, following *Westminster Bank Executor and Trustee Company (Channel Islands) v National Bank of Greece* 47 TC 472).

6.4.1   Double tax agreements

As noted, the normal requirement is for income tax to be deducted at source when interest is paid to a non-resident. Where the non-resident is entitled to relief by way of a lower rate of withholding tax than the basic rate of income tax, or where the non-resident is entitled to interest without any UK taxation, under the terms of a double tax agreement, he may reclaim the excess so deducted. It is possible to arrange with the Inland Revenue for the interest to be paid with the lower or nil rate of withholding tax provided for under the treaty – but only after authority has been received from the Inland Revenue – and the payer may otherwise have to account to the Inland Revenue for the full amount of taxation that he should otherwise have deducted.

Where income tax has been deducted at some lower rate (or no deduction) in accordance with the terms of a double tax treaty, it is nonetheless regarded as having been paid under deduction of tax for the purposes of relief under the rules outlined in this part of the chapter.

6.5   Other interest payable by individuals

This section deals with relief for interest payable by individuals that does not fall to be allowed as a deduction in computing trading profits or property letting business profits. In the context of commercial property transactions, there are two relevant cases. In either case, the individual may claim relief for interest paid in the tax year and the relief is available against his total income for the year (ICTA 1988, s. 353).

6.5.1   Loan to buy interest in close company

In two cases, interest on a loan applied in acquiring any part of the ordinary share capital of a close company, or in lending money to a close company, qualifies for relief (ICTA 1988, s. 360). In either case, the company must be either:

(a)   a trading company, or

(b)   a company whose business consists of investment in property that is let to unconnected persons.

As regards (b), the spouse, relative, or spouse of a relative of a connected person is a proscribed tenant (ICTA 1988, s. 13A).

A company that is the holding company of a group of qualifying companies qualifies, as does a company that co-ordinates the activities of two or more qualifying companies.

The company must qualify at the time the investment is made and at the time of payment of the interest. However, where a company that was close at the time the investment was made subsequently becomes non-close, interest will continue to qualify for relief provided that all other conditions are satisfied (SP 3/78).

In the case of a loan, the money must be used by the company for the purposes of its business.

The first case is where, at the time the interest is paid, the individual has a material interest in the company and that in a company within (b) none of the company's properties is used by the individual as his residence. The second case is where the individual has worked for the company for the greater part of his time in the actual management of the company's business from the time the investment was made to the time of payment of the interest.

Any capital recovered from the company is deemed to pay off an equivalent amount of the loan.

A material interest is a holding of more than 5 per cent of the ordinary share capital, provided that it entitles the holder to more than 5 per cent of any assets available for distribution in a winding up of the company (ICTA 1988, s. 360A).

A loan that replaces a qualifying loan qualifies to the extent that the first loan qualified.

6.5.2   Loan to buy into partnership

A loan qualifies if it is applied in:

- purchasing a share of a partnership;
- contributing capital into a partnership, or
- making a loan to a partnership, (ICTA 1988, s. 362).

The individual must be a member of the partnership other than a limited partner.

Any capital recovered from the partnership is deemed to pay off an equivalent amount of the loan.

The relief is not available in relation to an investment in an investment limited liability partnership (LLP) (ICTA 1988, s. 362(2)(a)(ii)).

An investment LLP is an LLP whose business consists wholly or mainly in the making of investments and the principal part of whose income is derived therefrom (ICTA 1988, s. 842B). Investments include property investments, but the definition of property investment LLP is relevant mainly in connection with the exemption for pension fund investment income.

6.6 Loan relationships

6.6.1 Introduction

The legislation discussed in this section applies for corporation tax purposes only. The legislation provides a new system for taxing interest and other sums receivable (whether of an income or capital nature), allowing interest, etc. payable, on bonds, loans and other money debts. It prescribes two alternative methods of calculating credits and debits relating to such debts. Where the company's accounts are drawn up in accordance with an 'authorised accounting method', the tax treatment will follow the accounting treatment (FA 1996, s. 82(1)).

Interest which falls to be treated as a distribution under the existing legislation continues to be so treated and is excluded from the loan relationships provisions (FA 1996, Sch. 9, (1)).

6.6.2 Trade interest

Bank interest and other short interest payable wholly and exclusively for the purposes of a trade continues to be allowed as a deduction in computing the profits of the trade, together with any related expenses, whether of an income or capital nature (FA 1996, s. 82(2), 84).

Similarly, where a trade consists of or includes the lending of money, or dealing in bonds or other corporate debt instruments, any interest receivable in the course of that trade is taxed as a trading receipt, together with any other sums received in respect of the debts.

Annual interest payable otherwise than to a bank has always been allowed under the 'charges' rules. Such interest will now be dealt with in the same way as non-trade interest (see below), except where it is payable wholly and exclusively for the purposes of a trade, in which case it will be allowed as a trading expense.

6.6.3 Non-trade interest

Interest and other sums receivable otherwise than in the course of a trade are taxed under Schedule D, Case III (FA 1996, s. 80(3)). As far as corporation tax is concerned, tax under Case III is charged on:

(a)   profits and gains on loan relationships;

(b)   annuities and annual payments,

(c)   discounts not falling within (a).

Case V now explicitly excludes income falling within (a) above (FA 1996, Sch. 14 (5) amending ICTA 1988, s. 18 for corporation tax purposes: the old Case III definition continues to apply for income tax purposes).

Interest and other sums payable on money debts otherwise than for the purposes of a trade are first deducted from any interest, etc. receivable. If the result is a net credit, that credit is taxed under Case III (FA1996, s. 82). If the result is a net debit, referred to as a 'deficit', that deficit, or any part of it, may be:

(a)   set off against the company's total profits for the accounting period in which it arises;

(b)   surrendered under the group relief provisions;

(c)   carried back against Case III profits for earlier periods, or

(d)   carried forward against any non-trading profits for the next accounting period (ICTA 1988, s. 403(1)(a) and 403ZC, and FA 1996, s. 83(2)).

A claim is required for any deficit to be set off under any of the above rules. Any unrelieved part of the deficit is carried forward and is allowed as a deduction in computing the Case III profit for the next accounting period. To the extent that this creates or increases a deficit for the next accounting period, it cannot be set off against total profits of that period, nor can it be surrendered under the group relief provisions for that period (FA 1996, s. 83).

However, it is available to be set off against non-trading profits of a subsequent accounting period, by means of a claim under (d) for the next period. It will be appreciated that non-trading profits include Schedule A profits, so the loan relationship deficit may be set off against future Schedule A profits.

The facility to set off only part of a loan relationship deficit allows a company to protect its tax credit relief on overseas income.

A claim under (a) to (c) above must be made within two years after the end of the accounting period in which the deficit arises. A claim under (d) must be made within two years after the end of the next accounting period (FA 1996, s. 83(6)). The claim should be made by being included in a return or amended return (FA 1998, Sch. 18, Paras. 55–58 and 67).

The Board has discretionary powers to extend the time limit.

6.6.4 Meaning of 'loan relationships'

A company has a loan relationship if it is either a creditor or a debtor in relation to any money debt arising from a transaction for the lending of money. A debt is a money debt if it falls to be settled by the payment of money or by the assignment of a debt which is a money debt. For this purpose, money includes foreign currency (FA 1996, s. 81). Therefore, the legislation covers interest that had hitherto been taxed under Case V as well as interest falling within Case III. However, it does not cover normal trading debts arising from the supply of goods or services. The main categories of loan relationships will be those created by gilts, corporate bonds and other loans made to or by companies, plus bank overdrafts. A shareholder is not in a loan relationship in respect of his rights as a shareholder.

6.6.5 Computation of Case III profits and deficits

In computing the profit or deficit arising on a company's loan relationships, there must be included:

(a) all interest payable and receivable under such relationships, together with any charges and expenses incurred for the purposes of such relationships;

(b) any other profits, gains and losses, including those of a capital nature, which arise from such relationships.

The expenses referred to at (a) include the expenses of establishing the loan, the costs of making any payments under the loan and the cost of collecting any interest and other receipts.

Receipts and expenses of 'related transactions' have to be included. Basically a related transaction is a purchase or sale of a loan debt (eg purchase or sale of a gilt, debenture, loan stock, etc.). Therefore, the profits and losses arising from the purchase and sale of a gilt, debenture, etc. will be taxed under Case III, except where the company deals in such debt, in which case the profits and losses will form part of its trading profits and losses.

The credits and debits for any accounting period must be ascertained in accordance with an 'authorised accounting method'. There are two such methods (FA 1996, s. 85):

- the accruals basis,
- the 'mark to market' basis.

The mark to market basis will be appropriate mainly for companies dealing in corporate or government debt. Property investment companies will normally use the accruals basis. In any event, the accruals basis must be used for intra-group borrowing and lending and other lending between companies under common control (FA 1996, s. 87).

It will be appreciated that property dealing and property development are regarded as trading activities, so any interest payable for the purposes of such activities will be dealt with as a trading expense.

Whichever basis is used, it must conform to normal accounting practice. Under the accruals basis, interest receivable and payable are apportioned on a time basis to the accounting periods to which they relate. Where capital expenses, such as arrangement fees and other setting up costs, are amortised over the term of the loan in the accounts, that pattern will be followed for tax purposes. Any provision against the principal or capital value of a debt is allowable only to the extent that the debt is bad or doubtful or has been released (FA 1996, Sch. 9, Para. 5).

Where the company is a debtor and the loan relates to the acquisition of a fixed asset or to some capital project, debits and credits relating to the loan are included in the Case III computation even if capitalised in the accounts (FA 1996, Sch. 9, Para. 14).

Where the company is a debtor and the loan is released either partially or fully, any amount which is released must be included in the Case III computation.

6.6.6   Pre-trade deficits

A company with a non-trade deficit relating to a trade that is commenced within seven years of the end of the accounting period may elect to take relief for the deficit in the period in which the trade commences. However, an election is required within two years of the end of the period in which the deficit arises (ICTA 1988, s. 401(1AB), (1AC)).

6.6.7   Case III deficits: order of set off

Where a claim is made to set off the deficit against total profits of the same accounting period, the set off is made:

- after relief for trading losses brought forward under ICTA 1988, s. 393(1);
- before relief for trading losses carried back from a later period under ICTA 1988, s. 393A,
- before relief given for a Case III deficit carried back from a later accounting period (FA 1996, Sch. 8 (1)).

Where part or all of a deficit is surrendered under the group relief provisions:

- it is treated as though it were a trading loss, and
- the restrictions for Case V losses under s. 403(2) do not apply (FA 1996, Sch.8 (2)).

Where part or all of a deficit is carried back against Case III profits of earlier periods:

1. Case III profits of a later period are set off in priority to Case III profits of an earlier period.

2. Any earlier period of set off must end within three years of the beginning of the deficit period.

3. If an earlier period begins before 1 April 1996, only the Case III profits of that part of the period which falls on or after that date may be included.

4. The following reliefs for any accounting period are given in priority to the relief for the Case III deficit carried back:

   (a) relief for Case III deficits brought forward from an earlier period and set off against non-trading profits of that period;
   (b) relief for 'charges' under ICTA 1988, s. 338;
   (c) relief for management expenses, capital allowances and charges of an investment company;
   (d) relief for trading losses carried back to that period under ICTA 1988, s. 393A,
   (e) relief against total profits for any Case III deficit of that period (FA 1996, Sch. 8 (3)).

Where part or all of a deficit is carried forward for set off against non-trading profits of the next accounting period, it is treated as reducing those non-trading profits. This set-off takes precedence over most items which are deductions against total profits (see ICTA 1988, s. 407 as regards group relief), but not claims under ICTA 1988, s. 573 for losses on unquoted shares in trading companies (ICTA 1988, s. 573(4)).

6.6.8 Change of accounting method, etc.

Where the company changes its accounting method from one authorised method to another, the prior year adjustment required to give effect to the change is a taxable receipt or allowable deduction, as the case may be, in the accounting period in which the change is effected (FA 1996, s. 84(4A)).

For accounting periods commencing on or after 1 October 2002, a similar rule applies where there is no actual change of accounting basis, but a change is required for tax purposes under the loan relationships legislation (FA 1996,

s. 90). The fair value of the loan relationship as at the date of the required change is brought into the tax computations as the closing and opening value for the purpose of the change.

6.6.9 Interest receivable: set off of tax deducted at source

Income tax deducted at source is set off against the corporation tax liability for the accounting period for which the interest is charged to corporation tax (ICTA 1988, s. 7(2) and 11(3)). Where the accruals basis applies, the income tax deductible from the accrued interest will be set off against corporation tax for the period in which it is accrued. However, for accounting periods beginning before 1 October 2002, if the interest is received later than two years after the end of the accounting period in which it is credited, the income tax may be set off against the corporation tax for the period in which the interest is received. A claim has to be made for this treatment (FA 1996, s. 91). The time limit is two years after the end of the accounting period in which it is received or six years after the end of the period in which it is credited, whichever is later. There are special rules for identifying payments of interest with outstanding amounts.

6.6.10 Late interest payable

Where the accruals basis is adopted for interest payable, but the recipient does not bring the full amount of interest into his computation, relief for interest payable is deferred until the accounting period in which it is paid (FA 1996, Sch. 9 (2)).

6.6.11 Transactions in land: gains taxed as income

There has always been doubt as to the deduction for interest payable in computing any gain which is taxed as income under ICTA 1988, s. 776. Subsection (6) allows 'only such expenses as are attributable to the land disposed of'. Therefore, relief for interest payable is available under the loan relationships rules for a Case III deficit.

6.6.12 Loan relationships for unallowable purposes

Where a company has a loan relationship that has an unallowable purpose, the allowable interest debits are not to include so much of those debits as is attributable to the unallowable purpose. There has to be a just and reasonable apportionment of the interest debits between the unallowable purpose and other (allowable) purposes. Any amount that is disallowed under this rule is not available for corporation tax relief at all (FA 1996, Sch. 9, Para. 13).

An unallowable purpose is a purpose that is not amongst the business and other commercial purposes of the company. In particular, the business and other commercial purposes do not include activities in respect of which the company is not within the charge to corporation tax (FA 1996, Para. 13(3)).

Where one of the purposes is tax avoidance, that is sufficient to disqualify the interest debits if the tax avoidance purpose was the main purpose, or one of the main purposes, of the loan relationship (FA 1996, Para. 13(4)). Tax avoidance includes obtaining a tax advantage (as defined in ICTA 1988, s. 709), whether for the company or for some other person (FA 1996, Sch.9, Para. 13 (5), (6)).

The Inland Revenue's *Company Taxation Manual* gives the following guidance on Para. 13 (see CT 12673ff).

'CT12674

You will note from the Economic Secretary's comments (see CT12673) that paragraph 13:

(a) will normally apply where UK branches of overseas companies borrow for overseas activities outside the UK tax net;

(b) will not normally apply where a company borrows to acquire shares in companies, whether in the United Kingdom or overseas, or to pay dividends, provided that the borrowings are not structured in an artificial way. See also CT12687(b) where the company cannot make a pre-tax profit. This approach is not affected by the substantial shareholdings rules; and

(c) will not normally apply where a company is choosing between different ways of arranging its commercial affairs, if it chooses the course that gives a favourable tax outcome, provided that tax avoidance is not the object, or one of the main objects, of the arrangements.

CT12686

Paragraph 13 would not normally apply to loan relationship debits:

(a) simply because a company is able to obtain relief for the same expenditure or loss on the borrowing to which the debits relate in more than one juris-diction. However, paragraph 13 would apply where the structure that has been adopted has one or more uncommercial features so that the loan relationship can be said to have an unallowable purpose and/or where, taking account of the overall position as regards the company or group, relief for interest and other finance costs might otherwise be available more than once in the UK in respect of the true economic costs of the borrowing;

(b) that relate to a borrowing from an exempt body (such as a pension fund), even if that exempt body is connected with the borrower, provided the arrangements are commercial;

(c) that relate to a straightforward borrowing by a UK Plc in order to fund a repurchase of its shares provided that there are no attempts to structure the arrangement in such a way as to provide a tax advantage for any other person and/or the amount borrowed – the level of gearing up – is dictated by market forces and hence is at arm's length;

(d) that relate to a third party borrowing undertaken by one group member, that fulfils the commercial borrowing requirements of the group, which it on lends interest-free (or at a rate not exceeding the costs of the third party borrowing) to other UK-resident group members. In such circumstances, paragraph 13 would not apply, provided that the group gets one and only one deduction for the costs associated with the true economic cost of the borrowing. For example, paragraph 13 will not normally apply where intra-group interest free loans are made primarily to enable borrowings to be matched with assets within the meaning of the Exchange Gains & Losses (Alternative Method) Regulations, or FA 1996, s. 84A (for periods beginning on or after 1 October 2002); or

(e) where a loan relationship debit in one UK-resident group company is matched by an equal and opposite loan relationship credit, which is fully taxed, in another UK-resident group company in respect of the same loan relationship. On the other hand, paragraph 13 is potentially in point if the main or one of the main purposes of the intra-group funding was to achieve a tax advantage for the group as a whole, in that the loan relationship credit on the intra-group funding is in some way shielded from tax. An example of the loan relationship credit being shielded would be by the soaking up of otherwise stranded surplus expenses of management etc. Where the loan relationships involve cross border transactions, thin capitalisation and transfer pricing legislation (ICTA 1988 s. 209 and Sch. 28AA) as well as the provisions of the Double Taxation Treaties may be applicable.

CT12687

Paragraph 13 would normally apply to loan relationship debits:

(a) that, subject to the comments at CT12686(d) and (e), relate to the write off of loans where the purpose of the loans was not amongst the business or other commercial purposes of a company. An example of a loan of this nature would be an interest free loan made by a company, whose business consists in operating a widgets retail outlet, which had lent the money to a football club supported by one of the directors of the company for the purpose of providing financial support to the football club. Furthermore, if the company borrowed to make the loan to the football club, then paragraph 13 would normally also apply to disallow the loan relationship debits relating to the interest or other finance costs on that borrowing;

(b) that, subject to the comments at CT12686(d) and (e), relate to a borrowing the proceeds of which are used in such a way that the company cannot or does not expect to make an overall pre-tax profit. An example would be where a company borrows at interest and on lends at a rate of interest that is less than the rate of interest on the borrowings; or

(c) where a company or a group of companies enters into one or more transactions or arrangements which have the main purpose or one of the main purposes of securing loan relationship debits for repayments of loan principal, in addition to payments of interest, on the true economic commercial borrowing to the company or group. An example of this would be where one group company undertakes a borrowing of £20 million at 8.4% for 5 years from a third party and at the same time a second group company pays that third party £13 million for preference shares of £20 million in the first group company to be delivered 5 years later. The effect of this is that, economically, the group borrows £7 million on an amortising basis at 8.4% but for lax purposes the group claims relief as loan relationship debits for both the interest of £1.4 million on the group amortised borrowing of £7 million and the repayment of the £7 million loan principal. In such circumstances paragraph 13 is likely to apply to disallow the amounts equivalent to repayments of principal.'

6.6.13 General

The above analysis deals with the loan relationships provisions only to the extent that they are likely to apply to property investment companies and property dealing and development companies. The full legislation runs to over 100 pages of the Finance Act 1996. In particular, there are special rules dealing with convertible securities, asset-linked securities, indexed securities, gilt strips, manufactured interest, collective investment schemes, insurance companies, financial instruments, discounted securities, etc. These rules are beyond the scope of this publication.

Further guidance will be found in the Inland Revenue's *Corporate Finance Manual.*

7 Construction Industry Scheme

7.1 Overview of the tax deduction scheme

The legislation discussed in this chapter was introduced in order to counter-act evasion of tax by sub-contractors in the construction industry. The legislation provides that if a *contractor* makes a payment to a *sub-contractor* in respect of *construction operations,* he must *deduct income tax* from the payment and account to the Revenue for that tax, unless:

- the sub-contractor has a valid *gross payment certificate*, and
- the contractor carries out certain *procedures* and keeps certain *records* relating to the payment (ICTA 1988, s. 559).

The legislation does not apply in relation to payments to employees but of course the PAYE regulations apply to such payments. If, through ignorance, a contractor fails to comply with the regulations discussed below, the Revenue will pursue him for the tax that he should have deducted at source. If, as is more than likely, the contractor is then unable to recover that tax from the sub-contractor, it will simply be an additional cost burden on his business. Similarly, if a sub-contractor fails to make a tax return or to pay his tax, or if the Revenue is unable to trace the sub-contractor, it will attempt to collect the tax from the contractor on the basis that he should have deducted tax from any payments made to the sub-contractor. It is up to the contractor to protect his own position by carrying out the procedures properly.

The terms shown in italic are defined in the following pages. There is a special section on the Revenue's website dealing with the Construction Industry Scheme.

A new CIS is to be introduced as from 6 April 2006 (FA 2004, ss. 57–77). The details will be included in the 2006–07 edition of this publication.

7.2 Contractors

7.2.1 Meaning of 'contractor'

The definition of 'contractor' encompasses companies that are not contractors in the ordinary sense of the word (ICTA 1988, s. 559(1)(b), 560(2) and SI 1993/743, Sch. A1). The following are contractors:

(a)   any person carrying on a business which includes *construction operations;*

(b)   any local authority;

(c)   any housing association or housing trust;

(d)   any development corporation or new town corporation;

(e)   the Commission for the New Towns;

(f)   the Housing Corporation, Housing for Wales, Scottish Homes and the Northern Ireland Housing Executive;

(g)   any NHS trust;

(h)   the Corporate Officers of the House of Commons and the House of Lords,

(i)   the Health and Social Services trusts established in Northern Ireland.

In addition, a person carrying on *any business* is a contractor at a particular time if his average annual expenditure on *construction operations* in the period of three years ending with the last period of account before that time exceeds £250,000. If he was not carrying on the business at the beginning of that three-year period, the £250,000 limit applies to one third of his total expenditure on construction operations for the part of the period during which he was carrying on the business. Thus a company carrying on the business of a large department store or chain of retail shops may well be a contractor. The limit of £250,000 was increased to £1 million as from 1 August 1999 (FA 1995, Sch. 27, Para. 2(2)).

Finally, a person is a contractor in relation to any particular contract if he is a *sub-contractor* in relation to that contract (as to which, see **7.3.1** below). In other words, if a sub-contractor has his own sub-contractors, payments that he makes to them are within the scheme. Bearing in mind the wide definition of construction operations, which includes repairs and refurbishment of premises (see **7.4.1** below), it is clear that the definition includes many companies that are not contractors in the usual sense of the word. For example, a company which purchases, refurbishes and sells properties is a contractor under (a) above.

7.2.2   Responsibilities of contractors

The Revenue issued the following summary:

'As a contractor you must–

- decide whether the person you are hiring should be treated as an employee or as self-employed (see our leaflet IR148/CA69 *Are your workers employed or self-employed?* for further details). If the person is an employee, then you are not a contractor but an employer and must operate PAYE – not CIS.

- if the contract is for self-employment, consider whether the work falls within the CIS. If it includes construction operations, then it is covered by the CIS. If it does not, then treat the person as you would any other self-employed person and pay him gross (that is, without taking off anything for tax or National Insurance contributions).
- check how your sub-contractors should be treated by inspecting their tax certificates or registration cards – you must not pay a sub-contractor who does not hold a valid certificate or card. If they have tax certificates, you should pay them gross (that is, with no deduction for tax or National Insurance contributions). If they have a registration card, you should pay them net (that is, after making a deduction for tax and National Insurance contributions).
- complete the correct type of monthly vouchers and send copies to us as explained in *What documents should be used for CIS?*
- gather together the information on the vouchers and enter it in your annual return.

7.3 Sub-contractors

7.3.1 Meaning of 'sub-contractor'

The term 'sub-contractor' is defined in relation to contracts relating to *construction operations* (ICTA 1988, s. 560(1)). However, contracts of employment are not within this definition.

Under such a contract, a person is a sub-contractor if he is under a duty to a contractor:

- to carry out the construction operations;
- to furnish his own labour or, in the case of a company, the labour of employees or officers of the company;
- to furnish the labour of others for the carrying out of the operations, or
- to arrange for the labour of others to be furnished for the carrying out of the operations.

He is also a contractor if he is answerable to the contractor for the carrying out of the operations by others, whether under the contract or under other arrangements made or to be made by him.

7.3.2 Film and TV industry

In *Tax Bulletin*, Issue 48 (August 2000) the Revenue restated its view that set construction workers are generally employees, subject to PAYE rather than CIS deductions.

7.3.3 Workers supplied by agencies

If a sub-contractor is supplied by an agency in circumstances where ICTA 1988, s. 134 applies, then the sub-contractors legislation does not apply. The result is that the agency has to apply PAYE to any payments to the sub-contractor (ICTA 1988, s. 559(1A)).

7.4 Meaning of 'construction operations'

The following are construction operations:

- construction, alteration, repair, extension, demolition or dismantling of buildings or structures (whether permanent or not), including offshore installations;
- construction, alteration, repair, extension or demolition of any works forming, or to form, part of the land, including (without prejudice to the foregoing) walls, roadworks, power-lines, telecommunication apparatus, aircraft runways, docks and harbours, railways, inland waterways, pipelines, reservoirs, water-mains, wells, sewers, industrial plant and installations for purposes of land drainage, coast protection or defence;
- installation in any building or structure of systems of heating, lighting, air-conditioning, ventilation, power supply, drainage, sanitation, water supply or fire protection;
- internal cleaning of buildings and structures, so far as carried out in the course of their construction, alteration, repair, extension or restoration;
- operations which form an integral part of, or are preparatory to, or are for rendering complete, such operations as are previously described in this subsection, including site clearance, earth-moving, excavation, tunnelling and boring, laying of foundations, erection of scaffolding, site restoration, landscaping and the provision of roadways and other access works,
- painting or decorating the internal or external surfaces of any building or structure.

Notwithstanding the above definition, the following are not construction operations:

- drilling for, or extraction of, oil or natural gas;
- extraction (whether by underground or surface working) of minerals; tunnelling or boring, or construction of underground works, for this purpose;
- manufacture of building or engineering components or equipment, materials, plant or machinery, or delivery of any of these things to site;
- manufacture of components for systems of heating, lighting, airconditioning, ventilation, power supply, drainage, sanitation, water supply or fire protection, or delivery of any of these things to site;

- the professional work of architects or surveyors, or of consultants in building, engineering, interior or exterior decoration or in the layingout of landscape;
- the making, installation and repair of artistic works, being sculptures, murals and other works which are wholly artistic in nature;
- signwriting and erecting, installing and repairing signboards and advertisements;
- the installation of seating, blinds and shutters,
- the installation of security systems, including burglar alarms, closed circuit television and public address systems.

The Inland Revenue's booklet IR14/15 gives the following examples of operations which are included in, and excluded from, the definition:

Operations included	Operations excluded
Planning	
• None	
Site preparation	
• Demolition of, for example, buildings, structures, tree-felling.	• Delivery of materials.
• Preparation of site and site clearance, earth-moving on site, excavation, tunnelling and boring.	• Transport of spoil from site.
Construction	
• Preparation and laying of foundations and piling.	• Manufacture or off-site fabrication of components or equipment, materials, plant or machinery and delivery of these to the site. For example:
• Actual construction, alteration and repair of a permanent or temporary building or civil or chemical engineering work or structure forming part of the land. For example:	

– storage tanks
  – silos
  – pylons
  – cranes or derricks
  – pumps.
	– traditional building materials
	  – prefabricated beams and panels
	  – ready mixed concrete
	  – concrete flooring units.

• Installation of prefabricated components or equipment under 'supply and fix' arrangements.	• Installation of security systems including burglar alarms, closed circuit television and public address systems.
• Installation of power lines, pipelines, gas mains, sewers, drainage, cable television and telecommunications distribution systems.	• Manufacture and delivery of prefabricated site facilities.
• Installation of public services.	• Running of site facilities such as canteens, hostels, offices, toilets and medical centres.
• Transport of materials on site.	
• Construction of site facilities.	

Operations included	Operations excluded
• Construction, repair and resurfacing of roads and bridges. • Provision of temporary and permanent roadways and other access works such as drives. • Erection or dismantling of scaffolding, falsework and formwork. • Plant hire with operator for use on site. • Internal cleaning of buildings and structures carried out in the course of, or on completion of, their construction, alteration, extension, repair or restoration. • Work done on installations (such as rigs, pipelines, construction platforms) maintained or intended to be established for underwater exploration for, or exploitation of, minerals where the work is on land or in the UK territorial waters (up to the 12 mile limit). • Installation of systems of heating, lighting, air conditioning, ventilation, power supply and distribution, drainage, sanitation, water supply and distribution, and fire protection works. • Installation of lifts, plant or machinery needed by the specification of a building under construction or alteration.	• Delivery of road-making materials. • The hire of scaffolding equipment (without labour). • Delivery, repair or maintenance of construction plant or hire equipment without an operator. For example, concrete mixers, pumps and skips. • External cleaning (other than painting or decorating) of buildings and structures. • Drilling for or extraction of oil or natural gas. • Extraction of minerals, boring or construction of underground works for this purpose. • Manufacture, delivery, repair or maintenance of these items. • Servicing, repair or maintenance of these items.

Finishing operations
 	
• Site restoration and landscaping.
• Installation, structural repair and painting of lamp standards, traffic lights, parking meters and street furniture.
• The fitting of flooring (other than carpets) where required by the specification of a building under construction, alteration or repair.
• Installation of
 	
  – double glazing
  – computer and instrumentation systems
  – thermal insulation materials
  – heating and ventilation systems
	• Tree planting and felling in the ordinary course of forestry or estate management.
	• Manufacture and delivery of lamp standards. Routine maintenance such as cleaning and general replacement.
	• Manufacture off-site and delivery of flooring materials.
	• Manufacture and delivery of
	
	  – glazing materials
	  – computer and instrumentation systems
	  – thermal insulation materials
	  – heating and ventilation systems
	  – doors and rolling grills
	  – painting or decorating materials.

Operations included	Operations excluded
– doors and rolling grills in a building under construction, alteration or repair – kitchens and bathrooms – doors and rolling grills – shop fittings and fixed furniture (except seating). • Painting and decorating the internal or external surfaces of any building or structure.	• Manufacture, delivery and installation of seating, blinds and shutters. • Manufacture, installation and repair of artistic work (for example sculptures and murals). • Signwriting and erecting. • Installation and repair of sign boards and advertisements.

7.5   Deduction of income tax

In general, where income tax is deductible, the contractor must deduct income tax at the prescribed rate from the gross amount of the payment. However, tax is not deductible from that part of the payment which represents the direct cost to the payee of materials used or to be used in carrying out the operations under the contract (ICTA 1988, s. 559(4)).

The prescribed rate is 18 per cent as from 6 April 2000 (SI 2000/921).

The amount of any payments that the sub-contractor may have to make to his own sub-contractors is not deductible from the amount from which the contractor must deduct tax. Thus, if the sub-contractor does not have a valid exemption certificate, he may be left in the position of having to pay his own sub-contractors out of his net of tax contract payments. In some cases, the exemption certificate will enable the contractor to make gross payments up to a certain limit. He must then deduct tax from the excess of any actual payments over that limit. Where the sub-contractor renders a VAT invoice, income tax is not deductible from the VAT.

The deduction of tax at source is without prejudice to the sub-contractor's liability to tax for the year concerned. If his actual tax liability exceeds the amount deducted, he may claim a refund of the excess, subject to first being set off against any liability to Class 4 NICs (ICTA 1988, s. 559(5)).

The contractor must account for tax deducted at source under the above rules on a monthly basis along with any PAYE deductions (see **7.9** below and Income Tax (Sub-contractors in the Construction Industry) Regulations 1993 (SI 1993/743), reg. 9).

7.6 Exemption certificates, etc.

7.6.1 General information

An exemption certificate entitles the holder to receive payments from contractors without deduction of tax subject to certain limits and to certain procedures being carried out. If a company is a sub-contractor, as defined above, it should obtain a certificate from the Inspector of Taxes. Application forms are obtainable from all tax offices. Exemption certificates look like credit cards.

Under the system that has applied since August 1999, qualifying individuals, companies or directors are issued with gross payment certificates.

Applications for gross payment certificates should be made to the local tax office as at present. Application should be made on Form CIS2 for a sole trader or partnership, CIS3 for a company, CIS8 for a company director or company secretary and CIS9 for a partner. These forms are obtainable from the local tax office.

There are four types of cards and certificates in use:

- **CIS 4(P)** – The permanent registration card issued to the majority of sub-contractors and entitling the holder to be paid with a deduction on account of tax and NIC. It has no expiry date and shows the photograph and signature of the authorised holder.
- **CIS 4(T)** – The temporary registration card issued to those sub-contractors who do not yet hold or do not know their valid NI number (eg people newly entering this country). This enables them, during the validity of the card, to be paid under deduction while they obtain a valid NINO from the Benefits Agency. The card bears an expiry date in the NINO field but in other respects is the same as the CIS4 (eg bears the photo and signature of the authorised holder).
- **CIS 5** – Construction certificate issued to certain companies, which because of their size, complexity of operations or geographical spread, cannot operate with a CIS 6. There is no photograph on the certificate and it bears the company secretary's signature. The company will be issued with an original card and a number of copies that will bear separate references. It entitles the subcontracting company to be paid gross during its validity.
- **CIS 5 (Partner)** – This is a certificate that is available to partnerships with an annual turnover of at least £1 million. The partnership can nominate one partner to apply for the certificate. Application should be made on Form CIS 3 (Partner). Once the certificate is granted, the partnership may use the certifying document method that is available to the larger companies. It must first complete Form CIS 14(P) and await authorisation from the Revenue.

- **CIS 6** – Sub-contractor certificate issued to qualifying individuals and partners in firms, and to the directors of most companies that qualify. It shows the photograph and signature of the authorised holder and entitles the holder to be paid gross during its validity.

7.6.2 The annual turnover test

Any person applying for a gross payment certificate will have to satisfy a minimum annual turnover test in addition to the requirements set out at **7.6.1** above. The minimum required annual turnover for an individual will be £30,000 (SI 1993/743, reg. 21A).

In the case of a company, the required minimum turnover will depend on the maximum number of directors and, in the case of a close company, beneficial shareholders in the three-year reference period. This number will be multiplied by the individual annual turnover requirement. In the case of a partnership, the required minimum turnover will depend on the maximum number of partners in the three-year reference period. This number will be multiplied by the individual annual turnover requirement.

By concession, where an application for a gross payment certificate is made before 1 August 2001, the maximum number of directors or partners is determined by reference to the last six months of the three-year reference period.

Example 7.1

A partnership draws up its accounts to 30 April each year. It applies for a new certificate and its reference period is the three-year period ending on 30 April 2004. At the start of the period, there were four partners, but one partner left on 31 October 2003.

The relevant turnover is as follows:

y/e 30 April 2002	£ 92,000
y/e 30 April 2003	£ 95.000
y/e 30 April 2004	£100,000

Under the above rule, the turnover requirement is based on there being three partners even though there were four in the years to 30 April 2002 and 30 April 2003 (implying a turnover requirement of £120,000 in each case) and four during part of the year to 30 April 2004.

Companies and partnerships may satisfy an alternative turnover test, which requires a turnover of £200,000. This limit applies to construction income, net of materials, whether or not it arises within the construction industry scheme (Inland Revenue Press Releases, 6 October and 23 October 1998, and reg. 21A(5), (6)).

The regulations provide that the Inspector may issue a CIS 5 certificate in any case where, in all the circumstances, he considers that the CIS 6 would be inappropriate (reg. 24(6)). The Revenue has applied this in the case of companies where the turnover exceeds £1 million. As from April 2001, the Revenue applies the same test to partnerships (Revenue Press Release, 8 November 2000). The main advantage of a CIS 5 certificate is that representatives of the business do not have to present the certificate to contractors in person in order to obtain payment without deduction of income tax.

The evidence required to demonstrate that the turnover test is satisfied is set out in new regs. 21B–21E.

Applications for registration cards should likewise be made to the local tax office.

7.6.3 Individuals

In order to obtain an exemption certificate, an individual must satisfy the conditions set out in ICTA 1988, s. 562.

The basic condition is that the individual must be carrying on a business in the UK, and that business must:

- consist of or include the carrying out of construction operations or the furnishing, or arranging for the furnishing, of labour in carrying out construction operations;
- to a substantial extent, be carried on by means of a bank account;
- be carried on with proper records, and
- be carried on from proper premises and with proper equipment, stock and other facilities.

In addition, unless the individual is renewing a certificate, or is able to provide a satisfactory guarantee to the Revenue, he must have been employed in the UK, or have carried on a trade or profession in the UK, for a period of three years ending with the date of his application for a certificate. This condition is satisfied if he was so occupied throughout a period of three years beginning not more than six years before the date of his application. However, if he was receiving full-time education at any time during the six-year period, he is treated as being so occupied whilst receiving full-time education.

Further, the individual must have complied fully with the tax and NIC regulations in respect of the period mentioned above. If he controlled a company at any time during the period, the company must also have complied fully with the tax regulations. In this connection, it is not sufficient to bring his tax affairs up to date just before applying: he must have complied during the period itself.

7.6.4 Partnerships

An application must be made by each individual partner who wishes to be paid gross. The conditions to be satisfied are set out in ICTA 1988, ss. 563 and 564. Essentially the conditions are the same as for individuals. In addition, the partnership must have complied with the requirements of the tax legislation throughout the three-year period.

7.6.5 Companies

In order to obtain a certificate, the company must be able to show that it has complied with all requirements under the tax and NIC legislation, and the Companies Act 1985, in relation to its accounting periods ending in a 'qualifying period'. The qualifying period is the period of three years ending with the date of the company's application for a certificate (ICTA 1988, s. 565).

In addition, the company's business must be carried on in the UK and must:

- to a substantial extent, be carried on by means of a bank account;
- maintain proper records, in particular records relating to its compliance with tax (including PAYE), NIC and company law, and
- be carried on from proper premises and with proper equipment, stock and other facilities.

7.6.6 Application to non-resident businesses

Set out below are details taken from the Inland Revenue's booklet IR 180 (CIS).

'The Scheme applies to any non-resident contractor that makes payments for construction work carried out in the UK or any non-resident sub-contractor being paid for carrying out construction work in the UK. There is no difference between the treatment of UK contractors and sub-contractors and non-resident contractors and sub-contractors. Companies that are contractors, engaging sub-contractors for construction work in the UK, and companies that are, or will be, sub-contractors in the UK should register with the Centre for Non-Residents (see below).

Partnerships and individuals wanting to operate as contractors or sub-contractors should register with the local Inland Revenue office responsible for the area in which the construction work is to be carried out. The address will be found in the local telephone book under "Inland Revenue".

All non-resident sub-contractors should apply for the necessary CIS documentation before work starts in the UK. as contractors are unable to make any payments before seeing the sub-contractor's Registration Card or Tax Certificate.

Unless the business is a company or a partnership applying for a Construction Tax Certificate CIS5 or CIS5 (Partner), an identity check will be required at a local UK Inland Revenue office before a Registration Card (CIS4) or Tax Certificate (CIS6) can be issued. Each director or company secretary applying to hold a Sub-contractors Tax Certificate or Registration Card on behalf of their company, and each partner or individual applying for a Sub-contractors Tax Certificate or Registration Card, will need to attend the identity check.

If the person carrying on the business is resident in a country that has a Double Taxation Agreement (DTA) with the UK it may be entitled to claim exemption from UK tax. This will be the case where the UK business profits are not attributable to a permanent establishment in this country through which the business is carried on. Claims for exemption under the terms of a DTA should be sent to the Centre for Non-Residents.

Company sub-contractors should set off any deductions made from payments they receive from contractors against their own liability for PAYE/NICs and sub-contractors' deductions, where they have such liabilities. Any balance of deductions that cannot be set off in this way may be repaid on submission of the company's end-of-year returns P35 and CIS36, where appropriate.

Individual and partnership sub-contractors wishing to claim a refund should contact the local UK Inland Revenue office responsible for issuing their Registration Card or Tax Certificate.

Where there is no Double Taxation Agreement, in the case of an individual or a partner in a partnership, the deductions made by contractors under the CIS are allowable against the sub-contractor's UK tax liability. If the deductions exceed that liability, the sub-contractor can claim a repayment of the excess deductions from the Inland Revenue. Companies may only claim a repayment of excess deductions on submission of their end of-year forms P35 and CIS36, where appropriate.

Details of the Centre for Non-Residents:

Centre for Non-Residents (Construction Industry Scheme)
Fitz Roy House
PO Box 46
Nottingham
NG2 1BD
England

E-mail: non-residents@inlandrevenue.gov.uk
Fax: 0115 974 2063.

You can telephone during office hours. The contact numbers are:

- 0115 974 1948 if you want information about Double Taxation Agreements or about how the Construction Industry Scheme applies to non-residents;
- 0115 974 1939 if you want to discuss registration, applications for certificates, vouchers or other matters relating to your operation of the Scheme. The Centre will be able to give you advice and send you the relevant forms and leaflets;
- 0115 974 1940 if you want to discuss a claim that you have made under a Double Taxation Agreement.'

7.6.7 Appeal against refusal of certificate

If the Revenue refuses to issue an exemption certificate, or cancel an existing certificate, it must give the applicant a written notice of refusal or cancellation. The company may appeal to the General or Special Commissioners against that notice. Written notice of appeal must be sent to the officer who issued the notice within 30 days of the dale of issue of the notice (ICTA 1988, s. 561(9)).

7.6.8 Further information

Further information is available in booklet IR40 (CIS) which can also be accessed on the Revenue's website at www.inlandrevenue.gov.uk.

7.6.9 Gross payment certificates

Under the new system, qualifying individuals, companies or directors will be issued with gross payment certificates.

Applications for gross payment certificates should be made to the local tax office as at present. Application should be made on Form CIS2 for a sole trader or partnership, CIS3 for a company, CIS8 for a company director or company secretary and CIS9 for a partner. These forms are obtainable from the local tax office.

The annual turnover test

Any person applying for a gross payment certificate will have to satisfy a minimum annual turnover test in addition to the requirements set out at **7.6.1** above. The minimum required annual turnover for an individual will be £30,000 (SI 1993/743, reg. 21A).

In the case of a company, the required minimum turnover will depend on the maximum number of directors and, in the case of a close company, beneficial shareholders in the three-year reference period. This number will be multiplied by the individual annual turnover requirement. In the case of a partnership, the required minimum turnover will depend on the maximum number of partners in the three-year reference period. This number will be multiplied by the individual annual turnover requirement.

7.6.10   Registration cards

Under the new system, if a contractor wishes to be paid as a self-employed person, but does not qualify for a gross payment certificate, he must apply for a registration card (Income Tax (Sub-contractors in the Construction Industry) Regulations 1993 (SI 1993/743), regs. 7A–7D). The contractor must inspect this card before making any payment subject to deduction of tax under the sub-contractors' scheme. A contractor who makes a payment to a sub-contractor without inspecting the registration card may be liable to a penalty of up to £3,000 (ICTA 1988, s. 566(2B)).

If the Revenue refuses to issue a registration card to any person, he may appeal to the General Commissioners within 30 days of the notice of refusal (reg. 7B).

7.7   Procedures

7.7.1   Inspection of gross payment certificates

Before a contractor may make a first payment to any sub-contractor without deducting tax at source, he must inspect the sub-contractor's gross payment certificate. The contractor should check that the certificate is in the name of the person to whom payment is being made. In the case of certificate CIS 6, he must check that the face on the certificate is that of the person to whom payment is being made. He must check the expiry date and the limit up to which payments may be made without deduction of tax (Income Tax (Sub-contractors in the Construction Industry) Regulations 1993 (SI 1993/743), reg. 33).

Having carried out the inspection, the contractor must make, and retain, a record of:

- the name and address of the sub-contractor;

- the name of the partner or officer of the company in the case of a certificate;
- the amount of the payment, including the cost of materials, subsistence and travelling expenses;
- the number of the certificate,
- the expiry date of the certificate.

For the second and subsequent payments, there is no need to inspect the certificate again unless the contractor has reason to believe that it may have been withdrawn. However, he will need to refer to the above records to check on the expiry date and upper limit for gross payment. The contractor will, of course, need to record the amount of the payment, cost of materials, etc.

7.7.2 Inspection of certifying document

Where a sub-contractor is a company holding a CIS 5 certificate, it may provide a 'certifying document' to the contractor, instead of submitting the actual certificate for inspection, in order to obtain payment without deduction of tax. The certifying document procedure is used mainly by larger companies that may have many contracts in progress at any given time. The following conditions must be satisfied before this procedure can be used:

- the contract under which the payment is due must be made or evidenced in writing;
- the sub-contractor must have notified the Revenue of details of a nominated bank account or accounts which must be held in the name of the company as registered with the Companies Registrar;
- the payment must be made for the company's own work and not to the company as nominee for another person,
- payment must be made either by a cheque made payable to the company and crossed 'account payee' or by credit transfer to the company's nominated bank account.

The certifying document is a document signed by the company's secretary certifying that the company is the user of a valid CIS 5 exemption certificate and giving the following information:

- the name of the user;
- the address of the user's registered office;
- the user's registration number;
- the number of the user's CIS 5 certificate;
- the date from which that certificate is valid;
- the expiry date;
- particulars of the nominated bank account,
- optionally, the name under which the user's business is carried on,

(SI 1993/743, reg. 34(4)).

The contractor should check that the details given on the document agree with the details on the contract. If he is in any doubt as to the validity of the document, or the sub-contractor's exemption certificate, he should check with the tax office dealing with the sub-contractor. Usually, the tax office is the office for the area in which the registered office is situated. The contractor can telephone that office for confirmation of the validity of the certificate.

Having inspected the document, the contractor must keep it readily available and must make and keep the same records of payments as for other payments to sub-contractors.

7.7.3   Registration cards

Before making any first payment to a sub-contractor as a self-employed person (ie without operating PAYE), the contractor must inspect the sub-contractor's registration card and satisfy himself that it is valid and that the person producing it is the user of the card. For the second and subsequent payments, it is not necessary to inspect the card if the contractor has no reason to doubt its continued validity (SI 1993/743, reg. 7F).

7.7.4   Vouchers for payments made without deduction of tax

The contractor must obtain a voucher for each payment made without deduction of tax. The voucher is a completed form CIS 23 or 24. The form must be completed and signed by the sub-contractor. Form CIS 23 is used where the exemption certificate is a CIS 5 certificate. Form CIS 24 is used where the exemption certificate is a CIS 6 certificate.

The following vouchers are currently in use:

- **CIS 23** – this is used to record payments to businesses holding CIS 5 or CIS 5 (Partner) certificates;
- **CIS 24** – this is used to record payments to holders of CIS 6 certificates,
- **CIS 25** – this is a Tax Payment Voucher that is used to record net payments to, and tax deductions from, holders of registration cards CIS 4.

The contractor must:

- in relation to gross payment certificates, endorse a completed gross payment voucher with his tax reference, give one part of the voucher to the sub-contractor and send one copy to the Revenue;
- in relation to company gross payment certificates, prepare a company gross payment voucher and send one copy to the Revenue,

- in relation to registration cards, prepare a taxed payment voucher, give the sub-contractor one copy and send one copy to the Revenue.

The Revenue has issued the following guidance on the completion of vouchers.

'CIS6 holders completing gross payment vouchers (CIS 24s)

Sub-contractors holding a CIS 6 certificate are required to complete a three part gross payment voucher (CIS 24) either for each payment in the income tax month or, if the contractor requests, on a one per month basis. Cheques posted by the contractor in the month should be taken as made in the month so it may be worth waiting a couple of days after the tax month end (the fifth) before completing vouchers if the contractor has asked you to complete vouchers monthly (as opposed to completing them as payments are received).

1. The sub-contractor should insert the contractor's name (but not the reference).
2. The month and year of payment (for example: payments between 6 August and 5 September are for the month ended 5 September).
3. The gross payment, the amount to be shown on the voucher is the gross payments made (cash received or cheques drawn) less VAT.
4. Sign.
5. Parts one and three of the voucher should be given to the contractor within 14 days of the month end (by the 19th). The sub-contractor will retain part two (the sub-contractor copy) for their own records.
6. The contractor should insert his/her reference and forward the Revenue part of the voucher to the Revenue by 19th of the following month. Contractors need to take all reasonable steps necessary to obtain vouchers corresponding to payments made in the month so that as far as is possible their end of year return tallies with the vouchers submitted.

Contractors

Contractors and vouchers from CIS 6 holders

A contractor must make every reasonable effort to obtain a fully completed voucher for every payment made to a CIS 6 holder. Where vouchers are not provided, or are incorrectly completed and further payments are due, the contractor should reconsider whether the certificate is in fact a valid one. If a fully completed voucher is not provided despite the contractor taking reasonable steps to obtain one, the contractor should report the matter to his Tax Office.

Vouchers for holders of construction certificates (CIS 5 holders)

A two part CGPV (CIS 23) should be completed for the total monthly gross payments (less VAT) to sub-contractors holding construction certificates (CIS 5) by inserting.

1. The company name as shown on the CIS 5 certificate (name will have a maximum length of 26 characters)
2. The certificate number as shown on the certifying document or CIS 5 certificate
3. The month and year in the format MM/YYYY
4. The gross amount of the payment (less VAT)
5. Certifying signature-by hand or secure stamp used for signing cheques.

Split the two parts-one for contractor records and one copy for Revenue-by 19th of the month.

Vouchers for registration card holders (CIS 6 holders):

A three part tax payment voucher (CIS 24) should be completed for each sub-contractor showing the total gross payments and deductions for the month as follows:

1. The sub-contractor's name as shown on the registration card (maximum of 26 characters) and optionally his address if you want to mail it to him using a window envelope
2. The card holder's reference from their registration card
3. National insurance number as shown on CIS 6
4. The month and year in the format MM/YYYY
5. Gross payments excluding VAT
6. Cost of materials
7. Amount liable to deduction
8. Amount deducted on account of tax
9. Signature.

The vouchers collected by a contractor in any tax month must be sent to the tax office within 14 days after the end of the month (SI 1993 No. 743, Regs. 35–39).

Tax deduction certificates

Conversely, where a contractor deducts tax from any payment to a sub-contractor, he must provide the sub-contractor with a certificate on CIS 25 showing:

(a) the sub-contractor's name and address, or the name and address of his nominee;
(b) the beginning and end of the period for which the payment is made;
(c) the gross amount of the payment;
(d) the amount relating to the cost of materials;
(e) the amount from which tax was deducted; and
(f) the amount of tax deducted;

(SI 1993 No. 743, reg. 7).

The contractor will need these certificates when completing his self-assessment return, since the tax deducted is credited against his tax liability for the year and may give rise to a refund.

If a contractor makes more than one payment to the same sub-contractor in any one year, he may, if the sub-contractor agrees, provide one tax deduction certificate covering all of the payments made in that year.'

7.8   Accounting for tax deducted

7.8.1   Payment of tax

In general, each contractor has to pay the tax deducted at source in any tax month to the Revenue within 14 days after the end of the month, the same deadline as for PAYE tax. Tax months run from 6th of one month to 5th of the next month (SI 1993/743, reg. 8).

Payments can be made by BACS, CHAPS, PC or Telephone Banking as well as by cheque. For details, contractors should contact the Inland Revenue Accounts Office at Shipley (Tel: 01274 539579) or Cumbernauld (Tel: 01236 783434).

However, if the contractor can show that the total of PAYE deductions, NICs and sub-contractors' deductions which he is liable to make will, on average, be less than £1,000 per month for tax months falling within the current tax year, he may make quarterly payments (SI 1993/743, reg. 9).

If the contractor fails to deduct the correct amount, he remains technically liable for the amount he should have deducted. However, the Revenue may, at its discretion, waive payment of the amount not actually deducted if the contractor can show that he took reasonable care to comply with the regulations and that either:

- the under-deduction was due to an error made in good faith, or
- despite taking reasonable care, he genuinely believed that no tax was deductible from part or all of a payment.

It will be appreciated that arguments about reasonable care are likely to arise long after the event. The contractor will almost certainly have to fall back on his record of inspection of the sub-contractor's exemption certificate and other records set up and maintained in accordance with the rules described above.

These records may be supplemented by oral evidence, but if the contractor has failed to create the proper written records, he will start at a disadvantage.

If the Revenue is not satisfied that the contractor has exercised reasonable care, the courts will not interfere with its refusal to exercise discretion (*Slater (HMIT) v Richardson & Bottoms* 53 TC 155).

Note that the above point is without prejudice to the question whether the contractor was liable to make the deduction of tax. It pre-supposes that he was, but failed to do so. If the Revenue claims tax that the contractor believes was not deductible, he can take the matter to appeal (see **7.9.1** below).

7.8.2 Returns

Annual returns

Each year, a contractor who has made payments under deduction of tax to sub-contractors must file a return on Form CIS 36. This requires the following information in relation to each such sub-contractor:

- the total amount of such payments made to him (or his nominee) in the year;
- the total amount within (a) which represents the cost of materials;
- the total amount of tax deducted from the above payments,
- the amounts in respect of which deduction certificates and CIS 25 have been given to the sub-contractor.

The above return must be filed within 44 days of the end of the tax year, ie by 19 May immediately following the end of the year (SI 1993/743, reg. 11).

In cases where the contractor has made payments without deduction of tax, the Revenue requires a return on Form CIS 36 of the total amounts paid to each sub-contractor without deduction of tax (reg. 40). No time limit is specified for the filing of this return, but if a contractor fails to make the return, he is liable for penalties in accordance with TMA 1970, s. 98. In practice, the return should be made at the same time as the return of gross payments.

Other returns

If a contractor fails to pay the tax deducted for any tax month within the 14-day time limit, or if the collector believes that the amount paid is less than the correct amount, the collector may require the contractor to make a return showing the amounts of tax deducted from payments to sub-contractors during the month concerned. A return may be required for a period of several consecutive months. The return must be filed within 14 days of the date of the collector's notice requiring it (SI 1993/743, reg. 12(2)). The tax shown by the return as being due is then collectible.

Electronic filing

The annual return on form CIS 36 and the accompanying Schedule on form CIS 36 CS may be filed electronically, but the form CIS 36 itself has to be submitted in hard copy.

The Construction Gross Payment Vouchers, forms CIS 23, may also be filed electronically, but the Sub-contractors Gross Payment Vouchers, forms CIS 24, can only be filed in hard copy. For details of electronic filing, contractors should contact:

Electronic Business Unit
Business and Management Services Division
Crown House
Victoria Street
Shipley
West Yorkshire
BD17 7TW

Tel: 01274 534555
Fax: 01274 534514
Email: ebu.ops.ir@gtnet.gov.uk

7.9   Enforcement

7.9.1   Notice of amount payable

If a contractor fails to pay the tax for any tax month or period of several months, or where the collector believes that the amount paid is less than the correct amount, the collector may issue a notice specifying the amount which he believes to be payable. This amount must be determined to the best of the collector's judgement by considering the contractor's record of past payments. If the contractor has paid some tax, the collector must seek an explanation from him before issuing any notice under the above rule.

Any notice issued under the above rule will give the contractor a period of seven days in which to respond by giving details of the correct amount of tax. If he fails to convince the collector, he may require the collector to inspect his records in order to determine the correct amount. Failing this, the amount shown by the notice becomes payable. However, this is without prejudice to the eventual determination of the correct amount. The amount paid in accordance with the notice becomes a payment on account of the correct amount (SI 1993/743, reg. 13).

7.9.2   Formal determination of the amount payable

The Inspector may issue a formal determination of the amount payable by a contractor for any period if:

(a)   there is a dispute between the contractor and the Revenue as to the amount of tax deductible from a payment to a sub-contractor;

(b)   the Inspector believes that the contractor's return for the period does not show the correct amount, or

(c)   the Inspector considers it necessary to do so in all the circumstances.

A formal determination may be made to the best of the Inspector's judgement.

A determination under the above rule operates like an assessment. There is the usual right of appeal to the Commissioners within 30 days of the date of issue of the notice of determination (SI 1993/743, reg. 14).

Where there is a dispute under (a), either the contractor or the sub-contractor may, by giving notice to the Inspector, apply to the General Commissioners to determine the matter. In the meantime, tax must be deducted pending the Commissioners' determination.

7.9.3   Interest on overdue tax

Interest on overdue payment of tax deducted from payments to sub-contractors runs from 19 April immediately following the end of the tax year concerned. This is, however, without prejudice to the right of the Revenue to collect the monthly tax liabilities when they become due (SI 1993/743, regs. 15–17).

7.9.4   Penalties

The penalty for late filing of returns of amounts paid under deduction of tax are the same as for late PAYE returns (TMA 1970, s. 98A). The amount of the penalty depends on the number of sub-contractors to be included in the return and the number of months by which the return is late. If the return is more than 12 months late, there is a tax-geared penalty.

The standard penalty is the 'relevant monthly amount' times the number of months late rounded up to the nearest month, up to a maximum of 12 months. The relevant monthly amount is £100 for each 50 persons rounded up to the nearest 50. Thus if there are 12 sub-contractors and the return is not submitted until 24 August, ie four months late, rounded up, the penalty is £400.

The tax geared penalty is a penalty not exceeding 100 per cent of the tax due. If a contractor fraudulently or negligently makes an incorrect return he is liable to a penalty of up to 100 per cent of the tax understated (TMA 1970, s. 98A(4)).

The Revenue has power to mitigate penalties. The amount of mitigation will depend on the circumstances of the particular case and the degree of co-operation given by the contractor in determining the correct liability (TMA 1970, s. 102).

The penalties for other returns are first a penalty of £300. If the failure continues after that penalty has been imposed, a further penalty of up to £60 per day may be incurred for each day on which the failure continues (TMA 1970, s. 98).

8 Capital gains

8.1 Introduction

8.1.1 The charge to tax on capital gains

Chargeable gains which accrue on the disposal of assets are liable to tax. Individuals, trustees and personal representatives are chargeable to capital gains tax in respect of chargeable gains less allowable losses arising in any year of assessment during any part of which they are either resident or ordinarily resident in the UK (TCGA 1992, ss. 1, 2).

Companies are chargeable to corporation tax on their chargeable gains. The chargeable gains which accrue in an accounting period are, after deducting any allowable losses, included in the computation of total profits for that accounting period (TCGA 1992, ss. 1(2), 8(1)).

Every gain which arises on the disposal of an asset is a chargeable gain unless it is covered by some exemption or relief (TCGA 1992, s.15(2)).

8.1.2 Assets

All forms of property are assets, whether situated in the UK or elsewhere (TCGA 1992, s. 21(1)). As well as tangible property, such as land and buildings, this includes:

- options, debts and incorporeal property generally – eg contractual rights (see, for example, *Marren v Ingles* (1980) 54 TC 76);
- any form of property created by the person disposing of it – eg goodwill, or a work of art or craft, and
- property coming to be owned without being acquired.

In considering whether a right is an asset, it is important to remember that an asset has the following attributes:

- it is capable of being owned by someone, and
- there is a possibility of value being realised from it (see Inland Revenue *Capital Gains Tax Manual*, paragraph CG12009ff).

However, the right need not necessarily be assignable to be an asset (see *O'Brien v Benson's Hosiery (Holdings) Ltd* (1979) 53 TC 241). A statutory right is an asset (see *Davenport v Chilver* (1983) BTC 223). Similarly, a right of action under the law of tort is an asset (see *Zim Properties Ltd v Proctor* (1985) BTC 42).

This chapter considers the following assets:

- an unencumbered freehold interest in land:
- a leasehold interest in land;
- a tenancy or licence to occupy land;
- an easement, or some other right in or over land – eg a right of way,
- a reversionary interest, being a freehold or leasehold interest which is subject to a lease, sub-lease or tenancy.

An interest in land may be held by one person, or by two or more persons jointly or as tenants in common. Each person's interest is an asset. 'Land' includes any buildings and structures standing on the land (TCGA 1992, s. 288). 'Buildings' includes any fixtures installed in the buildings. Land also includes any minerals below the surface of the land. However, the right of a mortgagee of land is not an interest in land, and the grant of a mortgage is not a disposal of an interest in that land (see **8.2.10**).

Ownership of assets

The tax on chargeable gains is normally levied on the beneficial owner of the asset disposed of. This may not be the same person as the legal owner. Thus, TCGA 1992, s. 60, provides that where legal ownership is held by a nominee, or by the trustee of a bare trust, it is the person beneficially entitled to the asset who is chargeable to tax.

In the case of settled property generally, the asset held by a beneficiary is his interest in the settlement, which is a right under the settlement deed, rather than any of the settled assets.

8.1.3   Reliefs

The reliefs and exemptions are many and varied – and so need to be noted carefully. Some apply to particular types of transactions, some to the disposal of certain types of asset, and others to particular classes of taxpayers. In addition there are a number of occasions where the liability arising on a disposal is deferred – although such gains may become liable to tax on some subsequent event, in some cases not necessarily involving a further disposal. Again the treatment of chargeable gains and the rate of tax applicable thereto may be modified in certain cases.

8.2 Disposals

8.2.1 Introduction

As noted at **8.1.1**, tax is charged on gains arising from the disposal of assets. This section will consider the general types of disposals which may be made by all classes of taxpayers. The special rules for companies will be covered in **8.6** and those for individuals, trustees and personal representatives in **8.7**.

What is a disposal?

There is no inclusive definition of 'disposal' in the legislation. The word has its ordinary meaning. However, this meaning is extended by certain statutory provisions, so that the following transactions are treated as disposals:

- an outright sale of an asset, whether for cash or for some other consideration;
- the exchange of an asset for another asset, which involves a disposal of the first asset and an acquisition of the second one;
- a part disposal (TCGA 1992, s. 21(2));
- the receipt of a capital sum which is derived from an asset, whether or not the person paying the sum acquires any interest in the asset (TCGA 1992, s.22);
- the loss, destruction or dissipation of an asset (TCGA 1992, s. 24);
- a gift or other disposition, including the transfer of an asset into a settlement;
- a change in the beneficial ownership of an asset, whether or not legal ownership changes;
- a partition of land between existing joint tenants or tenants in common;
- the appropriation of an asset to or from trading stock (TCGA 1992, s. 161);
- certain 'value shifting' transactions (TCGA 1992, s. 29),
- the occasion of an asset ceasing to be a chargeable asset on being removed from the UK (TCGA 1992, s. 25).

However, the grant of a mortgage over an asset is not a disposal (TCGA 1992, s.26).

Date of disposal

Contracts

In general the acquisition or disposal of a property for capital gains purposes takes place at the date when an unconditional contract for its acquisition or disposal is made, rather than the date when the property is actually conveyed or transferred. If the contract is conditional, for example upon the grant of planning permission, the acquisition or disposal is deemed to be made at the time when the condition is satisfied (TCGA 1992, s. 28 and *Hatt v Newman* [2000] BTC 42). A distinction is made however between a conditional contract and a contract which contains certain provisions to be carried out by the parties concerned (see *Eastham v Leigh, London & Provincial Properties Ltd* (1971) 46 TC 687).

A condition means a condition precedent under contract law. A mere breach of warranty by the vendor does not amount to the failure of a condition, since the contract stands and the purchaser can only sue for damages. An example of a conditional contract is an option. There are special rules for options and they are set out at **8.4.5**. The significance of the above rule was considered in the case of *Jerome v Kelly* [2004] BTC 176. In that case, contracts for the sale of three plots of land to a company C Ltd were signed in April 1987, but were not completed at that time. Although the contracts were unconditional, they could be rescinded by the purchaser if planning permission was not obtained. In December 1989, the vendors assigned part of their beneficial interests to the trustees of offshore settlements. The contracts were eventually completed in 1990. The House of Lords held that although the contracts fixed the time of disposal, they did not fix the parties to the transaction. Accordingly there had been a disposal by the vendors to the offshore settlements, and the sale to Company C Ltd had been made by the offshore settlements. The sale was to be treated as occurring when the offshore settlements had acquired the land, rather than the contract date, as the trusts had not then been created.

The fact that the vendor of land is permitted to remain at the land after the date of disposal does not serve to postpone that date for tax purposes (*Smith & Another v IRC* SpC 388 and SpC 389).

Compulsory purchases
If the property is compulsorily acquired, its disposal takes place at the time when the compensation is agreed or otherwise settled or, if earlier, at the time when the authority enters the land in pursuance of its powers (TCGA 1992, s. 246).

Capital receipts
In the case of a disposal arising upon the receipt of a capital sum, where no asset is acquired by the person paying that sum, the date of disposal is taken as the date of receipt of the monies concerned (TCGA 1992, s. 22(2)).

Premiums
Additional rules apply in the case of the receipt of a premium (see **8.4.2**).

Hire purchase

A hire purchase or similar agreement entailing the transfer of property at the end of a period, is treated as a disposal at the beginning of the period of use, but with any necessary subsequent adjustments if in fact no eventual transfer of ownership takes place (TCGA 1992, s. 27).

Notional disposals

Where a notional disposal is deemed to have occurred as a result of some event, the date of disposal is regarded as the date of the happening of that event.

Timing

The timing of a disposal for capital gains purposes requires careful consideration, particularly in the case of a company where trading or other losses may be available to set against general taxable profits in one accounting period but not in another. For instance, terminal trading losses cannot be offset against a chargeable gain arising after the trade had ceased (the end of an accounting period), so that an unconditional contract for the disposal should be entered into before cessation.

8.2.2 Outright sales and exchanges

In general, a disposal of a freehold or leasehold interest in land occurs when beneficial ownership of that interest changes hands. Legal title may or may not change hands at the same time. If legal title does not pass, then the transferor or vendor holds that title as nominee for the transferee or purchaser (TCGA 1992, s. 60). This situation may arise in non-commercial transactions, but is less likely now that Stamp Duty (which was a tax on documents) has been replaced by Stamp Duty Land Tax (which is a tax on transactions). Similarly, the situation may arise where A contracts to sell a property to B who then contracts to sell it on to C. On completion, there may be only one conveyance of legal title from A to C. A disposal can be made by means of a contract or a declaration of trust. Any contract for the sale or other disposition of an interest in land can only be made in writing and only by incorporating all the terms which the parties have expressly agreed (Law of Property (Miscellaneous Provisions) Act 1989, s.2(1)). A contract which is not in writing is not enforceable (Law of Property Act 1925, s. 40). Any subsequent conveyance of legal title must also be in writing (LPA 1925, s. 52).

A declaration of trust is usually in writing. However, the Revenue accepts that it can be made orally (*Capital Gains Tax Manual*, paragraph CG70291). A person can transfer beneficial ownership of his interest by declaring that he holds the interest for another person.

Disposal of reversionary interests

The owner of a freehold interest may wish to dispose of a reversionary interest in the land subject to a lease or tenancy in favour of himself. In the author's view, this involves a disposal of the freehold and an acquisition of the lease or tenancy. The same applies where the reversion is put into a settlement where the transferor has a life interest (TCGA 1992, s. 70, and *Berry v Warnett* (1982) BTC 239).

Exchange of properties

An exchange of properties involves the disposal of one property and the acquisition of another. Rollover relief under TCGA 1992, s. 152 may be available if the properties are occupied for the purposes of a trade or profession. The consideration for the disposal is the market value of the property received in exchange. However, if the transaction is between connected persons or is otherwise a non-arm's length transaction, then the gain is computed by reference to the market value of the property disposed of (TCGA 1992, ss. 17, 18).

8.2.3 Part disposals

A part disposal arises wherever there is an outright disposal of part of a property, with part being retained by the person making the disposal, such as the sale of a building plot out of a larger area of land. A part disposal also arises where there is a disposal of an interest in a property, and the person making the disposal retains an interest in the same property – including in particular the grant of a lease at a premium or the sale of a reversionary interest where a subsidiary leasehold interest is retained (TCGA 1992, s. 21).

A number of special rules relate to the computation of a chargeable gain on a part disposal, with further detailed rules applying on receipt of a premium, discussed at **2.6** and **8.4.2**. Note also the reliefs available for small part disposals; see **8.5.4**.

8.2.4 Capital receipts

The receipt of a capital sum in cash or kind, derived from property or other assets, is also treated as a disposal for capital gains purposes, even if no asset is acquired by the person paying out that capital sum.

Receipts covered

This rule applies to:

- capital receipts for damage or injury to assets, or for the loss, destruction or dissipation of assets, or depreciation of assets or the risk thereof;
- the proceeds of an insurance policy against such risks;
- capital sums received for the forfeiture or surrender of rights, or for refraining from exercising rights,
- capital sums received for the use or exploitation of an asset (TCGA 1992, s. 22(1) and (3)).

In the cases of *Zim Properties Ltd v Proctor* (1985) BTC 42, the company failed to complete the sale of properties through alleged negligence of its solicitors. The sum paid to it by the solicitors was in compromise of an action derived from its right to enforce a claim against them, not from a part disposal of the properties.

This means that in strictness there will often be no allowable acquisition cost and none of the reliefs or exemptions (eg rollover relief, principal residence exemption) that might apply if the receipt of the damages represented a disposal or part disposal of the underlying asset. Extra-Statutory Concession D33 allows the taxpayer to treat the damages as derived from a part disposal of the underlying asset, qualifying for any relevant reliefs or exemption. Where, however, there is no underlying asset at all, there is no asset regarded as having been disposed of for capital gains purposes and the capital sum is exempt from tax. The rule does not apply to payments made under a warranty or indemnity included as one of the terms of a contract of purchase and sale. Instead the consideration received by the vendor and paid by the purchaser are adjusted accordingly.

Treatment as disposals

Such capital receipts are regarded as the proceeds of a disposal for capital gains purposes, or of a part disposal, where the owner still retains the asset or an interest therein.

Deferment

In certain cases the chargeable gain arising on a part disposal of this nature is deferred, for example where the proceeds of an insurance policy are used to replace or restore the asset in question (see **8.5.3**).

Company distributions

Where a company transfers property to its shareholders by way of a dividend *in specie* or a distribution in liquidation, the property is treated, subject to certain exceptions, as being disposed of at its market value by the company or its liquidator and acquired by the shareholders at the same value (TCGA 1992, s. 17.). If it is a capital distribution it will also be regarded as a part disposal of the shareholding

If the distribution is within ICTA 1988, s. 209, then it is excluded from the computation of the chargeable gain by TCGA 1992, s. 37. However, if the recipient is another UK resident company then it is not excluded from the computation of the chargeable gain since it is excluded from the charge to tax as income by ICTA 1988, s. 208.

8.2.5 Loss, destruction, etc. of assets

A deemed disposal arises on the occasion of the entire loss, destruction, dissipation or extinction of an asset (TCGA 1992, s. 24(1)). If compensation is received (eg from an insurance policy) that compensation is a capital sum derived from the asset and, as such, will form consideration for the deemed disposal. Rollover relief may be claimed if a replacement asset is acquired (see **8.5.2**).

For the purposes of the above rule, a building is regarded as a separate asset from the site on which it stands. However, if the owner is treated as having disposed of the building under these provisions, he is also deemed to have sold and re-acquired at its market value the site and any other land occupied for purposes ancillary to the use of the building itself, so that the loss on the building may be offset by a gain on the land value (TCGA 1992, s. 24(1) and (3)). Theoretically this could lead to an overall gain arising. It is understood that the Revenue would normally only apply this provision in restricting any loss arising and would not impute a gain. This would also be a rational application of what is a relieving section (see *Elliss v BP Oil Northern Ireland Refinery* [1987] BTC 38). If the value of an asset becomes negligible, the taxpayer may claim that the asset should be treaded as if it had been sold and immediately reacquired for that value. This allows a capital loss to be generated (see **8.5.10**).

8.2.6 Gifts and gratuitous transfers of value

Gifts

A disposal may still arise for capital gains purposes, even where no consideration is received by the person making the disposal. Subject to certain exceptions, any bargain carried out otherwise than at arm's length, including a gift, is treated as a disposal and an acquisition of the asset concerned at its market value (TCGA 1992, s. 17, and see also *Turner v Follett* (1973) 48 TC 614 and **8.3.3**).

Part disposals

Similarly a part disposal not at arm's length is also treated as a disposal at the market value of the part disposed of. Thus for example the grant of a lease at less than its full market rent, where the landlord could require a premium or a larger premium in an arm's length transaction, is regarded as a part disposal for a consideration equal to the value of a premium forgone, as well as any premium actually received (TCGA 1992, Sch. 8, Para. 3(7)).

Connected persons

In particular, all transactions between connected persons are treated as taking place at other than arm's length, so that the market value is normally substituted for any actual proceeds of sale. See **8.3.3** for exceptions to the market value rule and for the special rules affecting the establishment of that market value (TCGA 1992, s. 18(2)).

For these purposes one person is connected with another person as follows (TCGA 1992, s. 286):

- an individual is connected with his spouse, with his relatives (brother, sister, ancestor or lineal descendant) and their spouses, and with his spouse's relatives together with their spouse;
- a trustee is connected with the settlor of a trust, and any persons connected with the settlor, and with a company deemed to be connected with the settlement (under the provisions of ICTA 1988, s. 660G);
- a partner is connected with his other partners, and with the husband or wife and relatives of such other partners (but not his partners' in-laws) – with one important exception, in connection with any dealings in partnership assets pursuant to bona fide commercial arrangements;
- a company is connected with another company if some person has control (see ICTA 1988, s. 416) of both, or if a person has control of one and persons connected with him (whether together with him or by themselves alone) have control of the other, or if a group of persons controlling each company is the same group, allowing the substitution of a person in one group for a connected person in the other group;
- a company is connected with another person if that person (together with others connected with him) has control of it,
- finally the members of any group of persons acting together to secure or exercise control of a company are treated, in relation to that company, as connected with each other and with anyone acting upon the directions of any of them to secure or exercise control.

Value shifting

The gratuitous transfer of value out of assets into assets owned by other persons may be regarded as a transaction not at arm's length and therefore normally treated as a part disposal at market value.

Under these rules, the variation of the terms of a lease, or the adjustment of the rights and liabilities under a lease, is a disposal by the lessor in certain circumstances. The circumstances are that:

(a)   the owner of land or any other description of property becomes the lessee of the property;

(b)   subsequently, there is a variation of the rights or liabilities under the lease, and

(c)   the variation as a whole is favourable to the lessor (TCGA 1992, s. 29(4)).

Circumstance (a) envisages a sale or transfer by the owner of his interest and a subsequent leaseback to him. The initial sale or transfer is a disposal under the normal rules. However, a gain may arise to the transferee (the lessor of the leaseback) on any subsequent variation of the lease (eg an increase in the rent payable). This variation may occur at a much later time.

The deemed disposal by the lessor is a part disposal for a deemed consideration equal to the value transferred to the lessor (again applying TCGA 1992, s.17). This is the value of the lease before the variation less the value afterwards (*Capital Gains Tax Manual*, paragraph CG72010ff). Similarly, if an asset (eg a freehold or leasehold interest in land) is subject to any description of right or restriction, then the extinction of that right or restriction either wholly or partly is a disposal by the person entitled to enforce it (TCGA 1992, s. 29(5)). This rule does not catch the surrender of a lease or tenancy, since such a surrender is a disposal under the normal rules.

Recipients of market value transfers

Where the market value of an asset is substituted in place of the proceeds of disposal in computing a chargeable gain, the cost of acquisition for the person acquiring that asset is similarly taken as that market value, in computing any chargeable gain arising on a subsequent disposal of the asset (but note the restriction to the application of this section set out at **8.3.3**).

8.2.7　Changes in beneficial ownership

The capital gains legislation is primarily concerned with the beneficial owner-ship of an asset, rather than the person in whom the registered ownership or legal title is vested.

Nominees and trustees

Thus a property held in the name of a nominee or a bare trustee is treated as if the asset belonged to the person absolutely entitled thereto (TCGA 1992, s. 60(1)). For this purpose one may disregard infancy as being a bar to being absolutely entitled to the assets (*Tomlinson v Glyns Executor and Trustee Co.* (1970) 45 TC 600).

In much the same way, assets held by a trustee or assignee in bankruptcy, or under a deed of arrangement, are treated as if still held by the bankrupt person himself (TCGA 1992, s. 66).

Change in nominees

Where property remains in the same beneficial ownership no disposal takes place for capital gains purposes, even if legal ownership is re-registered under some other nominee's name.

Change in beneficial ownership

On the other hand, where a nominee ceases to hold property on behalf of one person, but instead holds it to the order of or for the ultimate benefit of some other person, a disposal is deemed to take place even though legal ownership remains in the same name. There is a disposal of the property by the original beneficial owner and an acquisition by the new beneficial owner.

Similarly, where a beneficiary becomes absolutely entitled to trust property, there is a deemed disposal of that property even before it is actually handed over by the trustees. The trustees are deemed to sell the property at its market value and re-acquire it as bare nominees for the beneficiary concerned – again see **8.7.5** (TCGA 1992, s. 71(1)).

8.2.8　Appropriations to or from trading stock

Appropriation to trading stock

Where a capital asset is appropriated as trading stock, it is deemed to be disposed of at its market value and re-acquired as trading stock at the same value, even though it remains in the same beneficial ownership throughout (TCGA 1992, s. 161).

The election

An election may be made under which any chargeable gain arising from such a notional disposal of the property is deducted from the costs of acquisition of the trading stock. Where an allowable loss arises in place of a chargeable gain, it can similarly be treated as being an additional cost added to trading stock (TCGA 1992, s. 161(3)).

The result of such an election is that tax on the chargeable gain in question is deferred until the sale of the property as trading stock, but is then taxed as income, as part of the profits of the trade. In the case of an allowable loss, tax relief is similarly deferred, but is given as an income loss rather than as a capital loss.

Whether the election is beneficial will depend largely on what allowances and reliefs are available to the taxpayer. Converting a capital gain into an income profit will result in a loss of taper relief for individuals, and may increase the tax due. Trading losses are, however, generally preferable to capital losses for all taxpayers because of the wider ranging loss reliefs.

Appropriation from trading stock

Where property is appropriated from trading stock, to be held as a capital asset or used for the owner's private purposes, it is treated as acquired for that purpose at whatever value is credited to the trading accounts for tax purposes (TCGA 1992, s. 161(2)). Following *Sharkey v Wernher* (1955) 36 TC 275, that will normally be market value, although it has been suggested that as this would not be in accordance with generally accepted accounting practice this rule is no longer valid. There is no election similar to the one mentioned above that is available when property is appropriated to stock. Note also that appropriations from stock can also give rise to problems under ICTA 1988, s. 776, which can impose a charge to income tax on certain capital profits derived from 'artificial' transactions in land (see **Chapter 4**).

Example 8.1

Richard Sandys carries on the business of a property developer and dealer as well as owning a property investment, originally costing £110,000 in June 1999, but worth only £80,000 in June 2004. Having appropriated the property to his trading stock in July 2003, he spends a further £150,000 developing it before selling it for £280,000 in 2004/05. With no election, his tax position is calculated as follows:

Capital gains tax –

Proceeds (= value on appropriation)		£ 80,000
Cost of acquisition		£110,000
Allowable loss, carried forward		£ 30,000

Income tax –

Proceeds		£280,000
Cost of acquisition (= value on appropriation)	£ 80,000	
Cost of development	£150,000	£230,000
Trading profit		£ 50,000
Income tax at 40%		£ 20,000

If however he makes an election in respect of the appropriation as above, his tax position alters quite dramatically, as follows:

Capital gains tax –		£(30,000)

Allowable loss, as above

(Added to appropriation value rather than carried forward)

Income tax –

Proceeds		£280,000
Cost of acquisition (= value on appropriation)	£ 80,000	
Add: Allowable loss, per election	£ 30,000	
	£110,000	
Cost of development	£150,000	£260,000
Trading profit		£ 20,000
Income tax at 40%		£ 8,000

He thus achieves an immediate saving of income tax of £12,000 in place of a possible future saving of capital gains tax in the same amount (assuming tax rates remain unchanged).

8.2.9 Disposals by a series of transactions

These provisions are designed to counteract attempts to reduce the amount of any gain on disposal of an asset by splitting that overall disposal into a number of part disposals. The provisions apply only where the disposal is to a connected person or to two or more connected persons. The market value rule applies to such disposals (TCGA 1992, ss. 18(2), 17(1)(a)). The following are examples of the above technique:

- the owner of a freehold interest in a plot of land transfers that interest to his son by means of a series of transfers of the freehold interest in parts of the plot,
- the owner of a freehold interest in land grants a lease or tenancy of the land to his son and, at some later time, transfers the freehold reversion to his daughter.

The rationale for the technique is that the sum of the values of the part disposals is less than the value of the whole asset transferred. The legislation requires that the series of linked transactions should be considered as a whole. The value transferred by the series is ascertained as at the time of each actual disposal. The value of the actual disposal is then the appropriate part of the value of the whole (TCGA 1992, s. 19). The appropriate part is determined on a just and reasonable basis (TCGA 1992, s. 52(4)).

Two or more transactions are linked if they occur within six years of the date of the last one (TCGA 1992, s. 19(3)).

Example 8.2

On 1 May 2003, the owner of a freehold property granted a lease of that property to his son. At that time, the unencumbered freehold was worth £250,000, the leasehold was worth £50,000 and the freehold reversion £70,000. On 1 May 2004, he transferred the freehold reversion to his daughter. At that time, the values were £275,000, £50,000 and £80,000.

The consideration for the two part disposal is calculated as follows:

(a) grant of lease:
$$\frac{£50,000 \times £250,000}{£50,000 + £70,000} = £104,167$$

(b) transfer of freehold reversion
$$\frac{£80,000 \times £275,000}{£50,000 + £80,000} = £169,231$$

In other words, the value of the whole is apportioned pro rata to the values of the parts (see *Capital Gains Tax Manual*, paragraph CG14671).

8.2.10 Mortgages

The creation of a charge over an asset is not a disposal of that asset for the capital gains purposes, so that a mortgage of a property is not a disposal of that property. Indeed, even if the person having a charge over the property (or any person appointed to enforce or give effect to the charge) subsequently sells it, it is treated as a disposal of the property by the owner himself. Where an asset is acquired subject to a charge, then the full amount of the liability assumed by the person acquiring it forms part of the consideration (TCGA 1992, s. 26).

8.3 Computations

8.3.1 Introduction

The chargeable gain is computed by reference to the proceeds of disposal, or in the case of a disposal not at arm's length or other notional disposals by reference to the market value of the property, less any allowable expenditure incurred in respect of the acquisition or improvement of the property. Where appropriate an indexation allowance is also deducted, see **8.3.6**.

Assets held at 31 March 1982

Subject to a number of transitional provisions, gains and losses accruing on the disposal of assets held on 31 March 1982 are computed as if those assets had been acquired at their market value on that date (see **8.3.7**).

Assets held at 6 April 1965

Further rules apply to assets held on 6 April 1965, the day that capital gains tax was introduced, effectively ensuring that gains arising before that day are not taxed (see **8.3.8**).

Special rules

Special computational rules apply to certain disposals, such as part disposals, as explained in **8.4**.

Other points

One should also take into account any available exemptions or reliefs as explained at **8.5**. Any allowable losses arising during the chargeable period (the year of assessment or, in the case of a company, its accounting period), whether arising before or after the chargeable gain, together with any allowable losses brought forward unrelieved from previous chargeable periods, should also be ascertained. The chargeable gains less allowable losses are then aggregated and taxed accordingly.

8.3.2 Proceeds of disposal

Actual proceeds

The proceeds of disposal include any capital sum received by the person making the disposal, whether received in cash or in value. Moreover, where the purchaser or other person acquiring the property takes over any mortgage or liability secured thereon, the proceeds of disposal are increased by the amount of liability thus taken over (TCGA 1992, s. 22(3) and 26(3)).

Market value

In a number of instances it is necessary to treat the market value of the property as the proceeds of disposal for capital gains purposes. The occasions on which market value is substituted for the actual consideration, if any, and the way in which the market value is ascertained, is considered in greater detail at **8.3.3**.

Deferred proceeds and instalments

Where the right to receive the proceeds of disposal is postponed or deferred, for example where the proceeds are payable by instalments, no discount is allowed for such delay in receipt, nor is any account taken in the first instance of any risk that part of the proceeds may become irrecoverable. However the chargeable gain is subsequently adjusted if in fact part of the proceeds do prove to be irrecoverable, with the repayment of any tax overpaid. See also **8.4.24** for the possible relief by way of payment of tax in instalments (TCGA 1992, s. 48). If the outstanding instalments bear interest, the interest is of course taxable as income and excluded from capital gains. But if the instalments are interest-free, with a corresponding increase in the capital amount of the instalments, the additional amount falls into the capital gains computations. On the other hand, the payment of interest may give rise to an income deduction for the purchaser (see Chapter 6), whereas increased instalments only give him a higher cost of acquisition for capital gains purposes.

Contingent consideration

Where the consideration includes an amount that is ascertainable but is subject to a contingency then that amount will be brought into account with no discount for the postponement of the right to receive any part of it nor for the risk of any part of it being irrecoverable. An adjustment to the computation is made if any part of the consideration previously brought into account is irrecoverable (TCGA 1992, s. 48).

If the contingent consideration is unascertainable, then the proceeds of the original disposal must include the estimated value of the right to receive any further monies. Since this is a question of valuation, it follows that the value will take into account a discount for the fact that receipt is to be delayed, as well as for any uncertainties in the eventual amount itself.

The right to the contingent sum constitutes a separate asset acquired by the vendor at a cost equal to that discounted value. This asset, by nature a chose in action, will subsequently be disposed of for the sum actually received, giving rise to a further gain or loss (*Marren v Ingles* (1980) 54 TC 76 and *Marson v Marriage* (1980) 54 TC 59). The purchaser's acquisition cost for capital gains purposes includes all amounts paid out by him by way of deferred consideration.

Example 8.3

In October 2003 Mary Shires sells a property for a consideration of £100,000 plus a further sum payable one year later dependent upon the additional value created if planning consent is granted. The value of the contingent sum at the time of the sale is agreed to be £10,000, but in the event the actual payment comes to £70,000. For capital gains tax purposes Mary will have sold the property in 2003/04 for £110,000 (£100,000 cash plus £10,000 present value of the contingent sum) and will have acquired a chose in action for £10,000. In 2004/05 she will have made a gain of £60,000 on the chose in action (viz. proceeds of £70,000 less cost of £10,000).

If the chose in action realises only £2,000 then a loss of £8,000 would arise in 2004/05. In certain circumstances this loss may be carried back and set against the original gain.

If the £70,000 was not a contingent sum but instead a fixed sum deferred for a year she would be treated as having sold her property in 2003/04 for £170,000. This would have meant that she would have had an earlier liability to tax (and only one year's annual allowance).

Since the contingent consideration is a chose in action, it is arguable that no rollover relief is available in respect of that part of the consideration on the replacement of business assets (see **8.5.2**).

Future contingencies

No deduction is allowed at the outset in respect of the following specified contingent liabilities that arise on the disposal:

- the possibility of a default by an assignee under an assignment of a lease;
- an obligation assumed by the vendor in respect of a covenant for quiet enjoyment or of similar obligations,

- any warranty or obligation made on a disposal by way of sale or lease of any assets other than land, whether made to the purchaser or anyone else.

Again there is provision for the computations to be subsequently adjusted if the contingent liability, etc. becomes enforceable (TCGA 1992, s. 49).

These specified contingencies do not cover all contingent liabilities that might be assumed by the person making the disposal. Other contingencies therefore have to be dealt with by way of negotiation with the Inspector of Taxes and in particular the contingency may need to be taken into account in arriving at the market value of the asset in appropriate cases.

Compulsory acquisitions

Where compensation is received in respect of a compulsory acquisition, it can be apportioned to the disposal of goodwill or a payment for disturbance, etc. as appropriate, notwithstanding that the compulsory purchase is only made under statutory powers stating that the consideration may only be paid in respect of the land itself (TCGA 1992, s. 245(1)). If the compensation for compulsory acquisition includes any element of compensation for temporary loss of profits of a trade or business carried on at the acquired premises, the total amount of compensation may be apportioned between its capital and income elements, thus freeing the compensation for loss of profits of its capital nature and allowing that part to be treated as a trading receipt. In the case in question, the council and the owner of the property had agreed a 'gross' compensation figure and the council sought to deduct tax from the income element.

The court ruled against such deduction on the basis that TCGA 1992, s. 245(1) allowed an apportionment and the Inland Revenue would give no assurance that they would not seek to tax the income element as income (*Stoke-on-Trent City Council v Wood Mitchell & Co* (1979) 1 WLR 254). Following this decision the Inland Revenue announced that any element of compensation received for temporary loss of profits will be included as a receipt taxable under Schedule D Case I or II, including cases where compensation is paid but no property is acquired (for example, where planning control is exercised). Compensation for losses on trading stock and to reimburse revenue expenses, such as removal costs and interest, will be treated in the same way (Inland Revenue Statement of Practice SP8/79 dated 18 June 1979). This approach was confirmed in the case of *Donald Fisher (Ealing) v Spencer* (1989) BTC 112.

Statutory compensation payable under agricultural or business tenancy legislation does not give rise to a chargeable gain (nor to taxable income). It represents a reimbursement of capital expense or loss incurred by the tenant (see

Davis v Powell (1977) 51 TC 492 and *Drummond v Austin Brown* (1983) BTC 142. Note the treatment of a severance payment in respect of the diminution in value of adjoining land – treated as a part disposal as explained at **8.4.1**.

Note also the possibility of deferring the gain by reinvesting the proceeds of land compulsorily acquired in other land (see **8.5.5**).

Proceeds subject to other taxes

As seen in previous chapters, many of the special tax provisions relating to property transactions are aimed at taxing the proceeds of disposal, or a proportion thereof, as income in the hands of the recipient, rather than as a capital receipt. In order therefore to avoid a double assessment on the same proceeds, provision is made for the exclusion of such proceeds from the capital gains computation to the extent that they are taxed as income or brought into account in computing income, profits or losses for income tax or corporation tax purposes, or if they are received under deduction of tax.

However such proceeds are not excluded merely because they represent the capitalised value of the right to receive an annual income such as a rent, which is itself subject to income tax or corporation tax. This might be thought to mean that there should be double taxation: once on the capitalised value of the rents, and again on the rents actually received. In practice this point is not taken by the Revenue (TCGA 1992, ss. 37 and 52).

Trading transactions

In the case of a trading transaction, the normal rule applies, namely that the whole of the proceeds of disposal are taken into account in computing the Schedule D Case I profits and are therefore outside the scope of tax on capital gains (see **Chapter 3**).

A similar position applies in the case of a profit assessed under the provisions of ICTA 1988, s. 776 (again see **Chapter 6**) unless exceptionally that section only applies to a part of the transaction, when any part not so assessed has to be considered in terms of chargeable gains. An example here might be the acquisition of a property for retention and its subsequent development for re-sale, when s. 776 only applies to the profit accruing from the time when the taxpayer decides to develop the property and any gain accruing up to that time is taxable as a chargeable gain.

Sale and leaseback transactions

Chapter 4 outlines the situations in which a sale and leaseback transaction gives rise to a tax liability on an income basis, where a leasehold interest in land with an unexpired term of not more than 50 years is sold and leased back for a period of 15 years or less. The provisions operate to treat a proportion of the proceeds as an income profit, and to the extent that the proceeds are thus taxed as income they are excluded from the capital gains computation under the normal rule. Since the whole of the proceeds do not fall within the income computation (unless the leaseback is for a period of one year or less) the balance needs to be considered in terms of chargeable gains.

Assets qualifying for capital allowances

Where proceeds are brought into the computation of a balancing adjustment in respect of capital allowances as explained at **3.3.4** and **3.4.4**, they must still be brought into the capital gains computation (TCGA 1992, s. 37(2)).

Special rules apply to restrict a loss arising on the disposal of an asset qualifying for capital allowances.

Premiums

Where a premium is received in respect of a lease granted for a period of less than 50 years, a proportion of it may be taxed as if it were rental income under the provisions explained in **Chapter 2**. In this case the general rule for the exclusion of proceeds subjected to tax as income is replaced by a series of alternative specific provisions dealing with the treatment of such premiums. The main provisions are explained at **8.4.2**, in relation to part disposals involving the receipt of a premium.

Further detailed rules relating to premiums received by a leaseholder, where the unexpired term of his own lease is less than 50 years, are dealt with at **8.4.4**.

Value-shifting

Anti-avoidance provisions apply to the disposal of an asset where its value is materially reduced under some scheme or arrangement (whether carried out before or after the disposal) which also confers a tax-free benefit upon the taxpayer, or some connected person (see **8.2.6**) unless it can be shown that the avoidance of tax was not one of the main purposes of carrying out the scheme.

The provisions provide for the consideration for the disposal to be increased by such amount as is just and reasonable thereby increasing the chargeable gain, reducing the allowable loss, or converting the loss into a gain, as the case may be. A corresponding reduction is also to be made to the proceeds of a subsequent disposal of any other asset affected by the scheme or arrangement.

The details of these provisions are very complex and fall outside the main subject matter of this handbook (TCGA 1992, ss. 30 to 34 and Para. 10(1), Sch. 11).

8.3.3　Market value

As seen at **8.2**, certain disposals are treated as taking place for a consideration equal to the market value of the property in question, rather than the actual consideration received. The same market value is generally also used for the acquisition cost of the person acquiring the property.

Application

This rule generally applies to substitute market value in place of any actual proceeds of disposal in connection with the following types of transactions:

(a)　gifts and other transactions not at arm's length (TCGA 1992, s. 17);

(b)　distributions of company and trust assets (TCGA 1992, s. 17);

(c)　transactions where the actual consideration received cannot itself be valued, or where the disposal is to an employee in connection with services rendered or compensation for loss of office (TCGA 1992, s. 17);

(d)　transactions between connected persons (TCGA 1992, s. 18);

(e)　appropriations of capital assets to and from trading stock (TCGA 1992, s. 161);

(f)　gratuitous transfer of value into assets owned by other persons (TCGA 1992, s. 29),

(g)　where in certain cases relief from tax on capital gains has been given, but falls to be withdrawn under the provisions relating to that relief, sometimes involving a notional disposal and re-acquisition of the asset at its market value, such as a degrouping charge (TCGA 1992, s. 179).

To prevent the market value rule from being used to obtain a tax free uplift from the price paid to market value, there is a restriction to the rule when it is applied on account of TCGA 1992, s.17 (see (a), (b) and (c) above).

Market value is not applied on the acquisition if:

- there is no corresponding disposal of the asset, and
- there is no consideration or the consideration falls below market value.

Instead the actual consideration passing, if any, is treated as the acquirer's cost.

Valuations

The market value of an asset for this purpose is taken as the price which that asset might reasonably be expected to fetch on a sale in the open market. Whilst it is assumed that the whole of the relevant assets are placed on the market at one time, which might perhaps tend to depress that market value, no reduction is allowed in the valuation for such an assumption (TCGA 1992, s. 272).

On the other hand, the valuation is made on the assumption that the property in question has already been split up into the most likely saleable units, and that any preliminary work necessary for such a fragmentation has already been carried out (*Buccleuch v IR Commrs* (1967) 1 AC 506, and also see *Ellesmere v IR Commrs* (1918)).

If the property is treated as sold and reacquired on a notional basis, no deduction is allowed for any anticipated costs of sale or reacquisition, nor the cost of breaking down the property into suitable units (TCGA 1992, s. 38(4)). Thus the valuation arising on such a notional disposal is based on the method that gives rise to the highest notional proceeds of sale, without taking any account of the costs that might be incurred in effecting such a disposal in reality.

Series of transactions

Where, in a series of transactions taking place over six years, assets are disposed of to connected persons and the market value would be greater if dealt with as a single transaction, the market value is taken at that higher figure and apportioned rateably between the respective disposals (TCGA 1992, s. 19) (see **8.2.9**).

Restrictions in use

Where property is disposed of to a connected person subject to some right or restriction enforceable by the person making the disposal or someone connected with him, some adjustment to the market value may be required. Rights or restrictions in respect of a breach of covenant under a lease, or a mortgage or similar charge, are not covered by this special provision, and are ignored in establishing the market value. In other cases the market value is taken as the value of the unfettered interest in the property, less an amount equal to the lower of the market value of the right or restriction or the amount by which its removal would enhance the value of the property. Otherwise of course it would be possible to materially reduce the value of an asset by making it liable to some right or restriction which it was not really intended should ever be applied. If the right or restriction is such that its enforcement might effectively destroy or substantially impair the value of the property, without any corresponding advantage to the person making the disposal or any connected person, or if it is an option or right to reacquire the property or to extinguish it, etc., the restriction is ignored altogether and the market value established without any regard to it (TCGA 1992, s. 18).

> **Example 8.4**
>
> Colin West gives a building site to his sister (a connected person) coupled with a restriction forbidding her to carry out any development, which he never intends to enforce. The restriction is ignored and the disposal is treated as taking place at the full market value of the land as a building site.
>
> If however Colin West occupies an adjoining property and makes stipulations as to the way in which any development on the site is to be carried out, for example to protect his own property, the valuation of the gift takes into account the restrictions.

8.3.4 No gain/no loss disposals

Certain transactions are deemed to take place at no gain/no loss to the transferor. Most of these situations arise under the rules relating to exemptions and reliefs explained at **8.4**, such as a transfer between husband and wife, or a transfer within a 75%+ group of companies. The provisions operate to treat the property as being transferred for a consideration such that neither a gain nor a loss arises on the disposal, ie at cost plus indexation allowance. This deemed consideration is also treated as the transferee's acquisition cost in relation to any subsequent capital gains disposal by him.

8.3.5 Allowable deductions

General

In general terms the expenses allowed against proceeds of disposal in a capital gains computation consist of the following sums (TCGA 1992, s. 38):

- the cost of acquisition, ie the amount or value of any consideration given in cash or kind wholly and exclusively in respect of the acquisition of the asset, or in providing the asset, together with the incidental costs of acquisition;
- expenditure on improvements, ie any expenditure incurred by the taxpayer, or on his behalf, wholly and exclusively on the asset for the purpose of enhancing its value which is reflected in the state or nature of the asset at the time of its disposal, together with any expenditure incurred wholly and exclusively on establishing, preserving or defending title to, or rights over, the asset in question;
- the incidental costs of disposal.

Strictly, demolition would not constitute an improvement reflected in the state of the land when it is disposed of, unless the land was acquired with the building on it in the first place, although the Inland Revenue may not seek to disallow demolition costs when they are small in relation to costs of reconstruction.

It is hardly surprising to find that the deduction of expenditure is only allowed once in a capital gains computation (TCGA 1992, ss. 38 and 52(1)).

Where a gain results there may be a further deduction for the indexation allowance (see **8.3.6**) before arriving at the chargeable gain.

Incidental costs of acquisition

For the above purposes, the incidental costs of acquisition are taken as any fees, commissions or remuneration paid for the professional services of any surveyor, valuer, auctioneer, accountant, agent or legal adviser, together with the cost of transfer or conveyance (including stamp duty or stamp duty land tax), and the cost of advertising to find a seller (TCGA 1992, s. 38(2)).

Wholly and exclusively

The question as to whether expenditure is incurred wholly and exclusively on the acquisition or improvement of a property depends to a large extent on the interpretation given to this wording in respect of income tax. Where expenditure is incurred for some duality of purpose, it is not strictly allowable at all for income tax purposes (see *Bowden v Russell & Russell* (1965) 42 TC 301), although in practice the Inland Revenue often allows the deduction of an appropriate proportion of such expenditure. Nevertheless, for capital gains purposes, at least one more liberal interpretation has been given to allow expenditure that was incurred for the dual purpose of establishing title and of establishing the estate duty position (*IR Commrs v Richards' Executors* (1971) 46 TC 626).

It may not always be obvious which asset an item of expenditure relates to. For example, in the case of *Garner v Pounds Shipowners and Shipbreakers and Garner v Pounds* ([2000] BTC 190), the company and Mr Pounds granted options to M plc to purchase certain land. The option consideration payable by M plc was £399,750. The company procured the release of various restrictive covenants affecting the land for the sum of £90,000. In the event, M plc did not exercise the option. It was held that the sum of £90,000 could not be set off against the option consideration in computing the gain on the option. It did, however, enhance the value of the company's interest in the land itself and would be deductible on an eventual disposal of that interest.

Assets held on 31 March 1982

Subject to a number of special rules, if an asset was held by the taxpayer on 31 March 1982, the actual acquisition cost of the asset is ignored and the gain or loss accruing on a disposal is computed as if the asset had been acquired for its market value on that date. These rules are discussed in detail at **8.3.7**.

Market value

As noted at **8.3.3**, in a number of instances the disposal of a property is deemed to take place for a consideration equal to the market value of that asset, rather than the actual consideration given for the transaction. In such circumstances the transferee may also deduct the additional consideration deemed to be given by him, as well as any actual expenditure incurred on the acquisition.

Appropriations from trading stock

Assets appropriated from trading stock are treated as acquired at their market value at the date of appropriation. This same value is used as the proceeds of disposal in computing the trading profits arising from the appropriation (see **6.3.5**) (TCGA 1992, s. 161).

Liabilities assumed

The cost of acquisition also includes any liability secured on the property assumed by the person acquiring that asset, such as where a purchaser takes over an existing mortgage on the property (TCGA 1992, s. 26(3)).

Grants and other expenditure recovered

Expenditure is not allowed in the capital gains computation if it is recouped, directly or indirectly, from the Crown, or any government or public or local authority in the UK or elsewhere (TCGA 1992, s. 50).

Tenants' improvements

Where the owner of a property grants a lease of less than 50 years out of his interest in the property and, under the terms of the lease, the tenant is liable to carry out some improvements which have the effect of improving the value of the landlord's reversionary interest therein, the landlord is liable to tax on a deemed premium as if it were rental income, under the provisions explained at **2.6**. In such circumstances, in computing the capital gain arising on any subsequent disposal of his interest in the property, the landlord can claim a deduction equal to the amount on which tax was assessed under those provisions as if it were expenditure incurred by him on the improvement of the property (TCGA 1992, Sch. 8, Para. 7).

Shares in a close company

Where a close company transfers an asset to any person otherwise than by way of bargain at arm's length and the consideration received by the company is less than the market value of that asset the difference is apportioned between the shareholders of the close company. (This is in addition to including the difference in the company's capital gains computation, by substitution of the market value in place of the proceeds of sale as noted at **8.3.3**.)

The amount apportioned to each shareholder reduces the amount of expenditure incurred on the acquisition of shares in the company allowed in computing a gain on the subsequent disposal of those shares. There is however no provision to assess any surplus amount apportioned over and above the acquisition costs available, nor to deduct the amount from any 'improvement' costs, which are still allowed in full. The apportionment may be followed through a series of close companies for this purpose if necessary. However where the transfer of assets takes place within a 75%+ group of companies (under TCGA 1992, s. 171, see **8.6.3**), no apportionment is required (TCGA 1992, s. 125(4)).

Without such a provision, the shareholder's own tax liability arising on the disposal of his shareholding would be reduced to the extent that the company's assets were not disposed of for full value.

Part disposals

Special rules apply to the allocation of allowable expenditure in the case of a part disposal to establish the proportion of expenditure that may be offset against the proceeds derived from the part disposed of, and the proportion attributable to the part retained (see **8.4.1**). Particular problems arise in the case of a part disposal involving the receipt of a premium on the grant of a lease of less than 50 years (see **8.4.2**).

Wasting assets

Allowable expenditure incurred in respect of certain wasting assets, that is assets having a life expectancy of less than 50 years at the time of their disposal, is amortised over the last 50 years of the asset's expected life (see **8.4.3** and **8.44**). Such assets may include leasehold property. The amortisation in the case of a leasehold property is on a curved line basis, whereas in other cases it is on a straight line basis.

Incidental costs of disposal

Any incidental costs of disposal are allowed as a deduction in the computation of the chargeable gain. These include any fees, commission or remuneration paid for the professional services of a surveyor, valuer or auctioneer, accountant, agent or legal adviser, together with the costs of transfer or conveyance (including stamp duty or stamp duty land tax), and the cost of advertising to find a buyer. These incidental costs also include amounts reasonably incurred in making any valuation or apportionment required for the purposes of the capital gains computation, including the expenses of ascertaining the property's market value, but not the costs of preparing the capital gains computation itself (TCGA 1992, s. 38(2)).

Revenue expenses

Expenditure is not allowable as a deduction for capital gains purposes if it is already allowed in computing income, profits or losses for the purposes of income tax or corporation tax, or would be allowable but for some insufficiency of income. This proviso is extended to include expenditure that would be so allowable, even if the income profits are not actually chargeable to tax. In the same way no deduction is allowed for expenditure incurred in respect of a property in circumstances such that, if that property was held as a capital asset used in a trade, the expenditure would be available for deduction in computing the profits of that trade (TCGA 1992, s.39 and 52).

Thus for example where a tenant continues to pay rent under a lease after he has ceased to occupy the premises, in order to obtain the right to assign the lease and to avoid its forfeiture, the payments are not regarded as allowable deductions for capital gains purposes, despite arguments that the payments were made to preserve or enhance the value of the lease (*Emmerson v Computer Time International* (1977) 50 TC 628). The distinction between revenue and capital expenditure is discussed in greater detail at **2.2.2**. General maintenance expenditure is normally available against income profits, whereas improvement expenditure is allowed for capital gains purposes. However in certain circumstances expenses on renovations, etc. may be disallowed in computing income profits (for example where the property is acquired in a dilapidated state) and such expenditure can be claimed as a capital gains cost.

Tithe annuities

Whilst only five-sixths of a tithe annuity payment was allowed as a charge on income, the remaining one-sixth was treated as a capital payment and may be deducted for capital gains purposes. Tithe annuity payments were phased out in 1977, but one-sixth of any amount paid beforehand still qualifies for relief in computing the capital gain on a subsequent disposal of the property.

Capital allowances

Certain capital expenditure may qualify for capital allowances, or an allowance for renewals or replacements in lieu thereof, which are set off against income profits under the provisions explained in **Chapter 5**. Nonetheless such expenditure can still be deducted for capital gains purposes in computing any gain arising on a subsequent disposal of that asset (TCGA 1992, s.41).

If, however, a loss arises any expenditure for which capital allowances have been given is excluded in computing the capital loss, since tax relief on an income basis will already have been given for such expenditure.

If the asset was acquired from a connected person under an election whereby it was treated as transferred at its written-down value for capital allowances purposes, any expenditure for which allowances were previously made to the transferor is also excluded.

Again where the asset was transferred within a 75%+ group of companies on a no gain/no loss basis, any allowances made to the transferor company or other members of the group are also taken into account here.

The general provisions relating to the calculation of capital allowances are explained in **Chapter 5**.

Interest

Interest is not normally allowed as a deduction in a capital gains computation (TCGA 1992, s. 38(3)).

Exceptionally, however, interest paid by a company in accounting periods ending before 1 April 1996 on any sum borrowed to meet the costs of construction of a building, structure or other work may be allowed as a deduction if the interest did not qualify for relief as a trade expense or as a charge on income.

Insurance premiums

In no instance is a premium paid under any policy of insurance allowed in a capital gains computation (TCGA 1992, s. 205).

Merger or division of assets

Where assets are merged or divided or their nature is otherwise changed, or where interest or rights over the assets are created or extinguished, the costs attributable to the original assets are followed through onto the new assets (TCGA 1992, s. 43).

The surrender of one lease and the grant of a new lease may, in some circumstances be treated in this way. It is understood that it is the Inland Revenue's view that this will only apply if the extent of the property covered by the two leases does not differ in any way and if the terms of the leases are the same (except for duration and the amount of rent payable). In these circumstances, the surrender and re-grant will not be treated as a disposal and acquisition. The acquisition cost of the original lease will be attributed to the new lease (ESC D39).

Apportionments

Unless otherwise specifically provided, any apportionments required in computing chargeable gains are made as is just and reasonable in the circumstances (TCGA 1992, s. 52).

Personal labours

No deduction is available in respect of the value of the personal labour and skill of an individual taxpayer himself in enhancing the value of his asset (*Oram v Johnson* (1980) 53 TC 319).

8.3.6 Indexation allowance

The indexation allowance was first introduced in April 1982, in an attempt to remove the inflation element of gains by uplifting the monetary cost and any enhancement expenditure in line with inflation as measured by the Retail Prices Index. The inflation factor is not applied for any period of ownership before April 1982. The effect of this was broadly to eliminate the post-1982 inflationary element from gains arising on assets held in, or purchased after, 1982.

Example 8.5

Collins Ltd buys a plot of land in April 1994 for £30,000 and sells it in March 2005 for £45,000. The Retail Prices Index has increased by, say, 32 per cent between April 1994 and March 2005. The chargeable gain is computed as follows:

	£
Proceeds	45,000
Cost	30,000
Gain before indexation	15,000
Indexation allowance: £30,000 × 32%	9,600
Chargeable gain	5,400

If the land had only been sold for £35,000 Collins would have made a loss in real terms. However the indexation allowance cannot be used to turn a gain into a loss or to increase the loss. The chargeable gain would be nil.

From April 1988 capital gains were rebased to 31 March 1982 (see **8.3.7**), so that any earlier gains are taken out of the charge to tax.

In 1998 indexation allowance was withdrawn for individuals, trustees and personal representatives and replaced by taper relief. This was intended to encourage the long-term holding of assets by reducing the proportion of gain chargeable as time elapsed. Indexation is still given up until April 1998 in respect of any assets acquired before that date. Indexation allowance continues for companies within the charge to corporation tax (TCGA 1992, ss. 53(1A), 54(1A)).

The allowance

The indexation allowance is given where there is a disposal which gives rise to an *unindexed gain*, ie a chargeable gain computed under the general rules before adjusting for the allowance. The allowance is deducted from the unindexed gain in order to arrive at the chargeable gain (subject to any other reliefs) (TCGA 1992, s. 53). Since 29 November 1993 indexation allowance has not been available to create or increase a capital loss, although some loss may have been established where a no gain/no loss transfer occurred before then.

The allowance is given automatically, without a claim requiring to be made. It is available regardless of whether the asset is situated in the UK or overseas and is available not only to those who are resident or ordinarily resident, but also where gains made by those who are neither resident nor ordinarily resident are chargeable to tax, either because the asset is used in a UK trade or where the gains of a non-resident company or trust can be taxed on UK residents (see **8.9**).

The indexation allowance is arrived at by multiplying the *relevant allowable expenditure* on the asset by the increase in the Retail Prices Index (rounded where appropriate to the nearest third decimal place) between that for March 1982 (or, if later, that for the month in which the expenditure was incurred) and the month of the disposal of the asset (or, for individuals, trustees and personal representatives, April 1998 if earlier) (TCGA 1992, s. 54).

The indexation allowance is applied to the relevant allowable expenditure, except that where the asset was held on 31 March 1982 the indexation allowance is automatically given on the greater of the asset's acquisition cost and its market value on that date (TCGA 1992, s. 55(2), see **8.3.7**).

Expenditure

Relevant allowable expenditure is expenditure upon the acquisition of the asset together with any expenditure on improvements (see **8.3.5**) but does not include the incidental costs of disposal. Acquisition expenditure is treated for this purpose as having been incurred at the time when the asset was acquired. Enhancement expenditure is treated as having been incurred when the expenditure became due and payable. Either of these dates may differ from the actual payment date (TCGA 1992, ss. 53(2)(*b*) and 54(4)).

Relevant allowable expenditure is the expenditure that is deductible for capital gains purposes, which may not be the same as the expenditure actually incurred. Examples where the two may differ are the writing down of the cost of short leases and other wasting assets (see **8.4.3** and **8.4.4**); the substitution of market value for the cost of acquisition from a connected party and in other circumstances (see **8.3.3**); and the reduction of the allowable cost either of a replacement business asset where rollover relief has been claimed (see **8.5.2**) or of a gifted asset where 'holdover' relief has been claimed (see **8.7.8**).

Where expenditure is apportioned on a part disposal (see **8.4.1** and **8.4.2**), the indexation allowance is applied to the apportioned expenditure.

Disposals on a no gain/no loss basis

Certain transfers, for example between husband and wife or within a 75%+ group of companies, are deemed to take place at a value such that neither a gain nor a loss accrues (see **8.3.4**). In effect the transfer is regarded as taking place at the cost to the transferor plus the indexation allowance to the date of transfer (or April 1998, if earlier, for individuals), and the unindexed gain of the transferor will be reduced by the allowance to nil.

8.3.7 Assets held on 31 March 1982

Subject to the various special rules described below, gains and losses accruing on the disposal on or after 6 April 1988 of assets held on 31 March 1982 are computed as if those assets had been acquired at their market value on that date (TCGA 1992, s. 35(2), see examples 1 and 2 below) This is often referred to as 31 March 1982 rebasing.

There are a number of special provisions to accommodate conflicts between the old rules and the new:

- where there is a gain since 31 March 1982, but under the old rules there would have been a smaller gain, the rebasing rules will not apply (TCGA 1992, s. 35(3)(*a*), see example 3 below);
- the rebasing rules will not apply where a loss would result but the old rules would produce a smaller loss (TCGA 1992, s. 35(3)(*b*), see example 4 below);

- where the old rules (including those dealing with assets held on 6 April 1965, see **8.3.9**) would produce a no gain/no loss position, the rebasing rules will not apply to give a different result (TCGA 1992 s. 35(3)(c) and (d), see examples 5 and 6 below); and
- where the effect of the rebasing rules would be to substitute a gain for a loss, or vice versa, the relevant disposal will be deemed to give rise to neither gain nor loss (TCGA 1992, s. 35(4), see examples 7 and 8 below).

General examples

	Cost	31.3.82 MV	Indexed gain
	£000	£000	£000
Example 1			
Proceeds	500	500	
Cost	(100)		
31.3.82 MV		(200)	
Indexation	(250)	(250)	
Indexed gain	150	50	50
Example 2			
Proceeds	100	100	
Cost	(300)		
31.3.82 MV	—	(200)	
Loss	(200)	(100)	(100)
Example 3			
Proceeds	500	500	
Cost	(200)		
31.3.82 MV		(100)	
Indexation	(250)	(250)	
Indexed gain	50	150	50
Example 4			
Proceeds	100	100	
Cost	(200)		
31.3.82 MV	—	(300)	
Loss	(100)	(200)	(100)
Example 5			
Proceeds	200	200	
Cost	(200)		

31.3.82 MV	—	(300)	
No gain/no loss	Nil	(100)	Nil

Example 6

Proceeds	200	200	
Cost	(200)		
31.3.82 MV	—	(100)	
No gain/no loss	Nil	100	Nil

Example 7

Proceeds	200	200	
Cost	(300)		
31.3.82 MV	—	(100)	
No gain/no loss	(100)	100	Nil

Example 8

Proceeds	200	200	
Cost	(100)		
31.3.82 MV	—	(300)	
No gain/no loss	100	(100)	Nil

Previous no gain/no loss disposal

Where a person disposes of an asset, otherwise than by means of a *no gain/no loss disposal,* which he did not hold on 31 March 1982 but which he acquired by means of a no gain/no loss disposal, and all previous disposals of that asset since 31 March 1982 were no gain/no loss disposals, he is treated as having held the asset since 31 March 1982, so that the rebasing rules described above may apply to it (TCGA 1992, Para. 1, Sch. 3).

For these purposes, a 'no gain/no loss' disposal is one which is deemed by statute to give rise to neither gain nor loss for capital gains purposes, notably one between husband and wife (see **8.7.3**) or within a group of companies (see **8.6.3**) (TCGA 1992, Para. 2(3), Sch. 3).

Capital allowances

Where a loss would otherwise accrue on the disposal of an asset, expenditure on which attracted capital allowances, the amount which qualified for allowances cannot be deducted in computing that loss (TCGA 1992, s. 41, see **8.3.5**). The effect of the rebasing of capital gains, however, is that the asset is deemed to have been disposed of and immediately re-acquired for its market value on 31 March 1982, so that the cost deductible on the ultimate disposal of the asset *cannot* include expenditure which qualified for capital allowances before that date. Accordingly, such expenditure is deemed to have been incurred on the notional re-acquisition of the asset on 31 March 1982 (TCGA 1992, Sch. 3, Para. 3).

Example 8.6

Mike Jones purchased a machine for use in his business in 1980. It cost £15,000 and was worth £12,000 on 31 March 1982. Mike sells the machine in 2004 for £2,000. He does not, however, have an allowable loss since the rebased acquisition cost must, in so far as it does not exceed the original cost qualifying for capital allowances, be disallowed as if it had itself qualified for allowances.

The treatment of wasting assets qualifying for capital allowances (see **8.4.3**) is similarly modified.

Assets derived from other assets

Where an asset acquired since 31 March 1982 derives part of its value from an asset which was held on that date, as for example where a lease of land was acquired before that date and the freehold reversion thereafter, the cost allowed on a disposal of the second asset will need to reflect a deemed acquisition at market value of the first asset on 31 March 1982 (TCGA 1992, Sch. 3, Para. 5, amending TCGA 1992, s. 43).

Periods of ownership

A number of provisions only apply where the relevant asset is held or used for a particular purpose, such as principal private residence relief or rollover relief on the replacement of business assets. Periods before 31 March 1982 are disregarded, except that the occupation of a principal private residence before 31 March 1982 will enable periods after that date to qualify as periods of deemed occupation.

31 March 1982 election

If the taxpayer so elects, the gains and losses arising on all disposals by him of assets held by him on 31 March 1982 may be computed solely by reference to the assets' market value on that date, without comparison with any computation under the previous rules (TCGA 1992, s. 35(5)); pre 31 March 1982 records will not then have to be retained.

That election can only be made within one year from 31 January following the end of the year of assessment (capital gains tax) or two years of the end of the accounting period (corporation tax) in which the first such disposal takes place, so in most cases it will now be too late. The election is irrevocable once made (TCGA 1992, s. 35(6)).

Although, in general, the election affects all the elector's disposals, an election made by him in one capacity, for example as beneficial owner, does not affect assets held by him in some other capacity, for example as trustee or partner (TCGA 1992, s. 35(7)). Nor does a person's election affect the disposal of an asset acquired by him from his spouse (if he is an individual) or from another member of the same 75%+ group of companies (if a company). Rather, such an asset will be covered by any election made by the person from whom it was so acquired (TCGA 1992, Sch. 3, Para. 2).

The election does not affect any disposal of, or of an interest in, plant or machinery that is eligible for capital allowances, or any asset used in the working of mineral deposits (TCGA 1992, Sch. 3, Para. 8).

8.3.8 Assets held on 6 April 1965

Although capital gains are only chargeable to tax to the extent that they accrued since 31 March 1982 the original rules for computing chargeable gains arising on the disposal of assets held on 6 April 1965 may still be relevant in computing chargeable gains, and are briefly outlined here.

Gains accruing before 6 April 1965

Where an asset was acquired before 6 April 1965 and disposed of after that date, part of the gain arising on the disposal may have accrued before the introduction of capital gains tax. The overall gain is therefore reduced under the rules explained below, in order to eliminate that part of the gain that may be said to have arisen before 6 April 1965. This is, of course, subject to 31 March 1982 rebasing where the gain or loss under the 6 April 1965 rules must then be compared with the gain or loss over the 31 March 1982 value (TCGA 1992, Sch. 3, Para. 6).

Losses accruing before 6 April 1965

In the same way, capital losses are only allowable if they arise after 6 April 1965.

Time-apportionment

The normal rule for eliminating any pre-6 April 1965 gain is to allocate the overall gain arising on the disposal between, and in proportion to, the period from the acquisition of the asset to 6 April 1965 and the period from that date up until its disposal.

The time-apportionment rule does not apply to the disposal of an interest in land reflecting development value, nor to property that has been the subject of a material development commenced after 17 December 1973, nor to the disposal of quoted shares (TCGA 1992, Sch. 2, Paras. 1 and 9).

Otherwise, where an asset is acquired before 6 April 1965 and disposed of after that date, only so much of the gain as is apportioned to the period after 6 April 1965 is taxed as a chargeable gain. The gain is spread evenly over the period of ownership so that the gain is reduced by the fraction $T/(P + T)$ to arrive at the chargeable gain, where T is the period from 6 April 1965 to the date of disposal and P is the period from the date of acquisition to 6 April 1965 (TCGA 1992, Sch. 2, Para. 16).

Expenditure on improvements

Where any expenditure is incurred on the improvement of an asset, the overall gain is first allocated between the original cost of acquisition and the expenditure on improvements on a pro rata basis in ratio to those costs. Time apportionment is then applied to each element of the gain separately, depending on the date the relevant expenditure was incurred. Where the improvement expenditure was incurred on or after 6 April 1965, the corresponding part of the gain is not time apportioned.

Little or no acquisition costs

The allocation of the gain may be amended if there was no expenditure on the acquisition or creation of the asset in question, or the expenditure is small as compared with the value of the asset just before any expenditure is incurred on its improvement. In such circumstances the gain can be re-allocated so that the part attributed to the expenditure on improvements is on a realistic basis with any remaining gain being attributed to the original expenditure on acquisition; the gains then being time-apportioned separately (TCGA 1992, Sch. 2, Para. 16(5)).

Assets acquired before 6 April 1945

Any expenditure incurred on the acquisition or improvement of an asset before 6 April 1945 is deemed to be incurred on that date, so that P in the above formula has maximum value of 20 years (TCGA 1992, Sch. 2, Para. 16(6)).

Part disposals after 5 April 1965

Where there is a part disposal of an asset on or after 6 April 1965, and the asset was acquired before 6 April 1965, the time-apportionment formula in respect of the gain arising on the part disposal runs to the date of that disposal.

However, in considering the apportionment of any gain arising on a subsequent disposal of the part retained, the chargeable gain is calculated in two separate steps. This is achieved by assuming that the part retained had been sold and re-acquired at its market value at the time of the part disposal. The overall gain derived from the disposal of the part retained is thus broken down into two parts with time apportionment only applying to the gain accruing up to the date of the part disposal (TCGA 1992, Sch. 2, Para. 16(8)).

Merged or divided assets
Where assets are merged, or derived from other assets (see **8.3.5**, and TCGA 1992, s. 43), regard is taken of the total period of ownership of the original assets and the new assets (TCGA 1992, Sch. 2, Para. 16(9)).

In practice a period of occupation under a tenancy can be treated as one with a subsequent period of ownership. However, if the tenant is able to obtain a new lease under the provisions of the Landlord and Tenant Act 1954 upon the expiry of his old lease, the new lease is treated as a separate asset for this purpose (*Bayley v Rogers* (1980) 53 TC 420 and *Lewis v Walters* [1992] BTC 76).

No gain/no loss transfers
Where an asset is transferred between a husband and wife or within a 75%+ group of companies on a no gain/no loss basis, the transferor and transferee are treated as one person so that the transferor's acquisition is treated as the acquisition of the transferee (TCGA 1992, s. 58).

Indexation allowance
The indexation allowance is deducted before applying time apportionment in arriving at the chargeable gain see **8.3.6** (*Smith v Schofield* [1993] BTC 147).

Example 8.7

Bill Bridger acquires a property on 6 April 1932 for a consideration of £9,000. On 6 April 1960 he spends £81,000 on improvements. He subsequently sells the property for £304,230 (net of selling expenses) on 6 April 2004. His overall profit is calculated as follows:

		£304,230
	£9,000	
Proceeds of disposal	£81,000	
Less: Cost of acquisition		
Cost of improvements		
		£ 90,000
		£214,230
Unindexed gain		
Less indexation allowance £90,000 × 1.047		£ 94,230
Gain		£120,000

This overall gain is apportioned between the original cost of acquisition and the expenditure on improvements, and time apportioned accordingly as follows:

(a) Attributed to acquisition cost –

$$\frac{\text{Gain} \times \text{Cost of acquisition}}{\text{Total cost}}$$

$$\frac{£120,000 \times £9,000}{£90,000} \quad = \quad £ 12\,000$$

$$\frac{\text{Apportioned gain} \times T}{P + T}$$

$$\frac{£12,000 \times 39}{20 \text{ (max)} + 39} \quad = \quad £ 7,932$$

(b) Attributed to improvement expenditure –

$$\frac{\text{Gain} \times \text{Cost of improvement}}{\text{Total cost}}$$

$$\frac{£120,000 \times £81,000}{£90,000} \quad = \quad £108,000$$

$$\frac{\text{Apportioned gain} \times T}{P + T}$$

$$\frac{£108,000 \times 39}{5 + 39} \quad = \quad £ 95,727$$

Total time apportioned gains (a + b)   £ 76,000

The time apportioned gain will then be compared with the gain over 31 March 1982 under the rebasing provisions.

6 April 1965 value election

Instead of applying time apportionment the taxpayer may make an irrevocable election for the asset to be treated as having been disposed of and reacquired at its market value at 6 April 1965. This has the effect of increasing the acquisition cost of the asset to its market value as at that date.

Such an election must be made within one year from 31 January following the end of the year of assessment (capital gains tax) or two years of the end of the accounting period (corporation tax) in which the disposal takes place (or such longer time as may be allowed by the Inland Revenue) and is irrevocable, so that once made it cannot be withdrawn (TCGA 1992, Sch. 2, Para. 17(1), (3) and (4)).

The resulting gain or loss must still be compared with the gain or loss under 31 March 1982 rebasing.

Losses

The rule is modified if the election would increase a loss or substitute a loss for a gain.

Where the election would substitute a larger loss, only the smaller actual loss is available, but the whole of that loss is allowed without any time-apportionment.

Where the election substitutes a loss in place of a gain, the disposal is treated as taking place at no gain/no loss to the taxpayer, so that the deemed acquisition at 6 April 1965 is treated as if it were equal to the proceeds of disposal, less any post-6 April 1965 expenditure on improvement (TCGA 1992, Sch. 2, Para. 17(2)).

There is however no similar restriction to restrict a gain arising from such an election to the actual gain realised by the taxpayer, if less.

Valuations

The general rules for the valuation of property are dealt with at **8.3.3** in relation to transactions not at arm's length. These rules also apply in respect of a valuation at 6 April 1965, but having regard to the circumstances existing at that date.

Since an election is irrevocable and values can normally only be agreed with the Inland Revenue after the election has been made, it is important to be quite clear as to the likely effects of the election before making it.

Part disposals after 5 April 1965

Where there is a part disposal of an asset on or after 6 April 1965, the election can only be made on the occasion of that part disposal. If not made then, the election cannot be made in respect of a subsequent disposal of any part retained. Where the subsequent disposal of the part retained takes place within the time limit for an election in respect of the earlier part disposal, the position may be reconsidered and it may still be possible to make an election in respect of the asset covering both disposals (TCGA 1992, Sch. 2, Para. 17(5)).

Assets qualifying for capital allowances

Where an asset qualifies for capital allowances, there is a restriction in respect of losses arising on the disposal. In effect, any expenditure qualifying for capital allowances is excluded in computing the allowable loss for capital gains purposes. Where such an asset is also treated as sold and re-acquired at 6 April 1965, the restriction in allowable losses applies as if the actual capital allowances made for any period after 6 April 1965 in respect of the original acquisition were made in respect of the deemed acquisition at that date (TCGA 1992, Sch. 2, Para. 20).

Indexation allowance

Where the gain is calculated by reference to the value on 6 April 1965, including as mentioned above a value giving rise to no gain/no loss, the indexation allowance is calculated by reference to that value, not to the original expenditure incurred.

Land with development value

Time-apportionment does not apply to the disposal of an interest in land reflecting development value nor to property that has been the subject of a material development commenced after 17 December 1973.

Instead it is assumed that the land was sold and immediately reacquired at market value on 6 April 1965. The gain is then compared with the gain over cost (TCGA 1992, Sch. 2, Para. 9):

- if both calculations show a gain, the smaller gain is taken,
- if both calculations show a loss, the smaller loss is taken, or
- if one calculation shows a gain and the other a loss, the consideration for the deemed disposal on 6 April 1965 is adjusted so that neither a gain nor a loss accrues.

Quoted shares

Quoted shares are dealt with in the same manner as land with development value (TCGA 1992, Sch. 2, Paras. 1, 2). However a taxpayer may if he wishes make an umbrella election covering either all ordinary shares, or all fixed-rate preference shares and securities, or both, whereupon the chargeable gains or allowable losses arising from the disposal of quoted shares or securities covered by the election are calculated solely on the basis of the deemed re-acquisition of those assets at 6 April 1965, without any regard to the actual profit or loss made on the disposal. The election must be made within one year from 31 January following the end of the year of assessment (capital gains tax) or two years of the end of the accounting period (corporation tax) in which the first disposal of such shares or securities as are covered by the election are disposed of after 19 March 1968. The election is irrevocable. In most cases the time limit for an election will have long passed.

8.3.9 Losses

Computation of losses

An allowable loss is generally computed in the same way as a chargeable gain, unless otherwise specified (TCGA 1992, s. 16). The indexation allowance cannot, however, be given to the extent that it would create or augment a loss (TCGA 1992, s. 53).

Where a loss arises in circumstances such that it would be exempt if it were a gain, the loss is not an allowable loss. Similarly if only part of any gain would be a chargeable gain, only part of the loss is treated as an allowable loss (TCGA 1992, s. 16(2)).

Allowable losses may be restricted in other cases, such as depreciatory transactions, for example.

Notification of loss

Under self-assessment, a loss must be notified to the Revenue (TCGA 1992, s. 16(2A)). This is normally done by including it in the return for the period concerned, but a loss may be notified at any time provided it is within five years from the 31 January following the end of the year of assessment (capital gains tax) or within six years of the end of the accounting period (corporation tax).

Utilisation of losses

The amount of allowable loss for capital gains purposes is offset against any chargeable gains arising to the same person in the same chargeable period. For this purpose a chargeable period is:

- a year of assessment for individuals, trustees and personal representatives (TCGA 1992, s. 2(2)(a)), or
- an accounting period for companies within the charge to corporation tax (TCGA 1992, s. 8(1)(a)).

Any excess of loss over the gains of the same chargeable period is carried forward indefinitely against chargeable gains arising to the same person in subsequent periods (TCGA 1992, ss. 2(2)(b) and 8(2)(b)).

Allowable losses may not be carried back against chargeable gains arising in an earlier chargeable period, except in the case of a deceased person, where losses arising in the year of death can be carried back and set off against any chargeable gains arising in the three years immediately preceding the year of death (TCGA 1992, s. 62(2)).

Needless to say losses can only be allowed once (TCGA 1992, s. 2(3)).

Losses on transactions between connected persons

Where an asset is disposed of to a connected person, any gain or loss on disposal must be calculated on the basis that the asset was disposed of for a consideration equal to its market value (TCGA 1992, ss. 18(2) and 17(1) and see **8.2.6**).

Any loss arising on the disposal is only available for offset against any chargeable gains arising on some other disposal to the same person at a time whilst both persons are still connected in some capacity (but not necessarily by the same route of connection) (TCGA 1992, s. 18(3)).

This restriction does not apply to the disposal of an asset by way of gift where the asset, together with any income derived from it, is primarily applicable for educational, cultural or recreational purposes and the persons benefiting from the gift are members of the association for whose benefit the gift is made and most of them are not connected persons (TCGA 1992, s. 18(4)).

Options between connected persons

Where an option is granted between connected persons (see **8.2.6**), a loss arising from the disposal of that option is not available as an allowable loss unless it arises from an arm's length disposal of the option to a third party who is not connected with either of the parties to the option (TCGA 1992, s. 18(5)).

8.4   Computations – special rules

8.4.1   Part disposals – general rules

The part disposal of an asset is treated as a disposal for the capital gains purposes. The special rules relating to part disposals generally apply whenever the person making the disposal retains any interest in the asset in question. They also apply to the disposal of an interest in an asset created by the disposal itself, for example where a new lease is granted (TCGA 1992, s. 21).

Apportionment of expenditure

The incidental expenses incurred in making a part disposal are allowed in full. However, any costs incurred in the acquisition or improvement of the property are apportioned between the part disposed of and the part retained, and only those attributed to the part disposed of may be deducted in computing the chargeable gain arising from that part disposal.

The apportionment is generally made in ratio to the proceeds or value received from the part disposal and the market value of the property remaining undisposed of, under the formula $A/(A + B)$, where A is equal to the proceeds of disposal and B is the market value of the retained interest. For this purpose the proceeds of disposal are taken as the gross proceeds, before any deduction in respect of the incidental costs of disposal.

The formula is thus:

$$\frac{\text{Gross proceeds}}{\text{Gross proceeds} + \text{Market value of retained interest}}$$

No apportionment is required in respect of any item of expenditure incurred on the acquisition or improvement of the asset, if it is wholly attributed to the part disposed of or to the part retained.

Where there is a disposal of an identifiable part of a property, as opposed to an interest in a property, it may be possible to ascertain separately the costs attributable to the part disposed of and the part retained and to compute the gain on the basis that the part disposed of is a separate asset (Statement of Practice D1). This treatment cannot apply in the case of a disposal of an interest in a property where some other interest in the same property is retained.

Any expenditure allowed against the proceeds of the part disposal is excluded from further deduction in respect of any subsequent disposal of the retained part (TCGA 1992, s. 42).

Example 8.8

Ralph Woodhouse acquires a freehold factory, together with several out-buildings, at a cost of £300,000 for use in his trade. He later sells one of the larger outbuildings for a consideration of £40,000, involving costs of disposal of £1,000. The cost of acquisition attributable to the building sold cannot be ascertained separately, but the current value of the retained freehold is agreed at £360,000. The cost of disposal however, relates wholly to the part disposal. The capital gains computation in respect of the part disposal, ignoring the indexation allowance and taper relief, proceeds as follows:

Consideration for disposal	£40,000
Less: Incidental costs of disposal	£ 1,000
Net proceeds	£39,000
Less: Proportion of total costs of acquisition –	

$$\text{Total cost} \times \frac{\text{Gross proceeds}}{\text{Gross proceeds} + \text{Value retained}}$$

$= £300,000 \times \dfrac{£40,000}{£40,000 + £360,000} =$	£30,000
Chargeable gain	£9,000

The cost attributable to the factory, etc. to be offset in the computation of any gain arising from the subsequent disposal of the retained interest is reduced to £270,000 (£300,000 less £30,000 allowed as above).

Leases

Special considerations apply to the receipt of a premium. These are considered separately at **8.4.2** below. The granting of a lease gives rise to a part disposal even though no premium is received. The part disposal would thus give rise to a loss as the incidental expenses of making the part disposal are allowed in full.

No gain/no loss disposals

The apportionment of costs on the above basis is carried out before considering whether the part disposal falls within any of the no gain/no loss situations (for example transfers between husband and wife or within a 75%+ group of companies), so that the expenditure apportioned to the part disposed of follows the part disposal to the transferee, and reduces the allowable costs in respect of any subsequent disposal of the retained property by the transferor (TCGA 1992, s. 42(5)).

Compulsory purchases

Where, under a compulsory purchase, some additional payment is made in compensation for the severance of the land compulsorily acquired, ie for the diminution in value of the land retained, the disposal under the compulsory purchase is also treated as the part disposal of the retained land, so that a proportion of the allowable costs in respect of that land can be offset against the proceeds of disposal, together with the costs attributable to the land actually disposed of (TCGA 1992, s. 245(2)). This does not apply, however, where there is a claim for rollover relief on land compulsorily acquired under TCGA 1992, s. 247 (see **8.5.5**).

Small part disposals of land

Certain part disposals, where the consideration received does not exceed one-fifth of the value of the property in question, qualify for relief as explained at **8.5.4** (TCGA 1992, s. 242).

Indexation allowance

Any indexation allowance is applied to the part disposed of, but not (until its subsequent disposal) to the part retained (see **8.3.6**).

Rebasing of capital gains

Where an asset held on 31 March 1982 is the subject of a part disposal the 31 March 1982 market value is apportioned between the part disposed of and the part retained in the same way as the acquisition cost.

8.4.2 Part disposals – premiums, etc.

Premiums

Where a premium is required under the terms of a lease granted out of an interest in property, the premium is dealt with as the consideration for a part disposal for capital gains purposes. Subject to the special points mentioned below, the chargeable gain arising on the part disposal is otherwise computed as with any other part disposal except that the market value of the retained interest in the property, required in order to apportion the allowable deductions, is established by taking into account the landlord's rights to receive the rents provided for under that lease, but not the right to receive the premium (TCGA 1992, Sch. 8, Para. 2). For these purposes, a 'premium' is any sum paid by a tenant to his landlord, in his capacity as landlord, in consideration for the grant of a lease. For example, where the taxpayer agreed to grant a lease in consideration of the prospective tenant meeting his past and future costs of developing the site to be let, the total amount so received fell to be taxed as a premium (*Clarke v United Real (Moorgate)* (1988) BTC 49).

Other capital sums

A part disposal also arises for capital gains purposes where a tenant becomes liable to pay any capital sum under the terms of his lease in lieu of rent, or for the surrender of the lease, or where a capital sum becomes payable by the tenant as consideration for the variation or waiver of the terms of the lease. In such circumstances the lease is deemed to have required the payment of a premium of an amount equal to the capital sum (TCGA 1992, Sch. 8, Paras. 3(2) and (3)).

Part disposals out of short leases

Special provisions apply to the allocation of costs of acquisition and expenditure on improvements in respect of a part disposal out of a leasehold interest in land where the remaining term of the lease is less than 50 years. These rules are dealt with at **8.4.4**, including further provisions relating to the receipt of a premium on the grant of a sub-lease out of a short leasehold interest.

Premiums taxed as rental income

Where a premium or similar sum is received in respect of a lease granted for a period not exceeding 50 years, a proportion of that sum is taxable as rental income under the provisions explained in **Chapter 2**. Where an amount is taxed as rental income on this basis, including a sale and re-conveyance treated as a deemed premium (under ICTA 1988, s. 36), the amount assessed as rental income is deducted from the consideration received in calculating the chargeable gain arising on the part disposal. However, in arriving at the proportion of allowable deductions to be brought into the part disposal computation under the formula referred to at **8.4.1**, A in the numerator excludes that part of premium received that is assessed as rental income, whereas A in the denominator includes the full premium (TCGA 1992, Sch.8, Para. 5(1) and (3)). The formula is thus revised to –

$$\frac{\text{Cost} \times \text{Premium less amount assessed as rental increase}}{\text{Full premium} + \text{Value retained}}$$

Example 8.9

In 1999 Tom Ditchfield acquired a freehold property at a cost of £120,000. In 2004 he grants a lease of the property for a term of 31 years at a premium of £40,000. He is assessed to income tax on £16,000 as if it were rental income. The value of his reversionary interest in the property after the grant of the lease is established as £90,000. His capital gain arising on the part disposal (before taper relief) is calculated as follows:

Premium received	£40,000
Less: Taxed as rental income	16,000
Net proceeds	£24,000

Allowable costs –

$$\text{Cost} \times \frac{\text{Premium less assessed as rental income}}{\text{Full premium} + \text{Value retained}}$$

$$£120,000 \times \frac{£24,000}{£40,000 + £90,000} \qquad = \qquad 22,154$$

Chargeable gain	£1,846

Tenant's improvements

In addition a landlord is also assessable on a proportion of any value added to his reversionary interest in respect of improvements carried out by his tenant under the terms of a lease of not more than 50 years as if it were rental income (as explained in **Chapter 2**). Whilst such improvements are treated as a premium received by the landlord for the purposes of those provisions, there is no similar treatment for capital gains purposes, and the deemed premium does not give rise to a part disposal under the capital gains legislation. Therefore, in order to give the landlord some equivalent capital gains relief in respect of the amount assessed as income, provision is made for the deduction of that amount in computing the chargeable gain arising on a subsequent disposal of his retained interest – as noted at **8.3.5** (TCGA 1992, Sch. 8, Para. 7).

Leases not at arm's length

Where the landlord grants a lease at an under-value in circumstances where, if the same terms were provided in an arm's length lease, the landlord could command a premium (or a larger premium), he is treated as making a part disposal equivalent to the premium that he could charge. In the same way, in the case of a lease not at arm's length where the terms of that lease are varied or waived without adequate consideration, a part disposal arises on the basis of the market value of the consideration for the variation or waiver that the landlord might otherwise obtain (TCGA 1992, s.17 and Sch.8, Para. 3(7)).

As seen in **Chapter 2**, the tenant may be subject to income tax on a subsequent assignment of his leasehold interest in respect of the premium forgone by his landlord in such circumstances. As far as the tenant is concerned, such an assignment is also a disposal for capital gains purposes. However, the amount charged to tax as income in his own hands is not excluded from the capital gains computation in this particular case. On the other hand, since the landlord's part disposal is adjusted to market value under the normal rule, so is the tenant's acquisition cost, with the result that any actual costs of acquisition are increased by the amount of premium deemed to be received by the landlord, but subject to amortisation under the rules explained at **8.4.4** (TCGA 1992, s. 17 and Sch. 8, Para. 6(2), see also **8.2.6**).

Thus for income purposes the premium forgone is assessed on the tenant in the event that he assigns his lease for a capital sum, but for capital gains purposes it is assessed on the landlord at the time the lease was granted. Note the position of a third party who acquires the leasehold interest from the original tenant. Whilst he may be assessed for income purposes also, he is denied the relief normally given for proceeds taxed as income and is given no corresponding increase in acquisition costs, as the following example illustrates.

Example 8.10

James Moore grants a 21 lease to his sister Janet Moore, and having regard to the terms of the lease, he might otherwise have charged a premium of £20,000 but in fact charges none. Eight years later Janet Moore assigns the lease on an arm's length basis to Brian Wall for the sum of £15,000. Two years later Brian Wall sells the lease for £25,000, again at arm's length.

For capital gains tax purposes James Moore is treated as making a part disposal for a notional consideration equal to the amount of premium forgone of £20,000. Correspondingly Janet Moore is treated as paying a premium of £20,000. When she subsequently assigns her lease, Janet Moore's capital gains tax position is calculated as follows –

Proceeds of disposal		£15,000
Cost of acquisition (taken as premium that would have been paid if the lease was granted at arm's length)	£20,000	

Less: Amortisation (see **8.4.4**) –

$$\times \frac{P(1) - P(3)}{P(1)}$$

$$\times \frac{72.770 - 53.191}{72.770}$$

	= 5,381	14,619
Chargeable gain		£381

(Remembering also that she suffers income tax, as explained at **2.6** – but with no relief against the capital gains tax liability.)

Brian Wall, as the innocent third party, seems to suffer the most. His capital gain is calculated as follows:

Proceeds of disposal		£25,000
Cost of acquisition		
Less: Amortisation (see **8.4.4**) –	£15,000	

$$\times \frac{P(1) - P(3)}{P(1)}$$

$$\times \frac{53.191 - 46.695}{53.191}$$

	= 1,832	13,168
Chargeable gain		£11,832

He thus suffers tax on a capital gain of £11,832 (whilst his actual profit is only £10,000), and in addition pays income tax on a deemed premium as explained at **2.6**.

Date of deemed disposal

Where a premium is paid otherwise than in respect of the surrender of a lease, both the landlord and the tenant are treated as if the premium was paid as consideration, or additional consideration, for the lease due at the time the lease was granted, requiring a computation or re-computation of the chargeable gain arising on the part disposal by the landlord at that time (TCGA 1992, Sch. 8, Para. 3(4)).

In a case involving the payment of a premium in respect of the surrender of a lease, no computation or re-computation is required at the time the lease was granted. Instead the transaction is treated as a separate part disposal by the landlord of his interest in the property (TCGA 1992, Sch.8, Para. 3(6)).

8.4.3 Wasting assets – general

Depreciating values

Where an asset has a limited useful life, it tends to have a diminishing value in real terms, albeit that the diminishing value in monetary terms may be offset by inflation or other market influences. Thus if such a depreciating asset is disposed of towards the end of its useful life, the proceeds of disposal may well be considerably lower than its original cost of acquisition.

In order to avoid a virtually automatic allowable loss on the disposal of such assets towards the end of their useful life, provisions were incorporated into the capital gains legislation to ensure that the allowable costs of acquisition and improvement are written off in some appropriate manner over the life of the asset. Such assets are termed wasting assets and, apart from the special case of leasehold interest in property dealt with separately below, the allowable costs in respect of such assets are written off over the life of the asset.

Wasting assets

For this purpose a wasting asset is taken as any asset that has a predictable life of not more than 50 years. The predictable life of an asset is based on the position as known or ascertainable at the time it was acquired.

Freehold land is never regarded as a wasting asset for this purpose, whatever the nature of the building or works thereon (TCGA 1992, s. 44(1) and (3)).

Acquisition costs

The acquisition cost of a wasting asset, less the amount of any residual scrap value of that asset, is amortised and written off evenly on a day to day basis from the date of acquisition to the end of its predictable life, so as to reduce the expenditure allowed in any capital gains computation arising from the disposal of the asset. For this purpose the residual scrap value of a wasting asset is taken as the predictable value of the asset at the end of its predictable life, as ascertained at acquisition.

This straight line amortisation is overridden in the case of leases (see **8.4.4**).

Expenditure on improvements

In the same way any cost of improvement, less the enhancement to the residual or scrap value of that asset, is written off over the period from the date when the improvement is first reflected in the value of the asset to the end of its predictable life, evenly on a day to day basis, so as to reduce the expenditure allowed in the capital gains computation.

Again, this straight line amortisation is overridden in the case of leases (see **8.4.4**).

The formulae

For this purpose the acquisition cost, less the residual or scrap value, is reduced by $\dfrac{T(1)}{L}$ of the expenditure incurred on acquiring the asset.

Similarly any cost of improvement is reduced by $\dfrac{T(2)}{L - [T(1) - T(2)]}$ of the expenditure.

Where L is the predictable life of the asset at the time it was acquired, $T(1)$ is the period between the date of acquisition and disposal, and $T(2)$ is the period between the time when the improvement expenditure was first reflected in the value of the asset and the date of disposal (TCGA 1992, ss. 44(2) and 46).

Indexation allowance

Any indexation allowance is applied to the amortised cost of a wasting asset, not to the actual expenditure.

Capital allowances

Assets are not regarded as wasting assets for this purpose if:

- they are used for the purposes of a trade, profession or vocation (TCGA 1992, s. 47(1)(*a*));
- capital allowances have been, or could have been, claimed under the provisions explained in **Chapter 5** (TCGA 1992, s. 47(1)(*b*)), and

- all the conditions leading to the making of a capital allowance continue to be satisfied when the assets are disposed of (see *Burman v Westminster Press Ltd* (1987) BTC 516).

If the asset is used partly for the purposes of a trade, profession or vocation and partly for some other purpose, the expenditure thereon and proceeds of sale are apportioned as between, and in ratio to, the part qualifying for capital allowances and the part not. The provisions for amortising the allowable expenditure then only apply to that part not qualifying for capital allowances. The expenditure in respect of the qualifying part of the asset is allowed in full, with no amortisation (TCGA 1992, s. 47(2)).

Any other assets qualifying for capital allowances, whether used for the purposes of a trade carried on by the owner, or let to others, are similarly treated on the normal basis, rather than as wasting assets.

There may be some restriction in any allowable loss arising from the disposal of an asset qualifying for capital allowances.

8.4.4 Wasting assets – leasehold interests

General

A leasehold interest in property is treated as a wasting asset if at the time of its disposal it has an unexpired term of not more than 50 years. This provision applies regardless as to whether the lease was originally granted for a longer period, or if it had more than 50 years to run at the time it was acquired; one only looks at the outstanding term of the lease at the date of disposal. For these purposes a leasehold interest includes an underlease, sub-lease, tenancy, licence and an agreement for such a lease, etc. (TCGA 1992, Sch. 8, Para. 10(1)).

However, in place of the straight line basis for amortising allowable deductions used in the case of other wasting assets, a special 'curved line' basis is applied to such leasehold interests.

Term of lease

A leasehold interest in property only becomes a wasting asset on this basis at such time as its unexpired term becomes equal to or less than 50 years and special rules apply to ascertain the unexpired term (TCGA 1992, Sch. 8, Para. 1(1)).

For this purpose the end of the term of a lease is generally ascertained by reference to the facts known or obtainable at the time the lease is granted, but in any event is taken as ending on the earliest of the following dates:

- If the landlord can give notice to terminate the lease, the earliest date on which he can determine the lease.
- If the terms of the lease (for example in respect of forfeiture, etc.) or other circumstances render it unlikely that the lease will carry on beyond a date falling before the expiration of the term of the lease, not later than that date. This would particularly apply to rental increases or other onerous obligations imposed on the tenant under the terms of the lease, where the tenant has powers to give notice to determine, so that it is unlikely that the lease will be continued beyond that date.
- If the terms of the lease allow the tenant to extend the lease, the lease is taken as continuing for as long as it may be extended by the tenant, subject to any powers of the landlord to determine the lease as above (TCGA 1992, Sch. 8, Paras. 8 and 9(1)). In the case of *Lewis v Walters* [1992] BTC 76 it was held that the right to extend a lease under the Leasehold Reform Act 1967 was not a term of the lease, and even if it was then it was not a provision for the extension of the lease beyond a given date but, as in *Bayley v Rogers* (1980) (see below), the right to a new lease.

Where, upon the expiry of his lease, a tenant is able to obtain a new lease under the provisions of the Landlord and Tenant Act 1954, the new lease is to be treated as a separate asset (*Bayley v Rogers* (1980) 53 TC 420).

Existing sub-leases at acquisition

In certain circumstances a tenant may acquire a leasehold interest in property that is subject to a sub-lease, and pay a lower price for that leasehold interest than its value at the end of the sub-lease. Where the rent receivable under the sub-lease is less than a full rack rent and the reversionary value of the leasehold interest at the end of the term of the sub-lease (as ascertained at the time of the acquisition of the leasehold interest) is greater than the cost of acquisition of that lease, the leasehold interest is not in fact a wasting asset at all and is not treated as such until the end of that sub-lease (TCGA 1992, Sch. 8, Para. 1(2)).

Example 8.11

Rowena Rivers buys a leasehold interest in a property that is subject to a sub-lease at less than the rack rent at the time, in order to obtain vacant possession of the property at the end of that sub-lease so that she can then re-let the property at its full rack rent. Whilst the sub-lease continues she cannot obtain vacant possession nor does she receive a proper commercial return on the cost of her leasehold interest, so that she may well pay less than the anticipated value at the end of that sub-lease. In the meantime her leasehold interest will in fact increase in value, as the outstanding occupancy by the uneconomic sub-tenant decreases. Therefore it is not in fact a wasting asset and so is not treated as such.

This is however a specific provision, and not a general principle. Thus if the leasehold interest has an increasing value for other reasons, for example as a result of inflation or market influences, it is nonetheless still regarded as a wasting asset if the term of the leasehold interest is less than 50 years.

Acquisition of superior interests

Where a tenant acquires a superior interest in the property concerned, his lease merges with that superior interest and from that time onwards one looks at the superior interest to see whether the wasting asset rules apply.

Example 8.12

Alan Shepherd acquires a leasehold interest in a property with an unexpired term of 40 years at a cost of £75,000. Five years later he acquires the freehold reversion from his landlord. The two interests merge and thenceforth are no longer regarded as a wasting asset. His original expenditure on the acquisition of the leasehold still falls to be amortised as set out below for the first five years of his ownership of that interest (ie for five years out of 40), but thereafter the reduced cost is added to the cost of acquiring the freehold and no further amortisation is required.

Sale and leaseback

In the same way, where the owner of a freehold sells that freehold subject to a leaseback at less than a rack rent, the transaction is regarded as a part disposal, and part of the original cost of the freehold is allocated to his retained leasehold interest. In so far as the leasehold interest has an outstanding term of 50 years or less at the time of any subsequent disposal, the expenditure allocated thereto is amortised as explained below, even though it was incurred on the acquisition of a freehold in the first instance.

Amortisation of costs

Allowable expenditure on the acquisition or improvement of a leasehold interest in property is amortised on a 'curved line' basis, rather than the straight line basis used for other wasting assets. The curved line itself covers a period of 50 years. In fact the curved line is reduced to a table of figures, called 'percentages' in the legislation. The amortisation of expenditure is then calculated on a formula basis, using these percentages. In the case of expenditure on acquisition, the amortisation is taken as

$$\frac{P(1) - P(3)}{P(1)} \text{ of the acquisition cost.}$$

In the case of improvement expenditure, costs are reduced by

$$\frac{P(2) - P(3)}{P(2)} \text{ of the cost of improvement.}$$

The percentages are taken from Table 8.1 set out below, where $P(1)$ is the percentage figure appropriate to the outstanding term of the lease at the time of its acquisition; $P(2)$ is the percentage figure appropriate to the outstanding term of the lease at the time the cost of improvement is first reflected in the value of the leasehold interest; and $P(3)$ is the percentage figure appropriate to the outstanding term of the lease at the time of its disposal. Each occasion of improvement must be dealt with separately (TCGA 1992, Sch. 8, Para. 1(3) and (4)).

Table 8.1

Term of lease outstanding (in years)	Appropriate percentage	Term of lease outstanding (in years)	Appropriate percentage
50 or more	100.000	25	81.100
49	99.657	24	79.622
48	99.289	23	78.055
47	98.902	22	76.399
46	98.490	21	74.635
45	98.059	20	72.770
44	97.595	19	70.791
43	97.107	18	68.697
42	96.593	17	66.470
41	96.041	16	64.116
40	95.457	15	61.617
39	94.842	14	58.971
38	94.189	13	56.167
37	93.497	12	53.191
36	92.761	11	50.038
35	91.981	10	46.695
34	91.156	9	43.154
33	90.280	8	39.399
32	89.354	7	35.414
31	88.371	6	31.195
30	87.330	5	26.722
29	86.226	4	21.983
28	85.053	3	16.959
27	83.816	2	11.629
26	82.496	1	5.983
		0	0.000

If the unexpired term of the lease is not an exact number of years, one takes the appropriate percentage for the number of whole years of that term and adds to it one-twelfth of the difference between that percentage figure and the next highest percentage figure for each additional month. An odd 14 days or more is treated as equal to a whole month for this purpose and 13 days or less are ignored altogether (TCGA 1992, Sch. 8, Para.1).

Thus the annual reduction is fairly small in the case of a lease where there is more than 20 years to run at the date of disposal, but this increases sharply as the term of lease shortens. For example, if a 15-year lease is acquired and subsequently disposed of ten years later, when there is only five years to run, the cost of acquisition is reduced by

$$\frac{61.617 - 26.722}{61.617}$$

so that nearly 57 per cent of the original expenditure is written off by way of amortisation and disallowed, and only a little over 43 per cent can be deducted in the capital gains computation on the disposal of that lease.

Where the lease has an outstanding term of more than 50 years at the time of its acquisition, $P(1)$ in the above formula will be taken as 100.000. If therefore one is considering a 99-year lease, disposed of by the original grantee at a time when it only has 45 years to run (ie after 54 years of ownership), the allowable expenditure in respect of acquisition is reduced by

$$\frac{100.000 - 98.059}{100.000}$$

giving an amortisation figure equal to only 1.941 per cent of that original cost (TCGA 1992, Sch. 8, Para. 1(5)).

If a lease is assigned on say 31 March 2000 and the term of that lease expires on 24 June 2004, the lease is treated as having an outstanding term of four years and three months (the period of 24 days being treated as a whole month). $P(3)$ is then taken as 23.168, being 21.983 (as appropriate for four years) plus $3/12 \times 4.739$ (the difference between that and the next highest figure, ie $26.722 - 21.983$).

Example 8.13

Dennis Hylands purchases a lease by assignment for a consideration of £50,000. The original lease had been granted for a term of 70 years, but at the time of assignment only had 55 years left unexpired. Twenty-three years later he sells the lease for £70,000 (when the lease has only 32 years to run). Ignoring costs, indexation and taper relief, his chargeable gain is computed as follows –

Proceeds of disposal		£70,000
Cost of acquisition	£50,000	
Less: Amortisation –		

$$\text{Cost} \times \frac{P(1) - P(3)^*}{P(1)}$$

$£50,000 \times \dfrac{100.000 - 89.354}{100.000} =$	£ 5,323	
Allowable cost		£44,677
Chargeable gain		£25,323

* $P(1)$ is percentage for more than 50 years; $P(3)$ is percentage for 32 years.

Premiums paid by sub-tenants

Where a sub-tenant pays a premium on the grant of a lease (see **8.4.2**), that premium is of course regarded as the acquisition cost of his sub-lease for the above purposes. In addition certain capital sums paid by the sub-tenant to his immediate landlord are regarded as a deemed premium on a part disposal by that landlord when paid in lieu of rent or for the variation or waiver of the terms of the lease (but not in respect of the surrender of a lease) as explained above. Where the landlord is himself a tenant under a lease of not more than 50 years, the capital sum paid by the sub-tenant is amortised over the period in respect of which it was paid in computing the capital gains position of the sub-tenant on any disposal of his interest in the property. In the case of a payment for a variation or waiver of the terms of a lease, the payment is amortised over the period during which it has effect (TCGA 1992, Sch.8, Para. 3(2), (3) and (5)).

Example 8.14

If in the previous example Dennis Hylands pays a further sum of £15,000 to his own landlord ten years after acquisition (when the lease had only 45 years to run) in return for the landlord agreeing to reduce rents over the next 25 years, the allowable amount in respect of this expenditure is calculated by amortising it over the 25-year period, as follows –

Proceeds of disposal			£70,000
Allowable cost of acquisition (amortised as before)		£44,677	
Cost of improvement	£15,000		
Less: Amortisation –			

$$\text{Cost} \times \frac{P(2) - P(3)^*}{P(2)}$$

$£15,000 \times \dfrac{81.100 - 53.191}{81.100} =$	£5,162	£9,838	
Total allowable costs			£54,515
Chargeable gain (before indexation and taper relief)			£15,485

* $P(2)$ is percentage for 25 years and $P(3)$ is percentage for 12 years – ie the remaining period over which the lower rent is payable at the time of sale.

Premiums received by intermediate landlords

Special provisions apply to the allocation of any costs of acquisition and improvements for a part disposal consisting of the receipt of a premium on the grant of a lease out of a leasehold interest, where that leasehold interest itself has an unexpired term at the date of the part disposal of not more than 50 years.

The allocation is achieved by allowing the offset of expenditure equal to the amount of amortisation of the total expenditure that would be written off during the subsistence of the sub-lease. This is calculated by taking a fraction of these costs of

$$\frac{P(2) - P(3)}{P(1)}$$ where $P(1)$ is the percentage figure appropriate to the period of

the main lease outstanding at the time of the expenditure (ie at acquisition or at the time any improvements are first reflected in the value of the leasehold interest); $P(2)$ is the percentage figure appropriate to the period of the main lease outstanding at the time the sub-lease is granted; and $P(3)$ is the percentage figure appropriate to the period of the main lease outstanding at the time the sub-lease comes to an end, as taken from the table above.

Where however the amount of the premium received by the intermediate landlord is less than the premium that he could have obtained if that sub-lease had been granted at the same rent that he is paying to his own superior landlord (ie normally where the rents he receives are more than the rents he pays), the allowable expenditure thus calculated as above is further reduced by reference to the fraction that the amount of the premium actually received bears to the amount of premium that could have been obtained on that basis (TCGA 1992, Sch. 8, Para. 4(1) and (2)).

If the sub-lease only relates to a part of the property in question, the expenditure is first allocated between that part and the remaining property and these provisions then apply to the amount attributed to the sub-let part (TCGA 1992, Sch. 8, Para. 4(3)).

Premiums taxed as rental income in intermediate landlord's hands

Where the intermediate landlord receives a premium, part of which is taxed as rental income in his hands under the provisions explained in **Chapter 2**, and his own leasehold interest has an outstanding term not exceeding 50 years, the amount thus taxed as income is deducted from the chargeable gain arising from the part disposal as computed as above (rather than deducted from the amount of the premium itself), but not so as to turn a gain into a loss, nor to add to an allowable loss. This provision is also extended to cover capital sums received by the intermediate landlord in lieu of rent, or for the variation or waiver of the terms of the sub-lease, or as consideration for the surrender of that sub-lease.

The rule also applies to the sale of a leasehold interest with a right to reconveyance or leaseback, where the proceeds of sale are also treated as rental income under the provisions explained at **5.2.1** (TCGA 1992, Sch. 8, Para. 5(2) and (3)).

It does not however apply to a deemed premium resulting from improvements carried out by the sub-tenant, where the normal rule applies to treat such enhancement as if it were expenditure on improvements incurred by the intermediate landlord himself, as noted at **8.3.5**. Such an amount would therefore be amortised as with any other expenditure, but from the date such improvements are first reflected in his own interest in the property (which might be the date the tenant undertakes to carry out the improvements), so that only restricted relief is available.

Example 8.15

Gerald Rix purchases an existing lease that has an outstanding term of 40 years, at a cost of £90,000. He sub-lets the property five years later for a period of 15 years charging a premium of £40,000. Of this amount, £28,000 is taxable as rental income in his hands (see **2.6**).

Assuming that he could have charged a premium of £50,000 if he had let the property for a rent equal to the rent he pays under his own lease, the chargeable gain arising under the part disposal on the grant of the sub-lease is calculated as follows:

Premium received		£40,000
Cost of acquisition	£90,000	
Allowable cost –		

$$\text{Cost} \times \frac{P(2) - P(3)^*}{P(1)}$$

$$£90,000 \times \frac{91.981 - 72.770}{95.457} = \quad £18,113$$

Apportioned in ratio of premium received compared with notional premium –		

$$\frac{£18,113 \times £40,000}{£50,000} = \qquad £14.490$$

Gain	£25,510
Less: Taxed as rental income	28,800
Chargeable gain (loss ignored)	£ –

* $P(1)$ is percentage for 40 years, the term of the lease outstanding when the expenditure on acquisition was incurred; $P(2)$ is percentage for 35 years, the term of the headlease outstanding on the grant of the sub-lease; and $P(3)$ is percentage for 20 years, the term outstanding at the end of the sub-lease.

Premiums paid and taxed as income in superior landlord's hands

A further situation requiring special consideration arises in the case of an intermediate landlord who pays a premium for the grant of his leasehold interest where that lease is for a period of not more than 50 years. The superior landlord is taxed on that premium as if it were rental income, and the intermediate landlord is granted a deduction as if he pays an additional amount of rent, under the provisions explained in **Chapter 2**. Where the intermediate landlord then grants a sub-lease out of his own interest for a premium or otherwise so that it is regarded as a part disposal, he might have been in a position to realise an allowable loss without actually incurring any loss. To overcome this possibility, the legislation provides that any allowable loss arising on such a transaction is reduced by the total amount of additional rents deemed to be paid by him in respect of the premium assessed as rental income in the superior landlord's hands. This rule only operates to restrict an allowable loss, and may not convert a loss into a chargeable gain, or increase any gain (TCGA 1992, Sch. 8, Para. 6(1)).

Summary for premiums received by intermediate landlords

Thus the procedure relating to premiums received by intermediate landlords may be summarised as follows:

(a) Bring in the full premium received as the proceeds of disposal, with no deduction for any amount taxed as rental income.

(b) If the premium relates to only part of the property, allocate the total costs involved between that part and the part unaffected by the sub-lease.

(c) Calculate the proportion of costs available under the formula
$$\frac{P(2) - P(3)}{P(1)}$$

(d) Reduce (c) if the premium is less than that obtainable if the sub-lease were granted at the same rent as the headlease.

(e) Deduct (d) from (a) to arrive at the basic gain.

(f) If (e) gives rise to a loss, reduce the loss by the total of any additional 'rents' allowed to the taxpayer in respect of a premium paid to his own landlord, but not so as to turn the loss into a profit.

(g) If (e) gives rise to a gain, deduct the amount of premium assessed as rental income, but not so as to turn the gain into a loss.

Indexation allowance

Any indexation allowance is calculated on the amortised cost, not on the actual expenditure – see **8.3.6**.

Capital allowances

As in the case of other wasting assets, where the leasehold interest in a property qualifies for capital allowances, for example where the leasehold interest is the qualifying interest in an industrial building under the provisions explained in **Chapter 5**, that leasehold interest is not regarded as a wasting asset for this purpose (TCGA 1992, s. 47 and Sch. 8, Para. 1(6)).

8.4.5 Options (and forfeited deposits)

Special rules apply to options for capital gains purposes. In general the grant of an option is regarded as a separate disposal or part disposal and not the part disposal of the underlying asset, unless it is treated as merged with a larger transaction under the rules explained below.

For this purpose an option to grant a lease, or for any other transaction which is not a sale, is also included (TCGA 1992, s. 144(6)).

Grantors

Looking at the position from the grantor's point of view, if he agrees to sell an asset that he does not actually own, or he agrees to purchase an asset and because the option is abandoned he never becomes the owner of that asset, the transaction is nonetheless regarded as the creation and disposal of the option for capital gains purposes (TCGA 1992, s. 144(1)).

If the option is exercised, it is treated as a single transaction with any subsequent transaction fulfilling the option. Accordingly the consideration received for the option is added to the proceeds of sale, in a case where the grantee has an option to buy; or deducted from the costs of acquisition, in a case where the grantee has an option to sell (TCGA 1992, s. 144(2)).

Grantees

As far as the grantee is concerned, he may either abandon the option, sell it or otherwise dispose of it, or exercise it.

Options abandoned
In the case of the abandonment of an option, the normal rule is that the abandonment is not regarded as a disposal for capital gains purposes, so that no allowable loss can be claimed. If however the option is for the acquisition of assets intended for use in a trade, the abandonment of the option is treated as a disposal. In such circumstances, the option is not treated as a wasting asset, and there is no amortisation of the expenditure on its acquisition. If therefore an option to acquire trading premises is abandoned for no consideration, it gives rise to an allowable loss equal to the full price paid for the option (TCGA 1992, ss. 144(4) and 146).

Consideration received for relinquishing rights under an option is treated for capital gains purposes as a capital sum derived from an asset and is not treated as an abandonment of an option involving no disposal, see *Golding v Kaufman* (1985) BTC 92 and *Welbeck Securities v Powlson* (1987) BTC 316.

Options sold

Where the option is assigned or otherwise disposed of, it is regarded as a disposal for capital gains purposes. In general an option is regarded as a wasting asset, so that the cost of the option has to be amortised over its life as explained at **8.4.3** (but not the rules at **8.4.4**, even if the option relates to a leasehold interest in land). Again however the special rules relating to options to acquire assets for use in a trade apply to treat the option as not being a wasting asset and the full cost is deducted in computing any chargeable gain arising from the disposal (TCGA 1992, s. 146).

Options exercised

Where the option is exercised, it is treated as a single transaction with any subsequent transaction fulfilling that option. Thus the consideration given for the option is added to the cost of acquisition, in a case where the grantee has an option to buy; or it is deducted from the proceeds of sale, in a case where the grantee has an option to sell. In such circumstances one looks at the full cost of acquiring the option, with no amortisation even if it is only exercised at the end of the option period (TCGA 1992, s. 144(3)).

Exercise before sale

Where the option price is material to the overall transaction, and some third party is to acquire the property, consideration should be given to the grantee exercising the option and re-assigning the property to the third party, rather than assigning the option to that person, to give full relief for the cost of the option.

Example 8.16

Heather Ward grants Hugh Gardner an option to acquire her freehold shop at a cost of £70,000. The consideration for the option is £6,000 and it may be exercised at any time over a three-year period. Ignoring the indexation allowance, the following effects may occur:

- If the option is abandoned and never exercised Heather Ward is charged to capital gains tax on £6,000 as the proceeds of disposal of the option (not a part disposal of the shop) and there are no allowable costs of acquisition, apart from legal etc. fees, since it is created by her.
- If the option is exercised, by Hugh Gardner or an assignee, the option price is added to the sale price an she is taxed as if she sells the shop for £76,000.
- As far as Hugh Gardner is concerned, if he abandons the option he cannot claim £6,000 as an allowable loss unless he intended to occupy the shop for the purposes of his trade.
- If he sells the option for £8,000 after two years have elapsed, he can claim a deduction for only part of his cost, as follows:

	£	£
Proceeds of disposal		8,000
Cost of acquisition	6,000	
Less: $\dfrac{T(1) \times \text{cost}}{L}$		
$\dfrac{2}{3} \times £6,000 =$	4,000	2,000
Chargeable gain		£6,000

- But again, if he intended to occupy the shop for the purposes of his trade, he can offset the full cost of the option reducing the chargeable gain to £2,000 (£8,000 – £6,000).
- Finally, if he exercises the option, his cost of acquisition of the shop for capital gains tax purposes is increased to £76,000.

Options to buy or sell

An option to buy or sell is treated as two separate options, with half the consideration being applicable to each (TCGA 1992, s. 144(5)).

Forfeited deposits

A forfeited deposit of purchase money is similarly treated as if it were the abandonment of an option for this purpose (TCGA 1992, s. 144(7)).

Indexation allowance

The indexation allowance is available in respect of expenditure both upon the option and upon the acquisition of the asset upon exercising the option. Where the option is sold and the cost is amortised, the indexation allowance is based on the amortised cost.

Example 8.17

In March 2004 Bingham Developments Ltd acquires an option to buy a site, paying £1,000. In October 2004 it exercises the option and acquires the site for £50,000.

When the site is sold the indexation allowance will be calculated on the £1,000 paid for the option with effect from March 2004 and on the £50,000 paid for the site with effect from October 2004.

Taper relief

Where an asset is acquired on the exercise of an option taper relief runs only from the date of exercise, not from the date the option was granted (TCGA 1992, Sch. A1, Para. 13).

8.4.6 Reverse premiums

Grant of lease

Where a reverse premium is payable by the developer of a property to secure a desirable tenant, that premium is deductible in computing the Schedule D Case I profit which arises when the development is sold. If such a premium is payable on a property held as an investment, it will normally be regarded as enhancement expenditure falling within TCGA 1992, s. 38(1)(b), Whether it is reflected in the state or nature of the asset on any subsequent disposal depends on whether the lease is still current at the time of the disposal (see *Capital Gains Tax Manual,* paragraphs CG 78050, 78051).

As far as the recipient is concerned, the premium is normally taxable as income (FA 1999, Sch. 6; see **Chapter 2**). The VAT treatment is dealt with in **Chapter 11**.

However, the sum may be payable in respect of some other asset. For example, the tenant may have surrendered an old lease (whether of the same premises or some other premises), prior to taking the new lease. If the payment can be shown to relate to the surrender of the old lease, then it will give rise to a chargeable gain on the disposal of that lease.

Assignment of lease

Where the lessee, as assignor, pays a premium to the assignee for taking over the liabilities under the lease, such a payment is normally a capital sum, so it is not allowable in computing the assignor's business profits. Further, the payment does not, in the Revenue's view, enhance the value of the asset. Therefore, it is not deductible in computing any allowable loss on disposal of the lease (*Capital Gains Tax Manual*, paragraph CG 71264). The payment will usually be taxable as income in the hands of the recipient.

Surrender of lease

Where the lessee pays the landlord a premium to surrender a lease, the position is that:

(a) the sum is not an allowable expense of the lessee's business, being a capital sum;

(b) the sum is not allowable as enhancement expenditure under TCGA 1992, s. 38(1)(b), since it does not enhance the value of the asset,

(c) the landlord has derived a capital sum from his superior interest and that gives rise to a part disposal,

(*Capital Gains Tax Manual*, paragraphs CG 71264, 71280). As regards (c), part of the lump sum may be taxed as income under Schedule A, as explained at **2.6**. Such part is excluded from the part disposal consideration under TCGA 1992, s. 37.

8.5   Exemptions and reliefs generally

8.5.1   Introduction

There are numerous exemptions and reliefs available for capital gains purposes. The main ones that relate to tax on property taxpayers are summarised below.

Exempt assets

A disposal of the only or main residence of the person making the disposal is exempt (see **8.7.7**).

Exempt persons

The main exemptions are for charities and approved pension funds. It is important to note, however, that the exemption does not extend to trading profits, but only to investment income and capital gains.

Exempt transactions

The main exemptions are for:

- transfers on death (see **8.7.4**);
- gifts to charities (see **8.5.8**);
- gifts of works of art (see **8.7.10**),
- disposals of substantial shareholdings (see **8.6.7**).

Rollover and holdover reliefs

Some transactions may give rise to a deferment of the capital gains charge. The main examples are:

- the disposal of a business to a company in exchange for shares (see **8.7.9**);
- the replacement of business assets (see **8.5.2**),
- a gift of business assets (see **8.7.8**).

8.5.2 Replacement of business assets

A measure of relief is given in the case of a business asset, where the proceeds of disposal are applied in acquiring another asset for business use. The relief is generally referred to as rollover relief. Briefly the provisions allow a chargeable gain arising on the disposal of the first asset to be deferred until a subsequent disposal of the second asset.

Qualifying assets

The relief is available in respect of land and buildings occupied and used for the purposes of the trade, unless held as trading stock, as well as fixed plant and machinery, ships, aircraft, hovercraft, satellites and spacecraft. Goodwill and fish and agricultural quotas are also qualifying assets, except that companies instead obtain a similar rollover relief under the special rules applying to the taxation of intangible fixed assets.

It should be noted that the term 'fixed' applies to machinery (as well as plant). Moveable machinery is excluded (*Williams v Evans* (1982) BTC 155). It is understood that the Inland Revenue treats plant, which is static, or heavy, or forming part of a major new project, as 'fixed'. There is no requirement that these assets be situated in the UK (TCGA 1992, ss. 155 and 156).

The land must actually be both occupied and used for the purposes of the trade, and a mere intention to use it for such purposes is not sufficient (*Temperley v Visibell* (1974) 49 TC 129).

However, a gain arising from the sale of farmland could not be rolled over onto the cost of building two houses for the occupation of the taxpayer's sons who were partners in the farming partnership. Whilst the partnership required the sons to work full time on the farm, and the houses enabled them to work more efficiently, nevertheless the houses were not *occupied* by the partnership for the purposes of its trade since there was no requirement that the partners live there (*Anderton v Lamb* (1981) 55 TC 1).

Reinvestment of proceeds

Where the whole of the net proceeds of disposal of qualifying assets that were used solely throughout ownership for the purposes of the trade are reinvested in acquiring other qualifying assets for use in the same trade, the person making the disposal may claim that the proceeds are reduced to such an amount as gives rise to no gain/no loss on the disposal. The reference to 'assets' does not, however, prevent a claim from being made in respect of a single asset, even where more than one asset is disposed of on a single occasion. The claim needs to be made within six years of the end of the period in which the disposal takes place (corporation tax) or within five years from the 31 January following the end of the tax year in which the disposal occurred (capital gains tax). Provisional claims may be made where the taxpayer intends to reinvest the proceeds but has not actually done so by the time the tax otherwise due becomes payable. Provisional claims can be withdrawn or superceded by actual claims. Otherwise they lapse two years before the time limit of an actual claim expires (TCGA 1992, s. 153A).

When a claim is made the cost of the new assets acquired is reduced by the amount of chargeable gain that otherwise would be assessed on the earlier disposal in calculating a chargeable gain arising from a subsequent disposal of those new assets. For this purpose the net proceeds of disposal are taken after deducting any incidental costs of sale, etc. and the cost of acquiring new assets includes any incidental costs of acquisition (TCGA 1992, s. 152(1) and (2)).

The taxpayer does not have to keep the actual proceeds of sale separate, nor specifically to reinvest the actual proceeds. It is sufficient simply to show that a corresponding amount is reinvested. The proceeds may be in non-cash form such as the issue of shares, and provision is made for the relief to be granted in full even if part or all of the proceeds are notional, as on a gift (TCGA 1992, s. 152(10)). There has to be a disposal and this may include a notional disposal provided the legislation does not treat the asset as having been sold

341

and immediately re-acquired for the same consideration. Relief can therefore be claimed for a gain accruing when a capital asset is appropriated to trading stock, and a capital asset appropriated from trading stock may be treated as the 'new' asset for the purposes of rolling over a gain on an old asset (TCGA 1992 s. 161). Special rules apply to intra-group transfers (see **8.6.3**)

Similarly there is no necessity for the new asset to be a replacement of the original asset. Thus, for example, one could dispose of trade premises and apply the proceeds in the acquisition of an aircraft and still claim relief. Subject to the rules relating to groups, however, it is necessary that the person acquiring the 'new' asset is the same as the person disposing of the 'old' asset. This follows from the wording of TCGA 1992, s. 152(1), which refers to the situation where 'the consideration which a person carrying on a trade obtains from the disposal of . . . assets . . . is applied *by him* in acquiring other assets . . .'. This point was tested in the case of *Joseph Carter and Sons v Baird* [1998] BTC 3, where Park, J applied the law strictly. In that case, two UK companies owned by Mr Carter sold land. Subsequently, Mr Carter acquired a farm in France. This farm was then transferred to a French company owned by the two UK companies. Rollover relief was refused.

Strictly, the replacement asset must constitute an entirely *new* asset This requirement is relaxed by Extra-Statutory Concessions as follows:

- expenditure on improving an existing asset is treated as expenditure on a new asset (ESC D22);
- expenditure on acquiring an additional interest in an existing asset (such as buying in the freehold when the lease is already held) is also treated as expenditure on a new asset (ESC D25),
- where land is partitioned between partners on the dissolution of a partnership the land acquired by each partner is treated as a new asset (ESC D23).

The new asset has to be taken into use for the purposes of the trade at the time of acquisition. A delay between acquisition and use could frustrate the relief, though relief is given by concession if the asset is not ready for use when acquired, provided all reasonable steps are taken to make it ready for use as soon as practicable after acquisition and it is then brought into use without unnecessary delay (ESC D24). Such a situation might arise where there was a need to refurbish a property before it could be used for the purpose intended. The property must not be used for any other purposes, such as letting, before trade use commences. Relief is not available if the asset cannot be brought into use because it is already occupied by a third party paying rent, under a sub-lease (*Cambell Connolly v Barnett* [1994] BTC 12). The argument submitted on behalf of the Revenue in the *Cambell Connolly* case highlights the limitation of Revenue concessions and the narrowness of the legislative reliefs.

Partial reinvestment

If not all the proceeds are reinvested, partial relief is still available provided that the proceeds not so reinvested are less than the amount of the gain (the whole profit, not just the chargeable gain) arising on the disposal. In such circumstances the gain is treated as arising first out of the 'free' proceeds not so applied. The overall gain is reduced to an amount equal to that part of the proceeds not reinvested, and the chargeable gain calculated thereon (if say requiring a time-apportionment, in respect of an asset acquired before 6 April 1965, see **8.3.8**). The cost of the new asset is reduced by the resultant reduction in the chargeable gain (TCGA 1992, s. 153).

Time limit for reinvestment

For these purposes the new asset must be acquired under an unconditional contract entered into within 12 months before or three years after the date of disposal, unless the Inland Revenue allows a longer time, for example where it is not practicable to acquire the new asset within these time limits (s. 152(3) and (4)). The time limit may be extended where there is a firm intention to acquire the new asset(s) within the time limit but the taxpayer is prevented from doing so by circumstances outside his control.

The power to extend the time limit is a discretionary power exercisable by the Revenue. A decision by the Revenue not to extend the time limit is not subject to review by the Commissioners on appeal (*Steibelt v Paling* [1999] BTC 184 and *R (on the application of Barnett) v IR Commrs* [2004] BTC 247).

Compulsory acquisitions

Where a new town corporation or similar authority acquires property under a compulsory purchase in advance of its requirement, and then leases it back to the previous owner until required, the three-year time limit is extended to three years from the date the previous owner ceases to use the land for his trade. There must be a clear understanding that the proceeds will be used to acquire qualifying assets in due course (Inland Revenue Statement of Practice D6).

Interest in assets

The relief applies where not only an asset as such, but also an interest in an asset, is disposed of and acquired. This caters for leasehold and other interests as well as freeholds, therefore. Although at law an option to purchase an asset usually constitutes an equitable interest in the underlying asset, the grant of an option is regarded for capital gains purposes as the disposal of a separate asset unless and until the option is exercised, whereupon the grant of the option becomes part and parcel of the disposal of the underlying asset (TCGA 1992. s. 144(1) and see **8.4.5**). Despite this, rollover relief is available where an option is granted (giving rise to a part disposal of the grantor's equitable interest in the land) over land occupied as well as used for the purposes of the claimant's trade.

The same trade

Strictly the new asset should be used in the same trade. However, two or more trades carried on by the same person, whether successively or simultaneously, are treated as a single trade for this purpose (TCGA 1992, s. 152(8)). The Inland Revenue regards two trades as being carried on successively where there is an interval of up to three years between them (Inland Revenue Statement of Practice SP8/81).

An individual who sells an asset used in the trade of a partnership of which he is a partner is entitled to rollover relief. Rollover relief is also available in respect of assets owned by an individual but used in a trade carried on by his 'personal company' (TCGA 1992, s. 157). (A personal company is one in which the individual holds at least 5 per cent of the voting rights.) Both the 'old' and the 'new' assets must, however, be used in the trade of the personal company; it is not possible for someone carrying on a personal trade to sell an asset used in that trade and to reinvest the proceeds in an asset for use by his personal company.

Despite the normal rules for groups of companies (see **8.6.3**), the personal company using the replacement asset must be the same as the company which used the original one: relief would not be given if the new asset was acquired for use by a separate company in the same 75%+ group. Moreover, the company concerned must be a trading company and the one in which the individual holds the shares: the relief would not be given if the individual held the shares in a holding company and a subsidiary used the assets in its trade.

Rollover relief is not available if the assets was acquired wholly or partly for the purposes of realising a gain from the subsequent disposal of that new asset, in other words if there is some underlying non-trading motive in acquiring the new asset (TCGA 1992, s. 152(5)).

Other activities

The reference to a trade also covers the functions of a public authority, woodlands run on a commercial basis, professions, vocations and offices and employments. The activities of a trade association, not itself carrying on a trade for profit, are regarded as a trade for this purpose, if the association exists for the protection of members who are trading. An unincorporated association or other body charged to corporation tax, but not carrying on a trade, can still claim relief under these provisions as respects land and buildings occupied and used by the body concerned – as can a limited company owned by such an association or by its members (CCAB Guidance Note TR 489). The lessor of tied premises is treated as the occupier of his tied premises for the purposes of this relief (TCGA 1992, ss.156(4) and 158).

Furnished holiday lettings

Where the commercial letting of furnished holiday accommodation is treated as a trade (see **2.11.4**), rollover relief is available in respect of the accommodation in the same way as for any other qualifying assets used in a trade. Because such accommodation is not normally let throughout the year on this basis, it is necessary to import the assumption that once the accommodation qualifies as furnished holiday accommodation in any year it is used in the trade throughout the year. It cannot, however, qualify for any part of a year during which it is not available for letting (unless it is then undergoing repair) (TCGA 1992, s. 241(5)).

Partial use for a trade

Where the old asset was occupied or used only partly for the purposes of a trade, it is treated as if that part so occupied or used was a separate asset from the part not so used and relief is available in respect of the former. Similarly if the asset was acquired or used wholly for the purposes of a trade, but not throughout the whole period of ownership, the asset is again treated as two separate assets by apportioning the proceeds to reflect the time of qualifying occupation or use as a proportion of the whole period. Thus if a building is owned for eight years, but only occupied for the purposes of the trade during five of those eight years, it is treated as if five-eighths of the building was occupied for the purposes of that trade throughout the whole eight years (TCGA 1992, s. 152(6) and (7)). Periods of ownership before 31 March 1982 are disregarded (TCGA 1992, s. 152(9)).

Apportionments

Where required, any apportionment of the consideration for the disposal is dealt with on such basis as may be just and reasonable in the circumstances (TCGA 1992, s. 152(11)).

Reinvestment in depreciating assets

Apart from the special provisions explained hereunder, it might otherwise be possible for a chargeable gain to be rolled over onto a depreciating asset so that, if that asset were held long enough until scrapped, its ultimate disposal might not produce a chargeable gain (comparing the scrap value received on sale with the cost of the original acquisition less the gain rolled over), and tax on the original chargeable gain arising on the disposal of the first asset would be avoided altogether. To ensure that there is no avoidance of tax in this way, further provisions therefore deal with the situation where the second asset

345

acquired is a depreciating asset, ie one having a predictable life span of not more than 60 years. In this context, the Revenue has confirmed (Inland Revenue Tax Bulletin 7) its view that a building on a leasehold site with an unexpired period of 60 years or less is a depreciating asset whilst plant and machinery incorporated into a building on a freehold or long leasehold (in excess of 60 years) is not.

Where the second asset is a depreciating asset, the chargeable gain is only deferred until the earliest of the following events:

- the date of disposal of the depreciating asset; or
- the date when the depreciating asset ceases to be used for the purposes of the trade, or
- the tenth anniversary of the date of acquisition of the depreciating asset.

Where such an event occurs, the deferred chargeable gain becomes assessable in full. The chargeable gain on the disposal of the second asset is then calculated in the normal way without any reduction in the cost of acquisition for the gain rolled over. If however a third asset, not itself a depreciating asset, is acquired during the intervening period and before the original gain is thus deemed to arise, the trader can roll over the chargeable gain onto this third asset instead, even if its acquisition is outside the normal time limit for the reinvestment of proceeds of the original asset. The claim for rollover onto the depreciating second asset is then withdrawn, and the chargeable gain deferred until the ultimate disposal of the third asset (with no effect when the depreciating second asset is sold, etc.). Part of the gain may be rolled over in this way, leaving the balance of chargeable gain remaining rolled over against the depreciating asset (TCGA 1992, s. 154).

Example 8.18

Philip Burns carries on a manufacturing business in his own freehold premises. The adjoining factory becomes available and, since his own business is expanding, he takes the opportunity of purchasing the freehold of this property at a cost of £200,000. He does not require it immediately and so lets it for one year before going into occupation himself. At the end of that year he expands into the new factory, whilst retaining his original premises as well. Four years later business slumps and he sells the new factory, for a consideration of £300,000. During the same year he takes advantage of this slack period and the new cash resources to modernise and re-equip his original factory – spending £55,000 on structural improvements and a further £165,000 on new fixed plant and machinery. Some four years later he builds an extension at the rear of his factory – incurring £110,000 on building work.

Philip Burns therefore claims rollover relief as follows (ignoring indexation and taper relief):

	Total	Qualifying (4 years)	Non-qualifying (1 year)
	£	£	£
Proceeds of disposal of second factory	300,000	240,000	60,000
Cost of acquisition	200,000	160,000	40,000
Chargeable gain	100,000	80,000	20,000
Available gain		80,000	
Less: Proceeds not applied –			
Proceeds	240,000		
Less: Cost of reinvestment	220,000	20,000	
Rollover relief		60,000	

The relief is then rolled over as follows –

(a) Against structural alterations –

$$£60,000 \times \frac{£55,000}{£220,000} \qquad\qquad 15,000$$

(b) Against plant and machinery –

$$£60,000 \times \frac{£165,000}{£220,000} \qquad\qquad 45,000$$

But subsequently part re-applied
against factory extension –

$$£45,000 \times \frac{£110,000}{£165,000} \qquad \qquad 30,000$$

Philip Burns' capital gains tax position is then computed as follows –

	£
Chargeable gain on sale of second factory	100,000
Less: Rollover relief	60,000
Taxable at time of disposal	40,000
Gain rolled over on to structural improvements (deferred until original factory sold)	15,000
Gain rolled over on to plant machinery	45,000
Less: Withdrawn (below)	30,000
	15,000
(deferred until plant sold or ceases to be used, subject to a ten-year maximum)	
Gain subsequently rolled over on to factory extension (deferred until factory extension sold)	30,000

Available losses

It is normally beneficial to claim such rollover relief wherever possible, even if the taxpayer has allowable capital gains tax losses available to set off against the chargeable gain. This leaves the losses available to carry forward against any other chargeable gains, including particularly those gains for which no rollover relief is available, if they arise before the deferred gain becomes re-assessable by a disposal of the replacement asset, etc. If no such gain arises during the intervening period, the loss is carried forward and so is available against the ultimate charge on the rolled over gain.

Subsequent disposal of new asset

As noted, the cost of acquisition of the new asset is reduced by the rolled over gain in computing the capital gains position on the disposal of the new asset.

Where the disposal is occasioned by the death of the taxpayer, the death exemption explained at **8.7.4** applies, so the deferment has become permanent.

However, in the case of a gain held over in the case of a new *depreciating* asset, the death exemption will not be available because the heldover gain is triggered off by the taxpayer ceasing to use the asset for the purposes of a trade, and not by a disposal on death.

Indexation allowance

Where the relief is claimed, the reduction in the cost of the replacement asset will, of course, have the effect also of reducing any indexation allowance on disposal of that asset (see **8.3.6**).

This restriction does not apply where the replacement asset is a depreciating asset, as the gain is deferred, rather than deducted from the cost of the replacement asset.

Taper relief

The gain which is rolled over is the gain before taper relief. When the replacement asset is sold, the whole of the gain arising on disposal (including the rolled over gain) qualifies for taper relief. However, the period of ownership of the replacement asset is not deemed to include the period of ownership of the original asset. The percentage taper relief on disposal of the replacement asset may be less than the percentage which would have been obtainable had the rollover relief not been claimed. However, as the maximum rate of taper relief can be obtained after only two years, it may be obvious at the time the rollover relief claim has to be made whether the claim is beneficial. If necessary, a provisional claim could be made.

Where the new asset is a depreciating asset, the gain is not deducted from the cost of the replacement asset. In this case taper relief will be given on the gain when it crystallises at the rate due at the time of the original disposal. Thus if an asset which had been owned for 18 months is sold and the proceeds reinvested in a depreciating asset, 50 per cent taper relief will be available when the gain crystallises, whenever this occurs.

Other parties to the transactions

A claim for rollover relief does not affect the tax position of the other party to the transaction. In particular the person acquiring the first asset will, when he subsequently disposes of that asset, compute his chargeable gain on the basis of the consideration actually given by him.

Contingent consideration

When the consideration for the disposal of the old asset consists partly of contingent (as opposed to deferred) consideration, rollover relief may be restricted. Part of the initial consideration will consist of a chose in action (the contingent consideration) and it is difficult to see how this can be applied in acquiring a new asset, so qualifying for the relief. When the contingent consideration becomes payable, this is strictly consideration on the disposal of a chose in action rather than for the disposal of the original qualifying asset. Because the position is unclear, however, it is worth claiming rollover relief on the full consideration obtained, making the circumstances clear to the Inspector of Taxes.

Value added tax

Under an Inland Revenue Statement of Practice (D7), in cases where VAT adjustments have been made in relation to expenditure on chargeable assets, appropriate adjustments may be made to such expenditure in computing capital gains and losses. The capital gains adjustments will normally be made when the gain or loss on the disposal is calculated. In certain circumstances a VAT adjustment may have the effect of reducing the amount of the expenditure on an asset qualifying for rollover relief on the replacement of business assets. The Revenue has indicated, in a press release issued on 20 March 1990, that where a VAT adjustment is made after a claim for rollover relief has been determined, it will not normally seek to reopen the claim.

8.5.3 Application of compensation/insurance monies

Where the disposal consists of the receipt of a capital sum in respect of damage or injury to an asset or its loss, dissipation or destruction (within the provisions of TCGA 1992, s. 23(1)(*a*) to (*d*), see **8.2.4** and **8.2.5**) and the monies received are used to restore or replace the asset in question, relief is available whereby the chargeable gain arising on the disposal can be rolled over against the application of the proceeds, in accordance with the following provisions.

Restoration

Where the asset is not entirely lost and the capital sum received is applied wholly or mainly, apart from some small proportion, in restoring the assets, the receipt is not treated as a disposal for capital gains purposes. Instead it is deducted from any allowable expenditure in computing the chargeable gain arising on a subsequent disposal of that asset.

If only part of the monies received is applied in this way, the claim is restricted to the amount spent on restoration, which is deducted from allowable costs, with the balance of monies being treated as the proceeds of a part disposal.

A similar claim can be made when the amount received is only small in relation to the total value of the asset, even though no amount is applied in restoration. The Inland Revenue is prepared to accept that an amount of less than the greater of £3,000 and 5 per cent of the total value is small for these purposes.

Replacement

Where an asset is entirely lost, but the capital sum received is spent on a replacement asset, the taxpayer can claim that the consideration for the old asset is reduced so that no gain/no loss arises on the disposal (TCGA 1992, s. 23(4)). Correspondingly the consideration given for the acquisition of the new asset is reduced by an amount equal to the chargeable gain that would otherwise arise on the disposal of the old asset, ascertained by treating both the capital sum received and any residual or scrap value of that asset as the proceeds of that disposal.

For this purpose, a building may be regarded as a separate asset from the land on which it stands, so that expenditure on constructing or acquiring a building can be treated as expenditure on a replacement asset (TCGA 1992, s. 23(6)–(8).

A building includes any permanent or semi-permanent structure in the nature of a building.

Although the building and the land are treated as separate assets, expenditure on the acquisition of land on which a new building is constructed does not count as expenditure on replacing or restoring the old building (TCGA 1992, s. 23(7)(*b*)).

Any necessary apportionment of the base cost, and the compensation or insurance recoveries, as between land and buildings, is to be made on a just and reasonable basis (TCGA 1992, s. 23(7)(c)).

If only part of the capital sum is used to replace the old asset in this way and the unutilised balance is less than the amount of the overall gain arising on the disposal of the old asset, the gain is reduced to an amount equal to that unutilised balance (with a proportionate reduction in the chargeable gain if only part of the gain is a chargeable gain) and the cost of the new asset is correspondingly reduced by an amount equal to the reduction in the chargeable gain. If the unused balance exceeds the gain, no relief is available.

The above rules are modified in relation to wasting assets, ie where the property is held under a lease which has not more than 50 years to run. First, the rules apply only where the capital sum received is *wholly* applied in restoring the asset. Secondly, the amount of qualifying expenditure from which the capital sum may be deducted is the amount which would be allowable in computing a chargeable gain or allowable loss if the asset had been disposed of immediately after the expenditure was incurred (TCGA 1992, s. 23(8)).

Where expenditure of a revenue nature is covered by insurance monies, etc. the two are netted off under general income tax principles.

Example 8.19

Doris Camp purchases a freehold office block for the sum of £300,000. The offices are subsequently gutted by fire but not entirely destroyed and she recovers the sum of £360,000 from her insurers. The site and the gutted shell are worth £120,000. The following consequences may arise:

(a) She may sell the site – in which case her chargeable gain is calculated as follows:

	£
Proceeds –	
Sale of site –	120,000
Insurance recovery	360,000
Total proceeds	480,000
Cost of acquisition	300,000
Chargeable gain (subject to indexation relief)	180,000

(b) She may re-build, at a cost of £375,000. Thus she applies the whole of the insurance recovery and no chargeable gain arises. The cost allowed against a subsequent sale of the building is computed as follows:

	£
Cost of acquisition	300,000
Cost of re-building	375,000
	675,000
Less: Insurance recovery	360,000
Allowable cost	315,000

(c) She may re-build, but at a cost of only £345,000. Whilst not all the insurance recovery is utilised, the amount not applied in re-building (£15,000) is only small (ie not more than 5 per cent of £300,000). Again therefore no chargeable gain arises and the cost of the building available against the proceeds of a subsequent sale is computed as follows:

	£
Cost of acquisition	300,000
Cost of re-building	345,000
	645,000
Less: Insurance recovery	360,000
Allowable cost	285,000

(d) She may re-build, but more economically, at a cost of £240.000. A much larger proportion of the insurance monies is not used in restoration. As a result she is treated as making a part disposal of her original building, before re-building takes place, as follows:

	£
Insurance recovery	360,000
Less: Utilised in restoration	240,000
Restricted proceeds of part disposal	120,000
Less: Allowable costs –	

$$\text{Cost} \times \frac{\text{Proceeds}}{\text{Proceeds} + \text{Value retained}}$$

$$£300,000 \times \frac{£120,000}{£120,000 + (£120,000 + £240,000*)} = 75,000$$

Chargeable gain (subject to indexation relief)	45,000

(*Site value £120,000 as in (a), plus balance of insurance proceeds not treated as part disposal £240,000)

The cost of the re-built property, allowable against a subsequent disposal, is as follows:

	£	£
Original cost		300,000
Less: Allowed in part disposal computation as above		75,000
		225,000
Re-building costs		
Less: Insurance proceeds utilised	240,000	
Allowable costs	240,000	–
		225,000

Indexation allowance

Where the consideration for the disposal is treated as a reduction in the allowable costs in computing any gain on a subsequent disposal out of the retained interest, rather than as the proceeds of a part disposal, the indexation allowance on the subsequent disposal of the retained part is calculated as follows. In the first place the allowance is calculated on the actual expenditure for the whole of the period qualifying for the allowance: then there is deducted from this the allowance applied to the proceeds of the part disposal, by reference to the date of the part disposal (TCGA 1992, s. 57).

Example 8.20

Cartwright Manufacturing Ltd, which buys a factory for £200,000 in May 1992, suffers structural damage to it in a freak storm in July 1995. The insurance proceeds amount to £75,000 and £73,000 is spent in January 1986 to make good the damage. The company claims that the capital receipt should be deducted from the cost of the factory rather than giving rise to a possible chargeable gain on a part disposal. The factory is sold in December 2004. The indexation allowance to be set against the unindexed gain on the sale of the factory is:

- the increase in the RPI from May 1992 to December 2004 times the original cost of £200,000, *less*
- the increase in the RPI between July 1995 and December 2004 times the insurance proceeds of £75,000, *plus*
- the increase in the RPI between January 1996 and December 2004 times the improvement expenditure of £72,000.

Land values

Whilst a building is normally regarded as an asset separate from the land on which it stands, if the building is destroyed the land may also be deemed to be sold and re-acquired (see **8.2.5**).

8.5.4 Small part disposals of land

General

Relief may be available where the proceeds of a part disposal of land do not exceed one-fifth of the full value of the asset.

The relief operates to treat the consideration for the disposal as a reduction in allowable costs in computing any gain on a subsequent disposal out of the retained interest, rather than as the proceeds of a part disposal. Where the proceeds of the part disposal exceed the whole of the allowable costs of the asset, the total costs are used up by deduction from the proceeds, and only the balance is taxed as a chargeable gain. If no costs are available, then clearly no relief is available and the whole proceeds of the part disposal are taxed as a chargeable gain (TCGA 1992, s. 242).

Restrictions

The relief is normally available in respect of any part disposal of an interest in land, unless it is a part disposal out of a leasehold interest, where the lease has less than 50 years to run at that time (ie the relief is not available for a part disposal out of a leasehold interest that is a wasting asset). However the relief is not given in a no gain/no loss situation, as for example transfers between husband and wife or within a 75%+ group of companies.

The relief is not available if the proceeds for the part disposal, together with any other proceeds of disposal of land in the same chargeable period, exceed £20,000. Thus for example the grant of a lease at a premium of £8,000 out of freehold land, together with the outright sale of another plot of land for £14,000 in the same chargeable period, would deny relief (TCGA 1992, s. 242).

Example 8.21

Nicholas Weir owns a freehold shop valued at £50,000 which originally cost £30,000. He grants a 60-year lease at a premium of £2,000. He later sells the freehold reversion for £48,000 in a subsequent year.

Since the premium received is less than 20 per cent of the market value of the shop before the premium is received (£50,000) no taxable gain arises and the net amount is deducted from the cost of acquisition in computing the gain on the freehold reversion as follows:

Proceeds of freehold reversion		£48,000
Cost of acquisition	£30,000	
Less: Premium	£2,000	
		£28,000
Chargeable gain		£20,000

If however he sells another property for £19,000 in the year in which he receives the premium, his total proceeds then exceed £20,000 and no relief is available.

Compulsory purchases

Where the part disposal consists of a disposal to an authority with compulsory purchase powers, if no active steps are taken that might affect the sale by the person making the transfer, the vendor may claim a similar relief, but again not in the case of a leasehold interest in property where the lease has less than 50 years to run. There is however no restriction by reference to proceeds exceeding £20,000 (TCGA 1992, s. 243). A claim for rollover relief on land compulsorily acquired under TCGA 1992, s. 247, overrides this treatment (see **8.5.5**).

Compensation/insurance monies

Where the disposal consists of the receipt of a capital sum in respect of damage, etc. to an asset, and the monies are small in relation to the total value of the asset, a similar relief is available (see **8.5.3**).

Indexation allowance

The computation of the indexation allowance must take into account the reduction in the acquisition cost from the date of receipt of the proceeds.

8.5.5 Compulsory purchase rollover

Where land (including buildings) is disposed of involuntarily to a body having compulsory powers, and the rollover relief on the replacement of business assets described under **8.5.2** is not applicable, a similar form of rollover relief can be claimed.

Rollover relief

This relief requires that the proceeds are reinvested in new land, and that this should be done under an unconditional contract entered into within 12 months before or three years after the disposal. The new land does not have to be in the UK. Where the whole of the proceeds of the old land is so reinvested, the disposal is regarded as taking place at no gain or loss, and the cost of the new land is treated as being reduced by the chargeable gain otherwise arising on the old land.

There is no rollover relief where the amount reinvested is less than the cost of the old land: but where it falls between the cost and the proceeds of the old land, the overall gain (and pro rata the chargeable gain) is reduced to the amount not reinvested, and the cost of the new land is reduced by the resultant reduction in the chargeable gain (TCGA 1992, s. 247). The Inland Revenue is understood to accept that relief is also available to landlords receiving a premium, payable under the leasehold enfranchisement legislation – the Housing and Urban Development Act 1993, on the granting by the landlord of a long lease at a nominal rent.

Leasehold franchise

In certain circumstances, tenants may exercise their rights under the Leasehold Reform Act 1967 to acquire the freehold reversion of a property.

In such cases, when a landlord disposes of a freehold reversion, the Inland Revenue will be prepared to accept claims under TCGA 1992, s. 247 for any resultant gains to be rolled over against the cost of acquisition of new land. This is of course subject to the general conditions of s. 247 being satisfied.

Because of the five-year and ten-months or six-year time limit for claims referred to under **8.5.2**, this allows a claim to be made for a disposal that took place some considerable time earlier. Provisional claims may be made in anticipation of the reinvestment.

Reinvestment in dwelling house

The relief is not available if the proceeds are reinvested in a dwelling house which would give rise in whole or in part to a capital gains tax exemption for a private residence (see **8.7.7**), if it were disposed of at any time in the six years from acquisition. This would require a cancellation of rollover relief already given if such a dwelling house subsequently became an exempt residence within the six-year period (TCGA 1992, s. 248(1) and (2)).

Reinvestment in depreciating asset

If the asset in which the proceeds are reinvested is a depreciating asset (such as a leasehold interest with 60 years or less unexpired) there is an opportunity to claim rollover relief and thereby to defer the chargeable gain on the original land for a period of up to ten years in the manner described for business assets at **8.5.2**. Within that period it is possible to transfer the rollover relief into a non-depreciating asset, providing it is land not qualifying for a private residence exemption (TCGA 1992, s. 248(3)).

Other compensation provisions

Where the compensation payment is in part for the severance of other land retained, a rollover relief claim is valid for the whole of the compensation money and overrides the requirement under TCGA 1992, s. 245(2) (explained at **8.4.1**) to treat the retained land as being subject to a part disposal. It also overrides the part disposal treatment under TCGA 1992, s. 243 (described at **8.5.4**) (TCGA 1992, ss. 247(6) and 248(4)).

Indexation allowance

Where the indexation allowance is available and the rollover claim is made, the allowance is added to the cost of the old land. This ensures that the disposal is regarded as taking place at no gain or loss and that the cost of the new land is reduced by the chargeable gain after deducting the indexation allowance.

Where the replacement asset is a depreciating asset the gain is not deducted from the cost of the replacement asset, and therefore will not affect the indexation allowance on a later sale.

Taper relief

Taper relief is not available on the gain rolled over, although it is given in the normal manner when the replacement land is sold based on the period of ownership of the replacement land. Taper relief is, however, due on any gain remaining chargeable.

If the replacement asset is a depreciating asset, taper relief is given when the gain crystallises according to the ownership of the original land.

8.5.6 Political party constituency associations – succession

A form of rollover relief is available in the case of certain disposals made in consequence of an Order giving effect to Parliamentary constituency boundary changes. Such changes often make it necessary for land and buildings owned by a former local constituency association of a political party to be transferred to a successor association, or for the land and buildings to be sold by the former association and the proceeds to be transferred to the successor association for reinvestment in new assets for the association's use.

In the former case the successor association steps into the shoes of the former association, in that the former association is treated as having made the disposal on a no gain/no loss basis. In the latter case, to the extent that the proceeds are re-invested, rollover relief is available as though the two associations were a continuing trading body replacing its business assets (see **8.5.2**).

In either case the gain becomes chargeable on a subsequent disposal by the successor (TCGA 1992, s. 264).

8.5.7 Rollover on exchange of joint interests

On a division of joint interests in land a person who owned part of the whole comes to own the whole of a part. The strict position is that he has made a disposal of part of the land subject to his joint interest and an acquisition of a further interest in the remainder of the land in which he now has a sole interest. The consideration received for giving up the joint interest will, of course, include the market value of the additional interest acquired, as well as any sum actually received. Similarly the consideration given for the sole interest will include the market value of the joint interest given up as well as any payment actually made.

By extra-statutory concession, however, it is possible to claim that the gain on the disposal of the joint interest is rolled over into the cost of acquiring the sole interest so that the gain is deferred in a similar way to the rollover of gains on business assets replaced (Extra-Statutory Concession D26), (see **8.5.2**). Consequently, if the consideration given for the sole interest equals or exceeds the consideration received for the joint interest, the disposal of the joint interest is regarded as taking place at no gain or loss, and the cost of the sole interest is treated as being reduced by the chargeable gain otherwise arising on the joint interest. This concession was rendered unnecessary in certain circumstances by the cases of *Jenkins v Brown* (1989) and *Warrington v Sterland* (1989) BTC 281 in which it was held that where property is put into or taken out of the pool, with the result that the interest in the whole reflects precisely the individual interests before the relevant deed is entered into, there is no disposal for capital gains purposes.

There is no rollover relief where the consideration given for the sole interest is less than the cost of the joint interest: but where it falls between the cost and the consideration received for the joint interest, there is partial rollover relief, whereby the gain immediately chargeable is reduced to the amount not reinvested and the remainder of the gain is rolled over into the acquisition of the sole interest.

Example 8.22

Some years ago Susan Paris and her brother John inherited a field jointly and in equal shares, when the probate value of each share was £20,000. Later, when the value of each share had risen to £35,000, they split their interests – Susan taking the larger part worth £50,000, and John taking the smaller part worth £30,000, with Susan paying John £10,000 for the difference. (It will be seen that in this example splitting the interests has increased the overall value by £10,000.)

The rollover relief is calculated as follows (ignoring indexation):

	Susan (£000)	John (£000)
Proceeds – market value of additional interest 1/2 × 50/30	25	15
– cash transferred	(10)	10
	15	25
Less: Cost – probate value of joint interest given up	7.5	12.5
Chargeable gain	7.5	12.5
Less: proceeds not applied		
– proceeds as above	15	25
– less amount reinvested (below)	25	15
Gain not rolled over, subject to immediate CGT	–	10
Gain rolled over	7.5	2.5
Amount reinvested:		
– value of half share given	15	25
Add/Less – cash payment	10	(10)
	25	15

The gain is then rolled over as follows:

	Susan (£000)	John (£000)
Cost of sole interest		
– cost of part retained	12.5	7.5
– amount reinvested	25	15
– less gain on joint interest rolled over (above)	(7.5)	(2.5)
– adjusted cost carried forward	30	20

It can be seen that John is taxed on £10,000, the cash received, and the cost carried forward comprises the original probate value plus the £10,000 cash invested by Susan.

The relief is not generally available where on partition the sole interest retained is, or becomes, the individual's main residence. However, where individuals are joint owners of dwelling houses which are their respective principal residences, a similar rollover claim may be made if each individual takes a sole interest in his residence such that any gain arising on an immediate disposal would be exempt under the principal private residence exemption would usually apply (see **8.7.7**). Otherwise a claim for rollover into a dwelling house is not allowed. Each individual must accept that he takes over the other's cost and acquisition date.

Where an exchange of joint interests is accompanied by an exchange of associated milk or potato quotas, the concession also applies to those quotas.

See also **8.5.2** for the similar rollover relief where there is a partition of business assets on the dissolution of a partnership.

8.5.8 Gifts to charities and certain other exempt bodies

The general rule that the full market value of an asset is substituted in place of any actual proceeds of disposal in the case of a gift (see **8.3.3**) does not apply in the case of a gift to a charity, local authority, government department, university, the National Trust, or certain museums and galleries, etc. (see IHTA 1984, Sch. 3 for a full list). If it is a pure gift, or if the consideration is less than the allowable cost, it is treated as having been transferred at no gain/no loss to the donor. The chargeable gain arising on a subsequent disposal by the donee is calculated on the basis of the proceeds of disposal received by him, as compared with the donor's cost of acquisition and indexation allowance. If the consideration actually received by the donor exceeds his allowable cost, the gain must be calculated on the basis of this consideration, but again without increase to the full market value if more

The provisions also apply to similar transfers of assets from a trust to such persons, where again the market value would otherwise be substituted, unless the transfer is exempt anyway due to the termination of a life interest on the death of the person entitled (TCGA 1992, s. 257).

Note also that a gift to a charity may qualify as a deduction in computing a trader's taxable profits (ICTA 1988, s. 577). Furthermore an individual or charity may claim relief from income or corporation tax for a gift of a qualifying interest in land to a charity. This relief is in addition to the capital gains relief described above (ICTA 1988, s. 587B).

8.5.9   Housing associations, etc.

Transfer of property to tenant

Capital gains exemption is given to the transfer of property from a housing association (or a self-build society) to a tenant of the association (or a member of the society) (ICTA 1988, ss. 488(5) and 489(3)). Similarly disposals of land between the housing corporation and housing societies or registered housing associations are treated as disposed of and acquired at no gain/no loss to the person making the disposal (TCGA 1992, ss. 218, 219 and 220).

Gifts to housing association

Rollover relief may be claimed where an estate or interest in land in the UK is transferred to a relevant housing association in a non-arm's length transaction. In such a case, the transfer is deemed to be for such a consideration as to secure that no gain or loss arises (TCGA 1992, s. 259). A 'relevant housing association' means:

- a registered social landlord within the meaning of Part 1 Housing Act 1996;
- a registered housing association within the meaning of the Housing Associations Act 1985 (Scottish registered housing associations), or
- a registered housing association within the meaning of Part II of the Housing (Northern Ireland) Order 1992.

8.5.10   Negligible value claims

A loss may be claimed in respect of an asset if the value of the asset has become negligible. The loss is computed on the basis of a deemed disposal and re-acquisition of the asset at the value specified in the claim (TCGA 1992, s. 24(2)).

The date of the deemed disposal is either:

- the date of the claim, or
- an earlier time specified in the claim, provided certain conditions are satisfied and subject to the time limit set out below.

The required conditions are that at the earlier time specified in the claim:

- the claimant owned the asset, and
- the value of the asset had already become negligible.

For individuals and trustees, the earlier time may not be more than two years before the beginning of the tax year in which the claim is made. Thus a claim for an earlier time falling in 2004/05 must be made by 5 April 2007. For companies within the charge to corporation tax, the earlier time may not be more than two years before the beginning of the accounting period which ends more than two years from the time of the claim. Thus if a company makes up accounts to 31 December each year, the time limit for claims relating to the year ended 31 December 2004 is 31 December 2006 (TCGA 1992, s. 24(2)(c)).

A building is regarded as a separate asset from the site on which it is situated for the purposes of a negligible value claim. If a claim is made the person is also deemed to have disposed of and reacquired the site at market value, including any land used or occupied for purposes ancillary to the use of the building. Although a claim may be made in respect of a dilapidated building, the loss arising from the claim is automatically reduced or offset by any increase in the site value (TCGA 1992, s. 24(3)).

8.5.11 Deferred charges on gains before 31 March 1982

In a number of circumstances, the gain arising on the disposal of an asset may be *rolled over* into some other asset, the allowable cost of that asset being reduced by the amount of the gain, or *held over*, the gain effectively being transferred with the asset and reducing its allowable cost in the hands of its new owner. Similarly, the gains arising on certain disposals do not fall into charge to tax until the occurrence of some later event. Where such a deferral occurred between 31 March 1982 and 6 April 1988 and the relevant charge falls in after the later date, the rebasing of capital gains discussed at **8.3.7** affords no general relief, since rebasing did not apply to disposals before 6 April 1988 of an asset held on 31 March 1982.

Rollovers and holdovers

Where:

1. a person disposes of an asset on or after 6 April 1988 which he acquired *after* 31 March 1982; and

2. a deduction falls to be made from the allowable cost of that asset because of a roll-over or holdover election under:

    (a) TCGA 1992, s. 23(4) and (5) (roll-over where replacement asset acquired after receipt of compensation or insurance money, see **8.5.3**); or

    (b) TCGA 1992, s. 247 (roll-over where replacement land acquired on compulsory acquisition of other land, see **8.5.5**); or

    (c) TCGA 1992, s. 152 (roll-over where replacement asset acquired on disposal of business asset, see **8.5.2**); or

    (d) TCGA 1992, s. 162 (roll-over where shares acquired on disposal of business to company, see **8.7.9**), or

    (e) TCGA 1992, s. 165 (holdover where business asset acquired by gift, see **8.7.8**),

3. that deduction is attributable, directly or indirectly and whether in whole or in part, to a chargeable gain accruing on the disposal before 6 April 1988 of an asset which was acquired before 31 March 1982, the amount of that deduction is reduced by half (TCGA 1992, s. 36 and Sch. 4, Paras. 1 and 2). Relief cannot, however, be given more than once in respect of the same deferred gain, where, for example, tax is again deferred on another disposal on or after 6 April 1988 (TCGA 1992, Sch. 4, Para. 2(2)).

Example 8.23

In 1980, Michael Wilson purchased land for £10,000. In 1983, he gave the land to his niece Janice Fowler when it was worth £16,000 and they elected to holdover the gain. In 2004, Janice sells the land. Her base cost of £16,000 would normally be reduced by Michael's heldover gain of £6,000 (ignoring indexation). If, however, Janice claims relief under TCGA 1992, Sch 4 , her base cost will be reduced by only half of the heldover gain (£3,000).

Example 8.24

In 1980, John Gray acquired a business asset. In 1983, he gave the asset to Ian Post and they elected to holdover the gain. In 1985, Ian replaced the asset and rolled the gain into the new asset, which was itself replaced in 1987 (again under a roll-over election). Ian sells this final replacement asset in 2004.

The gain deferred in 1987 is in part attributable indirectly to John's disposal in 1983 of an asset which he acquired before 31 March 1982. Ian may therefore claim for the gain deferred in 1987 (which does of course include that deferred in 1983) to be halved.

Where the deferred gain arises from a roll-over election under TCGA 1992, s. 152, (see **8.5.2**), relief will be given under TCGA 1992, Sch. 4, provided the 'old asset' was disposed of before 6 April 1988, even though the replacement asset may not have been acquired until after that date.

Other postponed charges

Similar relief is given where (TCGA 1992, Sch. 4, Paras 1 and 4):

1. a gain is treated as accruing in consequence of an event occurring on or after 6 April 1988 by virtue of:

    (a) TCGA 1992, s. 140 (postponement of charge where securities are issued in exchange for business acquired by non-UK resident company, see **8.9.4**), or

(b) TCGA 1992, s. 154(2) (postponement of charge where depreciating asset acquired as replacement for business asset, see **8.5.2**), and

2. that gain is attributable, whether directly or indirectly and whether in whole or in part, to the disposal before 6 April 1988 of an asset acquired before 31 March 1982.

No gain/no loss disposals

Relief is also given where the asset giving rise to the deferred or postponed charge was not held by the taxpayer on 31 March 1982, but was acquired by him after that date in circumstances treated by the capital gains legislation as giving rise to neither gain nor loss, notably transfers between spouses or between companies within the same group (TCGA 1992, Sch. 4, Paras. 5 and 7).

Example 8.25

In 1980, Rodney Williams purchased some land. In 1983, he gave the land to his wife Martha, a no gain/no loss disposal. In 1985, Martha gave it to Christopher Hamilton and they elected to holdover the gain. When Christopher sells the land in 2004, he may claim relief under Sch. 9 even though Martha herself did not own the asset giving rise to the deferred gain on 31 March 1982.

Provision is also made to preserve the relief where a roll-over or holdover election is followed by a no gain/no loss disposal before the eventual chargeable disposal (TCGA 1992, Sch. 4, Paras. 6 and 7), and where the asset which is ultimately disposed of is derived from the asset giving rise to the deferred gain (TCGA 1992, Sch. 4, Para. 9).

Claims

In all cases, relief under Schedule 9 must be claimed within one year from 31 January following the end of the year of assessment (capital gains tax) or two years from the end of the accounting period (corporation tax) in which the event which causes the rolled-over or heldover gain to crystallise occurs (TCGA 1992, Sch. 4, Para. 9).

8.5.12 Default on mortgage granted by vendor

Where on the sale of an asset at arm's length there has been a default in respect of a loan granted by the vendor to the purchaser of all or part of the proceeds and, as a result, the vendor has regained the beneficial ownership of the interest which he had contracted to sell, there is an Extra-Statutory Concession (D18) under which the vendor may elect that for capital gains purposes the gain realised by him on that sale be limited to the amount of the proceeds (net of allowable incidental costs of disposal) retained by him and the loan be treated as having never having come into existence. Accordingly, the computation of the gain (or loss) on any later sale of that asset will be made by reference to the original date and cost of acquisition. The treatment for income tax purposes of any interest received in respect of the loan will remain unaltered.

8.5.13 Payment of tax by instalments

Relief is given by way of deferment of the payment of tax on capital gains where the full value of the consideration is not available to the taxpayer at the time of disposal because the consideration itself is received in instalments.

Considerations received in instalments

If any part of the consideration included in the capital gains computation is payable by instalments over a period exceeding 18 months from the date of the disposal, the taxpayer may opt to pay the tax in such instalments as the Inland Revenue may allow, over a period not exceeding eight years and not exceeding the period over which the instalments of consideration are receivable (TCGA 1992, s. 280). The Inland Revenue is normally prepared to agree that no more than half of each instalment should be used to settle the tax liability.

8.6 Companies

8.6.1 Introduction

The provisions regarding the taxation of chargeable gains discussed in **8.1** to **8.5** apply to taxpayers generally. There are some provisions which apply only to companies.

Most of the provisions apply to groups of companies, enabling the group as a whole to be taxed no less advantageously that if it were a single company.

8.6.2 Taxation of chargeable gains

The aggregate chargeable gains accruing to a company in any accounting period after reliefs and exemptions, less any allowable losses accruing during the same period or unused losses brought forward from earlier periods, are included in the company's total profits for that accounting period and are chargeable to corporation tax at the appropriate rate (ICTA 1988, s. 6(3), (4) and TCGA 1992, s. 8). For the purpose of the small companies' rate and the starting rate, the chargeable gains for any accounting period form part of the company's 'profits' and 'basic profits' (ICTA 1988, s. 13(8) and 13AA(7)).

Companies must include chargeable gains in their corporation tax self-assessment returns. The corporation tax for any accounting period is payable nine months after the end of the period. Large companies are required to make quarterly payments on account, based on an estimate of the corporation tax liability for the period including corporation tax on chargeable gains. This causes problems where a chargeable gain arises late in an accounting period. A company may simply not know in advance whether the gain will arise in the current period or in the next period. Nevertheless it will be charged interest if early payments on account turn out to be inadequate because of unforeseen gains arising late in the accounting period (see the Corporation Tax (Instalment Payments) Regulations 1998, SI 1998/3175).

Advance corporation tax

The surplus ACT brought forward which may be set off in any accounting period is set against the company's liability to corporation tax on *any profits* charged to corporation tax for that period (SI 1999/358, reg. 14). As noted above, profits include chargeable gains.

Liquidations

A liability to corporation tax on chargeable gains arising from a disposal of property by a liquidator in a winding up is a necessary disbursement of the liquidator (*Re Mesco Properties Ltd* (1979) 54 TC 238). As such, it ranks before the liquidator's fees under the Insolvency Rules 1986 (SI 1986/1925, reg. 4.218(a), (o)). However, the court has power to order that the liquidator's fees rank before the tax liability (IA 1986, s. 156).

Receiverships

Where a receiver appointed on behalf of secured creditors disposes of property which is subject to the security for the purposes of enforcing that security, his dealings are treated as dealings by the company (TCGA 1992, s. 26(2)). Any chargeable gain arising on disposal of the asset is a gain arising to the company and is chargeable to corporation tax in the normal way.

8.6.3   Groups of companies, general rules

Qualification as a group

Special capital gains rules apply to groups of companies.

A group of companies for this purpose includes a parent company, together with all its subsidiaries of which it owns at least 75 per cent of the equity (a 75%+ group) A company does not cease to be a member of a group of companies merely because it is put into liquidation, but care is needed in transactions carried out by the liquidator thereafter (TCGA 1992, s. 170). A group consists not only of a 'principal company' and all its 75 per cent subsidiaries, but also any 75 per cent subsidiaries of those subsidiaries and so on, but excluding any company that is not an *effective 51 per cent subsidiary* of the principal company of the group. Moreover a company cannot be a member of more than one group. Where a company otherwise would be a member of more than one group, it is necessary to determine to which group it belongs. A company is an 'effective 51 per cent subsidiary' of another company at any time if, and only if, the parent is beneficially entitled to more than 50 per cent of any profits available for distribution by the subsidiary as a dividend or on a winding up (TCGA 1992, s. 170).

Transfer of assets

The transfer of a chargeable asset from one member of a 75%+ group of companies to another member of the same group is deemed to take place at no gain/no loss to the transferor. Correspondingly the transferee is treated as acquiring the asset at the same cost as the transferor (TCGA 1992, s. 171). Any indexation allowance available to the transferor is included in the transfer price so that after deducting the allowance neither a gain nor a loss arises to him. The allowance is, however, eliminated from the acquisition cost to the transferee where he makes an election to have his allowance based upon the value at 31 March 1982 (see **8.3.6**).

The no gain-no loss rules cover the cases where:

- the transferor company is resident in the UK at the time of the transfer, or the asset is a chargeable asset immediately before that time in relation to the transferor company,
- the transferee company is resident in the UK at the time of the transfer, or the asset is a chargeable asset immediately after that time in relation to the transferee company,

(TCGA 1992, s. 171(1A)).

An asset is a chargeable asset in relation to a company if any gain arising on its disposal at that time would be a chargeable gain forming part of its profits liable to corporation tax under TCGA 1992, s. 10B. This includes assets owned by a non-resident company which are situated in the UK and are used for the purposes of a UK permanent establishment of that company.

The Revenue will accept that there is a no gain/no loss transfer when one group company grants a lease out of a freehold to another group company, although strictly the freehold and leasehold are separate interests, or where a leaseholder surrenders his lease to another group member which holds the freehold, or where the freeholder transfers the freehold to another group company which holds the lease.

Trading stock

If the asset is taken as the trading stock of the transferee, but not of the transferor, it is treated as the transfer of a chargeable asset from the one company to the other, followed by an appropriation to trading stock at market value by the transferee (see **8.2.8**). It is then possible for the transferee to elect that the resulting chargeable gain or allowable loss be rolled over into its trading stock.

Example 8.26

Crowsnest Investments Ltd acquires a property investment for £225,000. It sells the property later to its wholly-owned property dealing subsidiary company, Crowsnest Properties Ltd for £275,000 – the latter taking the property as dealing stock. At the time the property is valued at £260,000. Crowsnest Properties Ltd subsequently sells the property for £300,000.

The inter-company transfer price is ignored altogether and tax assessments are raised on Crowsnest Properties Ltd as follows:

	£
Capital gains –	
Proceeds of disposal (= value at time of 'appropriation' by Crowsnest Properties Ltd)	260,000
Cost (= cost to Crowsnest Investments Ltd)	225,000
Chargeable gain	35,000
Dealing profit –	
Proceeds of sale	300,000
Cost (= value at appropriation, as above)	260,000
Assessable profit	40,000

Alternatively, Crowsnest Properties Ltd could elect that the chargeable gain is rolled over into its trading stock. The result of this election is as follows:

		£
Capital gains –		
Chargeable gain as above		35,000
Less: Rolled over into trading stock		35,000
Chargeable gain		nil
Dealing profit –		
Proceeds of sale		300,000
Cost (= market value at appropriation)	260,000	
Less: Chargeable gain rolled over	35,000	
		225,000
Assessable profit		75,000

Where the asset consists of trading stock of the transferor, but not the trading stock of the transferee, it is treated as if the transferor appropriates the asset from trading stock immediately prior to the transfer (TCGA 1992, s. 173).

Property groups

It is not uncommon for groups in the property sector to have dealing companies, development companies and investment companies. Unrealised capital losses can, in principle, be converted into trading losses by means of intra-group transfers where a group of companies includes a property investment company and a property dealing company. The loss on an investment property would have to arise at a time when the company concerned was a member of the group. Further, the Revenue would naturally wish to satisfy itself, on the basis of the facts, that the dealing company acquired the asset as part of its trading stock. Decisions regarding the property, and the basis on which they were taken, would have to be properly documented.

On the other hand, taxable profits can be generated inadvertently if properties are acquired by a trading company, but a decision is made at a later stage to keep them as investment properties and to transfer them to a property investment company in the group and to re-categorise them in the accounts. Therefore, where a property is to be acquired in a group, it is important to ensure that it is acquired by the appropriate company.

See *Reed v Nova Securities Ltd* (1985) BTC 121 and *New Angel Court Ltd v Adam* [2004] EWCA Civ 242.

Deemed transfers

No group relief is available in respect of allowable capital losses. It is of course possible to transfer assets between group companies at no gain/no loss so as to match gains and losses, and indeed it used to be common for groups to hold their capital assets in one company so as to avoid the need to make such transfers.

Since 1 April 2002 it has not been necessary to make an actual transfer of an asset prior to its sale outside the group. Instead an election can be made to treat the asset as if all or part of it has been transferred to another group company immediately before the sale (TCGA 1992, s. 171A). The election must be made jointly by both companies within two years of the end of the accounting period of the company which actually made the sale to the third party, and the election can only be made if an actual transfer between the companies would have been on a no gain/no loss basis.

The election can be used to reallocate gains and losses, and can be restricted to part only of the asset, and hence part only of the gain or loss. It is made retrospectively, so that not only can gains and losses be matched, but gains not matched with capital losses can be reallocated to companies with trading or other losses eligible for relief, or to the companies with the lowest marginal corporation tax rates.

Note, however, the pre-entry losses and pre-entry gains provisions discussed at **8.6.5** which prevent groups from acquiring new subsidiaries to shelter gains or utilise losses.

Rollover relief for the replacement of business assets

For the purposes of a claim to rollover relief on the replacement of business assets (see **8.5.2**), all the trades carried on by members of a 75%+ group of companies are treated as one trade (TCGA 1992, s 175(1)). Furthermore a gain on a disposal by one company, which at the time of the *disposal* was a member of a group, may be rolled over against the cost of a replacement asset acquired by another company which at the time of the *acquisition* was a member of the same group. The two companies need not both be members of the group at the same time. The claim has to be made by both companies (TCGA 1992, s. 175(2A)).

Companies which are not themselves trading may claim rollover relief. Thus, if a group holds its land and buildings in a property investment company rollover relief will be available provided the relevant properties are used wholly for a trading purpose by other group members (TCGA 1992, s. 175(2B)).

A gain on a disposal by a group company cannot be rolled over against the acquisition of a qualifying asset *from* another group company which is a no gain/no loss transfer (TCGA 1992, s. 175(2C)).

Prior to 1 April 2002 it was not possible to roll over a gain arising when a company left a group within six years of acquiring an asset from another group company. (This gain is referred to as a degrouping charge.) This was because the proceeds of the deemed disposal were treated as immediately reinvested in acquiring the same asset. From 1 April 2002 rollover relief may be claimed, provided an appropriate reinvestment is made (TCGA 1992, s. 179B). Since the gain is deemed to arise at the start of the accounting period in which the company leaves the group, or at the time of the intra-group transfer if later, it is this date which sets the time limit for reinvestment. All or part of a degrouping charge may be reallocated to another company which was a member of the same group at the time the degrouping charge was made. In this case the company to which the degrouping charge is reallocated may claim rollover relief.

Compulsory sale of land

Where land is disposed of to an authority having compulsory purchase powers, the taxpayer can claim rollover relief against the acquisition of replacement land, even if the normal conditions of occupation, and usage, for the purpose of a trade are not present (see **8.5.5**). A claim can be made when the disposal to the relevant authority is made by one member of a group and the replacement land is acquired by another member of that same group.

Market value election

A taxpayer who held assets on 31 March 1982 can make an election under TCGA 1992, s. 35(5) under which all of the assets held on that date are treated as sold and immediately reacquired at market value on that date. In the case of a 75%+ group of companies, the general rule is that an election can only be made by the principal (ie parent) company of the group, and that its election will apply to all companies which are then members of the group. There are complicated rules for companies joining and leaving the group.

8.6.4   Groups of companies: de-grouping charge

There are however some anti-avoidance provisions that need to be borne in mind in relation to groups of companies. Thus it would be all too easy to transfer an asset to a subsidiary company for a full consideration left outstanding on a no gain/no loss basis for capital gains purposes and if that subsidiary company is then sold with the purchaser procuring the payment of the outstanding consideration for the transfer, tax might be avoided.

Companies leaving groups after inter-company transfers

To prevent such avoidance it is provided that, where a company ceases to be a member of a 75%+ group at a time that it owns an asset previously belonging to another member of the same group at some time during the previous six years, the company is treated as having sold and re-acquired the asset at its market value immediately after the time of the inter-company transfer (TCGA 1992, s. 179). Thus a purchaser of a company that has hitherto been a member of such a group should take care to ensure adequate protection against such a charge, by appropriate indemnities, etc.

The gain is deemed to arise at the start of the accounting period in which the company leaves the group or on the date of the intra-group transfer, if later (TCGA 1992, s. 179(4)).

This provision does not apply if the company leaves the group merely as a consequence of the winding up of that company or of its parent company, nor if both the transferor and the transferee companies leave the group at the same time and form a separate 75%+ group by themselves, unless of course the transferor company had similarly received the asset by transfer from a third member of the original group which did not leave the group at the same time. In that case the transferor company is assessed, based on the value of the asset at the time of the transfer to it from the third company.

The exception provided where both transferor and transferee companies leave the group at the same time does not apply to companies which cease to be a member of the second group if there is a connection between the group those companies left (the first group) and the one which they join (the second group). The critical test is whether, at the time the chargeable company leaves the second group, the principal company of that group is controlled (a 51 per cent test) by:

(a) the principal company of the first group; or

(b) if the first group no longer exists, the company which was the principal company of that group when the chargeable company left; or

(c) any company which also controls the principal company or which has done so at any time since the chargeable company left that group; or

(d) any other company which has at any time controlled a company which fell within (c) but no longer exists, and so on through any number of companies which have ceased to exist.

Nor does this provision apply where a company ceases to be a member of a group solely because the principal company of the group becomes a member of another group.

Furthermore this anti-avoidance provision does not apply where a company ceases to be a member of a 75%+ group as part of a merger carried out for bona fide commercial reasons, and not to avoid liability of tax, and that merger falls within certain prescribed terms (see TCGA 1992, s. 181). Nor does it apply where the company leaves the group as a result of an exempt distribution under the demerger provisions, provided no chargeable payment is made within five years of that exempt distribution (TCGA 1992 s. 192).

Example 8.27

Acrefield (Holdings) Ltd purchases a freehold property at a cost of £450,000. The property is subsequently transferred to a wholly-owned subsidiary company, Acrefield (Properties) Ltd, at its market value of £600,000 – satisfied by the issue of 100,000 shares of £1 each at a premium of £5 each. Two years later Acrefield (Holdings) Ltd sells its shares in Acrefield (Properties) Ltd for £635,000.

Acrefield (Holdings) Ltd realises a chargeable gain on the sale of shares (ignoring indexation) as follows:

	£
Proceeds of disposal	635,000
Cost of acquisition (= value of assets given for shares)	600,000
Chargeable gain	35,000

At the same time Acrefield (Properties) Ltd is assessed on a chargeable gain on leaving the Acrefield (Holdings) Ltd group under the above provisions (ignoring indexation) as follows:

	£
Proceeds of deemed disposal (= value of property immediately after transfer)	600,000
Cost of acquisition (= original cost to group – the inter-company transfer being on a no gain/no loss basis)	450,000
Chargeable gain	150,000

Note that indexation on this gain runs from the date of the original purchase to the date of the intra-group transfer.

The purchaser would take into account the tax payable by Acrefield (Properties) Ltd on the latter gain – which, if tax is levied at 30 per cent amounts to £45,000. This might be the case if, say, the real value of the property was £680,000, and the purchaser retains £45,000 to provide funds to Acrefield (Properties) Ltd to meet its corporation tax liability on the gain.

There is still some initial tax saving here, despite the anti-avoidance provisions, representing tax on tax (ie corporation tax on the amount of tax payable by Acrefield (Properties) Ltd), since tax is only paid on chargeable gains totalling £185,000 – instead of £230,000 (£680,000 – £450,000) arising if Acrefield (Holdings) Ltd sells the property for the full price direct. Nevertheless there is still a potential capital gain within Acrefield (Properties) Ltd of £80,000 (£680,000 – £600,000) on which tax more than wipes out the initial tax saving. Really therefore the purchaser should take into account not only the immediate tax liability in Acrefield (Properties) Ltd on leaving the group, but also the potential additional liability in the event of a disposal of the property for its full market value, albeit on a discounted basis.

Reallocation of de-grouping gain

In relation to de-grouping events occurring on or after 1 April 2002, the chargeable company, ie the company leaving the group, and any other company in its group may jointly elect that all or part of any gain or loss arising under the degrouping rules shall be treated as accruing to the other company (TCGA 1992, s. 179A). The other company must be resident in the UK or must be carrying on a trade in the UK so as to be within the charge to corporation tax.

The election may, for example, be made to ensure that responsibility for any tax liability on the gain remains within the vendor's group.

An election under TCGA 1992, s. 179A must be made within two years after the end of the accounting period of the chargeable company in which the gain was deemed to arise (TCGA 1992, s. 179A(10)).

Any payment made between the two companies in connection with the election is disregarded for tax purposes provided that it does not exceed the amount of the gain or loss arising (TCGA 1992, s. 179A(11)).

Rollover of de-grouping gain

Where a de-grouping event occurs on or after 1 April 2002 any de-grouping gain may be rolled over under the replacement of business assets rules if and to the extent that any gain arising on an actual disposal of the asset concerned could be rolled over (TCGA 1992, s. 179B, and Sch. 7AB). Rollover is also possible where the de-grouping gain has been reallocated.

8.6.5 Groups of companies, anti-avoidance rules

Depreciatory transactions

There are complicated rules under which an allowable loss arising from a disposal of shares in a company may be restricted if there has been some artificial reduction in the value of those shares resulting from the disposal of assets between members of a 75%+ group of companies at other than their market value, or where there has been some other 'depreciatory transaction' between members of a 75%+ group. There are no powers to turn a loss into a chargeable gain. Anti-avoidance rules may also apply if a distribution is made which materially reduces the value of the shareholding.

Although these rules are outside the scope of this work, care must be taken where there have been intra-group transfers of property at less than market value.

Pre-entry losses

The use of capital losses within a company where the loss arose or is attributable to a period whilst it was not in the same group, ie a pre-entry loss, is restricted (TCGA 1992, s. 177A and Sch. 7A). The provisions are extremely complex and necessitate the identification of losses accruing whilst the asset was in the ownership of a company outside the group. An outline of the rules is given below.

These rules come into operation if there is a company which is or has been a member of a group, the *relevant group*, and that company has *pre-entry losses* (TCGA 1992, Sch. 7A, Para. 1(1)). The rules also applies if a non-resident company becomes UK resident, so that all of its capital assets become chargeable assets, or if a non-resident company trading through a permanent establishment in the UK begins to use an asset for that trade so that the asset becomes a chargeable asset (TCGA 1992, Sch. 7A, Para. 1(3A)).

Certain terms are defined:

- a *pre-entry loss* is either one that arose before the company joined the group or the pre-entry part of a loss which arises on the disposal of a *pre-entry asset* (TCGA 1992, Sch. 7A, Para. 1(2));
- a *pre-entry asset* is one which the company owned immediately before it joined the group, or an asset which became a chargeable asset when a company became non-resident or commenced to use the asset for the purposes of a trade carried on through a UK permanent establishment. An asset remains within the definition even if it is transferred within the group in a no gain/no loss transaction under TCGA 1992, s. 171 (TCGA 1992, Sch. 7A, Para. 1(3), (3A), (4)), and

- the *relevant time* is the time at which the company owning a pre-entry asset joins the group; or earlier of the time a non-resident company first uses an asset for the trade of its UK permanent establishment or the time the non-resident company becomes UK resident. If there is more than one relevant time, the latest occasion is taken (TCGA 1992, Sch. 7A, Para. 1(5)).

The principal company of a group is treated as joining a new group if another company acquires the share capital of that principal company. So when there is a takeover of one group by another company, the companies in the group taken over will be treated as joining the new group at the date of that takeover. By contrast, when a new holding company is inserted over a group and its only assets are shares in the principal company of the first group and the ultimate shareholders of the group remain the same, the companies in the first group are treated as having joined the new group when they joined the first group (TCGA 1992, Sch. 7A, Para. 1(7)). Where an asset is derived from another asset, for example where a leasehold interest merges with the freehold when the latter is acquired, both assets are to be treated as the same asset. If one is a pre-entry asset, then the asset which derives value from it is also treated as a pre-entry asset.

Unrealised losses
Particular difficulty arises when the pre-entry loss is an unrealised loss. There is a pre-entry loss when a company joins a group holding an asset which, when subsequently sold, gives rise to a loss. In this situation, the basic rule is that the pre-entry loss (strictly the pre-entry proportion of the loss) is determined by time apportioning the loss into the period before and the period after the relevant time (ie when it joined the group). Alternatively, if the company so elects, the apportionment is based on the market value of the relevant asset at the relevant time (ie when it is brought into the group). Such an election has to be made within two years of the end of the accounting period in which the loss-making disposal occurs, or such longer period as the Revenue allows. Where the election is made, the pre-entry loss is the lesser of the actual loss and the loss which would have arisen on a market value disposal of the pre-entry asset at the relevant time. If, on the market value basis, no loss arises, it is to be assumed that there is no pre-entry loss (TCGA 1992, Sch. 7A, Para. 5(3)).

The details of the time apportionment rules applicable when no election has been made for the market value alternative are set out in Paragraph 2 of new Schedule 7A. Under these, the pre-entry loss on a pre-entry asset is given by the formula:

$$A \times \frac{B}{C} \times \frac{D}{E}$$

where:

A is the total amount of the allowable loss;

B is the *pre-entry* allowable expenditure on the asset;

C is the *total* allowable expenditure on the asset, pre-entry and post-entry;

D is the length of the period beginning with either the date of acquisition of the asset or 1 April 1982, whichever is the later, and ending at the relevant time, and

E is the length of the period beginning with the later of 1 April 1982 and the acquisition date and ending with the date of disposal (TCGA 1992, Sch. 7A, Para. 2(1) to 2(3), (8)).

The result of the application of this basic rule is that the total loss is apportioned into specific items of expenditure, that is, expenditure allowable under TCGA 1992, s. 38. These items are each then apportioned on a straight line basis between the periods before and after the relevant time. The sum total of times apportioned to the period before the relevant time is the pre-entry loss.

Example 8.28

Honey Ltd bought a property in July 2000 for £1 million. In July 2002 the company joined the Sweet-tooth Group. In July 2003 Honey Ltd built an extension for £100,000.

On 1 August 2004 Honey sold the property for £500,000 to Curd Ltd, an unconnected party.

The total allowable loss is:

	£	£
Sale price		500,000
Less: purchase price	1,000,000	
Enhancement expenditure	100,000	(1,100,000)
Total allowable loss		(600,000)

The calculation of the pre-entry proportion of the loss on the asset is:

$$A \times \frac{B}{C} \times \frac{D}{E}$$

$$\pounds600,000 \times \frac{\pounds1,000,000}{\pounds1,100,000} \times \frac{24}{49} = \pounds267,161$$

The pre-entry loss is therefore £267,161

Note 1: No apportionment of the enhancement expenditure is necessary, as it was incurred *after* Honey Ltd joined the Sweet-tooth Group.

Note 2: *D* is the period from July 2000–July 2003 (24 months)

Note 3: *E* is the period from July 2000–August 2004 (49 months).

Pre-entry losses: offset against gains

The main aim of the provisions is to ring-fence capital losses brought into a group. There are detailed rules which identify gains against which pre-entry losses may be set. Broadly, pre-entry losses can only be used against gains on the following kinds of assets (TCGA 1992, Sch. 7A, Para. 7):

(a) one disposed of by the relevant company before it joined the group;

(b) one held by the relevant company on entry into the group;

(c) one acquired by the relevant company from outside the group after entry and which throughout the period of ownership until disposal has been used for the purposes of a trade carried on by the company since before entry.

It should be noted that (c) above only refers to 'trade', not 'trade or business'. Nor does it extend to investment companies, such as a holding company in a trading group. Also, the ambit of the sub-paragraph is extremely narrow, depending as it does on the trade remaining in the same company even after a reconstruction.

Pre-entry losses which can be set off are deducted from a chargeable gain in priority to post-entry losses, and those arising in the same accounting period are before those carried forward from earlier accounting periods.

Pre-entry gains

The provisions were designed to counteract the perceived avoidance of tax where:

• a company (company A) has realised a substantial chargeable gain;
• an unrelated company (company B) has unrealised capital losses;

- company A is acquired by the group of which company B is a member;
- the assets with the unrealised losses are transferred intra-group to company A,
- company A disposes of the assets outside of the group in the same accounting period as that in which the chargeable gain was realised.

The provisions work by restricting the losses available for set off against gains which arise in a company before it joins a group (TCGA 1992, Sch. 7AA). The losses which may be set off are restricted to:

- losses which arose before the company joined the group, and
- losses which arise subsequently on assets which it held when it joined the group.

Given that capital losses may not be carried back to earlier periods, it is only necessary to deal only with the period in which company A joined the B group. Its chargeable gains for that period are computed separately for the parts of the period before and after joining the group, and therefore comprise:

- the adjusted pre-entry gains, and
- post-entry gains less post-entry losses (Sch. 7AA, Para. 2).

The adjusted pre-entry gains are the pre-entry gains less 'qualifying losses'. These are defined as:

- losses arising at or before the time when the gain arose;
- losses arising after that time but before the company joined the group, and
- losses arising after it joined the group on assets which it held when it joined the group,

(Para. 3).

8.6.6 Company reconstructions, etc.

Reorganisations

Whilst not within the scope of this work, it should be noted that relief by way of deferment of capital gains is given in respect of certain company re-organisations, reconstructions, amalgamations, etc.

Transfers of business

Where a scheme of reconstruction or amalgamation involves a transfer of the whole or part of a business from one company to another company, and the transferor company does not receive any consideration itself but the consideration is passed direct to the shareholders in that company, the assets transferred are treated as passing at no gain/no loss to the transferor company.

This relief however does not apply to trading stock or to assets acquired as trading stock. The relief applies whatever the consideration given to the shareholder, provided that at least some shares are given, although the shareholders themselves be treated as making a part disposal if they receive some cash (TCGA 1992, s. 139).

The no gain/no loss rules cover the cases where:

- the transferor company is resident in the UK at the time of the transfer, or the asset is a chargeable asset immediately before that time, or
- the transferee company is resident in the UK at the time of the transfer, or the asset is a chargeable asset immediately after that time.

A chargeable asset where, if it were disposed of, any gain would be chargeable, ie an asset situated in the UK and used for the purposes of a trade carried on by the transferor through a permanent establishment in the UK (TCGA 1992, ss. 10B and 139(1A).

Any indexation allowance available to the first company is added to the transfer price so that the assets are treated as passing at no gain/no loss.

Alteration of interests in company

The division of a company's business into two or more new companies owned by different sets of shareholders (having possibly reorganised the share capital of the original company into separate classes of shares to allow for this) would not in strictness rank as a reconstruction of this nature. However, where there is a genuine segregation of trades (as opposed to a segregation of assets only) into separate identifiable parts of the trade or business, each of which is capable of being carried on in its own right, and the division is carried out for bona fide commercial reasons, rather than just to facilitate a subsequent disposal of part of the trade, the Inland Revenue will accept it as a scheme of reconstruction for capital gains purposes (Inland Revenue Statement of Practice SP5/85).

Anti-avoidance and clearances

There is a proviso that the relief for such a transfer of assess is not to apply unless the reconstruction is carried out for bona fide commercial reasons and does not form part of a scheme or arrangement designed to avoid a tax liability. There is also a clearance procedure, whereby particulars of a proposed reconstruction may be submitted to the Inland Revenue in advance for a ruling as to whether the anti-avoidance provisions apply or not, but with no appeal against an adverse ruling, except against an ultimate assessment under the normal procedures, if the reconstruction is carried out anyway (TCGA 1992, s. 139(5)).

Intra-group transfers

The straightforward transfer of a trade or business or other assets between members of a 75%+ group of companies on a no gain-no loss basis has already been explained at **8.6.3**.

Demergers

The demerger provisions are designed to facilitate the division of trading activities carried on by a single company or group of companies into two or more independent companies or groups of companies. They are designed primarily to give income tax relief in respect of company distributions, but also have capital gains implications. The provisions are amplified by Inland Revenue Statement of Practice SP13/80.

Where a company makes an 'exempt distribution' of shares in a subsidiary company to its own shareholders, such distribution is not regarded as the proceeds of a part disposal by the recipient. Instead the distributing and distributed companies are treated as if they were a single company undergoing a reorganisation (TCGA 1992, s. 192).

Where a business is transferred as part of the deemed reconstruction the capital gains provisions for transfers of businesses as described above (TCGA 1992, s. 139) apply.

Relief under the demerger provisions only applies if the distributing company is a trading company or a member of a trading group, and any transferred subsidiary company must similarly be a trading company or a holding company of a trading group. Note however that dealing in land is specifically excluded from the definition of a trade for the purposes of this relief (ICTA 1988, ss. 213 and 218(1)).

8.6.7 Substantial shareholdings

As from 1 April 2002, where a company (company A) makes a disposal or part disposal of a 'substantial shareholding' in another company (company B), any gain arising on the disposal is exempt from corporation tax provided that certain conditions are met. These conditions relate to the period of ownership of the shares and the status of companies A and B (TCGA 1992, Sch. 7AC). Similarly, any loss arising on the disposal is not an allowable loss.

The rules are briefly outlined below, but it should be noted from the outset that as the rules only apply to trading companies/groups, property investment companies are excluded.

Meaning of 'substantial shareholding'

Company A has a substantial shareholding in company B if (TCGA 1992, Sch. 7AC, Para. 8):

- it holds not less than 10 per cent of the ordinary share capital of company B;
- it is beneficially entitled to not less than 10 per cent of the profits of company B that are available for distribution to equity-holders, and
- it would be beneficially entitled to not less than 10 per cent of the assets of company B that are available for distribution to equity holders in a winding up.

A company that is a member of a group is treated as holding shares held by other companies in the same group in determining whether it has a substantial shareholding (TCGA 1992, Sch. 7AC, Para. 9).

Disposals where qualifying conditions satisfied at an earlier time

A gain may also be exempt where company B satisfied the required conditions at some time within the period of two years ending with the disposal (TCGA 1992, Sch. 7AC, Para. 3). This covers the situation where company A or company B ceases to trade and goes into liquidation, for example.

No gain, no loss disposals

The legislation that treats disposals as being made for a consideration giving rise to neither gain nor loss takes precedence over this legislation, as does legislation providing for the exemption of a gain (TCGA 1992, Sch. 7AC, Para. 6).

Minimum period of ownership

In the case of a disposal of shares, company A must have held a substantial shareholding in company B throughout a 12-month period beginning not more than two years before the date of the disposal (TCGA 1992, Sch. 7AC, Para. 7). Where shares are acquired in tranches, the qualifying period starts once the combined shareholding exceeds the 10 per cent minimum required for the relief to operate. Once this minimum requirement is met, further additions to the (already substantial) shareholding qualify on acquisition. Similarly, part-disposals out of a substantial shareholding can be made within the exemption. Where the resulting shareholding immediately after a part-disposal is below the 10 per cent threshold, that shareholding can be disposed of within the next 12 months within the exemption, provided that the other qualifying conditions are satisfied.

Where the shares were acquired in a no gain/no loss transaction, or a series of no gain/no loss transactions, the holding period is extended by any earlier period during which the shares, or shares from which were derived, were held by a company from which they were transferred in the no gain/no loss transaction (TCGA 1992, Sch. 7AC, Para. 10). A similar rule applies where there has been a reconstruction or demerger that has been treated as not involving the disposal of any 'original holding' (TCGA 1992, Sch. 7AC, Paras. 14–16). However, the holding period cannot span a deemed disposal and reacquisition (TCGA 1992, Sch. 7AC, Para. 11).

Other qualifying conditions

Company A must have been a sole trading company or a member of a 'qualifying group':

- throughout the 'qualifying period, and
- immediately after the disposal of the shares or assets in company B (TCGA 1992, Sch. 7AC, Para. 18).

Company B must have been a trading company or a holding company of a trading group or sub-group throughout the qualifying period and must be such a company immediately after the disposal of the shares or assets in company B (TCGA 1992, Sch. 7AC, Para. 19).

A group 'qualifies' if is a trading group, or would be a trading group if the activities of non-profit-making members were disregarded so far as carried on otherwise than for profit.

The qualifying period is the period starting with the latest 12-month period by reference to which company A satisfies the minimum period of ownership requirement and ending with the date of the disposal of the shares in company B (TCGA 1992, Sch. 7AC, Para. 18).

Trading company and trading group

A trading company is one that carries on trading activities and does not carry on non-trading activities to any 'substantial extent' (TCGA 1992, Sch. 7 AC, Para. 20).

A trading group is a group in which:

- one or more members are carrying on trading activities, and
- the activities of the group as a whole do not include non-trading activities to any substantial extent (TCGA 1992, Sch. 7AC, Para. 21). Intra-group activities are ignored for this purpose.

A trading sub-group is a sub-group in which:

- one or more members are carrying on trading activities, and
- the activities of the sub-group as a whole do not include non-trading activities to any substantial extent, (TCGA 1992, Sch. 7AC, Para. 22).

It is understood that the Revenue will operate a 20 per cent rule of thumb in interpreting the 'substantial extent' requirement. This test may be applied to income, asset base, expenses incurred or time spent. Each case can only be decided on its own facts.

Interaction with gift relief

Where an asset is acquired by a company by way of a gift, then any gain rolled over on a TCGA 1992, s. 165 claim (see **8.7.8**) crystallises within the company and is not covered by this new exemption (TCGA 1992, Sch. 7AC, Para. 37).

8.7 Individuals, trustees and personal representatives

8.7.1 Introduction

The provisions regarding the taxation of chargeable gains discussed in **8.1** to **8.5** apply to taxpayers generally. There are some provisions which apply only to individuals, trustees and personal representatives, and they are discussed in this section.

They include:

- how capital gains tax is charged;
- the treatment of husband and wife;
- the exemption on death;
- occasions of charge for trustees;
- taper relief;
- principal private residence relief
- gift relief;
- incorporation relief;
- relief for works of art, etc.;
- enterprise investment scheme deferral relief,
- payment by instalments.

8.7.2 The charge to capital gains tax

Having ascertained the amount of any chargeable gain or allowable loss arising under the principles explained above and taking account of any reliefs or exemptions, the next step is to aggregate the total amount of chargeable gains less allowable losses accruing during the year of assessment and to deduct allowable losses brought forward from previous years, to find the net amount on which capital gains tax is chargeable (TCGA 1992, s. 2(2)). Note that the set off of brought forward losses is restricted so that the net gains are only reduced to the level of the annual exemption.

Allowable losses may not be carried back against chargeable gains arising in an earlier year, except in the case of a deceased person, where losses arising in the year of death can be carried back and set off against any chargeable gains arising in the three years immediately preceding the year of death (TCGA 1992, s. 62(2)). Again the set off is restricted to preserve the annual exemption.

Needless to say losses can only be allowed once (TCGA 1992, s. 2(3)).

Taper relief is applied to the net gains remaining after deducting losses (TCGA 1992, s. 2A).

Individuals

An individual's gains (after deducting the annual exemption) are charged to capital gains tax at rates equivalent to the rates of income tax that would apply if the gains were the top slice of his income and were savings income (but not dividends) (TCGA 1992, s. 4). Accordingly, depending on the level of that income, gains will be taxed in 2004/05 at 10 per cent, 20 per cent or 40 per cent, or at a combination of those rates.

Example 8.29

A taxpayer's gross income and gains for 2004/05 are as follows:

	£
Dividends	5,000
Interest	3,000
Other income net of reliefs and allowances	10,000
Chargeable gains after taper relief and annual exempt amount	50,000

The income tax on the chargeable gains is calculated as follows:

	£	
31,400 – 5,000 – 3,000 – 10,000	= 13,400 @ 20%	= 2,680
balance	36,600 @ 40%	= 14,640
	50,000	17,320

The taxpayer's unused personal allowances cannot be offset against his capital gains (TCGA 1992, s. 6(5)). Nor can capital losses be set against his income (with the exception on certain losses on shares subscribed for in unquoted trading companies). However, where an individual sustains a trading loss in any tax year, and that loss exceeds his income for the year, he may claim to set off the excess against his chargeable gain for the same year (FA 1991, s. 72).

Trusts and estates

The personal representatives of deceased estates and trustees of settlements are normally chargeable to capital gains tax at the rate applicable to trusts, ie 40 per cent in 2004/05 (TCGA 1992, s.4 (1AA)).

Trustees are entitled to an annual exemption of one half of the amount available to an individual. This may be restricted if the settlor has created more than one trust.

Personal representatives are entitled to an annual exemption equal to that for an individual for the first three years of the administration period, but none in subsequent years.

Settlements in which the settlor has an interest

There are complicated anti-avoidance rules for trusts which are beyond the scope of this work, but in general if the settlor or his spouse has an interest in the settlement the gains are taxed as the settlor's (TCGA 1992, s. 77).

Where these provisions apply, the settlor will be entitled to recover an amount equivalent to the tax paid from the trustees (TCGA 1992, s. 78).

8.7.3 Husband and wife

In the case of a husband and wife living together during the relevant year of assessment, any disposals between the two spouses are treated as made at no gain/no loss to the transferor (see **8.3.4**).

This relief is not available where the asset is treated as the trading stock of one spouse but a capital asset of the other spouse. Nor does the relief apply to gifts made in contemplation of death (*donatio mortis causa*). Since such gifts would be exempt in the same way as a disposal at death this ensures that the transferee's acquisition cost is uplifted to the market value of the asset free of capital gains tax, in the same way as for other donees in similar circumstances (TCGA 1992, s. 58).

Indexation relief

Any indexation allowance available to the transferor is included in the transfer price so that after deducting the allowance neither a gain nor a loss arises to him.

Taper relief

The transferee spouse's period of ownership, or deemed period of ownership, is deemed to include the transferor spouse's period of ownership (TCGA 1992, Sch. A1(15)). For assets other than shares, then whether or not the asset qualifies a business asset is determined as follows:

- prior to the transfer, by reference to either spouse, and
- after the transfer, only by reference to the transferee spouse.

Shares will only qualify as business assets for periods during which the company was a qualifying company for the transferee spouse.

8.7.4 Death

For capital gains tax purposes the death of an individual is treated as the occasion of the acquisition by his personal representatives or other persons on whom the assets devolve (such as joint owners) of all assets owned by him at that time. The acquisition is deemed to take place at the market values of those assets, being the value as applied for inheritance tax purposes. However, the event is not treated as a disposal by the deceased for capital gains tax purposes. Thus the effect is a tax-free gain to the deceased, and a higher capital gains tax acquisition cost to his successors (assuming that the property is worth more at the date of death than when it was originally acquired by the deceased) (TCGA 1992, ss. 62(1) and 274).

Personal representatives

The personal representatives are regarded as a continuing body of persons, so that there is no disposal for capital gains tax purposes, when there is a change in persons acting in this capacity (TCGA 1992, s. 62(3)).

Transfers to heirs

Where the personal representatives subsequently transfer property to a legatee in the ordinary course of dealing with the deceased's estate, it is not regarded as a disposal by the personal representatives for capital gains tax purposes. Where the legatee subsequently disposes of the property himself, he is regarded as having acquired it at the same time and cost as the personal representatives, namely at the probate value at the time of death of the original owner.

This covers the transfer of assets in kind in satisfaction of a cash legacy, as well as a legacy of assets themselves. The personal representatives might therefore give some consideration to the satisfaction of cash legacies in kind in this way, to avoid a capital gains tax liability on the sale of assets to provide the requisite cash (TCGA 1992, s. 62(4)).

Family arrangements

A deed of family arrangement, or disclaimer, or similar re-arrangement of the terms of the deceased's will or the laws of intestacy, is treated as altering the terms of the original will or intestacy, if made within two years of death and provided a statement to this effect is included in the deed. If under the terms of the deed the assets are held on trust the original beneficiary is, however, treated as the settlor of a trust (*Marshall v Kerr* [1994] BTC 258).

Such an arrangement can still be made, within the two-year limit, even if the estate has already been distributed. It should be noted that in times of falling prices this treatment may not be worthwhile.

The special rules will not apply if the arrangement is made for some consideration other than a consideration consisting of a variation or disclaimer in respect of another of the dispositions (TCGA 1992, s. 62(6) to (9)).

Gifts before death

Similar treatment is given to a disposal by way of gift in contemplation of death (*donatio mortis causa*), which is also treated as not giving rise to a chargeable gain and so is exempt from capital gains tax as far as the donor is concerned, but with an acquisition by the donee at full market value (TCGA 1992, s. 62(5)).

Trusts

Where the deceased had a life or other interest in a trust, further capital gains tax implications may apply (see **8.7.5**).

8.7.5 Trusts

Numerous special provisions relate to the capital gains tax position of trusts and their beneficiaries. It is therefore worthwhile considering the main points that may apply to property-owning trusts.

Transfer into trust

A transfer into a settlement is treated as a disposal for the capital gains purposes of the whole of any assets thus transferred. Even where the trust is a revocable trust or the transferor is a beneficiary or he otherwise retains some interest in the property, or where the transferor is one of the trustees or the sole trustee, the setting up of the trust is nevertheless regarded as a full disposal of those assets rather than a part disposal with a retained interest (TCGA 1992, s. 70). The transfer is normally regarded as taking place at market value (see **8.3.3**).

An individual transferor may be in a position to claim 'holdover' relief so that the resulting gain is deferred until the trustees make a disposal of the assets (see **8.7.8**).

Changes in trustees

The trustees are regarded as a continuing body of persons, so that a change in the persons acting as trustees does not result in a disposal for the capital gains purposes. If part of the property is vested in one set of trustees and part in another set (and in particular where settled land within the meaning of the Settled Land Act 1925 is vested in a tenant for life and investments representing capital monies are vested in the trustees of the settlement), the trustees are nevertheless treated as one single body of persons for this purpose (TCGA 1992, s. 69(1) to (3)).

Disposals of trust property to third parties

Where the trustees dispose of trust property by way of sale or otherwise, they are liable to capital gains tax on any chargeable gain realised by them, taking their acquisition cost as the market value of the property when transferred into the trust as reduced by any 'holdover' relief, or else any actual costs incurred by them in the acquisition of the asset.

Distribution of trust assets

Where a beneficiary becomes absolutely entitled to trust property as against the trustees (or would become so entitled but for being an infant or under a similar legal disability), the occasion is treated as a deemed disposal of the property by the trustees at its market value and a reacquisition by them as bare nominees for the beneficiary. A resulting gain may be deferred in certain circumstances by claiming 'holdover' relief (see **8.7.8**). Any subsequent transfer of the legal title to the property to the beneficiary is disregarded as being a transfer from a nominee to the beneficial owner (TCGA 1992, s. 71(1)).

If, however, a beneficiary becomes absolutely entitled to trust assets as a result of the death of the life tenant (again subject to being an infant or under some other disability) any gain arising on the disposal is not treated as a chargeable gain and is therefore exempt. If holdover relief had been claimed on the transfer of assets into the settlement, the gain is not exempt but is limited to the amount of the heldover gain (TCGA 1992, s.74). This gain may itself be eligible for further holdover. Normally the beneficiary treats the full market value of the property, less any 'holdover' relief claimed, as his acquisition cost in computing the capital gains tax liability on any subsequent disposal. If the settled property reverts back to the settlor on the death of the life tenant, the transfer is treated as taking place at such a value as would give rise to no gain/no loss to the trustees, so that the settlor takes the property at its original acquisition cost to them (plus indexation, if available) (TCGA 1992, s. 73(1)).

A beneficiary can claim any expenses incurred by the trustees in transferring the assets as if they were the incidental costs of his own acquisition.

If the deemed disposal gives rise to an allowable loss which cannot be set against gains on other assets vesting in the beneficiary or other gains realised by the trustees in the same year but before the deemed disposal, the loss can be transferred to the beneficiary. It can then only be set against future gains arising on that asset or, where the asset is an estate, interest or right in or over land, on any asset deriving from that asset (TCGA 1992, s. 71(2)–(2D)).

Termination of life interest, property remaining settled

The termination of a life interest other than on the death of the life tenant does not have any capital gains tax consequences if the property remains settled property.

Where a life interest in possession terminates on the death of a life tenant but remains settled property, the settled property is treated as if it is disposed of and reacquired by the trustees at its market value, but any gain arising is not chargeable (TCGA 1992 s. 72). If holdover relief had been claimed on the transfer of assets into the settlement, the gain is not exempt but is limited to the amount of the heldover gain (TCGA 1992, s.74). This gain may be the subject of a further holdover claim.

Partial interests

Where the life interest in possession relates only to part of the trust assets, or where it gives an entitlement to only part of the trust income, the notional disposal and re-acquisition is restricted to those assets that are the subject of that interest, or a corresponding part of the total trust assets as appropriate (TCGA 1992, ss. 72(1) and (5) and 73(2) and (3)). Thus the death of a person having a one-quarter interest in trust funds was held to be a deemed disposal of only one-quarter of those settled funds, rather than the whole of the assets forming the settlement (*Pexton v Bell and Another* (1976) 51 TC 457).

Annuitants

Where a beneficiary is entitled to an annuity out of trust income, this is not normally regarded as a limited life interest in possession, even if the annuity is charged on trust property, unless the trustees actually appropriate trust property for this purpose and the beneficiary has no recourse to any other trust assets.

Nevertheless, in the event of the death of an annuitant, a deemed disposal arises as if the annuitant had a limited interest in possession, with a corresponding deemed disposal of part of the trust assets taking place on his death, so that the capital gains tax exemption upon death can then apply to any such notional gain, and it will thus be exempt. Again the effect is to increase the acquisition cost of the trustees on a tax-free basis (TCGA 1992, ss. 72(4) and 75).

Holdover relief

Note however that the trustees and beneficiary may be able to jointly elect for the capital gain to be deferred under holdover relief, where a gain arises in connection with the transfer of business assets or shares in a trading company by way of distribution of trust assets or upon the termination of a life interest in possession (see **8.7.8**).

Discretionary and accumulating trusts

In a discretionary or accumulating trust, there are no beneficiaries entitled to income, and so no life interest in possession for the above purposes. There is thus no deemed disposal for capital gains tax purposes on a change in beneficiaries receiving income from the trust, even if occasioned by the death of such a beneficiary. Capital gains tax does however apply on the distribution of trust assets in specie to any beneficiary.

The rule in Crowe v Appleby

In *Crowe v Appleby* (1976) 51 TC 457, the testator's residuary estate, which comprised freehold property, was held in trust for the trustees to sell and hold the proceeds for his five children; each child's share was held on protective trust for their benefit for life. Two of the testator's children died and their shares devolved to their children absolutely. The freehold property was subsequently sold and the trustees assessed on the gain. The trustees contended that the gain on the ultimate sale should be computed on the basis that on the deaths of the children the beneficiaries to whom their shares passed were absolutely entitled. It was held that the children's shares in the property – being an undivided share of land – had not vested absolutely in the beneficiaries, so that they were unable to direct the trustees to transfer the assets to them.

The decision has important capital gains tax ramifications for any trust where there are undivided shares in land. The Inland Revenue's view (*Capital Gains Tax Manual*, CG 37520ff.), based on the High Court decision, is that each beneficiary should be regarded as having become absolutely entitled on the occurrence of each successive contingency to the appropriate share of assets which are readily divisible into shares, unless the trustees have an express power to decide which assets should go to a beneficiary in satisfaction of his beneficial interest. Where the trustees do have such a power, no beneficiary should be regarded as having become absolutely entitled to the appropriate share of any such assets until the last contingency is fulfilled, or (if sooner) until the trustees appropriate specific assets to a beneficiary whose share has vested. Thus, if the settled property is land in England or Wales, the Revenue takes the view that there is no occasion of absolute entitlement on the occurrence of any contingency other than the final one: the beneficiary has no right to call upon the trustees to transfer to him an undivided share of the land or to create a tenancy in common.

Charities

Charities are generally exempt *from* capital gains tax on any gain arising from the disposal of an asset, if the proceeds are applicable and applied for charitable purposes (TCGA 1992, s. 256(1)).

However where property previously held on charitable trusts ceases to be so held, it is treated as sold and re-acquired at its market value at that time. Any gain arising from this notional disposal is treated as accruing otherwise than to a charity, and so does not fall within this exemption. Moreover, where the consideration for an earlier actual disposal of an asset by the trustees has been applied in acquiring assets held at the time the trust ceases to be charitable, any gain arising from the earlier disposal also loses its exemption and tax is also assessed on that earlier gain. The time limit for assessments is extended to three years after the property ceases to be held on charitable trusts. The provision is to prevent avoidance of capital gains tax through the use of a trust set up for temporary charitable purposes, pending the realisation of a profit, ultimately destined for other non-charitable purposes (TCGA 1992, s. 256).

8.7.6 Taper relief

Introduction

Indexation relief is abolished for individuals, trustees and personal representatives as from 6 April 1998, and has been replaced by taper relief. Where an asset was acquired before that date, indexation relief is still given, but up to that date only. Indexation relief continues to apply for corporation tax purposes, so taper relief is not available for corporation tax purposes.

Taper relief applies in calculating the chargeable gains arising on disposals by individuals, trustees and personal representatives occurring on or after 6 April 1998 (TCGA 1992, s. 2A and Sch. A1). It works by restricting the chargeable gain to a percentage of the gain that would otherwise be chargeable. Losses are not tapered, but must be deducted from gains before taper relief is applied. The taxpayer can allocate losses against gains as he chooses, and should therefore allocate them against the gains eligible for the lowest rates of taper relief. Each gain remaining is then considered separately in order to determine whether it is eligible for taper relief and at what rate.

Gains arising on the disposal of the following assets are eligible for taper relief:

- a business asset with a qualifying holding period of at least one year,
- any other assets with a qualifying holding period of at least three years.

Taper relief reduces the eligible gain by a percentage which depends on the number of whole years comprised in the 'qualifying holding period'. The qualifying holding period begins on the later of the date of acquisition and 6 April 1998 and ends on the date of disposal. However, in the case of a non-business asset held on 16 March 1998, the start date is effectively 6 April 1997, giving the owner a 'bonus year' of ownership (TCGA 1992 s. 2A(8)).

Subject to that, however, periods of ownership before 6 April 1998 are ignored, being covered by indexation relief, as explained above. The percentage relief applying to disposals on or after 6 April 2002 is shown in the table set out below.

No. of whole years in qualifying holding period	Percentage of gain chargeable	
	Business assets	**Other assets**
1	50.0	100
2	25.0	100
3	25.0	95
4	25.0	90
5	25.0	85
6	25.0	80
7	25.0	75
8	25.0	70
9	25.0	65
10 or more	25.0	60

Business assets

The definition of business assets has changed significantly twice since taper relief was introduced. The changes are not retrospective, so an asset may change its status from a non-business asset to a business asset part of the way through the period of ownership. It is crucially important to review the status of the asset throughout its whole period of ownership to determine the available rate of taper relief (see below for computational examples).

Assets other than shares

From 6 April 1994 an asset is a business asset (TCGA 1992, Sch. A1, Para. 5):

(a) if it is used wholly or partly for a trade carried on by an individual, trustees or personal representatives, or a partnership whose members included an individual, trustees or personal representatives,

(b) if it is used wholly or partly for a trade carried on by a company which is:

    (i) a qualifying company in relation to the disposer; or

    (ii) a company which is a member of a trading group where the holding company is a qualifying company in relation to the disposer, or

    (iii) a partnership where one of the members is a qualifying company as in (i) or (ii) above.

The disposer may be an individual, trustees or personal representatives. If the disposal is made by trustees, (b) extends to cases where the appropriate company is a relevant company in relation to an eligible beneficiary;

(c) in the case of a disposal by an individual, if it is used by that individual for the purpose of an office or employment with a person carrying on a trade, or

(d) in the case of a disposal by trustees, if it is used by an eligible beneficiary individual for the purpose of an office or employment with a person carrying on a trade.

Before 6 April 2004, (a) above only applied if the trade was carried on by the individual, trustees (or an eligible beneficiary) or personal representatives who made the disposal, or a partnership of which they were a member. Thus a property let by an individual to an unconnected partnership is only a business asset from 6 April 2004.

Where a property is let to an unconnected company, however, it may qualify as a business asset from 6 April 2000 because of the change in definition of a qualifying company (see below)

Shares

Shares in a company qualify as business assets if the company is a 'qualifying company' by reference to the person making the disposal of the shares (TCGA 1992, Sch. A1, Para. 4).

Qualifying companies

From 6 April 2000, a company is a qualifying company for an individual, trustees or personal representatives in the following circumstances (TCGA 1992, Sch. A1, Para. 6):

(a) the company is a trading company or the holding company of a trading group and:

- is unlisted; or

- not less than 5 per cent of the voting rights are exercisable by the individual, trustees or personal representatives as appropriate, or

- the individual, or an eligible beneficiary in the case of a disposal by trustees, is an officer or employee of the company or of another company in the same group, or

(b) the company is a non-trading company or the holding company of a non-trading group where the individual, or an eligible beneficiary in the case of a disposal by trustees, is an officer or employee of the company or of another company in the same group and the individual, or trustees, do not have a material interest in the company. An interest is material if it comprises more than 10 per cent of the issued shares in a class, or the voting rights, or profits distributable or assets available on a winding up.

An unlisted company is one which has none of its shares or securities listed on a recognised stock exchange and which is not a 51 per cent subsidiary of a company which has any of its shares or securities so listed.

Prior to 6 April 2000 the company had to be a trading company or the holding company of a trading group and the individual, trustees or personal representatives had to have at least 25 per cent of the voting rights. If the individual, or in the case of a trustees disposal, and eligible beneficiary, was a full-time working officer or employee of the company (or another group company), then 5 per cent of the voting rights were sufficient.

The Revenue has provided guidance on the meaning of certain terms used in the legislation (*Tax Bulletin*, Issue 62, December 2002). Particular points to note are:

- A holding company is a company that has one or more 51 per cent subsidiaries (TCGA 1992, Sch. A1, Para. 22(1)).
- A trading company is defined as a company carrying on trading activities whose activities do not include to a substantial extent activities other than trading activities (TCGA 1992, Sch. A1, Para. 22A(1)). 'Substantial' is not defined, but the Revenue has indicated that it regards more than 20 per cent as substantial. This test may be applied to income, asset base, expenses incurred or time spent. Each case can only be decided on its own facts.
- A trading group is similarly defined as a group one or more of whose members carries on trading activities provided the activities of the group as a whole do not include, to a substantial extent, activities other than trading activities (TCGA 1992, Sch. A1, Para. 22B(1)). The activities of the group are regarded as a whole, and intra-group activities are ignored.

- Trade includes any activity treated as a trade, profession or vocation by the Taxes Acts that is conducted on a commercial basis (TCGA 1992, Sch. A1, Para. 22(1)). It includes furnished holiday lettings and farming and other commercial occupation of land regarded as a trade under ICTA 1988, s.53.
- Holding surplus trading property will not necessarily be treated as a non-trading activity. For example part of the trade premises may be let, property which has been used for trading may be temporarily let prior to sale or sublet where assignment or surrender of the lease is impracticable, or property may be purchased with the intention of using it for trade purposes. Again, each case will depend on the specific facts.

Eligible beneficiaries

A beneficiary is 'eligible' if he has a 'relevant interest in possession' in the asset concerned. This means any interest in possession other than a right to an annuity or a fixed-term entitlement. Where there are non-eligible and eligible beneficiaries in relation to a particular asset, any gain on disposal of the asset is apportioned by reference to the beneficiaries and the part relating to the eligible beneficiaries qualifies for taper relief. The apportionment is made by reference to entitlement to income (TCGA 1992, Sch. A1, Paras. 7 and 8).

Restriction for non-business use

Where an asset was a business asset throughout the period of ownership after 5 April 1998, the taper relief is available without restriction. Where it was a business asset for only part of that period, the gain is apportioned on a time basis between business use and non-business use. The part of the gain relating to business use then qualifies for business asset taper relief as if the period of ownership was the whole period, not just the part relating to business use. The balance of the gain qualifies for non-business asset taper relief on the same basis (TCGA 1992, Sch. A1, Para. 3).

Example 8.30

A freehold property is acquired on 1 April 1999 for £80,000. It is occupied for the purposes of a trade from that date until 31 March 2002. It is then let out to an unconnected partnership which uses it for trade purposes. The property is sold on 30 September 2007.

The total period of ownership is 8½ years. The period of business use is 3 years (1 April 1999–31 March 2002) plus 3½ years (6 April 2004–30 September 2007). Therefore the fraction of the gain on disposal which relates to business use is 6½/8½. If the net disposal consideration is £205,000, then the overall gain is £125,000. Of this, 78/102 × £125,000 = £95,588 is reduced by multiplying by 25% to £23,897 (business asset, 8 complete years of ownership). The balance of £125,000 – £95,588 = £29,412 is reduced to 70% of £29,412 =£20,588 (non-business asset, 8 complete years of ownership). Thus the net chargeable gain is £23,897 + £20,588 = £44,485.

Contrast this with the position had the property been let to an unquoted trading company. The property would have been a business asset throughout and the tapered gain would be 25% × £125,000 = £31,250.

Example 8.31

Harriet owned 10 per cent of the ordinary shares of U Ltd, an unquoted trading company. She had never worked for the company. She had held the shares since 1995 and sold them on 6 July 2004 making a gain (after indexation) of £50,000.

The total period of ownership since 6 April 1998 is 6¼ years, but the shares were not business assets prior to 6 April 2000. 4¼/6¼ × £50,000 = £34,000 is treated as a gain on a business asset, and is tapered to 25% × £34,000 = £8,500 (6 complete years of ownership). The remainder of the gain, £16,000, is treated as a gain on a non-business asset, and is tapered to 75% × £16,000 = £12,000 (7 complete years of ownership including the bonus year). The total chargeable gain is £8,500 + £16,000 = 24,500. Thus in total 49 per cent of the gain is chargeable. Contrast this with Harriet's sister, Jane. She also held 10 per cent of the shares in U Ltd, but had acquired them in May 2002. Only 25 per cent of her gain is chargeable, even though she had only held the shares for two years.

Asset used at the same time for different purposes

Any gain on disposal is apportioned by reference to business and non-qualifying use. The part relating to business qualifying use qualifies for taper relief at the business assets rate. Any apportionment is made on a just and reasonable basis (TCGA 1992, Sch. A1, Paras. 9 and 21).

Example 8.32

A freehold property is acquired on 1 June 1999 for £100,000. 75 per cent of the building is occupied for the purposes of a trade from that date until the date of disposal, 31 August 2007. The net sale consideration is £300,000. The period of ownership is 8 years and 3 months.

The gain before taper relief is £200,000. 75 per cent of this gain, ie £150,000, qualifies for business taper relief, and is reduced to 25% × £150,000 = £37,500. The balance of the gain, £200,000 – £150,000 = £50,000 is reduced to 70% × £50,000 = £35,000. Thus the net gain left in charge is £37,500 + £35,000 = £72,500.

Interaction with indexation allowance

Where an asset was acquired before 6 April 1998 and is sold after that date, the gain is computed giving indexation relief up to 5 April 1998 and then taper relief is applied to the gain remaining.

Anti-avoidance

Transactions reducing exposure to risk

Periods of ownership after 5 April 1998 during which the owner's exposure to risks of fluctuating values was limited by transactions entered into by the individual are excluded from taper relief altogether (Sch. A1, Para. 10).

Shareholdings in close companies: non-active periods of company

Any period of ownership of shares in a close company during which the company was not active does not count for taper relief purposes (TCGA 1992, Sch. A1, Para. 11A). A company is active at any time when:

- it is carrying on any business, whether or not on a commercial basis;
- it is preparing to carry on any business, or
- it or another person is winding up the affairs of a business that it has ceased to carry on.

Carrying on a business includes holding assets and managing them, but a company is not active merely by reason of:

- holding money in cash or on deposit;
- holding other assets whose total value is insignificant;
- holding shares or debentures in a non-active company;
- making loans to an associated company, or to a participator or associate thereof, or
- carrying out certain statutory administrative functions.

There is a useful article on this provision in *Tax Bulletin*, Issue 61 (October 2002).

Value shifting

Any part of the qualifying period falling before the time at which value is shifted into the asset is disqualified from taper relief. Where there is more than one occasion of value shifting, any period up to the latest occasion is disqualified (TCGA 1992, Sch. A1, Para. 12).

Options

Under TCGA 1992, s. 144, if an option is exercised, the grant of the option and the exercise are telescoped into one transaction. In such a case, the time of disposal is the date of disposal which results from the option being exercised. The time of acquisition is the date of exercise of the option (TCGA 1992, Sch. A1, Para. 13).

Assets derived from other assets

The asset disposed of is treated as acquired at the earliest time at which any asset from which its value is derived was acquired into the same ownership (TCGA 1992, Sch. A1, Para. 14).

Assets transferred between spouses

The transferee spouse's period of ownership, or deemed period of ownership, is deemed to include the transferor spouse's period of ownership. This applies both for the purposes of determining the amount of taper relief and, in the case of business assets other than shares, for determining whether the asset qualified as a business asset at any time (TCGA 1992, Sch. A1, Para. 15) (see **8.7.3**).

Heldover gains and postponed gains

A special rule is required for dealing with the situation where a gain which is held over eventually crystallises. The taper relief is not recalculated by reference to the date on which the gain crystallises. The original taper relief stands. This rule applies in particular to the following heldover gains (TCGA 1992, Sch. A1, Para. 16):

- gains falling within TCGA 1992, s. 10A (temporary non-residents);
- replacement of business assets where the new asset is a depreciating asset (TCGA 1992, s. 154(2) or (4)),
- EIS or VCT reinvestment (TCGA 1992, Sch. 5B or 5C).

Where relief is given by deducting a gain from the cost of another asset, such as under rollover relief on the replacement of business assets, holdover relief on gifts of business assets or incorporation relief, taper relief to that date is wasted. Taper relief is given on the disposal of the 'new' asset by reference only to its period of ownership.

Enhancement expenditure

Taper relief is given by reference to the period of ownership of the asset disposed of. Enhancement expenditure does not bring a separate asset into existence. Therefore the gain attributable to the enhancement expenditure is not treated separately for taper relief purposes, but is simply part of the single gain arising on disposal of the asset. Thus if an individual purchases a freehold property in say 2000 and has an extension built in 2005, taper relief on the entire gain arising on a subsequent disposal is calculated by reference to the year 2000 acquisition date.

It is, of course, a question of fact whether a person acquires a second asset or enhances an original asset. Under land law, however, a building forms part of the land on which it stands. It is the interest in that land which is enhanced by the expenditure.

Partnership assets

Each partner holds a proportionate interest in a partnership asset. He may first acquire an interest when he becomes a partner, but the partnership agreement may provide for asset-ownership sharing ratios which are different from the profit-sharing ratios. Where a partner's interest in an asset increases, the partner is generally deemed to incur enhancement expenditure equal to a proportion of the agreed value of the asset as at the date of the increase (see SP D12). Thus there is only one period of ownership for the purposes of taper relief and this period starts when the partner first acquired an interest in the asset.

See **8.8** for the treatment of partnerships.

8.7.7   Principal private residence relief

General

There is a complete exemption from capital gains tax for the disposal of a dwelling house which has been occupied by the owner as his only or main residence. The exemption may be restricted for periods of non-occupation, or if there has been business use (TCGA 1992, ss. 222–224).

House and grounds

'Dwelling-house' is not defined in the capital gains legislation and must therefore take on its normal meaning 'a house occupied as a place of residence'.

In most cases, whether or not the asset in question is a dwelling-house will not be in dispute. To come within the exemption, however, the dwelling-house must be used as a residence, mere ownership is insufficient (*Goodwin v Curtis (HMIT)* [1996] BTC 501).

In many cases, having determined that there is a 'dwelling-house', it is a straightforward exercise to identify how far the house extends, but in some cases it is not so simple. Exemption may, for example, be available in the case of separate premises occupied by a caretaker, gardener, etc. on the grounds that those premises are vicariously occupied by the owner as part of the main residence. Four cases have had a bearing on this: *Batey v Wakefield* (1981) 55 TC 550, *Markey v Sanders* (1987) BTC 176, *Williams v Merrylees* (1987) BTC 393 and *Lewis v Rook* [1992] BTC 102. The conclusion, based primarily on the decision of *Lewis v Rook*, to be drawn from these cases is that it is necessary for the premises to be close to the main residence. The correct test is whether the building is within the curtilage of, and appurtenant to, the main house so as to be part of the entity which constitutes the dwelling house occupied as the residence (see also the Revenue's comments in its *Tax Bulletin* August 1994).

The exemption extends to land which the individual has for his own occupation and enjoyment with that residence as garden and grounds up to the permitted area.

Occupation and enjoyment take their normal meanings, and entail unfettered possession and use of the land. Thus exemption is available for grounds which the individual holds under a lease or tenancy – no relief is available if the land is let to a third party, even on an informal licence.

'Garden' and 'grounds' are not defined in the statute and again must take their normal meaning. Each case can only be determined according to its particular facts.

The Revenue takes the word 'garden' to mean an enclosed piece of ground devoted to the cultivation of flowers, fruit or vegetables. The word 'grounds' is wider than this, and one dictionary definition of grounds is 'enclosed land surrounding or attached to a dwelling-house or other building serving chiefly for ornament or recreation'. In general, the Revenue accepts that land surrounding the residence and in the same ownership is the grounds of the residence, unless it is used for some other purpose. Thus land used for agriculture, commercial woodlands, trade or business would not be accepted as part of the garden or grounds. Land which has been earmarked for development and has been fenced off from the residence would not qualify.

Areas which have become neglected, paddocks and orchards may qualify, provided there is no business use. This also applies to buildings, such as summerhouses and greenhouses. Land which has some non-recreational use may qualify, such as the garden of a guest house which guests are allowed to use the garden.

It may be more difficult to obtain the benefit of the exemption if part of the land is separated from the main dwelling-house by other land which is not in the same ownership. In such a case, the Revenue will usually accept that land is part of the garden or grounds of the residence. However, it may be the case that the land is naturally and traditionally the garden or grounds of the house (for example, in some villages where it is common for the garden to be across the street from the dwelling-house) and in such a case, the physical separation should not of itself be regarded as a reason for denying relief (*Capital Gains Tax Manual*, 64369, 64370, *Wakeling v Pearce (HMIT)* (1995) Sp C 32).

The permitted area, including the site of the house, is an area of up to half a hectare (5,000 square metres). A greater area of land can be exempt if, having regard to the size and character of the house, a larger area is required for the reasonable enjoyment of that house as a residence (TCGA 1992, s. 222(3)).

What area of land an individual would require for the 'reasonable enjoyment' of his residence appears to import the concept of a 'reasonable person' and what such a person – as distinct from the particular taxpayer in question – would require (*Longson v Baker (HMIT)* [2002] BTC 356). This is a matter for negotiation with the Inspector of Taxes (who will take advice from the Valuations Office) and, failing agreement, an appeal before the commissioners.

On appeal, questions of valuation, as distinct from what constitutes the 'permitted area', are dealt with by the Lands Tribunal (TMA 1970, s. 47).

The Revenue has usually adopted a very restrictive view of the 'required' test and explained its views in the *Tax Bulletin* for February 1992, pp. 10–11. In particular, it relied on an old compulsory purchase case, Re *Newhill Compulsory Purchase Order* [1938] 2 All ER 163. The Revenue has tended to equate the term 'required' with something approaching 'indispensable'. Following the decision in Longson, it is likely that the Revenue will have become even more wedded to this view, even though there is an argument that this view is based on a mis-reading of *Newhill* and that the correct sense of 'required', in this context, should be somewhere between 'merely desirable' and 'essential'.

It is worth noting that the test of reasonableness is to be applied as at the time of the disposal; this may give a significantly different answer than that which would have been given when the property was acquired if the area has been the subject of radical change.

Where it is recognised that the area of land sold exceeds the 'permitted area', the calculation of the gain arising requires the following steps:

- identify the amount of the 'permitted area' and therefore by deduction the quantum of the excess area of land;
- determine which part or parts of the land is or are to be taken as making up the 'permitted area' (this is done by identifying which land would be the most suitable for occupation and enjoyment with the residence such that the total area of that land equals the 'permitted area'),
- value the land identified as the 'non-permitted area'; this exercise will not necessarily produce the same arithmetical result as a straight apportionment of the total gain based on size, as the 'permitted' and 'non-permitted' areas of land may have differing characteristics and therefore varying values per hectare.

If the property is sold in separate lots exemption is normally available for land sold before the house, provided the total area is less than half a hectare. If this area is exceeded, the Revenue may contend that exemption should not be available as the land being sold is not required for the reasonable enjoyment. Any part of the grounds disposed of after the main residence may not qualify for exemption (even if within the normal half hectare limit) since at the time of the disposal the house itself no longer qualifies since it is no longer owned (*Varty v Lynes* (1976) 51 TC 419 – see also the Revenue's comments in its *Tax Bulletin* August 1994).

Election

Where more than one residence is owned, an election may be made, within two years of the acquisition of the second residence, to determine which is the principal one (TCGA 1992, s. 222(5) and Extra-Statutory Concession D21, *Griffin v Craig-Harvey* [1993] BTC 3). Such an election need not accord with what is actually the principal residence, but if no election is made the question will be determined according to the facts. Following *Frost v Feltham* (1980) 55 TC 10, such a determination need not necessarily be based upon where the owner spends the greater part of his time. Once an election has been made it can be varied, and the variation can be retrospective, but not to a date more than two years prior to the variation.

Non-occupation

The rules are modified if only part of the property is occupied by the owner as a private residence. Such part occupation may apply in relation to a span of time or to the physical space occupied within the building. For example, where part of the house has been let, the exemptions would only apply to the unlet owner-occupied part (but see below for the letting exemption). Full exemption is, however, available in respect of occupation by a lodger who shares accommodation and takes meals with the owner and his family.

If the house has been an individual's main residence for only part of his ownership, only *part* of the gain is exempt. The exempt part is the proportion of the gain which the period when the house was his main residence bears to the total period of ownership. However, there are certain periods which are treated as if they had been periods when the house was the main residence. These periods include (TCGA 1992, s. 223(2), (3)):

(a)   up to three years of absence for any reason;

(b)   up to four years of absence whilst the individual is working elsewhere;

(c)   unlimited periods during which the individual is employed outside the UK, and

(d)   the last three years of ownership.

For the purposes of the capital gains tax legislation, 'periods of ownership' does not include any period before 31 March 1982 (TCGA 1992, s. 223(7)). Residence before 31 March 1982 will, however, establish the availability of the reliefs for periods of non-occupation. In cases (a) to (c) there must be periods of actual occupation both before and after the absence. By concession, the failure to re-occupy the property will be disregarded in cases (b) and (c) if the employee was prevented from resuming occupation because the terms of his employment required him to work elsewhere (ESC D4). If the individual builds a new house, or carries out renovations on buying a house, the fact that he does not take up immediate occupation is ignored, provided he moves in within 12 months of acquisition (ESC D49). It should be noted that the Revenue will allow the periods of non-occupation on a cumulative basis; they need not each be preceded and followed by actual occupation.

Business use

The relief may also be reduced where part of a house is occupied for the purposes of a trade. Claiming a deduction for the running expenses of using a room in the house as an office should not, however, lead to a restriction in the capital gains tax relief unless the room is used exclusively as an office. Using a room as an office during the working day and as a study in the evenings, for example, should not prejudice the relief.

Where the relief is restricted other reliefs may however be available, such as the rollover relief in respect of replacement of business assets (see **8.5.2**).

Where part of the property is used exclusively for business use throughout, the exemption for the last three years of ownership cannot apply to that part.

If the use was not exclusive throughout, the exemption for the last three years may apply.

Letting exemption

The owner-occupier exemption is extended to a residence that is partly let as residential accommodation, but the exemption for the let part of the house is limited to an amount equal to the amount exempted as occupied by the owner, subject to an overriding limit of £40,000. For this purpose the Inland Revenue will accept the letting of a part of a house, previously occupied by the owner and his family, as qualifying for relief when let as a flat or set of rooms, whether or not it has separate washing or cooking facilities, provided there are no major structural alterations, only minor adaptations.

Relief will not be available to property which, whilst forming part of the same building, affords completely separate accommodation to that occupied by the owner, such as a fully self-contained flat with its own access from the road (TCGA 1992, s. 223(4) and Inland Revenue Statement of Practice SP14/80).

In *Owen v Elliott* [1990] BTC 323, it was held by the Court of Appeal that the letting of rooms in a hotel was property 'let as residential accommodation' under TCGA 1992, s. 223(4), and therefore qualified for the relief from capital gains tax specified in the section, even where the guests stayed there (say) for holiday purposes.

Job-related accommodation

If an employee is required to live in accommodation provided by his employer under the terms of his employment, but owns another property which he intends to use as his only or main residence (eg in retirement) that property may be treated as occupied by him for the purpose of the capital gains tax exemption (TCGA 1992, s. 222(8)). This relief extends to a self-employed person required by contract to live on someone else's premises in order to carry on his trade, profession or vocation on land provided by that other person. Self-employed farmers and publicans living on tied premises are examples (ICTA 1988, s. 356(3)(*b*)).

Profit motive

The case of *Kirkby v Hughes* [1993] BTC 52 highlights the importance of the finding of facts when considering whether there is a profit motive. This relief is not available where the property is acquired or improved with a view to its disposal at a profit (TCGA 1992, s. 224(3).

Dependent relative

Gains arising on the disposal of property occupied by the taxpayer's dependent relative as his only or main residence are also exempt (wholly or in part) in certain circumstances, provided the property was so occupied on 5 April 1988, or at any earlier time during the tax-payer's ownership of the property since 31 March 1982 (TCGA 1992, s. 226).

Settlements and estates

Relief from capital gains tax may be claimed by trustees where a beneficiary occupies a dwelling house owned by the settlement as his only or main residence (TCGA 1992, s. 225).

Relief also extends to a house sold by personal representatives if it was both before and after death occupied by one or more beneficiaries, and those beneficiaries are together entitled to at least 75 per cent of the proceeds of sale TCGA 1992, s. 225A, previously ESC D5). This, for example, applies where a house left to the surviving spouse is sold by the personal representatives.

Claims for holdover relief

Relief for owner occupied property is not available for disposals by individuals or trustees after 10 December 2003 if a claim for holdover relief has been made under TCGA 1992 s. 260.

If the holdover claim had been made in respect of a disposal which occurred before 10 December 2003 then some transitional relief is allowed. Relief will be given on a time apportionment basis, assuming that the property did not qualify for relief after 9 December 2003, not even under the extension normally given for the last three years of ownership (TCGA 1992, s. 226A).

8.7.8 Holdover relief for gifts of business assets and agricultural property

Gifts of business assets and agricultural property

Holdover relief may be claimed where an individual makes a qualifying gift to another person (whether individual, trustees of a settlement or company). The relief may also be claimed in certain circumstances where trustees make a transfer out of a settlement to beneficiaries, as explained further on.

The relief is given by reducing the chargeable gain accruing to the donor on the disposal (calculated by reference to market value, see **8.2.6**) and a similar reduction is made to the allowable cost available to the donee on a subsequent disposal of the asset. This reduction is called the heldover gain.

Where the donee pays consideration for the asset which exceeds the donor's allowable cost, the heldover gain is the excess of the market value over the consideration given by the donee.

The relief must be claimed jointly by both parties to the transaction except where the gift is to trustees, in which case the claim need only be made by the donor (TCGA 1992, s. 165).

Where holdover relief is not available the tax may be paid in interest bearing instalments (see **8.7.11**).

Qualifying gift

The categories of gift qualifying for this relief are as follows:

- gift of business assets: this comprises assets used in a trade, profession or vocation carried on by the donor or by his personal company, or by a member of a trading group of which his personal company is the holding company. (A company is an individual's personal company if he holds at least 5 per cent of the voting rights.)
- gift of shares in a trading company or in a holding company of a trading group: the company must be either unquoted or the donor's personal company,
- gift of certain kinds of agricultural property (TCGA 1992, s. 165 and Part 1, Sch. 7).

For this purpose the definitions of holding company, trading company and trading group follow those used for taper relief purposes (TCGA 1992, s. 165(8) and Sch. A1, Para. 22) (see **8.7.6**).

Residence status

The donee must be resident or ordinarily resident in the UK, and therefore within charge to tax on capital gains. Moreover, where the donee is a company, the company must not at that time be under the control of a non-resident connected with the donor (TCGA 1992, ss. 166 and 167).

Where the donee is an individual who becomes neither resident nor ordinarily resident in the UK without having disposed of the asset the heldover gain becomes chargeable upon the donee (with provision for recovery of the tax from the donor) immediately before the change in status takes place. This charge is not made where the change in residence status occurs more than six years after the end of the fiscal year in which the original disposal took place: nor is it made where the change in status results from his taking up full-time employment overseas for a period of not more than three years, so long as at the end of the period he resumes residence or ordinary residence in the UK, still holding the asset in question (TCGA 1992, s. 168).

Partial business use

In normal circumstances in the case of an outright gift, the heldover gain is the full amount of the chargeable gain arising on the disposal. If however the asset is not used throughout the period of ownership for the purpose of a trade as above, the heldover gain is reduced in proportion to the period of qualifying use compared with the total period of ownership. Similarly, if the asset is a building or structure that is only partly used for the purposes of a trade as above, the heldover gain is reduced by such fraction as is reasonable in the circumstances.

If the asset consists of shares in a company and the donor held at least 25 per cent of the voting rights in the year before the gift, then if not all of the company's own assets are business assets, the heldover gain is reduced to the proportion that the company's chargeable business assets bear to the company's total chargeable assets. If the company is a holding company, the ratio applies to the group assets.

Receipt of consideration

In a case where the transferor actually receives some consideration for the disposal and that consideration exceeds the allowable costs available to him in computing his chargeable gain, the heldover gain is restricted to the unrelieved gain reduced by that excess. This restriction applies first, before applying any of the other fractions referred to above (TCGA 1992, Sch. 7, Paras. 5 to 7).

Transfers by trustees

The relief may also be claimed by trustees when making a transfer at an undervalue, eg when a beneficiary becomes absolutely entitled to assets of the trust.

The relief is available where the gift comprises either:

- assets used in a trade, profession or vocation carried on by the trustees or by a beneficiary with an interest in possession, or
- shares in a trading company or a holding company of a trading company where the company is unquoted or where the trustees hold at least 25 per cent of the voting rights (TCGA 1992, s. 165 and Sch. 7, Paras. 2 and 3).

Agricultural property

The relief described above is extended to non-arm's length disposals of agricultural property that would not otherwise qualify for business assets relief (TCGA 1992, Sch. 7, Para. 1). Agricultural property is that which would qualify for agricultural property relief if it was the subject of a transfer of value (see **Chapter 9**).

Time limit for claims

No specific time limit is mentioned so the general time limit in TMA 1970, s. 43 applies, ie five years after the 31 January following the tax year in which the disposal occurs.

Indexation allowance

Where the cost to the transferee has been reduced by holdover relief, the indexation allowance is calculated by reference to that reduced cost (see **8.3.6**).

Taper relief

Taper relief is wasted where holdover relief is claimed, as the ownership period for the donee runs from the date of the gift. If any part of the gain cannot be held over, taper relief is given according to the period of ownership and nature of the asset prior to the gift.

Gifts liable to inheritance tax

A similar relief is available for gifts between individuals and trustees on which inheritance tax is immediately chargeable. This would include a gift into a discretionary trust, even if covered by the nil rate band: whereas a potentially exempt transfer would not be included, even if it became chargeable as a result of the death of the donor within seven years (TCGA 1992, s. 260(2)(a)).

The relief is also available where the occasion of charge is a beneficiary of an accumulation and maintenance trust becoming absolutely entitled to an asset of the trust (TCGA 1992, s. 260(2)(d)).

The relief operates in the same was as the relief for gifts of business assets and with the same restriction on the residence status of the donee. There is, however, no restriction on the nature of the asset, and therefore no restriction when shares are gifted if the company holds non-business chargeable assets.

This relief is given in priority to the relief for business assets.

Gifts to settlor interested trusts

Holdover relief under TCGA 1992, s. 165 or s. 260 is not available if the recipient is a settlor interested trust (TCGA 1992, s. 169B). This anti-avoidance provision prevents a settlor interested trust from being used to reset the taper relief clock. The rules also prevent the assets from being routed via a third party, or the settlor later obtaining an interest in the trust.

8.7.9 Transfers of a business to a company for shares

Relief is available to an individual where he transfers a business to a company in exchange for new shares issued by that company (TCGA 1992, s. 162). The relief is given by way of a deduction from the chargeable gains arising on the disposal to the company, coupled with a corresponding reduction in the cost of the new shares acquired in the company, thus deferring the tax charge until a subsequent disposal of those shares. The relief only applies where the business is transferred as a going concern, together with the whole of the assets and undertaking of that business (except possibly cash). The relief was not prevented from applying where, prior to the transfer of farmland as part of the transfer of a business from a partnership to a company as a going concern, the company had agreed to sell the farmland to another party (*Gordon v IR Commrs* [1991] BTC 130).

Consideration for transfer

Where the consideration for the transfer consists wholly of new shares in the company, relief is given in respect of the whole of the chargeable gain arising from the disposal. If some other consideration is also received, other than new shares, the chargeable gain is allocated in proportion to the value of consideration received in shares and that other consideration and relief is restricted to that part allocated to the new shares.

Where the company takes over business liabilities as well as assets, the assumption of such liabilities is not regarded by the Inland Revenue as 'other consideration' for this purpose, although they will regard the transaction as the transfer of the whole of the business, even if not all the business liabilities are taken over (Inland Revenue Extra-Statutory Concession D32).

Deduction from chargeable gains

The amount for which relief is available is deducted from the chargeable gains arising on the disposal, so that capital gains tax only applies to the balance (ie that part of the chargeable gain allocated to consideration received other than in shares). Chargeable gains are taken as being the aggregate net gains, less allowable losses, arising on the disposal.

The relief is automatic but an election can be made to disapply the relief (TCGA 1992, s.162A). Such an election may be beneficial if, for example, the shares sold shortly after the transfer, before the top rate of business asset taper relief has applied, or if another relief is available, such as for the replacement of business assets (see **8.5.2**). The election must normally be made two years from the 31 January following the tax year in which the transfer occurred, but the time limit is shortened by one year if the shares are sold before the end of the tax year following the disposal.

New shares

The cost of acquisition of the new shares (which otherwise normally equals the value of the assets transferred or if not ascertainable equals the value of the shares received), under TCGA 1992, s. 17 (see **8.2.6**) is also reduced by a similar amount, so that the capital gains tax liability is thus deferred until those new shares are subsequently disposed of (TCGA 1992, s. 162).

Indexation allowance

The indexation allowance will be calculated by reference to the cost of acquisition of the new shares as reduced by the relief (see **8.3.6**).

Example 8.33

Diana Groves carries on a business which she transfers to Groves Ltd in exchange for 80,000 ordinary shares of £1 each (valued at £2 each) and £50,000 payable in cash – the company also taking over the liabilities of the business. The balance sheet of the business at the time of transfer may be summarised as follows:

	Cost	*Value*
	£	£
Freehold premises	70,000	180,000
Current assets	50,000	50,000
	120,000	230,000
Less: Current liabilities	20,000	20,000
Capital	100,000	210,000

If appropriate relief is claimed, the chargeable gain arising in respect of the premises is calculated as follows (ignoring indexation):

	£
Proceeds – taken as market value	180,000
Less: Cost of acquisition	70,000
Gain	110,000

Deferred gain:

$$\text{Gains} \times \frac{\text{Proceeds received in new shares}}{\text{Total proceeds}}$$

	£
$£110,000 \times \dfrac{£160,000}{£210,000} =$	83,810
Chargeable gain	26,190

When Diana Groves subsequently disposes of her shares in the new company, the cost allowable in computing the capital gains tax arising on that disposal is similarly reduced as follows:

	£
Cost of acquisition, at market value	160,000
Less: Deferred gain	83,810
Allowable cost	76,190

Gift of business assets

Another way for an individual to transfer business assets to a company is for that individual to gift them to the company. Holdover relief can then be claimed under TCGA 1992, s. 165 (see **8.7.8**).

Loss of taper relief

There is an effective loss of taper relief where gains are rolled over on incorporation of a business. This is because the gains which would otherwise arise are reduced, in some cases to nil, under TCGA 1992, s. 162(2). It is only the reduced gain which qualifies for taper relief. Thus the base cost of the shares in the company is reduced by the amount by which the untapered gains are reduced. However, the period of ownership of the shares starts on the actual date of acquisition (ie the date the shares were issued in exchange for the assets), there being no provision extending that period back to the date of acquisition of the transferred assets. The option to elect to disapply the relief (see above) mitigates the position if the shares are sold within two years of the transfer.

8.7.10 Works of art, etc.

A number of capital gains tax exemptions and reliefs apply which are basically related to the appropriate inheritance tax provisions (and see also Inland Revenue booklet IR67: *Capital Taxation and the National Heritage*).

Disposals to museums, etc.

Complete exemption is given in respect of assets which are disposed of by way of sale by private treaty to certain museums (IHTA 1984, Sch. 3) or where surrendered in satisfaction of inheritance tax (IHTA 1984, s. 230) and where a suitable undertaking has been given (TCGA 1992, s. 258(2)).

Treasury designations

Further relief is given, by treating the disposal and acquisition as taking place at no gain/no loss to the person making the disposal, in respect of heritage property where it is disposed of by way of gift, including gift into trust, or by transfer from a trust to the person becoming beneficially entitled, if the asset has been, or could be, designated by the Treasury under IHTA 1984, s. 31 and if an appropriate undertaking is given under that section (TCGA 1992, s. 258(3)).

Subsequent disposals or lapsed undertakings

Where a subsequent sale takes place and inheritance tax becomes payable under IHTA 1984, s. 32 (or would have become payable, if an inheritance tax undertaking had been given under IHTA 1984, s. 31), or where the terms of the undertaking are not observed, the asset is treated as if it were disposed of at its full market value for capital gains tax purposes, and re-acquired at that value if the undertaking was broken (TCGA 1992, s. 258).

8.7.11   Payment of tax by instalments on gifts

Subject to certain conditions, capital gains tax chargeable on a gift not eligible for holdover relief (see **8.7.8**) may, on election in writing, be paid by ten equal yearly instalments (in contrast to the eight-year spread where sales proceeds are paid in instalments). The first instalment is due on the ordinary due date and will be subject to the provisions regarding interest on overdue tax in the usual way. The outstanding balance, together with any accrued interest, may be paid at any time, and the balance becomes immediately payable if the subject matter is sold or is gifted to a connected party. The assets specified for these purposes are land, shares disposed of out of a controlling shareholding and unquoted shares (TCGA 1992, s. 281).

8.7.12   Enterprise investment scheme deferral relief

A chargeable gain on the disposal of any asset may be deferred if shares are subscribed for in a qualifying company under the enterprise investment scheme (TCGA 1992, Sch. 5B).

The conditions are complicated and are outside the scope of this work, but in broad terms a qualifying company is one which is unlisted at the time of the share issue and which uses the proceeds of the subscription to carry on a qualifying trade. There is a long list of non-qualifying trades, including in particular (ICTA 1988, s. 297(2)):

- dealing in land,
- property development,
- farming or market gardening,
- woodland and forestry activities,
- running hotels, and
- running residential care homes.

The reinvestment must be made within the period of one year before to three years after the date the gain which is to be deferred accrued (TCGA 1992, Sch. 5B, Para. 1(3)).

The gain which is to be deferred may be specified in the claim, but cannot exceed the lower of the amount of the chargeable gain (before taper relief) and the amount reinvested.

The deferred gain crystallises if the shares are disposed of (other than to the investor's spouse), or within three years the investor becomes non-resident or the shares cease to be qualifying shares (TCGA 1992, Sch. 5B, Para. 3). Taper relief is given on the gain according to the period of ownership of the original asset on which the gain was deferred.

8.8   Partnerships

8.8.1   General principles

A partnership is not deemed to be a separate person for capital gains purposes. Each partner is a separate taxable person and owns a share of each partnership asset. Partnership dealings are treated as dealings by the partners and not by the firm as such. Therefore, when there is a disposal of a partnership asset, each partner's gain is calculated separately (TCGA 1992, s. 59 and SP D12, paragraph 1).

Under self-assessment, the partnership statement for any accounting period must show the amount of the consideration which has accrued to the partnership in respect of each disposal of partnership property during that period and the apportionment of that consideration between the partners (TMA 1970, s. 12AB(1)(a)(ia), (b)). Each partner must show his capital gain on his tax return under TMA 1970, s. 8 or FA 1998, Sch. 18, Para. 3.

Ownership and valuation of partnership assets

The ratios in which partners own partnership assets is a matter for agreement between the partners. The ratios may not be the same as the profit sharing ratios. For example, it is not uncommon in smaller partnerships for the freehold or leasehold property from which the business is carried on to be owned by the founding partners, with incoming partners acquiring a share of profits but not any interest in the property. This may be reflected in the amount of capital which the incoming partners are required to subscribe. It is essential that the asset owning ratios are set out in the partnership agreement, especially if they are not the same as the profit sharing ratios.

The value of a partner's share in a partnership asset is his proportionate share of the value of the asset, without any discount for minority interests (SP D12, paragraph 1).

Partners are 'connected persons' for capital gains purposes except in relation to bona fide commercial arrangements (TCGA 1992, s. 286(4)). Therefore, the Revenue might insist on a revaluation of chargeable assets to open market value under TCGA 1992, s. 18 where there is a change in the ownership ratios or where a partner leaves the firm. However, in practice the Revenue will not invoke the market value rule where the partners are not otherwise connected with each other or, if they are, if the transaction is made on the same terms as it would have been had there been no connection (SP D12, paragraph 7).

The partners are not connected with a prospective new partner under TCGA 1992, s. 286(4) until he becomes a partner. However, if the partners make a bargain which is not at arm's length, the Revenue can intervene.

Chargeable occasions

Capital gains may arise in two types of circumstance:

(a)   a disposal of a chargeable asset by the partnership, or

(b)   a change in the composition of the partnership, or in the ratios in which the partners share in the ownership of the partnership assets.

As regards (a), a disposal by the partnership includes the case where a partner withdraws an asset from the partnership. This involves the other partners disposing of their interests in the asset to him (SP D12, paragraph 3).

Gains under (b) above can arise in the following circumstances:

- a partner leaves the partnership, thereby disposing of his interest in the partnership assets;
- a new partner joins the partnership and acquires from the other partners an interest in the partnership assets, or
- there is a change in the ratio in which the partners share in the ownership of the partnership assets. This involves acquisitions by partners whose shares increase and disposals by partners whose shares decrease.

If the assets concerned are revalued or consideration passes, this determines the disposal proceeds. If there is no revaluation and no consideration passes the disposal is treated as taking place for such consideration that no gain or loss accrues, ie at cost plus indexation.

It is important to note that gains under (b) above do not involve disposals of partnership property within the meaning of TMA 1970, s. 12AB(1)(ia) and will not, therefore, feature in any partnership statement under the self-assessment procedures. Nevertheless, partners to whom such gains arise are responsible for ensuring that those gains are included in their self-assessment tax returns.

Examples

The following examples illustrate the working of the above rules.

Example 8.34

A and B carried on business in partnership, sharing profits and assets equally. In 1999 the partnership acquired a freehold property for £100,000.

In 2002, C was taken into partnership and A, B and C agreed to share profits and assets equally. For the purposes of C's admission the property was valued at £180,000.

In 2004 the property is sold for £300,000.

In 2002, A and B each disposed of a 1/6th share in the property to C. Therefore, the gain arising to each is:

Part disposal	$1/6 \times 180,000 = £30,000$
Cost available for set off	$1/6 \times 100,000 = £16,667$
Gain before taper relief	£13,333

The capital gains base costs carried forward at that point are:

A 50,000 – 16,667	= £33,333
B 50,000 – 16,667	= £33,333
C 1/3 × £180,000	= £60,000

Therefore, the gains arising on the eventual disposal in 2004 are:

	A	B	C
Sale proceeds			
Cost			
	100,000	100,000	100,000
	33,333	33,333	60,000
Gain before taper relief	£66,667	£66,667	£40,000

Total gains arising before taper relief:

	A	B	C
In 2002	13,333	13,333	–
In 2004	66,667	66,667	40,000
	£80,000	£80,000	£40,000

These total gains are equal to the appreciation and profit on sale credited to the respective partners' accounts:

	A	B	C
In 2002 (180,000 – 100,000)	40,000	40,000	–
In 2004 (300,000 – 180,000	40,000	40,000	40,000
	£80,000	£80,000	£40,000

Notes

When C was admitted to the partnership, it was a matter for agreement between the partners as to whether C should subscribe capital in respect of his acquired interest in the freehold and whether A and B should withdraw capital equivalent to their part disposals to C. This would not affect the capital gains tax position.

However, if it was agreed that A, B and C would share profits equally but that C should not acquire any interest in the freehold property, then:

- no gains would have arisen in 2002, and
- the gain arising on the disposal of the freehold in 2004 would have been split equally between A and B.

Example 8.35

The facts are the same as in Example 8.34 except that the property is not sold. A retires in 2004 and relinquishes his share of all partnership assets. The property is valued at £300,000 for the purposes of his retirement. B and C share profits and assets equally after A's retirement.

Upon retirement, A disposes of his 1/3 share in the property to B and C equally.

A's chargeable gain (subject to indexation relief) is:

Value of disposal 1/3 × £300,000	= 100,000
Less capital gains cost B/F as before	33,333
	£66,667

B and C then have capital gains base costs C/F as follows:

	B	C
Cost B/F in 2002	33,333	60,000
Cost in 2004	50,000	50,000
Costs C/F	£83,333	£18,000

If the property is eventually sold for £360,000 the gains arising on sale, before taper relief, will be:

	B	C
Sale proceeds	180,000	180,000
Less capital gains cost	83,333	110,000
Unindexed	£96,667	£70,000

The total gains arising to B and C are:

	B	C
In 2002	13,333	70,000
On sale	96,667	
	£110,000	£70,000

Again these are equal to the total appreciation and profit on sale credited to the respective accounts of B and C:

	B	C
In 2002	40,000 ⎫	
In 2004	40,000 ⎬	40,000 as before
On sale (360,000 – 300,000)	30,000	30,000
	£110,000	£70,000

Notes

When A retires in 2004, a decision has to be taken as to whether he should withdraw the balance of his capital account at that point. If he did not withdraw it, the undrawn amount would have been transferred to a loan account. This would not, however, affect the CGT position.

In cases where the property is owned by the senior partner entirely, he may agree not to sell it immediately but to let it to the partnership for rent. Prior to 6 April 2004 the assets would not thereafter have qualified as a business asset for taper relief purposes. This drawback has been removed from 6 April 2004, provided the asset is used for trade purposes.

Example 8.36

The facts are the same as in Example 8.34 except that the property is not sold. In 2004 the partnership asset owning ratios are amended to the following:

A	1/5
B	2/5
C	2/5

The property is valued at £300,000 for this purpose. A has disposed of a 2/15 share (1/3–1/5) to B and C. A's gain is:

Value of disposal 2/15 of £300,000	=	£40,000
Allowable cost:		
40,000 × £33,333		
40,000 + 60,000	=	13,333
Gain before taper relief		£26,667
Capital gains cost C/F £33,333 – £13,333	=	£20,000

The capital gains cost C/F for B and C is:

	B	C
Cost B/F in 2002	33,333	60,000
Cost in 2004	20,000	20,000
	£53,333	£80,000

If the property is subsequently sold for £360,000 the gains arising on sale before taper relief are:

	A	B	C
Proceeds	72,000	144,000	144,000
Cost B/F	20,000	53,333	80,000
	£52,000	£90,667	£64,000

The total gains arising would then be:

	A	B	C
In 2002	13,333	13,333	–
In 2004	26,667	–	–
On sale	52,000	90,667	64,000
	£92,000	£104,000	£64,000

Once again the totals are equal to the total appreciation and profit on sale credited to each partner's account:

	A	B	C
In 2002 (90,000 – 100,000)	40,000	40,000	–
In 2004 (150,000 – 180,000)	40,000	40,000	40,000
On sale (360,000 – 300,000)	12,000	24,000	24,000
	£92,000	£104,000	£64,000

Partnership mergers and splits

The same principles apply where two partnerships merge or where a partnership splits into two or more separate firms (SP D12, paragraph 9). It is necessary to consider each partner separately and the disposals and acquisitions which he makes of interests in the partnerships' assets.

> ### *Example 8.37*
>
> Partnership X consists of partners, A, B and C sharing in the ratios 50 per cent, 30 per cent and 20 per cent. Partnership Y consists of partners D, E and F sharing in the ratios 40 per cent, 35 per cent and 25 per cent. They merge to form a new firm X, Y & Co. sharing profits as follows:
>
> | | |
> |---|---|
> | A | 30% |
> | B | 18% |
> | C | 12% |
> | D | 16% |
> | E | 14% |
> | F | 10% |
>
> A has disposed of a $(50\% - 30\%) = 20\%$ interest in the assets of Partnership X and has acquired a 30% interest in the assets of Partnership Y.
>
> B has disposed of a $(30\% - 18\%) = 12\%$ interest in the assets of Partnership X and has acquired a 12% interest in the assets of Partnership Y.
>
> C has disposed of a $(20\% - 12\%) = 8\%$ interest in the assets of Partnership X and has acquired an 8% interest in the assets of Partnership Y.
>
> D has disposed of a $(40\% - 16\%) = 24\%$ interest in the assets of Partnership Y and has acquired a 16% interest in the assets of Partnership X..
>
> E has disposed of a $(35\% - 14\%) = 21\%$ interest in the assets of Partnership Y and has acquired a 14% interest in the assets of Partnership X..
>
> F has disposed of a $(25\% - 10\%) = 15\%$ interest in the assets of Partnership Y and has acquired a 10% interest in the assets of Partnership X..
>
> Rollover relief is available under TCGA 1992, s. 152.

8.8.2 Limited Liability Partnerships (LLPs)

Where a limited liability partnership carries on a trade or business with a view to profit:

* assets held by the LLP shall be treated for the purposes of tax in respect of chargeable gains as held by its members as partners, and
* any dealings by the LLP shall be treated for those purposes as dealings by its members in artnership (and not by the LLP as such).

Accordingly, tax in respect of chargeable gains accruing to the members of the limited liability partnership on the disposal of any of its assets is assessed and charged on the partners separately (TCGA 1992, s. 59A).

This brings the tax treatment of LLPs into line with that of ordinary partnerships.

Where an LLP ceases to carry on its trade or business, it is treated as a company from the time of cessation. Gains on disposals made after that time are chargeable to corporation tax as though the LLP had always been a company. However, the cessation does not trigger any deemed disposal (TCGA 1992, s. 59A(2), (3)).

Where, immediately before the time of cessation of trade, a member of an LLP holds an asset, or an interest in an asset, acquired by him for a consideration treated as reduced under TCGA 1992, ss. 152 or 153 (replacement of business assets), he is treated as if a chargeable gain equal to the amount of the reduction accrued to him immediately before that time. If the previous gain was merely postponed under TCGA 1992, s. 154 it crystallises at that time (TCGA 1992, s. 156A).

8.9 Overseas elements

8.9.1 Non-residents generally

Individuals

An individual is liable to capital gains tax on the disposal of chargeable assets wherever situated if he is either resident or ordinarily resident in the UK during any part of the year of assessment in which the disposal takes place. This is subject to the rules discussed below regarding non-domiciled individuals (TCGA 1992, s. 2(1)).

By concession, a person who is treated as resident in the UK from the date of his arrival here, but who has not been regarded as resident in the UK at any time during the period of five years immediately preceding his or her arrival, is charged to tax only on gains arising after his arrival in the UK. Similarly, when a person leaves the UK, and is treated as neither resident nor ordinarily resident in the UK from the date of his departure, he is not charged tax on gains arising after the date of departure provided he had been not resident and not ordinarily resident for at least four complete tax years out of the previous seven (ESC D2). This concession does not extend to gains arising from assets held for the purposes of a trade carried on in the UK through a branch or agency.

Special rules apply to temporary non-residents (TCGA 1992, s.10A). If an individual is not resident and not ordinarily resident for a period of less than five complete tax years, and he had been resident and ordinarily resident for at least four out of the seven years prior to departure, then he will be taxed on his return on any gains made whilst non-resident. There is an exception for gains made on assets which were purchased after departure and sold before return. Note that such individuals do not come within ESC D2 and are not entitled to the split year treatment for the year of departure or return.

Where an individual is resident in the UK for a period of less than six months, and not with a view to establishing permanent residence here, he is not chargeable to capital gains tax except in relation to any branch or agency in the UK (TCGA 1992, s. 9).

An individual who is neither resident nor ordinarily resident in the UK, but who carries on a trade or profession through a branch or agency in the UK, is liable to capital gains tax on gains arising from the disposal of assets situated in the UK and either:

- used in or for the purposes of the trade at or before the time when the gain accrued, or
- used or held for the purposes of the branch or agency at or before that time, or acquired for use by or for the purposes of the branch or agency (TCGA 1992, s. 10).

Trustees

The trustees of a settlement are treated as a single and continuing body of persons. That body is regarded as resident and ordinarily resident in the UK unless the general administration of the settlement is carried on outside the UK and a majority of the trustees are not resident or not ordinarily resident in the UK (TCGA 1992, s. 69). As such it is liable to capital gains tax on the disposal of chargeable assets wherever situated. Professional trustees may still be regarded as not being resident here, even if themselves resident in the UK, if their business includes the management of trusts and they are acting as trustees in the course of that business. Provided that the settlor was himself domiciled, resident and ordinarily resident abroad at the time the assets were provided to the settlement, any professional trustees may be treated as non-resident also. If as a result a majority of trustees are then regarded as not resident in the UK, the general administration of the trust may also be treated as carried on outside the UK for this purpose (TCGA 1992, s. 69(1) and (2)).

Companies

A UK resident company is liable to corporation tax, and not capital gains tax, on chargeable gains arising from the disposal of assets wherever situated. The net gains form part of its profits for corporation tax purposes (ICTA 1988, s. 6).

A non-resident company which carries on a trade through a permanent establishment in the UK is chargeable to corporation tax on gains arising from the disposal of assets situated in the UK and either:

- used in or for the purposes of the trade at or before the time when the gain accrued, or
- used or held for the purposes of the permanent establishment at or before that time, or acquired for use by or for the purposes of the permanent establishment (TCGA 1992, s. 10B).

However, where such a non-resident company ceases to carry on the trade, there is a deemed disposal of the chargeable assets of that trade unless they are transferred to another company on a no gain/no loss basis under TCGA 1992, ss. 139 or 171.

UK branch or agency

Where an asset ceases to be chargeable because it is removed from the UK or because the trade ceases to be carried on in the UK through a branch or agency or, for a company, a permanent establishment, the non-resident is treated as having disposed of the asset and immediately reacquired it at its then market value (TCGA 1992, s. 25). Where a non-resident replaces a business asset within the charge to UK tax with a business asset outside the UK tax regime, no rollover relief (see **8.5.2**) is available unless the acquisition of the new asset occurs after the disposal of the old asset and at a time when the person has become resident or ordinarily resident in the UK.

Company migration

A company which is incorporated outside the UK will be UK resident if its central management and control is located within the UK. Such a company may emigrate by moving central management and control to outside the UK (Treasury consent is not required). Should they do so, however, all capital assets owned at the time of the cessation of residence will be deemed to be disposed of and immediately re-acquired at their market value immediately before that time. Chargeable gains arising on such a deemed disposal will be chargeable to corporation tax (TCGA 1992, s. 185(1) and (2)).

Gains arising on the disposal of the company's assets before its migration can only be rolled over (see **8.5.2**) into assets acquired after that time if the new assets are used for the purposes of a trade carried on by its UK permanent establishment (TCGA 1992, s. 185(3) and (4)).

If the company ceasing to be UK resident is carrying on a trade in the UK through a permanent establishment, any assets used or held for the purposes of that permanent establishment are excepted from the charge described above, such assets remaining within the charge to UK tax in any event (see **8.9.1**) (TCGA 1992, s. 185(4)).

Where the company ceasing to be resident in the UK is a direct 75%+ subsidiary of a UK resident company, the companies may jointly elect that the net capital gains are deferred until:

- the assets are actually disposed of within six years of the company's migration; or
- the parent company disposes of shares in the company which migrated and either it ceases to be a direct 75%+ subsidiary, or it has already ceased to be a 75% subsidiary, or
- the parent company itself ceases to be UK resident,

but the tax in respect of those gains then becomes chargeable on the parent company. Such an election must be made in writing within two years of the company's migration (TCGA 1992, s. 187). In these circumstances the companies may jointly elect that unutilised capital losses available to the migrating company may be utilised by the parent company to offset chargeable gains arising to it on the relevant event. Again, such an election must be made in writing within two years of that event (TCGA 1992, s. 187(5)). There is no provision allowing a net loss arising on the migration of a subsidiary to be set off against any later gains of its UK resident parent.

Transfer of a UK trade between EC companies

The legislation provides for a deferral of the corporation tax liability which would otherwise arise when a company transfers a trade carried on in the UK, or part of such a trade, to another EC company (TCGA 1992, s. 140A). The conditions for the deferral are that:

- the transferor company must be resident in a Member State:
- the transferee company must be resident in another Member State and incorporated under the laws of a Member State;
- the consideration for the transfer must take the form of securities issued by the transferee company to the transferor company:
- if the transferee company is not resident in the UK, it must use or hold any chargeable assets transferred for the purposes of a trade carried on in the UK, so as to be within the charge to corporation tax in respect of those assets, and
- if the transferee company is resident in the UK, the assets must not be outside the scope of UK tax by reason of any double taxation agreement.

Where the conditions are satisfied, the companies may claim that the consideration for the transfer of any chargeable assets is such an amount as secures that neither a chargeable gain nor an allowable loss arises on the transfer. This applies to determine both the transferor's disposal consideration and the

427

transferee's acquisition consideration, so the accrued gain crystallises when the transferee company disposes of the assets.

The deferral must be claimed jointly by transferor and transferee within six years after the end of the accounting period of the transferor in which the transfer takes place (TMA 1970, s. 43). Deferral is not available if the transfer is effected for tax avoidance purposes or is otherwise not effected for bona fide commercial reasons (TCGA 1992, s. 140B).

Losses

Any loss suffered on the disposal of an asset is an allowable loss for capital gains purposes where, if the disposal gave rise to a gain, that gain would be taxable as a chargeable gain (TCGA 1992, s. 16).

Partnerships

Any transaction carried out by a partnership is treated as carried out by the partners themselves. Thus a partner resident or ordinarily resident in the UK is taxable on his share of all the partnership gains, wherever the assets are situated, as if realised by him. On the other hand a non-resident partner is only chargeable on gains arising from the disposal of assets situated in the UK, and then only if arising in respect of a UK branch or agency of the partnership (TCGA 1992, s. 59).

Deceased persons

The personal representatives of a deceased person are treated as having the same residence and domicile status as that of the deceased at the time of his death, in relation to assets held by the deceased's estate, regardless of their own personal residence position (TCGA 1992, s. 62).

Anti-avoidance provisions

In two particular cases chargeable gains realised by a non-resident may be deemed to have been realised by UK residents. The rules relating to these provisions are set out at **8.9.2** and **8.9.3**.

8.9.2   Non-resident companies: apportionment of gains

Where a chargeable gain accrues to a non-resident company that would be a close company if it was resident in the UK, such gains may be apportioned to any shareholders in the company who are domiciled and resident or ordinarily resident in the UK, and taxed as if realised by them. The provisions apply whether the resident shareholder is an individual or a company (TCGA 1992, s. 13(1) and (2)).

Apportionments

The proportion of the gain chargeable on a UK resident participator depends on the extent of that person's interest as a participator in the non-resident company, but only if the interest is more than 10 per cent (TCGA 1992, s. 13(3) and (4)). A 'participator' is defined as in the corporation tax legislation dealing with close companies. Participators will, therefore, include people with existing or potential shareholdings and voting rights in a company, loan creditors of the company, and those entitled to distributions from the company or to benefit from its income or assets. A person's interest as a participator is his interest in the company as represented by all of the factors by reference to which he falls to be treated as a participator. The interests of other participators are ascertained on the same basis.

Where a person is chargeable on a gain, and is subsequently chargeable to tax on a distribution in respect of that gain within three years from the end of the period of account in which the gain accrued (or within four years from the date of accrual if earlier), any tax paid by that person on the gain will be available to reduce his liability to tax on the later distribution. This relief applies whether the distribution is income or capital in nature.

Where a shareholder who had paid tax on part of the gain of a non-resident company later disposes of his shares in the company, he is entitled to a deduction of the amount of tax paid on computing the gain on the disposal (TCGA 1992, s. 13(7)).

If the company pays the tax, the payment is not regarded as an income or capital distribution to the shareholder on whose behalf it is paid (TCGA 1992, s. 13(11)).

> ### *Example 8.38*
>
> Claud Beck purchases the whole of the share capital of a Bahamian company for a consideration of £400,000. The company in turn owns a holiday hotel in the Bahamas, which originally cost £300,000. The company sells the hotel in May 2004 for £500,000, thereby realising a capital profit of £200,000.
>
> If the company carries on the business of hotelier itself, the gain is not apportionable under these provisions (even if no replacement is purchased) since the hotel was used for the purpose of a trade.
>
> If however the hotel is merely leased to another operator, the profit is apportioned to Claud Beck. The following consequences might then arise (ignoring indexation relief):
>
> (a) Claud Beck could pay the tax himself – which at 40 per cent would cost £80,000. The tax paid is treated as expenditure on the improvement' of his shareholding. If he then sold his shares for say £500,000 he would deduct a cost of £480,000 and suffer tax on £20,000 – which at 40 per cent involves a further payment of £8,000. His tax bill on the transactions thus totals £88,000 on an actual realised gain of only £100,000!
>
> (b) Alternatively the company could pay the £80,000 tax on behalf of Claud Beck – reducing its value to £420,000 and still leaving a potential chargeable gain in the shareholder's hands of £20,000, so that there would be no overall saving.
>
> (c) Alternatively the company could distribute the whole of its profit of £200,000 as a dividend. Claud Beck would still be liable to tax of £80,000, but this would extinguish his income tax liability of £65,000 at 32.5 per cent, although there would be no repayment. There would be a potential capital loss of £100,000 on any subsequent realisation of the company.
>
> (d) Finally the company could be liquidated within three years. Again tax of £80,000 would be due by Claud Beck on the apportioned gain. This would be set against Claud's liability to capital gains tax of £40,000 on his actual profit of £100,000, thereby extinguishing it.,
>
> Clearly the latter two courses of action are preferable, as far as Claud Beck is concerned, with (c) being the better if he is able to make use of the capital gains tax loss. If however he does not control the whole of the shares in the Bahamian company, he might not be in a position to secure a sale of the shares or liquidation of the company.

Gains accruing before acquisition

A charge to tax arises even where the profit made by the non-resident company represents the realisation of a gain that accrued before the UK shareholder acquired his holding, and no allowance is made for any amounts paid by him towards such accrued value at the time of his acquisition of the shares.

Trading premises

Exemption from these provisions is given to gains arising from any tangible assets, whether moveable or immoveable, which are used solely for the purposes of a trade carried on by that company wholly outside the UK, and from foreign currency held in a foreign bank account for such purposes. Thus for example the exemption applies where a non-resident company carrying on a trade abroad disposes of its overseas trade premises. However, the shareholder of a non-resident property investment company is caught, whether the property investments are situated in the UK or abroad (TCGA 1992, s. 13(5)(*b*)).

UK permanent establishment

Where the chargeable gain arising from the disposal is already subject to tax as being the disposal of an asset of a UK permanent establishment, no further assessment is made on the shareholders under these provisions (TCGA 1992, s. 13(5)(*d*) and see **8.9.1**).

Overseas groups of companies

A number of capital gains exemptions and reliefs are available to a 75%+ group of companies resident in the UK see **8.6**. These provisions are adapted to apply to a non-resident 75%+ group of such companies, so that if a no gain/no loss situation thus arises, no gain is available to be apportioned to UK resident shareholders. However UK resident companies are excluded from such a non-resident group, so that if one of the companies involved is resident here, no such relief is available (TCGA 1992, ss. 14, 171, 173, 174 and 175).

Losses

Where an allowable loss arises to the non-resident company during the same chargeable period (the chargeable period of the UK taxpayer, not of the non-resident company), it may be deducted from an apportionment gain if the disposal, if it gave rise to a gain rather than a loss, would be an apportionable gain. However such losses are not available for apportionment themselves and there is no set-off against other chargeable gains accruing to the UK resident taxpayer, nor may they be set off against chargeable gains apportioned under these provisions from other foreign compaines, nor is any relief given for losses incurred by the same non-resident company in an earlier period (TCGA 1992, s. 13(8)).

431

Foreign subsidiary companies

A gain may be apportioned through a series of foreign companies if necessary, so that a gain realised by a foreign subsidiary company is apportioned to its non-resident parent company and thence to the UK resident shareholders (TCGA 1992, s. 13(9)). If the parent company is resident in the UK, the apportioned gain is assessed on that company (as opposed to its own individual shareholders).

8.9.3   Non-resident trusts

The provisions relating to non-resident trusts are extremely complicated and are outside the scope of this book. Points to watch out for are:

(a)   Gains may be charged on the settlor if the settlor, the settlor's spouse, or the settlor's children or grandchildren may be taxed on the settlor.

(b)   Where (a) does not apply gains may be apportioned to beneficiaries and charged to capital gains tax as and when capital distributions are made. A surcharge is levied on such gains if they are not distributed within one year from the end of the tax year in which they accrue.

(c)   Chargeable gains of non-resident companies can be apportioned to non-resident trustees.

A settlement which becomes non-resident is liable to an exit charge by treating it as if it had disposed of all the trust assets at market value and immediately reacquired them.

8.9.4   Overseas property

UK residents

The capital gains legislation applies generally to the worldwide assets wherever situated of a person who is resident or ordinarily resident in the UK (TCGA 1992, s. 2(1)).

Non-residents

Correspondingly a person who is neither resident nor ordinarily resident in the UK during the year of assessment in question is not normally subject to UK capital gains tax on property situated abroad. Indeed such a person is only liable to capital gains tax on property situated in the UK in the circumstances described at **8.9.1**, ie if that property is used by him for the purposes of a trade carried on here through a branch or agency.

If, however, an individual is only temporarily non-resident (ie for less than five complete tax years), chargeable gains made during the period of non-residence are charged to capital gains tax on his return to the UK (see **8.9.1**).

Foreign companies and trusts

However special provisions relate to capital gains realised by certain foreign companies and foreign trusts, where one or more shareholders or beneficiaries are both domiciled and resident or ordinarily resident in the UK, as noted at **8.9.2** and **8.9.3**. These provisions apply whether the non-resident company or trust disposes of assets situated within or outside the UK.

Persons domiciled abroad

Where a person is resident or ordinarily resident in the UK but not domiciled here, he is only liable to capital gains tax on the disposal of assets situated outside the UK to the extent that any amount representing the gain arising is received in the UK. The usual rules relating to constructive remittances, as provided for income tax purposes (see ICTA 1988, s. 65(5) to (9)), also apply to the remittance of capital gains. The remittance of the proceeds of sale of an asset brings into charge the gain derived not only from that sale but also from any earlier disposal, the proceeds of which were reinvested in that asset.

As a corollary, losses derived by such persons from the disposal of foreign assets are not available as allowable losses for capital gains tax purposes, since one cannot remit monies that have been lost (TCGA 1992, ss. 12 and 16).

Foreign currency assets

Since UK taxation is assessable in sterling, it follows that the foreign currency costs of acquisition and improvement and the proceeds of disposal have to be converted into sterling at the rate ruling on the date of expenditure or receipt (see *Bentley v Pike* (1981) 53 TC 590 and *Capcount Trading v Evans* [1993] BTC 3).

Incorporation of overseas branches

Some deferment of tax is available where a UK resident company transfers an overseas trading activity to an overseas company in exchange for shares or loan stock issued by that foreign company.

The relief is available where the UK company carried on a trade through a permanent establishment situated outside the UK and transfers the trade together with all the assets of that permanent establishment (except possibly cash) to a non-resident company in exchange for shares or loan stock issued by that company, so that the UK company ends up by owning at least 25 per cent of the equity of the non-resident company (whether received as consideration for the disposal, or received at some earlier time).

Any chargeable gain arising from the transfer of the assets (on an aggregated net basis, after deducting any losses arising on the transfer) is apportioned rateably between the consideration received in shares and loan stock, and any other consideration received. The liability arising on the gain apportioned to the shares or loan stock is deferred, whereas that part of the chargeable gain apportioned to any other consideration is subject to immediate taxation in the normal way.

The tax is deferred until such time as the shares, etc. received in exchange are disposed of. Upon such a disposal the deferred gain is added to the proceeds of that disposal – with provision for apportionment of the gain if only some of the shares are disposed of, based on the market value of the total holding immediately before the disposal.

An anti-avoidance provision deals with the disposal of the underlying assets by the non-resident company within six years of the transfer, again treating the deferred gain, or the appropriate part attributable to the assets disposed of, as arising to the transferor company on that occasion, unless already taken into account on an earlier disposal of shares, etc. For these purposes disposals of shares are ignored if they fall within the relief for transfers within a 75%+ group of companies (see **8.6.3**) – as are transfers of the overseas assets within a group that would qualify for such relief if it were a UK group. A subsequent disposal by the transferee then triggers off the charge on the deferred gain (TCGA 1992, s. 140). Such a transaction may require consent from HM Treasury (see ICTA 1988, ss. 765 to 766).

A somewhat similar relief is available to an individual on a more general basis, without a time limitation and whether the business is carried on abroad or not, see **8.7.9**.

Unremittable proceeds of disposal

Where a person is subject to tax on a capital gain derived from the disposal of assets situated outside the UK and he cannot, despite reasonable endeavours on his part, remit the proceeds to the UK due to the laws of the foreign country in which the gain arose, or to the executive action of its government, or to the impossibility of obtaining foreign currency in that territory, the taxpayer may claim to defer the tax liability arising. As a result, the chargeable gain in question is treated as arising in the period in which the condition blocking the remittance ceases to exist, rather than the period in which the gain originally arose.

Personal representatives may make a claim on behalf of a deceased person, if such a claim would be competent had he still been living. The claim must be made within five years from 31 January following the end of the year of assessment (capital gains tax) or within six years from the end of the accounting period (corporation tax) (TCGA 1992, s. 279).

Foreign taxes and double tax relief

In addition the disposal of an overseas property may give rise to a tax liability in the country in which it is situated. Such liability may be affected by the provisions of any double tax agreement between the UK and that foreign country, if it affords some exemption to a UK resident owner. Where no treaty is available, double taxation relief is given on a unilateral basis, as for taxes on income and income tax generally (achieved by substituting a reference to chargeable gains for a reference to income, and a reference to capital gains tax in place of income tax in the relevant double tax relief provisions of ICTA 1988, ss. 788 to 806). If relief is not available in this way for offset against the UK tax liability, the foreign tax is deducted in the capital gains computation itself as an expense (TCGA 1992, ss. 277 and 278 and ICTA 1988, s. 797).

A number of countries impose quite heavy transfer duties, equivalent to UK stamp duty land tax, which the taxpayer also needs to take into account. It is often found that such a duty does not qualify for double tax relief against UK tax on capital gains but may qualify as an incidental expense of acquisition or disposal, as appropriate.

Transfer of a non-UK trade

The provisions now contained in TCGA 1992, s. 140C and 140D were enacted in response to the EC Mergers Directive (90/434/EEC). They relate to transfers of non-UK trades. Provisions dealing with the transfer of UK trades are dealt with at **8.9.1**.

As far as non-UK trades are concerned, the legislation provides for a reduction of the corporation tax liability which would otherwise arise when a UK resident company transfers a trade carried on through a permanent establishment in a Member State, or part of such a trade, to a company resident in another Member State (TCGA 1992, s. 140C). The conditions for the relief are that:

- the transfer must include the whole of the assets of the transferor company used for the purposes of the trade or part, or the whole of those assets other than cash;
- at least part of the consideration for the transfer must take the form of securities issued by the transferee company to the transferor company, and

- the aggregate of the chargeable gains arising on the transfer must exceed the aggregate allowable losses so arising.

Where the conditions are satisfied, the transferor company may claim that the net chargeable gains arising be treated as a single chargeable gain, and that in computing the corporation tax payable on that gain, credit be given for the foreign tax which would be payable on that gain in the Member State in which the branch is situated but for the reliefs available under the Mergers Directive (TCGA 1992, s. 140C and ICTA 1988, s. 815A).

The claim must be made within six years after the end of the accounting period of the transferor in which the transfer takes place (TMA 1970, s. 43).

Relief is not available if the transfer is effected for tax avoidance purposes or is otherwise not effected for bona fide commercial reasons (TCGA 1992, s. 140D).

8.10 Miscellaneous

8.10.1 Co-ownership of property

It is possible for an interest in land to be held jointly by two or more persons. Where the number of co-owners exceeds four, the legal title must be registered in the names of not more than four of them as trustees or nominees for all of them (LPA 1925, ss. 34, 36 and Trustee Act 1925, s. 34). The named persons are then trustees under a trust for sale with power to postpone the sale.

On a disposal of the interest, there is only one sale contract and one conveyance. For tax purposes, however, each co-owner makes a disposal of his share in the interest. Therefore, there are as many computation of chargeable gains as there are co-owners. It will be appreciated that capital gains tax or corporation tax is chargeable on gains accruing to a 'person' on the disposal of assets (TCGA 1992, s. 1) and that all forms of property are assets for this purpose, including incorporeal property (TCGA 1992, s. 21). In the situation considered, each co-owner, as a person, disposes of his proportionate share in the freehold or leasehold interest.

Joint tenants and tenants in common

There are two forms of co-ownership: co-ownership as joint tenants or as tenants in common. In this context, the word tenant derives from tenure and does not imply that the co-owners are tenants in the ordinary sense of the word.

Under a joint tenancy:

- each co-owner has an equal share in the asset, and
- if a co-owner dies, his share passes automatically to the other co-owners.

A company can be a joint tenant. For this purpose, it 'dies' when it is dissolved (Bodies Corporate (Joint Tenancies) Act 1899, s. 1(1)). It will be appreciated that, if an individual joint tenant dies, no chargeable gain arises in respect of the devolution of his share of the property onto the other co-owners (TCGA 1992, s. 62 (1) and (10)).

Under a tenancy in common:

- the proportionate shares of the co-owners may be different, and
- each co-owner may deal independently with his share. In particular, each individual co-owner may leave his share separately in his will, there being no automatic devolution of his share onto the other co-owners on his death.

Severance

It is sometimes desirable to convert a joint tenancy into a tenancy in common with equal shares. This can only be done during the lifetime of the joint owner who wishes to sever his share in the asset. It requires that the joint owner give a written notice to the other joint owners in accordance with LPA 1925, s. 36(2). This does not involve any disposal or acquisition for capital gains purposes unless one or more of the former joint tenants have reduced their interests in the land (*Capital Gains Tax Manual*, CG70526).

Severance is often considered as an instrument of inheritance tax planning where a matrimonial home is held jointly by husband and wife and is their principal asset, so that each spouse may leave his share independently on death, thereby ensuring that the benefit of the nil rate band of IHT is not lost.

Partitioning

It is possible that the co-owners of a plot of land may wish to divide up the plot such that each co-owner owns outright a specific part of the plot. For each co-owner, this involves:

- a disposal of his share in the parts taken by the other co-owners, and
- an acquisition of the shares held by the other co-owners in the part which he takes.

Rollover relief under TCGA 1992, s. 152 or under ESC D26 (see **8.5.2**) may be available. Stamp duty land tax will be payable on a partition if any consideration (other than the value of the existing interest) changes hands (see **Chapter 10**).

8.10.2   Tax recoverable from others

In a number of instances, unpaid tax on chargeable gains may be recovered from other persons, as in the circumstances outlined hereunder.

Donors/donees

Where capital gains tax arising on the disposal of an asset by way of gift is not paid by the donor within 12 months of the due date, the gain may be assessed on the donee. The gain so assessed is limited to the chargeable gain assessed on the donor or, if less, the 'grossed up' amount of the capital gains tax remaining unpaid. The donee is entitled to recover any tax so paid from the donor or his personal representatives. Similar rules apply to any bargain not at arm's length, where the consideration for the disposal is less than full market value. There is no restriction to the difference between the consideration given and the market value, so that the transferee could be called upon to pay a total of consideration and tax under this provision in excess of the value of the asset acquired by him (TCGA 1992, s. 282).

Note that although the donor and donee may jointly elect for the gain charge to be deferred until a subsequent disposal by the donee, if the donee emigrates the chargeable gain crystallises in his hands, and if he does not pay the tax it can be recovered from the donor, as explained at **8.7.8**.

Trustees/beneficiaries

If the liability to pay capital gains tax on a disposal by trustees remains unpaid by them after six months from its due date, and the assets disposed of or the proceeds of disposal have been transferred to a beneficiary becoming absolutely entitled thereto, the tax may be charged on the beneficiary. No powers of recovery from the trustees are however given (TCGA 1992, s. 69).

Companies/shareholders

If a company makes a capital distribution (other than as a reduction in capital) arising from or constituting a disposal of assets, and the company fails to pay the tax liability on any chargeable gain arising as a result of that disposal within six months of the date it becomes due, the tax may be recovered from any shareholder participating in the distribution. The amount recovered from a shareholder cannot exceed the lower the amount of the capital distribution received by him or a proportion of the corporation tax based on his share of the chargeable gain. The shareholder is entitled to recover any tax so paid from the company (TCGA 1992, s. 189).

Groups of companies

If tax on a chargeable gain is not paid by a company which is a member of a 75%+ group of companies within six months of the due date, the tax may be recovered from the company that was the parent company of that group at the time the gain accrued, or from any other company which at some time within the previous 12 months was a member of the group and owned the asset. The tax so paid is recoverable from the company to which the gain accrued (TCGA 1992, s. 190).

Company reconstructions

In the case of a transfer of a business, where the transferor company has been wound up, the tax may be assessed on the transferee company or any other company acquiring the assets under a no gain/no loss disposal (TCGA 1992, s. 139(6) and (7)).

8.10.3   Appeals: valuations, etc.

Under self-assessment, where there is an appeal against an amendment of a self-assessment or the refusal of a claim, or indeed against an assessment made by an Inspector or the Board, any dispute relating to the taxation of chargeable gains or allowable capital losses is to be heard by the Special Commissioners (TMA 1970, s. 46B). The same applies in relation to partnerships, where the Inspector issues an amended partnership statement.

Where there is a dispute concerning the value of a freehold or leasehold interest in land, that dispute is heard and determined by the Lands Tribunal (TMA 1970, s. 46D). The decision of the Tribunal on the question of valuation is final. The value so determined is then fed back into the tax computation.

Valuations of land need to be agreed in any of the following circumstances:

- market value on 31 March 1982, on a disposal of an asset acquired before that date,
- the current market value in the case of:
    - a part disposal;
    - a non-arm's length disposal;
    - an appropriation from trading stock;
    - a company joining a group, where pre-entry losses may be determined by reference to the market value of assets on the date the company joined the group (TCGA 1992, Sch. 7A, Para. 5),
    - an apportionment of purchase consideration between building and plant (ie fixtures which qualify as plant).

Valuations are normally negotiated with the Valuations Agency. Only if agreement cannot be reached will the matter be referred to the Lands Tribunal.

It is important to ascertain the precise nature of the interest to be valued, especially when dealing with valuations as at 31 March 1982. The interest held at that date may not be the same as the interest disposed of. For example, a freehold interest may have been subject to a tenancy as at 31 March 1982 but may eventually be sold unencumbered. In this case, the March 1982 value will be the value of the freehold reversion subject to the tenancy (*Henderson v Exors of David Karmel (dec'd)* (1984) BTC 330). A lease held at March 1982 may have expired and the lease now being disposed of may be a new lease granted after the expiry of the old one, in which case the 31 March 1982 value will be irrelevant. Different interests may have been acquired at different times and subsequently merged. Where the vendor is a member of a group, different interests may have been acquired by different companies and transferred to the vendor by intra-group transfers. The 31 March 1982 valuation will relate to the interests actually held at that date by the vendor, or by a company in the same group which transferred its interest to the vendor by intra-group transfer.

Where land is held jointly or in common, the interest to be valued is the interest of the particular joint owner. This will not necessarily be ascertained by valuing the entire asset and taking the owner's proportionate share: some discounting factor may be involved. In the case of partnership assets, however, the usual practice is to value the entire asset and take the partner's proportionate share of that value (see SP D12, paragraph 1). The Inland Revenue's land valuation procedures are set out in the *Capital Gains Tax Manual*, paragraphs CG 74000–75820.

Guidance on property valuations

In some cases a surveyor may be instructed to prepare a valuation of property. The Royal Institute of Chartered Surveyors (RICS) have issued a guidance note, CGN21 which forms part of their Appraisal and Valuation manual (commonly called the Red Book). This guidance note gives advice to members of RICS about the meaning of market value for capital gains purposes, and has been approved by the Valuations Office Agency. The Valuations Office Agency also publish manuals containing guidance on property valuations.

9 Inheritance tax

9.1 Valuation

For inheritance tax (IHT) purposes, the value transferred is measured not by the value of the property itself but by the diminution in the value of the transferor's estate (IHTA 1984, s. 3(1)). However, it is specifically provided that the grant of a tenancy of agricultural property in the UK, the Channel Islands or the Isle of Man for use for agricultural purposes is not a transfer of value by the grantor if made for full consideration in money or money's worth (IHTA 1984, s. 16).

The concept of 'loss to the transferor's estate' is applied to transfers on death by s. 4(1), which charges tax as if, immediately before death, the deceased had made a transfer of value equal to the whole value of his estate. Clearly in this case the 'loss to the estate' is equal to the value of the estate when reckoned as a whole.

Where an entire asset leaves a person's estate the computation of the diminution in value entails the valuation of the asset which ceases to be comprised in it. Likewise, the valuation of a person's estate immediately before death necessitates putting a value to the particular assets that make up the estate.

The value at any time of any property for IHT purposes is the price the property might reasonably be expected to fetch if sold in the open market at that time (IHTA 1984, s. 160). However, that price is not assumed to be reduced on the ground that the whole property is to be placed on the market at one and the same time.

The Royal Institution of Chartered Surveyors has published a new edition of 'The Red Book', now known as the 'Appraisal and Valuation Standards'. Compliance with it is mandatory for Chartered Surveyors for the majority of valuation work from 1 May 2003. The new Red Book provides advice on the meaning of 'market value' as defined in s. 160 as a basis of valuation.

The Revenue has power to make a determination of a transfer of value where it appears to it that a transfer has been made (IHTA 1984, s. 221). There is a right of appeal to the Special Commissioners within 30 days of the date of the notice of determination (s. 222). Where the amount of the transfer depends on the value of any land, any appeal against the Revenue's valuation lies to the appropriate Lands Tribunal (s. 222(4), (4B)).

9.2 Sale of land from deceased's estate

9.2.1 Description of the relief

Where 'the appropriate person' makes a claim in respect of an interest in land which was comprised in the deceased's estate immediately before death, and which is sold within the period of three years following the date of death, the value of that interest for IHT purposes, and of any other interest in land comprised in that estate and sold within that period by the same person in the same capacity, is taken to be its sale value (IHTA 1984, s. 191(1)).

Example 9.1

An estate includes the following property sold within three years of death:

Interest in land	Value at death	Sale price
	£	£
Blackacre	300,000	240,000
Whiteacre	140,000	160,000
	440,000	400,000

If a claim is made by the 'appropriate person' (see below), the values of Blackacre and Whiteacre for inheritance tax purposes will be treated as £240,000 and £160,000 respectively. Hence, the total value of the estate is reduced by £40,000. However, it is not possible to substitute the sale price of Blackacre alone.

Before relief can be claimed, there must be a completed sale. In *Jones & Anor (Administrators of the Estate of Balls Deceased) v IR Commrs* [1997] BTC 8,003 a contract of sale of land at less than the probate value was made within three years after the date of the deceased's death. The purchaser failed to complete and the sale fell through. The property was eventually sold outside the three-year period. Lightman J held that it was clear from the context of IHTA 1984, ss. 190–198 that the word 'sold' meant 'conveyed or transferred on completion of a sale' and that relief was not available in respect of an abortive contract of sale.

It has been held by a Special Commissioner in *Stonor v IR Commrs* (2001) SpC 288 that s. 191 applies only where at least some inheritance tax is payable. Without any IHT liability, there is no 'appropriate person' to make a claim.

9.2.2 Sales in fourth year after death

Relief is also available in respect of sales in the fourth year after death (IHTA 1984, s. 197A(1)). The sale, which must be by the 'appropriate person', is deemed to have taken place within the three-year period. Accordingly, the relief applies in the same way as for sales within three years, except that:

- relief in the fourth year is not available in respect of acquisitions by compulsory purchase (s. 197A(1)(b));
- claims may not be made in respect of property sold at a profit (s. 197A(2));
- the adjustment for purchases by the appropriate person need not take account of sales in the fourth year (s. 197A(3)),
- the adjustment for collusive sales at a profit need not take account of any such sale in the fourth year (s. 197A(4)).

No claim may be made in respect of sales at a profit in the fourth year after death (s. 197A(2)).

9.2.3 Minimal difference

Where the difference between the value on death and the sale value is less than the lower of:

- £1,000, and
- 5 per cent of the value on death,

the value on death is not replaced by the sale value (s. 191(2)).

Example 9.2

If in Example 9.1 Whiteacre had been sold for £140,500, the difference would have been disregarded, so that the values of Blackacre and Whiteacre for tax purposes would have been £240,000 and £140,000 respectively.

Any number of minimal differences (whether up or down) in respect of different interests must be thus disregarded.

9.2.4 Exclusion of collusive sales

The above relief does not apply to the sale of any interest which is either:

1. A sale by a personal representative or trustee to:

    (a) a person who, at any time between the death and the sale, has been beneficially entitled to, or to an interest in possession in, property comprising the interest sold; or

    (b) the spouse of such a person or the child or remoter descendant of such a person, or

    (c) trustees of a settlement under which a person within (a) or (b) has an interest in possession in property comprising the interest sold; or

2. A sale in connection with which the seller or any person within (1) obtains a right to acquire the interest sold or any other interest in the same land.

In order to cover the question whether a beneficiary can be said to be beneficially entitled to property comprised in an unadministered estate, a person is treated as having the same interest therein as he would have if the administration had been completed (IHTA 1984, s. 191(3)).

Example 9.3

In terms of Bernard's will, his son Colin is entitled to Greenacre, valued on death at £320,000. As part of an arrangement between the beneficiaries in Bernard's estate, Colin agrees to purchase Greenacre from Bernard's executors for £120,000. Relief is not available and the sale price may not be substituted for the value on death in calculating the tax on Bernard's estate.

9.2.5 Application to compulsory acquisition

Relief may be claimed where the interest in land is acquired by an authority possessing powers of compulsory acquisition, provided that the notice to treat was served either before the death or within the three-year period after death (IHTA 1984, s. 197). It does not matter if the date of acquisition itself is outside the three-year period.

No account need be taken of compulsory acquisitions at a value higher than the value on death (s. 197(2)). Thus, there is no need to aggregate such acquisitions with those showing a loss, or with ordinary sales at a loss.

> ### Example 9.4
>
> Emma's estate includes Blackacre, valued at £320,000 and Whiteacre, valued at £280,000 on the date of Emma's death. Both properties are compulsorily acquired in pursuance of notices served within the three-year period. The prices paid are £360,000 and £200,000 respectively.

Relief may be claimed in respect of the £80,000 loss on Whiteacre, and the £40,000 gain on Blackacre may be disregarded.

9.2.6 Definitions

Interest in land

Land includes buildings and other structures, land covered with water, and any estate, interest, easement, servitude or right in or over land (Interpretation Act 1978, Sch. 1). 'Interest in land' does not include any estate, interest or right by way of mortgage or other security (IHTA 1984, s. 190(1)).

In Scotland, the phrase 'interest in land' is defined in three different ways in the Conveyancing and Feudal Reform (Scotland) Act 1970 and in the Land Registration Act 1979, generally in terms of an interest capable of being owned separately and of being recorded in the Register of Sasines or Land Register.

The appropriate person

The appropriate person is the person liable for tax attributable to the value of an interest in land comprised in an estate immediately before death. Where there is more than one such person, and one of them is in fact paying the tax, then that person is the appropriate person (IHTA 1984, s. 190(1)).

For these purposes, the deceased's personal representatives are treated as a single and continuous body of persons, distinct from the persons who may from time to time be the personal representatives. Trustees are treated in the same way (s. 190(3)). Hence a change in the composition of either body will not affect the identity of 'the appropriate person'.

Where liability for payment of tax on different parts of the estate falls on different persons, each of these will be 'the appropriate person' as regards the value of land comprised in that part of the estate.

The significance of the appropriate person is that it is he who must make the claim for relief, in respect of land sold by him. Thus, there must be identity between the person liable for (and paying) the tax, and the person selling the land. Otherwise, the relief is not available. For example, a legatee who sells at a loss land which has been made over to him by the executors cannot claim relief.

Sale price

'Sale price' is defined as the price for which the land is sold, or, if greater, the best consideration that could reasonably have been obtained for it at the time of the sale (IHTA 1984, s. 190(1)). In determining the best consideration obtainable, no account can be taken of expenses such as commission and stamp duty incidental to the sale or purchase. 'Sale value' means the sale price after adjustment up or down according to the provisions of ss. 190–198.

9.2.7　Claiming the relief

The relief must be claimed. The appropriate person must specify the capacity in which he is making the claim (IHTA 1984, s. 191(1)(b)), for example as executor, trustee or otherwise. There is no provision in the legislation for withdrawing a claim that turns out to be unfavourable; thus, no claim should be made until the aggregate effect of all sales within the three-year period is known.

The time limit is effectively four months after the date of the last relevant sales because of the rules for adjustment for purchases (see below). However, the Capital Taxes Office has issued the following practice note, which appeared in the *Law Society's Gazette* on 12 January 1994:

> **'Capital Taxes Office practice note: loss on sale relief: S191 IHTA 1984**
>
> Loss on sale relief cannot be formally granted until four months have elapsed from the date of the last sale of qualifying property, assuming all the other conditions are satisfied.
>
> In many estates there is one property and it has to be sold to give effect to the terms of the deceased's will. There is no prospect of a re-investment of the proceeds of sale in another property.
>
> The Capital Taxes Office (CTO) has received representations that having sometimes waited one or two years to achieve a sale it is unreasonable to compel personal representatives to wait another four months before lodging an application for loss on sale relief. The CTO will now accept and process a claim and, where appropriate, it will make a provisional repayment of inheritance tax.

Formal clearance on form Cap 30 will not be issued until the legal personal representatives have confirmed (after four months have elapsed from the sale) that there have been no changes to the information contained in their original application.'

9.2.8 Adjustment for changes to the interest between death and sale

An addition is made to the sale price of an interest in land if either:

- the interest is not the same in all respects and with the same incidents at the date of death and at the date of sale, or
- the land in which the interest subsists is not in the same state and with the same incidents at the date of death and at the date of the sale,

(IHTA 1984, s. 193(1)).

The meaning of 'incidents' was considered in *Re Johnston's Application* [1950] 1 All ER 613, in the context of the War Damage Act 1943, where Harman J defined an incident at p. 617 as '. . . any factor connected with the proprietary interests which . . .would have affected the value of each of them in the market'. In that case it was held that an option to the lessor to purchase the freehold reversion was an incident.

The amount of the addition is an amount equal to the difference between:

- the value on death of the interest, and
- what that value would have been if the changed circumstances (which caused the failure to satisfy the conditions) had prevailed immediately before the death.

Where the change of circumstances, had it occurred before death, would have increased the value of the interest, the sale price must be reduced to what it would have been had the change not occurred (IHTA 1984, s. 193(4)).

Example 9.5

Gregory's estate includes the freehold reversion of Hardacre, subject to a lease in favour of Tony. The value of the land with vacant possession would be £1,000,000; subject to the lease it is worth £600,000.

Within three years of Gregory's death, Tony vacates the property and shortly afterwards Gregory's executor sells it with vacant possession for £900,000.

Under s. 193(4) this figure is reduced to what it would have been had the change in circumstances (the obtaining of vacant possession) not occurred: say £500,000.

Relief under s. 191 may thus be claimed, giving Hardacre a value for inheritance tax of £500,000.

Compensation payments

Where compensation is payable under any enactment:

- because of the imposition of a restriction on the use or development of the land in which the interest subsists, or
- because the value of the interest is reduced for any other reason,

the sale price is simply increased by the amount of the compensation.

9.2.9 Leases with less than 50 years to run

Special provision is needed for leases moving toward expiry, because no other interest in land suffers an inevitable fall in value without some change to the property itself (such as the working of a quarry).

In the case of a lease which had 50 years or less to run at the date of death, the sale price is increased by an amount equal to the 'appropriate fraction' of the value on death (IHTA 1984, s. 194). The 'appropriate fraction' is:

$(P(1) - P(2))/P(1)$

where:

$P(1)$ is the percentage derived from the table in TCGA 1992, Sch. 8, Para. 1 for a lease of the duration as at the date of death, and

$P(2)$ is the percentage so derived for the duration of the lease as at the date of the sale.

> ### Example 9.6
>
> Henry's estate includes the leasehold of Brownacre, with 12 years of the lease still to run at the date of death. The interest is valued on death at £240,000. Henry's executors assign the lease exactly two years later for the sum of £200,000, and claim relief under s. 191. To the £200,000 must be added the 'appropriate fraction' of the value on death.
>
> From the table:
>
> $$P(1) = 53.191$$
> $$P(2) = 46.695$$
>
> The appropriate fraction is thus $(53.191 - 46.695)/53.191 = 0.122$
>
> Amount to be added $= £240,000 \times 0.122 = £29,280$.
>
> Relief may therefore be claimed on the difference between £240,000 and £229,280, ie £10,720, leaving IHT payable on £229,280.

9.2.10 Adjustment for exchange and collusive sales

Where the appropriate person, acting in the same capacity, has carried out one of the following transactions:

- a 'collusive' sale within s. 191(3) (see above), or
- within the period of three years after death, an exchange, whether with or without any equalising payment, of an interest in land comprised in the estate at death,

and the sale price, or in the case of an exchange the market value at the date of the exchange, of the interest exceeds the value on death, the sale price of any land for which relief is claimed must be increased by all or part of the excess (IHTA 1984, s. 196(2)). Where only one other interest is sold within the three-year period, its sale price is increased by the whole of the excess. Where more than one interest is sold, the sale price of each is increased by the 'appropriate fraction' of the excess (s. 196(3)).

The appropriate fraction is A/B, where:

- A is the difference (up or down) between the value on death and the sale price of that particular interest, and
- B is the aggregate of all differences (up or down) between the values on death and the sale prices of all interests sold within the period.

This is to prevent abuse of the relief by taking land showing a gain out of the claim by means of a non-qualifying sale or an exchange, leaving only land showing a loss to be sold by a qualifying sale. The effect of s. 196 is that the gain is brought back into the computation and reduces the relief available in respect of land sold at a loss.

Example 9.7

Jim's estate includes Blackacre, valued at £400,000, and Whiteacre, valued at £480,000 on the date of Jim's death. Within three years of Jim's death, his executors sell Blackacre to Zoe, at arm's length, for £300,000, and exchange Whiteacre for other property. At the date of the exchange Whiteacre is worth £600,000.

In the absence of s. 196, Jim's executors would be able to claim relief in respect of the loss of Blackacre. But to the sale price of Blackacre must be added the whole of the excess value of Whiteacre at the date of the exchange over its value at death. This indeed has the effect of turning the loss on Blackacre into a gain, and a claim under s. 191 would be unfavourable.

9.2.11 Adjustment for purchases

Relief under the above rules may be restricted or withdrawn if the person claiming relief purchases, in the same capacity, any interest in land within the period:

- beginning on the date of death, and
- ending four months after the date of the last sale made within three years of death (IHTA 1984, s. 192). Compulsory acquisitions are disregarded here (s. 197(3).

If the total amount invested in land within the period exceeds the total sale prices of land sold (as adjusted under ss. 193, 194 and 195), no relief is available at all. If the total purchases are less than the total sales, there is an addition to the sale price of each interest sold at a loss, and a reduction in the sale price of each interest sold at profit. The addition or reduction is the following fraction (the 'appropriate fraction') of the difference between the value on death and the sale price of each interest (as adjusted under ss. 193, 194 and 195):

$$\frac{\text{Aggregate of purchase prices}}{\text{Aggregate of sale prices}}$$

Example 9.8

Linda's estate includes the following properties, valued on death and sold within the three-year period as shown:

Property	Value at death £	Sale price £
Greenacre	400,000	320,000
Brownacre	280,000	300,000
	680,000	620,000

One month after the sale of Brownacre, Linda's executors purchase Yellowacre for a price of £124000. Relief under s. 191 is claimed.

The 'appropriate fraction' is $124,000/620,000 = 1/5$

	£
Sale price of Greenacre	320,000
Increased by $1/5 \times (£400,000 - £320,000)$	16,000
	334,000

	£
Sale price of Brownacre	300,000
Reduced by $1/5 \times (£300,000 - £280,000)$	4,000
	296,000

The overall effect is to reduce the total relief available from £60,000 to £48,000, ie a reduction of 1/5.

There is nothing to prevent the proceeds of sale of interests in land being reinvested in qualifying securities, or vice versa; any relief due in respect of a loss on sale would not be affected.

Sales in the fourth year after death are disregarded in determining whether or not a purchase has taken place within four months of the last sale. Where all sales have taken place during the fourth year, s. 192 does not apply at all (s. 197A(3)).

Compulsory acquisitions

If the claim relates solely to land which is compulsorily acquired, no adjustment is required if a purchase within the three-year period is made, ie no relief is lost (s. 197(3)).

9.2.12   Valuation: special provisions

In determining the purchase price or sale price any interest in land, or the best consideration that could reasonably have been obtained on sale, no account is taken of expenses which are incidental to the sale or purchase (IHTA 1984, s. 190(4)). Thus, no addition or reduction is made with regard to agents' commission, valuers' fees, stamp duty land tax, etc.

9.2.13   Date of sale or purchase

The date of sale or purchase of any interest in land is to be the date on which the appropriate person entered the contract of sale or purchase (s. 198(1)), ie the date of exchange of contracts (in Scotland, conclusion of missives). Where the sale or purchase results from the exercise of an option (whether by the appropriate person or by someone else) granted not more than six months earlier, the date of sale or purchase is taken to be the date on which the option was granted (s. 198(2)).

Compulsory purchase

If an interest in land is acquired in pursuance of a notice to treat served by an authority possessing powers of compulsory acquisition, the date of sale is taken to be the date on which compensation is agreed or determined (disregarding any variations on appeal), or, if earlier, the date when the authorities enter on the land in pursuance of their powers (s. 198(3)). Where, however, the interest is acquired by virtue of a general vesting declaration (or, in Northern Ireland, a vesting order), the date of sale is taken to be the last day of the period specified in the declaration (or, in Northern Ireland, the date on which the vesting order becomes operative) (s. 198(4)).

9.2.14   Valuation by reference to other interests

The sale price of an interest in land is to be increased by the difference between the value on death and what would have been the value on death if no other interests had been taken into account in determining that value.

Example 9.9

M's estate includes Goldenacre, which on its own is worth £240,000, but when valued along with 'related property' owned by M's spouse, is worth £360,000. Within the three-year period, M's executors sell the land for £220,000 and claim relief under s. 191. The amount of relief is not £360,000 − £220,000 but £240,000 − £220,000 = £20,000.

It may be held that, in circumstances such as these, it will be advantageous to make a claim for relief under s. 176 instead of s. 191.

9.3 Payment of IHT by instalments

9.3.1 The instalment option

In certain circumstances, the inheritance tax attributable to a particular asset is payable in ten equal yearly instalments (IHTA 1984, s. 227(1)).

This option is available in respect of all transfers on death. It is also available:

- on chargeable lifetime transfers (including potentially exempt transfers which become chargeable, and extra tax payable on a chargeable lifetime transfer because of the transferor's death within seven years) if the donee is bearing the tax, and
- on charges on settled property, if the property to which the charge relates continues to be comprised in the settlement, or if the beneficiary who becomes entitled to property bears the tax on it.

9.3.2 Transfers within seven years before death

In the case of tax (or extra tax) payable because the donor of a lifetime gift has died within seven years, there are further conditions to fulfil. The property must either:

- have been owned by the transferee throughout the period between the date of the gift and the donor's death (or, if earlier, the donee's own death), or
- fall within the 'replacement property' provisions in respect of agricultural property relief or business property relief.

If the property in question is unquoted shares or securities, there is an additional requirement that it remains unquoted throughout the period between the gift and the death (s. 228(3A)).

> ### Example 9.10
>
> Andrew makes a gift of Blackacre to Bob. Three years later Bob sells the land and invests the proceeds in quoted shares. Six months later, Andrew dies, and tax becomes chargeable on the gift to Bob. The instalment option is not available.

> ### Example 9.11
>
> The facts are as in Example 9.10, except that Bob invests the proceeds of sale in Whiteacre. The instalment option is available provided the requirements of the replacement property rules are satisfied.

Where the potentially exempt transfer was to the trustees of an accumulation and maintenance trust, 'transferee' in s. 227 is construed as meaning the trustees (s. 227(1B)). In other cases, 'transferee' means the person whose property the qualifying property became on the potentially exempt transfer.

9.3.3 Property qualifying for the instalment option

The following categories of property qualify for the instalment option.

Land

Land of any description, wherever situated (IHTA 1984, s. 227(2)(a)). 'Land' is defined as including buildings and other structures, land covered with water, and any estate, interest, easement, servitude or right in or over land, but not any estate, interest or right by way of mortgage or other security (s. 272; Interpretation Act 1978, Sch. 1). It therefore includes leasehold land, and it is generally accepted that it also includes land held on trusts for sale.

Controlling shareholding

These are shares or securities of a company, which gave the transferor control of the company immediately before the transfer (IHTA 1984, ss. 227(2)(b), 228).

A person has control at any time if he then has control of powers of voting on all questions affecting the company as a whole which, if exercised, would yield a majority of the votes capable of being exercised on them (IHTA 1984, s. 269). The words 'capable of being exercised' explain the category of votes being referred to, ie votes on questions affecting a particular class of shares only. They do not refer to the personal capacity of the shareholder. In

Walding v IR Commrs [1996] BTC 8003, it was argued successfully that where shares were owned by a four-year-old, the votes carried by those shares were not capable of being exercised, so that the holding should be ignored in determining whether or not another holding was a controlling shareholding for business property relief purposes.

This basic definition is supplemented by three deeming provisions (s. 269(2)–(4)):

- shares or securities are deemed to give a person control if, together with any related property, they would be sufficient to give control as above;
- where the trustees of a settlement in which an interest in possession subsists have powers of voting, these are deemed to be given to any individual (ie not a company) with an interest in possession, and
- where any class of shares or securities has powers of voting limited to the question of winding up the company or to questions primarily affecting the shares or securities of that class (or both), such voting powers are disregarded.

Other unquoted shares or securities

Unquoted shares or securities which did not give the transferor control of the company – provided one of three alternative conditions is satisfied (ss. 227(2)(b), 228(1)(b)–(d)). The alternatives are:

1. The Board is satisfied that the tax attributable to the shares cannot be paid in one sum without undue hardship. The Board's decision is final. In the cases of lifetime gifts and transfers of settled property, the question is determined on the assumption that the shares or securities concerned will be retained by the persons liable to pay the tax (s. 228(1)(c)).

2. The transfer is on death, and at least 20 per cent of the tax for which the same person is liable in the same capacity is attributable to assets (including the shares or securities) that qualify for the instalment option (s. 228(1)(b) and (2)).

3. The value transferred attributable to the shares (exclusive of inheritance tax) exceeds £20,000, and either:

   - their nominal value is at least 10 per cent of the nominal value of all the shares in the company at the time of the transfer, or

   - if the shares are ordinary shares, their nominal value is at least 10 per cent of the nominal value of the ordinary share capital. Ordinary shares means shares which carry either a right to dividends not restricted to dividends at a fixed rate, or a right to conversion to such shares (s. 228(1)(d), (3) and (4)).

The general definition of 'quoted' in s. 272 is overridden for the purposes of the instalment option by s. 228(5), which defines 'unquoted' as 'not listed on a recognised stock exchange'. Thus the instalment option for minority holdings is extended to shares dealt in on the Unlisted Securities Market. This presumably includes securities dealt in on the Alternative Investment Market (AIM).

Business or interest in a business

A business or interest in a business, including a business carried on in the exercise of a profession or vocation, but excluding a business carried on otherwise than for gain (IHTA 1984, s. 227(2)(c), (7)(d)).

The instalment option applies to tax attributable to the 'net value' of the business, meaning the value of assets used in the business (including goodwill), reduced by the aggregate amount of liabilities incurred for business purposes (s. 227(7)(a), (b)).

The net value of an interest in a business must be valued without regard to assets and liabilities which would not have been taken into account in valuing the whole business (s. 227(7)(c)). This subsection is capable of more than one interpretation. The view generally taken has been that this provision is intended to make it clear that assets and liabilities among the partners themselves, for example rights and obligations regarding pensions, should be disregarded. However, the meaning of this provision remains uncertain.

Woodlands

Woodlands which, having been the subject of a deferral of tax, are later the subject of a lifetime chargeable gift (s. 229 IHTA 1984). The instalment option is available in respect of the tax on the lifetime gift (although not the deferred tax), whether or not the trees are disposed of together with the land on which they are growing.

9.3.4   Payment of instalments

Notice in writing must be given to the Board if the person paying the tax elects to pay it by instalments (IHTA 1984, ss. 227(1), 229). In practice this is usually a matter of answering the appropriate question in the Revenue account form.

The first instalment is payable six months after the end of the month in which the death occurred, or in other cases on the date when tax would be due if it were not payable by instalments (s. 227(3)). Even if a person elects to pay by instalments he may at any time afterwards pay all the tax outstanding, together with any accrued interest, in one lump sum.

9.3.5 Sale of instalment option property

Where an election is made to pay tax by instalments, and the property in question is sold before the end of the instalment period, the tax unpaid at the date of the sale, together with any accrued interest, becomes payable forthwith (IHTA 1984, s. 227(4)). Where part of the property is sold, a proportionate part of the tax becomes payable.

Tax similarly becomes payable forthwith in any of the following circumstances (s. 227(5)):

- where, following an election made on a lifetime transfer on which the donee bore the tax, the donee makes a chargeable transfer of value wholly or partly attributable to the property in question (other than a transfer on death),
- where, following an election made when settled property remained settled, the property subsequently leaves the settlement.

> ### Example 9.12
>
> Land is settled on discretionary trusts. The trustees, in exercise of a power of appointment, appoint the property to Adam for life, and an election is made to pay the tax arising under the exit charge by instalments. Five years later Adam becomes absolutely entitled to the property under the terms of the trust.
>
> Unpaid tax arising under the exit charge, and any accrued interest, is now payable.
>
> The tax does not become payable under the above provisions where the donee predeceases the donor.
>
> A sale of an interest in a business (or part of an interest) is treated as a sale of part of the business (s. 227(6)(a)). A payment, for example under a partnership agreement, of a sum in satisfaction of an interest in a business is treated as a sale of an interest therein at the time of payment (s. 227(6)(b)).
>
> In Scotland, where missives of sale are concluded but the sale falls through because of litigation, it is understood that the official view is that s. 227(4) is not triggered and the instalment option continues to be available.

9.3.6 Subsequent disposal

If any property (other than woodlands) in respect of which the instalment option has been exercised is sold, the tax unpaid becomes payable forthwith, together with any accrued interest (s. 227(4)).

Where part only of the property is sold, a proportionate part of the tax becomes payable. In the case of a business, the sale of an interest (or part of an interest) in it is treated as a sale of part of the business (s. 227(6)(a)); and the payment under a partnership agreement or otherwise of any sum in satisfaction of the whole or part of an interest (otherwise than on a sale), is treated as a sale of that interest or part, at the time of payment (s. 227(6)(b)).

In cases where the instalment option was exercised in respect of a lifetime transfer, the tax unpaid becomes payable if the property is the subject of a further chargeable transfer, other than on death (s. 227(5)). The same applies where the instalment option was exercised in respect of property comprised in a settlement, and the property subsequently leaves the settlement. It does not, however, apply where a potentially exempt transfer becomes chargeable, and in the meantime the transferee has predeceased the transferor.

9.3.7 Interest on instalments

Interest is charged on the first instalment from the due date of payment until the actual date of payment. Subsequent instalments may or may not be 'interest-free'.

Interest-free instalments

Where instalments are interest-free, this means that no interest is payable on the instalments until they fall due. Once an instalment falls due, interest is payable on that instalment only, until it is paid. Thus, if all instalments are paid as they fall due, no interest ever becomes payable. Instalments on the following types of property are interest-free:

- shares and securities other than those listed below;
- business or interest in a business;
- the agricultural value of agricultural property qualifying for relief under IHTA 1984, s. 116,
- woodlands.

Instalments not interest-free

Where instalments are not interest-free, interest is charged:

- on the whole unpaid portion of tax for one year, and

- on each instalment from the due date of payment until the actual date of payment.

Instalments of the following types are not interest-free:

- land unless it falls within one of the categories listed above,
- shares and securities in a company whose business consists wholly or mainly in dealing in securities, stocks or shares, land or buildings, or in making or holding investments. However, a company will qualify if its business consists wholly or mainly in being a holding company of companies other than those mentioned above, or if its business is wholly that of a 'market maker' or of a discount house and (in either case) is carried on in the UK (s. 234(2) and s. 234(3)).

'Market maker' means a person who:

- holds himself out at all normal times in compliance with the rules of the Stock Exchange as willing to buy and sell securities, stocks or shares at a price specified by him; and
- is recognised as doing so by the Council of The Stock Exchange (s. 234(4)).

The Board is further empowered to make regulations extending the reference in IHTA 1984, s. 234(4) above to 'The Stock Exchange' to any recognised investment exchange, within the meaning of the Financial Services Act 1986, or to any exchanges specified in the regulations (FA 1986, s. 107(4)). That power has been exercised to extend the reference to LIFFE (Administration and Management) (SI 1992/3181).

'Holding company' is defined as in Companies Act 1985, s. 736(1).

In some cases an item of property will fall within both categories, for example land which represents part of the value of a business. It is obviously important to ensure that interest-free instalments are claimed wherever possible, as the saving over ten years is considerable.

9.4 Business property relief

9.4.1 Description of the relief

Relief from inheritance tax is given where value transferred by a transfer of value is attributable to 'relevant business property' (IHTA 1984, s. 104). There are six types of relevant business property, attracting relief at the following rates:

- a business or an interest in a business (100 per cent);
- a controlling shareholding in an unquoted company (100 per cent);
- a minority shareholding of shares in an unquoted company (100 per cent);
- a controlling shareholding in a quoted company (50 per cent);
- land, buildings, machinery or plant used in a business carried on by a company controlled by the transferor or by a partnership of which he is a partner (50 per cent), and
- land, buildings, machinery or plant in which the transferor has an interest in possession and which is used in his business (100 per cent if transferred with the business; 50 per cent if not).

The relief is also applied to transfers by the trustees of a settlement in which no interest in possession subsists, including maintenance funds (IHTA 1984, s. 103(1)).

The percentage reduction is made before any available exemptions are taken into account, and before any necessary grossing up is made (s. 104(2)).

In general, relief is not confined to property situated in the UK.

Relief is not available:

- where the business consists of dealing in securities or land, or of holding investments;
- where the property transferred is subject to a binding contract for sale;
- in respect of shares in a company in liquidation,
- in respect of assets not used wholly or mainly for business purposes.

As a general rule, the transferor must have owned the property for at least two years before the transfer. This requirement is adapted where, within the two-year period, the property has replaced other business property, or there have been two transfers, one of which was on death.

Shares and securities

In the application of the relief to shares and securities, the expressions 'holding company' and 'subsidiary' are defined as in CA 1985, s. 736(1), which provides that a company is a 'subsidiary' of another company, its 'holding company', if the latter company:

- holds a majority of the voting rights in it;
- is a member of it and has the right to appoint or remove a majority of its board of directors; or
- is a member of it and controls alone, pursuant to an agreement with other shareholders or members, a majority of the voting rights in it,
- or if it is a subsidiary of a company which is itself a subsidiary of the holding company.

This definition is supplemented by s. 736A, which applies it to circumstances such as nominees, trustees, security-holders, conditional rights, etc. In case of doubt, reference should be made to the wording of s. 736A itself.

A 'group' consists of a company and all its subsidiaries (IHTA 1984, s. 103(2)).

Claiming the relief

Relief is given automatically where it is due. In practice, the benefit of the relief is obtained by making an appropriate deduction (with accompanying explanation) in the account by which a transfer of value is notified to the Revenue. So far as transfers on death are concerned, this is done on page 10 of Cap Form 200 or, in Scotland, on page 10 of Cap Form A-3. In respect of chargeable lifetime transfers, relief is taken into account on page 3 of Cap Form C5.

9.4.2   A business or an interest in a business

Rate of relief

Where property consists of a business, or an interest in a business, it qualifies for relief at 100 per cent (IHTA 1984, s. 105(1)(a)).

Meaning of 'a business'

The only guidance given by the legislation as to the meaning of 'business' is that it includes a business carried on in the exercise of a profession or vocation, but does not include a business carried on otherwise than for gain (s. 103(3)). This at least indicates that the word is treated as having a wide meaning: wider, for example, than the word 'trade'. It includes farming, commercial management of woodlands, and other activities charged to tax under Schedule D, Case I by ICTA 1988, s. 55 (mines, quarries and other concerns).

Distinction between 'a business' and the assets of a business

A distinction must be drawn between a business or interest in a business on the one hand, and the assets of a business on the other. In *McGregor v Adcock* (1977) 51 TC 692, the taxpayer disposed of an area of farmland and claimed the relief from capital gains tax given in respect of disposal of a business on retirement. Rejecting the claim, Fox J said (at page 68):

> 'In the ordinary use of language land is not the same thing as a business. A business connotes an activity; land is merely an asset of a business ... A business connotes a distinct entity which is separate from its parts.'

In *Baytrust Holdings Ltd v IR Commrs* [1971] 1 WLR 1333, Plowman J put it another way (at page 95):

'A greengrocer's business is no doubt to sell fruit, but the pound of apples which you buy can hardly be described as a purchase of part of the green-grocer's business.'

The legislation does not provide specifically that 'business' includes part of a business that is capable of separate operation as a business. In this respect it resembles the capital gains tax relief for the transfer of a business to a company, and differs from the VAT transfer of going concern rules (which enable part of a business to be transferred). Suppose, for example, that Albert owns a chain of shoe shops situated in several towns. Albert wishes to make a gift of one of the shops to his son Bruce, with the intention that Bruce will take over the business in that town. Is this a gift of a business or merely of business assets? Does the shop transferred constitutes a separate business, which has been wholly transferred?

Whether there is a single business or more than one business seems to be one of fact, to be determined by the Commissioners. In the Privy Council case of *River Estates Sdn Bhd v Director General of Inland Revenue (Malaysia)* [1984] BTC 20, the appellant company carried on operations on three estates which included logging and planting, timber operations on another estate where they did not own the land, and logging without plantation on a further estate. The Special Commissioners found that the company was carrying on three separate businesses. The Privy Council took the view that it was open to the Commissioners to conclude either that there was a single business or three separate businesses, and refused to interfere with their finding of fact. In the inheritance tax context, the case may afford useful authority for an argument that what has been sold is a business, rather than a collection of business assets; it also demonstrates the importance of the Commissioners' findings in this regard.

Meaning of 'an interest in a business'

The transferor need not be the sole proprietor. The interest of a partner, or other joint owner, qualifies as an 'interest in a business'. The interest of a loan creditor does not qualify.

In *Beckman v IR Commrs* (2000) Sp C 226, the deceased had carried on business in a partnership until four years before her death. Her capital account as a partner was derived from the capital which she introduced into the business and from accumulated profits which had not been withdrawn. At the time of her death the sum of £112,800 was standing to the credit of her capital account. The Special Commissioner held that this was not an 'interest in a business': after her retirement her rights were simply those of a creditor of the business.

Farming quotas

The value of a farming business may include producer quotas such as cow and sheep quotas. Their value will be included in the value qualifying for business property relief. Milk quotas will, however, attach to agricultural land and qualify for agricultural property relief.

Amount on which relief given

Relief is given on the net value of the business, as defined in IHTA 1984, s. 110: the value of the assets used in the business (including goodwill) reduced by the aggregate amount of any liabilities incurred for business purposes. No regard is had to assets or liabilities other than those by reference to which the entire business would be valued.

9.4.3 Controlling shareholdings

Shares in, or securities of, a company qualify for relief if, either alone or together with other such shares or securities, they gave the transferor control of the company immediately before the transfer.

Where the shares are unquoted, relief is at 100 per cent (IHTA 1984, s. 105(1)(b)). Where the shares are quoted, relief is at 50 per cent (s. 105(1)(cc)).

Controlling shareholdings in AIM companies qualify for 100 per cent relief, whereas controlling shareholdings in companies quoted on a recognised stock exchange attract only 50 per cent relief.

'Control' is defined broadly as control of powers of voting on all questions affecting the company as a whole which, if exercised, would yield a majority of votes capable of being exercised on them (IHTA 1984, s. 269). A director with a holding a 50 per cent of the shares plus a casting vote at general meetings has control of the company for the purposes of this provision: *Walker's Exors v IR Commrs* (2001) Sp C 275, applying *IR Commrs v BW Noble Ltd* (1926) 12 TC 911.

The words 'capable of being exercised' explain the category of votes being referred to, ie votes on questions affecting the company as a whole, as opposed to questions affecting a particular class of shares only. They do not refer to the personal capacity of the shareholder. In *Walding v IR Commrs* [1996] BTC 8,003, it was argued unsuccessfully that where shares were owned by a four-year-old, the votes carried by those shares were not capable of being exercised, so that the holding should be ignored in determining whether or not another holding was a controlling shareholding for business property relief purposes.

The full definition in s. 269 includes control resulting from valuation along with 'related property'. Where, however, relief under s. 176 (sale of related property) is obtained, so that the shares are revalued as a minority holding of 25 per cent or less, the 100 per cent relief is withdrawn (s. 105(2)), but the 50 per cent relief may be available.

Example 9.13

Cecil dies leaving an estate which includes a 20 per cent shareholding in Buildnot Ltd (an unquoted company), in which his wife also owns a 40 per cent holding. Cecil's shares are valued as one-third of a 60 per cent holding worth (say) £300,000; ie at 1/3 × £300,000 = £100,000. Cecil's executors sell the shares for £60,000. There would be no point in making a claim under s. 176 because although the value would be reduced from £100,000 to 350,000, relief at 100 per cent would cease to be available, although relief at 50 per cent would probably be available under s. 105(1)(c).

The relief for a controlling holding applies only to shares which were part of the holding which gave the transferor control. If, in addition, he transfers shares of another class, eg non-voting preference shares, these do not attract 100 per cent relief, although if the company is unquoted they will obtain 50 per cent relief. Moreover, quoted and unquoted shares cannot be aggregated in determining whether the transferor's holding (of either category) was a controlling holding.

Control may be derived indirectly. For example, if P owns 40 per cent of the shares in X Ltd, plus all the shares in Y Ltd, which in turn owns 30 per cent of the shares in X Ltd, P will be treated as having control of X Ltd, for purposes of both valuation and business relief.

The size of the transferor's holding after the transfer is irrelevant, except in so far as it will determine the rate of relief applicable to any further transfers of shares out of it.

Example 9.14

David owns 90 per cent of the shares in Zap Ltd, an unquoted company. He gives a 30 per cent holding to Elaine, and soon afterwards gives a 40 per cent holding to Fiona. A year later he gives the remaining shares to Guy. Two years later David dies, and it becomes necessary to determine the value transferred by the two gifts.

The transfers to Elaine and Fiona attract relief at 100 per cent. The transfer to Guy does not, although it will attract relief at 50 per cent under s. 105(1)(c).

9.4.4   Minority holding of unquoted shares

Unquoted shares in a company qualify for relief at 100 per cent, regardless of the size of the holding (IHTA 1984, s. 105(1)(bb)).

However, the relief extends only to shares and not to recognised securities (although securities giving the transferor control may qualify for relief under s. 105(1)(b): see above).

'Quoted' means 'listed on a recognised stock exchange', and 'unquoted' means any shares not so listed (s. 105(IZA)). Securities dealt in on the Alternative Investment Market (AIM) are treated as unquoted for these purposes (Revenue Press Release, 20 February 1995).

9.4.5   Property of the transferor used by his company or partnership

Land or buildings and machinery or plant owned by the transferor qualify for relief at 50 per cent if, immediately before the transfer, they were used wholly or mainly for the purposes of a business carried on by:

- a company controlled by the transferor, or
- a partnership of which the transferor was then a partner (s. 105(1)(d) IHTA 1984).

Example 9.15

Henry is the senior partner in a firm of accountants who carry on business in office premises owned by Henry. Henry dies and leaves both the building and his interest in the firm to his son James, one of the junior partners.

Henry's interest in the business qualifies for relief at 100 per cent under s. 105(1)(a). The building qualifies for relief at 50 per cent under s. 105(1)(d).

The land, building, machinery or plant do not qualify as relevant business property unless the transferor's interest in the partnership or shareholding in the company is itself relevant business property (s. 105(6)). This does not mean that relief is excluded unless the transferor's interest (or share-holding) is transferred at the same time as the underlying assets. Rather, relief is excluded where the interest (or shareholding) would fail to qualify if it were transferred.

> ### Example 9.16
>
> Kenneth is the owner of a factory in which the company he controls carries on a manufacturing business purchased less than two years ago from the former tenant. Kenneth transfers the factory into trust for his son Luke for life.
>
> The property does not qualify for 50 per cent relief because Kenneth's shares in the company would fail to satisfy the two-year ownership requirement of s. 106.

It is considered that where, following a transfer of land, buildings, machinery or plant within s. 105(1)(d), the transferor retains his controlling interest or partnership share, as the case may be, this is not a gift subject to reservation, bringing FA 1986, s. 102 into play.

9.4.6 Settled property used in a life tenant's business

Land or buildings and machinery or plant qualify for relief at 50 per cent if, immediately before the transfer, they were:

- used wholly or mainly for the purposes of a business carried on by the transferor, and
- settled property in which the transferor was entitled to an interest in possession,

(IHTA 1984, s. 105(1)(d), (e)).

> ### Example 9.17
>
> Mark is the life tenant of premises in which he carries on trade as a motor dealer. In terms of the settlement, the property passes to Paul after Mark's death.
>
> On the occasion of Mark's death, the property is aggregated with his free estate. It will attract relief under s. 105(1)(e) at 50 per cent.

The land, building, machinery or plant does not qualify as relevant business property unless the life tenant's business is itself relevant business property (s. 105(6)). This does not mean that relief is excluded unless the life tenant's business is transferred at the same time as the settled property: rather, relief is excluded where the business would fail to qualify if it were transferred.

Property and business both settled

In contrast to the above, where the business itself is settled property as well as the underlying assets, relief is available at 100 per cent. This follows from the fact that IHTA, s. 49(1) 1984 treats the life tenant as beneficially entitled to the business (including the assets).

9.4.7 Property excluded from relief

Dealing in land or shares, or holding investments

Relief is not available in respect of a business or interest in a business, or shares in or securities of a company, if its business consists wholly or mainly of one or more of the following:

- dealing in securities, stocks or shares;
- dealing in land or buildings,
- making or holding investments,

(s. 105(3) IHTA 1984).

The property of such businesses is not 'relevant business property'. Thus, where a business falls foul of s. 105(3), its whole value is disqualified, and not just that part attributable to investments.

Example 9.18

Philip's business consists mainly of dealing in land, but also includes the management of commercial woodlands.

Under s. 105(3) the business is not 'relevant business property' and does not qualify for relief, not even the proportion attributable to the woodlands. Philip may, however, be able to establish, on the basis of factual evidence, that he has two separate businesses, one qualifying and one non-qualifying.

Does property letting qualify for relief?

The issue of whether the letting of property of itself constitutes a business qualifying for business property relief is one which recurs regularly, but which has not yet been the subject of a court decision. It will be excluded from relief by s. 105(3) if it is no more than the making or holding of investments. The Revenue's view is understood to be that the exclusion applies unless substantial additional services are provided by the landlord. This view is supported by decisions of the Special Commissioners (see, for example, *Executors of Moore (deceased) v IR Commrs* (1995) Sp C 2, *Executor of Burkinyoung (deceased) v IR Commrs (1995) Sp C* 3, *Hall & Anor v IR Commrs* (1997) Sp C 114, and *Powell & Anor v IR Commrs* (1997) Sp C 120.

In *Weston v IR Commrs* [2000] BTC 8,041, the issue was appealed to the High Court for the first time. The caravan site in question was wholly residential and looked like a miniature suburban residential development. The three employees spent 75 per cent of their time on park maintenance and 25 per cent on sales activities. Profits from pitch fees exceeded profits from caravan sales. The Special Commissioner held that in these circumstances the caravan sales were ancillary to the pitch fees and that the business therefore consisted wholly or mainly of making investments. On appeal, this decision was upheld. The taxpayer argued unsuccessfully that the profit and loss account was not a reliable indication of the relative contributions to the business of pitch fees on the one hand and caravan sales on the other, and that a greater proportion of the site expenditure should have been allocated to pitch income. Collins J held that the Special Commissioner could not be faulted in the weight which he attached to the various factors in holding that the business of pitch letting was not ancillary to caravan sales.

In *IR Commrs v George (executors of Stedman dec'd)* [2004] BTC 8,003, the deceased held a majority shareholding in a company which carried on the business of running a residential caravan park and various other activities connected therewith. The Special Commissioners held that, in reality, the owners of caravans on the site were paying for the services provided by the company, rather than the mere right to enjoy the pitch. The High Court disagreed and allowed the Revenue's appeal on the basis that the core and main activity of the company was the holding of investments in land. In the Court of Appeal Carnwath LJ, allowing the executors' appeal, said that the question was whether the business was 'mainly' that of holding investments. The High Court had placed too much reliance on the decision in *Weston v IR Commrs* [2000] BTC 8,041 that land was generally held as an investment where gain was derived from payment to the owner for use of the property, and so a landlord would normally hold his property as an investment, even if he had to engage in activities of maintenance and management which were required by the lease or were incidental to the letting. While that was fair as a statement related to the facts in that case, in the present case what was meant by 'management' and the relevance to that question of the requirements of the lease had to be considered in more detail.

Both the Commissioners and the High Court had referred to *Cook v Medway Society Ltd* [1997] BTC 63, where the judge said that the critical question was whether the holding of assets to produce a profitable return was merely incidental to the carrying on of some other business, or was the very business carried on by the taxpayer. However, it was doubtful if the judge in that case intended to lay down a general statement of principle. If he did, it was open to the criticism that it excluded the third possibility where the holding of investments was neither 'merely incidental' nor 'the very business', but was simply one of a number of components of a composite business. In the present case, the holding of property as an investment was only one component of the business and, on the findings of the Commissioners, it was not the main component.

The case of *Furness v IR Commrs* (1999) Sp C 202, also concerned the management of a caravan park. In this case the business consisted to some extent of running activities on the site for the entertainment of residents, and there was also a business of sale of static caravans from which a substantial part of the profits was derived. Looking at the business as a whole, and in particular the amount of activity of the proprietors, the Special Commissioner held that it did not consist wholly or mainly of holding investments.

On the whole, therefore, the Revenue's view has been borne out by the series of published Special Commissioners' decisions.

Parks industry: Revenue practice

In addition to the guidance afforded by the Special Commissioners' decisions referred to above, an indication of the official view regarding the availability of business property relief to holiday and home parks is afforded by a statement provided by the Capital Taxes Office (CTO) to the British Holiday and Home Parks Association Ltd in February 1999. The guidance in the statement is obviously in general terms and must be read subject to the Revenue's usual warning that each case must be looked at on its own facts and its own merits. In summary, the guidance is to the following effect:

- In determining whether or not relief is denied by IHTA 1984, s. 105(3), regard will be had to the amalgam of the preponderant activities, assets and sources of income or gains of the business at the time of the transfer and over a reasonable period leading up to it. A reasonable period in this context is likely to mean more than two or three years, and it could be necessary to look back ten or even 15 years. A decline in activity due to the owner's age, ill health or changed family circumstances will not necessarily preclude relief.
- 'Mainly' means in excess of 50 per cent. Regard will ordinarily be had to profit rather than to turnover, but profit is only one measure of the business activities. The 'mainly' test does not apply where the activity is so intense as to be wholly of a non-investment nature, such as a hotel, motel or short-term holiday operation of a similar nature.
- Short-term holiday letting: the CTO will draw a distinction between the mere exploitation of a view or location (indicative of investment) and attractions provided or enhanced and actively managed by, or on behalf

of, the owner (indicative of non-investment). The latter may range from swimming pools to managed nature reserves or walks. Provision of tourist information services is a relevant factor on the non-investment side where the 'mainly' test is applied. Where there is a mix of investment and non-investment activity the 'mainly' test will be applied.

Where cottages, chalets or caravans owned by the proprietor are let on short term holiday lets, the CTO will consider, among other things, whether there are services such as cleaning, provision of bed linen, towels, etc. in addition to furnishings. Subject to the caveat that each case must be considered individually, the CTO states that in practice relief has been available for businesses that consist of letting such properties with 'ample services'.

As regards touring caravan and camping sites, there can be a wide spectrum of businesses, ranging from relatively simple fields up towards holiday camps. Where the income is derived from allowing the use of land without substantial services, there will be presumption in favour of investment, but in some cases the other facilities will swing the 'mainly' test in favour of allowing relief.

- Holiday caravan and chalet sites where the units are owner occupied: there will require to be a substantial range of facilities and income from services to tilt the balance in favour of allowing relief.
- Residential caravan sites: again the level of services and facilities will be relevant. A large and unresolved issue is the treatment of profits from the sale of caravans, either outright or on commission.

Finally the CTO warns that where any change in operations is considered, other taxes should be taken into account, especially VAT.

'Wholly or mainly'

The meaning of 'wholly or mainly' was considered in the inheritance tax context by a Special Commissioner in *Farmer's Executors v IR Commrs* (1999) Sp C 216. This case concerned a farming business. At the time of the deceased's death there were 23 tenancies of land or buildings previously used in farming operations, all for short periods. It was common ground that the in hand farmland, farmhouse, etc. qualified for agricultural property relief, and the question was whether the remaining land qualified for business property relief. The Special Commissioner held that the level of net profits of the business was not the only, or even the principal, factor in deciding whether a business consisted wholly or mainly of the making of investments. She took into account a number of factors, including:

- the overall context of the business, including the fact that the qualifying activities had been carried on in a businesslike way, employing managers and consultants;
- capital employed;
- time spent by employees, casual staff and consultants;
- turnover,
- profit.

Of these factors only attribution of profit supported the conclusion that the business did not consist mainly of farming. That was outweighed by the other factors that supported the opposite conclusion. Clearly the case was decided on its own facts, but the decision affords useful guidance as to the approach to be adopted in applying the phrase 'wholly or mainly' in this context.

Where an unincorporated business consists mainly of qualifying activities, a further question may arise as to whether the non-qualifying activities constitute a separate business or a minor part of a larger single business. This is essentially a question of fact, to be decided on the basis of available evidence.

Where the business is incorporated, the position is more clear-cut. If the business of the company is wholly or mainly a qualifying one, all its business assets are included in the value of the shares for business relief. If, on the other hand, the business of the company is wholly or mainly a non-qualifying one, the value of its shares is entirely disqualified. The dividing line could conceivably be quite narrow, and will depend upon the circumstances of each case.

9.4.8 Groups of companies

Shares in a holding company are not disqualified if its subsidiaries carry on qualifying businesses (IHTA 1984, s. 105(4)(b)).

Where a company (A), whose shares are transferred, is a member of a group which also includes a member (B) whose business falls foul of s. 105(3), the shares of Company A are valued for business relief as if Company B were not a member of the group (IHTA 1984, s. 111). This ensures that the value qualifying for relief is not 'tainted' by non-qualifying activities, and may reduce it substantially.

Section 111 does not apply where Company B's business consists wholly or mainly in the holding of land or buildings which are wholly or mainly occupied by other group members whose businesses qualify.

9.4.9 Property subject to a contract for sale

Where the property transferred is subject to a binding contract for sale, it is not relevant business property in relation to the transfer (IHTA 1984, s. 113). There are two exceptions to this, in which the relief is not lost:

- where the sale is to a company which is to carry on the business, and is made wholly or mainly in consideration of shares in or securities of the company, ie where a trader incorporates his business,
- where the sale is of shares in or securities of a company, and is made for the purpose of reconstruction or amalgamation.

No indication is given as to whether a conditional contract is 'binding' before the condition is purified, but it is thought that there is no reason why it should not be so. For example, if A agrees to purchase a hotel business from B on condition that the necessary licences are transferred, the contract is binding when entered into, so that prior to transfer of the licence neither party may resile unilaterally. Accordingly, if in the meantime B gives the property to C, the hotel is not relevant business property, and relief is not available.

The exclusion applies to any of the classes of 'relevant business property' in s. 105(1). Thus, for example, if D enters into a contract for sale of a building used for business purposes by his partnership, the building ceases to be relevant business property under s. 105(1)(d).

The purchaser's equitable interest during the period between the contract and completion of the sale may qualify for relief as an interest in a business. The value of his interest will be approximately equivalent to the value of the business itself, less a discount reflecting uncertainties such as the risk of the seller's bankruptcy, or the risk of the seller being unwilling to complete the sale without litigation. The purchaser's interest may therefore qualify for relief at 100 per cent, provided the other requirements are satisfied. In particular, the requirement of s. 106 as to minimum period of ownership may be satisfied if the purchase is made as a replacement of another qualifying interest in a business.

In Scotland, where the concept of an equitable interest is unknown, the same result is achieved by valuing the contractual right of the purchaser to have the business conveyed to him. The remarks above as to availability of relief apply.

Section 113 does not apply where the transfer is of a business whose value is partly attributable to assets that are subject to a contract of sale at the time of the transfer. The proceeds of sale will, after all, later form part of the assets of the business that is being transferred.

Example 9.19

Andrew owns a business comprising of a chain of retail shops. On 1 October he contracts to sell one of the shops to Bob. The transaction is completed on 1 December. On 1 November Andrew makes a gift to Clive of a one-half share of the business.

The value attributable to the shop subject to contract of sale is not excluded by s. 113 from the value of the 'interest in a business' qualifying for 100 per cent relief, provided that it can be shown that the proceeds of sale will be reinvested in the business (whether or not for the purchase of a new shop). This represents a continuation of a previous estate duty practice.

'Buy and sell' agreements and accruer arrangements

'Buy and sell' agreement is the name commonly given to an agreement between the partners of a partnership, or the shareholder directors of a company, whereby, on the death of one of them before retirement, the deceased's personal representatives are obliged to sell, and the survivors are obliged to buy, the deceased's interest or shares. Funds for the purchase are often provided by appropriate life assurance policies.

In Statement of Practice 12/80, the Revenue stated its view that such an agreement, requiring as it does a sale and purchase and not merely conferring an option to sell or buy, is a binding contract for sale within s. 113.

It is understood that business relief remained available in the following cases:

- partnership terminating on death; partnership assets realised and estate entitled to deceased's share of proceeds;
- partnership continuing; estate entitled to represent deceased;
- partnership continuing; partnership share falling into deceased's estate but with option for other partners to acquire either on valuation or formula,
- partnership continuing; deceased partner's share accruing to surviving partners with estate entitled to payment either on valuation or formula,

(see article in the *Law Society's Gazette*, 6 May 1981).

This article subsequently received Revenue approval, most recently in an article in the *Law Society's Gazette*, 4 September 1996.

9.4.10   Shares in a company in liquidation

Shares in or securities of a company are not relevant business property, and are thus disqualified from relief, if at the time of the transfer any of the following apply:

- a winding-up order has been made in respect of the company;
- the company has passed a resolution for voluntary winding-up,
- the company is otherwise in process of liquidation,

(IHTA 1984, s. 105(5)).

However, they are not disqualified if:

- the business of the company is to continue to be carried on after a reconstruction or amalgamation, and
- the reconstruction or amalgamation either is the purpose of the winding-up or liquidation, or takes place within one year after the transfer of value.

Example 9.20

Angus and Bruce each own 50 per cent of the shares in two companies, Brick Ltd, and Timber Ltd. It is agreed to restructure the holdings so that Angus obtains control of the business of Brick Ltd, and Bruce obtains control of the business of Timber Ltd. As part of the reconstruction, both the original companies are put into voluntary liquidation. Before the reconstruction is completed. Angus dies leaving his shares in Brick Ltd (in liquidation) to Carol.

Business relief is available on the transfer because s. 105(5) does not apply if the liquidation is part of the reconstruction.

9.4.11   Assets not used in the business

Excepted assets

Any value attributable to 'excepted assets' is to be left out of account in determining the value of relevant business property that qualifies for relief (IHTA 1984, s. 112(1)). In general terms, 'excepted assets' are assets that have not been used for the purposes of the transferor's business during the specified period. The effect of s. 112 is that the value of any such assets is deducted from the value of relevant business property before the relief is calculated.

Example 9.21

Adam owns property worth £200,000 which is used by his company for business purposes; £10,000 comprises 'excepted assets'. Adam transfers a one-half share of the property into a discretionary trust. Adam's remaining one-half share is valued at £90,000.

	£
Value transferred (£200,000 − £90,000)	110,000
Less: business relief at 50 per cent on	
£110,000 − (1/2 × £10,000)	52,500
Reduced value transferred	57,500

An asset is deemed not to have been used wholly or mainly for business purposes at any time where it was used wholly or mainly for the benefit of the transferor or any person connected with him (s. 112(6)).

Where a business consists partly, but not wholly or mainly, of non-qualifying activities such as dealing in land or holding investments, an asset that is predominantly used for the dealing or investment activities is not an excepted asset, and is not excluded from relief by s. 112. This is because s. 112(2) simply requires the asset to be used or required for the purposes of the business, as opposed to personal benefit, and does not require it to be used for the part of the business consisting of non-dealing or investment activities.

Transfer of business or interest in a business

Where the transfer concerned is of a business or an interest in a business, an asset is excepted unless either:

- it was used wholly or mainly for the purposes of the business throughout the whole of its ownership by the transferor or the last two years, whichever is the shorter, or
- it was required at the time of the transfer for future business use (IHTA 1984, s. 112(2) and (5)).

Example 9.22

Arthur dies, leaving his business to his son Ben. At the date of Arthur's death, the assets of the business include the following:

- an item of machinery purchased five years ago and always used for business purposes;
- a word-processing machine purchased one year ago and always used for business purposes;
- a car purchased four years ago and used for the past year for business purposes,
- a data retrieval system purchased a few weeks ago for business purposes, not yet in use.

The first two avoid being excepted because of past use. The last two will avoid being excepted if it can be shown that they are required for future use in the business.

Transfer of shares or securities

Where the transfer concerned is of shares or securities in a company (whether a controlling shareholding or not), an asset is excepted unless either:

1. it was used wholly or mainly for the purposes of the business carried on by the company (or by another company in the same group) throughout the whole of its ownership by the company or another group member, or the last two years, whichever is the shorter; or

2. it was required at the time of the transfer for future business use,

(IHTA 1984, s. 112(2) and (5)).

For the purposes of 1 above, use or ownership by a non-qualifying group member is disregarded.

Example 9.23

If in Example 9.22, Arthur's business had been a company, and the bequest to Ben had been shares in the company, the four assets mentioned would be treated in exactly the same way.

In *Barclays Bank Trust Co Ltd v IR Commrs* (1998) Sp C 158, a somewhat restrictive interpretation was given by a Special Commissioner to the words 'required . . . for future business use'. 'Required' implied some imperative that the money would be used on a given project, or for some palpable business purpose. It was not enough to show that there was a possibility that the money might be required should an opportunity arise at some unspecified time in the future. In that case a sum of cash held by a company which was not in fact used for business purposes until 1997 was held not to have been 'required for future business use' at the time of a transfer of shares in 1990.

It is understood that if during the two-year period a trader incorporates his business, s. 112(2) will be treated as satisfied if the combined period of use before and after incorporation meets its requirements.

Transfer of assets used by transferor's partnership or company

Where the transfer concerned is of land, buildings, machinery or plant used by the transferor's partnership or controlled company (ie an asset qualifying for 50 per cent relief under IHTA 1984, s. 105(1)(d)), the rules are slightly different from those for an interest in a business itself. An asset in this category is not relevant business property unless either:

- it was used wholly or mainly for the purposes of the business carried on by the partnership or company throughout the last two years, or
- it replaced another asset so used, and it and the other asset and any asset replaced in turn by the other asset were together so used for two out of the last five years,

(IHTA 1984, s. 112(3)).

Example 9.24

Charles is the controlling shareholder of Sales Ltd, a retail business. Charles owns the premises and most of the shop fittings used for Sales Ltd's business. In 2001, Charles purchased a new supermarket to replace one he had owned for many years and sold in 1999. At the same time Charles purchased some new shop fittings. In 2002, Charles dies.

The building qualifies for relief because of the replacement rules: the present building and the one it replaced have been in use for more than two out of the last five years.

The new shop fittings are disqualified since they do not fulfil either requirement as to use.

An asset in this category cannot qualify on the basis of requirement for future business use.

In the case of successive transfers within two years, the condition in s. 112(3) is satisfied if the asset (and any other asset it replaced) was so used throughout the period between the transfers, or throughout the part of that period during which it was owned by the transferor or his spouse.

> ### Example 9.25
>
> Dennis and Eric carry on business in partnership, in an office owned by Dennis. On 1 June 1999 Dennis dies, leaving the office to Eric and his interest in the business to his son Fred. On 1 May 2000, Eric sells the office to a third party, and two months later purchases new premises with the proceeds of sale. On 1 October 2001 Eric makes a gift of one-half share of the new office to Fred. Eric dies in 2004 and it is necessary to determine whether business relief is available in respect of the gift by Eric to Fred.
>
> By virtue of s. 109, the 'ownership' requirement of s. 106 is satisfied. By virtue of the proviso to s. 112(3), the 'business use' requirement is also satisfied and the office qualifies for relief.

Deemed transfer of settled property used by life tenant's business

No special provision is made in IHTA 1984, s. 112 for settled property used for the purposes of a business carried on by the life tenant. Such property is covered by the general provisions relating to interests in a business.

> ### Example 9.26
>
> Peter is the life tenant of a building and machinery, which he uses for the purposes of a manufacturing business. Some of the items of machinery are mainly used by Peter's son for do-it-yourself car repairs.
>
> On Peter's death these items will be excepted assets.

Possible treatment of land, etc. as separate assets

Where a part of any land or building which would otherwise be an excepted asset, or would fail to qualify as business property, is used exclusively for business purposes, the part used for business and the remainder may be treated as separate assets, so that the former qualifies for relief (IHTA 1984, s. 112(4)). The value of the part used for business shall (if it would otherwise be less) be taken to be a just proportion of the value of the whole.

> **Example 9.27**
>
> Roger owns a house, the basement of which he uses for the making and selling of pottery. The basement comprises about one-third of the total floor space of the house. Roger makes a gift of the whole house to Stephen.
>
> Were it not for s. 112(4), that part of Roger's house used for business would not qualify for business relief. The effect of s. 112(4) is that Roger will be given relief on approximately one-third of the value transferred to Stephen.

9.4.12 Minimum period of ownership

General: two-year requirement

Property is not relevant business property unless it was owned by the transferor for at least two years prior to the transfer (s. 106 IHTA 1984).

'Ownership' is not defined in the Act. In particular, no indication is given as to whether legal or beneficial ownership is envisaged. The official view appears to be that for the purposes of business relief, 'ownership' includes both legal and beneficial ownership so that either is sufficient on its own (Official Report, Standing Committee E, 24 June 1976, col. 1275–76). The effect is that the ownership requirement is capable of being satisfied by a life tenant under either a trust for sale (on the basis of his equitable interest) or a strict settlement (on the basis of his legal title and his equitable interest).

The position of a life renter in Scotland (including a life renter under a proper life rent) is discussed in relation to the parallel ownership requirement for agricultural relief, where the conclusion is reached that the ownership requirement is capable of being satisfied.

As regards settled property in which no interest in possession subsists, 'transferor' means the trustees, who are capable of qualifying on the basis of their legal ownership. In Scotland, no difficulty arises because the trustees are the owners of the trust property, and qualify on that basis.

Replacements of property

Relief is not lost if, during the two-year period, the transferor has sold qualifying property and replaced it with the property which he now transfers, provide that the transferred property, the other property, and any property directly or indirectly replaced by the other property, were owned by the transferor for a total of at least two out of the five years before the transfer (IHTA 1984, s. 107).

Example 9.28

In 2001, Adam sells a building he has owned for some years, and used for a business carried on by the company he controls. In 2003, he reinvests the proceeds of sale in a new building, which he transfers to Bob in 2004.

The ownership requirement is treated as satisfied.

Section 107 does not apply to minority shareholdings in unquoted companies.

Restriction on relief for replacements

Relief on replacement property is limited to what would have been obtained had the replacement (or replacements if more than one) not taken place (s. 107(2)).

Doubts have been expressed as to the meaning of this provision. Read literally, it requires a valuation of the replaced property at the date of the gift, even though the taxpayer no longer owns it. If the old property is worth less than the value of the new property, relief is given at the appropriate percentage on the value of the old property.

Example 9.29

Colin, who has been a partner in Chester & Co for some years, sells his share to the other partners for £100,000 and shortly thereafter buys a share in the business of York & Co, for £200,000. Less than two years later, Colin dies, at a time when his interest in York & Co is worth £250,000.

On a literal interpretation of s. 107(2), it is necessary to obtain a valuation of what Colin's shares in Chester & Co would have been had he still been a partner at the date of his death. If this is less than £250,000, business relief is given at 100 per cent on this lower amount.

An alternative, less literal construction of IHTA 1984, s. 107(2) is to interpret it as a restriction of relief to the proportion of the value of the new property attributable to the proceeds of sale of the old property. Hence, in the above example relief would be available at 100 per cent on £250,000 × 100,000/200,000 = £125,000.

It is understood that, in practice, the Revenue allows relief to be calculated according to the alternative construction outlined above.

On a different reading of s. 107(2), it prevents relief at 100 per cent being obtained if the replaced property would only have received 50 per cent relief, for example where a minority shareholding is replaced by a controlling holding. There has, as yet, been no judicial or official support for this reading.

Any change resulting from the formation, alteration or dissolution of a partnership is disregarded for the purposes of the restriction on relief (s. 107(3)). In other words, such a change is not treated as a 'replacement' bringing s. 107(2) into effect.

Minority shareholdings in unquoted companies

Where the relevant business property consists of a minority shareholding in an unquoted company (whether of more or less than 25 per cent), special provisions apply to replacements within the two-year period, in order to determine whether relief is available, and if so, at what rate. The period of ownership of the old shares is added to the period of ownership of the new shares, provided that the latter would be identified with the former under any of the provisions of TCGA 1992, ss. 126–136 (IHTA 1984, s. 107(4)). This applies in place of the normal qualification rule for replacements within the two years before the transfer.

Successions

There are two relaxations of the ownership requirement, in respect of transfers on death.

Deemed ownership

Where a person becomes entitled to property on the death of another person, he is treated as having owned it:

- from the date of death, and
- if the deceased person was the new owner's spouse, for any period during which the spouse owned it,

(IHTA 1984, s. 108).

Example 9.30

On 1 February 2002, Adam purchased business property. On 1 October 2002, Adam died, leaving the property to his wife Jane. On 1 September 2003, Jane transferred the property to Beth.

In determining whether Jane's ownership fulfils the two-year requirement, she is deemed to have owned the property throughout Adam's period of ownership, and also since the date of Adam's death. This second point ensures that the period during which Adam's estate was being administered counts towards the two-year period.

Second transfer within two years

Where two transfers are separated by a period of less than two years, and one of the transfers is on death, the two-year requirement does not apply if:

- the first transfer qualified for business relief (or would have qualified if business relief had existed at that time);
- the relevant business property became the property of the transferor of the second transfer, or of his spouse;
- the property (or any property replacing it) would, apart from the two-year ownership requirement, have been relevant business property in relation to the second transfer, and
- one or other transfer was made on the death of the respective transferor (or both were),

(IHTA 1984, s. 109(1)).

Example 9.31

Charles dies and leaves his business to his son David. The business is 'relevant business property'. Less than two years later, David gives a share in the business to Edward. In spite of the fact that David has not owned the business for two years, relief is available.

A similar rule applies where:

- only part of the value transferred by the first transfer qualified for relief (as will normally be the case where the first transfer is on death);
- only part of the subjects qualifying on the first transfer became the property of the second transferor, and
- the value transferred by the first transfer represents only part of the value of the business property. This would occur where the first transfer was not a gift but a sale at an undervalue. Section 109(3) provides that relief on the second transfer is restricted to the same proportion of the value thereby transferred.

Example 9.32

Frank sells a business worth £400,000 to his son George for £100,000. Less than two years later, George dies, leaving the business to Harry, at a time when it is worth £500,000. Relief is available in respect of George's death only on:

£500,000 × 300,000/400,000 = £375,000 at 100 per cent.

Relief is available under s. 109 even if the subjects of the first transfer have been sold and replaced before the second transfer. In such cases the relief is not to exceed what it would have been had the replacement (or replacements if more than one) not taken place (s. 109(2)).

9.4.13 Transfers within seven years before death

General: additional conditions to fulfil

Where a lifetime transfer of business property is followed within less than seven years by the death of the transferor, tax (or additional tax) may become chargeable.

In calculating the amount of such tax (or extra tax), business relief will only be available if the following conditions are fulfilled:

- the 'original property' must have been owned by the transferee throughout the period between the date of the transfer and the death of the transferor,
- the 'original property' would have qualified as relevant business property on a notional transfer of value by the transferee immediately before the transferor's death,

(IHTA 1984, s. 113A(3)).

In summary, the general conditions for business relief must continue to be satisfied throughout the period from the date of the transfer until the date of death.

> ### Example 9.33
>
> Jack makes a lifetime gift of his haulage business to his son Kevin. The transfer is potentially exempt and no tax is payable at this time.
>
> Five years later Kevin sells the business and invests the proceeds of sale. One more year later, Jack dies. Tax becomes chargeable on Jack's gift within seven years before death. Business property relief is not available in respect of this transfer because the business was not owned by Kevin throughout the period between the gift and Jack's death.

> ### Example 9.34
>
> Les makes a lifetime gift of his forestry business to Martin. The transfer is potentially exempt and no tax is payable at this time.
>
> Four years later Les dies and the potential exemption is lost. During this period, Martin has changed the nature of the business so that it now consists wholly of dealing in land.
>
> Business property relief is not available in respect of Les's gift because the property would not be 'relevant business property' on a notional transfer immediately before Les's death.

'Original property' means the property which was relevant business property in relation to the lifetime gift (s. 113A(8)).

'Transferee' means the person who received the property on the lifetime transfer. Where it becomes or remains settled property in which no interest in possession subsists, 'transferee' means the trustees of the settlement. Where business property is settled on accumulation and maintenance settlements and, prior to the settlor's death within seven years, a beneficiary becomes entitled to the property (or to an interest in possession therein), relief will be lost. If however the property had initially been settled on the beneficiary for life, relief would not be lost.

A similar anomaly arises where the transferee makes a further transfer to his or her spouse within the seven-year period. Once again, relief would be lost.

In determining for these purposes whether or not there was a potentially exempt transfer which has proved to be chargeable, the percentage reduction in value transferred given on the original transfer must be ignored (s. 113A(7A)). This provision prevents an argument that the charge under s. 113A can never apply, because there has been no PET capable of becoming chargeable.

Controlling shareholdings: special provisions

Where the property transferred consists of shares out of a controlling shareholding, special provision is necessary to preserve relief in cases where control is not passed to the transferee.

For example, where A owns 60 per cent of the shares in a quoted company and transfers half his shares to B, in the absence of specific provision the 30 per cent holding now owned by B would fail to qualify as 'relevant business property' on A's death within seven years. Such special provision is made by IHTA 1984, s. 113A(3A), which provides that the second condition above (ie that the 'original property' must qualify as relevant business property at the transferor's death) need not be fulfilled as regards either:

- shares quoted at the time of the gift, or
- shares which gave the transferor control at the time of the gift, and which have remained unquoted throughout the period until death.

Example 9.35

Nigel makes a lifetime gift of a controlling shareholding in Hawk Ltd, an unquoted company, to the trustees of a discretionary trust. The transfer is chargeable at the time when it is made, and attracts business property relief at 100 per cent.

Two years later Hawk Ltd makes a rights issue, which the trustees do not take up. After the issue, the trustees' holding no longer gives them control of the company. Three years later, Nigel dies, and extra tax becomes chargeable on his transfer into trust.

In calculating the extra tax, business relief is available because the conditions in s. 113A(3) are fulfilled. Relief will still be at the rate of 100 per cent, despite the fact that at the time of Nigel's death the trustees have only a minority shareholding in Hawk Ltd.

The same would apply if in this example Nigel made a gift of one-quarter of a 60 per cent holding to the trustees.

The effect of s. 113A(3) is that transfers out of quoted shareholdings which qualified for relief at the date of the gift continue to qualify even if the transferee never has control. On the other hand, transfers out of unquoted shareholdings that qualified at the date of the gift because the transferor had control continue to qualify even if the transferee never has control, but only if the shares remain unquoted. Thus where an unquoted company becomes quoted during the intervening period, relief is lost.

'Quoted' means listed on a recognised stock exchange (IHTA 1984, s. 113A(3B)).

'Unquoted' means any shares not so listed.

Death of transferee before transferor

Special provision is made for the case where a transferor dies within seven years after making a gift of business property, but in the meantime the transferee has also died. In these circumstances the lifetime gift will attract relief if the qualifying conditions have been satisfied during the period ending with the transferee's death, rather than the transferor's (s. 113A(4)).

Part only of property qualifying

Where, at the time of the transferor's death within seven years, the conditions for relief continue to be fulfilled in respect only of part of the original property, then relief is given in respect of such a proportionate part in calculating the tax (or extra tax) chargeable (IHTA 1984, s. 113A(5)).

Example 9.36

Paul makes a gift of his catering business to his son Oliver. The transfer is potentially exempt, and no tax is chargeable at this time.

Three years later Oliver enters into partnership with Roger, an unconnected person, and sells him a 25 per cent share of the catering business. Six months later Paul dies, and tax becomes chargeable in respect of Paul's gift to Oliver.

Provided Oliver's interest in the business at the time of Paul's death is 'relevant business property', the tax is calculated on the basis that 75 per cent of the value transferred by Paul's gift qualified for business relief.

Company reconstructions

Where a company undergoes a reorganisation or reconstruction of shares during the period between the date of the gift and the donor's death, business relief is not necessarily lost in calculating the tax (or extra tax) due on death. Where shares owned by the transferor immediately before his death would, under TCGA 1992, ss. 126–136, be identified with the shares gifted (or part of them), then they are treated as the 'original property' and relief remains available (IHTA 1984, s. 113A(6)(a)).

Incorporation of business

Where a business is incorporated between the date of the gift and the donor's death, the shares issued in consideration of the transfer of business property contained in the original gift are treated as the 'original property', and relief remains available (IHTA 1984, s. 113A(6)(b)).

Replacement of property

Where, during the period between the date of the gift and the death of the transferor, the original property comprised in the gift has been replaced by other property, business relief in respect of the tax (or extra tax) chargeable as a result of the death is not lost, provided the following six conditions are satisfied:

1. the whole of the consideration received by the donee for the property sold must have been applied in acquiring replacement property;

2. the replacement property must have been acquired, or a binding contract for its acquisition entered into, within three years (or such longer period as the Board may allow) after the disposal of the original property;

3. both the disposal and acquisition are made in arm's length transactions, or on terms such as might be expected to be included in an arm's length transaction;

4. the replacement property must be owned by the transferee immediately before the transferor's death;

5. throughout the period from the gift to the date of death (other than any period between the disposal and acquisition), either the original property or the replacement property must have been owned by the transferee, and

6. the replacement property must have qualified as 'relevant business property' immediately before death,

(IHTA 1984, s. 113B).

Example 9.37

In 1999 Kenneth makes a gift of his haulage business to his son Len.

In 2002 Len decides to move from haulage to manufacturing, and in September of that year sells the haulage business to an unconnected purchaser. In February 2003 Len purchases a manufacturing business, from an unconnected seller. In 2004 Kenneth dies, and the gift to Len in 1999 becomes chargeable to tax.

The six conditions above are fulfilled, and therefore in calculating the value transferred by Kenneth's lifetime gift, relief at 100 per cent is available.

The following points concerning the six conditions should be noted:

- Sales and purchases between connected persons are not ruled out absolutely, but in such cases it must be shown that the terms of the bargain are such as might be expected to be included in an arm's length sale or purchase.
- The property sold may be either all or only part of the original property. What matters is that the whole proceeds of sale, of however much is sold, are reinvested in the replacement property.
- There is nothing to preclude the acquisition of replacement property before the disposal of the original property. It would have to be shown, however, that the two transactions were linked, and that the proceeds of sale were 'applied' in the acquisition: this would seemingly cover repayment of a bridging loan.
- Although the legislation does not provide specifically for the situation where business property is replaced by agricultural property, the official view, confirmed in the Inland Revenue *Tax Bulletin*, December 1994, is that in such a case business property relief will be available on the donor's death within seven years, provided the replacement property would qualify for relief if agricultural property relief did not take precedence. Thus, if, in the above example, Len had sold the haulage business and purchased a farm, business relief would have been available in respect of the value transferred by Kenneth's gift, provided that the farm fell within one of the categories of 'relevant business property' in s. 105.

For the purposes of s. 113B, the date when a binding contract is entered into is taken to be the date of disposal (s. 113B(7)).

Death of transferee before transferor

Where the transferor dies within seven years predeceased by the transferee, relief is available provided the conditions have been fulfilled during the period up to the transferee's death (s. 113B(4)). It is not necessary that they continue to be fulfilled during the period between the two deaths.

Sale and repurchase in progress at time of death

Special provision is made for the case where, at the time of the transferor's death, the original property has been disposed of or is subject to a binding contract for sale, but no re-acquisition by the transferee has yet taken place. Provided the replacement property is acquired, or a binding contract for purchase is entered into, within three years (or such longer period as the Board may allow) after the date of disposal (albeit after the transferor's death), condition 4 above does not apply, and relief is available (s. 113B(5)). The other conditions have effect as if references to the transferor's death were references to the date of acquisition of the replacement property. Prior to 30 November 1993, the period specified was 12 months.

Share reconstructions, etc.

The provisions of s. 113A(6), described above, are applied to replacement property by s. 113B(6). Thus if, after a replacement, a business is incorporated or a share reorganisation takes place, relief is not lost.

9.4.14   Gifts subject to reservation of benefit

Special provision is necessary for agricultural or business property disposed of subject to a reservation of benefit. Although the charge to tax is on the donor, in most circumstances ownership will have passed to the donee after the gift. In the absence of any relieving provision, such property would fail to qualify for the appropriate relief.

Accordingly, it is provided that the questions of qualification for relief and the rate of relief are to be determined as if the transfer in question has been made by the donee, instead of the donor. The question whether a holding is a controlling holding or a substantial minority holding (so as to qualify for 100 per cent or 50 per cent relief as the case may be) is determined as if the shares were still owned by the donor and had been since the date of the gift. In other words the donor's and donee's holdings are aggregated to ascertain what rate of relief, if any, is available (FA 1986, Sch. 20 Para. 8). This is discussed in detail, in the context of agricultural property.

9.4.15   Interaction with other reliefs and exemptions

Agricultural property relief

It will often be the case that relevant business property will also be agricultural property qualifying for relief under IHTA 1984, s. 116. As might be expected, both reliefs cannot be claimed in respect of the same property. Agricultural property relief takes precedence over business property relief (IHTA 1984, s. 114(1)).

Business relief may be claimed, in appropriate cases, on the non-agricultural value of agricultural property. It will also generally be claimed in respect of movable assets, which do not fall within the definition of 'agricultural property' (eg stock, crop and implements).

Woodlands

The value of commercial woodlands may form part of the value of a business that is relevant business property.

Where tax on the value of woodlands transferred on death is deferred, the benefit of business relief is not lost. The interaction of the two reliefs is explained and illustrated under **9.7** below. It is worth noting here that woodlands relief only applies where the property in the deceased's estate is the woodlands themselves, and not where the deceased owned company shares, whose value is wholly or partly attributable to the value of trees.

Exemptions

Property qualifying for business relief may be the subject of an exempt or partly-exempt transfer. Since business relief consists of a reduction of the value transferred by a transfer of value, the percentage reduction is made before any available exemptions are taken into account, an order of treatment that favours the taxpayer.

Example 9.38

Alfred makes a gift to Bill of business property worth £300,000 and qualifying for relief at 50 per cent. Alfred dies a year later, and it becomes necessary to calculate tax on Alfred's gift.

	£
Value transferred	30,000
Less: relief at 50 per cent	(15,000)
Reduced value transferred	15,000
Less: annual exemption	(3,000)
Chargeable transfer	12,000

National heritage property

Business property may in appropriate cases qualify for conditional exemption under IHTA 1984, s. 30, where, for example, a building of outstanding historic interest is used for the transferor's business (whether or not that business has anything to do with the character of the building). The conditional exemption will, of course, override any business relief, since the property is removed from charge altogether.

If conditional exemption is subsequently lost on the occurrence of a chargeable event, there is no provision in the legislation for the amount chargeable to be reduced by business relief. This seems somewhat harsh, and should be borne in mind when a claim for conditional exemption is contemplated.

9.5 Agricultural property relief

9.5.1 Outline of the relief

Relief from IHT is given on the 'agricultural value' of 'agricultural property'. It only extends to land and buildings, and not to movable property (which must rely on business property relief: see **9.4**). It applies to transfers of value, to events upon which tax is charged as if a transfer of value had been made (eg death, or the coming to an end of an interest in possession), and to transfers by the trustees of a settlement in which no interest in possession subsists (IHTA 1984, s. 115(1)).

The relief consists of a percentage reduction in the value transferred. Where the transferor has the right to vacant possession, or the right to obtain it within 12 months, the percentage is 100 per cent. In other cases, the percentage is 50 per cent. A transitional provision extends the 100 per cent rate to certain property which, if disposed of before the 1981 amendment, would have attracted relief at 50 per cent and which would between 1981 and 1992 otherwise have attracted relief at only 30 per cent (IHTA 1984, s. 116).

A person may qualify for relief in two ways (IHTA 1984, s. 117):

- by occupying land himself for two years before the transfer for the purposes of agriculture, or
- by owning land for seven years before the transfer which is occupied for the purposes of agriculture by himself or someone else.

Thus, the relief is not restricted to 'working farmers', but is also available to landowners of tenanted land. In certain circumstances, a person may qualify through occupation or ownership by a spouse. The legislation also contains provisions applying the relief to partnerships and shares in farming companies.

For transfers of agricultural property within seven years before death (whether potentially exempt or not), although the transfer may qualify for relief at the time when it is made, relief is lost if the property transferred (or other qualifying property replacing it) is not owned by the transferee; and occupied by someone for agricultural purposes, throughout the intervening period (IHTA 1984, s. 124A).

9.5.2 Claiming the relief

Agricultural property relief is given automatically where it is due. One result of this is that where property qualifies both for agricultural property relief and for business property relief, it is the agricultural and not the business relief which is given (IHTA 1984, s. 114(1)).

In practice, the benefit of the relief is obtained by making an appropriate deduction in the account by which a transfer of value is notified to the Revenue. So far as transfers on death are concerned, this is done on page 10 of Cap Form 200 or, in Scotland, on page 10 of Cap form A-3. In respect of chargeable lifetime transfers, relief is taken into account on page 3 of Cap Form C5.

9.5.3 Meaning of 'agricultural property'

The relief applies to agricultural property situated in the UK, the Channel Islands or the Isle of Man (IHTA 1984, s. 115(5)).

'Agricultural property' means:

- agricultural land or pasture;
- woodland ancillary to agricultural land or pasture occupied with it;
- buildings used in connection with the intensive rearing of livestock or fish, provided such a building is ancillary to agricultural land or pasture occupied with it,
- cottages, farm buildings and farm-houses, together with land occupied with them, provided they are of a character appropriate to the property,

(s. 115(2)).

Woodlands which qualify for relief (eg shelter belts) are excluded from woodlands relief under s. 125.

Buildings cannot qualify for relief on their own but only if ancillary to, or occupied with, agricultural land or pasture which qualifies. Thus buildings used for the intensive rearing of livestock which are not attached to agricultural land do not qualify.

In *Starke & Anor v IR Commrs* [1994] BTC 8,029, the appellants sought to argue that the word 'land' in the expression 'agricultural land' used in s. 115(2) had the meaning given to it by the Interpretation Act 1978, Sch.1, so that it included buildings and other structures. Thus, it was contended, a 2½-acre site, consisting of a large dwelling house, many farm outbuildings, and a small area of enclosed land, owned by the deceased and occupied and used by him in conjunction with a farm owned by a farming company, fell within the scope of the expression. It was held, however, that the expression 'agricultural land' must refer to undeveloped land used for agricultural purposes such as cultivation of crops, since the meaning contended for by the appellants would render much of the remainder of s. 115(2) and (4) otiose. The finding of the High Court was upheld by the Court of Appeal – see [1995] BTC 8,028; (1995) 1 CTC 619.

Despite the decision in *Starke* above, it is thought that in certain circumstances, a building could itself be argued to be 'agricultural land', where it is devoted to a crop that must be grown indoors. The most obvious example is a glasshouse used for growing tomatoes and other fruits. There seems no reason why such buildings should have to be occupied along with other agricultural land in order to qualify for relief. It is understood that buildings used for intensive mushroom cultivation will also qualify.

'Agriculture' includes fruit growing. However, the fact that fruit is grown on a property does not of itself permit the property to qualify for agricultural property relief if its true nature as a matter of fact is residential. In *Dixon v IR Commrs* (2001) Sp C 297, it was unsuccessfully argued that a cottage and orchard planted with damson trees, from which surplus fruit was sold, and on which neighbours' animals were sometimes grazed, was agricultural property. The Special Commissioner held that as a matter of fact and degree the land was not agricultural land or pasture, and the cottage was not a farmhouse.

In *Higginson v IR Commrs* (2002) Sp C 337, the Special Commissioner concluded that a house set in a landed estate of 134 acres, including 63 acres of agricultural land, was not a farmhouse 'of a character appropriate to the property' within IHTA 1984, s. 115(2).

While the land and the house formed a unit, the house being integral to it, for the purposes of IHTA 1984, s. 115(2), the unit had to be an agricultural unit, and within the unit the land had to predominate. The farmhouse had to be ancillary to the land (*Starke v IR Commrs* [1994] BTC 8,029).

On the evidence, within this particular unit, it was the house that predominated. It was, therefore, a house with farmland and not vice versa.

The decision in *Higginson v IR Commrs* (2002) Sp C 337 can be contrasted with that in *Lloyds TSB (personal representative of Antrobus dec'd) v IR Commrs* (2002) Sp C 336, where the Special Commissioner held that a house surrounded by 126 acres of freehold land and 6.54 acres of tenanted land, all of which was agricultural land or pasture, was 'of a character appropriate to the property' within IHTA 1984, s. 115(2).

The Special Commissioner said that the principles that had to be considered when deciding whether a farmhouse was 'of a character appropriate to the property' were:

- whether the house was appropriate by reference to its size, content and layout, with the farm buildings and the particular area of farmland being farmed;

- whether the house was proportionate in size and nature to the requirements of the farming activities conducted on the agricultural land or pasture in question;
- although it might not be possible to describe a farmhouse which satisfied the 'character appropriate' test, the principle was that you would know one when you saw it;
- whether the educated rural layman would regard the property as a house with land or a farm, and
- how long the house in question had been associated with the agricultural property and whether there was a history of agricultural production (*Korner v IR Commrs* (1969) 45 TC 287; *Starke v IR Commrs* [1994] BTC 8,029; and *Dixon v IR Commrs* (2002) Sp C 297 considered).

The Special Commissioner said that applying those principles to this case, there had been a house on the site since 1242 and the present house had been a working asset, and integral to the farm, for at least 100 years. On the evidence, the farmhouse and the land occupied with it was of a character appropriate to the property within IHTA 1984, s. 115(2).

The reference in s. 115(2) to the intensive rearing of fish does not extend to the stocking of ponds or rivers for sporting purposes. Sporting rights, including fishing rights, are not agricultural property; in *Earl of Normanton v Giles* [1980] 1 WLR 28 it was held that breeding pheasants for shooting was not agriculture.

Where a farmhouse fails to meet the requirement of appropriate character, it would appear to be excluded altogether from relief. There is no provision for giving relief to the extent that a farmhouse of appropriate character would have qualified.

In *Rosser v IR Commrs* (2003) Sp C 368 a Special Commissioner concluded that a house did not attract relief as agricultural property, as it was not a farmhouse within IHTA 1984, s. 115(2). However, a barn was eligible for relief, as it was 'of a character appropriate' to the two acres of agricultural land on which both the buildings were situated.

In this case, the deceased and her husband had farmed the 41 acres for 30 years until 39 acres were gifted to their daughter. The deceased and her husband continued to live in the house on the farm. The remaining two acres were subsequently gifted to the daughter.

The Special Commissioner, following the decision in *Starke v IR Commrs* [1995] BTC 8,028, said that the Interpretation Act 1978, Sch. 1 required the word 'land' to be read as including 'buildings or other structures' unless the contrary intention appeared. Such a contrary contention could be read into

s. 115(2) sufficient to exclude from the word 'land ' the words 'buildings or other structures'. Accordingly, in this case the house and barn were not agricultural land within s. 115(2).

Considering the question as to whether the house or barn were of a character appropriate to the property, the Special Commissioner concluded that if the person making the deemed disposition at death legally owned the farm buildings and had a legal interest such as a right of profit in the property to which the character of the farm buildings was appropriate, then the farm buildings and property would be part of the estate. Thus in the present case the property in s. 115(2) was the two acres of agricultural land upon which the house and the barn were built.

Moreover, the house had changed from a farmhouse to a retirement home for the deceased and her husband. It was therefore not necessary to decide whether the house was of a character appropriate to the two acres of agricultural land.

With regard to the barn, after weighing up all the facts and their application to the principles enunciated in Lloyds TSB (*personal representative of Antrobus dec'd) v IR Commrs* (2002) Sp C 336, the Special Commissioner concluded that the barn was of a character appropriate to the agricultural land comprised in the two acres.

Stud farms

The breeding and rearing of horses on a stud farm, and the grazing of horses in connection with those activities, are to be taken as agriculture. Accordingly, land used for such activities qualifies for relief. Buildings used in connection with those activities qualify as farm buildings (s. 115(4)).

A meadow let for grazing horses was held by a Special Commissioner not to qualify for relief as agricultural property in *Wheatley's Executors v IR Commrs* (1998) Sp C 149. Although it was common ground that the field was 'pasture', it was not occupied for the purposes of agriculture, and the Special Commissioner held that in order for the field to qualify the horses would have had to have some connection with agriculture.

Short rotation coppice

The cultivation of short rotation coppice is, with effect from 6 April 1995, regarded as agriculture. Accordingly, land on which short rotation coppice is cultivated is regarded as agricultural land, and buildings used in connection with the cultivation of short rotation coppice are regarded as farm buildings (FA 1995, s. 154(2)). 'Short rotation coppice' is defined as a perennial crop of tree species planted at high density, the stems of which are harvested above ground levels at intervals of less than ten years (FA 1995, s. 154(3)). The cuttings, normally of willow or poplar, are used as fuel for biomass-fed power stations.

Agricultural land 'set aside'

In certain circumstances compensation payments may be obtained where agricultural land is 'set aside', ie where land is left lying fallow to reduce over-production of a particular crop. It is understood that in the official view 'set-aside' does not disqualify the land from being agricultural property for the purposes of the relief, provided the intention is not to set aside the land permanently from agriculture, following the set-aside with some non-agricultural use such as development.

Land in habitat schemes

Land in a 'habitat scheme' is regarded for the purposes of the relief as agricultural land (IHTA 1984, s. 124C(1)). Management of the land in accordance with the requirements of the scheme is regarded as agriculture, and buildings used in connection with such management are regarded as farm buildings. Land is in a habitat scheme for these purposes if (s. 124C(2), (3)):

- an application for aid under any of the following regulations has been accepted in respect of the land:

  the Habitat (Water Fringe) Regulations 1994, reg. 3(1);
  the Habitat (Former Set-Aside Land) Regulations 1994;

- the Habitat (Salt-Marsh) Regulations 1994;
- the Habitats (Scotland) Regulations 1994, if an undertaking has been given under reg. 3(2)(a);
- the Habitats Improvement Regulations Northern Ireland) 1995, if an undertaking has been given under reg. 3(1)(a), and
- the undertakings to which the acceptance relates have been neither terminated by the expiry of the period to which they relate, nor treated as terminated.

Milk and other quotas

In *Faulks v Faulks* [1992] 15 EG 82 (a non-tax case) it was held that a milk quota was not a separate asset from the land to which it attached. This contrasts with the Revenue view, reflected in the specific inclusion of milk quotas among assets qualifying for CGT roll-over relief. In the inheritance tax context, the value of a milk quota will usually be reflected in the value of agricultural land which is the subject of a lifetime gift or transfer on death. Agricultural property relief will be available on the enhanced value, including the element attributable to the milk quota. Where, unusually, a milk quota has to be valued separately, the official view is that agricultural property relief is available (Inland Revenue Tax Bulletin, February 1993).

The position is otherwise as regards other quotas, such as cow and sheep quotas. These quotas attach to the producer, rather than the land, and it is understood that the official view is that they attract business and not agricultural property relief.

9.5.4 Meaning of 'agricultural value'

Under IHTA 1984, s. 115(3), the agricultural value of any agricultural property is the value which it would have if it were subject to a perpetual covenant prohibiting its use otherwise than as agricultural property. The intention is to exclude any element of development value which the land may have.

Example 9.39

Ashley is a farmer who owns a field worth £5,000 at current use value, in respect of which planning permission for development has been obtained. As a result, its open market value is £80,000. If Ashley makes a transfer of value of the field, agricultural property relief is available only at the appropriate percentage of £5,000, leaving the balance of the open market value chargeable.

The agricultural value includes the value of growing crops, provided that they have not been severed. The same applies to trees and underwood, and to cultivations and unexhausted manures.

9.5.5 Agricultural tenancies

The fact that agricultural property is subject to a tenancy does not disqualify it from relief, although it is likely that relief will only be available at the lower rate of 50 per cent, at least in so far as the landlord's interest is concerned.

It is now established that a tenant's interest in agricultural property has a value and is capable of being the subject of a transfer of value. One might think that such an interest was not 'agricultural property' so as to qualify it for relief under s. 115(2), although it could qualify for business property relief. Potatoes are grown in the ground, not in a tenancy. However, it is understood that the official view is that the appropriate relief for the interest of a tenant is agricultural property relief. This will be at the higher, 100 per cent rate.

9.5.6 Property subject to a contract for sale

Relief is not available in respect of agricultural property if, at the time of the transfer, the transferor has entered into a binding contract for its sale. Since agricultural property is invariably realty (in Scotland, heritable property), this means that relief ceases to be available at the moment when (in England) contracts for sale are exchanged, or (in Scotland) missives of sale are concluded (IHTA 1984, s. 124).

There are two exceptions to s. 124, in which the relief is not lost:

- where the sale is to a company, and is made wholly or mainly in consideration of shares in or securities of the company which will give the transferor control of the company, ie where the farmer incorporates his farming business,
- where the sale is of shares in a farming company to which relief is applied by s. 122, and is made for the purpose of reconstruction or amalgamation.

9.5.7 Persons qualifying for relief

Qualification by occupation for two years

The first route to qualifying for relief is where the transferor has occupied the property for the purposes of agriculture throughout the period of two years ending with the date of the transfer (IHTA 1984, s. 117(a)). 'Occupation' is not defined in the legislation, but is a question of fact. It is taken to mean the legal right to physical possession of the property. If a person owns land that he farms for his profit, he is treated as occupying the property whether or not he actually resides there. Occupation is not disturbed by the letting of grazing rights for less than a year (which do not constitute an agricultural holding).

Where, however, relief is claimed in respect of a farmhouse, it is necessary to show that it was physically occupied by the transferor. This is illustrated by the Special Commissioner's decision in *Harrold's Executors v IR Commrs* (1996) Sp C 71, where a father and son bought a farm which included a large farmhouse in need of substantial renovation. At the time when the father made a lifetime gift of his share to his son, work was still in progress and continued for a further two years before the son moved in. When the father died four years after making the gift, it was held by the Special Commissioner that the farmhouse had not been occupied by the transferor and, accordingly, that relief was not available in respect of its value.

Farm workers' cottages

In certain circumstances, farm cottages inhabited by currently employed or retired farm workers will be treated by the Revenue as occupied by the owner of the land. A tied cottage inhabited by a person who is actually employed in agriculture on the land in question will clearly satisfy the condition. Beyond that situation, the Revenue practice is set out in Extra-statutory Concession

F16, which states that the occupation requirement will be regarded as satisfied with respect to a cottage if either:

- the occupier is a statutorily protected tenant, or
- the occupation is under a lease granted to the farm employee for his life and that of any surviving spouse as part of the employee's contract of employment by the landlord for agricultural purposes.

The benefit of the published concession does not extend to cottages occupied by retired farm workers who continue to live in their cottages with the owner's informal permission, but without any statutory or contractual right to do so. So far as is known, however, the Revenue does not normally refuse relief in respect of the value of such cottages.

Example 9.40

Derek is the owner of a farm which is farmed by Farmstead Ltd, a company in which Derek owns a 75 per cent shareholding. Derek dies, leaving the farm to his daughter Emily.

Derek is treated as occupying the farm.

Replacements of property

Relief is not necessarily lost if, during the two-year period, the transferor has sold qualifying property and replaced it with the property which he now transfers. The occupation condition is satisfied if the transferred property, the original qualifying property, and any agricultural property directly or indirectly replaced by that qualifying property, were occupied by the transferor for the purposes of agriculture for a total of at least two out of five years ending with the date of the transfer (IHTA 1984, s. 118(1)).

Example 9.41

In 1984, Gilbert sells agricultural property he has owned for some years. In 1986, he reinvests the proceeds of sale in new agricultural property, which he transfers to Harry in 1987.

The occupation requirement is treated as satisfied.

Relief is, however, limited to what would have been obtained had the replacement (or replacements, if more than one) not taken place (s. 118(3)). In practical terms, this will require a valuation of the replaced farm to be obtained, even though the taxpayer no longer owns it. If it is worth less than the value of the new farm, relief is given at the appropriate percentage on the value of the old farm.

> **Example 9.42**
>
> Henry, who has farmed Blackacre for some years, sells it for £400,000, and shortly thereafter buys Whiteacre for £800,000. Less than two years later, Henry gives Whiteacre to his son Jeremy, at a time when it is worth £1,000,000. On the date of the transfer, Blackacre is valued at £450,000. Henry dies one year later and the conditions for relief are still fulfilled.
>
> Relief is given at the appropriate percentage of whichever has the lower value, ie on £450,000 only.

Any change resulting from the formation, alteration or dissolution of a partnership is disregarded for the purposes of the restriction on relief (s. 118(4)). In other words, such a change is not treated as a 'replacement' bringing s. 118(3) into effect.

Qualification by ownership for seven years

The second route to qualifying for relief is where the transferor has owned the property throughout the period of seven years ending with the date of the transfer, and during that period the property was occupied (by him or by someone else) for the purposes of agriculture (IHTA 1984, s. 117(b)). This route to qualification opens up the relief to landowners who do not themselves farm the land. It also serves as a safety net for working farmers who, for some reason, fail to fulfil the two-year occupation route to qualifying for relief.

'Ownership' is not defined in the legislation. In particular, no indication is given as to whether legal or beneficial ownership is envisaged. This becomes significant when the application of the provisions to partnership, company or settled property is considered. The ordinary meaning of 'ownership' might be regarded as including both legal and beneficial ownership, so that one or the other is in itself insufficient.

However, it is understood that the Revenue takes a broader view, and regards either interest as ownership for the purposes of s. 117(b). The basis of this is a Treasury statement made in connection with the use of the word 'ownership' in the business property relief provisions of what is now IHTA 1984, s. 103–114 (Official Report, Standing Committee E, 24 June 1976, col. 1275–76).

'Occupation' has the same meaning as for s. 117(a), discussed above. The provisions of s. 119(1) and (2) regarding occupation by a partnership or a company controlled by the transferor apply equally to s. 117(b).

> ### Example 9.43
>
> Paul, a farmer who owns his farm, decides to retire, and transfers his business to his sons John and Matthew. Paul retains the ownership of the farm. Five years later, Paul dies. Provided the property was occupied for agricultural purposes, by Paul before the transfer and by his sons after the transfer, relief is available at the appropriate rate.

Replacements of property

Relief is not necessarily lost if, during the seven-year period, the transferor has sold qualifying property and replaced it with other property which he now transfers. The occupation condition is satisfied if the transferred property, the original qualifying property, and any agricultural property directly or indirectly replaced by that original qualifying property, were owned by the transferor and occupied for the purposes of agriculture for a total of at least seven out of the ten years ending with the date of the transfer (IHTA 1984, s. 118(2)).

> ### Example 9.44
>
> In 1995, Christopher sells agricultural property he has owned and farmed for some years. In 1996 he invests the proceeds of sale in a tenanted farm, which he resells in 1999. In 2000 he purchases another tenanted farm that he gives to his son Donald in 2003.
>
> The requirements of s. 117(b) are treated as satisfied.

Relief is limited to what would have been obtained had the replacement (or replacements if more than one) not taken place (s. 118(3)). This provision operates in the same way as the corresponding provision for two-year occupation explained above.

Where agricultural property is sold and replaced by non-agricultural business property, the replacement property will clearly not qualify for agricultural property relief. However, for the purposes of the qualifying periods for business property relief, the official view is that the period of ownership of the agricultural property may be taken into account. Similarly, where non-agricultural business property is sold and replaced by agricultural property, if on a subsequent transfer of the replacement property agricultural relief is not available (because the minimum period has not elapsed), business relief may be available: Inland Revenue *Tax Bulletin*, December 1994.

Occupation by a partnership

Occupation by a partnership (including a Scottish partnership, treated by the Partnership Act 1890, s. 4(2) as a separate legal person) is treated as occupation by the partners (IHTA 1984, s. 119(2)).

Occupation by a company

Occupation by a company controlled by the transferor is treated as occupation by the transferor (IHTA 1984, s. 119(1)).

Transfers on death

There are three relaxations of the occupation or ownership requirements, in respect of transfers on death.

First, where a person becomes entitled to property on the death of another person, he is treated as owning it (and, if he subsequently occupies it, as occupying it) from the date of the death (IHTA 1984, s. 120(1)(a)). This ensures that the period during which the deceased's estate is being administered counts, where appropriate, towards the qualifying period.

Secondly, where a person inherits property on the death of his spouse, he is treated as having occupied it for the purposes of agriculture for any period for which the spouse so occupied it, and as having owned it for any period for which the spouse owned it (s. 120(1)(b)).

Thirdly, s. 121 provides for cases where two transfers are separated by a period less than the qualifying period of two or seven years, and one of the transfers is on death. In such cases, the minimum period does not apply. More precisely, the two-year or seven-year period requirement does not apply if:

- the first transfer qualified for relief (or would have qualified if relief according to s. 116 had existed at that time) (s. 121(1)(a));
- the subjects transferred thereby became the property of the transferor of the second transfer, or of his spouse (s. 121(1)(b));
- at the time of the second transfer, the subjects are occupied for the purposes of agriculture by the second transferor or by the personal representatives of the first transferor (s. 121(1)(b));
- the subjects (or any property replacing them) would, apart from the minimum period requirement, have qualified for relief on the second transfer (s. 121(1)(c)),
- one or other transfer was made on the death of the respective transferor (or both were) (s. 121(1)(d)).

Example 9.45

Alexander dies and leaves a farm to his son Boris, which qualifies for relief. Less than two years later, Boris gives the property to Carl, having in the meantime occupied the farm for agricultural purposes.

In spite of the fact that Boris has not occupied the farm for two years, relief is available.

Example 9.46

Dennis makes a chargeable gift (qualifying for relief) of a one-half share of a farm to his daughter Elizabeth. Dennis continues to carry on the farming business alone. Five years later, Elizabeth dies, leaving her share of the farm to Fiona. Relief is not available because Elizabeth has not occupied the farm for the purposes of agriculture.

There is partial relief where:

- only part of the value transferred by the first transfer qualified for relief (as will normally be the case where the first transfer is on death);
- only part of the subjects qualifying on the first transfer become the property of the second transferor, and
- the value transferred by the first transfer represents only part of the value of the subjects, for example where the first transfer was not a gift but a sale at an undervalue.

Relief on the second transfer is restricted to the same proportion of the value thereby transferred (s. 121(3)).

Example 9.47

Graham sells a farm worth £400,000 to his son Hector for £100,000. This transfer qualifies for relief. Less than two years later, Hector dies, leaving the farm to Johan, at a time when it is worth £500,000.

Relief is available only on £500,000 × 300,000/400,000 = £375,000, at the appropriate rate.

Replacements of property

Because of s. 121(1)(c) above, relief is available under s. 121 even if the subjects of the first transfer have been sold and replaced before the second transfer. Section 121(2) provides that in such cases the relief is not to exceed what it would have been had the replacement (or replacements it more than one) not taken place. This provision is equivalent to s. 118(3) explained above. Section 118(4) also applies.

9.5.8 Amount of the relief

The 100 per cent rate
Relief is available at 100 per cent in four sets of circumstances.

1 Right to vacant possession
Where the interest of the transferor in the property immediately before the transfer carries the right to vacant possession, or the right to obtain it within the next 12 months, relief is at 100 per cent (s. 116(2)(a) IHTA 1984).

The question whether or not the transferor's interest carries vacant possession is a matter of general law. The minimum period of notice required to terminate a lease of an agricultural holding is one year (Agricultural Holdings Act 1986, s. 25; Agricultural Holdings (Scotland) Act 1991, s. 21(3)). Accordingly, land subject to an agricultural tenancy would not, in the absence of the concession discussed below, qualify for 100 per cent relief unless a valid notice to quit has already been served. In Scotland, the same applies to leases for one year that are continued by tacit relocation.

Where the transfer is on death, it may be that the death of the transferor results in the termination of a tenancy. For example, where land is let by A to a partnership of A and B, the death of A will terminate the partnership and hence the lease. Since changes in value of a person's estate by reason of death are deemed to occur before it (IHTA 1984, s. 171), the land will be valued with vacant possession, and 100 per cent relief will be available.

Extra-statutory Concession F17, first published on 13 February 1995, states that 100 per cent relief will be given where the transferor's interest in the property carries the right to vacant possession within 24 months of the date of the transfer. The period is thus extended from one to two years. It appears that the reason for the concession is to recognise the difficulty mentioned above with regard to the 12-month notice period, and to make 100 per cent relief available in cases where, at the date of the transfer, notice to quit has not yet been served. The concession also makes relief available in the first year of a tenancy for a period of more than one but less than two years (sometimes referred to in England and Wales as a *Gladstone v Bower* arrangement).

The statutory 12-month cut-off is thus overridden by the extension of the period by concession to 24 months.

The interest of one of two or more joint tenants or tenants in common (in Scotland, joint or common owners) is taken to carry a right to vacant possession if the interests of all of them together carry such a right (s. 116(6)).

2 Certain land let prior to 10 March 1981

Relief at 100 per cent is available if the following three conditions are fulfilled (IHTA 1984, s. 116(2),(3)):

- the transferor has been beneficially entitled to the interest transferred since before 10 March 1981;
- if the transferor had disposed of the interest by a transfer of value immediately before 10 March 1981, and made a claim under FA 1975, Sch. 8, Para. 1, relief at 50 per cent under the old provisions would have been given,
- the transferor's interest did not at any time since 10 March 1981 carry a right to obtain vacant possession, and did not fail to carry such a right by reason of any act or deliberate omission of the transferor during that period.

Under the pre-1981 provisions, relief was restricted to transfers of property not exceeding a total of £250,000 in value or 1,000 acres, whichever was the greater. This restriction is carried into the transitional relief, so that the 100 per cent rate applies only to the extent that the property would have attracted relief under the old system. Any excess receives only 50 per cent relief (IHTA 1984, s. 116(4)).

In determining whether or not a transferor's cumulative total exceeds the limit, the reference to previous chargeable transfers in the old legislation is treated as including chargeable transfers made since 10 March 1981 (s. 116(5)).

The transitional relief also applies where, since 1981, the property has been transferred on death by one spouse to the other. For the purposes of satisfying the first condition above, the transferor may count the period during which the deceased spouse was beneficially entitled to the property, provided that the other two conditions were both satisfied by the deceased spouse before his death (s. 120(2)).

3 Property subject to tenancy beginning on or after 1 September 1995

Relief at 100 per cent is available in respect of property subject to a tenancy, provided the property is let on a tenancy beginning on or after 1 September 1995 (IHTA 1984, s. 116(2)(c)). The purpose of increasing the rate of relief on tenanted land to 100 per cent was to boost the government's reforms of the law in England and Wales on agricultural tenancies, contained in the Agricultural Tenancies Act 1995. The increased rate is not however restricted to tenancies falling within that Act (Revenue Interpretation, Inland Revenue *Tax Bulletin*, Issue 18, August 1995, page 241).

Statutory succession on death: England and Wales

Where, on the death of a tenant, a tenancy of the property is obtained by a person by virtue of a statutory entitlement, or is obtained by a person who would at some later date have become entitled to it by statute, or is granted to a person who is, in terms of statute in question, the only eligible or only remaining applicant, that tenancy is treated as a tenancy beginning on the date of death (s. 116(5B)). The landlord's interest accordingly begins to qualify for 100 per cent relief from the date of death.

Statutory succession on death: Scotland

Scottish law differs from English law in the respect that where, in Scotland, a tenant with security of tenure dies, his statutory successor is treated as holding the property under the same tenancy as his deceased predecessor. In order to ensure that 100 per cent relief is available to the landlord from the date of the predecessor's death, s. 116(5A) provides that where on the tenant's death the tenancy becomes vested in a person, in terms of the deceased's will or on intestacy, or where otherwise the tenancy becomes binding on the landlord and the successor (eg because the landlord objected to the proposed successor and the transfer had to be confirmed by the Land Court), the successor's tenancy is treated as a tenancy beginning on the date of death.

Death following notice of intention to retire

In certain circumstances a tenant may, on retirement, give notice to the landlord that a particular person shall thereafter become tenant of the property. The tenancy in favour of the successor may then become binding on the landlord. Sections 116(5D) and (5E) deal with the situation where, after having given such notice, the tenant dies, and the 'retirement' in favour of the new tenant takes place after his death but within 30 months of the giving of the notice. In these circumstances, the new tenant is treated as having been granted or assigned a tenancy that began immediately before the transfer of value deemed to occur immediately before the original tenant's death. The effect is to ensure that the landlord's interest qualifies for 100 per cent relief from the date of the old tenant's death.

4 Tenanted land with a vacant possession value

The above three categories exhaust the statutory alternatives for obtaining 100 per cent relief. There is, however, a fourth category of land in respect of which 100 per cent relief is given by extra-statutory concession. The concession in question (ESC F17) states that 100 per cent relief will be available where the transferor's interest in the property is, notwithstanding the terms of a tenancy, valued at an amount broadly equivalent to the vacant possession value of the property.

The 50 per cent rate

Relief is available at 50 per cent in all circumstances except the four specified above.

It is understood to be the official view that a farm worker's cottage which is occupied by the employee as the 'representative occupier', and accordingly under an assured agricultural occupancy in terms of the Rent (Agriculture) Act 1976, s. 2 and Sch. 1, qualifies for relief at the lower 50 per cent rate.

9.5.9 Transfers within seven years before death

Additional conditions to be fulfilled

Where a lifetime transfer of agricultural property is followed within less than seven years by the death of the transferor, tax (or additional tax) may become chargeable. In calculating the amount of such tax (or additional tax) agricultural relief will only be available if the following conditions are fulfilled (IHTA 1984, s. 124A):

- The 'original property' must have been owned by the transferee throughout the period between the date of the transfer and the death of the transferor. The property must not, at the time of death, be subject to a binding contract of sale. (This is subject to the relaxation in s. 124B permitting replacements of property, see below.)
- Unless the 'original property' was shares or securities, it must have been agricultural property immediately before the transferor's death, and must have been occupied (by someone) for the purposes of agriculture throughout the intervening period.
- Where the 'original property' was shares or securities, the agricultural property which qualified them for relief must have been owned by the company and occupied (by someone) for the purposes of agriculture throughout the intervening period.

In summary, therefore, the general conditions for agricultural relief must continue to be satisfied throughout the period from the date of transfer until the date of death.

Example 9.48

Angus, who has been a farmer for many years, makes a lifetime gift of the farm to his son Bob. The transfer is potentially exempt and no tax is payable at this time.

Four years later, Bob decides to stop farming and emigrate to Australia. Bob sells the farm. Six months later, Angus dies. Tax becomes chargeable on Angus's gift within seven years before death. Agricultural property relief is not available in respect of this transfer because the farm was not owned by Bob throughout the period between the gift and Angus's death.

Liability for tax on the transfer falls primarily on Bob. If in this example it proves impossible to recover tax from Bob because he is in Australia, the Revenue may recover it from Angus's personal representatives instead. It is clearly important for Angus's adviser to draw to everyone's attention the potential tax consequences of Bob's sale of the farm.

Example 9.49

Colin, who has been a farmer for many years, transfers his farm to trustees to hold it on discretionary trusts for the benefit of his children and various other persons. The trust is not an accumulation and maintenance settlement.

The transfer is not potentially exempt, but all the conditions for relief at 100 per cent are fulfilled.

Shortly after the transfer, the trustees let the farm to Donald, an unconnected tenant. Three years later Colin dies. Extra tax becomes chargeable on Colin's transfer into trust. In calculating the extra tax, agricultural relief is available because the conditions in s. 124A(3) are fulfilled. Relief will still be at the rate of 100 per cent despite the fact that at the time of Colin's death the trustees do not have vacant possession of the farm.

'Original property' means the property which was transferred by the lifetime gift, whether agricultural property or shares deriving their value from agricultural property (s. 124A(8)).

'Transferee' means the person who received the property on the lifetime transfer. Where it becomes or remains settled property in which no interest in possession subsists, 'transferee' means the trustees of the settlement.

In determining for these purposes whether or not there was a potentially exempt transfer which has proved to be chargeable, the percentage reduction in value transferred given on the original transfer must be ignored (s. 124A(7A)). This provision prevents an argument that the charge under s. 124A can never apply, because there has been no potentially exempt transfer (PET) capable of becoming chargeable.

Death of transferee before transferor

Special provision is made for the case where a transferor dies within seven years after making a gift of agricultural property, but in the meantime the transferee has also died. In these circumstances the lifetime gift will attract relief if the conditions in s. 124A(3) have been satisfied during the period ending with the transferee's death, rather than the transferor's (s. 124A(4)).

Example 9.50

Edgar makes a lifetime gift of his farm to Frank. The transfer is potentially exempt. Three years later, Frank dies, and a further two years later, Edgar dies.

On Edgar's death, the gift to Frank becomes chargeable. Agricultural relief will be available provided the conditions in s. 124A(3) were satisfied up to the time of Frank's death. It makes no difference whether they ceased to be satisfied during the period between the two deaths.

Part only of property qualifying

Where, at the time of the transferor's death within seven years, the conditions for relief continue to be fulfilled in respect only of part of the original property, then relief is given in respect of such a proportionate part in calculating the tax (or extra tax) chargeable (IHTA 1984, s. 124A(5)).

> ### *Example 9.51*
>
> Gregory, who has for many years owned 90 per cent of the shares in Farrow Ltd, a farming company, transfers all his shares to the trustees of a discretionary trust. The transfer is not potentially exempt, and tax is chargeable (at half rates) at the time when it is made. Assume that all the conditions for relief at 100 per cent are fulfilled, and that the whole value of the shares can be attributed to the agricultural value of agricultural property.
>
> Four years later, the trustees sell half of the shares, leaving them with a 45 per cent holding. Two years after the sale, Gregory dies, and extra tax becomes chargeable on the gift into trust.
>
> Provided the 'occupation' requirement in s. 124A(3) has been fulfilled throughout the intervening period, the extra tax is calculated on the basis that half the value transferred by Gregory's gift qualified for agricultural relief.
>
> It appears that this proportion is not affected by the fact that the value of the trustees' holding at the time of Gregory's death is less than half the value of the holding transferred to them, because control has been lost.

Company reconstructions

Where a company undergoes a reorganisation or reconstruction during the period between the date of the gift and the donor's death, agricultural relief is not necessarily lost in calculating the tax (or extra tax) due on death. Where shares owned by the transferor immediately before his death would, under any of TCGA 1992, ss. 126–136, be identified with the shares gifted (or part of them), then the donee's period of ownership of the original shares is treated as including his period of ownership of the new shares, and relief remains available (IHTA 1984, s. 124A(6)(a)).

Incorporation of business

Where a farming business is incorporated between the date of the gift and the donor's death, the donee's period of ownership of the shares issued in consideration of the transfer of agricultural property is treated as included in his period of ownership of the property contained in the original gift, and relief remains available (IHTA 1984, s. 124A(6)(b)).

Example 9.52

Harold makes a lifetime gift of his farm to his son John. The whole value transferred is attributable to agricultural property. Harold dies four years later.

In the meantime, John has incorporated the farming business. Relief is available to John in respect of the tax payable on the gift by Harold within seven years before death.

Replacement of property

Where, during the period between the date of the gift and the death of the transferor, the original property comprised in the gift has been replaced by other property, agricultural relief in respect of the tax (or extra tax) chargeable as a result of the death is not lost, provided the conditions in IHTA 1984, s. 124B are fulfilled.

There are seven conditions, as follows:

1. The whole of the consideration received by the donee for the property sold must have been applied in acquiring replacement property.

2. The replacement property must have been acquired, or a binding contract for its acquisition entered into, within three years (or such longer period as the Board may allow) after the disposal of the original property.

3. Both the disposal and acquisition are made in arm's length transactions, or on terms such as might be expected to be included in an arm's length transaction.

4. The replacement property must be owned by the transferee immediately before the transferor's death, and not then be subject to a binding contract for sale.

5. Throughout the period from the gift to the disposal, the original property must have been owned by the transferee and occupied (by someone) for the purposes of agriculture.

6. Throughout the period from the acquisition to the death, the replacement property must have been similarly owned and occupied.

7. The replacement property must have qualified as 'agricultural property' immediately before death.

> ### Example 9.53
>
> In 1997 Keith makes a gift of his dairy farm, Blackacre, to his son Louis. The whole value transferred is attributable to the agricultural value of agricultural property.
>
> In 2000 Louis decides to move from dairy to arable farming, and in September of that year sells Blackacre to an unconnected purchaser. In February 2001 Louis purchases Whiteacre, from an unconnected seller, and begins to farm it immediately. In 2002 Keith dies, and the gift to Louis in 1997 becomes chargeable to tax.
>
> The seven conditions above are fulfilled, and therefore in calculating the value transferred by Keith's lifetime gift, relief at 100 per cent is available.

The following points concerning the seven conditions should be noted:

- Sales and purchases between connected persons are not ruled out absolutely, but in such cases it must be shown that the terms of the bargain are such as might be expected to be included in an arm's length sale or purchase.
- The property sold may be either all or only part of the original property. What matters is that the whole proceeds of sale, of however much is sold, are reinvested in the replacement property.
- There is nothing to preclude the acquisition of replacement property before the disposal of the original property. It would have to be shown, however, that the two transactions were linked, and that the proceeds of sale were 'applied' in the acquisition: this would seemingly cover repayment of a bridging loan. Also, the requirements of ownership and occupation would have to be fulfilled in respect of both properties during any overlap period.
- Although the legislation does not provide specifically for the situation where agricultural property is replaced by business property the official view is that in such a case business property relief will be available on the donor's death within seven years, if the original property would have qualified for business property relief, had agricultural property relief not taken precedence. Thus, if in the above example Louis had sold the farm and acquired an agricultural machinery business, business property would have been available in respect of the value transferred by Keith's gift, provided the conditions for business property relief were met by that transfer.

The date when a binding contract is entered into is taken to be the date of disposal (s. 124B(7)). This coincides with the date of disposal for capital gains tax purposes (TCGA 1992, s. 28).

Death of transferee before transferor

Where the transferor dies within seven years predeceased by the transferee, relief is available provided the conditions have been fulfilled during the period up to the transferee's death (s. 124B(4)). It is not necessary that they continue to be fulfilled during the period between the two deaths.

Sale and repurchase in progress at time of death

Special provision is made for the case where, at the time of the transferor's death, the original property has been disposed of or is subject to a binding contract for sale, but no re-acquisition by the transferee has yet taken place. Provided the replacement property is acquired, or a binding contract for purchase is entered into, within three years (or such longer period as the Board may allow) after the date of disposal (albeit after the transferor's death), conditions (4) and (6) above do not apply, and relief is available (s. 124B(5)). The other conditions have effect as if references to the transferor's death were references to the date of acquisition of the replacement property

Reconstructions, etc.

The provisions of s. 124A(6) (see above) are applied to replacement property by s. 124B(6). Thus if, after a replacement, a farming business is incorporated or a share reorganisation takes place, relief is not lost.

9.6 Woodlands

9.6.1 Introduction

Where a person's estate at death includes non-agricultural woodlands, an election may be made to have the value of the trees or underwood (but not the land itself) left out of account in calculating IHT on the estate (IHTA 1984, s. 125). In effect, the relief operates as a deferment of tax until a subsequent disposal of the trees. If no disposal occurs before the next transfer on death, the relief becomes absolute.

An election under IHTA 1984 must be made by the person who would otherwise be liable for the whole or part of the tax. The election must be made in writing, within two years of the death or such longer time as the Board may allow (s. 125(3)).

It is understood that the official view is that it is possible to make an election in respect of part only of the woodlands in a person's estate at death, provided they can be identified as separate viable areas; thus it might be advantageous to make an election only in respect of those areas of woodland which have reached maturity and are unlikely to undergo any further substantial increase in value.

9.6.2 Conditions for relief

Property qualifying

The relief applies to the value of trees or underwood, where part of the value transferred by a chargeable transfer on death is attributable to land in the UK on which trees or underwood are growing, but which is not agricultural property. Thus, the following are excluded from relief:

- woodlands outside the UK,
- 'agricultural woodlands', ie woodlands occupied with agricultural land or pasture, where the occupation is ancillary to that of the agricultural land or pasture (s. 115(2)). Shelter belts and the like are envisaged here, but such property may qualify for agricultural property relief.

The legislation uses the words 'trees or underwood', and not the word 'timber'; hence, the relief extends to trees, which would not fall within a strict definition of timber.

Minimum period of ownership

Relief is available only if the deceased either:

- was beneficially entitled to the land (or to an interest in possession in it) throughout the five years before his death, or
- became beneficially entitled to it otherwise than for a consideration in money or money's worth (s. 125(1)).

9.6.3 Tax charge on disposal

General

Once relief under s. 125 has been given, a charge to tax will accrue on the occurrence of the first disposal of the trees or underwood, unless:

- the disposal is on the occasion of another death. If so, tax will never become chargeable by reference to the first death, and the relief becomes absolute,
- the disposal is by a person to his or her spouse. In this case the disposal is disregarded, so that the tax charge may crystallise later when the recipient spouse in turn makes a disposal. This is not restricted to cases where the recipient spouse is domiciled in the UK, since it will make no difference

to the charge if the timber happens to be excluded property at the time of the disposal which causes it,

(s. 126 IHTA 1984).

In any other circumstances a charge will be made, regardless of whether the trees are sold separately or with the underlying land. References to a disposal of trees include references to the disposal of any interest in the trees (s. 130(1)(c)). Thus, a disposal of an interest that is less than full (eg the granting of a tenancy, or the creation of a life interest) is an occasion of charge. However, any particular trees or underwood (or an interest therein) can only be charged once with reference to the same death (s. 126(3)).

Amount chargeable

The amount chargeable on the disposal depends upon whether or not the disposal is a sale for full consideration in money or money's worth. If so, the amount chargeable is the net proceeds of sale. If not, the amount chargeable is the net value of the trees or underwood at the time of the disposal (IHTA 1984, s. 127(1)).

'Net proceeds of sale' and 'net value' are the proceeds of sale value less the following expenses (so far as these are not allowable for income tax purposes):

- expenses incurred in disposing of the trees or underwood, including felling and removal of the timber, expenses of sale, and costs of office administration and expert supervision attributable to the disposal;
- expenses incurred in replanting within three years of the disposal (or such longer time as the Board may allow) to replace the trees or underwood disposed of. It is understood that the period will be extended where the replanting is delayed by circumstances beyond the taxpayer's control, such as planning approval,
- expenses incurred in replanting to replace trees or underwood previously disposed of, so far as not allowed on the previous disposal (s. 130(2)). This would include replanting expenses incurred too late to be set off against an earlier disposal,

(IHTA 1984, s. 130(1)(b)).

Rate of tax

The rate chargeable on the disposal is intended to be that which would have applied had the property not been left out of account on death. Thus the amount chargeable is treated as the top slice of the deceased's estate (including any amount which has previously become chargeable under s. 126) and tax is payable at the full rate applicable at the time of the disposal (s. 128 and Sch. 2, Para. 4).

Example 9.54

Andrew died on 1 March 1999, leaving a chargeable estate valued at £500,000, plus woodlands which are left out of account. There were no transfers within seven years of the date of death. The woodlands are left to Graham and Craig.

In July 2001, Graham fells the trees on his land and sells the timber for £75,000. Allowable expenses amount to £10,000.

In January 2004, Craig makes a gift of his woodlands to David at a time when they are worth £160,000 (including £50,000 attributable to the underlying land). There are no allowable expenses.

Sale by Graham	£	£
Andrew's chargeable estate at death		500,000
Proceeds of sale	75,000	
Less: allowable expenses	(10,000)	65,000
		565,000
Tax thereon at 1998–99 rates		136,800
Less: tax on Andrew's estate		110,800
IHT payable on disposals		26,000

Gift by Craig		
Andrew's cumulative total		565,000
Value at date of disposal	160,000	
Less: value of land (which would not be left out of account on Andrew's death)	50,000	110,000
		675,000
Tax thereon at 1998–99 rates		180,800
Less tax on £565,000		136,800
Tax on gift		44,000

9.6.4 Interaction with business property relief

In some circumstances, the value of woodlands that are left out of account on death would otherwise have qualified for business property relief. The benefit of such relief is not lost if tax is deferred until disposal. Instead, the amount chargeable under on the disposal is reduced by the appropriate percentage (IHTA 1984, s. 127(2)).

> ### Example 9.55
>
> If in the above example the woodlands were, on Andrew's death, relevant business property, and met all other conditions for business property relief, the net proceeds of sale on Graham's disposal, and the net value at the date of Craig's disposal, will each be reduced by the appropriate percentage (100 per cent in each case).

> ### Example 9.56
>
> The facts are as in the above example, except that Andrew had an interest in possession in the woodlands which, on his death, passed to Graham and Craig absolutely.
>
> If no election under s. 125 is made, the woodlands will attract business relief at a rate of 50 per cent. However, if the woodlands pass to Graham and Craig and are subsequently disposed of, the amount chargeable is reduced by 100 per cent.
>
> As noted above, s. 125 does not apply to agricultural woodlands, so there is no interaction between woodlands relief and agricultural property relief.

Credit against tax on disposal

If the disposal that triggers the charge under the above rules is itself a chargeable transfer (including a potentially exempt transfer which becomes chargeable), the tax chargeable on the disposal may be set against the value transferred by the disposal.

Liability

Liability for the tax payable on a disposal of trees or underwood rests upon the person who is entitled to the proceeds of sale, or who would be so entitled if the disposal were a sale (IHTA 1984, s. 208).

9.7 Gifts with reservation of benefit

9.7.1 Introduction

The main thrust of the rules considered under this heading is to treat property which is given away subject to a reservation as continuing to form part of the donor's estate until his death, or alternatively until the reservation is released by him during his lifetime (FA 1986, s. 102 and Sch. 20).

In order to escape the charge under these rules, two conditions must be satisfied:

- Possession and enjoyment of the property which is given away must have been bona fide assumed by the donee.
- The property must be enjoyed to the entire exclusion, or virtually to the entire exclusion, of the donor and of any benefit to him by contract or otherwise.

Matters have been further complicated by the enactment in 1999 of provisions applying specifically to gifts of interests in land, intended to put an end to avoidance schemes which permitted the owner of property to give away the freehold reversion and yet remain in occupation without falling foul of the reservation of benefit rules.

Anti-avoidance legislation was enacted in the Finance Act 2003 following the Court of Appeal's decision in *IR Commrs v Eversden (executors of Greenstock dec'd)* [2003] BTC 8,028, to disapply the exemption from s. 102 for gifts to a spouse in certain circumstances.

Schedule 20 contains provisions for tracing property which may no longer be owned by the donee when the charge under s. 102 arises. It also contains important exceptions from charge. No tax is chargeable:

- if the donor has given full consideration for the benefit reserved, or
- where, following a change of circumstances, the donor has to re-occupy property due to old age or infirmity.

'Disposal'

Unlike the rest of the inheritance tax legislation, the gifts subject to reservation rules apply to 'disposals'. Thus the fact that the section applies to gifts as distinct from transfers of value means that the exceptions from charge for dispositions that are not transfers of value are of no assistance. A disposition of excluded property could also fall within s. 102 as a disposal by way of gift, even if it is not a transfer of value.

It would, however, be misleading to assume that any inheritance tax provisions that apply to 'dispositions' (such as the associated operations rules) cannot apply to 'disposals'. The better view seems to be that the term 'disposition' is wide enough to cover 'disposals by way of gift' falling within s. 102.

9.7.2 Meaning of 'gift'

Common law background

In *In re Earl Fitzwilliam's Agreement* [1950] Ch 448, Danckwerts J held that the word 'gift' retained its ordinary meaning. He said at p. 455:

> 'If it was the intention of the legislature to make such a striking change as to include sales for full monetary value in the former provisions relating to gifts, it certainly seems that an odd method of carrying out such a change was adopted. So long as the provisions were dealing with gifts and purely voluntary transactions, the words "gift", "donor" and "donee" were the natural words to use and were entirely logical. It seems to me that it would have been perfectly simple (if it had been desired to include sales) to have substituted the word "assurance" for "gift" and "grantor" and "grantee" or "transferor" and "transferee" for the words "donor" and "donee".'

In *Berry v Warnett* [1982] BTC 239, a capital gains tax case, Lord Wilberforce, with whom Lords Scarman and Bridge agreed, felt unable to accept the Revenue argument. He said (page 241):

> 'The natural meaning of gift in settlement seems to me to be related to beneficial interests created, not to the legal transfer of title. I find the same words used in s. 31(3) together with "gift" where the latter is clearly directed towards the donee, suggesting that the former are similarly directed. So, however much I may suspect (as I do) that "gift" is a draftsman's error for "transfer", I am reluctant, in a taxing Act, to depart from the natural meaning of the words.'

His Lordship thus took a similar view as to the meaning of 'gift' as did Danckwerts J in Fitzwilliam.

It seems clear, therefore, that the Revenue must show that there is an element of bounty in a transaction before s. 102 can apply. This is more onerous than the objective test of showing that a transferor's estate is diminished: the Revenue must show that the transferor intended to benefit the transferee. (This appears to have been conceded by the Revenue at a meeting with the ICAEW on 4 June 1986: see notes published by ICAEW as TR 631 in September 1986.)

> ### Example 9.57
>
> Adrian owns a dwelling-house worth £400,000. He transfers three one-quarter shares in the house to his three adult children, reserving the right to occupy the house from time to time, whenever he chooses. In consideration of the transfers, each child pays Adrian £60,000, representing the full value of a one-quarter share subject to Adrian's right of occupation. The value of Adrian's remaining one-quarter share, plus the reserved right, is £120,000, and hence Adrian's estate has been diminished by £100,000 (ie £400,000 − £120,000 + 3 × £60,000).
>
> Since there is no element of bounty in the transaction, Adrian's children having given full value for what they received, this is not a disposal 'by way of gift', and, despite Adrian's reservation of benefit, and the loss to Adrian's estate, s. 102 does not apply.

It is essential that full consideration must be given by the transferee. Once the Revenue can show that there is any element of bounty, the whole gift will fall within s. 102.

Assumption by donee of possession and enjoyment

To escape the gifts with reservation rules, it must be shown that possession and enjoyment of the property has been bona fide assumed by the donee at or before the beginning of the relevant period (s. 102(1)(a)). The 'relevant period' means seven years before the donor's death or, if shorter, the period between the gift and the death.

The phrase 'possession and enjoyment' should be understood as a composite expression (see *Commissioner for Stamp Duties of New South Wales v Perpetual Trustee Co Ltd* [1943] AC 425 (PC)). In that case, the deceased settled property on accumulation and maintenance trusts for his son, with provision for capital and accumulated income to be made over to the son in the event of his attaining 21. With the exception of payment of life policy premiums, the whole income was accumulated until the son attained 21. Lord Russell of Killowen said (pp. 439–440):

> 'The donee was the recipient of the gift: whether the son alone was the donee (as their Lordships think) or whether the son and the body of trustees together constituted the donee, seems immaterial. The trustees alone were not the donee. They were in no sense the object of the settlor's bounty. Did the donee assume bona fide possession and enjoyment immediately upon the gift? The linking of possession with enjoyment as a composite object which has to be assumed by the donee indicates that the possession and enjoyment contemplated is beneficial possession and enjoyment by the object of the donor's bounty. This question therefore must be answered in the affirmative, because

the son was (through the medium of the trustees) immediately put in such bona fide beneficial possession and enjoyment of the property comprised in the gift as the nature of the gift and the circumstances permitted.'

Thus a donee can be said to have assumed possession and enjoyment even though the whole income of the property in question is being accumulated on his behalf.

9.7.3 Exclusion of donor and of any benefit to him

General

In order to escape the consequences of the gifts with reservation rules, it must be shown that throughout the relevant period the property was enjoyed to the entire exclusion, or virtually to the entire exclusion, of the donor and of any benefit to him by contract or otherwise (s. 102(1)(b)). The 'relevant period' means seven years before the donor's death, or the period between the gift and the death, if shorter.

If and so long as any property is not enjoyed to the entire exclusion of the donor and of any benefit to him, the property is referred to (in relation to the gift and the donor) as property subject to a reservation (s. 102(2)).

'Virtually to the entire exclusion'

Some official guidance has been given as to when property will be regarded as being enjoyed 'virtually to the entire exclusion' of benefit to the donor. The official view, set out in Issue 9 of the Inland Revenue's *Tax Bulletin* (November 1993), is as follows:

'The word "virtually" in the *de minimis* rule in Section 102(1)(b) is not defined and the statute does not give any express guidance about its meaning. However, the shorter OED defines it as, amongst other things, "to all intents" and "as good as". Our interpretation of "virtually to the entire exclusion" is that it covers cases in which the benefit to the donor is insignificant in relation to the gifted property.

It is not possible to reduce this test to a single crisp proposition. Each case turns on its own unique circumstances and the questions are likely to be ones of fact and degree. We do not operate Section 102(1)(b) in such a way that donors are unreasonably prevented from having limited access to property they have given away and a measure of flexibility is adopted in applying the test.

Some examples of situations in which we consider that Section 102(1)(b) permits limited benefit to the donor without bringing the GWR provisions into play are given below to illustrate how we apply the *de minimis* test:

- a house which becomes the donee's residence but where the donor subsequently stays, in the absence of the donee, for not more than 2 weeks each year, or
- stays with the donee for less than one month each year;
- social visits, excluding overnight stays made by a donor as a guest of the donee, to a house which he had given away. The extent of the social visits should be no greater than the visits which the donor might be expected to make to the donee's house in the absence of any gift by the donor;
- a temporary stay for some short term purpose in a house the donor had previously given away, for example
- while the donor convalesces after medical treatment,
- while the donor looks after a donee convalescing after medical treatment,
- while the donor's own home is being redecorated;
- visits to a house for domestic reasons, for example baby-sitting by the donor for the donee's children;
- a house together with a library of books which the donor visits less than 5 times in any year to consult or borrow a book;
- a motor car which the donee uses to give occasional (ie less than 3 times a month) lifts to the donor;
- land which the donor uses to walk his dogs or for horse riding provided this does not restrict the donee's use of the land.

It follows, of course, that if the benefit to the donor is, or becomes, more significant, the GWR provisions are likely to apply. Examples of this include gifts of:

- a house in which the donor then stays most weekends, or for a month or more each year;
- a second home or holiday home which the donor and the donee both then use on an occasional basis;
- a house with a library in which the donor continues to keep his own books, or which the donor uses on a regular basis, for example because it is necessary for his work;
- a motor car which the donee uses every day to take the donor to work.'

The above guidance demonstrates that the Revenue take a strict view of the meaning of the phrase 'virtually to the entire exclusion'. For example, if X gives away his holiday villa in Spain to his son Y, but reserves the right to occupy it for one week in September each year, it seems that this may be sufficient to constitute a reservation of benefit, unless the house in Spain becomes the usual residence of Y. The question is, as the official view recognises, one of fact and degree, but one suspects that it would not be easy to persuade a court, in a marginal situation, to reverse a refusal by the Revenue to apply the *de minimis* rule.

'By contract or otherwise'

In *A-G v Seccombe* [1911] 2 KB 688, it was held in the High Court that the words 'or otherwise' were to be construed *eiusdem generis* with the word 'contract', and that they covered contracts between the parties to the gift and third parties, and any other transactions enforceable at law or in equity which, though not in the form of a contract, may confer a benefit, such as a lien. The Crown's contention that the words covered unenforceable arrangements was rejected. In *Seccombe* it was held that in the absence of an enforceable agreement the donor's presence in a house after giving it away did not amount to a reservation.

It appears that the interpretation of the phrase in *Seccombe* is still authoritative, and on this basis unenforceable agreements are not covered.

Associated operations

A benefit which the donor obtained by virtue of any associated operations, of which the disposal by way of gift is one, is treated as a benefit to him by contract or otherwise (FA 1986, Sch. 20, Para. 6(1)(c)). It could be argued that Para. 6(1)(c) overrides the *eiusdem generis* construction of the words 'or otherwise' discussed above. Thus where a benefit was reserved by associated operations, it would not matter whether all or any of them were enforceable agreements. At present it is not clear whether this is what is intended, but it is important to be aware of the possibility.

Gift with reservation or absolute gift of part?

The important distinction between a gift subject to reservation on the one hand, and an absolute gift of part of the donor's interest on the other, is illustrated by the cases of *Chick v Commissioner of Stamp Duties* [1958] AC 435 and *Munro & Ors v Commissioner of Stamp Duties* [1934] AC 61. In *Chick*, the owner of a farm transferred it to his son absolutely. Some 17 months later, the father, son and another son entered into partnership to carry on the business of graziers and stock dealers. The father was to be manager of the business, with the final decision on all matters. The business was conducted on the respective holdings of the three partners, including the farm that was the subject matter of the gift. The agreement continued up to the date of the father's death. The Privy Council held that the subject matter of the gift had not been enjoyed to the entire exclusion of the father, and that it fell to be included in his estate for the purposes of death duty. It was of no consequence that the partnership agreement was an independent commercial transaction for full consideration, or that it was in no way related to the enjoyment of the gift by the donee.

By way of contrast, in the earlier case of *Munro*, a farmer agreed with his six children that his business would thereafter be carried on by them as partners, the business to be solely managed by him and each to receive a specified share of the profits. Four years later he made a gift to each child of a portion of the land, subject to the partnership agreement but on the understanding that each could withdraw and work his land separately. This understanding was later revoked. On the donor's death, it was held that the subject matter of the gifts had been the land, shorn of the partnership's rights, and that any benefit remaining in the donor was referable to the partnership agreement and not to the gifts. Accordingly, they did not fall to be included in his estate for death duty.

This distinction gave rise in the estate duty era to the principle of 'carving out' a separate interest to be given away, and this principle is once again relevant for the purposes of inheritance tax. If it can be shown that what is given away is a separate interest in property in which the donor may have retained another interest, then this is not a gift subject to reservation, even if the interest disposed of was carved out by the donor. What is important is that the separation of the interests should take place before the gift is made (as was the case in *Munro*, but not in *Chick*).

This principle was applied to settled property in *Commissioner for Stamp Duties of New South Wales v Perpetual Trustee Co Ltd* [1943] AC 425. A settlor created an accumulation and maintenance settlement in favour of his son, with capital and accumulated income vesting in the son absolutely on his attaining 21. In the event of the son failing to attain 21 the settled property would have re-vested in the settlor under a resulting trust. The Privy Council held that this was not a gift with reservation. What was given was the equitable interest in the assets settled, and this was given without reservation.

The decisions in *Munro* and *Perpetual Trustee Co Ltd* were referred to at length by the House of Lords in *St. Aubyn & Ors v A-G* [1952] AC 15, and the principle was stated by Lord Simonds at page 29 as follows:

> 'In the simplest analysis, if A gives to B all his estates in Wiltshire except Blackacre, he does not except Blackacre out of what he has given: he just does not give Blackacre. And if it can be regarded as a "benefit" to him that he does not give but keeps Blackacre, it is a benefit which is in no relevant sense (to use the language of Lord Tomlin [in Munro]) "referable" or (to use that of Lord Russell of Killowen [in Perpetual Trustee Co. Ltd.]) "attributable" to the gift that he made of the rest of the Wiltshire estate.'

In the same case, Lord Radcliffe said at page 49:

> 'All these decisions [ie *Munro, Perpetual Trustee Co Ltd* and *Re Cochrane* [1906] 2 IR 200] proceed upon a common principle, namely, that it is the possession and enjoyment of the actual property given that has to be taken account of, and that if that property is, as it may be, a limited equitable interest or an equitable interest distinct from another such interest which is not given or an interest in property subject to an interest that is retained, it is of no consequence for this purpose that the retained interest remains in the beneficial enjoyment of the person who provides the gift.'

So far as interests in land are concerned, all of the above must now be read subject to the provisions of s. 102A–102C, which are discussed in detail below.

Occupation of land

This paragraph examines the circumstances in which the entitlement or ability of a donor to occupy land, or otherwise enjoy land, can cause it to be treated as property subject to a reservation of benefit (FA 1986, s. 102A).

1 Reservation of rent-free occupation

A donor who disposes of an interest in land by way of gift on or after 9 March 1999 will be treated as having reserved a benefit in the land if he or his spouse enjoys a 'significant right or interest' or is party to a 'significant arrangement' in relation to the land. A right, interest or arrangement is 'significant' if it entitles or enables the donor to occupy all or part of the land, or to enjoy some right in relation to the land, otherwise than for full consideration in money or money's worth (s. 102A(1)–(3)).

Example 9.58

Peter is the owner of the house in which he lives with his wife, Rachel. Peter grants a lease of the house to Rachel and then makes a gift of the freehold reversion, to his two adult children Sally and Thomas. Peter and Rachel continue to live in the house; Sally and Thomas do not.

It is considered that the informal basis upon which Rachel permits Peter to remain resident is an 'arrangement' which 'enables' (even though it does not 'entitle') Peter to occupy the house otherwise than for full consideration in money or money's worth, and accordingly Peter's gift of the reversion is a gift subject to reservation of benefit.

Section 102A will not take effect in the following circumstances:

- where the right, interest or arrangement does not and cannot prevent the enjoyment of the land to the entire exclusion, or virtually to the entire exclusion, of the donor (s. 102A(4)(a));
- where the right, interest or arrangement does not entitle or enable the donor to occupy the land immediately after the disposal, but would do so were it not for the interest disposed of: for example, where the donor makes a gift of a leasehold interest but retains the freehold reversion (s. 102A(4)(b));
- where any of the exemptions listed below (s. 102C(2));

- where the donor's occupation results from an unforeseen change of circumstances, at a time when the donor has become unable to maintain himself, representing a reasonable provision for his maintenance by a donee who is a relative of his (s. 102C(3)), or
- where the right or interest was granted or acquired more than seven years before the date of the gift (s. 102A(5)).

As regards the last of these exceptions, where a farmer grants a lease of the farm to a partnership which includes himself, and then more than seven years later makes a gift of the reversion to members of his family (who will probably also be members of the partnership), the gift will not be treated as made subject to a reservation. It appears however that if seven years have not elapsed by the time of the gift, s. 102A will apply. The partnership agreement is treated as a 'significant arrangement', ie an arrangement enabling the farmer to continue to occupy and/or enjoy rights in relation to the farm. (The position will be otherwise when the farm is also occupied by the donees: see point (5) below.)

Where there is more than one disposal by way of gift, whether at the same time or to the same donee or not, each is considered separately in determining whether s. 102A applies (s. 102A(6)).

The 'tracing' provisions in FA 1986, Sch. 20 apply. Where property other than an interest in land is treated by the tracing provisions as if it had been comprised in the gift, the general provisions in s. 102 take over in determining whether the property in question is subject to a reservation (s. 102C(5)).

Any property falling within s. 102A is excluded from the more general provisions of s. 102 (s. 102C(7)).

2 Reservation of occupation at less than market rent

The position in relation to occupation of land at less than market rent is the same as for occupation rent-free: under s. 102A, the right or ability to do so will be treated as a reservation of benefit.

3 Reservation of occupation at full market rental

Where the donor's entitlement or ability to occupy the land, or to enjoy a right in relation to it, is retained or obtained for full consideration in money or money's worth, FA 1986, s. 102A does not apply (s. 102A(3)).

In a letter dated 18 May 1987 to the Law Society, the Revenue expressed the following view:

> 'Whether an arrangement is for full consideration will of course depend on the precise facts. But among the attributes of an acceptable arrangement would be the existence of a bargain negotiated at arm's length by parties who were independently advised and which followed the normal commercial criteria in force at the time it was negotiated.'

The same letter states elsewhere:

'In applying the test [ie of "full consideration"] we shall take account of all the circumstances surrounding the arrangement including the sharing of profits and losses, the donor's and the donee's interests in the land, and their respective commitment and expertise.'

In a Revenue interpretation published in Issue 9 of the Inland Revenue's *Tax Bulletin* (November 1993, page 98), it is recognised that there is generally no single value at which the consideration can be fixed as 'full'. The Revenue accepts that what constitutes full consideration in any case lies within a range of values reflecting normal valuation tolerances, and that any amount within that range can be accepted as satisfying the Para. 6(1)(a) test.

It is assumed that the same applies for the purposes of interpreting the 'significance' test in s. 102A(3). The problem with this test is that it is an all-or-nothing exception. Where a leaseback is taken at what is intended to be a full market rent, but the consideration is subsequently proved to be inadequate, the whole gift is treated as having been made subject to reservation.

4 Occupation by donor without enforceable right
As discussed under 1 above, it seems clear, with regard to gifts made on or after 9 March 1999, that the absence of any entitlement of a donor to retain or resume occupation of property which he has disposed of by way of gift does not prevent him from being held to have reserved a benefit in the property, if there is any 'arrangement', however informal, which enables him to occupy it.

5 Gift of undivided share; occupation by donor and donee
A gift of an undivided share of an interest in land is treated as a gift subject to reservation unless either:

- the donor does not at the material time occupy the land, or
- the donor occupies the land to the exclusion of the donee for full consideration in money or money's worth (FA 1986, s. 102B(1)–(3)).

Where a donor gives away an undivided share of property and remains in occupation along with the donee, the official view is that this does not fall foul of s. 102. During the Committee stage debate of what became FA 1986, Sch. 20, the Treasury Minister of State said (Standing Committee G, 10 June 1986, col. 425), in reply to a back-bench query on this point:

'It may be that my hon. Friend's intention concerns the common case where someone gives away an individual share in land, typically a house, which is then occupied by all the joint owners including the donor. For example, elderly

527

parents make unconditional gifts of undivided shares in their house to their children and the parents and the children occupy the property as their family home, each owner bearing his or her share of the running costs. In those circumstances, the parents' occupation or enjoyment of the part of the house that they have given away is in return for similar enjoyment of the children of the other part of the property. Thus the donors' occupation is for a full consideration.

Accordingly, I assure my Hon. Friend that the gift with reservation rules will not be applied to an unconditional gift of an undivided share in land merely because the property is occupied by all the joint owners or tenants in common, including the donor.'

This statement was expanded to some extent in a letter by the Inland Revenue to The Law Society dated 18 May 1987. where it is stated:

'If, and for so long as, all the joint owners remain in occupation, the donor's occupation will not be treated as a reservation provided the gift is itself unconditional and there is no collateral benefit to the donor. The payment by the donee of the donor's share of the running costs, for example, might be such a benefit. An arrangement will not necessarily be jeopardised merely because it invoves a gift of an unequal share in a house.'

This favourable treatment of property of which the donor remains in occupation along with the donee is continued by s. 102B(4), which provides that property will not be treated as gifted subject to reservation where:

- the donor and the donee occupy the land, and
- the donor receives no benefit, other than a negligible one, which is provided by or at the expense of the donee for some reason connected with the gift.

During the passage of the 1999 Finance Bill through Parliament, the Paymaster-General gave assurances that what was said by the Treasury Minister in 1986 still held good, and that the new rules were the same as the old ones on undivided shares (Hansard, Standing Committee B, 15 June 1999, col. 552–556). Nor will s. 102B(1) and s. 102B(2) apply:

- where any of the exemptions listed above apply (s. 102C(2)),
- where the donor's occupation fulfils the conditions in FA 1986, Sch. 20, Para. 6(1)(b), listed at point (6) below: ie where it results from an unforeseen change of circumstances, at a time when the donor has become unable to maintain himself, representing a reasonable provision for his maintenance by a donee who is a relative of his (s. 102C(3)).

The 'tracing' provisions in FA 1986, Sch. 20 apply for the purposes of s. 102B(s. 102C(4)). Where property other than an interest in land is treated by the tracing provisions as if it had been comprised in the gift, the general provisions in s. 102 take over in determining whether the property in question is subject to a reservation (s. 102C(5)).

Any property falling within s. 102B is excluded from the more general provisions of s. 102 and s. 102A (s. 102C(6)).

6 Occupation following change of circumstances

Occupation of land by the donor is disregarded if the following four conditions are fulfilled:

- the occupation results from a change of circumstances of the donor since the time of the gift, being a change which was unforeseen at that time and was not brought about by the donor to receive the benefit of an exclusion;
- the occupation occurs at a time when the donor has become unable to maintain himself through old age, infirmity or otherwise;
- the occupation represents a reasonable provision by the donee for the care and maintenance of the donor, and
- the donee is a relative of the donor or his spouse.

This is clearly an exception of very limited scope. It is intended to prevent a charge arising where, through unforeseen circumstances with no tax avoidance motive, a donor has had to resume occupation of a house or land that he had earlier given away. It should be noted that it is necessary both that the donor has become unable to maintain himself due to old age, infirmity, etc., and that other circumstances have rendered it necessary for him to move back in, ie the old age or infirmity is not enough on its own.

7 Reservation of other specific rights

In a number of cases a gift has been held to be subject to reservation because of the retention by the donor of lesser rights than indefinite or fixed-term occupation. In *Earl Grey v A-G* [1900] AC 124 the donor conveyed an estate to the donee subject to payment of a rent charge to the donor during his life. The charge was released within seven years before the donor's death and the gift was held to be chargeable to estate duty. In an Irish case, *Revenue Commissioners v O'Donoghue* [1936] IR 342, certain rights of lodging were reserved, and the donor was held not excluded from benefit.

In *Nichols v IR Commrs* [1975] 1 WLR 534, the deceased gave an estate to his son and immediately took a lease back in favour of himself and his wife, at a full market rent. The property was held to be dutiable for two different reasons. First, the lease contained a full repairing covenant by the son, and the Court of Appeal regarded this as a benefit taken by the donor which did not exist before the gift was made. Secondly, the lease was amended to shift liability for a tithe redemption annuity from the deceased to his son, which represented a cutting down of the original gift and hence a reservation of benefit. See also *Oakes v Commissioner of Stamp Duties of New South Wales*

[1954] AC 57, in which receipt of remuneration for management of the property given was held to be a reservation of benefit.

8   Easements and servitudes

The estate duty case law contains no specific guidance as to whether reservation of an easement, such as a right of way, is to be regarded as falling foul of the gifts subject to reservation rules. However, there are dicta in *Perpetual Trustee Co* and in *St Aubyn v A-G* to suggest that it would not. Further, in *Commissioner for Stamp Duties of New South Wales v Perpetual Trustee Co Ltd* [1943] AC 425, Lord Russell of Killowen said, at page 446:

> '. . . the entire exclusion of the donor from possession and enjoyment which is contemplated by s. 11 , sub-s. 1, of the Act of 1889, of the Act of 1889 is entire exclusion from possession and enjoyment of the beneficial interest in property which has been given by the gift, and. . . possession and enjoyment by the donor of some beneficial interest therein which he has not included in the gift is not inconsistent with the entire exclusion from possession and enjoyment which the sub-section requires.'

Example 9.59

A owns a house set in a large area of garden. He makes a gift to his daughter of part of the garden, lying between his own house and the public road, but reserves a right of access over the land which he has given away.

On the authority of *Perpetual Trustee Co* and *St. Aubyn* the enjoyment by A of the right of access over B's land is not inconsistent with his entire exclusion from the subject-matter of the gift, namely the land subject to a right of access.

It is considered that in the above example A's daughter would be regarded as enjoying the land 'virtually to the entire exclusion' of A, so that by virtue of s. 102A(4) A's right of access would not be regarded as 'significant' for the purposes of s. 102A.

---

9   Shooting and fishing rights

Under English law, shooting and fishing rights are species of *profits à prendre* which may be enjoyed either appurtenant to a nearby dominant tenement, or 'in gross', ie independent of any other interest in land. They may be created either by grant or by reservation. To the extent that they may exist independently of any dominant tenement, the argument is slightly stronger than for easements above, that they may be reserved without falling foul of FA 1986, s. 102. Thus, for example, A may give land to B but reserve the shooting rights over it, and on A's death the land would not be treated as property subject to reservation.

Under Scottish law, salmon fishings are a separate feudal right. It seems clear, therefore, that a proprietor may give away land, but reserve the salmon fishing rights (whether on one or both banks) without falling foul of s. 102. Other fishing rights and shooting rights are granted (or reserved) by way of lease, and hence the discussion at 1–3 above of leases is applicable.

9.7.4 Exemptions

The gifts with reservation rules do not apply to:

- transfers between spouses, subject to the proviso mentioned below;
- small gifts (currently up to £250);
- gifts to charities;
- gifts to political parties;
- gifts to housing associations;
- gifts for national purposes;
- gifts to maintenance funds for historic buildings, and
- gifts to employee trusts

(FA 1986, s. 102(5)).

Transfers between spouses

The exemption for transfers between spouses does not apply if, or to the extent that:

- the property becomes settled property by virtue of the gift;
- the transfer remains an exempt inter-spouse transfer because the spouse has an interest in possession;
- the spouse 's interest in possession comes to an end before the death of the donor, and
- when it comes to an end, the spouse does not become beneficially entitled to the settled property,

(FA 1986, s. 102(5A)).

Where this rule applies, the gift is treated as made when the spouse's interest in possession comes to an end (s. 102(5B)).

10   Stamp duty land tax (SDLT)

10.1   The charge to SDLT

10.1.1   Scope of SDLT

Stamp duty land tax (SDLT) is charged on land transactions. It is chargeable:

- whether or not there is any instrument effecting the transaction;
- if there is such an instrument, whether or not it is executed in the UK, and
- whether or not any party to the transaction is present, or resident, in the UK,

(FA 2003, s. 42).

It applies to transactions effected on or after 1 December 2003 (FA 2003, Sch. 19, Para. 2, and SI 2003/2899).

10.1.2   Land transactions

A 'land transaction' means any acquisition of a chargeable interest (FA 2003, s. 43(1)).

A charge to SDLT is imposed however the acquisition is effected, whether by act of the parties, by order of a court or other authority, by or under any statutory provision or by operation of law (s. 43(2)).

In particular:

- the creation of a chargeable interest is:

  an acquisition by the person becoming entitled to the interest created, and
  a disposal by the person whose interest or right is subject to the interest created;

- the surrender or release of a chargeable interest is:

  an acquisition of that interest by any person whose interest or right is benefited or enlarged by the transaction, and
  a disposal by the person ceasing to be entitled to that interest, and

- the variation of a chargeable interest is:

  an acquisition of a chargeable interest by the person benefiting from the variation, and a disposal of a chargeable interest by the person whose interest is subject to or limited by the variation,

(s. 43(3)).

10.1.3 Purchaser and vendor

The 'purchaser' and 'vendor', in relation to a land transaction, are respectively the person acquiring and the person disposing of the subject matter of the transaction (s. 43(4)).

These expressions apply even if there is no consideration given for the transaction. However, a person is not treated as a purchaser unless he has given consideration for, or is a party to, the transaction (s. 43(5)).

References to the subject matter of a land transaction are to the chargeable interest acquired (the 'main subject matter'), together with any interest or right appurtenant or pertaining to it that is acquired with it (s. 43(6)).

10.1.4 Chargeable interest

The term 'chargeable interest' means:

- an estate, interest, right or power in or over land in the UK, or
- the benefit of an obligation, restriction or condition affecting the value of any such estate, interest, right or power,

(s. 48(1), FA 2003).

However, the following are exempt interests:

- any security interest;
- a licence to use or occupy land,
- in England and Wales or Northern Ireland:

  a tenancy at will,
  an advowson, franchise or manor,

(s. 48(2)).

A 'security interest' is an interest or right (other than a rentcharge) held for the purpose of securing the payment of money or the performance of any other obligation.

A 'franchise' is a grant from the Crown such as the right to hold a market or fair, or the right to take tolls (s. 48(3)).

In Scotland the reference to a rentcharge is treated as a reference to a feu duty or a payment mentioned in s. 56(1) of the Abolition of Feudal Tenure, etc. (Scotland) Act 2000 (s. 48(4)).

The Treasury may by regulations add to the list of exempt interests (s. 48(5)).

10.1.5 Fixtures and chattels

The Revenue has issued the following guidance on fixtures and chattels (SDLT Bulletin Issue 6).

'For an item to be regarded as a fixture or part of the land (chargeable to tax), as opposed to a chattel or moveable in Scotland (not chargeable), the item must, as a starting point, be annexed to the property. The issue then turns on the degree and purpose of the annexation, with greater emphasis being placed (in the more recent cases) to purpose. Where a purchaser agrees to buy a property for a price that includes an amount properly attributed to chattels or moveables, that amount will not be charged to Stamp Duty Land Tax.

. . . .

Under paragraph (4) of Schedule 4 Finance Act 2003, a "just and reasonable apportionment" is required where a price is paid partly for a land transaction and partly for a non-land transaction such as the purchase of chattels. It does not matter that the parties to a transaction may agree a particular apportionment, which is then documented in the contract. The apportionment will not be correct unless it was arrived at on a "just and reasonable" basis.

. . . .

We are unable to provide a comprehensive list of items that we accept as chattels or moveables. This is because each case must be considered on its own merits and because this is an area of the law that continues to evolve.

The following are, however, confirmed as being items that will normally fall to be regarded as chattels:

- carpets (fitted or otherwise)
- curtains and blinds
- free standing furniture
- kitchen white goods
- electric and gas fires (provided that they can be removed by disconnection from the power supply without causing damage to the property)
- light shades and fittings (unless recessed).

On the other hand, the following will not normally be regarded as chattels:

- fitted kitchen units, cupboards and sinks
- agas and wall mounted ovens

- fitted bathroom sanitary ware
- central heating systems
- intruder alarm systems.

Externally any plants, shrubs or trees growing in the soil form part of the land and are not regarded as chattels. A deduction would, however, be possible for amounts properly apportioned to any plants growing in pots or containers.

The above guidance is written primarily in the context of sales of residential property. The same principles apply when considering the purchase of industrial or commercial property in which the sale may also involve the acquisition of plant, machinery or equipment.'

10.2　Contract and conveyance

10.2.1　Effective date – general rule

Where a contract for a land transaction is entered into under which the transaction is to be completed by a conveyance, the general rule is that the contract and the transaction effected on completion are treated as parts of a single land transaction. In this case the effective date of the transaction is the date of completion (FA 2003, s. 44(3)).

However, if the contract is substantially performed without having been completed, the contract is treated as if it were itself the transaction provided for in the contract. In this case the effective date of the transaction is when the contract is substantially performed (s. 44(4)).

10.2.2　Substantial performance

A contract is 'substantially performed' when:

- the purchaser, or a person connected with the purchaser, takes possession of the whole, or substantially the whole, of the subject matter of the contract, or
- a substantial amount of the consideration is paid or provided.

For this purpose, possession includes receipt of rents and profits or the right to receive them. It is immaterial whether possession is taken under the contract or under a licence or lease of a temporary character (s. 44(4),(5)).

10.2.3　Substantial amount of consideration

If none of the consideration is rent, a substantial amount of the consideration is paid or provided where the whole or substantially the whole of the consideration is paid or provided.

If the only consideration is rent, a substantial amount of the consideration is paid or provided when the first payment of rent is made.

If the consideration includes both rent and other consideration, a substantial amount of the consideration is paid or provided when:

- the whole or substantially the whole of the consideration other than rent is paid or provided, or
- the first payment of rent is made,

(s. 44(7)).

10.2.4   Subsequent completion or annulment

In a case of substantial performance, if the contract is subsequently completed by a conveyance both the contract and the transaction effected on completion are notifiable transactions. Tax is chargeable on the conveyance to the extent (if any) that the amount of tax chargeable on it is greater than the amount of tax chargeable on the contract. If the contract is (to any extent) afterwards rescinded or annulled, or is for any other reason not carried into effect, the tax paid on substantial performance is repayable accordingly (s. 44(8), (9)). Repayment must be claimed by amendment of the relevant land transaction return (s. 44(10)).

10.2.5   Definitions

Completion means completion of the land transaction proposed, between the same parties, in substantial conformity with the contract.

The term 'contract' includes any agreement and 'conveyance' includes any instrument (s. 44(10)).

The ICTA 1988, s. 839 definition of connected persons applies for the purposes of the above rules (s. 44(11)).

10.3   Assignments and sub-sales

10.3.1   Relief for sub-sales

A special rule, effectively giving relief from a double charge to SDLT, applies where:

- a contract for a land transaction ('the original contract') is entered into under which the transaction is to be completed by a conveyance – say from A to B, and

- there is an assignment, sub-sale or other transaction (relating to the whole or part of the subject matter of the original contract) as a result of which a person other than B (say C) becomes entitled to call for a conveyance from A to him,

(FA 2003, s. 45(1)).

The transferee C is not regarded as entering into a land transaction by reason of the transfer of rights, but the above rules have effect as if there were a contract for a land transaction (a 'secondary contract') under which:

- the transferee C (rather than B) is the purchaser, and
- the consideration for the transaction is:

  so much of the consideration under the original contract (between A and B) as is referable to the subject matter of the transfer of rights and is to be given (directly or indirectly) by C or a person connected with him, and
  the consideration (by C to B) given for the transfer of rights,

(s. 45(2), (3)).

The substantial performance or completion of the original contract at the same time as, and in connection with, the substantial performance or completion of the secondary contract is disregarded (s. 45(3)).

Where there are successive transfers of rights, this special rule has effect in relation to each of them. The substantial performance or completion of the secondary contract arising from an earlier transfer of rights at the same time as, and in connection with, the substantial performance or completion of the secondary contract arising from a subsequent transfer of rights is disregarded (s. 45(4)).

Where a transfer of rights relates to part only of the subject matter of the original contract, the restriction of charge to tax on the subsequent conveyance has effect as if the reference to the amount of tax chargeable on that contract were a reference to an appropriate proportion of that amount (s. 45(5)).

However, if the original contract between A and B is substantially performed, then B is treated as having acquired a chargeable interest, in relation to which the effective date is the date on which it is substantially performed (s. 44A). This is a notifiable acquisition.

Where C assigns its rights, or there is some other transaction as a result of which D becomes entitled to exercise any of B's rights, D is treated as if it had entered into a contract in the same terms as the original contract, except with D as a party instead of B. D's chargeable consideration is deemed to be the sum of the consideration given for the transfer of rights and so much of the consideration under the original contract as is referable to the transfer of rights and is to be given by D or a person connected with D (s. 45A).

10.3.2 Definitions

Completion means completion of the land transaction proposed, between the same parties, in substantial conformity with the contract.

The term 'contract' includes any agreement and 'conveyance' includes any instrument (s. 45(7)).

The ICTA 1988, s. 839 definition of connected persons applies for the purposes of the above rules (s. 45(6)).

10.4 Options and pre-emption rights

The acquisition of an option binding the grantor to enter into a land transaction is treated as a land transaction distinct from any land transaction resulting from the exercise of the option.

Similarly, the acquisition of a right of pre-emption preventing the grantor from entering into, or restricting the right of the grantor to enter into, a land transaction, is also treated as a land transaction distinct from any land transaction resulting from the exercise of the right (FA 2003, s. 46(1)).

An option binding the grantor to enter into a land transaction includes an option requiring the grantor either to enter into a land transaction or to discharge his obligations under the option in some other way (eg by the payment of cash).

The effective date of the transaction in the case of the acquisition of such an option or right is when the option or right is acquired, as opposed to when it becomes exercisable (s. 46(3)).

Where an option is exercised, the grant and exercise of the option may be regarded as a single transaction in accordance with the 'linked transactions' rules (s. 108). This affects the rate of SDLT that is chargeable on the exercise, because the consideration for the grant of the option and the consideration payable on exercise have to be aggregated (s. 55(4)). In practice, the tax on the grant is calculated without having regard to the amount payable on exercise.

The tax payable on exercise is then the difference between tax on the combined consideration and the tax paid on the grant.

Example 10.1

An option is granted for the purchase of a freehold office building. The option consideration is £80,000 and the exercise price is £1,600,000.

The tax payable on the grant is nil, because the option consideration falls within the £150,000 nil rate band for commercial buildings.

The tax payable on exercise is 4 per cent of £1,680,000 = £67,200.

10.5   Exchanges

10.5.1   The general rule

Where a land transaction is entered into by a purchaser (alone or jointly) wholly or partly in consideration of another land transaction being entered into by him (alone or jointly) as vendor, each transaction is treated as distinct and separate from the other (FA 2003, s. 47(1)).

This rule applies in particular where an obligation to give consideration for a land transaction that a person enters into as purchaser is met wholly or partly by way of that person entering into another transaction as vendor.

The SDLT liability on each transaction is the appropriate percentage of the market value of the property (Sch. 5, Para. 5).

Where one of the transactions consists of the grant of a lease, the rent payable under the lease is included in the chargeable consideration for the acquisition (Para. 5(3)).

10.5.2   Part-exchange of residential property

Acquisition by house-building company from individual acquiring new dwelling

Where a dwelling ('the old dwelling') is acquired by a house-building company, or a company connected with it, from an individual (whether alone or with other individuals), the acquisition is exempt from SDLT if the following conditions are met (Sch. 6A, Para. 1):

- the individual (whether alone or with other individuals) must acquire a new dwelling from the house-building company;
- the individual:

  must have occupied the old dwelling as his only or main residence at some time in the period of two years ending with the date of its acquisition by the house-building company, and
  must intend to occupy the new dwelling as his only or main residence;
- each acquisition must be entered into in consideration of the other, and
- the area of land acquired by the house-building company must not exceed the permitted area.

If the area of land acquired by the house-building company exceeds the permitted area, the chargeable consideration for the acquisition is taken to be the amount calculated by deducting the market value of the permitted area from the market value of the old dwelling.

Acquisition by property trader from individual acquiring new dwelling

Where a dwelling ('the old dwelling') is acquired by a property trader from an individual (whether alone or with other individuals), the acquisition is exempt from charge if the following conditions are met (Sch. 6A, Para. 2):

- the acquisition must be made in the course of a business that consists of or includes acquiring dwellings from individuals who acquire new dwellings from house-building companies;
- the individual (whether alone or with other individuals) must acquire a new dwelling from a house-building company;
- the individual:

  must have occupied the old dwelling as his only or main residence at some time in the period of two years ending with the date of its acquisition, and
  must intend to occupy the new dwelling as his only or main residence;
- the property trader must not intend:

  to spend more than the permitted amount on refurbishment of the old dwelling; or
  to grant a lease or licence of the old dwelling, or
  to permit any of its principals or employees (or any person connected with any of its principals or employees) to occupy the old dwelling, and
- the area of land acquired by the property trader does not exceed the permitted area.

If the area of land acquired by the property trader exceeds the permitted area, the chargeable consideration for the acquisition is taken to be the amount calculated by deducting the market value of the permitted area from the market value of the old dwelling.

Relief is withdrawn if the property trader:

- spends more than the permitted amount on refurbishment of the old dwelling; or
- grants a lease or licence of the old dwelling, or
- permits any of its principals or employees (or any person connected with any of its principals or employees) to occupy the old dwelling;

(Sch. 6A, Para. 11).

Acquisition by property trader from personal representatives

Where a dwelling is acquired by a property trader from the personal representatives of a deceased individual, the acquisition is exempt from charge if the following conditions are met (Sch. 6A, Para. 4):

- the acquisition must be made in the course of a business that consists of or includes acquiring dwellings from personal representatives of deceased individuals;
- the deceased individual must have occupied the dwelling as his only or main residence at some time in the period of two years ending with the date of his death;
- that the property trader must not intend:

  to spend more than the permitted amount on refurbishment of the dwelling;
  to grant a lease or licence of the dwelling, or
  to permit any of its principals or employees (or any person connected with any of its principals or employees) to occupy the dwelling, and

- the area of land acquired must not exceed the permitted area.

If the area of land acquired exceeds the permitted area, the chargeable consideration for the acquisition is taken to be the amount calculated by deducting the market value of the permitted area from the market value of the dwelling.

Relief is withdrawn if the property trader:

- spends more than the permitted amount on refurbishment of the dwelling; or
- grants a lease or licence of the dwelling, or

- permits any of its principals or employees (or any person connected with any of its principals or employees) to occupy the dwelling,

(Sch. 6A, Para. 11).

Acquisition by property trader from individual where chain of transactions breaks down

Where a dwelling ('the old dwelling') is acquired by a property trader from an individual (whether alone or with other individuals), the acquisition is exempt from charge if:

- the individual has made arrangements to sell a dwelling ('the old dwelling') and acquire another dwelling ('the second dwelling');
- the arrangements to sell the old dwelling fail;
- the acquisition of the old dwelling is made for the purpose of enabling the individual's acquisition of the second dwelling to proceed;
- the acquisition is made in the course of a business that consists of or includes acquiring dwellings from individuals in those circumstances;
- the individual:

  occupied the old dwelling as his only or main residence at some time in the period of two years ending with the date of its acquisition, and
  intends to occupy the second dwelling as his only or main residence;

- the property trader does not intend:

  to spend more than the permitted amount on refurbishment of the old dwelling;
  to grant a lease or licence of the old dwelling, or
  to permit any of its principals or employees (or any person connected with any of its principals or employees) to occupy the old dwelling, and

- the area of land acquired does not exceed the permitted area,

(Sch. 6A, Para. 5).

If the area of land acquired exceeds the permitted area, the chargeable consideration for the acquisition is taken to be the amount calculated by deducting the market value of the permitted area from the market value of the old dwelling.

Relief is withdrawn if the property trader:

- spends more than the permitted amount on refurbishment of the old dwelling, or
- grants a lease or licence of the old dwelling, or

- permits any of its principals or employees (or any person connected with any of its principals or employees) to occupy the old dwelling,

(Sch. 6A, Para. 11).

Definitions

A 'house-building company' means a company that carries on the business of constructing or adapting buildings or parts of buildings for use as dwellings.

The acquisition of the new dwelling means the acquisition, by way of grant or transfer, of a major interest in the dwelling.

The acquisition of the old dwelling means the acquisition, by way of transfer, of a major interest in the dwelling.

'Dwelling' includes land occupied and enjoyed with the dwelling as its garden or grounds.

A building or part of a building is a 'new dwelling' if:

- it has been constructed for use as a single dwelling and has not previously been occupied, or
- it has been adapted for use as a single dwelling and has not been occupied since its adaptation.

The 'permitted area', in relation to a dwelling, means land occupied and enjoyed with the dwelling as its garden or grounds that does not exceed:

(a)   an area (inclusive of the site of the dwelling) of 0.5 of a hectare, or

(b)   such larger area as is required for the reasonable enjoyment of the dwelling as a dwelling having regard to its size and character.

Where (b) applies, the permitted area is taken to consist of that part of the land that would be the most suitable for occupation and enjoyment with the dwelling as its garden or grounds if the rest of the land were separately occupied (Sch. 6A, Para. 7).

A 'property trader' means:

- a company,
- a limited liability partnership, or
- a partnership whose members are all either companies or limited liability partnerships,

that carries on the business of buying and selling dwellings.

In relation to a property trader a 'principal' means:

- in the case of a company, a director;
- in the case of a limited liability partnership, a member,
- in the case of a partnership whose members are all either companies or limited liability partnerships, a member or a person who is a principal of a member.

Anything done by or in relation to a company connected with a property trader is treated as done by or in relation to that property trader.

The principals or employees of a property trader include the principals or employees of any such company (Sch. 6A, Para. 8).

'Refurbishment' of a dwelling means the carrying out of works that enhance or are intended to enhance the value of the dwelling, but does not include:

- cleaning the dwelling, or
- works required solely for the purpose of ensuring that the dwelling meets minimum safety standards.

The 'permitted amount', in relation to the refurbishment of a dwelling, is:

- £10,000, or
- 5 per cent of the consideration for the acquisition of the dwelling,

whichever is the greater, but subject to a maximum of £20,000,

(Sch. 6A, Para. 8).

10.6 Exempt transactions

10.6.1 General exemptions

The following transactions are exempt, and no return is required in respect of them (FA 2003, Sch. 3). However, a self-certificate may be required.

No chargeable consideration

A land transaction is exempt from charge if there is no chargeable consideration for the transaction (eg a gift or transfer on death).

Grant of certain leases by registered social landlords

The grant of a lease of a dwelling is exempt from charge if the lease:

(a) is granted by a registered social landlord to one or more individuals, and

(b) is for an indefinite term or is terminable by notice of a month or less.

This exemption applies to arrangements between a registered social landlord and a housing authority under which the landlord provides, for individuals nominated by the authority in pursuance of its statutory housing functions, temporary rented accommodation which the landlord itself has obtained for a term of five years or less.

A 'housing authority' means:

- in relation to England and Wales:

  a principal council within the meaning of the Local Government Act 1972 (c 70), or
  the Common Council of the City of London;

- in relation to Scotland, a council constituted under s. 2 of the Local Government etc (Scotland) Act 1994 (c 39),
- in relation to Northern Ireland:

  the Department for Social Development in Northern Ireland, or
  the Northern Ireland Housing Executive.

Transactions in connection with divorce, etc.

A transaction between one party to a marriage and the other is exempt from charge if it is effected:

- in pursuance of an order of a court made on granting a decree of divorce, nullity of marriage or judicial separation;
- in pursuance of an order of a court made in connection with the dissolution or annulment of the marriage, or the parties' judicial separation, at any time after the granting of such a decree;
- in pursuance of:

  an order of a court made at any time under s. 22A, 23A or 24A, Matrimonial Causes Act 1973, or
  an incidental order of a court made under s. 8(2), Family Law (Scotland) Act 1985 by virtue of s. 14(1) of that Act,

- at any time in pursuance of an agreement of the parties made in contemplation or otherwise in connection with the dissolution or annulment of the marriage, their judicial separation or the making of a separation order in respect of them.

Variation of testamentary dispositions, etc.

A transaction following a person's death that varies a disposition (whether effected by will, under the law relating to intestacy or otherwise) of property of which the deceased was competent to dispose is exempt from charge if the following conditions are met:

(a) the transaction must be carried out within the period of two years after a person's death, and

(b) no consideration in money or money's worth other than the making of a variation of another such disposition must be given for it.

This exemption applies whether or not the administration of the estate is complete or the property has been distributed in accordance with the original dispositions.

This provision is drawn in terms similar to the provisions of IHTA 1984, s.142 and facilitates the variation of a will after the death of the deceased in a tax-effective way.

10.6.2 Exemptions granted by the Stamp Duty Land Tax (Consequential Amendment of Enactments) Regulations 2003 (SI 2003/2867)

A land transaction effected by or in pursuance of an agreement made or confirmed or used under the following enactments is exempt from SDLT:

- Inclosure Act 1845, s. 163A;
- Metropolitan Commons Act 1866, s. 33;
- Chequers Estate Act 1917, s. 3A;
- Chevening Estate Act 1959, s. 2A,
- Friendly Societies Act 1974, s. 105A.

10.6.3 Other statutory exemptions

A land transaction under which the purchaser is any of the following is exempt from SDLT (s. 107, FA 2003):

Government

- A Minister of the Crown
- The Scottish Ministers
- A Northern Ireland department

Parliament, etc.

- The Corporate Officer of the House of Lords
- The Corporate Officer of the House of Commons
- The Scottish Parliamentary Corporate Body
- The Northern Ireland Assembly Commission
- The National Assembly for Wales

The powers of entry with warrant to obtain information are not exercisable in relation to premises occupied for the purposes of the Crown.

10.7 Exempt but notifiable transactions

In the cases mentioned below, relief must be claimed in a land transaction return or an amendment of such a return.

10.7.1 Visiting forces and allied headquarters

A land transaction entered into with a view to building or enlarging barracks or camps for a force, or to facilitating the training in the UK of a force, or to promoting the health or efficiency of a force, is exempt from charge for the purposes of SDLT (FA 1960, s. 74A).

Various terms are defined for this purpose.

10.7.2 Welsh Development Agency

A land transaction by which property is transferred to the Agency is exempt from SDLT if immediately before the transfer the property was held:

- by or on behalf of the Crown, or
- by a company all of whose shares are held by or on behalf of the Crown or by a wholly owned subsidiary of such a company,

(Welsh Development Act 1975, Sch. 1, Para. 20A).

10.7.3 National Health Service (Scotland)

A land transaction effected by virtue of an order under National Health Service (Scotland) Act 1978, s. 12D(1) is exempt from SDLT (s. 12DA).

A land transaction effected by a conveyance, agreement or assignation made, or an instrument executed, solely for the purpose of giving effect to any transfer of property, rights or liabilities held upon trust under s. 82 of the above Act is exempt from SDLT (s. 104A).

10.7.4   National Heritage

A land transaction:

- which is entered into under s. 9 of the above Act and by which property is transferred to any such institution or body mentioned in subsection (2) of that section, or
- which is entered into under subsection (4) of that section,

is exempt from SDLT (National Heritage Act 1980, s. 11A).

10.7.5   Industry Act 1980

A land transaction:

- by which property is transferred under Industry Act 1980, s. 2, and
- which is not exempt from charge by virtue of s. 66(1), FA 2003 (transfers between public bodies in consequence of reorganisation),

is exempt from SDLT (s. 2A).

10.7.6   Highways

A land transaction to which the Minister is a party is exempt from SDLT if:

- the transaction relates to a highway or proposed highway which is, or is to become, a trunk road, and
- but for this section stamp duty land tax would be payable in respect of the transaction as an expense incurred by the Minister under this Act,

(Highways Act 1980, s. 281A).

10.7.7   Airports

A land transaction which:

- is effected by or in pursuance of a scheme under s. 15, or
- is entered into in pursuance of Transport Act 1968, Sch. 4 as it applies in relation to any such scheme by virtue of s. 75(3),

is exempt from charge for the purposes of stamp duty land tax (Airports Act 1986, s. 76A).

10.7.8 Building societies

A land transaction effected by or in consequence of:

- an amalgamation of two or more building societies under Building Societies Act 1986, s. 93, or
- a transfer of engagements between building societies under s. 94,

is exempt from SDLT (s. 109A).

10.7.9 Health service bodies

A land transaction is exempt from SDLT where the purchaser is one of the following bodies:

- a National Health Service trust established under Part 1 of this Act or under the National Health Service (Scotland) Act 1978;
- a Health and Social Services trust established under the Health and Personal Social Services (Northern Ireland) Order 1991;
- a Primary Care Trust, or
- a Local Health Board,

(National Health Service and Community Care Act 1990, s. 61A).

10.7.10 Ports

A land transaction effected under the Ports Act 1991 is exempt from SDLT (s. 36A).

10.7.11 Water resources

A land transaction by which property is vested in the Agency by virtue of an order or agreement under this schedule is exempt from SDLT (Water Resources Act 1991, Sch. 2, Para. 8(3)).

10.7.12 Further and higher education

A land transaction effected under or by virtue of ss. 25, 27, 32 or 34 of the Further and Higher Education Act 1992 is exempt from SDLT (s. 88).

10.7.13 Further and higher education (Scotland)

Any land transaction effected under or by virtue of any of the provisions of the Further and Higher Education (Scotland) Act 1992 is exempt from SDLT (s. 58A).

10.7.14   Friendly societies

A land transaction effected by or in consequence of:

- an amalgamation of two or more friendly societies under Friendly Societies Act 1992, s. 85;
- a transfer of the engagements of a friendly society under s. 86, or
- a transfer of the engagements of a friendly society pursuant to a direction given by the Authority under s. 90,

is exempt from SDLT (s. 105A).

10.7.15   Museums and galleries

A land transaction by which land occupied wholly or partly for the purposes of an institution specified in column 1 of Sch. 6 to the Museums and Galleries Act 1992 is transferred by the Secretary of State to the body specified in relation to that institution in column 2 of that schedule is exempt from SDLT (s. 8A).

10.7.16   Health authorities

A land transaction effected by virtue of Health Authorities Act 1995, Sch. 2, Para. 2 is exempt from SDLT.

10.7.17   Merchant shipping

Any land transaction entered into by or under the direction of any general lighthouse authority for the purposes of carrying on those services is exempt from SDLT (Merchant Shipping Act 1995, s. 221(2A)).

Any land transaction entered into by or under the direction of the Secretary of State for the purposes of carrying this part into effect is exempt from SDLT (s. 221(4A)).

10.7.18   Broadcasting

A land transaction that is effected by a restructuring scheme, or effected in accordance with, or in pursuance of an obligation imposed by a restructuring scheme is exempt from SDLT (Broadcasting Act 1996, Sch. 7, Para. 25).

10.7.19 Education

A land transaction effected by virtue of Education Act 1997, s. 30 is exempt from SDLT (s. 53A).

10.7.20 Regional Development Agencies

A land transaction effected by or in pursuance of a transfer scheme under the Regional Development Agencies Act 1998 is exempt from charge (s. 39A).

10.7.21 School standards and framework

A land transaction entered into by virtue of any of the provisions mentioned in School Standards and Framework Act 1998, s. 79(1) is exempt from SDLT.

10.7.22 Access to justice

A land transaction effected by or in pursuance of a scheme under Access to Justice Act 1999, Sch. 14, Para. 33 is exempt from SDLT (Para. 34A).

10.7.23 Criminal justice and court services

A land transaction effected by virtue of Criminal Justice and Court Services Act 2000, s. 19 under which the purchaser is the service, is exempt from SDLT.

10.7.24 Learning and skills

A land transaction effected by a scheme under Learning and Skills Act 2000, ss. 92 or 93 is exempt from SDLT (s. 94A).

10.7.25 Transport

A land transaction which is effected by, or in pursuance of a scheme under Transport Act 2000, Sch. 15, Para. 1, Sch. 17, Para. 31, or Para. 1 of Sch. 19, 21 or 25, is exempt from SDLT (Sch. 26, Para. 40A).

10.7.26 Communications

A land transaction effected by, or for the purposes of, or for purposes connected with, a transfer scheme under the Transport Act 2000 is exempt from SDLT (Sch. 2, Para. 5A).

10.8   Computation of SDLT liability

10.8.1   General rules

The amount of tax chargeable on a chargeable transaction is a percentage of the relevant consideration for the transaction. The percentages depend on whether the 'relevant land' is residential or commercial, and are as follows (FA 2003, s. 55(1), (2)):

Table A: Residential

Relevant consideration	Percentage
Not more than £60,000	0
More than £60,000 but not more than £250,000	1
More than £250,000 but not more than £500,000	3
More than £500,000	4

Table B: Non-residential or mixed

Relevant consideration	Percentage
Not more than £150,000	0
More than £150,000 but not more than £250,000	1
More than £250,000 but not more than £500,000	3
More than £500,000	4

The slab scale principle applies: that is to say that the percentage shown in the right-hand column applies to the whole of the consideration, not just to the excess over the threshold for that percentage. So if the consideration is say £275,000, then the SDLT is 3 per cent of £275,000 = £8,250.

The relevant consideration is the chargeable consideration for the transaction. However, if the transaction in question is one of a number of linked transactions:

- the relevant land is any land an interest in which is the main subject matter of any of those transactions, and
- the relevant consideration is the total of the chargeable consideration for all those transactions.

The chargeable consideration is the consideration in money or money's worth given for the subject matter of the transaction, directly or indirectly by the purchaser or a person connected with him (ICTA 1988, s. 839 definition) (FA 2003, Sch. 4, Para. 1).

The relevant land is the land an interest in which is the main subject matter of the transaction (s. 55(3)).

There are special rules for collective enfranchisement by leaseholders, and for the crofting community's right to buy (see below).

Where the whole or part of the chargeable consideration is rent, additional liability arises as explained below.

10.8.2 Chargeable consideration

Money or money's worth

The general rule is that chargeable consideration for a transaction is any consideration in money or money's worth given for the subject matter of the transaction, directly or indirectly, by the purchaser or a person connected with him.

VAT

The chargeable consideration for a transaction includes any VAT chargeable in respect of the transaction, other than VAT chargeable as a result of the 'vendor' opting for taxation after the effective date of the transaction (FA 2003, Sch. 4, Para. 2).

Postponed consideration

The amount or value of the chargeable consideration for a transaction is determined without any discount for deferred payment (Sch. 4, Para. 3).

Just and reasonable apportionment

A just and reasonable apportionment of the consideration is required where consideration is attributable:

- to two or more land transactions; or
- in part to a land transaction and in part to another matter, or
- in part to matters making it chargeable consideration and in part to other matters,

whether or not the consideration is actually apportioned by the parties to the transaction (Sch. 4, Para. 4).

Any consideration given for what is in substance one bargain is treated as attributable to all the elements of the bargain, even though:

- separate consideration is, or purports to be, given for different elements of the bargain, or

- there are, or purport to be, separate transactions in respect of different elements of the bargain,

(Sch. 4, Para. 4(3)). This gives the Revenue power to apportion the consideration on a just and reasonable basis where the apportionment agreed between the parties is artificial.

The Revenue has provided the following guidance on how the apportionment rules work in the case of a sale of land with associated construction, etc. contracts (Press Release 5 April 2004):

> 'We have been asked how to determine the chargeable consideration for Stamp Duty Land Tax purposes where V agrees to sell land to P and V also agrees to carry out work (commonly works of construction, improvement or repair) on the land sold. Our view is that the decision in *Prudential Assurance Co Ltd v IR Commrs* [1992] BTC 8,094 applies for the purposes of Stamp Duty Land Tax as it does for stamp duty. This is because the basis of the decision was the identification of the subject matter of the transaction and this is as relevant for Stamp Duty Land Tax as it is for stamp duty.
>
> It follows that SP8/93 will be applied for Stamp Duty Land Tax as it was for stamp duty. The paragraphs on "contracts already entered into" and "procedure for submitting documents" are, however, not relevant to Stamp Duty Land Tax.
>
> Where, however, the sale of land and the construction, &c, contract are in substance one bargain (as they were in the *Prudential* case) there must be a just and reasonable apportionment of the total consideration given for all elements of the bargain in order to arrive at the chargeable consideration for Stamp Duty Land Tax purposes.'

Exchanges

Where one or more land transactions are entered into by a person as purchaser (alone or jointly) wholly or partly in consideration of one or more other land transactions being entered into by him (alone or jointly) as vendor, a market value rule applies. The rule differs for transactions that involve major interests in land and those that do not (Sch. 4, Para. 5).

In a case involving a 'major interest', where a single relevant acquisition is made, the chargeable consideration for the acquisition is the market value of the subject matter of the acquisition. If the acquisition is the grant of a lease at a rent, the rent is included.

Where two or more relevant acquisitions are made, the chargeable consideration for each relevant acquisition is the market value of the subject matter of that acquisition. If the acquisition is the grant of a lease at a rent, the rent is included.

If major interests in land are not involved, then the market value of asset disposed of in exchange is effectively ignored. If two or more acquisitions are made, the chargeable element of the consideration is apportioned between them by reference to market values, in accordance with the following formula:

$$\frac{MV}{TMV}$$

where:

- *MV* is the market value of the subject matter of the acquisition for which the chargeable consideration is being determined, and
- *TMV* is the total market value of the subject matter of all the relevant acquisitions.

Partition, etc.: disregard of existing interest

In the case of a land transaction giving effect to a partition or division of a chargeable interest to which persons are jointly entitled, the share of the interest held by the purchaser immediately before the partition or division does not count as chargeable consideration (FA 2003, Sch. 4, Para. 6). In a simple partition, with no other consideration being given (eg by one party to another) no SDLT liability arises. Where consideration is given as between the parties, SDLT will be payable on that consideration.

Valuation of non-monetary consideration

The value of any chargeable consideration for a land transaction, other than money (whether in sterling or another currency), or debt (as defined below), is its market value at the effective date of the transaction (FA 2003, Sch. 4, Para. 7).

Debt as consideration

Where the chargeable consideration for a land transaction consists in whole or in part of the satisfaction or release of debt due to the purchaser or owed by the vendor, or the assumption of existing debt by the purchaser, the amount of debt satisfied, released or assumed is part of the chargeable consideration for the transaction (FA 2003, Sch. 4, Para. 8).

If the effect of this rule would be that the amount of the chargeable consideration for the transaction exceeded the market value of the subject matter of the transaction, the amount of the chargeable consideration is treated as limited to that value.

'Debt' means an obligation, whether certain or contingent, to pay a sum of money either immediately or at a future date.

'Existing debt', in relation to a transaction, means debt created or arising before the effective date of, and otherwise than in connection with, the transaction.

References to the amount of a debt are to the principal amount payable plus any interest that has accrued due on or before the effective date of the transaction.

Consideration in foreign currency

Currency is translated into sterling at the London closing exchange rate on the effective date of the transaction unless the parties have used a different rate for the purposes of the transaction (FA 2003, Sch. 4, Para. 9).

Carrying out of works

Where the whole or part of the consideration for a land transaction consists of the carrying out of works of construction, improvement or repair of a building or other works to enhance the value of land, the value of the works is taken into account as chargeable consideration (FA 2003, Sch. 4, Para. 10).

However, the value of works is not taken into account if the following conditions are satisfied:

(a)   the works must be carried out after the effective date of the transaction;

(b)   the works must be carried out on land acquired or to be acquired under the transaction or on other land held by the purchaser or a person connected with him, and

(c)   it is not a condition of the transaction that the works are carried out by the vendor or a person connected with him.

The reference in (b) to 'land acquired' is to the acquisition of a major interest in the land.

The value of the works is the amount that would have to be paid in the open market for the carrying out of the works in question.

Provision of services

Where the whole or part of the consideration for a land transaction consists of the provision of services (other than the carrying out of works referred to in the preceding paragraph), the market value of the services is taken into account as chargeable consideration (FA 2003, Sch. 4, Para. 11).

Land transaction entered into by reason of employment

Where a land transaction is entered into by reason of the purchaser's employment, or that of a person connected with him, and it gives rise to a taxable fringe benefit, then the cash equivalent chargeable under the fringe benefit legislation is treated as rent.

However, in the case of representative accommodation, the consideration for the transaction is the actual consideration (if any).

If neither of the above rules apply, the consideration for the transaction is taken to be not less than the market value of the subject matter of the transaction as at the effective date of the transaction (FA 2003, Sch. 4, Para. 12).

Indemnity given by purchaser

Where the purchaser agrees to indemnify the vendor in respect of liability to a third party arising from breach of an obligation owed by the vendor in relation to the land that is the subject of the transaction, neither the agreement nor any payment made in pursuance of it counts as chargeable consideration (FA 2003, Sch. 4, Para. 16).

Major interest

In England and Wales, a major interest is a fee simple (freehold) or a term of years absolute (lease). In Scotland, it is the interest of the owner of the land or the tenant's right over, or interest in, a property subject to a lease. In Northern Ireland it is a freehold or leasehold estate, whether subsisting at law or in equity (FA 2003, s. 117).

Connected persons

The ICTA 1988, s. 839 definition of connected persons applies.

10.8.3   Rules applicable to lease rents

Introduction

SDLT is chargeable so much of the chargeable consideration for the grant of a lease or sub-lease consists of rent (FA 2003, Sch. 5, Para. 1). The amount of tax is a percentage of the net present value of the rent payable over the term of the lease. The percentages are as follows.

Table A: Residential land

Relevant rental value	Percentage
Not more than £60,000	0
More than £60,000	1

Table B: Non-residential or mixed use land

Relevant rental value	Percentage
Not more than £150,000	0
More than £150,000	1

The relevant rental value is the net present value of the rent payable over the term of the lease (FA 2003, Sch. 5, Para. 2). However the slice scale principle applies, so that if the NPV exceeds the 0 per cent threshold, SDLT is charged only on the excess. Thus, in the case of a commercial lease, if the NPV is £500,000, then the SDLT is 1% × (£500,000 − £150,000) = £3,500.

However, if the lease in question is one of a number of linked transactions for which the chargeable consideration consists of or includes rent, the relevant rental value is the total of the net present values of the rent payable over the terms of those leases. This total liability is then apportioned between the leases concerned in proportion to the net present values of those leases, as follows:

First, calculate the amount of the tax that would be chargeable if the linked transactions were a single transaction, so that:

- the relevant rental value is the total of the net present values of the rent payable over the terms of all the leases, and
- the relevant land is all land that is the subject of any of those leases.

Then, multiply that amount by the fraction:

$$\frac{NPV}{TNPV}$$

where:

NPV is the net present value of the rent payable over the term of the lease in question, and

TNPV is the total of the net present values of the rent payable over the terms of the all the leases.

Net present value

The net present value (v) of the rent payable over the term of a lease is calculated by applying the formula:

where–

r is the rent payable in year i;

i is the first, second, third, etc. year of the term;

n is the term of the lease, and

T is the temporal discount rate,

(FA 2003, Sch. 5, Para. 3).

However, all rent changes taking effect more than five years after the start of the lease are ignored for the purposes of the NPV calculation.

The Revenue's website contains a calculator for working out NPVs. This can be accessed from the Stamp Taxes website, which is at www.inlandrevenue. gov/so/index.htm

Temporal discount rate

In the NPV formula set out above, the 'temporal discount rate' is 3.5 per cent or such other rate as may be specified by regulations made by the Treasury (FA 2003, Sch. 5, Para. 8).

Liability where premium and other consideration is payable

Where a lease is granted and the consideration includes a premium or other consideration as well as rent, SDLT is chargeable on that consideration in relation to the other chargeable consideration. The tax chargeable in respect of the rents is in addition to any tax chargeable in respect of the other consideration (FA 2003, Sch. 5, Para. 9).

If there is other consideration and the annual rent exceeds £600 a year, the 0 per cent band in the tables set out above does not apply and any case that would have fallen within that band is treated as falling within the 1 per cent band.

The 'annual rent' means the average annual rent over the term of the lease. If different amounts of rent are payable for different parts of the term, and those amounts (or any of them) are ascertainable at the effective date of the transaction, then the average annual rent over the period for which the highest ascertainable rent is payable is taken.

Variation of lease

Where a lease is varied so as to increase the amount of the rent, the variation is treated as if it were the grant of a lease in consideration of the additional rent made payable by it.

This rule does not apply to an increase of rent in pursuance of a provision already contained in the lease (FA 2003, Sch. 5, Para. 10).

Revenue guidance

The Revenue has provided the following guidance in SDLT Bulletin Issue 6.

'SDLT due on the rental element

SDLT is . . . . charged at a flat rate of 1% of the Net Present Value (NPV) of the rental stream over the term (period) of the lease. NPV depends on the term (period) of the lease and the amount of rent payable in the first five years.

To calculate the NPV, determine what the amount of rent payable for each of the first five years of the term (period) of the lease is. If this cannot be determined, for example, if it depends fully or to some extent on turnover, or some other unknown amount, you should make a reasonable estimate of what you expect the rent to be each year. Once you have determined what the rental payments in the first five years are (or are likely to be) you need to determine what the highest rent payable in any continuous twelve month period is (this will usually, but not always, be the highest annual rent payable). This amount should be used in the calculation for all years after the first five.

The tables *[set out below]* give factors to apply for all years from 1 to 99 for leases of up to 99 years. There are two columns: Individual year Factor and Cumulative Factor. The column called Individual year Factor should be used where the rent payable in the first five years varies, that is, the yearly rent is not the same in the first five years of the lease.

The column called Cumulative Factor should be used where the rent does not vary in the first five years, that is, the same amount of rent is payable for each of the first five years of the lease.

How to use the column called Individual year Factor

1) Determine the rental payable for each of the first five years:-

    i)   Apply year one factor (0.966183575) to the rent for year one. So, for example, if the rent payable in year one was £20,000 the figure to use would be £20,000 × 0.966183575 = £19323.71;

ii) Apply year two factor (0.9335107) to the rent for year two. So for example, if the rent payable in year two was £25,000 the figures to use would be £25,000 × 0.9335107 = £23,337.76

iii) Continue similarly until year six is reached.

2) For years six onwards only one calculation is needed:-

i) The rent used for year six should be the highest rent payable in any continuous twelve month period in the first five years. This will normally (but not always) be the highest rent payable in any of the first five years. This rent applies for all subsequent years. The factor to apply to this rent depends on the term (period) of the lease. If you have a six year lease, apply the factor for year six (0.81350064) to the rent used for year six. So, for example, if the rent used for year six was £32,500, the figure to use would be £32,500 × 0.81350064 = £26,438.77. If you have a twenty year lease, apply the factor for year twenty (9.69735093) to the rent used for year six. So, for example. If the rent used for year six was £32,500, the figure to use would be £315,163.90.

3) Calculate the NPV

i) Add together the figures obtained for years one to five (five figures) and the figure obtained for year six onwards. This will be a maximum of six figures to add together. This total is the NPV of the rent.

4) Calculate the SDLT due on the NPV

i) If the NPV (calculated at step (3) above) is greater than the relevant threshold (£60,000 for residential leases and £150,000 for commercial and mixed use leases), SDLT is due at 1% of the excess of the NPV above the relevant threshold. For example, if a residential lease has an NPV of £72,500 (the residential threshold being £60,000) tax would be due on £72,500 − £60,000 = £15,000 × 1% = £150.

How to use the column called Cumulative Factor

This column should only be used where the rent doesn't vary during the first five years, that is, it is the same amount for each of the first five years of the lease.

1) Use the factor for the term (period) of the lease with the rent payable in year one. For example, if you have a six year lease, the factor is 5.32855302. The NPV of a lease paying a rent of £30,000 for six years is, therefore, £159,856. If the lease was for twenty years, the factor is 14.21240330 and the NPV is £426,372.

EXAMPLES

1) *A residential lease for 99 years with a premium of £50,000 and an annual rent of £200 for the first 25 years, £400 for the next 25 years and £800 thereafter.*

A) The average annual rent is £547 and so the premium thresholds aren't affected. The premium is below the residential threshold and so no SDLT is due on the premium

B) As the rent doesn't change in the first five years, use the cumulative table. The factor for 99 years is 27.62336529 and the rent to be used for year six is £200. The NPV is, therefore, £5,524. As this is below the residential threshold, no SDLT is due on the rental element.

C) The total SDLT due is nil. However, a land transaction return is still required as the term of the lease is for seven years or more.

2) *A residential lease for 25 years with a premium of £50,000 and an annual rent of £1,000 reviewable after five years*

A) The average annual rent is £1,000 (which is more than £600) and so the premium threshold becomes £0. SDLT is due on the premium at a rate of 1% (as the premium is not more than £250,000). The SDLT due is £500.

B) As the rent doesn't change in the first five years, use the cumulative table. The factor for 25 years is 16.48151459 and the rent to be used for year six is £1,000. The NPV is, therefore, £16,481. As this is below the residential threshold, no SDLT is due on the rental element.

C) The total SDLT due is £500. This should be included on a land transaction return.

3) *A commercial lease for 20 years with a premium of £50,000 and an annual rent of 10% of turnover. There is no minimum rent. Rent payable in the first five years is estimated to be £100,000 each year.*

A) The average annual rent is £0 (as there is no ascertainable rent) and so the premium thresholds aren't affected. The premium is below the commercial threshold and so no SDLT is due on the premium

B) As the rent doesn't change in the first five years, use the cumulative table. The factor for 20 years is 14.2124033 and the rent to be used for year six is £100,000. The NPV is, therefore, £1,421,240. This is above the commercial threshold and SDLT is due on the excess of (£1,421,240 − £150,000 = £1,271,240) at 1%, that is SDLT of £12,712.40 is due

C) The total SDLT due is £12,712.40 (rounded down to £12,712). This should be included on a land transaction return.

4) *A commercial lease for 35 years with a premium of £125,000 and an annual rent based on 10% of turnover or £38,000, whichever is the greater. Rent payable in the first five years is estimated to be £38,000 for years one and two £40,000 for year three and £45,000 for years four and five.*

A) The average annual rent is £38,000 (as this is the ascertainable rent) and so the premium threshold becomes £0. SDLT is due on the premium at a rate of 1 per cent (as the premium is not more than £250,000). The SDLT due is £1,250

B) As the rent changes in the first five years, use the Individual year table. The factor for year one is 0.96618357 and the NPV for this year is £38,000 × 0.96618357 = £36,714.97. The factor for year two is 0.9335107 and the NPV for this year is £38,000 × 0.9335107 =

£35,473.40. The factor for year three is 0.90194271 and the NPV for this year is £40,000 × 0.90194271 = £36,077.70. The factor for year four is 0.87144223 and the NPV for this year is £45,000 × 0.87144223 = £39,214.90. The factor for year five is 0.84197317 and the NPV for this year is £45,000 × 0.84197317 = £37,888.79. The highest rent payable in any twelve month period is £45,000 and this is used as the rent for year six onwards. The factor for a thirty-five year lease is 15.48560872 and the NPV for the balance of the term of the lease is £45,000 × 15.48560872 = £696,852.39. The total NPV is, therefore, £36,714.97 + £35,473.40 + £36,077.70 + £39,214,.90 + £37,888.79 + £696,852.39 = £882222.15. This is above the commercial threshold and SDLT is due on the excess of (£882,222 − £150,000 = £732,222) at 1%, that is SDLT of £7,322.22 is due

C) The total SDLT due is £1,250.00 + £7,322.22 = £8,572.22 (rounded down to £8,572). This should be included on a land transaction return.'

Tables of Individual year Factors and Cumulative Factors

Year	Individual year Factor	Cumulative Factor
1	0.96618357	0.96618357
2	0.93351070	1.89969428
3	0.90194271	2.80163698
4	0.87144223	3.67307921
5	0.84197317	4.51505238
6	0.81350064	5.32855302
7	1.59949160	6.11454398
8	2.35890316	6.87395554
9	3.09263413	7.60768651
10	3.80155295	8.31660532
11	4.48649866	9.00155104
12	5.14828196	9.66333433
13	5.78768611	10.30273849
14	6.40546790	10.92052028
15	7.00235852	11.51741090
16	7.57906443	12.09411681
17	8.13626821	12.65132059
18	8.67462935	13.18968173
19	9.19478504	13.70983742

Year	Individual year Factor	Cumulative Factor
20	9.69735093	14.21240330
21	10.18292183	14.69797420
22	10.65207246	15.16712484
23	11.10535809	15.62041047
24	11.54331523	16.05836760
25	11.96646222	16.48151459
26	12.37529989	16.89035226
27	12.77031213	17.28536451
28	13.15196647	17.66701885
29	13.52071463	18.03576700
30	13.87699304	18.39204541
31	14.22122338	18.73627576
32	14.55381309	19.06886547
33	14.87515581	19.39020818
34	15.18563186	19.70068423
35	15.48560872	20.00066110
36	15.77544144	20.29049381
37	16.05547305	20.57052542
38	16.32603499	20.84108736
39	16.58744749	21.10249987
40	16.84001996	21.35507234
41	17.08405133	21.59910371
42	17.31983043	21.83488281
43	17.54763633	22.06268870
44	17.76773864	22.28279102
45	17.98039788	22.49545026
46	18.18586575	22.70091813
47	18.38438543	22.89943780
48	18.57619188	23.09124425
49	18.76151212	23.27656450
50	18.94056550	23.45561787
51	19.11356392	23.62861630

Year	Individual year Factor	Cumulative Factor
52	19.28071217	23.79576454
53	19.44220805	23.95726043
54	19.59824272	24.11329510
55	19.74900086	24.26405323
56	19.89466089	24.40971327
57	20.03539523	24.55044760
58	20.17137043	24.68642281
59	20.30274744	24.81779981
60	20.42968174	24.94473412
61	20.55232358	25.06737596
62	20.67081812	25.18587049
63	20.78530559	25.30035796
64	20.89592150	25.41097388
65	21.00279678	25.51784916
66	21.10605792	25.62111030
67	21.20582714	25.72087951
68	21.30222252	25.81727489
69	21.39535815	25.91041052
70	21.48534427	26.00039664
71	21.57228738	26.08733975
72	21.65629038	26.17134275
73	21.73745270	26.25250508
74	21.81587040	26.33092278
75	21.89163630	26.40668868
76	21.96484006	26.47989244
77	22.03556834	26.55062072
78	22.10390484	26.61895721
79	22.16993044	26.68498281
80	22.23372329	26.74877567
81	22.29535890	26.81041127
82	22.35491021	26.86996258
83	22.41244770	26.92750008

Year	Individual year Factor	Cumulative Factor
84	22.46803949	26.98309186
85	22.52175136	27.03680373
86	22.57364688	27.08869926
87	22.62378749	27.13993986
88	22.67223252	27.18728489
89	22.71903931	27.23409168
90	22.76426326	27.27931564
91	22.80795790	27.32301028
92	22.85017494	27.36522732
93	22.89096436	27.40601673
94	22.93037442	27.44542680
95	22.96845178	27.48350415
96	23.00524149	27.52029387
97	23.04078711	27.55583948
98	23.07513070	27.59018308
99	23.10831292	27.62336529

10.8.4   Leases: further provisions

Meaning of 'lease'

In relation to England and Wales or Northern Ireland 'lease' means:

- an interest or right in or over land for a term of years (whether fixed or periodic), or
- a tenancy at will or other interest or right in or over land terminable by notice at any time,

(FA 2003, Sch. 17A, Para. 1).

Leases for a fixed term

In the case of a lease for a fixed term, no account is taken of:

- any contingency as a result of which the lease may determine before the end of the fixed term, or
- any right of either party to determine the lease or renew it,

(FA 2003, Sch. 17A, Para. 2).

Leases that continue after a fixed term

If a lease is for a fixed term and thereafter until determined, or for a fixed term that may continue beyond the fixed term by operation of law, it is treated in the first instance as if it were a lease for the original fixed term and no longer. A return should be made, and the tax calculated on that basis (FA 2003, Sch. 17A, Para. 3).

If the lease continues after the end of that term, it is treated as a lease for a fixed term one year longer than the original fixed term.

If the lease continues after the end of that extended term, it is treated as a lease for a fixed term two years longer than the original fixed term, and so on.

The effect of the above rules is that a transaction that was not notifiable at the outset may become notifiable, or that additional tax may be payable in respect of a transaction, or that tax is payable in respect of a transaction where none was payable before. In this case, the purchaser must deliver a return or further return in respect of that transaction within 30 days after the end of that term, and must pay any tax, or additional tax, at the same time.

Treatment of leases for indefinite term

A lease for an indefinite term is treated in the first instance as if it were a lease for a fixed term of one year. If it continues after the end of that one-year period, it is treated as if it were a lease for a fixed term of two years, and so on (FA 2003, Sch. 17A, Para. 4). No account is taken of any other statutory provision in England and Wales or Northern Ireland deeming a lease for an indefinite period to be a lease for a different term.

The effect of the above rules is that a transaction that was not notifiable at the outset may become notifiable, or that additional tax may be payable in respect of a transaction, or that tax is payable in respect of a transaction where none was payable before. In this case, the purchaser must deliver a return or further return in respect of that transaction within 30 days after the end of that term, and must pay any tax, or additional tax, at the same time.

A lease for an indefinite period includes:

- a periodic tenancy or other interest or right terminable by a period of notice;
- a tenancy at will in England and Wales or Northern Ireland, or
- any other interest or right terminable by notice at any time.

Treatment of successive linked leases

If successive leases are granted or treated as granted (whether at the same time or at different times) of the same or substantially the same premises, and those grants are linked transactions, the series of leases is treated as a single lease:

- granted at the time of the grant of the first lease in the series;
- for a term equal to the aggregate of the terms of all the leases, and
- in consideration of the rent payable under all of the leases.

Further returns may be required in respect of the second and any subsequent lease (FA 2003, Sch. 17A, Para. 5).

Rent

A single sum expressed to be payable in respect of rent, or expressed to be payable in respect of rent and other matters but not apportioned, is treated as entirely rent. This is without prejudice to the rules requiring just and reasonable apportionment of consideration where separate sums are expressed to be payable in respect of rent and other matters (FA 2003, Sch. 17A, Para. 6).

Variable or uncertain rent

The following rules apply to determine the amount of rent payable under a lease where that amount varies in accordance with provision in the lease, or is contingent, uncertain or unascertained (FA 2003, Sch. 17A, Para. 7).

As regards rent payable in respect of any period before the end of the fifth year of the term of the lease the normal rules for uncertain or contingent consideration apply.

As regards rent payable in respect of any period after the end of the fifth year of the term of the lease, the annual amount is assumed to be, in every case, equal to the highest amount of rent payable in respect of any consecutive 12-month period in the first five years of the term.

No account is taken of any provision for rent to be adjusted in line with the retail price index.

Where the above rules apply and the end of the fifth year of the term of the lease is reached, or the amount of rent payable in respect of the first five years of the term of the lease ceases to be uncertain at an earlier date, the SDLT liability on the lease rents has to be recomputed (FA 2003, Sch. 17A, Para. 8).

If the result is that a transaction becomes notifiable, or that additional tax is payable in respect of a transaction or that tax is payable where none was payable before, the purchaser must make a return to the Revenue and pay the tax, or additional tax. The time limit is 30 days from the earlier of:

- the end of the fifth year, and
- the date when the rent ceases to be uncertain.

If the result is that less tax is payable in respect of the transaction than has already been paid, the purchaser may claim repayment of the amount overpaid together with interest as from the date of payment.

Rent for overlap period in case of grant of further lease

Where:

- A surrenders an existing lease to B ('the old lease') and in consideration of that surrender B grants a lease to A of the same or substantially the same premises ('the new lease'), or
- the tenant under a lease ('the old lease') of premises to which Part 2 of the Landlord and Tenant Act 1954 or the Business Tenancies (Northern Ireland) Order 1996 applies makes a request for a new tenancy ('the new lease') which is duly executed,

the rent payable under the new lease in respect of any period falling within the overlap period is treated as reduced by the amount of the rent that would have been payable in respect of that period under the old lease (FA 2003, Sch. 17A, Para. 9).

The overlap period is the period between the date of grant of the new lease and what would have been the end of the term of the old lease had it not been terminated.

The rent that would have been payable under the old lease is the amount taken into account in determining the tax chargeable in respect of the acquisition of the old lease.

The above rule does not have effect so as to require the rent payable under the new lease to be treated as a negative amount.

Tenants' obligations, etc. that do not count as chargeable consideration

In the case of the grant of a lease none of the following counts as chargeable consideration:

- any undertaking by the tenant to repair, maintain or insure the demised premises (in Scotland, the leased premises);
- any undertaking by the tenant to pay any amount in respect of services, repairs, maintenance or insurance or the landlord's costs of management;

- any other obligation undertaken by the tenant that is not such as to affect the rent that a tenant would be prepared to pay in the open market;
- any guarantee of the payment of rent or the performance of any other obligation of the tenant under the lease,
- any penal rent, or increased rent in the nature of a penal rent, payable in respect of the breach of any obligation of the tenant under the lease,

(FA 2003, Sch. 17A, Para. 10).

A payment made in discharge of any of the above obligations does not count as chargeable consideration.

The release of any such obligation does not count as chargeable consideration in relation to the surrender of the lease.

Assignment of lease treated as grant of lease: claw back of earlier relief

If the grant of a lease ('the original lease') is exempt from charge by virtue of any of the provisions specified below, the first assignment of the lease that is not exempt from charge by virtue of any of those provisions is treated as if it were the grant of a lease by the assignor. Thus any relief given is effectively clawed back, wholly or partly, on the first assignment (FA 2003, Sch. 17A, Para. 11).

The provisions are:

- sale and leaseback arrangements;
- group relief or reconstruction or acquisition relief;
- transfers involving public bodies;
- charities relief,
- regulations providing for exemption from stamp duty.

The grant is treated as being for a term equal to the unexpired term of the original lease, and on the same terms as those on which the assignee holds that lease after the assignment.

This charge does not arise where the relief in question is group relief, reconstruction or acquisition relief, or charities relief and is withdrawn as a result of a disqualifying event (eg a degrouping event) occurring before the effective date of the assignment.

Assignment of lease: responsibility of assignee for returns, etc.

Where a lease is assigned, the assignee is responsible for making any further returns and paying any further tax resulting from:

- an adjustment where a contingency ceases or consideration is ascertained;
- a later linked transaction;

- a lease for an indefinite period continuing, or
- an adjustment where rent ceases to be uncertain,

(FA 2003, Sch. 17A, Para. 12).

Anything previously done by or in relation to the assignor is treated as if it had been done by or in relation to the assignee.

This provision does not apply if the assignment falls to be treated as the grant of a lease by the assignor under the claw-back rules discussed above.

Increase of rent treated as grant of new lease: variation of lease

Where a lease is varied so as to increase the amount of the rent, the variation is treated for as if it were the grant of a lease in consideration of the additional rent made payable by it except where it occurs in pursuance of a provision contained in the lease (FA 2003, Sch. 17A, Para. 13).

Increase of rent treated as grant of new lease: abnormal increase after fifth year

If, after the end of the fifth year of the term of a lease:

- the amount of rent payable increases (or is increased) in accordance with the provisions of the lease, and
- the rent payable as a result ('the new rent') is such that the increase is 'abnormal',

then the increase in rent is treated as if it were the grant of a lease in consideration of the 'excess rent' (FA 2003, Sch. 17A, Para. 14).

The excess rent is the difference between the new rent and the rent previously taxed.

The rent previously taxed is the rent that is assumed to be payable after the fifth year of the term of the lease. However, where this rule has previously been applied, the rent previously taxed is the rent payable as a result of the last such increase.

The deemed grant is treated as being made on the date on which the increased rent first became payable, for a term equal to the unexpired part of the original lease. It is also treated as linked with the grant of the original lease (and with any other transaction with which that transaction is linked).

Whether an increase in rent is to be regarded as abnormal is determined as follows (FA 2003, Sch. 17A, Para. 15):

'*Step one*

Find the start date, which is the beginning of the period by reference to which the rent assumed to be payable after the fifth year of the term of the lease is determined. However, where the above rules have previously been applied, the start date is the date of the last increase in relation to which the provisions of that paragraph applied.

Step two

Divide the period between the start date and the date on which the new rent first becomes payable ('the reference period') into:

(a) successive periods of twelve months running from the start date (if any); and
(b) any remaining period which does not fall within paragraph (a).

Step three

Find the factor by which the retail prices index has increased over each period identified in step two.

This is a figure expressed as a decimal and determined by the formula:

(RD – RI)/RI

where:

RD is the retail prices index for the month in which the last day of the period in question falls; and

RI is the retail prices index for the month in which the first day of the period in question falls.

If, in relation to any period, *RD* is equal to or less than *RI*, the increase in the retail prices index over the period in question is nil.

If, in relation to any period, the figure determined in accordance with the formula, would be a figure having more than three decimal paces, round it to the nearest third decimal place.

Step four

Find the relevant factor for each period identified in step two.

This is a figure expressed as a decimal and determined by the formula:

where:

m is the number of months in the period in question (treating part of a month as a whole month); and *r* is the increase in the retail price index over the period in question, determined under step four.

If, in relation to any period, the figure determined in accordance with the formula would have more than three decimal places, round it to the nearest third decimal place.

Step five

Find the uplift factor for the reference period as follows.

If there is only one period identified in step two, the uplift factor for the reference period is the relevant factor for that period.

If there are only two periods identified in step two, the uplift factor for the reference period is calculated by multiplying the relevant factors for those periods.

If there are more than two periods identified in step two, the uplift factor for the reference period is calculated by:

(a) multiplying the relevant factors for the first two periods;
(b) multiplying the result by the relevant factor for the next period;
(c) if there are further periods, multiplying the result by the relevant factor for the next period;

until all periods have been taken into account.

Step six

The rent increase is regarded as abnormal if the new rent is greater than:

$R \times UF$

where:

R is the rent previously taxed, and

UF is the uplift factor for the reference period.'

Surrender of existing lease in return for new lease

Where a lease is granted in consideration of the surrender of an existing lease between the same parties:

- the grant of the new lease does not count as chargeable consideration for the surrender, and
- the surrender does not count as chargeable consideration for the grant of the new lease,

(FA 2003, Sch. 17A, Para. 16).

Assignment of lease: assumption of obligations by assignee

In the case of an assignment of a lease the assumption by the assignee of the obligation to pay rent, or to perform or observe any other undertaking of the tenant under the lease, does not count as chargeable consideration for the assignment (FA 2003, Sch. 17A, Para. 17).

Reverse premium

In the case of the grant, assignment or surrender of a lease a reverse premium does not count as chargeable consideration (FA 2003, Sch. 17A, Para. 18).

A 'reverse premium' means:

- in relation to the grant of a lease, a premium moving from the landlord to the tenant;
- in relation to the assignment of a lease, a premium moving from the assignor to the assignee,
- in relation to the surrender of a lease, a premium moving from the tenant to the landlord.

Provisions relating to leases in Scotland

In relation to Scotland:

- any reference to the term of a lease is to the period of the lease, and
- any reference to the reversion on a lease is to the interest of the landlord in the property subject to the lease,

(FA 2003, Sch. 17A, Para. 19).

Where tax has been paid in respect of a land transaction ('the first transaction') that involves missives of let in Scotland that constitute a lease, and subsequent to those missives of let a lease is granted ('the second transaction') which either:

- is in conformity with the missives of let, or
- relates to substantially the same property and period as the missives of let,

the tax that would otherwise be charged in respect of the second transaction is reduced by the amount of tax paid in respect of the first transaction in respect of the missives of let.

10.8.5 Contingent, uncertain or unascertained consideration

Where the whole or part of the chargeable consideration for a transaction is contingent, the amount or value of the consideration is determined in the first instance on the assumption that the consideration is payable or, as the case may be, does not cease to be payable (FA 2003, s. 51).

Where the whole or part of the chargeable consideration for a transaction is uncertain or unascertained, its amount or value is determined in the first instance on the basis of a reasonable estimate.

If:

- in the case of contingent consideration, the contingency occurs or it becomes clear that it will not occur, or
- in the case of uncertain or unascertained consideration, an amount relevant to the calculation of the consideration, or any instalment of consideration, becomes ascertained,

then the liability to SDLT has to be recomputed (FA 2003, s. 80).

If the effect of the new information is that:

- a transaction becomes notifiable or chargeable;
- additional tax is payable in respect of a transaction, or
- tax is payable where none was payable before,

then the purchaser must make a return or further return to the Revenue within 30 days and pay any additional tax due.

If the effect of the new information is that less tax is payable in respect of a transaction than has already been paid, the taxpayer may claim repayment of the mount overpaid.

'Contingent', in relation to consideration, means:

- that it is to be paid or provided only if some uncertain future event occurs, or
- that it is to cease to be paid or provided if some uncertain future event occurs.

'Uncertain', in relation to consideration, means that its amount or value depends on uncertain future events.

The above rules do not apply in relation to tax on lease rents.

10.8.6 Consideration consisting of annuities

Where the chargeable consideration for a land transaction consists of or includes an annuity payable:

- for life;
- in perpetuity;
- for an indefinite period, or
- for a definite period exceeding 12 years,

the consideration to be taken into account is limited to 12 years' annual payments (FA 2003, s. 52).

Where the amount payable varies, or may vary, from year to year, the 12 highest annual payments are taken.

No account is taken for the purposes of this schedule of any provision for adjustment of the amount payable in line with the retail price index.

The relevant annual payments are payments in respect of each successive period of 12 months beginning with the effective date of the transaction.

The rules relating to contingent, uncertain or unascertained consideration apply, but the adjustment where contingency ceases or consideration is ascertained does not apply and no application to defer payment may be made.

An 'annuity' includes any consideration (other than rent) that falls to be paid or provided periodically.

10.8.7   Connected company: market value rule

Where the purchaser is a company and:

- the vendor is connected with the purchaser, or
- some or all of the consideration for the transaction consists of the issue or transfer of shares in a company with which the vendor is connected,

the chargeable consideration for the transaction is deemed to be not less than the market value of the subject matter of the transaction as at the effective date of the transaction (FA 2003, s. 53). Market value is determined as for capital gains tax purposes (FA 2003, s. 118 applying TCGA 1992, ss. 272–274).

The exemption for transactions for which there is no chargeable consideration does not apply, but the benefit of any other relevant exemption is not denied.

Thus there continues to be a charge to tax where property is transferred to a company as part of the incorporation of a business, except in the case of a transfer to an LLP.

The market value rule does not apply in the following cases (FA 2003, s. 54).

'*Case 1:*

where immediately after the transaction the company holds the property as trustee in the course of a business carried on by it that consists of or includes the management of trusts.

Case 2:

where immediately after the transaction the company holds the property as trustee, and the vendor is connected with the company only because of being the settlor or person connected with the settlor (s. 839(3), ICTA 1988).

Case 3:

where the vendor is a company and the transaction is, or is part of, a distribution of the assets of that company (whether or not in connection with its winding up), provided that neither the subject matter of the transaction nor an interest from which that interest is derived has, within the period of three years immediately preceding the effective date of the transaction, been the subject of a transaction in respect of which group relief was claimed by the vendor.'

'Company' means any body corporate and 'shares' includes stock.

'The company' means the company that is the purchaser in relation to the transaction in question.

The ICTA 1988, s. 839 definition of connected persons applies.

Power to inspect premises

If the Board authorise a Revenue officer to inspect any property for the purpose of ascertaining its market value, the person having custody or possession of the property must permit the officer to inspect it at such reasonable times as the Board may consider necessary (FA 2003, s. 94).

A person who wilfully delays or obstructs a Revenue officer inspecting the property commits an offence and is liable on summary conviction to a fine not exceeding level 1 on the standard scale.

10.8.8   Residential and non-residential property

'Residential property' means:

(a)   a building that is used or suitable for use as a dwelling, or is in the process of being constructed or adapted for such use; and

(b) land that is or forms part of the garden or grounds of a building within (a) (including any building or structure on such land), or

(c) an interest in or right over land that subsists for the benefit of a building within (a) or of land within (b),

(FA 2003, s. 116).

'Non-residential property' means any property that is not residential property.

A building used for any of the following purposes is used as a dwelling:

* residential accommodation for school pupils;
* residential accommodation for students, other than a hall of residence for students in further or higher education;
* residential accommodation for members of the armed forces,
* an institution that is the sole or main residence of at least 90 per cent of its residents and does not fall within any of the exclusions set out below.

A building used for any of the following purposes is not used as a dwelling:

* a home or other institution providing residential accommodation for children;
* a hall of residence for students in further or higher education;
* a home or other institution providing residential accommodation with personal care for persons in need of personal care by reason of old age, disablement, past or present dependence on alcohol or drugs or past or present mental disorder;
* a hospital or hospice;
* a prison or similar establishment,
* a hotel or inn or similar establishment.

Where a building is used for an excluded purpose, no account is taken of its suitability for any other use.

Where a building that is not in use is suitable for use for at least one of the qualifying purposes and at least one of the excluded purposes:

* if there is one such use for which it is most suitable, or if the uses for which it is most suitable are either all qualifying or all excluded, no account shall be taken of its suitability for any other use,
* otherwise, the building is treated as suitable for use as a dwelling.

'Building' includes part of a building.

Where six or more separate dwellings are the subject of a single transaction involving the transfer of a major interest in, or the grant of a lease over, them, those dwellings are treated as not being residential property.

10.8.9   Private finance initiatives (PFIs)

Chargeable consideration

In determining the chargeable consideration for certain land transactions entered into in pursuance of a PFI project, the market value of the subject matter of:

- the transfer or lease of the transferred land;
- the lease or under-lease of the leased-back land, and
- any transfer or lease of surplus land,

is taken to be nil (FA 2003, Sch. 4, Para. 17).

Similarly, none of the following are regarded as rent:

- the carrying out of works, or the provision of services, and
- any consideration in money or money's worth given by the transferor for the carrying out of those works or the provision of those services.

Qualifying transactions

The above relief applies in any case where arrangements are entered into under which:

- a qualifying body ('A') transfers, or grants or assigns a lease of, any land ('the transferred land') to a non-qualifying body ('B');
- in consideration (whether in whole or in part) for that transfer, grant, or assignment, B grants A a lease or under-lease of the whole, or substantially the whole, of that land ('the leased-back land');
- B undertakes to carry out works or provide services to A, and
- some or all of the consideration given by A to B for the carrying out of those works or the provision of those services is consideration in money,

whether or not A also transfers, or grants or assigns a lease of, any other land ('surplus land') to B.

Qualifying bodies

The following are qualifying bodies:

- public bodies;
- institutions within the further education sector or the higher education sector within the meaning of Further and Higher Education Act 1992, s. 91;
- further education corporations within the meaning of s. 17 of that Act;
- higher education corporations within the meaning s. 90 of that Act;
- persons who undertake to establish and maintain, and carry on, or provide for the carrying on, of an Academy within the meaning of Education Act 1996, s. 482, and

- in Scotland, institutions funded by the Scottish Further Education Funding Council or the Scottish Higher Education Funding Council.

Application to Scotland

The above rules apply to Scotland as if:

- references to A transferring land to B were references to A transferring the interest of an owner of land to B, and
- 'assignment' means 'assignation'.

Until the appointed day for the purposes of the Abolition of Feudal Tenure etc. (Scotland) Act 2000, the reference to the interest of the owner is to be read, in relation to feudal property, as a reference to the estate or interest of the proprietor of the *dominium utile*.

10.9 Reliefs

10.9.1 Sale and leaseback

The leaseback element of a sale and leaseback arrangement is exempt from SDLT if:

- the property is not residential property;
- the consideration for the sale does not consist of or include anything other than the payment of money or the assumption, satisfaction or release of a debt, and
- the leaseback is of the same premises that were the subject of the sale,

(FA 2003, s. 57A).

Where the leaseback element of a sale and leaseback arrangement qualifies for relief under this rule (whether or not relief is claimed), the chargeable consideration for the sale is taken to be not less than the market value of the interest transferred (calculated as if it were not part of a sale and leaseback arrangement).

A 'sale and leaseback' arrangement means an arrangement under which:

- A transfers to B a major interest in land (the 'sale'), and
- out of that interest B grants a lease to A (the 'leaseback').

'Debt' means an obligation, whether certain or contingent, to pay a sum of money either immediately or at a future date; and 'money' means money in sterling or another currency.

10.9.2   Disadvantaged areas

Meaning of 'disadvantaged area'

A 'disadvantaged area' means an area designated as a disadvantaged area by the Stamp Duty (Disadvantaged Areas) (Application of Exemptions) Regulations 2003 (SI 2003/1056) as applied by FA 2003, Sch. 6, Para. 2. A comprehensive list is available on the Inland Revenue Stamp Taxes website, which is at www.inlandrevenue.gov.uk/so/index.htm The Revenue has issued the following Statement of Practice (SP 1/2003).

'**SP1/2003: Stamp duty: Disadvantaged Areas Relief**

This Statement of Practice is intended as guidance for those claiming exemption from stamp duty in respect of transfers of property situated in designated areas ("Disadvantaged Areas Relief") and explains how Inland Revenue Stamp Taxes will interpret the extension to the relief introduced with effect from 10 April 2003.

The relief is one of a number of measures set out in the Government's Urban White Paper *"Our Towns and Cities: The Future: Delivering an Urban Renaissance"* published in November 2000. The measure is designed to stimulate the physical, economic and social regeneration of the UK's most disadvantaged areas by attracting development and by encouraging the purchase of residential and commercial property by individuals and businesses. The areas eligible for relief were designated "Enterprise Areas" by the Chancellor in his 2002 Pre-Budget Report. In addition to the relief, a range of other Government policies designed to support enterprise and economic regeneration, including the Community Investment Tax Relief, will benefit these areas, helping to support the development of new and existing businesses.

Introduction

1. Disadvantaged Areas Relief (provided for by section 92 of, and Schedule 30 to, the Finance Act 2001) was introduced on 30 November 2001 and was initially only available for conveyances or transfers on sale (of both residential and commercial property) for which the consideration did not exceed £150,000. Stamp duty in respect of conveyances or transfers of commercial property in disadvantaged areas was abolished in consequence of the Stamp Duty (Disadvantaged Areas) (Application of Exemptions) Regulations 2003 ("the Regulations"), which have effect in relation to instruments executed on or after 10 April 2003. Thereafter the £150,000 limit applies only in relation to residential property.

2. Finance Act 2002 inserted the following provisions in Finance Act 2001 to distinguish residential from other property and to provide for differing stamp duty exemptions:

    –   Section 92A which enables stamp duty relief in designated disadvantaged areas in respect of all properties to be varied depending on whether or not the property is "residential";

    – Section 92B which defines "residential property" for the purposes of the relief. Non-residential property, in respect of which unlimited relief is available, is therefore defined in the Act by exclusion. The section also sets out particular building uses that are specifically included within, or specifically excluded from, the definition.

3. In most cases there will be no difficulty in practice in establishing whether or not a property is "residential". This statement sets out in more detail the Stamp Office's approach to borderline cases and gives guidance on the practical application of the legislation. The annexed flowchart provides a quick guide for simpler cases as to whether property constitutes "residential property".

Certification

4. Claims for unlimited relief must be accompanied by a certificate stating either that none of the land in question is residential property or, if part is residential, the proportion that is non-residential (together with the usual certificate of value for the remainder).

    – Residential property: Section 92A(4) of Finance Act 2001, together with the Regulations, provides that the exemption will only apply if the document is certified to the effect that the amount or value of the consideration does not exceed £150,000.

    – Non-residential property: Subsection (2) of section 92 of Finance Act 2001 provides that the exemption will only apply if the document is certified to the Commissioners as being an instrument on which stamp duty is not chargeable by virtue of subsection (1) of that section.

5. The following are suggested forms of words for particular certificates:

    – Residential Property: "I/We hereby certify that the transaction effected by this instrument does not form part of a larger transaction or series of transactions in respect of which the amount or value of the consideration exceeds £150,000 and that stamp duty is not chargeable thereon by virtue of the provisions of sections 92 and 92A of the Finance Act 2001."

    – Non-residential Property: "I/We hereby certify that this is an instrument in respect of non-residential property on which stamp duty is not chargeable by virtue of the provisions of section 92 of the Finance Act 2001."

    – Mixed Use Property: "I/We hereby certify that the transaction effected by this instrument is in respect of property part of which is residential property, and which does not form part of a larger transaction or series of transactions in respect of which the amount or value of the consideration relating to the residential part exceeds £150,000 so that stamp duty is not chargeable by virtue of sections 92 and 92A of the Finance Act 2001, and part of which is non-residential property on which stamp duty is not chargeable by virtue of the provisions of section 92 of the Finance Act 2001. The basis upon which the allocation between residential and non-residential parts has been made is as follows: . . ."

6. While the legislation does not specifically require the certificate to be included as part of the document, it is suggested that it should be so included. If the person submitting the document for stamping does not provide a certificate, either in the document or separately in writing, exemption will not be granted.

7. Appropriate contemporaneous evidence should be retained to support any certificate provided. Estate agents' specifications, site plans, planning applications or permissions, marketing material and photographs may all provide relevant information.

8. Anyone falsely certifying a document with a view to obtaining relief that is not due will be committing a stamp duty fraud.

The meaning of residential property

9. Section 92B defines "residential property" as a building which:

   - is used as a dwelling, **or**
   - is suitable for use as a dwelling, **or**
   - is in the process of being constructed or adapted for such use.

If a property meets any one of these separate tests it will be treated as residential property and be subject to the £150,000 limit for relief, as will any garden or grounds belonging to it or any interests or rights attaching to it. Each element of the definition is considered in turn below.

The question of whether and to what extent a building and grounds are defined as residential property for stamp duty purposes may also have implications for its treatment for capital gains tax and local authority rates.

Use as a dwelling

10. Where a building is in use at the date of execution of the relevant instrument, it will be a question of fact whether and to what extent it is used as a dwelling. Use at the date the instrument is executed overrides any past or intended future uses for this purpose.

11. Where the property in question is in use as a dwelling at the date of execution, it is residential property for the purposes of the relief unless it is part of a multiple transaction qualifying for relief under the Regulations (see paragraphs 35 to 39 below).

12. For the treatment of buildings put to both residential and non-residential use, see paragraphs 17 and 18 below.

Suitable for use as a dwelling

13. The suitability test applies to the state of the building at the time the instrument is executed, having regard to the facilities available and any history of use. For example, the Inland Revenue will not regard an office block as "suitable for use as a dwelling", but a house which has been used as an office without particular adaptation may well be so.

14. If a building is not in use at the date of execution but its last use was as a dwelling, it will be taken to be "suitable for use as a dwelling" and treated

as residential property for the purposes of the relief, unless evidence is produced to the contrary (see paragraph 15).

15. Whether a building is suitable for use as a dwelling will depend upon the precise facts and circumstances. The simple removal of, for example, a bathroom suite or kitchen facilities will not be regarded as rendering a building unsuitable for use as a dwelling. Where it is claimed that a previously residential property is no longer suitable for use as a dwelling, perhaps because it is derelict or has been substantially altered, the claimant will need to provide evidence that this is the case. See also paragraph 29.

16. Where a building has been used partly for residential purposes and partly for another purpose, its overall suitability for use as a dwelling will be judged from the facilities available at the date of execution of the relevant document. For example, if two rooms of a house were in use as a dentist's surgery and waiting room at the date of execution, the Inland Revenue would nevertheless normally consider this property suitable for use as a dwelling unless the claimant provided evidence to the contrary. In other words, the interaction of the Regulations with section 92B(1) enables a building that is used only partly as a dwelling to be nevertheless suitable for use wholly as a dwelling, with the effect that the £150,000 limit applies to the whole of the consideration. Where only a distinct part of the building is used and suitable for use as a dwelling, that part will be residential property for the purposes of the relief and the mixed use provisions will apply (paragraphs 17 and 18 below).

Mixed use

17. Where only part of a building (and land or interest relating to it) is "residential property" within section 92B(1), the consideration "shall be apportioned on such basis as is just and reasonable" between the residential and non-residential elements. The £150,000 limit is then applied only to the residential portion, in accordance with the appropriate certification (regulation 5 of the Regulations).

For example:

A property situated wholly within a disadvantaged area is bought for

a) £200,000
b) £400,000

50% of the property is "residential property" on the basis of a just and reasonable apportionment.

Relief is conferred by section 92 FA 2001, applied in conjunction with regulation 5 of the Regulations. Paragraph (3) of regulation 5 calls for an apportionment of the total consideration between residential and non-residential elements. Paragraph (4) confirms that relief applies to the residential property element only where the consideration attributed to it does not exceed £150,000. In these examples:

a) £100,000 is attributed to the residential property element, so relief is due. The part of the land that is not residential property is also exempt under the normal operation of section 92 FA 2001. So no duty is payable.

b) the £200,000 attributed to the residential property element is not exempt, because of regulation 5(4), but attracts duty at the rate of 1% (stamp duty payable £2,000). The non-residential property element is exempt as above.

18. The "just and reasonable" test is necessarily subjective, and each case will be considered on its merits. Apportionment might be on the basis of the percentage areas quoted in planning applications, where appropriate, or alternatively of floor space relating to the respective uses. Other methods of apportionment will be considered as part of a claim.

Specific cases

19. Some types of communal or institutional building are used neither as dwellings nor for commercial purposes. The legislation therefore outlines how these are classified for the purposes of relief, specifically including some such buildings within the definition of "dwelling" (section 92B(2)) and specifically excluding others (section 92B(3)). If they do not fall within any of the specific categories of section 92B(3), most residential institutions will come within section 92B(2)(d) and will be treated as dwellings by default.

20. Categories of building use specifically included within the definition of "use as a dwelling" (so that transfers of such buildings only qualify for relief if the consideration does not exceed £150,000) (section 92B(2)) are:

a) residential accommodation for school pupils, for example accommodation blocks in boarding schools;

b) residential accommodation for students, other than that within section 92B(3)(b). Student accommodation provided by private landlords is "a dwelling", as is accommodation leased to students by universities or colleges in flats or houses rather than in halls of residence (see section 92B(3)(b));

c) residential accommodation for members of any of the armed forces, including accommodation for their families (section 92B(2)(c));

d) an institution that is the sole or main residence of at least 90 per cent of its residents and does not fall within any of the categories referred to in section 92B(3) (see section 92B(2)(d) and also paragraph 21 below).

This would include, for example,

– sheltered accommodation for the elderly where no nursing or personal care is provided

– accommodation for religious communities (subject to the rules regarding mixed use; see paragraphs 17 and 18).

21. Categories of building use specifically excluded from the definition of "use as a dwelling" (so that transfers of such buildings in a disadvantaged area will qualify for unlimited relief) (section 92B(3)) are:

a) a home or other institution providing residential accommodation for children;

b) a hall of residence for students in further or higher education. This is not defined in the legislation but in practice property provided by a university or similar establishment will be judged on the facts (number of inhabitants, type of facilities, availability of communal areas);

c) a home or other institution providing residential accommodation with personal care for persons in need of personal care by reason of old age, disablement, past or present dependence on alcohol or drugs or past or present mental disorder;

d) a hospital or hospice;

e) a prison or similar establishment, or

f) a hotel or inn or similar establishment.

22. The specific inclusions and exclusions set out in paragraphs 20 and 21 above apply not only to a building's actual use at the date of the transfer, but to the uses for which it is suitable at that date. Where, however, a building is being put to one of the non-residential uses specified in section 92B(3), this overrides any suitability for another use (section 92B(4)). For example, a building used as a children's home may also be suitable for use as a school boarding house, but this will not preclude a claim to unlimited relief.

23. Where a vacant building is suitable for at least one of the uses specified in section 92B(2) and at least one specified in section 92B(3), the tiebreaker in section 92B(5) determines, for the purposes of the relief, the use for which it is "most suitable". Whether or not a vacant building has one or more uses for which it is most suitable is a question of fact. Evidence supporting such uses should be provided with the claim for relief.

24. Where there is a single use for which a building is most suitable, the fact that it is also suitable for another use will be discounted.

25. If there are a number of uses for which a building is most suitable and they all come within either of the two subsections, any other use for which the building is suitable will be discounted.

26. Where no most suitable use can be shown, the default will be to classify the building as residential property and apply the £150,000 limit.

27. Land and buildings that are not suitable for any use at the date of execution will be treated as residential property if they are "in the process of being constructed or adapted for such use" – see paragraphs 28 and 29 below.

Process of being constructed or adapted for use as a dwelling

28. Undeveloped land is in essence non-residential, but land may be "residential property" for the purposes of disadvantaged areas relief if a residential building is being built on it at the date the instrument is executed. The process of construction is taken as commencing when the builders first start work. A development of six or more dwellings is deemed to be non-residential under regulation 6 of the Regulations, even if in the process of construction at the date of the instrument (see paragraph 35 below).

29. Where (at the date the relevant instrument is executed) an existing building is being adapted for, or restored to, domestic use, it is "residential property" for the purposes of the relief. This may apply, for example, where a derelict building is being made fit for habitation, or where a previously non-residential building is being converted to a dwelling. Again, the process is taken as commencing when the builders start work.

The garden or grounds of a building used etc. as a dwelling

30. Section 92B(1)(b) includes within the definition of residential property "land that is or forms part of the garden or grounds of a building within paragraph (a) (including any building or structure on such land)". The test the Inland Revenue will apply is similar to that applied for the purposes of the capital gains tax relief for main residences (section 222(3) of the Taxation of Chargeable Gains Act 1992). The land will include that which is needed for the reasonable enjoyment of the dwelling having regard to the size and nature of the dwelling.
31. A caravan or houseboat is not a "building" for this purpose.
32. Commercial farmland is not within the definition of residential property. A farmhouse situated on agricultural land would be dealt with under the mixed use provisions (paragraphs 17 and 18 above).
33. Outhouses on land within the section 92B(1)(b) definition will also be "residential property" unless it can be demonstrated that they have a specific non-residential purpose. Where a distinct non-residential use can be demonstrated, the mixed use provisions will apply.

Interest in or rights over residential property

34. The treatment of interests in, or rights over, land or buildings for the purposes of disadvantaged areas relief will follow that of the land or buildings to which they relate.

Six or more separate dwellings transferred by single contract

35. The Regulations provide that "where there is a single contract for the conveyance, transfer or lease of land comprising or including six or more separate dwellings, none of that land counts as residential property ..." Accordingly the transaction will qualify for unlimited relief. This recognizes that commercial developers and institutional landlords, for example, frequently deal in numerous properties at one time. The fact that those properties may individually be "residential property" does not detract from the inherently commercial nature of the transaction itself.
36. To qualify as "separate", the dwellings must be self-contained. So for example, flats within a block, sharing some common areas but each with their own amenities, will qualify as separate dwellings. Rooms let within a house will not constitute separate dwellings if tenants share amenities such as a kitchen and bathroom.
37. A transaction in respect of six or more such dwellings must be carried out by means of a single contract in order to qualify for relief. Several instru-

ments may however be presented for stamping if the properties are held under separate title.

38. Qualifying multiple transactions will be treated as non-residential property for the purposes of relief, even where the proportionate consideration for individual dwellings exceeds the £150,000 limit for residential property. It is not a condition of relief that multiple transactions comprise only dwellings.

39. The fact that some of the six or more dwellings within the single contract are outside a designated disadvantaged area will not prevent them from constituting a non-residential transaction. However relief will only be available for the portion of the land situated within the disadvantaged area.

Property only partly within a disadvantaged area

40. Schedule 30 to Finance Act 2001, together with the Regulations, determines how property situated partly within and partly outside a designated disadvantaged area is to be treated for the purposes of the relief. Such cases are relatively rare in practice. Queries may be referred to Inland Revenue (Stamp Taxes) for guidance.

Lease Duty

41. Relief is also available from duty on the rental element of new leases executed on or after 10 April 2003. Rental leases of residential property shall be eligible for relief where the average annual rent is no more than £15,000 and/ or where any premium does not exceed £150,000. For nonresidential property, full relief is available for the rental element of leases as well as for any premium.

Other issues

42. The extended relief applies to documents executed on or after 10 April 2003, irrespective of whether the contract was entered into before or after that date. There is no scope to reclaim stamp duty already paid in respect of transfers executed on or before 9 April 2003.'

Land wholly situated in a disadvantaged area

Land all non-residential
If all the land is non-residential property, the transaction is exempt from charge (FA 2003, Sch. 6, Para. 4).

Land all residential
If all the land is all residential property and:

- the consideration for the transaction does not include rent and the relevant consideration does not exceed £150,000, or
- the consideration for the transaction consists only of rent and the relevant rental value does not exceed £150,000,

the transaction is exempt from charge,

(FA 2003, Sch. 6, Para. 4).

If the consideration for the transaction includes rent and the relevant rental value does not exceed £150,000, the rent does not count as chargeable consideration.

If the consideration for the transaction includes consideration other than rent, and if:

- the annual rent does not exceed £600, and
- the relevant consideration does not exceed £150,000,

then the consideration other than rent does not count as chargeable consideration.

If the annual rent exceeds £600, the 0 per cent band in Table A above does not apply in relation to the consideration other than rent and any case that would have fallen within that band is treated as falling within the 1 per cent band.

Land partly non-residential and partly residential

Where the land is partly non-residential property and partly residential property, the consideration attributable to non-residential property does not count as chargeable consideration (FA 2003, Sch. 6, Para. 5).

If the consideration attributable to residential property:

- does not include rent, and the 'relevant consideration' does not exceed £150,000, or
- consists only of rent, and the 'relevant rental value' does not exceed £150,000,

none of that consideration counts as chargeable consideration.

If that consideration includes rent (together with other consideration) and the relevant rental value does not exceed £150,000, the rent attributable to non-residential property does not count as chargeable consideration.

The consideration other than rent does not count as chargeable consideration if:

- the annual rent so attributable does not exceed £600, and
- the relevant consideration does not exceed £150,000.

If the annual rent attributable to non-residential property exceeds £600, the 0 per cent band in the Tables does not apply in relation to the consideration other than rent and any case that would have fallen within that band is treated as falling within the 1 per cent band.

In determining the consideration attributable to land that is non-residential property or land that is residential property (or to the rent or annual rent so attributable), a just and reasonable apportionment of the total consideration is required.

Land partly situated in a disadvantaged area

In determining the consideration attributable to land situated in a disadvantaged area and to land not so situated (or to the rent or annual rent so attributable), a just and reasonable apportionment of the total consideration is required (FA 2003, Sch. 6, Para. 7(2)).

Land all non-residential
If all of the land situated in a disadvantaged area is non-residential property, the consideration attributable to that land does not count as chargeable consideration (FA 2003, Sch. 6, Para. 8).

Land all residential
If all the land situated in a disadvantaged area is residential property and:

- the consideration attributable to that land does not include rent and the relevant consideration does not exceed £150,000, or
- the consideration attributable to that land consists only of rent and the relevant rental value does not exceed £150,000,

none of the consideration so attributable counts as chargeable consideration,

(FA 2003, Sch. 6, Para. 9).

If the consideration attributable to land situated in a disadvantaged area includes rent (together with other consideration) and the relevant rental value does not exceed £150,000, the rent so attributable does not count as chargeable consideration.

The consideration other than rent does not count as chargeable consideration if:

- the annual rent so attributable does not exceed £600, and
- the relevant consideration does not exceed £150,000.

If the annual rent so attributable exceeds £600, the 0 per cent band in Table A does not apply in relation to the non-rent consideration so attributable and any case that would have fallen within that band is treated as falling within the 1 per cent band.

Land partly non-residential and partly residential

In determining the consideration attributable to non-residential property or residential property (or to the rent or annual rent so attributable), a just and reasonable apportionment of the total consideration is required (FA 2003, Sch. 6, Para. 10).

The consideration attributable to land that is non-residential property does not count as chargeable consideration.

None of the consideration attributable to residential property counts as chargeable consideration if:

- the consideration so attributable does not include rent and the relevant consideration does not exceed £150,000, or
- the consideration so attributable consists only of rent and the relevant rental value does not exceed £150,000.

If that consideration includes rent (together with other consideration) and the relevant rental value does not exceed £150,000, the rent so attributable does not count as chargeable consideration.

The consideration other than rent does not count as chargeable consideration if:

- the annual rent attributable to residential property does not exceed £600, and
- the relevant consideration does not exceed £150,000.

If the annual rent attributable to residential property exceeds £600, the 0 per cent band in the Tables does not apply in relation to the consideration other than rent and any case that would have fallen within that band is treated as falling within the 1 per cent band.

Definitions

Relevant consideration and relevant rental value

The 'relevant consideration' in relation to a transaction means the amount falling to be taken into account in determining the rate of tax chargeable on the consideration other than rent apart from any relief under the above provisions (whether in relation to that or any other transaction) (FA 2003, Sch. 6, Para. 11).

The 'relevant rental value' in relation to a transaction means the amount falling to be taken into account in determining the rate of tax chargeable in respect of consideration consisting of rent apart from any relief under the above provisions (whether in relation to that or any other transaction).

Rent and annual rent

These terms have the same meaning as in Schedule 5 (FA 2003, Sch. 6, Para. 12).

10.9.3 Employees: relocation relief

Acquisition by employer in case of relocation of employment

Where a dwelling is acquired from an individual (whether alone or with other individuals) by his employer, the acquisition is exempt from SDLT if the following conditions are met (FA 2003, Sch. 6A, Para. 5):

- the individual must have occupied the dwelling as his only or main residence at some time in the period of two years ending with the date of the acquisition;
- the acquisition must made in connection with a change of residence by the individual resulting from relocation of employment;
- the consideration for the acquisition must not exceed the market value of the dwelling, and
- the area of land acquired must not exceed the permitted area.

If the area of land acquired exceeds the permitted area, the chargeable consideration for the acquisition is taken to be the amount calculated by deducting the market value of the permitted area from the market value of the dwelling, ie it is the value attributable to the excess over the permitted area.

Acquisition by property trader in case of relocation of employment

Where a dwelling is acquired by a property trader from an individual (whether alone or with other individuals), the acquisition is exempt from SDLT if:

- it is made in the course of a business that consists of or includes acquiring dwellings from individuals in connection with a change of residence resulting from relocation of employment;
- the individual occupied the dwelling as his only or main residence at some time in the period of two years ending with the date of the acquisition;
- the acquisition is made in connection with a change of residence by the individual resulting from relocation of employment;
- the consideration for the acquisition does not exceed the market value of the dwelling;
- the property trader does not intend:

  to spend more than the permitted amount on refurbishment of the dwelling;

to grant a lease or licence of the dwelling, or

to permit any of its principals or employees (or any person connected with any of its principals or employees) to occupy the dwelling, and

- the area of land acquired does not exceed the permitted area,

(FA 2003, Sch. 6A, Para. 6).

If the area of land acquired exceeds the permitted area, the chargeable consideration for the acquisition is taken to be the amount calculated by deducting the market value of the permitted area from the market value of the dwelling, ie it is the value attributable to the excess over the permitted area.

Withdrawal of relief

Relief is withdrawn if the property trader:

- spends more than the permitted amount on refurbishment of the old dwelling; or
- grants a lease or licence of the old dwelling, or
- permits any of its principals or employees (or any person connected with any of its principals or employees) to occupy the old dwelling,

(FA 2003, Sch. 6A, Para. 11).

Definitions

'Relocation of employment' means a change of the individual's place of employment due to:

- his becoming an employee of the employer;
- an alteration of the duties of his employment with the employer, or
- an alteration of the place where he normally performs those duties.

A 'property trader' means:

- a company;
- a limited liability partnership, or
- a partnership whose members are all either companies or limited liability partnerships,

that carries on the business of buying and selling dwellings.

In relation to a property trader a 'principal' means:

- in the case of a company, a director;
- in the case of a limited liability partnership, a member,
- in the case of a partnership whose members are all either companies or limited liability partnerships, a member or a person who is a principal of a member.

Anything done by or in relation to a company connected with a property trader is treated as done by or in relation to that property trader.

The principals or employees of a property trader include the principals or employees of any such company (FA 2003, Sch. 6A, Para. 8).

'Refurbishment' of a dwelling means the carrying out of works that enhance or are intended to enhance the value of the dwelling, but does not include:

- cleaning the dwelling, or
- works required solely for the purpose of ensuring that the dwelling meets minimum safety standards.

'The permitted amount', in relation to the refurbishment of a dwelling, is:

- £10,000, or
- 5 per cent of the consideration for the acquisition of the dwelling,

whichever is the greater, but subject to a maximum of £20,000,

(FA 2003, Sch. 6A, Para. 8).

A change of residence is one 'resulting from' relocation of employment if:

- the change is made wholly or mainly to allow the individual to have his residence within a reasonable daily travelling distance of his new place of employment, and
- his former residence is not within a reasonable daily travelling distance of that place.

The individual's 'new place of employment' means the place where he normally performs, or is normally to perform, the duties of his employment after the relocation.

The acquisition of the dwelling means the acquisition, by way of transfer, of a major interest in the dwelling.

The market value of the dwelling and of the permitted area mean, respectively, the market value of that major interest in the dwelling and of that interest so far as it relates to that area (FA 2003, Sch. 6A, Paras. 5, 6).

'Dwelling' includes land occupied and enjoyed with the dwelling as its garden or grounds.

A building or part of a building is a 'new dwelling' if:

- it has been constructed for use as a single dwelling and has not previously been occupied, or

- it has been adapted for use as a single dwelling and has not been occupied since its adaptation.

'The permitted area', in relation to a dwelling, means land occupied and enjoyed with the dwelling as its garden or grounds that does not exceed:

(a) an area (inclusive of the site of the dwelling) of 0.5 of a hectare, or

(b) such larger area as is required for the reasonable enjoyment of the dwelling as a dwelling having regard to its size and character.

Where (b) applies, the permitted area is taken to consist of that part of the land that would be the most suitable for occupation and enjoyment with the dwelling as its garden or grounds if the rest of the land were separately occupied (FA 2003, Sch. 6A, Para. 7).

10.9.4 Compulsory purchase facilitating development

A compulsory purchase facilitating development is exempt from SDLT (FA 2003, s. 60).

'Compulsory purchase facilitating development', in relation to England and Wales or Scotland, means the acquisition by a person of a chargeable interest in respect of which that person has made a compulsory purchase order for the purpose of facilitating development by another person. It does not matter how the acquisition is effected, so the provision applies where the acquisition is effected by agreement.

In relation to Northern Ireland, it means the acquisition by a person of a chargeable interest by means of a vesting order made for the purpose of facilitating development by a person other than the person who acquires the interest. A 'vesting order' means an order made under any statutory provision to authorise the acquisition of land otherwise than by agreement.

'Development', in relation to England and Wales, means the carrying out of building, engineering, mining or other operations in, on, over or under land, or the making of any material change in the use of any buildings or other land (Town and Country Planning Act 1990, s. 55).

The following operations or uses of land are deemed not to involve development of the land:

- the carrying out for the maintenance, improvement or other alteration of any building of works which:

  affect only the interior of the building, or
  do not materially affect the external appearance of the building,

and are not works for making good war damage or works begun after 5 December 1968 for the alteration of a building by providing additional space in it underground;

- the carrying out on land within the boundaries of a road by a local highway authority of any works required for the maintenance or improvement of the road;
- the carrying out by a local authority or statutory undertakers of any works for the purpose of inspecting, repairing or renewing any sewers, mains, pipes, cables or other apparatus, including the breaking open of any street or other land for that purpose;
- the use of any buildings or other land within the curtilage of a dwelling house for any purpose incidental to the enjoyment of the dwelling house as such;
- the use of any land for the purposes of agriculture or forestry (including afforestation) and the use for any of those purposes of any building occupied together with land so used,
- in the case of buildings or other land which are used for a purpose of any class specified by Regulations, the use of the buildings or other land or, subject to the provisions of the order, of any part of the buildings or the other land, for any other purpose of the same class.

The use as two or more separate dwellinghouses of any building previously used as a single dwellinghouse involves a material change in the use of the building and of each part of it which is so used.

The deposit of refuse or waste materials on land involves a material change in its use, notwithstanding that the land is comprised in a site already used for that purpose, if:

- the superficial area of the deposit is extended, or
- the height of the deposit is extended and exceeds the level of the land adjoining the site.

In relation to Scotland, development has the same meaning as in the Town and Country Planning (Scotland) Act 1997 (see s. 26 of that Act).

In relation to Northern Ireland, it has the same meaning as in the Planning (Northern Ireland) Order 1991 (SI 1991/1220) (see Art. 11 of that Order).

10.9.5 Compliance with planning obligations

Exemption from SDLT

A land transaction that is entered into in order to comply with a planning obligation or a modification of a planning obligation is exempt from SDLT if:

- the planning obligation or modification is enforceable against the vendor;
- the purchaser is a 'public authority', and
- the transaction takes place within the period of five years beginning with the date on which the planning obligation was entered into or modified,

(FA 2003, s. 61).

Planning obligation

In relation to England and Wales, 'planning obligation' means either of the following:

- a planning obligation within the meaning of s. 106 Town and Country Planning Act 1990 that is entered into in accordance with s. 106(9), or
- a planning obligation within the meaning of s. 299A of that Act that is entered into in accordance with s. 299A(2).

'Modification' of a planning obligation means modification as mentioned in s. 106A(1) of that Act.

In relation to Scotland, 'planning obligation' means an agreement made under Town and Country Planning (Scotland) Act 1997, s. 75 or s. 246.

In relation to Northern Ireland 'planning obligation' means a planning agreement within the meaning of Art. 40 of the Planning (Northern Ireland) Order 1991 (SI 1991/1220 (NI 11)) that is entered into in accordance with Para. (10) of that Article. 'Modification' of a planning obligation means modification as mentioned in Art. 40A(1) of that Order.

Public authorities

The following are public authorities for the above purposes:

Government

- A Minister of the Crown or government department
- The Scottish Ministers
- A Northern Ireland department
- The National Assembly for Wales

Local government: England

- A county or district council constituted under, Local Government Act 1972, s. 2
- The council of a London borough
- The Common Council of the City of London
- The Greater London Authority
- Transport for London
- The Council of the Isles of Scilly

Local government: Wales
A county or county borough council constituted under Local Government Act 1972, s. 21.

Local government: Scotland
A council constituted under Local Government, etc. (Scotland) Act 1994, s. 2.

Local government: Northern Ireland
A district council within the meaning of the Local Government Act (Northern Ireland) 1972.

Health: England and Wales
- A Strategic Health Authority or Health Authority established under National Health Service Act 1977, s. 8
- A Special Health Authority established under s. 11 of that Act
- A Primary Care Trust established under s. 16A of that Act
- A Local Health Board established under s. 16BA of that Act
- A National Health Service Trust established under National Health Service and Community Care Act 1990, s. 5

Health: Scotland
- The Common Services Agency established under National Health Service (Scotland) Act 1978, s. 10(1)
- A Health Board established under s. 2(1)(a) of that Act
- A National Health Service Trust established under s. 12A(1) of that Act
- A Special Health Board established under s. 2(1)(b) of that Act

Health: Northern Ireland
- A Health and Social Services Board established under Art. 16 of the Health and Personal Social Services (Northern Ireland) Order 1972 (SI 1972/1265)
- A Health and Social Services Trust established under Art. 10 of the Health and Personal Social Services (Northern Ireland) Order 1991 (SI 1991/194)

Other planning authorities
Any other authority that:

- is a local planning authority within the meaning of the Town and Country Planning Act 1990, or
- is the planning authority for any of the purposes of the planning Acts within the meaning of the Town and Country Planning (Scotland) Act 1997.

Prescribed persons

Other persons 'prescribed' as public authorities by Treasury order.

10.9.6   Islamic mortgages, etc.

Land sold to financial institution and leased to individual

Relief from SDLT is granted for certain transactions carried out in pursuance of Islamic mortgages (FA 2003, s. 72).

The steps envisaged are:

- the purchase by a financial institution of a major interest in the property concerned (the 'first transaction');
- the grant to an individual out of that interest of a lease (if the interest acquired is freehold) or a sub-lease (if the interest acquired is leasehold) (the 'second transaction'), and
- the grant to the individual of a right to require the institution or its successor in title to transfer the major interest to that individual (the exercise of this right being the 'third transaction').

The effect of the provisions is to exempt the second and third transactions, so that only one charge to SDLT arises, being the charge on the first transaction, ie the original acquisition of the major interest by the financial institution.

The first transaction is also exempt from SDLT if the vendor is the individual concerned (eg in the case of a remortgage) or another financial institution by whom the interest was acquired under similar arrangements between it and the individual.

The second transaction is exempt from SDLT if the provisions relating to the first transaction are complied with (including the payment of any tax chargeable).

The third transaction is exempt from SDLT if:

- the provisions relating to the first and second transactions are complied with, and
- at all times between the second and third transactions:

    the interest purchased under the first transaction is held by a financial institution, and
    the lease or sub-lease granted under the second transaction is held by the individual.

The agreement relating to the third transaction is not treated as substantially performed unless and until the third transaction is entered into. It is not treated as a distinct land transaction by virtue of the rules relating to options and rights of pre-emption.

The reliefs do not apply if:

- the individual enters into the arrangement, or holds the lease or sub-lease, as trustee and any beneficiary of the trust is not an individual, or
- the individual enters into the arrangements, or holds the lease or sub-lease, as partner and any of the other partners is not an individual.

Land sold to financial institution and re-sold to individual

A similar relief is available where a financial institution purchases a major interest in land ('the first transaction'), and sells that interest to an individual ('the second transaction'), and where the individual grants the institution a legal mortgage over that interest. The effect is to relieve the second transaction from SDLT (FA 2003, s. 73).

The first transaction is also exempt from SDLT if the vendor is:

- the individual concerned, or
- another financial institution by whom the interest was acquired under other similar arrangements.

The second transaction is exempt from SDLT if the financial institution complies with the provisions relating to the first transaction (including the payment of any tax chargeable).

The reliefs do not apply if:

- the individual enters into the arrangements as trustee and any beneficiary of the trust is not an individual, or
- the individual enters into the arrangements as partner and any of the other partners is not an individual.

Definitions

'Financial institution' means:

(a) a bank within the meaning of ICTA 1988, s. 840A;

(b) a building society within the meaning of the Building Societies Act 1986, or

(c) a wholly-owned subsidiary of a bank within (a) or a building society within (b).

For this purpose, a company is a wholly-owned subsidiary of a bank or building society ('the parent') if it has no members except the parent and the parent's wholly-owned subsidiaries or persons acting on behalf of the parent or the parent's wholly-owned subsidiaries.

In relation to Scotland:

(a)   the reference to a freehold interest is a reference to the interest of the owner, and

(b)   the reference to a leasehold interest is to a tenant's right over or interest in a property subject to a lease.

Until the appointed day for the purposes of the Abolition of Feudal Tenure, etc. (Scotland) Act 2000, the reference in point (a) to the interest of the owner shall be read, in relation to feudal property, as a reference to the estate or interest of the proprietor of the *dominium utile*.

References to an individual, in relation to times after the death of the individual concerned, are references to his personal representatives.

'Legal mortgage':

- in relation to land in England or Wales, means a legal mortgage as defined in Law of Property Act 1925, s. 205(1)(*xvi*);
- relation to land in Scotland, means a standard security,
- in relation to land in Northern Ireland, means a mortgage by conveyance of a legal estate or by demise or sub-demise or a charge by way of legal mortgage.

Meaning of 'major interest' in land

In relation to land in England or Wales, a major interest is:

- an estate in fee simple absolute, or
- a term of years absolute,

whether subsisting at law or in equity.

In relation to land in Scotland, a major interest is:

- the interest of an owner of land, or
- the tenant's right over or interest in a property subject to a lease.

Until the appointed day for the purposes of the Abolition of Feudal Tenure, etc. (Scotland) Act 2000, the reference to the interest of the owner, in relation to feudal property, is a reference to the estate or interest of the proprietor of the *dominium utile*.

In relation to land in Northern Ireland, a major interest is:

- any freehold estate, or

- any leasehold estate,

whether subsisting at law or in equity (FA 2003, s. 117).

10.9.7 Charities relief

Exemption from SDLT

A land transaction is exempt from SDLT if the purchaser is a charity and the following conditions are met (FA 2003, Sch. 8, Para. 1).

The first condition is that the purchaser must intend to hold the subject matter of the transaction for qualifying charitable purposes, that is:

- for use in furtherance of the charitable purposes of the purchaser or of another charity, or
- as an investment from which the profits are applied to the charitable purposes of the purchaser.

The second condition is that the transaction must not have been entered into for the purpose of avoiding SDLT (whether by the purchaser or any other person).

A 'charity' means a body or trust established for charitable purposes only.

Withdrawal of relief

Relief is withdrawn if a disqualifying event occurs:

- before the end of the period of three years beginning with the effective date of the transaction, or
- in pursuance of, or in connection with, arrangements made before the end of that period,

(FA 2003, Sch. 8, Para. 2).

However, relief is not withdrawn unless at the time of the disqualifying event the purchaser holds a chargeable interest:

- that was acquired by the purchaser under the relevant transaction, or
- that is derived from an interest so acquired.

An appropriate proportion of the relief is withdrawn where the purchaser continues to hold only part of the interest purchased for which relief was obtained.

The amount chargeable on withdrawal of relief is the amount that would have been chargeable in respect of the relevant transaction but for charities relief or, as the case may be, an appropriate proportion of the tax that would have been so chargeable.

Definitions

Disqualifying event

A 'disqualifying event' means:

- the purchaser ceasing to be established for charitable purposes only, or
- the subject matter of the transaction, or any interest or right derived from it, being used or held by the purchaser otherwise than for qualifying charitable purposes.

Appropriate proportion

An 'appropriate proportion' means an appropriate proportion having regard to:

- what was acquired by the purchaser under the relevant transaction and what is held by the purchaser at the time of the disqualifying event, and
- the extent to which what is held by the purchaser at that time becomes used or held for purposes other than qualifying charitable purposes.

10.9.8 Right to buy transactions and shared ownership leases

Right to buy transactions

In the case of a right to buy transaction, the provisions relating to contingent consideration do not apply. Any consideration that would be payable only if a contingency were to occur, or that is payable only because a contingency has occurred, does not count as chargeable consideration (FA 2003, Sch. 9, Para.1).

A 'right to buy transaction' means:

- the sale of a dwelling at a discount, or the grant of a lease of a dwelling at a discount, by a 'relevant public sector body', or
- the sale of a dwelling, or the grant of a lease of a dwelling, in pursuance of the 'preserved right to buy'.

'Relevant public sector bodies'

The following are relevant public sector bodies:

Government

- A Minister of the Crown
- The Scottish Ministers
- A Northern Ireland department

Local government

- A local housing authority within the meaning of the Housing Act 1985
- A county council in England
- A council constituted under Local Government etc. (Scotland) Act 1994, s.2, the common good of such a council or any trust under its control
- A district council within the meaning of the Local Government Act (Northern Ireland) 1972

Social housing

- The Housing Corporation
- Scottish Homes
- The Northern Ireland Housing Executive
- A registered social landlord
- A housing action trust established under Part 3 of the Housing Act 1988

New towns and development corporations

- The Commission for the New Towns
- A development corporation established by an order made, or having effect as if made, under the New Towns Act 1981
- A development corporation established by an order made, or having effect as if made, under the New Towns (Scotland) Act 1968
- A new town commission established under, New Towns Act (Northern Ireland) 1965, s. 7
- An urban development corporation established by an order made under Local Government, Planning and Land Act 1980, s.135
- The Welsh Development Agency

Police

- A police authority within the meaning of Police Act 1996, s.101(1)
- A police authority within the meaning of Police (Scotland) Act 1967, s.2(1) or 19(9)(b)
- The Northern Ireland Policing Board

Miscellaneous

- An Education and Libraries Board within the meaning of the Education and Libraries (Northern Ireland) Order 1986 (SI 1986/594)
- The UK Atomic Energy Authority
- Any person mentioned in Housing (Scotland) Act 1987, s.61(11) (g), (k), (l) or (n)
- A body prescribed by Treasury order

Preserved right to buy

The transfer of a dwelling, or the grant of a lease of a dwelling, is made in pursuance of the preserved right to buy if:

- the vendor is:

  in England and Wales, a person against whom the right to buy under Part 5 Housing Act 1985 is exercisable by virtue of s.171A of that Act, or
  in Scotland, a person against whom the right to buy under s.61 of the Housing (Scotland) Act 1987 is exercisable by virtue of s.81A of that Act,

  (which provide for the preservation of the right to buy on disposal to a private sector landlord);
- the purchaser is the qualifying person for the purposes of the preserved right to buy, and
- the dwelling is the qualifying dwelling-house in relation to the purchaser.

Purchase grants

A grant under Housing Act 1996, s.20 or 21 (purchase grants in respect of disposals at a discount by registered social landlords) does not count as part of the chargeable consideration for a right to buy transaction in relation to which the vendor is a registered social landlord.

Shared ownership lease: election for market value treatment

In certain circumstances, a purchaser may elect for SDLT to be charged on:

- the market value of the dwelling, or
- the sum calculated by reference to that value,

as stated in the lease (FA 2003, Sch. 9, Para.2).

The circumstances are that a lease is granted by a qualifying body, or in pursuance of the preserved right to buy, and the lease:

- is of a dwelling;
- gives the lessee or lessees exclusive use of the dwelling;
- provides for the lessee or lessees to acquire the reversion;
- is granted partly in consideration of rent and partly in consideration of a premium calculated by reference to:

  the market value of the dwelling, or
  a sum calculated by reference to that value,

- contains a statement of:

  the market value of the dwelling; or
  the sum calculated by reference to that value,

by reference to which the premium is calculated.

An election under the above provisions must be included in the land transaction return made in respect of the grant of the lease, or in an amendment of that return, and is irrevocable.

The statutory definition of 'market value' does not apply for the above purposes.

Transfer of reversion under shared ownership lease where election made for market value treatment

The transfer of the reversion to the lessee or lessees under the terms of a qualifying shared ownership lease is exempt from charge if:

- an election was made for tax to be charged in accordance with that paragraph, and
- any tax chargeable in respect of the grant of the lease has been paid,

(FA 2003, Sch. 9, Para.3).

Shared ownership lease: election where 'staircasing' allowed

Where a lease is granted by a qualifying body or in pursuance of a preserved right to buy, the purchaser may elect for SDLT to be charged on the basis that:

- the rent in consideration of which the lease is granted is taken to be the minimum rent stated in the lease, and
- the chargeable consideration for the grant other than rent is taken to be the amount stated in the lease,

(FA 2003, Sch. 9, Para.4).

The conditions under which such an election may be made are as follows:

(a) the lease must be of a dwelling;

(b) the lease must give the lessee or lessees exclusive use of the dwelling;

(c) the lease must provide that the lessee or lessees may, on the payment of a sum, require the terms of the lease to be altered so that the rent payable under it is reduced;

(d) the lease must be granted partly in consideration of rent and partly in consideration of a premium calculated by reference to:

    (i) the premium obtainable on the open market for the grant of a lease containing the same terms as the lease but with the substitution of the minimum rent for the rent payable under the lease, or

    (ii) a sum calculated by reference to that premium,

(e) the lease must contain a statement of the minimum rent and of:

    (i)   the premium obtainable on the open market, or

    (ii)   the sum calculated by reference to that premium,

by reference to which the premium is calculated.

An election under the above provisions must be included in the land transaction return made in respect of the grant of the lease, or in an amendment of that return. It is irrevocable.

The 'minimum rent' means the lowest rent which could become payable under the lease if it were altered in accordance with (c) above at the date when the lease is granted.

Meaning of 'qualifying body' and 'preserved right to buy'

A 'qualifying body' means:

- a local housing authority within the meaning of the Housing Act 1985;
- a housing association within the meaning of:

  the Housing Associations Act 1985, or
  Part 2 of the Housing (Northern Ireland) Order 1992 (SI 1992/1725);

- a housing action trust established under Part 3 of the Housing Act 1988;
- the Northern Ireland Housing Executive;
- the Commission for the New Towns,
- a development corporation established by an order made, or having effect as if made, under the New Towns Act 1981,

(FA 2003, Sch. 9, Para.5).

A lease is granted 'in pursuance of the preserved right to buy' if:

- the vendor is a person against whom the right to buy under Part 5 of the Housing Act 1985 is exercisable by virtue of s. 171A of that Act (preservation of right to buy on disposal to private sector landlord);
- the lessee is, or lessees are, the qualifying person for the purposes of the preserved right to buy, and
- the lease is of a dwelling that is the qualifying dwelling-house in relation to the purchaser.

Rent to mortgage or rent to loan: chargeable consideration

The chargeable consideration for a rent to mortgage or rent to loan transaction is equal to the price that, by virtue of Housing Act 1985, s. 126 would be payable for:

- a transfer of the dwelling to the person (where the rent to mortgage transaction is a transfer), or

- the grant of a lease of the dwelling to the person (where the rent to mortgage transaction is the grant of a lease),

if the person were exercising the right to buy under Part 5 of that Act,

(FA 2003, Sch. 9, Para.6).

A 'rent to mortgage transaction' means:

- the transfer of a dwelling to a person, or
- the grant of a lease of a dwelling to a person,

pursuant to the exercise by that person of the right to acquire on rent to mortgage terms under Part 5 of the Housing Act 1985.

A 'rent to loan transaction' means the execution of a heritable disposition in favour of a person pursuant to the exercise by that person of the right to purchase a house by way of the rent to loan scheme in Part 3 of the Housing (Scotland) Act 1987.

The chargeable consideration for such a transaction is equal to the price that, by virtue of Housing (Scotland) Act 1987, s. 62, would be payable for the house if the person were exercising the right to purchase under s.61 of that Act.

10.9.9   Other reliefs

Demutualisation of insurance company

A land transaction is exempt from SDLT if it is entered into for the purposes of or in connection with a qualifying transfer of the whole or part of the business of a mutual insurance company ('the mutual') to a company that has share capital ('the acquiring company') (FA 2003, s. 63).

Various terms are defined for this purpose.

Demutualisation of building society

A land transaction effected by Building Societies Act 1986, s. 97(6) or (7) (transfer of building society's business to a commercial company) is exempt from SDLT (FA 2003, s. 64).

Transfers involving public bodies

A land transaction entered into on, or in consequence of, or in connection with, a reorganisation effected by or under a statutory provision is exempt from SDLT if the purchaser and vendor are both public bodies (FA 2003, s. 66).

The Treasury may by order extend the exemption to a transaction effected by or under a prescribed statutory provision where either the purchaser or the vendor is a public body.

Various terms are defined for this purpose.

Transfer in consequence of reorganisation of parliamentary constituencies

Where an Order in Council is made under the Parliamentary Constituencies Act 1986 (orders specifying new parliamentary constituencies), and an existing local constituency association transfers a chargeable interest to:

- a new association that is a successor to the existing association, or
- a related body that as soon as practicable transfers the interest or right to a new association that is a successor to the existing association,

the transfer (or transfers) is exempt from SDLT (FA 2003, s. 67).

Various terms are defined for this purpose.

Acquisition by bodies established for national purposes

A land transaction is exempt from SDLT if the purchaser is any of the following:

- the Historic Buildings and Monuments Commission for England;
- the National Endowment for Science, Technology and the Arts;
- the Trustees of the British Museum;
- the Trustees of the National Heritage Memorial Fund,
- the Trustees of the Natural History Museum,

(FA 2003, s. 69).

Certain acquisitions by registered social landlord

A land transaction under which the purchaser is a registered social landlord is exempt from SDLT if:

- the registered social landlord is 'controlled by its tenants';
- the vendor is a 'qualifying body', or
- the transaction is funded with the assistance of a 'public subsidy',

(FA 2003, s. 71).

A registered social landlord is 'controlled by its tenants' if the majority of its board members are tenants occupying properties owned or managed by it.

'Board member', in relation to a registered social landlord, means:

(a) if it is a company, a director of the company;

(b) if it is a body corporate whose affairs are managed by its members, a member;

(c) if it is body of trustees, a trustee;

(d) if it is not within paragraphs (a) to (c), a member of the committee of management or other body to which is entrusted the direction of the affairs of the registered social landlord.

'Qualifying body' means:

- a registered social landlord;
- a housing action trust established under Part 3 of the Housing Act 1988;
- a principal council within the meaning of the Local Government Act 1972;
- the Common Council of the City of London;
- the Scottish Ministers;
- a council constituted under Local Government etc (Scotland) Act 1994, s. 2;
- Scottish Homes;
- the Department for Social Development in Northern Ireland, or
- the Northern Ireland Housing Executive.

'Public subsidy' means any grant or other financial assistance:

- made or given by way of a distribution pursuant to National Lottery, etc. Act 1993, s. 25 (application of money by distributing bodies);
- under Housing Act 1996, s. 18 (social housing grants);
- under Housing Grants, Construction and Regeneration Act 1996, s. 126 (financial assistance for regeneration and development);
- under Housing (Scotland) Act 1988, s. 2 (general functions of the Scottish Ministers), or
- under Art. 33 of the Housing (Northern Ireland) Order 1992 (SI 1992/1725).

Collective enfranchisement by leaseholders

Where a chargeable transaction is entered into by an RTE company in pursuance of a right of collective enfranchisement, the rate of SDLT is determined by dividing the total amount of the consideration by the number of flats in respect of which the right of collective enfranchisement is being exercised (FA 2003, s. 74).

'RTE company' has the meaning given by Leasehold Reform, Housing and Urban Development Act 1993, s. 4A.

'Right of collective enfranchisement' means the right exercisable by an RTE company under:

- Part 1 of the Landlord and Tenant Act 1987, or
- Chapter 1 of Part 1 of the Leasehold Reform, Housing and Urban Development Act 1993.

'Flat' has the same meaning as in the Act conferring the right of collective enfranchisement.

Crofting community right to buy

Where a chargeable transaction is entered into in pursuance of the crofting community right to buy, and under that transaction two or more crofts are being bought, the total amount of that consideration is divided by the number of crofts being bought for the purpose of determining the rate of SDLT chargeable on each croft (FA 2003, s. 75).

'Crofting community right to buy' means the right exercisable by a crofting community body under Part 3 of the Land Reform (Scotland) Act 2003.

10.10 Company reorganisations, reconstructions, acquisitions, etc.

10.10.1 Intra-group transfers

Group relief

A transaction is exempt from SDLT if the vendor and purchaser are companies that are members of the same group as at the effective date of the transaction (FA 2003, Sch. 7, Para. 1).

For this purposes 'company' means a body corporate, so unincorporated associations are not covered.

Companies are members of the same group if one is the 75%+ subsidiary of the other or both are 75%+ subsidiaries of a third company.

A company ('company A') is the 75%+ subsidiary of another company ('company B') if company B:

- is beneficial owner of not less than 75%+ of the ordinary share capital of company A;
- is beneficially entitled to not less than 75%+ of any profits available for distribution to equity holders of company A, and
- would be beneficially entitled to not less than 75%+ of any assets of company A available for distribution to its equity holders on a winding-up.

The group relief rules apply for this purpose.

Restrictions on availability of group relief: 'arrangements'

Group relief is not available if, at the effective date of the transaction, there are 'arrangements' in existence by virtue of which, at that or some later time, a person has or could obtain, or any persons together have or could obtain, control of the purchaser but not of the vendor (FA 2003, Sch. 7, Para. 2).

This does not apply to arrangements entered into with a view to an acquisition of shares by a company in relation to which stamp duty acquisition relief will apply.

Group relief is not available if the transaction is effected in pursuance of, or in connection with, arrangements under which:

- the consideration, or any part of the consideration, for the transaction is to be provided or received (directly or indirectly) by a person other than a group company, or
- the vendor and the purchaser are to cease to be members of the same group by reason of the purchaser ceasing to be a 75%+ subsidiary of the vendor or a third company.

A 'group company' means a company that at the effective date of the transaction is a member of the same group as the vendor or the purchaser.

'Arrangements' includes any scheme, agreement or understanding, whether or not legally enforceable.

'Control' has the meaning given by ICTA 1988, s. 840.

Withdrawal of group relief on degrouping event

Group relief is withdrawn if the purchaser ceases to be a member of the same group as the vendor:

- before the end of the period of three years beginning with the effective date of the transaction, or
- in pursuance of, or in connection with, arrangements made before the end of that period,

(FA 2003, Sch. 7, Para. 3).

However, it is withdrawn only if at the time of the degrouping event ('the relevant time'), the purchaser or a relevant associated company holds a chargeable interest:

- that was acquired by the purchaser under the intra-group transaction, or
- that is derived from a chargeable interest so acquired,

and that has not subsequently been acquired at market value under a chargeable transaction for which group relief was available but was not claimed. There is a proportionate withdrawal if part only of the asset is held at the date of the degrouping event.

The amount chargeable is the tax that would have been chargeable in respect of the relevant transaction if the chargeable consideration had been an amount equal to the market value of the subject matter of the transaction, or an appropriate proportion of that tax.

'Arrangements' includes any scheme, agreement or understanding, whether or not legally enforceable.

'Relevant associated company', in relation to the purchaser, means a company that:

- is a member of the same group as the purchaser immediately before the purchaser ceases to be a member of the same group as the vendor, and
- ceases to be a member of the same group as the vendor in consequence of the purchaser so ceasing.

Cases in which group relief not withdrawn

Group relief is not withdrawn in the following cases (FA 2003, s. 7, Para. 4).

The first case
This is where the purchaser ceases to be a member of the same group as the vendor because the vendor leaves the group. The vendor is regarded as leaving the group if the companies cease to be members of the same group by reason of a transaction relating to shares in:

- the vendor, or
- another company that as a result of the transaction ceases to be a member of the same group as the purchaser.

The second case
This is where the purchaser ceases to be a member of the same group as the vendor by reason of anything done for the purposes of, or in the course of, winding up the vendor or another company that is above the vendor in the group structure. A company is 'above' the vendor in the group structure if the vendor, or another company that is above the vendor in the group structure, is a 75%+ subsidiary of the company.

The third case
This is where the purchaser ceases to be a member of the same group as the vendor as a result of an acquisition of shares by another company ('the

acquiring company') in relation to which stamp duty acquisition relief applies.

However, the degrouping rules apply if the purchaser ceases to be a member of the same group as the acquiring company:

- before the end of the period of three years beginning with the effective date of the relevant transaction, or
- in pursuance of, or in connection with, arrangements made before the end of that period.

The degrouping rules do not apply unless at the time the purchaser ceases to be a member of the same group as the acquiring company, it or a relevant associated company holds a chargeable interest:

- that was acquired by the purchaser under the relevant transaction, or
- that is derived from an interest so acquired,

and that has not subsequently been acquired at market value under a chargeable transaction for which group relief was available but was not claimed.

'Arrangements' includes any scheme, agreement or understanding, whether or not legally enforceable.

'Relevant associated company', in relation to the purchaser, means a company that is a member of the same group as the purchaser that ceases to be a member of the same group as the acquiring company in consequence of the purchaser so ceasing.

Recovery of group relief from another group company or controlling director

Where tax is chargeable as a result of the withdrawal of group relief, the amount of tax has been finally determined, and the whole or part of that amount is unpaid six months after the date on which it became payable, the unpaid tax can be recovered from the following persons (FA 2003, Sch. 7, Para. 5):

- the vendor;
- any company that at any relevant time was a member of the same group as the purchaser and was above it in the group structure,
- any person who at any relevant time was a controlling director of the purchaser or a company having control of the purchaser.

Recovery procedure
The Revenue must serve a notice on any person from whom it is seeking to recover the tax requiring him within 30 days of the service of the notice to

pay the amount that remains unpaid (FA 2003, Sch. 7, Para. 6). It must state the amount required to be paid by the person concerned.

Any such notice must be served before the end of the period of three years beginning with the date of the final determination of the tax due. It is treated as if it were a notice of assessment and as if the amount were an amount of tax due from that person. Accordingly, there is the normal right of appeal.

A person who has paid an amount in pursuance of such a notice is entitled to recover it from the purchaser.

A payment in pursuance of such a notice is not allowed as a deduction in computing any income, profits or losses for any tax purpose.

Definitions

A 'relevant time' means any time between the effective date of the relevant transaction and the purchaser ceasing to be a member of the same group as the vendor.

A company ('company A') is 'above' another company ('company B') in a group structure, is a 75%+ subsidiary of company A.

'Director', in relation to a company, has the meaning given by Income Tax (Earnings and Pensions) Act 2003, s. 67(1) (read with subsection (2) of that section) and includes any person falling within ICTA 1988, s. 417(5) (read with subsection (6) of that section).

'Controlling director', in relation to a company, means a director of the company who has control of it (construing control in accordance with ICTA 1988, s. 416).

Revenue guidance

There is a useful article on group relief in *Tax Bulletin*, Issue 70 (April 2004).

10.10.2 Reconstruction relief

A land transaction entered into for the purposes of, or in connection with, the transfer of an undertaking or part of an undertaking in a reconstruction is exempt from SDLT (FA 2003, Sch. 7, Para. 7).

The envisaged circumstances are that a company ('the acquiring company') acquires the whole or part of the undertaking of another company ('the target company') in pursuance of a scheme for the reconstruction of the target company, and the conditions set out below are met.

The first condition

This is that the consideration for the acquisition consists wholly or partly of the issue of non-redeemable shares in the acquiring company to all the shareholders of the target company. Where the consideration for the acquisition consists only partly of the issue of non-redeemable shares, the rest of the consideration must consist wholly of the assumption or discharge by the acquiring company of liabilities of the target company.

The second condition

This is that after the acquisition has been made:

- each shareholder of each of the companies is a shareholder of the other, and
- the proportion of shares of one of the companies held by any shareholder is the same, or as nearly as may be the same, as the proportion of shares of the other company held by that shareholder.

Thus the relief is not available in the context of company partitions, but acquisition relief may be available.

The third condition

This is that the acquisition is effected for bona fide commercial reasons and does not form part of a scheme or arrangement of which the main purpose, or one of the main purposes, is the avoidance of liability to stamp duty, income tax, corporation tax, capital gains tax or SDLT.

10.10.3   Acquisition relief

A land transaction entered into for the purposes of or in connection with the transfer of the undertaking or part is charged to SDLT at the rate of 0.5 per cent (FA 2003, Sch. 7, Para. 8). The envisaged circumstances are that a company ('the acquiring company') acquires the whole or part of the undertaking of another company ('the target company'), and the conditions set out below are met.

The first condition

This is that the consideration for the acquisition consists wholly or partly of the issue of non-redeemable shares in the acquiring company to the target company, or all or any of the target company's shareholders.

Where the consideration for the acquisition consists partly of the issue of non-redeemable shares, the rest of the consideration must consist wholly of:

- cash not exceeding 10 per cent of the nominal value of the non-redeemable shares so issued;
- the assumption or discharge by the acquiring company of liabilities of the target company, or
- both of those things.

The second condition

This is that the acquiring company is not associated with another company that is a party to arrangements with the target company relating to shares of the acquiring company issued in connection with the transfer of the undertaking or part.

Companies are associated if one has control of the other or both are controlled by the same person or persons.

'Arrangements' includes any scheme, agreement or understanding, whether or not legally enforceable.

The ICTA 1988, s. 416 definition of control applies.

10.10.4   Withdrawal of reconstruction or acquisition relief

Relief is withdrawn if control of the acquiring company changes:

- before the end of the period of three years beginning with the effective date of the transaction, or
- in pursuance of, or in connection with, arrangements made before the end of that period,

(FA 2003, Sch. 7, Para. 9).

However, it is withdrawn only if at the time control of the acquiring company changes ('the relevant time'), it or a relevant associated company holds a chargeable interest:

- that was acquired by the acquiring company under the relevant transaction, or
- that is derived from an interest so acquired,

and that has not subsequently been acquired at market value under a chargeable transaction in relation to which reconstruction or acquisition relief was available but was not claimed,

The amount chargeable is the tax that would have been chargeable in respect of the relevant transaction if the chargeable consideration had been an amount equal to the market value of the subject matter of the transaction or an appropriate proportion of that tax.

'Relevant associated company', in relation to the acquiring company, means a company:

- that is controlled by the acquiring company immediately before the control of that company changes, and
- of which control changes in consequence of the change of control of that company.

'Arrangements' includes any scheme, agreement or understanding, whether or not legally enforceable.

'Control' is construed in accordance with ICTA 1988, s. 416.

Control of a company changes if the company becomes controlled:

- by a different person;
- by a different number of persons, or
- by two or more persons at least one of whom is not the person, or one of the persons, by whom the company was previously controlled.

Cases in which reconstruction or acquisition relief not withdrawn

Reconstruction or acquisition relief is not withdrawn in the following cases.

The first case: divorce
This is where control of the acquiring company changes as a result of a share transaction that is effected in connection with divorce, etc.

The second case: variation of testamentary disposition
This is where control of the acquiring company changes as a result of a share transaction that is effected in pursuance of the variation of a testamentary disposition.

The third case: exempt intra-group transfer
This is where control of the acquiring company changes as a result of an exempt intra-group transfer.

The fourth case: acquisition relief
This is where control of the acquiring company changes as a result of a transfer of shares to another company in relation to which share acquisition relief applies.

The fifth case: control by loan creditor

This is where:

- control of the acquiring company changes as a result of a loan creditor becoming, or ceasing to be, treated as having control of the company, and
- the other persons who were previously treated as controlling the company continue to be so treated.

'Loan creditor' is defined in ICTA 1988, s. 417(7)–(9).

Withdrawal of reconstruction or acquisition relief on subsequent non-exempt transfer

In the third case referred to above, reconstruction or acquisition relief in relation to the relevant transaction, or an appropriate proportion of it, is withdrawn if a company holding shares in the acquiring company to which the exempt intra-group transfer related, or that are derived from shares to which that transfer related, ceases to be a member of the same group as the target company:

- before the end of the period of three years beginning with the effective date of the relevant transaction, or
- in pursuance of or in connection with arrangements made before the end of that period,

(FA 2003, Sch. 7, Para. 11).

However, relief is withdrawn only if the acquiring company or a relevant associated company, at that time ('the relevant time'), holds a chargeable interest:

- that was transferred to the acquiring company by the relevant transaction, or
- that is derived from an interest that was so transferred, and that has not subsequently been transferred at market value by a chargeable transaction in relation to which reconstruction or acquisition relief was available but was not claimed.

In the fourth case referred to above, reconstruction or acquisition relief in relation to the relevant transaction, or an appropriate proportion of it, is withdrawn if control of the other company mentioned in that provision changes:

- before the end of the period of three years beginning with the effective date of the relevant transaction, or
- in pursuance of or in connection with arrangements made before the end of that period,

at a time when that company holds any shares transferred to it by the exempt transfer, or any shares derived from shares so transferred.

However, relief is withdrawn only if the acquiring company or a relevant associated company, at that time ('the relevant time'), holds a chargeable interest:

- that was transferred to the acquiring company by the relevant transaction, or
- that is derived from an interest that was so transferred,

and that has not subsequently been transferred at market value by a chargeable transaction in relation to which reconstruction or acquisition relief was available but was not claimed.

The amount chargeable is the tax that would have been chargeable in respect of the relevant transaction if the chargeable consideration had been an amount equal to the market value of the subject matter of the transaction, or an appropriate proportion of that tax.

Definitions
'Relevant associated company', in relation to the acquiring company, means a company:

- that is controlled by the acquiring company immediately before the control of that company changes, and
- of which control changes in consequence of the change of control of that company.

'Arrangements' includes any scheme, agreement or understanding, whether or not legally enforceable.

'Control' is construed in accordance with ICTA 1988, s. 416.

References to control of a company changing are to the company becoming controlled:

- by a different person;
- by a different number of persons, or
- by two or more persons at least one of whom is not the person, or one of the persons, by whom the company was previously controlled.

Recovery of reconstruction or acquisition relief from another group company or controlling director

Where tax is chargeable as a result of the withdrawal of reconstruction or acquisition relief, the amount of tax has been finally determined, and the whole or part of that amount is unpaid six months after the date on which it became payable, the unpaid tax can be recovered from the following persons:

- any company that at any relevant time was a member of the same group as the acquiring company and was above it in the group structure,

- any person who at any relevant time was a controlling director of the acquiring company or a company having control of the acquiring company,

(FA 2003, Sch. 7, Para. 12).

Recovery procedure

The Revenue must serve a notice on the relevant person requiring him within 30 days of the service of the notice to pay the amount that remains unpaid. The notice must state the amount required to be paid by the person on whom the notice is served (FA 2003, Sch. 7, Para. 13).

The notice must be served before the end of the period of three years beginning with the date of the final determination of the tax due.

The notice is treated as if it were a notice of assessment. Therefore, the normal right of appeal applies.

A person who has paid an amount in pursuance of such a notice is entitled to recover that amount from the acquiring company.

A payment in pursuance of such a notice is not allowed as a deduction in computing any income, profits or losses for any tax purpose.

Definitions

The 'relevant time' means any time between effective date of the relevant transaction and the change of control by virtue of which tax is chargeable.

A company ('company A') is 'above' another company ('company B') in a group structure if company B, or another company that is above company B in the group structure, is a 75%+ subsidiary of company A.

'Director', in relation to a company, has the meaning given by, ITEPA 2003, s. 67(1) and includes any person falling within ICTA 1988, s. 417(5).

'Controlling director', in relation to a company, means a director of the company who has control of it (construing control in accordance with ICTA 1988, s. 416).

10.10.5 Incorporation of an LLP

A transaction by which a chargeable interest is transferred by a person ('the transferor') to a limited liability partnership in connection with its incorporation is exempt from SDLT if the following conditions are met (FA 2003, s. 65).

The effective date of the transaction must be not more than one year after the date of incorporation of the LLP.

At the 'relevant time' the transferor:

- must be a partner in a partnership comprised of all the persons who are or are to be members of the LLP (and no-one else), or
- must hold the interest transferred as nominee or bare trustee for one or more of the partners in such a partnership.

The proportions of the interest transferred to which the partners are entitled immediately after the transfer must be the same as those to which they were entitled at the relevant time. Alternatively, if there are differences, none of them must have arisen as part of a scheme or arrangement of which the main purpose, or one of the main purposes, is avoidance of liability to any duty or tax.

'The relevant time' means:

- where the transferor acquired the interest after the incorporation of the limited liability partnership, immediately after he acquired it, and
- in any other case, immediately before its incorporation.

'Limited liability partnership' (LLP) means a limited liability partnership formed under the Limited Liability Partnerships Act 2000 or the Limited Liability Partnerships Act (Northern Ireland) 2002.

10.11   Administration

10.11.1   General

Care and management of SDLT

The tax is under the care and management of the Commissioners of Revenue ('the Board') (FA 2003, s. 42(3)).

Unlike Stamp Duty, SDLT is a tax on transactions rather than on documents. It works on the self-assessment principle. Many of the rights, duties and procedures relating to Income Tax Self-Assessment and Corporation Tax Self-Assessment are reproduced in the SDLT legislation.

Readers are referred to the Stamp Taxes website, which is at www.inland revenue.gov.uk/so/index.htm.

Details of Stamp Office addresses, SDLT forms, booklets, etc. are available from this website, as is access to the Revenue's SDLT Manual.

Delivery and service of documents

A notice or other document to be served on a person may be delivered to him or left at his usual or last known place of abode (FA 2003, s. 84).

A notice or other document to be given, served or delivered may be served by post. Such a notice is properly addressed if it is addressed to that person:

- in the case of an individual, at his usual or last known place of residence or his place of business,
- in the case of a company:

  at its principal place of business,
  if a liquidator has been appointed, at his address for the purposes of the liquidation.

See also **10.11.5** regarding distraint proceedings.

Power to allow further time and reasonable excuse for failure

The Revenue has a general discretionary power to extend the time limit for doing 'anything required to be done' for SDLT purposes within a limited time (FA 2003, s. 97).

Where a person had a reasonable excuse for not doing anything required to be done for SDLT purposes, he is deemed not to have failed to do it if he did it without unreasonable delay after the excuse had ceased to be valid.

10.11.2 Returns and Revenue certificates

Requirement to file return

In the case of every 'notifiable transaction', the purchaser must file a 'land transaction return' with the Revenue. The time limit is 30 days after the effective date of the transaction (FA 2003, s. 76). Form SDLT1 should be used. This return should be sent to:

Rapid Data Capture Centre
DX 725593
Bootle 9

or by post to:

Revenue
Stamp Taxes
Comben House

Farriers Way
Netherton
Merseyside
L30 4RN.

The land transaction return includes a 'self-assessment' of the SDLT charge-able on the transaction. The tax is payable at the time the return is submitted and the payment should be sent with the return.

Where additional information is required, the following additional forms may need to be completed:

- SDLT2 – where there are more than two vendors and/or two purchasers;
- SDLT3 – where land is involved and further space is required in addition to the space provided on SDLT1,
- SDLT4 – for complex commercial transactions and leases.

The above forms are prescribed in accordance with the Stamp Duty Land Tax (Administration) Regulations 2003 (SI 2003/2837), reg. 9 and Sch. 2. Supplies of these returns are obtainable by telephoning 0845 3021472 or faxing 01726 201015; e-mail: saorderline.ir @gtnet.gov.uk; or by post:

IRCC
PO Box 37
St Austell
PL35 5YN.

Photocopies of the return are not acceptable since each return form carries a unique reference number.

Notifiable transactions

It is important to note that a transaction may be notifiable even though no SDLT is payable on it.

Grant of lease

The grant of a lease for a contractual term of seven years or more for chargeable consideration is notifiable (FA 2003, s. 77).

The grant of a lease is for a contractual term of less than seven years is notifiable if either:

- the chargeable consideration consists or includes a premium in respect of which tax is chargeable at a rate of 1 per cent or higher, or
- the chargeable consideration consists of or includes rent in respect of which tax is chargeable at a rate of 1 per cent or higher.

In either of the above cases, the grant is notifiable if the consideration would be chargeable but for a relief.

Acquisition of major interest

Any other acquisition of a major interest in land is notifiable unless it is an exempt transaction (as to which, see **10.6** above).

Acquisition of other interest

An acquisition of a chargeable interest other than a major interest in land is notifiable if there is chargeable consideration in respect of which tax is chargeable at a rate of 1 per cent or higher, or in respect of which tax would be so chargeable but for a relief.

Meaning of filing date and delivery of return

The filing date, in relation to a land transaction return, is the last day of the period within which the return must be delivered (FA 2003, Sch. 10, Para. 2).

A return must be signed by the 'purchaser' in relation to the transaction concerned.

In the case of an individual, a person acting under power of attorney for that individual may sign (FA 2003, s. 81B).

A return is not properly delivered unless it is accompanied by payment of any SDLT chargeable on the transaction.

Issue of certificate by the Revenue

When the Revenue has processed a return satisfactorily, it will issue a certificate (form SDLT5) to the effect that the provisions of the SDLT legislation have been complied with in respect of the transaction covered by the return. This certificate, or a self-certificate (as to which, see **10.11.5** below), is required if the transaction is to be registered at the Land Registry (FA 2003, s. 79). Certificates are issued in accordance with SI 2003/2837, regs. 4–6.

The return will not be processed unless it contains:

- a unique reference number;
- the liable person's name and address;
- a signed declaration, signed by all purchasers, and
- the effective date of the transaction.

The certificate will not be issued unless:

- all relevant information is provided;

- the Revenue's system check verifies the calculation of SDLT, and
- payment of the SDLT is enclosed,

(reg. 4).

If the Revenue is satisfied that a certificate has been lost or destroyed, it will issue a duplicate (reg. 6).

If a return is made that relates to more than one transaction, the Revenue will issue only one certificate in respect of all of the transactions covered by the one return. However, the Revenue may provide separate certificates for each transaction if requested by the purchaser (reg. 7).

Loss or destruction of, or damage to, return, etc.

Where a return delivered to the Revenue, or any other document relating to tax made by or provided to the Revenue, has been lost or destroyed (ie by the Revenue), or been so defaced or damaged as to be illegible or otherwise useless, the Revenue may treat the return as not having been delivered or the document as not having been made or provided (FA 2003, s. 82).

However, if as a result a person is charged with SDLT but proves to the satisfaction of the General or Special Commissioners that he has already paid tax in respect of the transaction in question, the charge must be reduced, or a repayment made, as the case may require.

Meaning of 'effective date' of a transaction

The general rule is that the effective date of a land transaction is the date of completion (FA 2003, s. 119).

See **10.2** regarding the case where a contract is substantially performed without having been completed.

See **10.4** regarding options and pre-emption rights.

SDLT codes
Type of property (Question 1)

Residential	01
Mixed	02
Non-residential	03

Description of transaction (Question 2)

Conveyance/transfer	F
Grant of lease	L
Other	O

Estate or interest transferred (Question 3)

Freehold with vacant possession	F P
Freehold subject to a long lease or leases each reserving a ground rent or nominal rent (for example, the acquisition of the freehold ground rents from a block of flats let on 99 year leases at £50 per annum each)	F G
Freehold subject to a lease or tenancy to an occupier (for example, the acquisition of a freehold house subject to a tenancy or a shop subject to a lease to the occupier)	F T
Long leasehold at a ground rent or nominal rent with vacant possession (for example, the acquisition of a vacant possession flat held on a 99 year lease at a ground rent of £50 per annum)	L G
Long leasehold subject to a lease or leases to an occupier (for example, the acquisition of the 99 year leasehold interest in a shop subject to a lease to the occupier)	L T
A lease to an occupier, for instance, with vacant possession and not at a ground rent or nominal rent (for example, the grant of a new lease of a shop to an occupier or the assignment of such a lease)	L P
All other interests (for example the acquisition of a share of any legal interest, – or the acquisition of an easement)	O T

Scottish transactions

Owner's interest with vacant possession	F P
Superior's interest, including minutes of waiver	F G
Owner's interest subject to tenancy	F T
Leasehold/tenant's interest	L P

Reliefs (Question 9)

Designated disadvantaged areas (residential)	05
Designated disadvantaged areas (non-residential)	06
Designated disadvantaged areas (mixed)	07
Part-exchange (house-building company)	08
Re-location of employment	09
Compulsory purchase facilitating development	10
Compliance with planning obligations	11
Group relief	12
Reconstruction relief	13
Acquisition relief (tax at 0.5 per cent)	14
Demutualisation of insurance company	15
Demutualisation of building society	16

Incorporation of limited liability partnership	17
Transfers involving public bodies	18
Transfer in consequence of reorganisation of parliamentary constituencies	19
Charities	20
Acquisition by bodies established for national purposes	21
Right to buy transactions	22
Registered social landlords	23
Alternative property finance	24
Collective enfranchisement by leaseholders (does not apply in Scotland)	25
Crofting community right to buy (applies in Scotland only)	26
Diplomatic privileges	27
Other	28
Combination of reliefs	29

Form of consideration (Question 12)

Cash	30
Debt (includes assumption by the purchaser of outstanding mortgage)	31
Building works	32
Employment	33
Other (such as an annuity)	34
Shares in a quoted company	35
Shares in an unquoted company	36
Other land	37
Services	38
Contingent	39

Type of lease (Question 16)

Residential	R
Non-residential	N
Mixed	M

Mineral rights reserved (SDLT3 Question 7)

More than one type shown below	01
Anhydrite	02
Barytes	03
Brickearth	04
Calcite	05
Chalk	06
Chert	07

Clay – ball	08
Clay – brick	09
Clay – cement	10
Clay – china	11
Clay – silica	12
Coal	13
Fieldspar	14
Fireclay	15
Flint	16
Fluorspar	17
Fullers Earth	18
Granite	19
Gypsum	20
Ironstone	21
Lead	22
Limestone	23
Marl	24
Oil	25
Peat	26
Potash	27
Salt	28
Sand	29
Sand and gravel	30
Sandstone	31
Shale	32
Slate	33
Tin	34
Vein minerals	35
Other	36

Other considerations (SDLT4 Question 18)

Debt (includes assumption by the purchaser of outstanding mortgage)	01
Building works	02
Employment	03
Other (such as an annuity)	04
Shares in a quoted company	05
Shares in an unquoted company	06
Other land	07
Services	08
Contingent	09

Local authority codes (SDLT3 Question 29)

Aberdeen	9051
Aberdeenshire	9052
Adur	3805
Allerdale	0905
Alnwick	2905
Amber Valley	1005
Angus	9053
Antrim	7005
Argyll and Bute	9054
Ards	7010
Armagh	7015
Arun	3810
Ashfield	3005
Ashford	2205
Aylesbury Vale	0405
Babergh	3505
Ballymena	7020
Ballymoney	7025
Banbridge	7030
Barking and Dagenham	5060
Barnet	5090
Barnsley	4405
Barrow in Furness	0910
Basildon	1505
Basingstoke and Deane	1705
Bassetlaw	3010
Bath and North-East Somerset	0114
Bedford	0205
Belfast	7035
Berwick-upon-Tweed	2910
Bexley	5120
Birmingham	4605
Blaby	2405
Blackburn with Darwen	2372
Blackpool	2373
Blaenau Gwent	6910
Blyth Valley	2915
Bolsover	1010
Bolton	4205
Borders, The	9055

Boston	2505
Bournemouth	1250
Bracknell Forest	0335
Bradford	4705
Braintree	1510
Breckland	2605
Brent	5150
Brentwood	1515
Bridgend	6915
Bridgnorth	3205
Brighton and Hove	1445
Bristol	0116
Broadland	2610
Bromley	5180
Bromsgrove	1805
Broxbourne	1905
Broxtowe	3015
Burnley	2315
Bury	4210
Caerphilly	6920
Calderdale	4710
Cambridge	0505
Camden	5210
Cannock Chase	3405
Canterbury	2210
Caradon	0805
Cardiff	6815
Carlisle	0915
Carmarthenshire (Carmarthen)	6825
Carmarthenshire (Dinefwr)	6828
Carmarthenshire (Llanelli)	6829
Carrick	0810
Carrickfergus	7040
Castle Morpeth	2920
Castle Point	1520
Castlereagh	7045
Ceredigion	6820
Charnwood	2410
Chelmsford	1525
Cheltenham	1605
Cherwell	3105

Chester	0605
Chester-le-Street	1305
Chesterfield	1015
Chichester	3815
Chiltern	0415
Chorley	2320
Christchurch	1210
Clackmannan	9056
Colchester	1530
Coleraine	7050
Congleton	0610
Conwy	6905
Cookstown	7055
Copeland	0920
Corby	2805
Cotswold	1610
Coventry	4610
Craigavon	7060
Craven	2705
Crawley	3820
Crewe and Nantwich	0615
Croydon	5240
Dacorum	1910
Darlington	1350
Dartford	2215
Daventry	2810
Denbighshire	6830
Derby	1055
Derbyshire Dales	1045
Derry	7095
Derwentside	1315
Doncaster	4410
Dover	2220
Down	7065
Dudley	4615
Dumfries and Galloway	9058
Dundee	9059
Dungannon	7070
Durham	1320
Ealing	5270
Easington	1325

East Ayrshire	9060
East Cambridgeshire	0510
East Devon	1105
East Dorset	1240
East Dunbartonshire	9061
East Hampshire	1710
East Hertfordshire	1915
East Lindsey	2510
East Lothian	9062
East Northamptonshire	2815
East Renfrewshire	9063
East Riding of Yorkshire	2001
East Staffordshire	3410
Eastbourne	1410
Eastleigh	1715
Eden	0925
Edinburgh	9064
Ellesmere Port and Neston	0620
Elmbridge	3605
Enfield	5300
Epping Forest	1535
Epsom and Ewell	3610
Erewash	1025
Exeter	1110
Falkirk	9065
Fareham	1720
Fenland	0515
Fermanagh	7075
Fife	9066
Flintshire	6835
Forest Heath	3510
Forest of Dean	1615
Fylde	2325
Gateshead	4505
Gedling	3020
Glasgow	9067
Gloucester	1620
Gosport	1725
Gravesham	2230
Great Yarmoth	2615
Greenwich	5330

Guildford	3615
Gwynedd	6810
Hackney	5360
Halton	0650
Hambledon	2710
Hammersmith and Fulham	5390
Harborough	2415
Haringey	5420
Harlow	1540
Harrogate	2715
Harrow	5450
Hart	1730
Hartlepool	0724
Hastings	1415
Havant	1735
Havering	5480
Herefordshire	1850
Hertsmere	1920
High Peak	1030
Highland	9068
Hillingdon	5510
Hinckley and Bosworth	2420
Horsham	3825
Hounslow	5540
Huntingdonshire	0520
Hyndburn	2330
Inverclyde	9069
Ipswich	3515
Isle of Anglesey	6805
Isle of Wight	2100
Isles of Scilly	0835
Islington	5570
Kennet	3905
Kensington and Chelsea	5600
Kerrier	0815
Kettering	2820
Kings Lynn and West Norfolk	2635
Kingston-upon-Hull	2004
Kingston-upon-Thames	5630
Kirklees	4715
Knowsley	4305

Lambeth	5660
Lancaster	2335
Larne	7080
Leeds	4720
Leicester	2465
Lewes	1425
Lewisham	5690
Lichfield	3415
Limavady	7085
Lincoln	515
Lisburn	7090
Liverpool	4310
London	5030
Luton	0230
Macclesfield	0630
Magherafelt	7100
Maidstone	2235
Maldon	1545
Malvern Hills	1860
Manchester	4215
Mansfield	3025
Medway	2280
Melton	2430
Mendip	3305
Merthyr Tydfil	6925
Merton	5720
Mid-Bedfordshire	0215
Mid-Devon	1135
Mid-Suffolk	3520
Mid-Sussex	3830
Middlesbrough	0734
Midlothian	9070
Milton Keynes	0435
Mole Valley	3620
Monmouthshire	6840
Moray	9071
Moyle	7110
Neath Port Talbot	6930
New Forest	1740
Newark and Sherwood	3030
Newcastle-under-Lyme	3420

Newcastle-upon-Tyne	4510
Newham	5750
Newport	6935
Newry and Mourne	7105
Newtonabbey	7115
North Ayrshire	9072
North Cornwall	0820
North Devon	1115
North Dorset	1215
North Down	7120
North-east Derbyshire	1035
North-east Lincolnshire	2002
North Hertfordshire	1925
North Kesteven	2520
North Lanarkshire	9073
North Lincolnshire	2003
North Norfolk	2620
North Shropshire	3210
North Somerset	0121
North Tyneside	4515
North Warwickshire	3705
North-west Leicestershire	2435
North Wiltshire	3910
Northampton	2825
Norwich	2625
Nottingham	3060
Nuneaton and Bedworth	3710
Oadby and Wigston	2440
Oldham	4220
Orkney Islands	9000
Omagh	7125
Oswestry	3215
Oxford	3110
Pembrokeshire	6845
Pendle	2340
Penwith	0825
Perthshire and Kinross	9074
Peterborough	0540
Plymouth	1160
Poole	1255
Portsmouth	1775

Powys (Montgomeryshire)	6850
Powys (Radnorshire)	6853
Powys (Breconshire)	6854
Preston	2345
Purbeck	1225
Reading	0345
Redbridge	5780
Redcar and Cleveland	0728
Redditch	1825
Reigate and Banstead	3625
Renfrewshire	9075
Restormel	0830
Rhondda, Cynon, Taff	6940
Ribble Valley	2350
Richmond-upon-Thames	5810
Richmondshire	2720
Rochdale	4225
Rochford	1550
Rossendale	2355
Rother	1430
Rotherham	4415
Rugby	3715
Runnymede	3630
Rushcliffe	3040
Rushmoor	1750
Rutland	2470
Ryedale	2725
Salford	4230
Salisbury	3915
Sandwell	4620
Scarborough	2730
Sedgefield	1330
Sedgemoor	3310
Sefton	4320
Selby	2735
Sevenoaks	2245
Sheffield	4420
Shepway	2250
Shetland Islands	9010
Shrewbury and Atcham	3220
Slough	0350

Solihull	4625
South Ayrshire	9076
South Bedfordshire	0220
South Buckinghamshire	0410
South Cambridgeshire	0530
South Derbyshire	1040
South Gloucestershire	0119
South Hams	1125
South Holland	2525
South Kesteven	2530
South Lakeland	0930
South Lanarkshire	9077
South Norfolk	2630
South Northamptonshire	2830
South Oxfordshire	3115
South Ribble	2360
South Shropshire	3225
South Somerset	3325
South Staffordshire	3420
South Tyneside	4520
Southampton	1780
Southend-on-Sea	1590
Southwark	5840
Spelthorne	3635
St Albans	1930
St Edmundsbury	3525
St Helens	4315
Stafford	3425
Staffordshire Moorlands	3435
Stevenage	1935
Stirling	9078
Stockport	4235
Stockton-on-Tees	0738
Stoke-on-Trent	3455
Strabane	7130
Stratford-upon-Avon	3720
Stroud	1625
Suffolk Coastal	3530
Sunderland	4525
Surrey Heath	3640
Sutton	5870

Swale	2255
Swansea	6855
Swindon	3935
Tameside	4240
Tamworth	3445
Tandridge	3645
Taunton Deane	3315
Teesdale	1335
Teignbridge	1130
Telford and Wrekin	3240
Tendring	1560
Test Valley	1760
Tewkesbury	1630
Thanet	2260
Three Rivers	1940
Thurrock	1595
Tonbridge and Malling	2265
Torbay	1165
Torfaen	6945
Torridge	1145
Tower Hamlets	5900
Trafford	4245
Tunbridge Wells	2270
Tynedale	2925
Uttlesford	1570
Vale of Glamorgan	6950
Vale of White Horse	3120
Vale Royal	0635
Wakefield	4725
Walsall	4630
Waltham Forest	5930
Wandsworth	5960
Wansbeck	2930
Warrington	0655
Warwick	3725
Watford	1945
Waveney	3535
Waverley	3650
Wealden	1435
Wear Valley	1340
Wellingborough	2835

Welwyn Hatfield	1950
West Berkshire	0340
West Devon	1150
West Dorset	1230
West Dunbartonshire	9057
West Lancashire	2365
West Lindsey	2535
West Lothian	9079
West Oxfordshire	3125
West Somerset	3320
West Wiltshire	3925
Western Isles	9020
Westminster	5990
Weymouth and Portland	1235
Wigan	4250
Winchester	1765
Windsor and Maidenhead	0355
Wirral	4325
Woking	3655
Wokingham	0360
Wolverhampton	4635
Worcester	1835
Worthing	3835
Wrexham	6955
Wychavon	1840
Wycombe	0425
Wyre	2370
Wyre Forest	1845
York	2741

NLPG UPRN (Question 31)

The Revenue's guidance note reads as follows:

'NLPG UPRN stands for "National Land and Property Gazetteer Unique Property Reference Number". This reference is increasingly used as a common property address reference by many public authorities. If you know the number or know you can find it, then please enter it here. You can obtain the UPRN from any of the three National Land Information Service (NLIS) Licensed Channels:

- NLIS Searchflow: Tel 0870 755 9940 www.searchflow.co.uk
- TM Property Service: Tel 0800 068 1272 www.tmproperty.co.uk
- Transaction Online: Tel 0800 0854 951 www.transaction-online.co.uk

In Northern Ireland the equivalent is "Pointer". For Northern Ireland properties enter prefix NI in the first two boxes in all cases, followed by the 12 digit Pointer UPRN. Note that 'Pointer' UPRN's do not cover undeveloped land and are not available from the NPLG sources. You can get them directly from "Pointer" or the Valuation and Lands Agency website from mid-2004.

Some providers may make a charge for this service. You are advised to check with the provider.'

10.11.3   Further return on withdrawal of relief, etc.

Further return where relief withdrawn

Where group relief, reconstruction relief, acquisition relief, or charities relief is withdrawn to any extent by reason of a degrouping event or some other disqualifying event, the purchaser must deliver a further return before the end of the period of 30 days after the date on which the disqualifying event occurred (FA 2003, s. 81).

The return must include a self-assessment of the amount of tax chargeable, and must be accompanied by payment of that tax.

Return or further return in consequence of later linked transaction

Where the effect of a transaction ('the later transaction') that is linked to an earlier transaction is that the earlier transaction becomes notifiable, or that SDLT or additional SDLT is payable in respect of the earlier transaction, the purchaser under the earlier transaction must deliver a return or further return in respect of that transaction before the end of the period of 30 days after the effective date of the later transaction (FA 2003, s. 81A).

The return must include a self-assessment of the amount of tax chargeable as a result of the later transaction and must be accompanied by payment of that tax. That tax is calculated by reference to the rates in force at the effective date of the earlier transaction.

10.11.4   Late and incorrect returns

Failure to deliver return: flat-rate penalty

A person who fails to deliver a land transaction return by the filing date is liable to a flat-rate penalty of:

- £100 if the return is delivered within three months after the filing date; and
- £200 in any other case,

(FA 2003, Sch. 10, Para. 3).

Failure to deliver return: tax-related penalty

A purchaser who fails to deliver a land transaction return within 12 months after the filing date is liable to a penalty not exceeding 100 per cent of the amount of tax chargeable in respect of the transaction. This is in addition to any flat-rate penalty that may be imposed (FA 2003, Sch. 10, Para. 4).

Formal notice to deliver return: daily penalty

If it appears to the Revenue that a purchaser has failed to deliver a land transaction return in respect of a chargeable transaction, and that the filing date has now passed, it may issue a notice requiring him to deliver a land transaction return in respect of the transaction (FA 2003, Sch. 10, Para. 5). The Revenue must give at least 30 days' notice for filing the return.

If the purchaser does not comply with the notice within the specified period, the Revenue may apply to the General or Special Commissioners for an order imposing a daily penalty. The Commissioners may impose a penalty or penalties not exceeding £60 for each day on which the failure continues after the day on which he is notified of the direction.

This penalty is independent of the above flat-rate and tax-related penalties.

Amendment of return by purchaser

The purchaser may amend a land transaction return within 12 months after the filing date (FA 2003, Sch. 10, Para. 6).

Correction of return by Revenue

The Revenue may amend a land transaction return so as to correct obvious errors or omissions in the return, whether errors of principle, arithmetical mistakes or otherwise (FA 2003, Sch. 10, Para. 7). Any such correction must be notified to the purchaser.

No such correction may be made more than nine months after the day on which the return or amended return was delivered.

A correction by the Revenue is of no effect if the purchaser:

(a)   amends the return so as to reject the correction, or

(b) after the end of the period within which he may amend the return, but within three months from the date of issue of the notice of correction, gives notice rejecting the correction.

Notice under (b) must be given to the officer of the Board by whom notice of the correction was given.

Penalty for incorrect or uncorrected return

A purchaser who fraudulently or negligently delivers a land transaction return that is incorrect is liable to a tax-related penalty (FA 2003, Sch. 10, Para. 8).

Similarly, if a purchaser discovers that a land transaction return delivered by him neither fraudulently nor negligently is incorrect and does not remedy the error without unreasonable delay, he is liable to a tax-related penalty.

The penalty is an amount not exceeding 100 per cent of the tax understated.

Penalty for assisting in preparation of incorrect return, etc.

A person who assists in or induces the preparation or delivery of any information, return or other document that he knows will be, or is likely to be, used for any purpose of tax, and he knows to be incorrect, is liable to a penalty not exceeding £3,000 (FA 2003, s. 96).

10.11.5   Registration of land transactions

A land transaction may not be registered, recorded or otherwise reflected in an entry made in a land register unless there is produced, together with the relevant application, a certificate as to compliance with the requirements of the SDLT legislation in relation to the transaction (FA 2003, s. 79).

The certificate must be either:

- a certificate issued by the Revenue (a 'Revenue certificate' – see **10.11.2** above) that a land transaction return has been delivered in respect of the transaction, or
- a certificate issued by the purchaser (a 'self-certificate' – see **10.12** below) that no land transaction return is required in respect of the transaction.

A land register means:

- in England and Wales, in the register of title maintained by the Chief Land Registrar;
- in Scotland, in any register maintained by the Keeper of the Registers of Scotland, or

- in Northern Ireland, in any register maintained by the Land Registry of Northern Ireland or in the Registry of Deeds for Northern Ireland.

The registrar (in Scotland, the Keeper of the Registers of Scotland):

- must allow the Revenue to inspect any certificates or self-certificates produced to him under the above rules and in his possession, and
- may enter into arrangements for affording the Revenue other information and facilities for verifying that the requirements of this Part have been complied with.

The requirement for a certificate does not apply where the entry is required to be made without any application, or so far as the entry relates to an interest or right other than the chargeable interest acquired by the purchaser under the land transaction that is to be registered.

The requirement applies to every land transaction other than:

- a contract for a land transaction under which the transaction is to be completed by a conveyance, in which case it applies in relation to the conveyance, or
- a transfer of rights under such a contract.

10.11.6   Record-keeping requirements

A purchaser who is required to deliver a land transaction return must keep such records as may be needed to enable him to deliver a correct and complete return. These records must be preserved for six years after the effective date of the transaction. The six-year period may be extended until any later date on which:

- an enquiry into the return is completed, or
- if there is no enquiry, the Revenue no longer has power to enquire into the return,

(FA 2003, Sch. 10, Para. 9).

The records required to be kept and preserved include:

- relevant instruments relating to the transaction, in particular, any contract or conveyance, and any supporting maps, plans or similar documents, and
- records of relevant payments, receipts and financial arrangements.

Preservation of information instead of original records

The duty to preserve records may be satisfied by the preservation of the information contained in them (FA 2003, Sch. 10, Para. 10).

Where information is preserved, a copy of any document forming part of the records is admissible in evidence in any proceedings before the Commissioners to the same extent as the records themselves.

Penalty for failure to keep and preserve records

A person who fails to comply with the above requirements in relation to a transaction is liable to a penalty not exceeding £3,000 (FA 2003, Sch. 10, Para. 11).

However, no penalty is incurred if the Revenue is satisfied that any facts that it reasonably requires to be proved, and that would have been proved by the records, are proved by other documentary evidence provided to it.

10.11.7   Enquiries into returns

Notice of enquiry

The Revenue may enquire into a land transaction return if it gives notice to the purchaser before the end of the period of nine months:

- after the filing date, if the return was delivered on or before that date;
- after the date on which the return was delivered, if the return was delivered after the filing date,
- after the date on which the amendment was made, if the return is amended by the purchaser,

(FA 2003, Sch. 10, Para. 12).

A return that has been the subject of one notice of enquiry may not be the subject of another, except one given in consequence of an amendment of the return by the purchaser.

An enquiry is deemed to commence when a notice under the above rule is issued.

Scope of enquiry

An enquiry may extend to anything contained in the return, or required to be contained in the return, that relates:

- to the question whether tax is chargeable in respect of the transaction, or
- to the amount of tax so chargeable,

(FA 2003, Sch. 10, Para. 13).

However, if the notice of enquiry is given as a result of an amendment of the return by purchaser:

- at a time when it is no longer possible to give notice of enquiry under the nine-month rule, or
- after an enquiry into the return has been completed,

the enquiry into the return is limited to matters to which the amendment relates or that are affected by the amendment.

Notice to produce documents, etc. for purposes of enquiry

In pursuance of an enquiry, the Revenue may by notice in writing require the purchaser:

- to produce to it such documents in his possession or power, and
- to provide it with such information, in such form,

as it may reasonably require for the purposes of the enquiry (FA 2003, Sch. 10, Para. 14).

The Revenue must allow at least 30 days for the production of these items.

Copies of documents may be produced instead of originals, but:

- the copies must be photographic or other facsimiles, and
- the Revenue may by notice require the original to be produced for inspection.

The Revenue must allow at least 30 days for the production of the original documents.

The Revenue may take copies of, or make extracts from, any documents produced to it under this paragraph.

A purchaser is not obliged to produce documents or provide information relating to the conduct of:

- any pending appeal by him, or
- any pending referral of a question to the Special Commissioners during an enquiry to which he is a party.

Appeal against notice to produce documents, etc.

There is a right of appeal against a requirement imposed by a notice to produce documents or provide information. Notice of appeal must be given in writing, within 30 days after the issue of the notice to produce documents, etc. It must be sent to the officer of the Board by whom that notice was given.

An appeal against such a notice is heard and determined in the same way as an appeal against an assessment (FA 2003, Sch. 10, Para. 15).

On appeal the Commissioners must set aside the notice so far as it requires the production of documents, or the provision of information, that appears to them not reasonably required for the purposes of the enquiry, but must otherwise confirm the notice. Once a notice is confirmed by the Commissioners (or so far as it is confirmed), it has effect as if the 30-day compliance period runs from the determination of the appeal.

The decision of the Commissioners is final.

Penalty for failure to produce documents, etc.

A person who fails to comply with a notice to produce documents, etc. for purposes of enquiry is liable to a penalty of £50. If the failure continues after the £50 penalty is imposed a daily penalty may be imposed for each day on which the failure continues. The amount of the daily penalty is:

- £30 if the penalty is determined by an officer of the Board, and
- £150 if the penalty is determined by the court,

(FA 2003, Sch. 10, Para. 16).

No penalty may be imposed after the failure has been remedied.

Amendment of self-assessment during enquiry to prevent loss of tax

When an enquiry is in progress, the Revenue may amend the purchaser's self-assessment to make good any deficiency if it forms the opinion that unless the assessment is immediately amended there is likely to be a loss of tax to the Crown. Notice of the amendment must be given to the purchaser (FA 2003, Sch. 10, Para. 17).

Amendment of return by taxpayer during enquiry

If a return is amended by the purchaser at a time when an enquiry is in progress into the return, it does not restrict the scope of the enquiry but may be taken into account (together with any matters arising) in the enquiry (FA 2003, Sch. 10, Para. 18).

So far as the amendment affects the amount of tax stated in the self-assessment, it does not take effect while the enquiry is in progress. If the Revenue states in the closure notice that it has taken the amendment into account in formulating the amendments contained in the notice, or that the amendment is incorrect, the amendment does not take effect. Otherwise, it takes effect when the closure notice is issued.

Referral of questions to Special Commissioners during enquiry

At any time when an enquiry is in progress, any question arising in connection with the subject matter of the enquiry may be referred to the Special Commissioners for their determination (FA 2003, Sch. 10, Para. 19).

Notice of referral must be given:

- jointly by the purchaser and the Revenue;
- in writing,
- to the Special Commissioners.

The notice of referral must specify the question or questions being referred.

More than one notice of referral may be given under this paragraph in relation to an enquiry.

Withdrawal of notice of referral

The Revenue or the purchaser may withdraw a notice of referral by notice given:

- in writing;
- to the other party to the referral and to the Special Commissioners,
- before the first hearing by the Special Commissioners in relation to the referral,

(FA 2003, Sch. 10, Para. 20).

Effect of referral on enquiry

While proceedings on a referral are in progress in relation to an enquiry:

- no closure notice may be given in relation to the enquiry, and
- no application may be made for a direction to give a closure notice,

(FA 2003, Sch. 10, Para. 21).

Proceedings on a referral are in progress until the questions referred have been finally determined, or the referral has been withdrawn.

A question referred is finally determined when:

- it has been determined by the Special Commissioners, and
- there is no further possibility of the determination being varied or set aside (disregarding any power to grant permission to appeal out of time).

Effect of determination

The determination of a question referred to the Special Commissioners is binding on the parties to the referral in the same way, and to the same extent, as a decision on a preliminary issue in an appeal (FA 2003, Sch. 10, Para. 22).

Accordingly, it must be taken into account by the Revenue in reaching its conclusions on the enquiry, and in formulating any amendments of the return required to give effect to those conclusions.

The right of appeal against an assessment may not be exercised so as to reopen the question determined except to the extent (if any) that it could be reopened if it had been determined as a preliminary issue in that appeal.

Completion of enquiry

An enquiry is completed when the Revenue issue a 'closure notice' to inform the purchaser that it has completed its enquiries. The notice must state its conclusions and make any necessary amendments of the return required to give effect to its conclusions (FA 2003, Sch. 10, Para. 23).

Direction to complete enquiry

The purchaser may apply to the General or Special Commissioners for a direction that the Revenue gives a closure notice within a specified period (FA 2003, Sch. 10, Para. 24).

Any such application is heard and determined in the same way as an appeal.

The Commissioners hearing the application must give a direction unless they are satisfied that the Revenue has reasonable grounds for not giving a closure notice within a specified period.

Revenue practice
Inland Revenue practice in relation to enquiries is set out in Code of Practice 24. Enquiries into companies and partnerships are dealt with in Code of Practice 25.

10.11.8 Revenue determinations

Power to make determination

Where no land transaction return for a chargeable transaction is delivered by the filing date, the Revenue may make a determination to the best of its information and belief of the amount of tax chargeable in respect of the transaction (FA 2003, Sch. 10, Para. 25). The time limit for such a determination is six years from the effective date of the transaction.

Notice of the determination must be served on the purchaser, stating the date on which it is issued.

A determination is treated as if were a self-assessment by the purchaser for the purposes of:

- the provisions relating to tax-related penalties;
- interest on unpaid tax, and
- collection and recovery of unpaid tax, etc.,

(Sch. 10, Para. 26).

However, there is no right of appeal against the determination. The appropriate remedy is to file the relevant return (see below).

This is without prejudice to any liability of the purchaser to a penalty for failure to deliver a return.

A determination is not ineffective:

- for want of form, or
- by reason of any mistake, defect or omission in it,

if it is substantially in conformity with the SDLT legislation and its intended effect is reasonably ascertainable by the person to whom it is directed.

The validity of a determination is not affected:

- by any mistake in it as to the name of a person liable; or the amount of the tax charged, or
- by reason of any variance between the notice of assessment or determination and the assessment or determination itself,

(FA 2003, s. 83).

Subsequent filing of return

If after a Revenue determination has been made the purchaser files a land transaction return in respect of the transaction concerned, the self-assessment included in that return supersedes the determination (FA 2003, Sch. 10, Para. 27).

This does not apply to a return delivered:

- more than six years after the day on which the power to make the determination first became exercisable (which is generally 30 days after the effective date of the transaction), or
- more than 12 months after the date of the determination,

whichever is the later.

Where proceedings have been begun for the recovery of any tax charged by a Revenue determination, and before the proceedings are concluded the determination is superseded by a self-assessment, the proceedings may be continued as if they were proceedings for the recovery of any unpaid tax charged by the self-assessment.

10.11.9   Revenue assessments

Assessment where loss of tax discovered

If the Revenue discovers as regards a chargeable transaction that:

- an amount of tax that ought to have been assessed has not been assessed; or
- an assessment to tax is or has become insufficient, or
- relief has been given that is or has become excessive,

it may make an assessment (a 'discovery assessment') in the amount or further amount that ought in its opinion to be charged in order to make good to the Crown the loss of tax (FA 2003, Sch. 10, Para. 28).

Assessment to recover excessive repayment of tax

If an amount of tax has been repaid to any person that ought not to have been repaid to him, that amount may be assessed and recovered as if it were unpaid tax (FA 2003, Sch. 10, Para. 29).

Where the repayment was made with interest, the amount assessed and recovered may include the amount of interest that ought not to have been paid.

Restrictions on assessment where return delivered

If the purchaser has delivered a land transaction return in respect of the transaction in question, an assessment in respect of the transaction may only be made in the following cases (FA 2003, Sch. 10, Para. 30):

First case
This is where the situation is attributable to fraudulent or negligent conduct on the part of:

- the purchaser;
- a person acting on behalf of the purchaser, or
- a person who was a partner of the purchaser at the relevant time.

Second case

This is where the Revenue, at the time it ceased to be entitled to give a notice of enquiry into the return, or completed its enquiries into the return, could not have been reasonably expected, on the basis of the information made available to it before that time, to be aware of the situation.

Information is regarded as made available to the Revenue if:

(a)   it is contained in a land transaction return made by the purchaser;

(b)   it is contained in any documents produced or information provided to the Revenue for the purposes of an enquiry into any such return, or

(c)   it is information the existence of which, and the relevance of which as regards the situation:

    (i)   could reasonably be expected to be inferred by the Revenue from information falling within (a) or (b) above, or

    (ii)   are notified in writing to the Revenue by the purchaser or a person acting on his behalf.

No assessment may be made if:

- the situation is attributable to a mistake in the return as to the basis on which the tax liability ought to have been computed, and
- the return was in fact made on the basis or in accordance with the practice generally prevailing at the time it was made.

Time limit for assessment

The general rule is that no assessment may be made more than six years after the effective date of the transaction to which it relates (FA 2003, Sch. 10, Para. 31).

However, the six-year period is increased to 21 years in a case involving fraud or negligence on the part of:

- the purchaser;
- a person acting on behalf of the purchaser, or
- a person who was a partner of the purchaser at the relevant time.

An assessment to recover excessive repayment of tax is not out of time:

- in a case where notice of enquiry is given into the land transaction return delivered by the person concerned, if it is made before the enquiry is completed,
- in any case, if it is made within one year after the repayment in question was made.

Where the purchaser has died:

- any assessment on the personal representatives of the deceased must be made within three years after his death, and
- an assessment may not be made in respect of a transaction of which the effective date was more than six years before the death.

Any objection to the making of an assessment on the ground that the time limit for making it has expired can only be made on an appeal against the assessment.

Assessment procedure

Notice of an assessment must be served on the purchaser stating:

- the tax due;
- the date on which the notice is issued, and
- the time within which any appeal against the assessment must be made,

(FA 2003, Sch. 10, Para. 32).

After notice of the assessment has been served on the purchaser, the assessment may not be altered except in accordance with the express provisions of the SDLT legislation.

Where an officer of the Board has decided to make an assessment to tax, and has taken all other decisions needed for arriving at the amount of the assessment, he may entrust to some other officer of the Board responsibility for completing the assessing procedure, whether by means involving the use of a computer or otherwise, including responsibility for serving notice of the assessment.

An assessment is not ineffective:

- for want of form; or
- by reason of any mistake, defect or omission in it,

if it is substantially in conformity with the SDLT legislation and its intended effect is reasonably ascertainable by the person to whom it is directed.

The validity of an assessment is not affected:

- by any mistake in it as to the name of a person liable, or the amount of the tax charged, or
- by reason of any variance between the notice of assessment or determination and the assessment or determination itself,

(FA 2003, s. 83).

10.11.10   Relief for excessive assessment

Relief in case of double assessment

A person who believes he has been assessed to tax more than once in respect of the same matter may make a claim for relief. The claim must be made by notice in writing given to the Revenue (FA 2003, Sch. 10, Para. 33).

If the Revenue is satisfied that the person has been assessed to tax more than once in respect of the same matter, it must amend the assessment or assessments concerned or give relief by way of discharge or repayment of tax or otherwise, to eliminate the double charge.

An appeal against the Revenue's decision may be brought to the Commissioners having jurisdiction to hear an appeal relating to the assessment, or the later of the assessments, to which the claim relates.

Relief in case of mistake in return

A person who believes he has paid tax under an assessment that was excessive by reason of some mistake in a land transaction return may make a claim for relief. The claim must be made by notice in writing given to the Revenue not more than six years after the effective date of the transaction (FA 2003, Sch. 10, Para. 34).

The Revenue must then enquire into the matter and give, by way of repayment, such relief in respect of the mistake as is reasonable and just.

No relief is given:

- in respect of a mistake as to the basis on which the liability of the claimant ought to have been computed when the return was in fact made on the basis or in accordance with the practice generally prevailing at the time when it was made, or
- in respect of a mistake in a claim or election included in the return.

In determining a claim, the Revenue must have regard to all the relevant circumstances of the case and must consider whether the granting of relief would result in amounts being excluded from charge to tax.

An appeal against the Revenue's decision on the claim lies to the Special Commissioners.

10.11.11 Appeals

Right of appeal

An appeal may be brought against:

(a) an amendment of a self-assessment by Revenue during an enquiry to prevent loss of tax;

(b) a conclusion stated or amendment made by a closure notice;

(c) a discovery assessment, or

(d) an assessment to recover an excessive repayment of tax,

(FA 2003, Sch. 10, Para. 35).

The appeal lies to the General or Special Commissioners.

An appeal against an amendment of a self-assessment made while an enquiry is in progress may not be heard and determined until the enquiry is completed.

Notice of appeal

Notice of an appeal must be given in writing to the relevant officer of the Board within 30 days after the 'specified date' (FA 2003, Sch. 10, Para. 36). The notice of appeal must specify the grounds of appeal. However, on the hearing of the appeal, the Commissioners may allow the appellant to put forward grounds not specified in the notice, and take them into consideration, if satisfied that the omission was not deliberate or unreasonable.

Specified date

In relation to an appeal under (a) above – an amendment of a self-assessment by Revenue during an enquiry to prevent loss of tax:

- the specified date is the date on which the notice of amendment was issued, and
- the relevant officer of the Board is the officer by whom the notice of amendment was given.

In relation to an appeal under (b) above – conclusion stated or amendment made by a closure notice:

- the specified date is the date on which the closure notice was issued, and
- the relevant officer of the Board is the officer by whom the closure notice was given.

In relation to an appeal under (c) or (d) above – discovery assessment or assessment to recover excessive repayment:

- the specified date is the date on which the notice of assessment was issued, and
- the relevant officer of the Board is the officer by whom the notice of assessment was given.

Settling of appeals by agreement

If, before an appeal is determined, the appellant and the Revenue reach agreement on the matter under appeal, the same consequences follow, for all purposes, as if, at the time the agreement was come to, the Commissioners had determined the appeal in accordance with the agreement (FA 2003, Sch. 10, Para. 37).

This does not apply if, within 30 days from the date when the agreement was arrived at, the appellant gives notice in writing to the Revenue that he wishes to withdraw from the agreement.

Where the agreement is not in writing the details must be confirmed by notice in writing given by the Revenue to the appellant or by the appellant to the Revenue. The time when the agreement was reached is to the time when the notice of confirmation was given.

Where the appellant notifies the Revenue, orally or in writing, that he does not wish to proceed with the appeal, the appeal is treated as withdrawn unless the Revenue gives the appellant notice in writing within 30 days after that notification indicating that it is unwilling that the appeal should be withdrawn.

Notices may be given by or to a person acting on behalf of the appellant in relation to the appeal.

Payment of tax in an appeal

Where there is an appeal to the Commissioners, the tax charged by the amendment or assessment in question remains due and payable as if there had been no appeal (FA 2003, Sch. 10, Para. 38).

However, if the appellant has grounds for believing that he is overcharged to tax by the decision appealed against, he may by notice in writing apply to the Commissioners for a direction that payment of an amount of tax should be postponed pending the determination of the appeal (FA 2003, Sch. 10, Para. 39).

The notice must:

- be given to the relevant officer of the Board within 30 days after the specified date, and

- state the amount by which the appellant believes himself to be over-charged to tax, and his grounds for that belief.

An application may be made more than 30 days after the specified date if there is a change in the circumstances of the case as a result of which the appellant has grounds for believing that he is overcharged to tax by the decision appealed against.

If, after any determination of the amount of tax the payment of which should be postponed, there is a change in the circumstances of the case as a result of which either party has grounds for believing that the amount so determined has become excessive or insufficient, he may, by notice in writing given to the other party at any time before the determination of the appeal, apply to the Commissioners for a further determination of that amount.

An application for postponement is heard and determined by the Commissioners in the same way as an appeal. The fact that any such application has been heard and determined by any Commissioners does not preclude them from hearing and determining the appeal or any further application for postponement.

In determining the amount to be postponed, the Commissioners must have regard to the representations made and any evidence adduced, and must be satisfied that there are reasonable grounds for believing that the appellant is overcharged.

The date on which any tax not postponed is due and payable is determined as if the tax were charged by an amendment or assessment that was issued on the date on which the application was determined.

On the determination of the appeal, the date on which any tax postponed becomes payable in accordance with that determination is determined as if the tax were charged by an amendment or assessment that was issued on the date on which the Revenue issues to the appellant a notice of the total amount payable in accordance with the determination. Any tax overpaid must be repaid.

Agreement to postpone payment of tax

If the appellant and the Revenue agree that payment of an amount of tax should be postponed pending the determination of the appeal, that is treated in the same way as a determination by the Commissioners of an amount to be postponed (FA 2003, Sch. 10, Para. 40). This is without prejudice to the making of a further agreement or of a further direction.

Where the agreement is not in writing it must be confirmed by notice in writing given by the Revenue to the appellant or by the appellant to the Revenue officer. The agreement is then treated as having been reached when notice of confirmation was given.

An agreement may be reached by a person acting on behalf of the appellant in relation to the appeal.

Appeal procedures

The procedures for the hearing of appeals are set out in the Stamp Duty Land Tax (Appeals) Regulations 2004 (SI 2004/1363). These regulations deal with the assignment of appeals to commissioners, questions to be determined by the Lands Tribunal, transfer of complex cases to the Special Commissioners and the application of the provisions of the Taxes Management Act 1970.

10.12 Liability for, and payment of, SDLT

10.12.1 Persons liable

The general rule is that the purchaser is liable to pay the SDLT in respect of a chargeable transaction (FA 2003, s. 85(1)).

Where there are two or more purchasers who are or will be jointly entitled to the interest acquired, any liability of the purchaser in relation to the transaction is a joint and several liability of the purchasers (FA 2003, s. 103(2)(c)).

Where a person acquires a chargeable interest as bare trustee, the rules apply as if the interest were vested in, and the acts of the trustee in relation to it were the acts of, the person or persons for whom he is trustee. This means that the person beneficially entitled is liable for the SDLT (FA 2003, Sch. 16, Para. 3).

Where persons acquire a chargeable interest as trustees of a settlement, they are treated as purchasers of the whole of the interest acquired, including the beneficial interest (FA 2003, Sch. 16, Para. 4).

10.12.2 Due date for payment

General rule

The general rule is that SDLT payable on a land transaction must be paid at the same time that a land transaction return is made – ie within 30 days of the effective date of the transaction (FA 2003, s. 86).

Tax payable as a result of the withdrawal of group relief, reconstruction or acquisition relief, or charities relief must be paid at the same time that a return is made in respect of the withdrawal, ie within 30 days of the event giving rise to the withdrawal.

Tax payable as a result of the amendment of a return must be paid forthwith or, if the amendment is made before the filing date for the return, not later than that date.

Tax payable in accordance with a determination or assessment by the Revenue must be paid within 30 days after the determination or assessment is issued.

Payment may be deferred on application in cases of contingent or uncertain consideration, or on application for postponement of payment pending determination of appeal. However, this does not affect the date from which interest is payable.

Effective date

The general rule is that the effective date of a land transaction is the date of completion (FA 2003, s. 119).

See **10.1.2** regarding the case where a contract is substantially performed without having been completed.

See **10.1.4** regarding options and pre-emption rights.

10.12.3   Interest on overdue and overpaid tax

Interest on unpaid tax

Interest on any unpaid tax runs from 30 days after the relevant date until the date of payment (FA 2003, s. 87).

'The relevant date' is normally the effective date of the transaction. This applies in particular in a case where the rules relating to contingent, uncertain or unascertained consideration apply unless payment is deferred.

In the case of an amount payable because of the withdrawal of group relief, reconstruction or acquisition relief, or charities relief, it is the date of the disqualifying event.

In the case of a deferred payment (see **10.12.4**), it is the date when the deferred payment is due.

In the case of an amount payable because of the effect of a later linked transaction it is the effective date of the later transaction.

If an amount is lodged with the Revenue in respect of the tax, the amount on which interest is payable is reduced by that amount.

Where payment is made by cheque, and the cheque is paid on its first presentation to the banker on whom it is drawn, the payment is treated as made on the day on which the cheque was received by the Revenue (FA 2003, s. 92).

Interest on penalties

A penalty imposed under the SDLT legislation carries interest from the date it is determined until payment (FA 2003, s. 88).

Interest on repayment of tax overpaid, etc.

A repayment of SDLT by the Revenue carries interest for the period between the relevant time and the date when the order for repayment is issued. The same applies to the repayment of a penalty or an amount lodged with the Revenue (FA 2003, s. 89).

The relevant time is the date on which the payment of tax or penalty was made.

No interest is payable in respect of a payment made in consequence of an order or judgment of a court having power to allow interest on the payment.

Interest paid to any person under this section is not income of that person for any tax purposes.

Rates of interest

Interest is calculated at the rate applicable under FA 1989, s. 178 (see SI 1989/1297 and the relevant Revenue Press Releases).

10.12.4 Deferred payment of tax

Application to defer payment in case of contingent or uncertain consideration

The purchaser may apply to the Revenue to defer payment of SDLT in a case where the amount payable depends on the amount or value of chargeable consideration that:

* at the effective date of the transaction is contingent or uncertain, and

- falls to be paid or provided on one or more future dates of which at least one falls, or may fall, more than six months after the effective date of the transaction,

(FA 2003, s. 90).

An application under this section does not affect the purchaser's obligations as regards payment of tax in respect of chargeable consideration that has already been paid or provided or is not contingent and whose amount is ascertained or ascertainable at the time the application is made.

When application to be made

An application must be made on or before the last day of the period within which the land transaction return relating to the transaction in question must be delivered (SI 2003/2837, reg. 11).

Form and contents of application

An application must be in writing and must set out all the facts and circumstances relevant to it (SI 2003/2837, reg. 12). In particular, it must specify:

- the consideration to which it relates;
- the respects in which that consideration is contingent or uncertain; and
- the events ('relevant events') on the occurrence of which the whole or any part of that consideration will cease to be contingent, or become ascertained.

Additional contents of application where consideration consists of works or services

The application must contain a scheme for payment of tax, which must include a proposal for the payment of tax in respect of the consideration, or element of the consideration, consisting of the carrying out of such works, or the provision of such services, within 30 days after the carrying out or provision is substantially completed (SI 2003/2837, reg. 13).

If the carrying out of such works or the provision of such services is expected to last for more than six months, it must contain proposals for a scheme of payment of tax at intervals of not more than six months.

The works referred to are works of construction, improvement or repair of a building or other works to enhance the value of land.

Provision of information

The Revenue may by notice in writing require the applicant to provide such information as it may reasonably require for the purposes of determining whether to accept the application (SI 2003/2837, reg. 14). It must give at least 30 days' notice to provide the information.

Recovery of tax not postponed by application

Where an application has been made but has not been accepted by the Revenue, payment of an amount of such tax as would not be due and payable if the application were accepted is postponed pending the reaching of a decision on the application. Otherwise, the tax in respect of the chargeable consideration to which the application relates remains due and payable as if there had been no application (SI 2003/2837, reg. 15).

If an application is refused by the Revenue, the date on which any tax the payment of which had been postponed under the above rule becomes due and payable is determined as if it were charged by an assessment of which notice was issued on the date on which the Revenue issues a notice of the total amount payable in consequence of the refusal of the application (see **10.12.2**).

Notice of decision on an application

The Revenue must give notice in writing to the person by whom the application was made of its decision whether to accept or refuse an application (SI 2003/2837, reg. 16).

Where the Revenue accepts an application, the notice must set out the terms on which the application has been accepted and must specify:

- any tax payable in accordance with a land transaction return relating to the transaction in question;
- the nature of any relevant events, and
- the dates of any relevant events (if known).

The tax is then payable within 30 days after the occurrence of a relevant event.

Where the Revenue refuses an application, the notice must set out:

- the grounds for the refusal, and
- the total amount of tax payable in consequence of the refusal.

Grounds on which application may be refused

An application may be refused by the Revenue if:

- the conditions for making an application are not met;
- the application does not comply with the requirements of the regulations;
- there are tax avoidance arrangements in relation to the transaction in question;
- the application, or information provided in connection with it, is incorrect, or
- information required to be provided to the Revenue is not provided within such time as the Revenue reasonably required,

(SI 2003/2837, reg. 17).

Tax avoidance arrangements

Arrangements are tax avoidance arrangements in relation to a transaction if their main objective or one of their main objectives is:

- to enable payment of the tax payable in respect of the transaction to be deferred, or
- to avoid the amount or value of the whole or part of the chargeable consideration for the transaction being determined,

(SI 2003/2837, reg. 19).

'Arrangements' includes any scheme, agreement or understanding, whether or not legally enforceable.

Right of appeal

An applicant may appeal to the General or Special Commissioners against a refusal by the Revenue to accept an application (SI 2003/2837, reg. 19).

Notice of appeal must be given:

- in writing;
- within 30 days after the date on which the notice of the decision to refuse the application was issued, and
- to the officer of the Board by whom that notice was given,

(SI 2003/2837, reg. 20).

The notice of appeal must specify the grounds of appeal. However, on the hearing of the appeal, the Commissioners may allow the appellant to put forward grounds not specified in the notice, and take them into consideration, if satisfied that the omission was not deliberate or unreasonable.

Settling of appeals by agreement

If before an appeal is determined, the appellant and the Revenue agrees that the decision appealed against:

- should be upheld without variation;
- should be varied in a particular manner, or
- should be discharged or cancelled,

that is treated as if the Commissioners had determined the appeal in accordance with the agreement (SI 2003/2837, reg. 21).

However, the appellant may withdraw from the agreement within 30 days from the date when the agreement was come to, by giving notice in writing to the Revenue.

Further, if the agreement is not in writing it must be confirmed by notice in writing given by the Revenue to the appellant or by the appellant to the Revenue. The time when agreement was come to is the time when the notice of confirmation is given.

The appellant may notify the Revenue, orally or in writing, that he does not wish to proceed with the appeal. The Revenue may, within 30 days after that notification, give the appellant notice in writing indicating that it is unwilling that the appeal should be withdrawn, failing which the appeal is treated as withdrawn.

An agreement may be reached, or notice or notification may be given by or to, a person acting on behalf of the appellant in relation to the appeal.

Direction by Commissioners postponing payment

An appellant may apply to the Commissioners in writing for a direction that payment of an amount of tax which would not have been due and payable had the application been accepted be postponed pending the determination of the appeal. The notice must be given within 30 days after the date on which the refusal notice was issued by the Revenue. It must be sent to the Revenue and must state the amount of tax to be postponed (SI 2003/2837, reg. 22).

If there is a change in the circumstances of the case, as a result of which either party has grounds for believing that the amount postponed has become excessive or insufficient, he may, by notice in writing given to the other party at any time before the determination of the appeal, apply to the Commissioners for a further determination of that amount.

An application is heard and determined by the Commissioners in the same way as an appeal.

The fact that any such application has been heard and determined by any Commissioners does not preclude them from hearing and determining the appeal or any further application under this regulation.

The amount of tax postponed is the amount (if any) that appears to the Commissioners to be appropriate.

The date on which any tax not postponed is due and payable is determined as if the tax were charged by an assessment issued on the date on which the application was determined.

On the determination of the appeal, the date on which any postponed tax becomes payable is determined as if the tax were charged by an assessment issued on the date on which the Revenue issues a notice of the total amount payable in accordance with the determination. Any tax overpaid is repaid.

Agreement to postpone payment

If the appellant and the Revenue agree that payment of an amount of tax should be postponed pending the determination of the appeal, this is treated as if the Commissioners had made a direction to the same effect. This is without prejudice to the making of a further agreement or of a further direction (SI 2003/2837, reg. 23).

If the agreement is not in writing, it must be confirmed by notice in writing given by the Revenue in question to the appellant or by the appellant to the Revenue. The time when the agreement was reached is the time when notice of confirmation was given.

An agreement may be reached, or notice given to or by a person acting on behalf of the appellant in relation to the appeal.

Payments and returns

Where the Revenue accepts an application. the purchaser must make a return or further return ('the return') within 30 days after the occurrence of a relevant event (SI 2003/2837, reg. 24).

If the application relates to deferring the payment of tax that has already been paid, the amount already paid is repayable together with interest as from the date of payment.

In the case of consideration consisting of works or services, a return must be filed within the period of 30 days following substantial completion of the works or services.

A return is also required in accordance with the scheme for payment where works, etc. extend over a period of more than six months.

A return is also required after the final payment has been made in accordance with that scheme, within 30 days after the purchaser obtains new information the effect of which is that additional tax or less tax is payable in respect of the transaction than has already been paid.

The return must be accompanied by payment of any tax or additional tax payable.

If the effect of the return is that less tax is payable in respect of a transaction than has already been paid, the amount overpaid shall on a claim by the purchaser be repaid together with interest as from the date of payment.

A return under the above rules must contain the following information:

- a self-assessment of the amount of tax chargeable in respect of the transaction as a whole on the basis of information contained in the return,
- a statement of the amount of tax payable in respect of so much of the chargeable consideration for the transaction as is not, or is no longer, contingent or uncertain,

(SI 2003/2837, reg. 25).

The tax must be calculated by reference to the rates in force at the effective date of the transaction.

Adjustment of payments made on certain or ascertained consideration

Where tax is paid on consideration that is certain or ascertained, and an application is accepted in respect of other chargeable consideration, the adjustment provisions mentioned above do not apply in relation to that payment. Instead, any necessary adjustment is made in accordance with the above rules (SI 2003/2837, reg. 26).

Returns and payments where consideration consists of works or services

Where the carrying out of the works or provision of the services in question is expected to be substantially completed within a period of less than six months after the date on which the return or further return is required, the applicant and the Revenue may agree that the scheme of payment should be varied so that the next return or further return may be made within 30 days after the substantial completion of the carrying out of the works or the provision of the services (SI 2003/2837, reg. 27).

If the carrying out of the works or provision of the services in question is not substantially completed within that period of six months:

- the variation ceases to have effect, and
- returns or further returns must continue to be made in accordance with the rules described above.

Applications accepted by the Revenue having no effect

An application that has been accepted by the Revenue has no effect if it contains false or misleading information; or any facts or circumstances relevant to it are not disclosed to the Revenue. An application ceases to have any effect if the facts and circumstances relevant to it materially change (SI 2003/2837, reg. 28).

10.12.5   Collection and recovery

Issue of tax demands and receipts

Where tax is due and payable, a collector may demand the sum charged from the person liable to pay it. On payment of the tax, the collector must, if so requested, give a receipt (FA 2003, Sch. 12, Para. 1).

Recovery of tax by distraint

In England and Wales or Northern Ireland, if a person neglects or refuses to pay the sum charged, upon demand made by the collector, the collector may distrain upon the goods and chattels of that person. He is referred to as 'the person in default' (FA 2003, Sch. 12, Para. 2).

For the purposes of levying such distress a justice of the peace, on being satisfied by information on oath that there is reasonable ground for believing that a person is neglecting or refusing to pay a sum charged, may issue a warrant in writing authorising a collector to break open, in the daytime, any house or premises, calling to his assistance any constable. Every such constable must, when so required, assist the collector in the execution of the warrant and in levying such distress in the house or premises. The procedure for applying for a warrant is set out in SI 2003/2837, regs. 33–38.

A levy or warrant to break open must be executed by, or under the direction of, and in the presence of, the collector.

A distress levied by the collector must be kept for five days, at the costs and charges of the person in default.

If the person in default does not pay the sum due, together with the costs and charges, the distress will be appraised by one or more independent persons appointed by the collector, and will be sold by public auction by the collector.

Any surplus resulting from the distress, after the deduction of the costs and charges and of the sum due, must be restored to the owner of the goods distrained.

The fees, costs and charges that may be recovered are as set out in the tables below (SI 2003/2837, Sch. 3).

Fees chargeable on or in connection with the levying of distress

'Action taken in connection with the levying of distress

Fees

For making a visit to premises with a view to levying distress (whether the levy is made or not).

A sum not exceeding £12.50.

Levying distress where the total sum charged is £100 or less.

£12.50.

Levying distress where the total sum charged is more than £100.

12.5% on the first £100 of the amount to be recovered; 4% on the next £400; 2.5% on the next £1,500; 1% on the next £8,000; 0.25% on any additional sum.

Costs and charges recoverable where distress has been levied

Action taken where distress has been levied	**Costs and charges**
1. Taking possession.	
– Where close possession is taken.	£4.50 for the day of levy only.

– Where walking possession is taken.	45p per day, payable for the day the distress is levied and up to 14 days thereafter.
2. Removal and storage of goods.	The reasonable costs and charges of removal and storage.
3. Appraisement.	The reasonable fees, charges and expenses of the person appraising.

4. Sale.

Where the sale is held on the auctioneer's premises, for the reasonable cost of advertising, auctioneer's commission (to include all out-of-pocket expenses other than charges for advertising, removal and storage).	15% of the sum realised plus the reasonable cost of advertising, removal and storage.
Where the sale is held on the debtor's premises, for the auctioneer's commission (not to include out-of-pocket expenses or charges for advertising).	7.5% of the sum realised plus out-of-pocket expenses actually and reasonably incurred and the reasonable costs of advertising.'

In the event of a dispute regarding the fees, etc. recoverable, an assessment is made by:

- in England and Wales, the district judge of the county court for the district in which the distress is, or is intended to be, levied,
- in Northern Ireland, the Master (Taxing Office),

(SI 2003/2837, reg. 32).

Recovery of tax by diligence in Scotland

In Scotland, where any tax is due and has not been paid, the sheriff, on an application by the collector accompanied by a certificate will grant a summary warrant in a form prescribed by Act of Sederunt authorising the recovery, by any of the following diligences mentioned in sub-paragraph (2), of the amount remaining due and unpaid (FA 2003, Sch. 12, Para. 3):

- an attachment;
- an earnings arrestment,
- an arrestment and action of furthcoming or sale.

The sheriff officer's fees, together with the outlays necessarily incurred by him, in connection with the execution of a summary warrant are chargeable against the debtor. However, no fee is chargeable by the sheriff officer against the debtor for collecting, and accounting to the collector for, sums paid to him by the debtor in respect of the amount owing.

Civil proceedings in magistrates' court or court of summary jurisdiction

An amount of tax not exceeding £2,000 is, in England and Wales or Northern Ireland, recoverable summarily as a civil debt in proceedings brought in the name of the collector (FA 2003, Sch. 12, Para. 4).

Proceedings in England and Wales may be brought at any time within one year from the time when the matter included in the complaint arose.

Proceedings in county court or sheriff court

Tax due and payable may be sued for and recovered from the person charged as a debt due to the Crown by proceedings brought in the name of a collector in a county court, or in a sheriff court (FA 2003, Sch. 12, Para. 5).

An Revenue officer authorised by the Board may address the court in any proceedings under this paragraph in England and Wales or Scotland.

Proceedings in High Court or Court of Session

Tax may be sued for and recovered from the person charged by proceedings in the High Court or, in Scotland, in the Court of Session sitting as the Court of Exchequer (FA 2003, Sch. 12, Para. 6).

Evidence of unpaid tax

A certificate of a Revenue officer that tax is due and payable, and that to the best of his knowledge and belief payment of the tax has not been made, is sufficient evidence that the sum mentioned in the certificate is unpaid and is due to the Crown (FA 2003, Sch. 12, Para. 7).

A document purporting to be such a certificate is deemed to be such a certificate unless the contrary is proved.

10.13   Self-certification

10.13.1   Certificate issued by purchaser

Certificate where no SDLT payable

Most land transactions, even those where there is no liability to SDLT, must be notified to the Revenue on a Land Transaction Return form (Form SDLT 1 – see **10.11.2** above). In some cases, however, where no SDLT is payable, a return is not required. In such cases, the purchaser must give a 'self-certificate' to the appropriate land registry on form SDLT 60 if he wants his title to the property concerned registered (FA 2003, s. 79 and SI 2003/2837, reg. 8 and Sch. 1). The Revenue may inspect the self-certificate and may obtain from the Land registry 'information and facilities' for verifying that the SDLT requirements have been met (s. 79(6)).

Land transactions not requiring a return

The Revenue's guidance notes indicate that the following transactions need to be self-certified:

'•   the acquisition of a freehold or leasehold interest in land (in Scotland, the acquisition of ownership of land, including the interest of the proprietor of the *dominium utile*, or of the tenant's interest in property subject to a lease) where there is no chargeable consideration;

•   the grant of a lease (including, in Scotland, the exchange of missives of let) where all the following conditions are satisfied:

the term of the lease is less than seven years;

   •   the amount of any premium (in Scotland, grassum) is not such as to attract a charge to SDLT at a rate of 1% or more, ignoring the availability of any relief; and

   •   the amount of any rent is not such as to attract a charge to SDLT at a rate of 1% or more, ignoring the availability of any relief;

•   any other acquisition of an interest in land (for example, the acquisition of an easement or servitude) where the chargeable consideration is not such as to attract a charge to SDLT at a rate of 1% or more, ignoring the availability of any relief;

•   transactions exempt from SDLT as being in connection with divorce or the variation of a testamentary disposition.'

Signature of self-certificate

The certificate must be signed by the purchaser or transferee. If there is more than one purchaser or transferee then all must sign. The Revenue will not accept signature by an agent such as a solicitor, licensed conveyancer or accountant unless the purchaser has been recognised by a Court as mentally incapable of understanding his affairs. A parent or guardian may sign on behalf of a minor.

Where the purchaser or transferee is a company, the Company Secretary or any person having express, implied or apparent authority to act on behalf of the company may sign. If the company is in liquidation, the liquidator must sign.

Where the purchaser or transferee is a partnership, the self-certificate may be signed by one or more nominated partners.

Where the purchasers or transferees enter into the transaction as trustees (other than bare trustees), any one or more of them may sign.

In the case of an individual, a person acting under power of attorney for that individual may sign (FA 2003, s. 81B).

Penalty for fraud or negligence

A person who fraudulently or negligently gives a self-certificate in respect of a chargeable transaction is liable to a penalty not exceeding 100 per cent of the amount of tax chargeable in respect of the transaction (FA 2003, Sch. 11, Para. 3).

If a person discovers that a transaction in respect of which he has given a self-certificate neither fraudulently nor negligently is a chargeable transaction, and does not remedy the error without unreasonable delay, he is liable to a similar penalty.

10.13.2   Record-keeping requirements

Duty to keep records

A purchaser who is required to give a self-certificate must keep such records as may be needed to enable him to deliver a correct and complete certificate. Those records must be preserved for six years after the effective date of the transaction. If an enquiry is in progress at that time, they must be preserved until the enquiry into the certificate is completed. If the time limit for starting an enquiry has not expired at that time, the records must be preserved until the time limit for the Revenue to start an enquiry expires (FA 2003, Sch. 11, Para. 4).

The records required include:

- relevant instruments relating to the transaction, in particular, any contract or conveyance, and any supporting maps, plans or similar documents, and
- records of relevant payments, receipts and financial arrangements.

The duty to preserve records may be satisfied by the preservation of the information contained in them (FA 2003, Sch. 11, Para. 5). Where information is so preserved, a copy of any document forming part of the records is admissible in evidence in any proceedings before the Commissioners to the same extent as the records themselves.

Penalty for failure to keep and preserve records

A person who fails to comply with the above requirements is liable to a penalty not exceeding £3,000 (FA 2003, Sch. 11, Para. 6). However, no penalty is incurred if the Revenue is satisfied that any facts that it reasonably require to be proved, and that would have been proved by the records, are proved by other documentary evidence provided to it.

10.13.3 Enquiries into certificates

Revenue enquiry power

The Revenue may enquire into a self-certificate by giving notice to the purchaser before the end of the period of nine months after the date on which the self-certificate was produced (FA 2003, Sch. 11, Para. 7).

A self-certificate that has been the subject of one notice of enquiry may not be the subject of another.

An enquiry may extend to anything contained in the certificate, or required to be contained in the certificate, that relates to the question whether the transaction to which the certificate relates is chargeable or notifiable, or to the amount of SDLT chargeable in respect of it (FA 2003, Sch. 11, Para. 8).

Notice to produce documents, etc.

In pursuance of an enquiry, the Revenue may by notice in writing require the purchaser:

- to produce to them such documents in his possession or power, and
- to provide them with such information, in such form,

as they may reasonably require for the purposes of the enquiry (FA 2003, Sch. 11, Para. 9).

Any such notice must give at least 30 days for the purchaser to comply with it.

In complying with a notice, copies of documents may be produced instead of originals, but:

- the copies must be photographic or other facsimiles, and
- the Revenue may by notice require the original to be produced for inspection within 30 days.

The Revenue may take copies of, or make extracts from, any documents produced to it.

The purchaser is not obliged to produce documents or provide information relating to the conduct of any pending appeal by him, or any pending referral to the Special Commissioners to which he is a party.

There is a right of appeal against a notice under the above rules (FA 2003, Sch. 11, Para. 10). Notice of appeal must be given in writing, within 30 days after the issue of the notice appealed against. It must be sent to the Revenue officer who issued the notice. An appeal is heard and determined in the same way as an appeal against an assessment.

On appeal, the Commissioners must set aside the notice so far as it requires the production of documents, or the provision of information, that appears to them not reasonably required for the purposes of the enquiry, but must otherwise confirm it.

Once a notice is confirmed, the period for complying with it is 30 days from the determination of the appeal.

The decision of the Commissioners on an appeal against such a notice is final.

Penalties

A person who fails to comply with a notice to produce documents, etc., for the purposes of an enquiry is liable to a penalty of £50 (FA 2003, Sch. 11, Para. 11). If the failure continues after this penalty is imposed, he is liable to a further penalty or penalties not exceeding £30 per day if the penalty is determined by the Revenue, or £150 per day if the penalty is determined by the court, for each day on which the failure continues.

However, no penalty may be imposed in respect of a failure at any time after the failure has been remedied.

Referral of questions to Special Commissioners during enquiry

At any time when an enquiry is in progress, any question arising in connection with the subject matter of the enquiry may be referred to the Special Commissioners for their determination (FA 2003, Sch. 11, Para. 12).

The notice of referral must be given in writing to the Special Commissioners jointly by the purchaser and the Revenue and must specify the question or questions being referred. More than one notice of referral may be given in relation to an enquiry.

The Revenue or the purchaser may withdraw a notice of referral. Notice of withdrawal must be given in writing to the other party to the referral and to the Special Commissioners before the first hearing in relation to the referral (FA 2003, Sch. 11, Para. 13).

While proceedings on a referral are in progress in relation to an enquiry:

- no closure notice may be given in relation to the enquiry, and
- no application may be made for a direction to give such a notice (see below),

(FA 2003, Sch. 11, Para. 14).

Proceedings on a referral are in progress until the questions referred have been finally determined.

The determination of a question referred to the Special Commissioners is binding on the parties to the referral in the same way, and to the same extent, as a decision on a preliminary issue in an appeal (FA 2003, Sch. 11, Para. 15). The determination must be taken into account by the Revenue in reaching its conclusions on the enquiry, and in formulating any amendments of the self-certificate required to give effect to those conclusions.

Any right of appeal against an assessment may not be exercised so as to reopen the question determined except to the extent (if any) that it could be reopened if it had been determined as a preliminary issue in that appeal.

Completion of enquiry

An enquiry is completed when the Revenue issues a 'closure notice' to the purchaser (FA 2003, Sch. 11, Para. 16).

A closure notice must state whether in the opinion of the Revenue the self-certificate was correct, and if the Revenue's opinion is that it was not, whether in its opinion the transaction to which it relates was chargeable or notifiable.

The purchaser may apply to the General or Special Commissioners for a direction to the Revenue to issue a closure notice within a specified period (FA 2003, Sch. 11, Para. 17). An application is heard and determined in the same way as an appeal.

The Commissioners must give a direction unless they are satisfied that the Revenue has reasonable grounds for not giving a closure notice within a specified period.

10.14   Enforcement

10.14.1   Revenue information powers: information from taxpayer

An authorised Revenue officer may, by notice in writing, require a person to deliver such documents as are in his possession or power and (in the officer's reasonable opinion) contain, or may contain, information relevant to his liability to SDLT. The notice may also require the person to provide the Revenue with such information as may reasonably be required as being relevant to, or to the amount of, any such liability (FA 2003, Sch. 13, Para. 1). At least 30 days' notice must be given for the production of this material (Sch. 13, Para. 3).

Before a person is given such a notice, he must be given a reasonable opportunity to deliver the documents or provide the information in question.

The consent of a General or Special Commissioner is required for the giving of such a notice. Consent may not be given unless the Commissioner is satisfied that in all the circumstances the Revenue officer is justified in issuing the notice (Sch. 13, Para. 2).

A Commissioner who has given such consent may not take part in, or be present at, any proceedings on, or related to, any appeal brought by the person to whom the notice applies if the Commissioner has reason to believe that any of the required information is likely to be adduced in evidence in those proceedings.

The Revenue may take copies of any documents submitted (Sch. 13, Para. 5).

An officer who gives such a notice must also give a written summary of his reasons for applying for consent to the notice (Sch. 13, Para. 4).

This does not require the disclosure of any information:

- that would, or might, identify any person who has provided the officer with any information which he took into account in deciding whether to apply for consent, or
- that the General or Special Commissioner giving consent directs need not be disclosed.

A Commissioner must not give any such direction unless he is satisfied that the officer has reasonable grounds for believing that disclosure of the information in question would prejudice the assessment or collection of tax.

A person is not obliged to provide any information relating to the conduct of any pending appeal (Sch. 13, Para. 21).

Photocopies or facsimile copies of documents may be produced, but the originals must be available for inspection (Sch. 13, Para. 23).

The provisions described above do not apply to documents that are personal records or journalistic material, or to information contained in any personal records or journalistic material (Sch. 13, Para. 20).

'Personal records' means personal records as defined in Police and Criminal Evidence Act 1984, s. 12 or, in Northern Ireland, in Police and Criminal Evidence (Northern Ireland) Order 1989 (SI 1989/1341), Art. 14.

'Journalistic material' means journalistic material as defined in s. 13 or, in Northern Ireland, in Art. 15.

10.14.2　Revenue information powers: information from third party

An authorised Revenue officer may for the purpose of enquiring into the tax liability of any person ('the taxpayer') by notice in writing require any other person to deliver to him or to make available for inspection such documents as are in that person's possession or power and (in the officer's reasonable opinion) contain, or may contain, information relevant to the taxpayer's liability to SDLT (FA 2003, Sch. 13, Para. 6). The notice must name the taxpayer to whom it relates.

Before a person is given such a notice, he must be given a reasonable opportunity to deliver or make available the documents in question.

The persons who may be treated as 'the taxpayer' for the purposes of this paragraph include a company that has ceased to exist and an individual who has died. However, a notice in relation to a taxpayer who has died may not be given more than six years after his death.

At least 30 days' notice must be given for the production of this material (Sch. 13, Para. 8).

Requirement of consent of General or Special Commissioner

The consent of a General or Special Commissioner is required for the giving of such a notice. Consent may not be given unless the Commissioner is satisfied that in all the circumstances the officer is justified in issuing the notice (Sch. 13, Para. 7).

A Commissioner who has given such consent may not take part in, or be present at, any proceedings on, or related to, any appeal brought by the taxpayer concerned if the Commissioner has reason to believe that any of the documents that were the subject of the notice is likely to be adduced in evidence in those proceedings.

Copy of notice to be given to taxpayer

Unless the Commissioner directs otherwise, a copy of the notice must be given to the taxpayer to whom it relates (Sch. 13, Para. 9). Such a direction may be given only if the Commissioner is satisfied that the officer has reasonable grounds for suspecting the taxpayer of fraud.

Summary of reasons to be given

An officer who gives a notice under the above rules must also give the taxpayer concerned a written summary of his reasons for applying for consent to the notice (Sch. 13, Para. 10). This is not required if a copy of the notice need not be given to the taxpayer.

This does not require the disclosure of any information:

- that would, or might, identify any person who has provided the officer with any information which he took into account in deciding whether to apply for consent, or
- that the General or Special Commissioner giving consent directs need not be disclosed.

A Commissioner may not give such a direction unless he is satisfied that the officer has reasonable grounds for believing that disclosure of the information in question would prejudice the assessment or collection of tax.

Power to give notice relating to unnamed taxpayer or taxpayers

If a Special Commissioner gives his consent, the Revenue officer may issue a notice without naming the taxpayer to whom it relates (Sch. 13, Para. 11).

Consent may not be given unless the Commissioner is satisfied:

- that the notice relates:

  to a taxpayer whose identity is not known to the officer, or
  to a class of taxpayers whose individual identities are not so known;

- that there are reasonable grounds for believing that the taxpayer, or any of the class of taxpayers, to whom the notice relates may have failed or may fail to comply with any provision of the SDLT legislation;
- that any such failure is likely to have led or to lead to serious prejudice to the proper assessment or collection of tax, and
- that the information that is likely to be contained in the documents to which the notice relates is not readily available from another source.

Before a person is given such a notice, he must be given a reasonable opportunity to deliver or make available the documents in question.

A person to whom there is given such a notice may, by notice in writing given to the officer within 30 days after the date of the notice, object to it on the ground that it would be onerous for him to comply with it. If the matter is not resolved by agreement it must be referred to the Special Commissioners who may confirm, vary or cancel the notice.

At least 30 days' notice must be given for the production of the material concerned (Sch. 13, Para. 12).

A person is not obliged to provide any information relating to the conduct of any pending appeal by the taxpayer concerned (Sch. 13, Para. 21).

Photocopies or facsimile copies of documents may be produced, but the originals must be available for inspection (Sch. 13, Para. 23).

The provisions described above do not apply to documents that are personal records or journalistic material, or to information contained in any personal records or journalistic material (Sch. 13, Para. 20).

'Personal records' means personal records as defined in Police and Criminal Evidence Act 1984, s. 12 or, in Northern Ireland, in Police and Criminal Evidence (Northern Ireland) Order 1989 (SI 1989/1341), Art. 14.

'Journalistic material' means journalistic material as defined in s. 13 or, in Northern Ireland, in Art. 15.

Power to take copies of documents, etc.

The Revenue may take copies of any documents submitted in accordance with a notice under the above rules (Sch. 13, Para. 13, FA 2003).

Barristers

Any notice given to a barrister, advocate or solicitor must be given by the Board (Sch. 13, Para. 22).

Documents subject to legal privilege

A barrister, advocate or solicitor is not obliged to deliver or make available, without his client's consent, any document that is subject to legal privilege (Sch. 13, Para. 25).

The following items are subject to legal privilege:

- communications between a professional legal adviser and his client or any person representing his client made in connection with the giving of legal advice to the client;
- communications between a professional legal adviser and his client or any person representing his client, or between such an adviser or his client or any such representative and any other person, made in connection with or in contemplation of legal proceedings and for the purposes of such proceedings,
- items enclosed with or referred to in such communications and made:

  in connection with the giving of legal advice, or
  in connection with or in contemplation of legal proceedings and for the purposes of such proceedings,

when they are in possession of a person entitled to possession of them (Sch. 13, Para. 35).

However, items held with the intention of furthering a criminal purpose are not subject to legal privilege.

Documents originating more than six years before date of notice

A person is not obliged to deliver or make available a document the whole of which originates more than six years before the date of the notice (Sch. 13, Para. 24).

This restriction does not apply where the notice is so expressed as to exclude it. However, the restriction can be excluded only:

- in the case of a notice given by an authorised officer, if the General or Special Commissioner giving consent to the notice has also given approval to the exclusion,
- in the case of a notice given by the Board, if they have applied to a General or Special Commissioner for, and obtained, that approval.

Approval may only be given if the Commissioner is satisfied, on application by the officer or the Board, that tax has been, or may have been, lost to the Crown owing to the fraud of the taxpayer.

Documents belonging to auditor or tax adviser

An auditor is not obliged to deliver or make available documents that are his property and were created by him or on his behalf for or in connection with the performance of his statutory functions as auditor (Sch. 13, Para. 26). Similarly, a tax adviser is not obliged to deliver or make available documents that are his property and consist of 'relevant communications'.

'Relevant communications' means communications between the tax adviser and:

- a person in relation to whose tax affairs he has been appointed, or
- any other tax adviser of such a person,

the purpose of which is the giving or obtaining of advice about any of those tax affairs.

Notwithstanding the above rule, the auditor or tax advisor must deliver a document or make it available for inspection if it contains:

- information explaining any information, return or other document that the tax accountant, assisted any client of his in preparing for, or for delivering to, the Revenue, or
- in the case of a notice in respect of unnamed taxpayer or taxpayers, information as to the identity or address of any taxpayer to whom the notice relates or any person who has acted on behalf of any such person,

(Sch. 13, Para. 27).

Information is regarded as having been made available to the Revenue if it is contained in some other document and:

- that other document, or a copy of it, has been delivered to the officer or the Board, or
- that other document has been inspected by a Revenue officer.

10.14.3 Revenue information powers: information from tax accountant

Where a tax accountant is convicted of an offence in relation to tax by or before a court in the UK, or has a penalty imposed on him for assisting in preparation of incorrect returns, etc., an authorised Revenue officer may by notice in writing require him to deliver such documents as are in his possession or power and (in the officer's reasonable opinion) contain information relevant to the SDLT liability of any of his clients (Sch. 13, Para. 14, FA 2003). At least 30 days' notice must be given for the production of this material (Sch. 13, Para. 17).

The tax accountant must first be given a reasonable opportunity to deliver the documents in question.

No notice may be given for so long as an appeal is pending against the conviction or penalty (Sch. 13, Para. 15).

No notice may be given after the end of the period of 12 months beginning with the date of that conviction or penalty.

A notice may not be given without the consent of the appropriate judicial authority, namely:

- in England and Wales, a circuit judge;
- in Scotland, a sheriff,
- in Northern Ireland, a county court judge,

(Sch. 13, Para. 16).

Consent may not be given unless that authority is satisfied that in all the circumstances the officer is justified in issuing the notice.

The Revenue may take copies of, or of extracts from, any documents submitted in response to a notice under the above provisions (Sch. 13, Para. 18).

A person is not obliged to provide any information relating to the conduct of any pending appeal by the taxpayer concerned (Sch. 13, Para. 21).

Photocopies or facsimile copies of documents may be produced, but the originals must be available for inspection (Sch. 13, Para. 23).

The provisions described above do not apply to documents that are personal records or journalistic material, or to information contained in any personal records or journalistic material (Sch. 13, Para. 20).

'Personal records' means personal records as defined in Police and Criminal Evidence Act 1984, s. 12 or, in Northern Ireland, in Police and Criminal Evidence (Northern Ireland) Order 1989 (SI 1989/1341), Art. 14.

'Journalistic material' means journalistic material as defined in s. 13 or, in Northern Ireland, in Art. 15.

Barristers

Any notice given to a barrister, advocate or solicitor must be given by the Board (Sch. 13, Para. 22, FA 2003).

Documents subject to legal privilege

A barrister, advocate or solicitor is not obliged to deliver or make available, without his client's consent, any document that is subject to legal privilege (Sch. 13, Para. 25).

The following items are subject to legal privilege:

- communications between a professional legal adviser and his client or any person representing his client made in connection with the giving of legal advice to the client;
- communications between a professional legal adviser and his client or any person representing his client, or between such an adviser or his client or any such representative and any other person, made in connection with or in contemplation of legal proceedings and for the purposes of such proceedings,
- items enclosed with or referred to in such communications and made:

  in connection with the giving of legal advice, or
  in connection with or in contemplation of legal proceedings and for the purposes of such proceedings,

when they are in possession of a person entitled to possession of them (Sch. 13, Para. 35).

However, items held with the intention of furthering a criminal purpose are not subject to legal privilege.

10.14.4 Information powers exercisable by the Board

The Board may by notice in writing require a person:

- to deliver to a named Revenue officer such documents as are in the person's possession or power and (in the Board's reasonable opinion) contain, or may contain, information relevant to his SDLT liability, or

- to provide to a named Revenue officer such information as the Board may reasonably require as being relevant to, or to the amount of, any such liability,

(Sch. 13, Para. 28, FA 2003).

Notice may not be given unless the Board has reasonable grounds for believing:

- that the person to whom it relates may have failed, or may fail, to comply with any provision of the SDLT legislation, and
- that any such failure is likely to have led, or to lead, to serious prejudice to the proper assessment or collection of tax.

A notice must specify the time within which the documents, etc. are to be provided (Sch. 13, Para. 29).

The Revenue may take copies of, or of extracts from, any documents submitted to them (Sch. 13, Para. 30).

The above rules do not apply to documents that are personal records or journalistic material (Sch. 13, Para. 31).

'Personal records' means personal records as defined in Police and Criminal Evidence Act 1984, s. 12 or, in Northern Ireland, in Police and Criminal Evidence (Northern Ireland) Order 1989 (SI 1989/1341), Art. 14.

'Journalistic material' means journalistic material as defined in s. 13 or, in Northern Ireland, in Art. 15.

10.14.5   Information powers exercisable by judicial authority

Order for the delivery of documents

The 'appropriate judicial authority' may make an order requiring the person who appears to the authority to have in his possession or power the documents specified or described in the order to deliver them to a Revenue officer within ten working days after the day on which notice of the order is served on him, or such shorter or longer period as may be specified in the order (Sch. 13, Para. 32, FA 2003).

An order may not be made unless the authority is satisfied on information on oath given by an authorised Revenue officer:

- that there is reasonable ground for suspecting that an offence involving serious fraud in connection with, or in relation to, SDLT has been or is about to be committed, and

- that documents that may be required as evidence for the purposes of any proceedings in respect of such an offence are or may be in the power or possession of any person.

For this purpose a 'working day' means any day other than a Saturday, Sunday or public holiday.

The appropriate judicial authority is:

- in England and Wales, a circuit judge;
- in Scotland, a sheriff,
- in Northern Ireland, a county court judge.

Where in Scotland the information relates to persons residing or having places of business at addresses situated in different sheriffdoms:

- an application for an order may be made to the sheriff for the sheriffdom in which any of the addresses is situated, and
- where the sheriff makes an order in respect of a person residing or having a place of business in his own sheriffdom, he may also make orders in respect of all or any of the other persons to whom the information relates (whether or not they have an address within the sheriffdom).

Approval of decision to apply for an order

Before the hearing of an application for an order, an officer of the Board who is a member of the Senior Civil Service in:

- the Cross-Cutting Policy branch of the Revenue, or
- the Special Compliance Office of the Revenue,

must approve in writing the decision to apply for that order (SI 2003/2837, reg. 34).

Complying with an order

A person complies with an order by producing the documents specified or described in the order to the specified Revenue officer within the period of ten working days, or longer period, mentioned above, or such further period, if any, as is agreed with that officer.

Documents are produced to an Revenue officer if they are either delivered to the officer; or left for the officer at an address specified in the relevant order.

Where documents are sent to an officer of the Board at the address specified in the relevant order by post, they shall be treated, unless the contrary is proved, as having been produced to the officer:

- if first class post is used, on the second working day after posting,

- if second class post is used, on the fourth working day after posting,

(SI 2003/2837, reg. 37).

Notice of application for order

A person is entitled to notice of the intention to apply for an order against him under FA 2003, Para. 32, and to appear and be heard at the hearing of the application, unless the appropriate judicial authority is satisfied that this would seriously prejudice the investigation of the offence (Sch. 13, Para. 33).

Notice of application must be given in writing and must contain the following details:

- the date, time and place of the hearing of the application;
- the specifications or descriptions of documents which are the subject of the application;
- a description of the suspected offence to which the application relates, and
- the name of the person suspected of committing, having committed or being about to commit the suspected offence,

(SI 2003/2837, reg. 35).

Notice of application must be given to the person entitled to it not less than five working days before the hearing of the application.

Notice of an order, or notice of an application, treated as having been given

Where notice of an order, or notice of application, is delivered to a person, or left at his proper address, it is treated as having been given to that person on the day on which it is delivered or left or, where that day is not a working day, on the next working day (SI 2003/2837, reg. 36).

Where notice of application, or notice of an order, is sent to a person's proper address by facsimile transmission or other similar means which produce a document containing a text of the communication, it is treated as given when the text is received in a legible form.

A person's proper address is:

- the usual or last known place of residence, or the place of business or employment, of that person;
- in the case of a company, the address of the company's registered office, or
- in the case of a liquidator of a company, the liquidator's address for the purposes of the liquidation.

Obligations of person given notice of application

A person who has been given notice of intention to apply for an order under the above rules must not:

- conceal, destroy, alter or dispose of any document to which the application relates, or
- disclose to any other person information or any other matter likely to prejudice the investigation of the offence to which the application relates,

(FA 2003, Sch. 13, Para. 34).

However, this does not prevent anything being done:

- with the leave of the appropriate judicial authority;
- with the written permission of an officer of the Board;
- after the application has been dismissed or abandoned, or
- after any order made on the application has been complied with.

Also, it does not prevent a professional legal adviser from disclosing any information or other matter:

- to, or to a representative of, a client of his in connection with the giving by the adviser of legal advice to the client, or
- to any person:

   in contemplation or, or in connection with, legal proceedings, and
   for the purposes of those proceedings.

However, information may not be disclosed with a view to furthering a criminal purpose.

Exception of items subject to legal privilege

Items subject to legal privilege do not have to be disclosed to the Revenue (FA 2003, Sch. 13, Para. 35).

Items 'subject to legal privilege' means:

- communications between a professional legal adviser and his client or any person representing his client made in connection with the giving of legal advice to the client;
- communications between a professional legal adviser and his client or any person representing his client, or between such an adviser or his client or any such representative and any other person, made in connection with or in contemplation of legal proceedings and for the purposes of such proceedings,
- items enclosed with or referred to in such communications and made:

   in connection with the giving of legal advice, or

in connection with or in contemplation of legal proceedings and for the purposes of such proceedings,

when they are in possession of a person entitled to possession of them.

Items held with the intention of furthering a criminal purpose are not subject to legal privilege.

Resolution of disputes as to legal privilege

Where there is a dispute as to whether a document, or part of a document, is an item subject to legal privilege, the person against whom an order has been made may apply to the appropriate judicial authority to resolve the dispute (SI 2003/2837, reg. 38).

All the disputed documents must be lodged in the court at the same time as the application is made and are held by the court until the appropriate judicial authority resolves the dispute.

The court must give the Board notice of any such application not less than five working days before the hearing of the application, and the Board may appear and be heard at that hearing in addition to the person making the application.

On hearing the application, the appropriate judicial authority must:

- resolve the dispute by deciding whether the document, or part of the document, is or is not an item subject to legal privilege, and
- order the costs of the application to be met by the Board except where it holds that no document, or no part of any document, to which the application relates is an item subject to legal privilege.

Where a person makes such an application within the permitted period, he is treated as having complied with the order in relation to the documents to which the application relates until the appropriate judicial authority resolves the dispute.

A dispute may be resolved at any time by agreement between the Board and the person against whom the order has been made.

Complying with an order

A person complies with an order by producing the documents specified or described in the order to the Revenue officer specified in the order within:

- the period of ten working days mentioned above, or
- such further period, if any, as is agreed with that officer.

Documents are produced to an Revenue officer if they are either delivered to the officer, or left for the officer at an address specified in the relevant order.

Where documents are sent to an Revenue officer at the address specified in the relevant order by post, they are treated, unless the contrary is proved, as having been produced to the officer:

- if first class post is used, on the second working day after posting,
- if second class post is used, on the fourth working day after posting,

(SI 2003/2837, reg. 37).

Where an order relates to a document in electronic or magnetic form, the order shall be taken to require the person to deliver the information recorded in the document in a form in which it is visible and legible (FA 2003, Sch. 13, Para. 37).

Document not to be retained if photograph or copy sufficient

Where a document delivered to a Revenue officer is of such a nature that a photograph or copy of it would be sufficient for use as evidence at a trial for an offence, or for forensic examination or for investigation in connection with an offence, it must not be retained longer than is necessary to establish that fact and to obtain the photograph or copy (FA 2003, Sch. 13, Para. 38).

Access to or supply of photograph or copy of documents delivered

If a request for permission to be granted access to a document that:

- has been delivered to an officer of the Board under this Part of this Schedule, and
- is retained by the Board for the purposes of investigating an offence,

is made to the officer in overall charge of the investigation by a person who had custody or control of the document immediately before it was so delivered, or by someone acting on behalf of any such person, the officer must allow the person who made the request access to it under the supervision of a Revenue officer (FA 2003, Sch. 13, Para. 39).

If a request for a photograph or copy of any such document is made to the officer in overall charge of the investigation by a person who had custody or control of the document immediately before it was so delivered, or by someone acting on behalf of any such person, the officer must:

- allow the person who made the request access to it under the supervision of an officer of the Board for the purpose of photographing or copying it, or
- photograph or copy it, or cause it to be photographed or copied.

Where a document is photographed or copied, the photograph or copy must be supplied to the person who made the request within a reasonable time from the making of the request.

There is no duty to grant access to, or to supply a photograph or copy of, a document if the officer in overall charge of the investigation for the purposes of which it was delivered has reasonable grounds for believing that to do so would prejudice:

(a) that investigation;

(b) the investigation of an offence other than the offence for the purposes of the investigation of which the document was delivered, or

(c) any criminal proceedings that may be brought as a result of:

    (i) the investigation of which he is in charge, or
    (ii) any investigation in (b).

Failure to comply with order

A person who fails to comply with an order under the above rules may be dealt with as if he had committed a contempt of the court (FA 2003, Sch. 13, Para. 40).

10.14.6   Serious fraud: entry of premises

Power to issue warrant

The 'appropriate judicial authority' may issue a warrant in writing authorising a Revenue officer to enter premises, if necessary by force, at any time within 14 days from the time of issue of the warrant, and search them.

The appropriate judicial authority is:

- in England and Wales, a circuit judge;
- in Scotland, a sheriff,
- in Northern Ireland, a county court judge.

Before issuing the warrant, however, the judge or sheriff must be satisfied, on information on oath given by a Revenue officer, that:

- there is reasonable ground for suspecting that an offence involving serious fraud in connection with, or in relation to, tax is being, has been or is about to be committed and that evidence of it is to be found on the premises, and

- the officer is acting with the approval of the Board given in relation to the particular case,

(FA 2003, Sch. 13, Para. 43).

Where in Scotland the information relates to premises situated in different sheriffdoms:

- petitions for the issue of warrants in respect of all the premises to which the information relates may be made to the sheriff for a sheriffdom in which any of the premises is situated, and
- where the sheriff issues a warrant in respect of premises situated in his own sheriffdom, he shall also have jurisdiction to issue warrants in respect of all or any of the other premises to which the information relates.

This does not affect any power or jurisdiction of a sheriff to issue a warrant in respect of an offence committed within his own sheriffdom.

Meaning of offence involving serious fraud

Fraud is a common law offence. The basic definition was given by Lord Herschell in the case of *Derry v Peek* ([1889] 14 AC 337 HL). He said that fraud is proven when it is shown that a false representation has been made knowingly, or without belief in its truth, or recklessly, careless whether it be true or false. Without prejudice to the common law, or to the provisions of the Theft Acts, the Perjury Act 1911 or the Forgery and Counterfeiting Act 1981, the SDLT legislation gives the following specific instance of serious fraud.

An offence involves serious fraud if its commission has led, or is intended or likely to lead, either:

- to substantial financial gain to any person, or
- to serious prejudice to the proper assessment or collection of tax,

(FA 2003, Sch. 13, Para. 44).

An offence that, if considered alone, would not be regarded as involving serious fraud may nevertheless be so regarded if there is reasonable ground for suspecting that it forms part of a course of conduct that is, or but for its detection would be, likely to result in serious prejudice to the proper assessment or collection of tax.

Approval of application by Board

The Board may not approve an application for a warrant unless it has reasonable grounds for believing that use of the order for delivery of documents procedure might seriously prejudice the investigation (Sch. 13, Para. 45).

The Board may not delegate the responsibility of giving approval for an application for a warrant.

Powers conferred by warrant

The warrant may specify:

- the number of Revenue officers by whom it may be exercised;
- the times of day during which it may be exercised, and
- whether a constable in uniform must be present,

(Sch. 13, Para. 46).

A Revenue officer seeking to exercise the powers conferred by a warrant, or the officer who is in charge of the search, must supply a copy of the warrant endorsed with his name to the occupier if the occupier of the premises concerned is present at the time the search is to begin. If at that time the occupier is not present but a person who appears to the officer to be in charge of the premises is present, the officer must supply such a copy to that person. In any other case, the officer must leave such a copy in a prominent place on the premises (Sch. 13, Para. 47).

An officer who enters the premises under the authority of a warrant may:

- take with him such other persons as appear to him to be necessary;
- seize and remove any things whatsoever found there that he has reasonable cause to believe may be required as evidence for the purposes of proceedings in respect of the suspected offence, and
- search or cause to be searched any person found on the premises whom he has reasonable cause to believe to be in possession of such things.

However, no person may be searched except by a person of the same sex.

In the case of information contained in a computer, the power of seizure includes a power to require the information to be produced in a form in which it can be taken away and in which it is visible and legible. This applies where the officer who enters the premises has reasonable cause to believe that the information may be required as evidence for the purposes of his investigation and is accessible from the premises,

Items subject to legal privilege

Items that are subject to legal privilege may not be seized (Sch. 13, Para. 48).

The following items are subject to legal privilege:

- communications between a professional legal adviser and his client or any person representing his client made in connection with the giving of legal advice to the client;

- communications between a professional legal adviser and his client or any person representing his client, or between such an adviser or his client or any such representative and any other person, made in connection with or in contemplation of legal proceedings and for the purposes of such proceedings,
- items enclosed with or referred to in such communications and made:

in connection with the giving of legal advice, or
in connection with or in contemplation of legal proceedings and for the purposes of such proceedings,

when they are in possession of a person entitled to possession of them (Sch. 13, Para. 35).

However, items held with the intention of furthering a criminal purpose are not subject to legal privilege.

Procedure where documents, etc. are removed

A Revenue officer who removes anything in the exercise of the above powers must, if so requested by the occupier of the premises or the person having custody or control of it immediately before the removal, provide that person with a record of what he removed. This must be provided within a reasonable time (Sch. 13, Para. 49). The Revenue must allow the person access to it under the supervision of an officer of the Board on request. If a request is made before removal, the Revenue must allow the person to copy it or photograph it under Revenue supervision (Sch. 13, Para. 51).

Where anything that has been removed is of such a nature that a photograph or copy of it would be sufficient:

- for use as evidence at a trial for an offence, or
- for forensic examination or for investigation in connection with an offence,

it must not be retained longer than is necessary to establish that fact and to obtain the photograph or copy (Sch. 13, Para. 50).

There is no duty to grant access to, or to supply a photograph or copy of, anything if the officer in overall charge of the investigation has reasonable grounds for believing that to do so would prejudice:

(a) that investigation;

(b) the investigation of an offence other than the offence for the purposes of the investigation of which the thing was removed, or

(c) any criminal proceedings that may be brought as a result of:

    (i) the investigation of which he is in charge, or
    (ii) any such investigation as is mentioned in paragraph (b).

Endorsement and custody, etc. of warrant

Where entry has been made with a warrant, and the officer making the entry has seized any things under the authority of the warrant, he must endorse on or attach to the warrant a list of the things seized (Sch. 13, Para. 52).

10.14.7 Criminal offences

Fraudulent evasion of tax

A person who is knowingly concerned in the fraudulent evasion of tax by him or any other person is liable:

- on summary conviction to imprisonment for a term not exceeding six months or a fine not exceeding the statutory maximum, or both,
- on conviction on indictment, to imprisonment for a term not exceeding seven years or a fine, or both,

(FA 2003, s. 95).

Falsification, etc. of documents

A person who has been required to produce documents commits an offence if he intentionally:

- falsifies, conceals, destroys or otherwise disposes of, or
- causes or permits the falsification, concealment, destruction or disposal of,

any such document (Sch. 13, Para. 53).

A person does not commit an offence if he acts:

- with the written permission of a General or Special Commissioner or a Revenue officer;
- after the document has been delivered or inspected, in the case of a document required from a third party, or
- after a copy has been delivered and the original has been inspected.

A person does not commit an offence in relation to documents required to be produced if he acts after the end of the period of two years beginning with the date on which the notice is given or the order is made, unless before the end of that period the Revenue has notified him, in writing, that the notice or order has not been complied with to its satisfaction.

A person does not commit an offence in relation to documents that he is given the opportunity to produce if he acts:

- after the end of the period of six months beginning with the date on which an opportunity to deliver the document was given, or
- after an application for consent to a notice being given in relation to the document has been refused.

A person guilty of an offence is liable:

- on summary conviction, to a fine not exceeding the statutory maximum,
- on conviction on indictment, to imprisonment for a term not exceeding two years or a fine or to both.

10.14.8   Penalties

Determination of penalty by Revenue officer

An 'authorised' Revenue officer may make a determination imposing the penalty, and setting it at such amount as in the officer's opinion is correct or appropriate (FA 2003, Sch. 14, Para. 2).

Notice of the determination must be served on the person liable to the penalty. He has the right of appeal within 30 days of the date of the notice (see below).

A penalty determined under this paragraph is due and payable at the end of that 30-day period.

Alteration of penalty determination

After a penalty notice has been served, the determination cannot be altered except on appeal or in the circumstances set out below (Sch. 14, Para. 3).

If it is discovered by an authorised officer that the amount of the penalty is or has become insufficient, the officer may make a determination in a further amount.

If it is discovered by an authorised officer that the amount of SDLT on which a tax-related penalty is calculated is or has become excessive, he may revise the determination so that the penalty is set at the amount that is correct. Any amount overpaid is then repaid.

Liability of personal representatives

If a person liable to a penalty has died:

- any determination that could have been made in relation to that person may be made in relation to his personal representatives, and
- any penalty imposed on them is a debt due from and payable out of the person's estate,

(Sch. 14, Para. 4).

Appeal against penalty determination

An appeal may be made to the General or Special Commissioners against the determination of a penalty. Notice of appeal must be given in writing to the Revenue officer by whom the determination was made within 30 days of the date of issue of the notice of determination (Sch. 14, Para. 5).

The notice of appeal must specify the grounds of appeal, but on the hearing of the appeal the Commissioners may allow the appellant to put forward a ground not specified in the notice of appeal, and take it into consideration, if satisfied that the omission was not deliberate or unreasonable.

On appeal, the Commissioners may confirm, increase or reduce the amount of the penalty as they consider appropriate.

An appeal against the Commissioners' determination may be made to the High Court or, in Scotland, to the Court of Session sitting as the Court of Exchequer (Sch. 14, Para. 6).

Penalty proceedings before the court

Where, in the opinion of the Board, the liability of a person for a penalty arises by reason of his fraud, or the fraud of another person, proceedings for the penalty may be brought in the High Court or, in Scotland, in the Court of Session sitting as the Court of Exchequer (Sch. 14, Para. 7).

Court proceedings in England and Wales must be brought:

- by and in the name of the Board, or
- in the name of the Attorney General.

Any such proceedings are deemed to be civil proceedings by the crown.

Proceedings in Scotland must be brought in the name of the Advocate General for Scotland.

Proceedings in Northern Ireland must be brought:

- by and in the name of the Board, or
- in the name of the Advocate General for Northern Ireland.

Any such proceedings are deemed to be civil proceedings.

If the court does not find that fraud is proved, but considers that the person concerned is nevertheless liable to a penalty, the court may determine a penalty notwithstanding that, but for the opinion of the Board as to fraud, the penalty would not have been a matter for the court.

Time limit for determination of penalties

The general rule is that:

- no penalty may be determined by a Revenue officer, and
- no proceedings for a penalty may be brought before the court,

more than six years after the date on which the penalty was incurred or, in the case of a daily penalty, began to be incurred (Sch. 14, Para. 8).

However, in the case of a tax-geared penalty, a determination may be made, or proceedings commenced at any time within three years after the final determination of the amount of tax involved. This does not apply where a person has died, and the determination would be made in relation to his personal representatives, if the tax was charged in an assessment made more than six years after the effective date of the transaction to which it relates.

A penalty for assisting in the preparation of incorrect return may be determined by a Revenue officer, or proceedings for such a penalty may be commenced before a court, at any time within 20 years after the date on which the penalty was incurred.

10.15 Partnerships

10.15.1 The general rule

A chargeable interest held by or on behalf of a partnership is treated as held by or on behalf of the partners and not by or on behalf of the partnership as such. Accordingly, a land transaction entered into for the purposes of a partnership is treated as entered into by or on behalf of the partners (FA 2003, Sch. 15, Para. 2). This rule applies even if the partnership is regarded as a legal person, or as a body corporate, under the law of the country or territory under which it is formed.

A partnership is treated as the same partnership notwithstanding a change in membership if any person who was a member before the change remains a member after the change (Sch. 15, Para. 3).

A partnership is not to be regarded as a unit trust scheme or an open-ended investment company (Sch. 15, Para. 4).

Ordinary partnership transactions

Anything required or authorised to be done by or in relation to the purchaser under a transaction entered into by or on behalf of the members of a partnership is required or authorised to be done by or in relation to all the responsible partners (Sch. 15, Para. 6). They are:

- the partners as at the effective date of the transaction, and
- any person who becomes a partner after the effective date of the transaction.

Any SDLT charged on such a transaction, including any interest and penalty, is a joint and several liability of the responsible partners (Sch. 15, Para. 7).

However, no penalty may be recovered from a person who did not become a responsible partner until after the 'relevant time'. This is:

- in relation to a daily penalty, including any interest thereon, the beginning of that day,
- in relation to any other penalty, or interest on such a penalty, the time when the act or omission occurred that caused the penalty to become payable.

The responsible partners may, by a majority, nominate a specific partner to be the representative partner for SDLT purposes (Sch. 15, Para. 8). He may, in particular, sign the declaration that a return or self-certificate is complete and correct.

Any such nomination may be revoked. The nomination or revocation has effect only after notice of it has been given to the Revenue.

10.15.2   Transactions excluded from SDLT up to 22 July 2004

The old stamp duty legislation continues to apply to transactions that are excluded from SDLT under the provisions set out below (FA 2003, Sch. 15, Para. 13(2)).

A transaction by which:

- a partner transfers an interest in land to a partnership, or
- a person transfers an interest in land to a partnership in return for an interest in the partnership,

whether in connection with the formation of the partnership or in a case where the partnership already exists, is excluded from SDLT (Sch. 15, Para. 10). There is a transfer of an interest in land to a partnership in any case where an interest in land that was not partnership property becomes partnership property.

An acquisition of an interest in a partnership is excluded from SDLT (Sch. 15, Para. 11).

A transaction by which an interest in land is transferred from a partnership to a person in consideration of his ceasing to be a member of the partnership or reducing his interest in the partnership is excluded from SDLT (Sch. 15, Para. 12).

There is a transfer of an interest in land from a partnership in any case where an interest in land that was partnership property ceases to be partnership property. For this purpose, property that was partnership property before the partnership was dissolved or otherwise ceased to exist shall be treated as remaining partnership property until it is distributed.

A transaction that is excluded from SDLT under the above rules is treated as if it were not a land transaction at all (Sch. 15, Para. 13).

10.15.3   Partnership transactions: rules applying from 23 July 2004

Transfer of interest in land into a partnership

There is a transfer of an interest in land to a partnership in any case where an interest in land that was not partnership property becomes partnership property (FA 2003, Sch. 15, Para. 35).

A transfer of an interest in land includes:

- the grant or creation of an interest in land;
- the variation of an interest in land, and
- the surrender, release or renunciation of an interest in land,

(Sch. 15, Para. 9(2)).

The responsible partners are:

- those who were partners immediately before the transfer and who remain partners after the transfer, and
- any person becoming a partner as a result of, or in connection with, the transfer.

The exemption of transactions for which there is no chargeable consideration does not apply; nor do the group relief rules.

The ICTA 1988, s. 839 definition of connected persons applies.

The consideration for the above transfer is taken to be the sum of two parts (Sch. 15, Para. 10).

The first part is $RCP \times MV$.

MV is the market value of the interest transferred. *RCP* is the "relevant chargeable proportion", being the proportion that is effectively held by the other partners (Sch. 15, Paras. 11, 12, 34). So if an individual who owns a freehold property transfers it to a partnership in which he has a 25 per cent interest and the other partners 75 per cent, then this part of the deemed consideration is 75 per cent of the market value of the property on the date of the transfer.

The second part is $RCP \times AC$.

AC is the actual consideration for the transaction. In this formula, however, *RCP* means effectively the transferring partner's interest in the partnership, ie the proportionate interest in the asset that remains with him: 25 per cent in the above example. This part is not understood. It appears to envisage that the individual, as partner, pays himself, as transferor, actual consideration. This appears to be inconsistent with the general rule explained at **10.15.1** above. It is hoped that the Revenue will provide clarification of what is involved here.

Where the transferring partner grants a lease to the partnership for rent, a charge arises in respect of the relevant chargeable proportion of the net present value of the rent, being the proportion that is effectively held by the other partners.

If there is chargeable consideration other than rent, then once again there are two parts to the charge, as explained above (Sch. 15, Para. 11).

Transfer of partnership interest

A transfer of an interest in a partnership is a chargeable transaction if:

- consideration is given for the transfer, and
- the relevant partnership property includes an interest in land,

(Sch. 15, Para. 14).

The purchaser under the transaction is the person who acquires an increased partnership share or, as the case may be, becomes a partner in consequence of the transfer.

There is a transfer of an interest in a partnership where arrangements are entered into under which:

(a) a partner transfers the whole or part of his interest as partner to another person (who may be an existing partner), or

(b) a person becomes a partner and an existing partner reduces his interest in the partnership or ceases to be a partner,

(Sch. 15, Para. 36).

Consideration is regarded as given for the transfer:

- in a case within (a) above, if consideration in money or money's worth is given by or on behalf of the person acquiring the interest,
- in a case within (b) above, if there is a withdrawal of money or money's worth from the partnership by the person reducing his interest or ceasing to be a partner,

(Sch. 15, Para. 14(4)).

The 'relevant partnership property', in relation to a transfer of an interest in a partnership, is every interest in land held as partnership property immediately after the transfer, other than any interest that was transferred to the partnership in connection with the transfer (Sch. 15, Para. 14(5)).

The chargeable consideration for the transfer is taken to be equal to a proportion of the market value of the relevant partnership property. That proportion is:

- if the person acquiring the interest in the partnership was not a partner before the transfer, his partnership share immediately after the transfer.
- if he was a partner before the transfer, the difference between his partnership share before and after the transfer,

(Sch. 15, Para. 14(6), (7)).

'Arrangements' includes any scheme, agreement or understanding, whether or not legally enforceable (Sch. 15, Para. 40).

The exemption for transactions for which there is no chargeable consideration does not apply (Sch. 15, Para. 25).

Application of provisions about exchanges, etc.

Where rules relating to exchanges apply to the acquisition of an interest in a partnership in consideration of entering into a land transaction with an existing partner, the interest in the partnership is treated as a major interest in land if the relevant partnership property includes a major interest in land (Sch. 15, Para. 16).

The provisions relating to partitions, etc. do not apply where the above rules apply.

Transfer of interest in land out of a partnership

Where an interest in land is transferred:

- from a partnership to a partner (or a person connected with a partner), or

- from a partnership to a former partner (or a person connected with a former partner),

the chargeable consideration for the transaction is taken to be the 'chargeable proportion' of the market value of the interest transferred (Sch. 15, Paras. 18–22).

There is a transfer of an interest in land from a partnership in any case where an interest in land that was partnership property ceases to be partnership property.

As in the case of a transfer into a partnership, there are two elements to the chargeable consideration, the first being $RCP \times MV$, which corresponds to the market value of the interest acquired by the transferee partner(s) from the other partners. The second part is $RCP \times AC$, which appears to be a deemed payment of consideration by the transferee partners as transferees to themselves as partners, and which appears to be inconsistent with the general rule explained at **10.15.1** above.

The exemption of transactions for which there is no chargeable consideration does not apply.

Property that was partnership property before the partnership was dissolved or otherwise ceased to exist is treated as remaining partnership property until it is distributed.

Where the partnership grants a lease to the transferee partners for rent, a charge arises in respect of the relevant chargeable proportion of the net present value of the rent, being the proportion that is effectively held by the other partners.

If there is chargeable consideration other than rent, then once again there are two parts to the charge, as explained above (Sch. 15, Para. 19).

The ICTA 1988, s. 839 definition of connected persons applies.

Special provisions

The above rules are adapted to cover the transfer of an interest from one partnership to another (Sch. 15, Para. 23) and the transfer from a partnership consisting wholly of corporate bodies (Sch. 15, Para. 24). As regards the latter, group relief is potentially available in relation to transfers between partners that are corporate bodies (Sch. 15, Para. 27).

Disadvantaged area relief may be available where the land is situated in a disadvantaged area (Sch. 15, Para. 26) and charities relief may be available where the land is transferred to a charity (Sch. 15, Para. 28).

Acquisition of interest in partnership not chargeable except as specially provided

Except in the case of a transfer of land into partnership or a transfer of partnership interest, the acquisition of an interest in a partnership is not a chargeable transaction, even if the partnership property includes land (Sch. 15, Para. 29).

Transactions that are not notifiable

A transfer of partnership interest is not a notifiable transaction unless the consideration for the transaction exceeds the zero-rate threshold (Sch. 15, Para. 30).

The consideration for a transaction exceeds the zero-rate threshold if:

- the relevant consideration is such that the rate of tax chargeable under that s. 55 is 1 per cent or higher, and/or
- the relevant rent value is such that the rate of tax chargeable under Sch. 5 is 1 per cent or higher.

Definitions

An interest in land includes any interest or right that would be a chargeable interest but for being excluded from SDLT.

The transfer of an interest in land includes:

- the grant or creation of an interest in land;
- the variation of an interest in land, and
- the surrender or release of an interest in land,

(s. 43).

A 'partnership' means:

- a partnership within the Partnership Act 1890;
- a limited partnership registered under the Limited Partnerships Act 1907, or
- a limited liability partnership formed under the Limited Liability Partnerships Act 2000 or the Limited Liability Partnerships Act (Northern Ireland) 2002,

or a firm or entity of a similar character to any of the above formed under the law of a country or territory outside the UK (Sch. 15, Para. 1).

Partnership property means an interest or right held by or on behalf of a partnership, or the members of a partnership, for the purposes of the partnership business (Sch. 15, Para. 34).

A person's partnership share at any time is the proportion in which he is entitled at that time to share in the profits of the partnership (Sch. 15, Para. 34).

10.16 Special provisions

10.16.1 Companies

Everything to be done by a company is to be done by the company acting through:

- the 'proper officer' of the company, or
- another person having for the time being the express, implied or apparent authority of the company to act on its behalf for the purpose,

(FA 2003, s. 100).

Service on a company of any document may be effected by serving it on the proper officer.

Tax due from a company that is not a body corporate, or is incorporated under the law of a country or territory outside the UK, may be recovered from the proper officer of the company. The proper officer may retain, out of any money coming into his hands on behalf of the company, sufficient sums to pay that tax and, so far as he is not so reimbursed, he is entitled to be indemnified by the company in respect of the liability imposed on him.

'Company' means any body corporate or unincorporated association, but does not include a partnership.

Proper officer

The proper officer of a body corporate is the secretary, or person acting as secretary, of the company.

The proper officer of an unincorporated association, or of a body corporate that does not have a proper officer as defined above, is the treasurer, or person acting as treasurer, of the company.

However, if a liquidator or administrator has been appointed for the company, then:

- the liquidator or, as the case may be, the administrator is the proper officer, and
- if two or more persons are appointed to act jointly or concurrently as the administrator of the company, the proper officer is:

such one of them as is specified in a notice given to the Revenue by those persons for the purposes of this section, or

where the Revenue is not so notified, such one or more of those persons as the Revenue may designate as the proper officer for those purposes.

10.16.2   Unit trust schemes

Initial transfer of assets to trustees of unit trust scheme

The acquisition of a chargeable interest by trustees of a unit trust scheme is exempt from charge if:

- immediately before the acquisition there were no assets held by the trustees for the purposes of the scheme, and there were no units of the scheme in issue;
- the only consideration for the acquisition is the issue of units in the scheme to the vendor, and
- immediately after the acquisition the vendor is the only unit holder of the scheme,

(FA 2003, s. 64A).

Treatment as company

For SDLT purposes a unit trust scheme is treated as if:

- the trustees were a company, and
- the rights of the unit holders were shares in the company,

(s. 101).

Each of the parts of an umbrella scheme is regarded for SDLT purposes as a separate unit trust scheme and the scheme as a whole is not so regarded.

An 'umbrella scheme' means a unit trust scheme:

- that provides arrangements for separate pooling of the contributions of participants and the profits or income out of which payments are to be made for them, and
- under which the participants are entitled to exchange rights in one pool for rights in another.

A 'part' of an umbrella scheme means such of the arrangements as relate to a separate pool.

'Unit trust scheme' has the same meaning as in the Financial Services and Markets Act 2000.

'Unit holder' means a person entitled to a share of the investments subject to the trusts of a unit trust scheme.

A court common investment fund is treated as a unit trust (the provisions of ICTA 1988, s. 469A being applied for this purpose).

However, a unit trust scheme is not treated as a company for the purposes of:

- the deemed market value rule for transactions with connected companies, or
- group relief, reconstruction relief or acquisition relief.

10.16.3   Open-ended investment companies (OEICs)

Regulations will make provision for the application of the SDLT legislation to OEICs (FA 2003, s. 102).

'Open-ended investment company' has the meaning given by Financial Services and Markets Act 2000, s. 236.

'Unit trust scheme' and 'umbrella scheme' have the same meaning as in 10.15.2 above.

10.16.4   Joint purchasers

Where there are two or more purchasers who are or will be jointly entitled to the interest acquired:

- any obligation of the purchaser under the SDLT legislation in relation to the transaction is an obligation of the purchasers jointly, but may be discharged by any of them;
- anything required or authorised to be done in relation to the purchaser must be done by or in relation to all of them, and
- any SDLT liability of the purchaser (including any interest and penalty) in relation to the transaction is a joint and several liability of the purchasers,

(FA 2003, s. 103).

If the transaction is a notifiable transaction, a single land transaction return is required. However, the declaration that return or self-certificate is complete and correct must be made by all the purchasers.

Enquiries

Any enquiry notice must be given to each of the purchasers.

The powers of the Revenue as to the production of documents and provision of information for the purposes of the enquiry are exercisable separately (and differently) in relation to each of the purchasers.

Any of the purchasers may apply for a direction that a closure notice be given, and all of them are entitled to appear and be heard on the application.

Any closure notice must be given to each of the purchasers.

Determinations and assessments

A Revenue determination or discovery assessment relating to the transaction must be made against all the purchasers and is not effective against any of them unless notice of it is given to each of them whose identity is known to the Revenue.

Appeals

An appeal may be brought by any of the purchasers.

Notice of the appeal must be given to any of them by whom it is not brought.

The agreement of all the purchasers is required if the appeal is to be settled by agreement.

If it is not settled, any of them are entitled to appear and be heard, and the decision on the appeal binds all of them.

10.16.5 Trustees

Bare trustee

Where a person acquires a chargeable interest as bare trustee, the interest is treated as if it were vested in, and the acts of the trustee in relation to it were the acts of, the person or persons for whom he is trustee (FA 2003, Sch. 16, Para. 3).

Trustees of settlement

Where persons acquire a chargeable interest as trustees of a settlement, they are treated, as purchasers of the whole of the interest acquired, including the beneficial interest (FA 2003, Sch. 16, Para. 4).

Where the trustees of a settlement are liable:

- to make a payment of tax or interest on unpaid tax;

- to make a payment in accordance with an assessment to recover an excessive repayment, or
- to a penalty or to interest on such a penalty,

the payment, penalty or interest may be recovered (but only once) from any one or more of the responsible trustees (FA 2003, Sch. 16, Para. 5).

No amount of penalty or interest thereon may be recovered from a person who did not become a responsible trustee until after the 'relevant time'.

The responsible trustees, in relation to a land transaction, are the persons who are trustees at the effective date of the transaction and any person who subsequently becomes a trustee.

The relevant time is:

- in relation to a daily penalty, or to interest thereon, the beginning of that day,
- in relation to any other penalty, or interest thereon, the time when the act or omission occurred that caused the penalty to become payable.

Relevant trustees for purposes of return, etc.

A return or self-certificate may be made or given by any one or more of the trustees who are the responsible trustees in relation to the transaction (Sch. 16, Para. 6). They are referred to below as 'the relevant trustees'.

A declaration that a return or self-certificate is complete and correct must be made by all the relevant trustees.

If the Revenue gives notice of an enquiry into the return or self-certificate:

- the notice must be given to each of the relevant trustees;
- the powers of the Revenue as to the production of documents and provision of information for the purposes of the enquiry are exercisable separately (and differently) in relation to each of the relevant trustees;
- any of the relevant trustees may apply for a direction that a closure notice be given (and all of them are entitled to appear and be heard on the application), and
- the closure notice must be given to each of the relevant trustees.

However, a notice is not invalidated if it is given to each of the relevant trustees whose identity is known to the Revenue.

A Revenue determination or discovery assessment relating to the transaction must be made against all of the relevant trustees and is not effective against any of them unless notice of it is given to each of them whose identity is known to the Revenue.

In the case of an appeal:

- the appeal may be brought by any of the relevant trustees;
- notice of the appeal must be given to any of them by whom it is not brought;
- the agreement of all the relevant trustees is required if the appeal is to be settled by agreement;
- if it is not settled, any of them are entitled to appear and be heard, and
- the decision on the appeal binds all of them.

Consideration for exercise of power of appointment or discretion

Where a chargeable interest is acquired by virtue of:

- the exercise of a power of appointment, or
- the exercise of a discretion vested in trustees of a settlement,

there is treated as consideration any consideration given for the person in whose favour the appointment was made, or the discretion was exercised, becoming an object of the power or discretion (Sch. 16, Para. 7).

Meaning of 'settlement' and 'bare trust'

'Settlement' means a trust that is not a bare trust (Sch. 16, Para. 1).

A 'bare trust' means a trust under which property is held by a person as trustee:

- for a person who is absolutely entitled as against the trustee, or who would be so entitled but for being a minor or other person under a disability, or
- for two or more persons who are or would be jointly so entitled,

and includes a case in which a person holds property as nominee for another.

A person is absolutely entitled to property as against the trustee if he has the exclusive right, subject only to satisfying any outstanding charge, lien or other right of the trustee, to resort to the property for payment of duty, taxes, costs or other outgoings or to direct how the property is to be dealt with.

'Minor', in relation to Scotland, means a person under legal disability by reason of nonage.

Scottish and overseas trusts

Where property is held in trust under the law of Scotland, or of a country or territory outside the UK, on terms such that, if the trust had effect under the law of England and Wales, a beneficiary would be regarded as having an equitable interest in the trust property:

- that beneficiary is treated as having such an interest even if no such interest is recognised by the law of Scotland or, as the case may be, the country or territory outside the UK, and
- an acquisition of the interest of a beneficiary under the trust is treated as involving the acquisition of an interest in the trust property,

(Sch. 16, Para. 2).

10.16.6   Personal representatives

The person having the direction, management or control of the property of an incapacitated person is responsible for discharging any obligations under the SDLT legislation, in relation to a transaction affecting that property, to which the incapacitated person would be subject if he were not incapacitated. He may retain, out of money coming into his hands on behalf of the incapacitated person, sums sufficient to meet any payment he is liable to make and is entitled to be indemnified in respect of any such payment (FA 2003, s. 106).

The parent or guardian of a minor is responsible for discharging any obligations of the minor under the SDLT legislation that are not discharged by the minor himself.

The personal representatives of a purchaser under a land transaction are responsible for discharging the obligations of the purchaser in relation to the transaction. They may deduct any payment made by them out of the assets and effects of the deceased person.

A receiver appointed by a court in the UK having the direction and control of any property is responsible for discharging any obligations under the SDLT legislation in relation to a transaction affecting that property.

10.16.7   Demutualisations

Demutualisation of insurance company

A land transaction is exempt from SDLT if it is entered into for the purposes of or in connection with a 'qualifying transfer' of the whole or part of the business of a mutual insurance company ('the mutual') to a company that has share capital ('the acquiring company') (FA 2003, s. 63).

A transfer is a qualifying transfer if:

- it is a transfer of business consisting of the effecting or carrying out of contracts of insurance and takes place under an insurance business transfer scheme, or

- it is a transfer of business of a general insurance company carried on through a permanent establishment in the UK and takes place in accordance with authorisation granted outside the UK for the purposes of the Life Assurance Directive, Art. 14 or the Third Non-life Insurance Directive, Art. 12.

In either case, however, the following requirements must be met in relation to the shares of a company ('the issuing company') which is either the acquiring company or a company of which the acquiring company is a wholly-owned subsidiary.

Shares in the issuing company must be offered, under the scheme, to at least 90 per cent of the persons who are members of the mutual immediately before the transfer.

Under the scheme all of the shares in the issuing company that will be in issue immediately after the transfer has been made, other than shares that are to be or have been issued pursuant to an offer to the public, must be offered to the persons who (at the time of the offer) are:

- members of the mutual;
- persons who are entitled to become members of the mutual, or
- employees, former employees or pensioners of the mutual, or a wholly-owned subsidiary of the mutual.

A company is the wholly-owned subsidiary of another company ('the parent') if the company has no members except the parent and the parent's wholly-owned subsidiaries or persons acting on behalf of the parent or the parent's wholly-owned subsidiaries.

Various terms are defined in the legislation.

Demutualisation of building society

A land transaction effected in pursuance of the transfer of a building society's business to a commercial company is exempt from SDLT (FA 2003, s. 64).

10.16.8 Transitional rules

Contract entered into before 11 July 2003

A transaction is not an SDLT transaction if it is effected in pursuance of a contract entered into before 11 July 2003 (FA 2003, Sch. 19, Para. 3).

However, this exclusion does not apply:

- if there is any variation of the contract or assignment of rights under the contract on or after that date;

- if the transaction is effected in consequence of the exercise after that date of any option, right of pre-emption or similar right,
- where the purchaser under the transaction is a person other than the purchaser under the contract because of a further contract made on or after that date.

Contract substantially performed before 1 December 2003

A transaction that is effected in pursuance of a contract entered into and substantially performed before 1 December 2003, and is completed on or after that date is not an SDLT transaction if the contract was substantially performed before 11 July 2003 (Sch. 19, Para. 4).

In any other case, the fact that the contract was substantially performed before the implementation date does not affect the matter. Accordingly, the effective date of the transaction is the date of completion.

Contracts substantially performed after 1 December 2003

Where:

- a transaction is effected in pursuance of a contract entered into before 11 July 2003;
- the contract is substantially performed, without having been completed, after 1 December 2003, and
- there is subsequently an exclusion event by virtue of which the transaction is an SDLT transaction,

the effective date of the transaction is the date of the exclusion event and not the date of substantial performance (Sch. 19, Para. 4A).

Application of provisions in case of transfer of rights

In the case of an assignment or sub-sale, the date of the deemed secondary contract with transferee is the date of the assignment, sub-sale or other transaction in question (Sch. 19, Para. 4B).

Credit for ad valorem stamp duty paid

Where a transaction chargeable to SDLT is effected in pursuance of a contract entered into before 1 December 2003, any *ad valorem* stamp duty paid on the contract is offset against the amount of SDLT payable, but not so as to give rise to any repayment (Sch. 19, Para. 5).

Where the application or operation of any exemption or relief from SDLT turns on whether tax was paid or payable in respect of an earlier transaction, that requirement is treated as met if *ad valorem* stamp duty was paid or payable on the instrument by which that transaction was effected.

Effect for stamp duty purposes of SDLT being paid or chargeable

Where in the case of a contract that, apart from the provisions relating to contracts chargeable as conveyances on sale, would not be chargeable with stamp duty:

- a conveyance made in conformity with the contract is effected after 1 December 2003, and
- SDLT is duly paid in respect of that transaction or no tax is chargeable because of an exemption or relief,

the contract is deemed to be duly stamped (Sch. 19, Para. 6).

There are provisions dealing with cases where a transaction occurring before 1 December 2003 qualified for group relief or acquisition relief, but a disqualifying event occurs after that date.

Earlier related transactions under stamp duty

There is a provision dealing with the case where a transaction occurring before 1 December 2003 is linked to a transaction occurring on or after that date (Sch. 19, Para. 7).

There is a provision dealing with the case where the transfer of a reversion under shared ownership lease occurs on or after 1 December 2003, but where an election made for market value treatment was made before that date.

In construing the exceptions from the deemed market value rule for transactions with a connected company, Case 3 applies as if the reference to group relief included a reference to the old stamp duty group relief.

Stamping of contract where transaction on completion subject to SDLT

The following rule applies where:

- a contract that apart from the stamp duty rules relating to contracts chargeable as conveyances on sale would not be chargeable with stamp duty is entered into before 1 December 2003;
- a conveyance made in conformity with the contract is effected on or after that date, and
- the transaction effected on completion is an SDLT transaction or would be but for an exemption or relief from SDLT,

(Sch. 19, Para. 7A).

If the contract is presented for stamping together with a Revenue certificate as to compliance with the SDLT provisions in relation to the transaction effected on completion:

- the payment of SDLT on that transaction or, as the case may be, the fact that no such tax was payable must be denoted on the contract by a particular stamp, and
- the contract is deemed thereupon to be duly stamped.

'Conveyance' includes any instrument.

Time for stamping agreement for lease: lease subject to SDLT

The following rule applies where:

- an agreement for a lease is entered into before 1 December 2003;
- a lease giving effect to the agreement is executed on or after that date,
- the transaction effected on completion is an SDLT transaction or would be but for an exemption or relief from stamp duty land tax,

(Sch. 19, Para. 8).

If the agreement is presented for stamping together with a Revenue SDLT certificate in relation to the grant of the lease:

- the payment of SDLT in respect of the grant of the lease or, as the case may be, the fact that no such tax was payable must be denoted on the agreement by a particular stamp, and
- the agreement is deemed thereupon to be duly stamped.

A lease gives effect to an agreement if the lease either is in conformity with the agreement or relates to substantially the same property and term as the agreement.

An agreement for a lease includes a missive of let in Scotland.

Exercise of option or right of pre-emption acquired before 1 December 2003

The following rules apply where:

- an option binding the grantor to enter into a land transaction, or
- a right of pre-emption preventing the grantor from entering into, or restricting the right of the grantor to enter into, a land transaction,

is acquired before 1 December 2003 and exercised on or after that date.

Where the option or right was acquired on or after 17 April 2003, any consideration for the acquisition is treated as part of the chargeable consideration for the transaction resulting from the exercise of the option or right.

Where the option or right was varied on or after 17 April 2003 and before the implementation date, any consideration for the variation is treated as part of the chargeable consideration for the transaction resulting from the exercise of the option or right (Sch. 19, Para. 9).

Whether or not the above rules apply, the acquisition of the option or right and any variation of the option or right is treated as linked with the land transaction resulting from the exercise of the option or right. However, this does not require the consideration for the acquisition or variation to be counted twice in determining the rate of tax chargeable on the land transaction resulting from the exercise of the option or right.

Any *ad valorem* stamp duty paid on the acquisition or variation of the option or right goes to reduce the amount of tax payable on the transaction resulting from the exercise of the option or right (but not so as to give rise to any repayment).

Contract

'Contract' includes any agreement (Sch. 19, Para. 10).

11 Value Added Tax

11.1 General principles and terms of VAT

11.1.1 Introduction

Value Added Tax (VAT) is a tax ultimately paid by the final consumer of goods or services on a supply made for a consideration. It is charged as *output tax* by each supplier at each stage of production. A VAT registered trader who has been charged VAT by a supplier can reclaim this tax as *input tax*. Each VAT registered trader submits a quarterly or monthly *VAT return* to HM Customs and Excise, the government department charged with overseeing VAT. This VAT return summarises the VAT charged by the trader to customers and the VAT it has paid to suppliers. The result is either an amount that is due to and is paid to the Government or when the input tax exceeds the output tax, a repayment to the trader from the Government.

That is the very simplistic outline of the system. As with all taxes the complications arise in the detail of the rules and legislation that mean certain amounts of input tax are not reclaimable and that certain goods and services are charged at different rates of VAT, or are not subject to VAT at all. If a trader does not have to charge VAT on his supplies then in general the input tax paid by the trader cannot be reclaimed.

11.1.2 European law

The source of VAT law in this country is now the EC Sixth Council Directive No. 77/388/EEC (the Sixth Directive). The Court of Justice of the European Communities (CJEC) has held that 'wherever the provisions of a Directive appear, as far as their subject matter is concerned, to be unconditional and sufficiently precise their provisions may . . . be relied upon as against any national provision which is incompatible with the Directive or in so far as the provisions define rights which individuals are able to assert against the state' (*Ursula Becker v Finanzamt Munster-Innenstadt* [1982] ECR 53). This applies to the Sixth Directive and thus to the UK's VAT legislation which is intended to implement the Sixth Directive in the UK.

11.1.3 Registration

A person carrying on a business in the UK must consider whether he is liable to register for VAT or if it would be beneficial to so do.

Past annual threshold (past turnover rule)

A person is liable to register if, at the end of any calendar month, the value of his taxable supplies which were made in the UK in the course or furtherance of a business during the year then ending exceeded £58,000 (from 1 April 2004) (VATA 1994, Sch. 1, Para. 1(1)(a)). For example, if a person's past supplies exceeded the limit by the end of March, Customs must be notified by 30 April in that year and registration takes effect from 1 May in that year.

Future turnover threshold (future-prospects rule; 30-day look-ahead test)

A person is immediately liable to register if at any time there are reasonable grounds for believing that the value of his taxable supplies, which will be made in the UK in the 30 days then beginning, will exceed £58,000 (from 1 April 2004) (VATA 1994, Sch. 1, Para. 1(1)(b)). This is sometimes known as the 'future prospects rule' or the '30-day look-ahead test' and aims to stop a large business from having a month's grace before accounting for output tax. The 30 days do not start at the beginning of each month, they start at any time.

Voluntary registration

A person, whose turnover does not reach the registration threshold, may register voluntarily. At the request of such a person, Customs must register that person if he makes taxable supplies in the course or furtherance of a business (VATA 1994, Sch. 1, Para. 9).

Registration before making taxable supplies

A person can register before making taxable supplies as an 'intending trader'. Customs wants to be satisfied that a person intends to trade in the future and is setting up a bona fide business.

11.1.4 Outputs and output tax

All supplies of goods and services made *by* a taxable person in the course or furtherance of a business are referred to as outputs of that business. The VAT chargeable on any standard-rated and reduced-rated supplies is output tax.

Where a supply includes both taxable and exempt items or supplies taxed at different rates, it is necessary to determine whether there is a mixed supply or a single composite supply. If there is a mixed supply, then VAT is chargeable only on the consideration for the taxable items, but if there is a composite supply, the output tax liability has to be determined for the supply as a whole. This also affects the recovery of input tax.

In the case of a mixed supply, if the apportionment of the consideration for the supply cannot be ascertained directly, it must be made on a just and reasonable basis.

Mixed and composite supplies

The distinction between mixed and composite supplies is not always easy to make, and a number of cases have been heard by the tribunals and the courts on this matter. The leading case on this is now *Card Protection Plan v C&E Comrs* 96 [1999] BVC 155. The Court held that there is a single composite supply if one or some elements constitute the principal service and others are merely ancillary. Services are ancillary if they do not constitute, for customers, aims in themselves, but imply a means of better enjoying the principal service. The fact that a single price is charged for a service consisting of several elements might suggest that there is a single supply, but is not decisive.

11.1.5   Inputs and input tax

All supplies of goods and services made *to* a taxable person for the purposes of a business are referred to as *inputs* of that business. Tax charged on such supplies is input tax.

Most input tax incurred in making taxable supplies is recoverable as credit against output tax, whereas input tax incurred in making exempt supplies is only recoverable in certain, limited circumstances.

Credit is technically only available for input VAT correctly charged (*Genius Holdings BV v Staatssecretaris van Financien* [1991] BVC 52).

Where VAT is charged and collected incorrectly on a supply, that VAT may be collected from the supplier (VATA 1994, Para. 5, Sch. 11) but credit refused to the customer. For example, credit for VAT charged incorrectly on a transfer of a going concern has been refused (*C&E Commrs v Dearwood* (1986) 2 BVC 200, 222).

The input tax must relate to goods or services which are used or to be used for the purpose of any business carried on or to be carried on by the taxable person. Thus the claim to input tax does not have to be limited to a business carried on only in the UK (VATA 1994, s. 26). The test of whether goods or services are used or to be used for the purposes of a business is a subjective one. It is the taxable person's objective that is important, and it does not matter that the intention may have been misconceived. Accordingly the purchase of a racing horse for publicity purposes by a company manufacturing plastic tubes was held to be wholly for business purposes, despite the fact that the commercial logic behind the purchase was extremely doubtful (*Ian Flockton Developments v Customs & Excise Commissioners* (1987) 3 BVC 23).

There is a right of appeal against any refusal by Customs to allow a set off of input tax. However, in relation to appeals relating to a set off of input tax on expenditure in 'the nature of luxury amusement or entertainment' the tribunal may amend the decision of Customs only if that decision was unreasonable (VATA 1994, ss. 83(c) and 84(4)). The leading case on what is unreasonable is the case of *Associated Provincial Picture Houses v Wednesbury Corporation* [1948] 1 KB 223. In that case, Lord Greene MR set out the circumstances in which an authority might be held to have acted unreasonably as follows:

- where it has not directed itself properly in law;
- where it has failed to take into account relevant considerations;
- where it has taken into account irrelevant considerations;
- where it has acted in bad faith, or
- where it has acted in disregard of public policy.

Allowable input tax is input tax relating to supplies made to the taxable person. Input tax on supplies made to other persons is not available for set off.

11.1.6   Accounting for VAT

A taxable person is required, in respect of supplies of goods and/or services made in the course or furtherance of the business for each 'prescribed accounting period', to account for and pay to Customs & Excise the difference between:

- the output tax charged on standard-rated and reduced-rated supplies made in that period, and on acquisitions and importations in the period, and
- the input tax attributable to standard-rated, reduced-rated and zero-rated supplies made in the period (VATA 1994, s. 25).

11.1.7   Tax invoices

Although it is not necessary in itself to validate a transaction as between the supplier of taxable goods or services and the recipient, the issue of a *tax invoice* in approved form by the supplier is obligatory in many circumstances, thus providing the recipient with evidence as to the amount of VAT charged on that particular transaction and the time of supply and his entitlement to credit for that tax as input tax in his hands (SI 1995/2518, reg. 13). Failure by the recipient to produce such an invoice on enquiry by Customs & Excise (eg on one of its control visits) may lead to the tax claimed being disallowed as a deduction.

Authenticated receipt

Sometimes in the building industry an authenticated receipt of payment takes the place of an invoice. Providing it contains all the required information it will be treated as a tax invoice. This procedure is not always satisfactory for the payer, since if the recipient delays sending him the authenticated receipt he cannot be certain that the payment has been received and the tax point established.

Request for payment

In order to avoid having to pay VAT when issuing a rent invoice where there is risk of non-payment by the tenant, a landlord may issue a request for payment instead. This would show the VAT-inclusive sum but would not include the landlord's VAT number, and would clearly be marked: 'This is not a VAT invoice.' The VAT invoice can then be issued on receipt of the rent.

Items to be included

Regulations made by Customs & Excise lay down that a tax invoice should include the following details:

- identifying number:
- date of supply and. if different, issue:
- supplier's name, address and VAT registration number:
- recipient's name and address;
- type of supply, eg sale;
- description of goods or services supplied;
- (for each item) quantity of goods or extent of services, rate of tax and net amount payable excluding tax;
- total amount payable, excluding tax;
- rate of any cash discount offered;
- amount of tax chargeable at each rate,
- total amount of tax chargeable.

With effect from January 2004, the EU Invoicing Directive is in force. Invoices should show the above information and in addition:

- The type of supply or the amount of VAT charged at each rate no longer has to be shown although the trader may chose to continue giving this information.

- The unit price must be shown. This applies to countable goods or services. It may be the hourly rate or standard service charge. It will not be a requirement if it is not normally provided in that business sector *and* is not required by the customer.
- VAT exclusive amounts may be in any currency but the total amount of VAT must continue to be shown in sterling.

Customs is looking at invoices issued in 2004 'with a light touch' but are expected to decide that incorrect invoices issued after 2004 are invalid and this may give rise to disallowance of input tax.

A tax invoice showing details of items charged at the standard-rate may also include items that are exempt or zero-rated, provided that these are clearly distinguished and the gross amount payable under each head is shown (VATA 1994, Para. 2, Sch. 11; SI 1995/2518, reg. 14).

Note that an invoice for most zero-rated and/or exempt supplies alone is not a tax invoice (SI 1995/2518, reg. 20).

A substituted invoice must be issued where a continuous supply of services spans a change in the rate of tax (SI 1995/2518, reg. 90(3)).

11.1.8 The person making or receiving the supply

It is essential to determine who is making or receiving the supply. This is important because it will govern who is responsible for accounting for output tax, the person entitled to reclaim input tax and on some occasions the place of supply. There are some instances when it will also determine the liability of the supply when this depends on the status of the recipient.

11.1.9 Goods or services

It is often necessary to determine whether one is dealing with a supply of goods or a supply of services. VATA 1994 states that anything done for a consideration that is not a supply of goods is a supply of services (VATA 1994, s. 5 (2) (b)).

11.1.10 Rates of VAT

There are currently three rates of VAT in use in the UK; zero-rate, reduced rate and standard-rate. The goods and services liable to zero-rate and reduced rate are defined in VATA 1994, Sch. 8 and Sch. 7A respectively. Taxable supplies not listed in these schedules are standard-rated.

A trader making supplies subject to any of these rates of VAT may reclaim input tax paid on supplies except for a few general exceptions that will not be discussed in this work. Details may be found in works specifically devoted to VAT such as *The British VAT Reporter*.

11.1.11 Exempt from VAT

There are some supplies that are exempt from VAT. The relevant supplies are listed in VATA 1994, Sch 9. A trader making such supplies cannot reclaim the input VAT paid on supplies except in a few cases.

11.1.12 Supplies outside the scope of VAT

Some supplies are outside the scope of UK VAT altogether. These include non-business activities and supplies where the 'place of supply' is outside the UK. If the place of supply is another Member State, VAT may be payable in that Member State. Input tax relating to business supplies made outside the UK may be reclaimed if those supplies would be taxable if made in the UK.

11.1.13 Place of supply/residence

The concept of residence is not directly relevant for VAT purposes. What matters is the place of supply of goods or services. If that place is the UK, then VAT is chargeable, subject to exemption and zero-rating. If the place of supply is in another Member State, then the supply is outside the scope of VAT in the UK, but it may be within the scope of VAT in the country in which the place of supply exists.

The place of supply for land and services relating to land, are dealt with below. For information about the place of supply of other goods or services see *The British VAT Reporter*.

Installed goods

Goods are treated as supplied in the UK where their supply involves their installation or assembly at a place in the UK to which they are removed. This applies, in particular, to building materials, etc. taken to a site in the UK and used in the construction, alteration, etc. of a building on that site and to fixtures and plant installed in such a building (VATA 1994, s. 7(3) following Sixth Directive, Art. 8, Para. 1(a)).

Similarly, goods are treated as supplied outside the UK where their supply involves their installation or assembly at a place outside the UK to which they are removed. This applies, in particular to building materials, etc. taken to a site outside the UK and used in the construction, alteration, etc. of a building on that site and to fixtures and plant installed in such a building.

11.1.14   Time of supply/tax point

Determining the time of supply, called the 'tax point', is important because it may affect the rate of tax applicable to the supply. It determines when the supplier is liable to account for VAT on a supply by him and it determines when the recipient may be able to claim credit for input tax.

General rules

In the case of goods supplied in the UK the primary tax point is when they are removed, or if this is not applicable when they are made available to the recipient. In the case of services the primary tax point is when they are performed, which is normally when they are completed (VATA 1994, s. 6).

Where the supplier issues a tax invoice (see below) or receives a payment *before* this primary point, the payment creates a tax point for the amount received. The tax point is thus the earlier of the issue of the invoice or the receipt of the money.

Where within 14 days (or such longer period as Customs may agree) *after* the primary point the supplier issues a tax invoice, then providing a payment has not been received, the tax point becomes the date of the issue of the invoice – though the supplier may elect for this rule not to apply and it should be noted that a tax invoice may not be issued in respect of a zero-rated supply.

In practice this means that there may be more than one tax point for a supply.

Continuous supply of services

Where there is a continuous supply of services over a period during which payments are made periodically or from time to time, a tax point arises with each payment, so that tax is chargeable each time a payment is received or an invoice is issued, whichever is earlier. The same applies where services are supplied under a building contract. Where invoices are issued periodically (at least once a year) in advance, setting out amounts payable and due dates, the time of supply is the due date set out in the summary invoice or the date of receipt, whichever is earlier (SI 1995/2518, reg. 90).

Annual tax point

With effect from 1 October 2003, there is a fall-back provision triggering an annual tax point in respect of supplies where no tax point is triggered under the above rules (SI 1995/2518, reg. 94B and VAT Information Sheet 14/03).

The new tax point applies to the following supplies:

(a) supplies involving land and property, where the supply is standard-rated otherwise than by reason of the exercise of the option for taxation;

(b) supplies of water, gas, or any form of power, heat, refrigeration or ventilation, and

(c) continuous supplies of services, other than exempt supplies (see above);

Examples of (a) are car parking, holiday accommodation and fishing and shooting rights.

The new tax point only applies to those supplies where the supplier and the recipient are connected or are group undertakings. Further, it applies only if the supplier is unable to demonstrate that the recipient is able to fully recover all the VAT on the supply as input tax.

The way in which this relates to land, see below; for other details see *The British VAT Reporter*.

11.1.15 Consideration for a supply

VAT is chargeable on 'everything which constitutes the consideration which has been or is to be obtained by the supplier from the purchaser, the customer or a third party for [the supply] including subsidies directly linked to the price of [the supply]' (Sixth Directive, Art. 11(1)(a)). There are some exceptions to this general rule, notably the market value rule, which is considered below insofar as it is relevant to property transactions. In the UK, the rules are incorporated into VATA 1994, s. 19 and Sch. 6.

If the consideration is in money, the value of the supply is 'such amount of money as, with the addition of the VAT chargeable, is equal to the consideration' (s. 19(2)). If the consideration is not wholly in money, the value of the supply is 'such amount of money as, with the addition of the VAT chargeable, is equivalent to the consideration' (s. 19(3)). The consideration includes any taxes, duties, levies or charges on the supplies other than VAT itself. It also normally includes any incidental expenses such as commission, packing, transport and insurance costs that are passed on to the customer, and expenses reimbursed by the customer. The taxable amount does not include price reductions by way of discount for early payment, or discounts or rebates allowed at the time of the supply (VATA 1994, Sch. 6, Para. 4 following Sixth Directive, Art. 11, Para. 3).

Where the consideration relates partly to the supply and partly to other matters, only the amount 'properly attributable' to the supply is subject to VAT (VATA 1994, s. 19(4)).

Commissions payable by a supplier to a sales agent do not reduce the consideration received for the supply. The commission is merely an expense incurred by the supplier.

In the case of *Naturally Yours Cosmetics v C&E Commrs* (1988) 3 BVC 428, the ECJ held that 'consideration' included not just the amounts paid by the agents to the supplier (ie excluding any commission deductible) but the value of the services provided by the agents to the supplier.

Third party consideration

An example of third party consideration will be found in the case of *C&E Commrs v Battersea Leisure* [1992] BVC 23. The company agreed to purchase the old power station from the Central Electricity Generating Board and to remove asbestos and asbestos-related plant from the site. The CEGB made a contribution of £2 million towards the cost of removal of the asbestos and related plant. This was held to be consideration for the supply of services.

Market value rule

Customs and Excise may direct that the value of a supply is to be the open market value where:

- the parties to a transaction are connected;
- the actual consideration is less than the market value, and
- the purchaser is not entitled to deduct all of the VAT chargeable on the supply (VATA 1994, Sch. 6, Para. 1). A direction must be by written notice given to the supplier within three years after the time of the supply. There is a right of appeal to the VAT Tribunal (VATA 1994, s. 83(v)). This rule is authorised by Sixth Directive, Art. 27, Para. 1 as an anti-avoidance measure.

The connected persons rules of ICTA 1988, s. 839 apply for this purpose (VATA 1994, Sch. 6, Para. 1(4)).

11.1.16 Bad debts

Relief is available where a business makes taxable supplies and accounts to Customs & Excise for the output VAT, but part or all of the consideration is written off as a bad debt. Relief is available in only two circumstances. The first of these is where the trader is operating under the cash accounting scheme where relief will automatically be available. The second is a comprehensive scheme giving relief from VAT when claimed in the following circumstances:

- the debt is more than six months old, and
- the debt has been written off (wholly or partially) in the accounts (ie books and records but not necessarily the financial accounts) of the business (VATA 1994, s. 36).

Relief is available only if the debt remains outstanding six months after the due date for payment (Value Added Tax Regulations 1995 (SI 1995/2518), reg. 172(1A)) or six months after the time of supply if that is later.

Where the consideration for taxable supplies received is not paid within six months from the date of the supply or, if later, the date it became payable, the customer concerned will have to repay any input tax claimed in respect of the supplies concerned (VATA 1994, s. 26A). In relation to supplies made on or after 1 January 2003, Customs & Excise will accept the invoice date as the due date, ie the date from which the six months runs (Business Brief 23/02).

Repayment of the relief, or part of the relief, will be required where the debt is subsequently paid in whole or in part. Similarly, the customer will be entitled to deduct input tax relating to the amount paid. The issue of a credit note to cancel output tax otherwise irrecoverable is not accepted by Customs.

The regulations provide that specified information relating to the supply must be maintained, for example date and number of invoice, any payment received, etc, and these records are collectively referred to as a 'refunds for bad debts account'. Writing off the debt in the accounts merely requires the making of a further entry in the 'refunds for bad debts account' and does not also necessitate an entry in the financial (double entry) accounting system (Value Added Tax Regulations 1995 (SI 1995/2518), regs.168, 172(2)).

11.2 Input tax concerns

11.2.1 Business/private use

Problems have arisen in the past in relation to the acquisition of freehold or leasehold premises for a capital sum which has attracted VAT at the standard-rate, and where the premises are used partly for private purposes. It has been possible for the business to claim all of the input tax at the point of acquisition provided that it made a separate standard-rated charge for the private use element (see *Lennartz v Finanzamt Munchen III*, [1993] BVC 202). The net effect was to spread the disallowance of the original input tax over several years. This technique is stopped as from 9 April 2003 by an amendment to VATA 1994, Sch. 4, Para. 5 the effect of which is that the supply of the private use of an interest in land, building or civil engineering work is not to be treated as a supply (see now Para. 5(4A)).

11.2.2 Partial exemption: the problem

Under the European Sixth VAT Directive, a VAT registered business is normally entitled to claim input tax incurred in the making of taxable business supplies (EC Sixth Council Directive, No. 77/388/EEC (the Sixth Directive) Art. 17). It does not matter if the supplies by the business are of goods or services or a combination of the two, if the end product is taxable and the business is VAT registered, input tax should be reclaimable.

There is no general right to input tax recovery on purchases used to generate either exempt or non-business supplies. Thus a business that has taxable and exempt supplies has a problem as does a business that generates non-business supplies. Perhaps the most complex is the organisation that has taxable and exempt supplies and in addition is involved in non-business activities. Charities often feature these special complexities.

Non-business supplies

Charities and voluntary organisations often make taxable supplies through shops, etc. alongside their ordinary charitable activities. The provision of any free charitable services or maintaining an historic site to which there is no entry charge are usually considered to be non-business activities. There is no right to reclaim input tax incurred in connection with these supplies.

An organisation that is involved with non-business supplies and is also registered for VAT because of taxable activities has to be able to separate the input tax linked to taxable supplies from that linked to the non-business activity. Although there is no official method of doing this, the methods used are often very similar to those used in partial exemption.

If an organisation has non-business activities, exempt supplies and taxable supplies the apportionment of input tax should take place in the following order:

- analyse input tax attributable to non-business activities,
- separate remaining input tax into that attributable to taxable supplies and that attributable to exempt supplies in order to quantify the reclaimable input tax.

What are exempt supplies?

VAT is not charged on exempt supplies. If a business makes entirely exempt supplies, it can neither register for VAT nor claim credit for input tax incurred on purchases.

Exempt supplies are defined in VATA 1994, Sch. 9.

The general categories are:

- Land
- Insurance
- Postal services
- Finance
- Education
- Health and welfare
- Burial and cremation
- Trade unions and professional bodies
- Sport, sports competitions and physical education
- Works of art
- Cultural services.

It can immediately be seen that this list needs clarification. For example, although land is exempt, there are cases where 'land' is zero-rated (new homes), taxable (new commercial buildings), either taxable or exempt depending on the owner (commercial buildings where the 'option to tax' may be used). The above list merely gives an overview of the exemptions.

There is no VAT on a funeral. The family that pays the undertaker therefore does not pay VAT on his services. This seems at first sight to be similar to the person buying a book – there is no VAT charged on books. The real difference is to the business making the supply. The undertaker cannot reclaim VAT charged on such items as telephone charges, advertising or the coffin. The bookseller is able to reclaim the VAT on all his overheads, subject to the normal rules in such areas as the fuel scale charge, entertainment, etc.

Recoverable input tax

In general it is only possible to reclaim input tax directly and exclusively linked to taxable supplies. (VATA 1994, s. 26). It may be easy to decide that certain purchases are for goods or services directly linked to making a taxable supply whilst other purchases are linked only to the making of exempt supplies. However if a business makes both taxable and exempt supplies there is a problem about how to treat the mixed input tax, that for example on charges for the telephone that is used in both parts of the business.

Step one is to analyse the input tax into three sections (VAT Regulations 1995 (SI 1995/2518), reg. 101):

- tax on purchases used or to be used exclusively in making exempt supplies;
- tax on purchases used or to be used exclusively in making taxable supplies,
- tax on purchases used for both taxable and exempt supplies, so-called residual input tax.

The next step is to apportion the residual input tax between taxable and exempt supplies. The aim of this is to achieve a 'fair and reasonable result' – fair and reasonable to both Customs and to the trader!

Attributing residual input tax

In the absence of permission from Customs, this must be done using a standard method (reg. 101(2) (d)).

The residual input tax is divided in the proportion of

$$\frac{\text{Value of taxable supplies}}{\text{Value of taxable supplies plus value of exempt supplies.}}$$

This is calculated as a percentage and if the result is not a whole number it is rounded up to the next whole number (reg. 101(4)).

The calculation is carried out each VAT return period as a provisional measure. The provisional calculations are then finalised at the end of each VAT year by an annual adjustment. The VAT year ends on March 31, April 30, May 31 dependent upon when the VAT periods end.

The following are excluded from the fraction in order not to distort the figures (reg. 101 (3)):

- capital goods
- incidental property or financial transactions
- self supplies
- goods/services that are not taxable or exempt (eg the sale of a going concern)
- imported services
- supplies made outside the UK
- non-business supplies.

Special methods

If it is considered that the standard method of attribution fails to achieve a fair and reasonable result, the trader may apply to Customs to be allowed to use a special method (reg. 102). There are still elements of the standard method that are included.

Customs prefers that there is some method of separating the input tax directly and exclusively used in the making of either taxable or exempt supplies. There will still be an annual adjustment. The essential difference is that a 'special method' is likely to be a special method of attributing residual input tax.

If the standard method does not give a fair and reasonable result, special methods of apportionment include:

- using the ratio of taxable transactions to total transactions;
- cost centred ratio;
- the area of the building used to generate taxable supplies as a ratio of the total area of the building,
- value of goods used in producing taxable supplies to the total value of goods used.

The above are only examples. It is the responsibility of the trader and or his advisors to calculate the most appropriate method and agree it with Customs before putting it into practice.

Insignificant exempt input tax

Partially exempt businesses that incur a small or *de minimus* amount of exempt input tax may reclaim this provided that certain parameters are not exceeded (reg.106).

In order to be considered insignificant the exempt input tax must:

- not exceed £625 per month AND
- not exceed 50 per cent of the total input tax.

The calculation is carried out each VAT period and then is recalculated for the annual adjustment. Businesses may find that they have to repay over-claimed input tax or are able to claim under-claimed input tax at the end of each VAT year.

Further information

Further information about this complex situation may be found in *The British VAT Reporter*, and/or VAT Notice 706.

11.3 Transfer of a business as a going concern

11.3.1 The no supply rule

In certain circumstances, the supply of assets which takes place in the case of a transfer of a business as a going concern is treated as being neither a supply of goods nor a supply of services (VAT Regulations 1995 (SI 1995/2518), reg. 5). This means that:

- no VAT is chargeable on the assets, etc. transferred, and
- if VAT is charged incorrectly, it is not available for set off as input tax in the hands of the transferee.

The circumstances in which the no supply rule applies are that:

- the assets are to be used by the transferee in carrying on the same kind of business as that of the transferor, and
- if the transferor is a taxable person, then the transferee must also be a taxable person or must register as a taxable person with effect from the time of the transfer.

The circumstances cover the case where the transferee uses the assets as part of an existing business provided that it is the same kind of business as that of the transferor.

It is important to note that the regulation refers to the transfer of a business rather than a trade. Thus an investment business can be the subject of the going concern transfer rules. In particular, the letting of property can be a business, as discussed below.

Where the going concern basis does not apply, the grant or transfer of an interest in land might be exempt, zero-rated or standard-rated according to the circumstances (as to which, see **11.5** later), assuming that the transferor is or becomes a taxable person.

11.3.2 Transfer of part of a business

The supply of assets which takes place in the case of the transfer of part of a business as a going concern is within the no supply rule if:

- that part is capable of separate operation;
- the assets are to be used by the transferee in carrying on the same kind of business as that of the transferor in respect of the part transferred, and
- the registration requirement is satisfied as for the transfer of a business.

Once again, the no supply rule applies if the transferee carries on the business as part of an existing business. In particular, the transfer of a let property can amount to the transfer of part of a business.

11.3.3 Meaning of 'going concern'

A large number of cases have come before the tribunals on the question of whether a transfer of assets amounts to the transfer of a going concern.

Many of these cases relate to the disallowance of input tax by Customs when it considers that there has been merely a transfer of assets. The following rules have emerged from the case law:

- The effect of a transfer must be to put the new owner in possession of a business that can be operated as such. Thus a mere sale of assets may not be a transfer of a going concern, but if assets are sold at different dates to the same person, the overall effect may amount to a transfer of a going concern.
- The business must be a going concern at the time of the transfer. This may be the case even if it has closed temporarily (eg for repairs), or is being operated by a liquidator or administrator. However, if it has ceased permanently, then any sale of assets will be within the scope of VAT. This will usually be the case where assets are sold by a liquidator, since a liquidator is not permitted to carry on a business except for the beneficial realisation of the assets (Insolvency Act 1986, Sch. 4, Para. 5).

11.3.4 Transfer of property rental business

The transfer of an interest in land with vacant possession is unlikely, by itself, to amount to the transfer of a business. However, if the owner of a freehold property which it let sells the freehold subject to, and with the benefit of, the lease (so that the transferee takes over an ongoing stream of rental income), that is a transfer of a going concern even if the property is only partly tenanted. Similarly, the assignment of a lease subject to, and with the benefit of, a sub-lease is the transfer of a going concern. This applies even if the sale occurs during a rent-free period, or if the tenants have not yet taken up occupation. This will be the transfer of part of a business if the vendor has other properties or businesses. However, where a property developer sells a site as a package to a single buyer and part of it is occupied on a temporary basis whilst the property is marketed, that is not a going concern transfer.

Similarly, if the owner of a freehold grants a long lease to a person with vacant possession, that is not a going concern transfer. This applies in particular if the property was let, but the tenant surrendered his interest before the grant of the new lease, since the letting business had ceased with the surrender of the tenant's interest.

If a freehold reversion is sold to the leaseholder, this is not a going concern transfer, since the tenant/transferee is not carrying on the same business as that of the transferor.

Customs provides examples of what they consider to be transfers of property rental businesses in Notice 700/9 'Transfer of a business as a going concern'.

11.3.5   Option for taxation

In relation to:

- land or buildings in respect of which the transferor has exercised the option for taxation, and
- new and unfinished buildings and civil engineering works ordinarily liable at the standard-rate, it is necessary for the transferee to exercise the option for taxation and to notify Customs prior to the 'relevant date' if the no supply rule is to operate (reg. 5(2)). Failing this, the transfer is a standard-rated supply. For further information see **11.6**.

11.3.6   Transfer of VAT registration

The transferee may apply to take over the transferor's VAT registration in the case of the transfer of a whole business (VATA 1994, s. 49 and SI 1995/2518, reg. 6). This is not necessarily appropriate, since the transferee will become liable for any unpaid VAT of the transferor in respect of the business transferred.

11.3.7   Anti-avoidance measures

Transfer to partially exempt group

There is a deemed self-supply to and by the representative member when a business or part of a business is transferred as a going concern to a VAT group.

Notice to be given to transferor

In respect of transfers on or after 18 March 2004 there are particular conditions applying to 'new' commercial buildings and buildings subject to an option to tax which are transferred as, or as part of, a transfer of a going concern. The transferee must notify the transferor that the transferee's election to 'waive the exemption' will not be nullified because of another anti-avoidance measure (VAT (Special Provisions) Order 1995 (SI 1995/1268), Para. 5(2B)(b)). The other anti-avoidance measure is in VATA 1994, Sch. 10, Para. 2(3AA). That paragraph provides that a supply is exempt if:

- the grant giving rise to the supply is made by a developer of the land, and
- at the time of the grant it is the intention or expectation of the grantor or the person financing the development that the land will become exempt

land (SI 2004/779 amending SI 1995/1268 – and see also Business Brief 12/04).

If the transferee does not give such a notification, the transfer is a taxable transaction.

11.4 Place of supply of land, construction services, etc.

11.4.1 Supplies relating to land

The grant, assignment or surrender of an interest in land is treated as made where the land is situated (SI 1992/3121, reg. 5(a)).

The basic principle is that the VAT treatment of the supply is determined by reference to the country in which the land is located. Under UK VAT legislation, the sale of the freehold of a building, or the granting of a long lease, is treated as a supply of goods. The sale of UK land to a non-resident, therefore, would not be eligible for zero-rating since it is possible to zero-rate a supply of goods only when they have been physically exported (VATA 1994, s. 30).

Where, for example, a UK resident company grants a long lease of a factory in the UK to a Jersey-resident company, such a supply will be taxable at the standard-rate if the UK company has opted to tax. If the Jersey company then wished to recover the VAT charged to it, it would need to register for VAT purposes in the UK. In these circumstances, it could appoint the managing agent to act as an agent on its behalf in VAT matters. This should be a simple procedure to operate since the managing agent will be responsible for collecting the rent and will therefore have sufficient funds with which to account for the VAT.

11.4.2 Services relating to land

The following services relating to land are likewise treated as made where the land is situated:

- works of construction, demolition, conversion, reconstruction, alteration, enlargement, repair or maintenance (including painting and decorating) of a building or civil engineering work,
- services such as are supplied by estate agents, auctioneers, architects, surveyors, engineers and others involved in matters relating to land this includes the management, conveyancing, survey or valuation of property by a solicitor, surveyor or loss adjuster (see, for example, *Brodrick Wright*

& *Strong Ltd,* LON/86/461, which concerned the survey of damage to a jetty and dock in the UK for companies registered abroad),

(SI 1992/3121, reg. 5(b), (c) following Sixth Directive, Art. 9, Para. 2(a) – and see VAT Notice 741).

The above principles apply only to defined services relating to land. Notice 741 gives examples of services that are not land related for these purposes and for which the place of supply and tax treatment is determined according to other rules and conditions. The examples are as follows:

- Repair and maintenance of machinery which is not installed as a fixture. This is work on goods, the hiring out of civil engineering plant on its own, which is the hire of goods; or the secondment of staff to a building site, which is a supply of staff.
- The legal administration of a deceased person's estate which happens to include property. These are lawyers' services.
- Advice or information relating to land prices or property markets as they do not relate to specific sites.
- Feasibility studies assessing the potential of particular businesses or business potential in a geographic area. Such services do not relate to a specific property or site.
- Provision of a recording studio where technicians are included as part of the supply. These are engineering services.
- Services of an accountant in simply calculating a tax return from figures provided by a client, even where those figures relate to rental income.

11.4.3 Working on overseas land

One danger area here is that a person who carries out construction work in a different country will be making potentially taxable supplies in that country and may have to register and account for VAT there.

For example, an English person purchases a derelict property in France. He instructs UK builders to carry out the renovation work. The UK builders are registered for UK VAT. The work is on a property outside the UK and thus the builders do not charge UK VAT on their services. However, if the work, together with any other work they do in France, is above the French VAT threshold, they will have to register in France (VAT (Place of Supply of Services) Order 1992 (SI 1992/3121), Art. 5(b)).

Building materials

A second danger area is that a trader carrying out construction services in a different Member State may decide to take their own materials to the place where the work is to be carried out. Tax is payable on those materials either in the UK or in the country where the work is carried out. Further advice needs to be taken because circumstances vary.

Building materials taken to a non-EU state are subject to the normal export rules. They may be zero-rated provided all the necessary conditions are fulfilled.

This is an area where British tradesmen do not realise that they are liable to register for VAT in any country in which they work and thus problems arise. Other Member States have different VAT registration thresholds and different penalty systems. A British builder falling foul of the French rules for example, may be liable to stringent penalties. An estate agent or auctioneer working in the UK but dealing with properties in, for example, Spain may well be liable to be registered for Spanish VAT. Any client appearing in danger of falling foul of the rules should be warned at the earliest opportunity.

Transactions in overseas land

Land situated outside the UK is not subject to UK VAT. If it is located in another EU State it will be subject to the VAT regime in that State.

Non-residents and UK land

A non-resident owner of UK land or supplying the land related services described above is subject to UK VAT. Therefore it may be necessary for the person to register for UK VAT. These registrations are dealt with by the Aberdeen office of Customs (HM Customs & Excise, 28 Guild Street, Aberdeen, AB9 2YD).

11.5 General principles of transactions in land

11.5.1 Introduction

Transactions in land are normally exempt from VAT unless specifically standard or zero-rated. Certain transactions may be converted to standard-rated supplies by use of the 'option to tax' provisions. The reduced rate of VAT does not apply to land transactions.

It should be appreciated that VAT does not in general recognise the distinction between capital and revenue that is fundamental in other areas of taxation. Thus the supply of an interest may be in consideration of a lump sum (eg as on the sale of the freehold), or in consideration of a series of payments amounting to a continuous supply of goods or services (eg as on the grant of a lease at a rental), or a combination of the two (eg as on the grant of a lease at a premium). In any event, the supply will be exempt, zero-rated, standard-rated or outside the scope depending on the particular circumstances.

In most cases the distinction between supplies of land that are to be treated as supplies of goods and those that are to be treated as supplies of services is not particularly significant. The rules governing the time of supply (see **11.1.14** above) are different but this is unlikely to be of much practical importance. If however different rates of tax for goods and services were brought in, the distinction could be vital.

11.5.2 Legislative framework

Articles 13–16 of the Sixth Directive provide that Member States must exempt certain supplies from VAT 'under conditions which they shall lay down for the purpose of ensuring the correct and straightforward application of such exemptions and of preventing any possible evasion, avoidance or abuse'. Article 13 provides for the following exemptions, *inter alia:*

'B(b) the leasing or letting of immovable property excluding:

- the provision of accommodation, as defined in the laws of the Member States, in the hotel sector or in sectors with a similar function, including the provision of accommodation in holiday camps or on sites developed for use as camping sites;
- the letting of premises and sites for parking vehicles;
- lettings of permanently installed equipment and machinery; and
- hire of safes.

B(g) the supply of buildings or parts thereof, and of land on which they stand, other than:

- the supply of such buildings before first occupation; and
- the supply of building land (as defined).

B(h) the supply of land which has not been built on other than building land. Member States may add to the exclusions in B(b).'

For this purpose, 'building land' means any unimproved or improved land defined as such by the Member State (VATA 1994, Art. 4(3)(b)).

Under UK law, VATA 1994, Sch. 9, gp. 1 deals with the exemption for supplies of interests in land. The rules are described at **11.5** below. Those supplies which are excluded from the exemption remain taxable unless covered by the zero-rating provisions.

Article 28(2)(a) allows Member States to continue to zero-rate supplies which were zero-rated as at 1 January 1991. As far as the UK is concerned, this covers, *inter alia*, the construction of certain residential and charitable buildings and certain grants and alterations to protected buildings (VATA 1994, Sch. 8, gp. 5, 6). This is considered at **11.7** below.

Supply of goods

Article 5 of the EC Sixth Directive provides that 'supply of goods' shall mean the transfer of the right to dispose of tangible property as owner. Paragraph 3 then provides that Member States may consider the following to be tangible property:

- certain interests in immovable property (eg freehold or leasehold interests in land and buildings);
- rights *in rem* giving the holder thereof a right of user over immovable property (eg easements and wayleaves),
- shares or interests equivalent to shares giving the holder thereof *de jure* or *de facto* rights of ownership or possession over immovable property or part thereof.

Option for taxation

Article 13C provides that Member States may allow taxpayers a right of option for taxation in cases of:

- letting and leasing of immovable property, and
- the transactions covered in B(g) and B(h) in the quote above.

Under UK law, VATA 1994, Sch. 10, deals with the option for taxation referred to above. The rules are dealt with at **11.6** below.

Time of supply for land

In the case of a sale or assignment of a freehold interest, the time of supply is usually the date of completion of the transaction. However, an earlier time of supply arises if a deposit is paid or if an invoice is issued before completion day (see Customs and Excise Notice 700). The same considerations apply in relation to the assignment of a lease.

Example 11.1

A developer sells a freehold property for £1 million, payable as to £100,000 on exchange of contracts and the balance on completion. He elects to waive exemption in accordance with VATA 1994, Sch. 10, Para. 2. The price of £1 million is agreed to be exclusive of VAT.

The tax points and VAT liabilities are as follows:

- on exchange 17.5 per cent × £100,000 = £17,500
- on completion 17.5 per cent × £900,000 = £157,500.

The total sale consideration including VAT is, therefore, £1,000,000 + £175,000 = £1,175,000.

In the case of a compulsory purchase, if the consideration for the purchase is not agreed at the time of the purchase, then supplies are deemed to be made at the earliest of the following times:

- each time that a part of the consideration is received by the vendor,
- each time the vendor issues a VAT invoice in respect of such part (SI 1995/2518, reg. 84(1)).

Similarly, where a person grants or assigns a fee simple (ie a freehold interest) in land and, at the time of the grant or assignment the total consideration is not determinable, then goods are treated as supplied at the following times:

(a)   the time when the land is made available to the grantee or assignee;

(b)   the date of issue of an invoice;

(c)   the receipt of consideration not covered by an invoice issued prior to the receipt, but subject to the 14-day rule in VATA 1994, s. 6(5);

(d)   the time directed by Customs & Excise under s. 6(10),

(e)   as regards the initially undetermined amount, the earlier of (b) and (c),

(SI 1995/2518, reg. 84(2)).

However, as from 28 November 2002, (e) does not apply in relation to:

- land which includes a new building or new civil engineering work;
- land which includes a building which has not been completed or a civil engineering work which has not been completed, or
- land on which the grantor intends or expects to construct a new building or new civil engineering work, unless the grantor or assignor has opted for taxation under VATA 1994, Sch. 10, Para. 2 and in consequence any supply is a taxable supply (SI 2002/2918 amending reg. 84).

The purpose of the amendment is to prevent any time of supply falling outside the three-year period in Sch. 9, gp. 1, note (4), where completion occurs before the end of that period. The amendment does not apply in relation to a building designed as a dwelling or number of dwellings, or intended for use solely for a relevant residential purpose or a relevant charitable purpose. It is intended to counteract certain tax avoidance schemes. Where it applies, the amount of undetermined consideration will, apparently, have to be estimated and corrected later, but this is not made clear by Customs & Excise. Where a lease or tenancy of more than 21 years is granted and the whole or part of the consideration is payable periodically or from time to time, supplies are deemed to be made at the earlier of the following times:

- each time that a part of the consideration is received by the grantor,
- each time the grantor issues a VAT invoice in respect of such part,

(SI 1995/2518, reg. 85).

Clearly, this covers the receipt of any premium or rent, for example. Such supplies may be exempt or taxable depending on whether the grantor exercises his option for taxation. It will be appreciated that the grant of a lease of 21 years or less is a supply of services. Therefore, the rules relating to continuous supplies of services apply in relation to rents under such leases.

The subsequent assignment of a lease does not disturb the operation of the general rules as regards the payment of rent.

11.5.3 Land and interests in land

'Land' includes any buildings and structures standing on the land (IA 1978, Sch 1).

Customs guidance indicates that the term 'land' includes 'any structures and natural objects attached to the land so long as they remain attached'. The legal understanding of 'land' is such that it includes buildings and other structures and any estate, interest, easement, servitude or right in or over land or land covered with water.

Hence the following are considered 'land':

- undeveloped land including that covered by water;
- buildings;
- civil engineering works;
- walls, fences and other structures fixed permanently to the land or sea bed;
- plant, machinery or equipment which is a fixture in a building or is an installation or edifice in its own right;
- North Sea oil rigs – they are within the UK if within 12 miles territorial waters limit,
- the Channel Tunnel – this is regarded as being in the UK as far as its mid-point.

Fixtures that are attached to land and buildings are regarded as forming part of the property. When a supply is made of an interest in the property, therefore, the VAT treatment of the fixtures is at one with the treatment of the interest in the property.

Major interest

As far as the UK is concerned, VATA 1994, Sch. 4, Para. 4 provides that the grant of a major interest in land is a supply of goods. The grant of any other interest in land for a consideration is a supply of services (VATA 1994, Art. 6 and s. 5(2)(b)).

A major interest means a freehold interest or a lease or tenancy for a term exceeding 21 years. In Scotland, 'freehold interest' is replaced by the interest of the proprietor of the *dominum utile* or, in the case of land not held on feudal tenure, the estate or interest of the owner (VATA 1994, s. 96(1)).

For the above purpose, 'grant' includes an assignment or surrender following Sch. 8, gp. 5, note (1) – see VAT Notice 742, paragraph 2.5.1).

Beneficial interests

A beneficial owner who directly receives the benefit of the proceeds from selling, leasing or letting land or buildings is treated for VAT purposes as the person making the supply. For example in the case of a bare trust, although the trustee is the legal owner of the land the beneficial owner is another person. This is the person treated as making the supply. The normal rules regarding registration, etc. apply (VATA 1994, Sch. 10, Para. 8)

Joint ownership

Where several persons (eg a site owner, a builder and a financier) join together in a joint venture to construct a building, the land is usually held in trust for the benefit of the parties. Any grant of a major interest in the building which the joint venture has constructed, or in its site, would have to be made by the trustees on the venturer's behalf. However, provided that the benefit of the consideration accrues to the venturers, they and not the trustees will be treated as making the grant of the major interest so that in the case of a non-commercial building it will be zero-rated (VATA 1994, Sch. 10, Para. 8).

Partnerships

A partnership is treated as a separate entity for VAT purposes, unlike the treatment for direct tax purposes (VATA 1994, s.45). In the case of *Fengate Developments v C&E Commrs* [2004] BVC 4,020, a plot of land was sold by one partnership to another. The land was worth £250,000 and the sale was recorded in the vendor's accounts at that value. The vendor had opted for taxation in respect of the land. It so happened that a particular individual had a 50 per cent interest in each partnership, the other 50 per cent interest being held by his first and second wives respectively. He argued that only a 50 per cent interest had been transferred and that VAT was payable on only £125,000. Customs & Excise assessed VAT on the full £250,000 and the taxpayer's appeal was dismissed.

It is not uncommon for premises occupied by a partnership to be owned by a particular partner or partners who allow the partnership to occupy the premises. Sometimes no rent is charged, but the landlord partners receive a prior share, or greater share, of profits by way of compensation. In other cases, a rent may be charged. In the case *of Staatssecretaris van Financien v Heerma* (Case C-23/98), the ECJ held that the letting of property by a partner to a partnership of which he was a member, under a lease which provided for rent to be payable, was an independent economic activity of the partner. This does not cause a problem unless the partner exercises the option for taxation of the rents and the partnership has exempt turnover.

If the landlord does not charge rent, but the partnership has exempt turnover, it is doubtful whether Customs & Excise would invoke the market value rule set out above. A partner is connected with a partnership of which he is a member except in relation to acquisitions and disposals of partnership assets pursuant to bona fide commercial arrangements (ICTA 1988, s. 839(4)). Clearly, the exception does not apply because the asset concerned is owned by a specific partner or partners individually.

However, Customs & Excise would have to deem the landlord partners to have exercised the option for taxation in respect of the property in order to increase the amount of VAT collectible, and there is no provision enabling it to do that.

Licence to occupy land

A licence to occupy land is a licence falling short of a legal interest in the land. It must relate primarily to occupation of the property rather than to doing something else which happens to involve going on to the land, and it must be possible to identify the land concerned.

Sinclair Collis Ltd provided, operated and maintained cigarette vending machines for the sale of cigarettes in public houses, clubs and the like. Sinclair Collis could select the site for the machines and under the agreement the site owner could not unreasonably refuse permission for any change of siting. The agreement was for a period of two years during which time Sinclair Collis had the right to install and operate the machines which remained the property of Sinclair Collis.

In 1996 Customs decided that these agreements should be exempt under Art. 13(B)(b) of the Sixth Directive. Sinclair Collis appealed saying that the supplies were taxable. The VAT and Duties Tribunal agreed with Sinclair Collis, this was overturned by the High Court. The Court of Appeal subsequently agreed with the High Court and so Sinclair Collis appealed to the House of Lords. The House of Lords sent a reference for a preliminary ruling to the ECJ asking if such an agreement was capable of amounting to the letting of immovable property within the meaning of Art. 13(B)(b).

The ECJ found that . . .

'it is settled that the fundamental characteristic of the letting of immovable property for the purposes of Art. 13(B)(b) of the Sixth Directive lies in conferring on the person concerned, for an agreed period and for payment, the right to occupy property as if that person were the owner and to exclude any other person from enjoyment of that right (see to that effect *Goed Wonen para 55 and C & E Commrs v Cantor Fitzgerald International Case C-108/99* [2002] BVC 9).'

Thus the arrangement between Sinclair Collis and the site owners was not the letting of immovable property. There were no rights of possession or control to Sinclair Collis other than those expressly set out in the agreement between the parties (*Sinclair Collis Ltd v C & E Commrs Case C-275/01* [2003] BVC 374).

Summary of the main characteristics of a 'licence to occupy land'

- The agreement must be for a set duration of time.
- It must be possible to identify the parcel or area of land concerned.
- It must include the right to occupy the land as owner.
- It should include the right to exclude others from the enjoyment of the property.

11.5.4 Zero-rated supplies of land

In order to qualify for zero-rating the land transaction must involve the first grant of a major interest in a *new* dwelling, relevant residential building or building for charitable use. Within each category there are certain conditions and reservations.

Anyone dealing with potentially zero-rated land transactions should check the following carefully:

- the required grant of a major interest is made by the appropriate person;
- that a *new* dwelling, relevant residential building or building for charitable use is being created,

- the required certificate is obtained for relevant residential buildings or buildings for charitable use.

What is 'new'?

New is not defined in the legislation.

For the purposes of the zero-rating schedule a 'new' building may be created by the following:

- the creation of an entire building;
- the demolition, or almost complete demolition, of an existing building and the erection of another building;
- an enlargement to an existing building to the extent that the enlargement creates an additional dwelling or dwellings;
- certain annexes to buildings used for charitable purposes;
- conversion of a non-residential building;
- renovation of a disused residential building,
- a substantially reconstructed protected building.

The creation of an entirely new building

This is self-evident. If there has been a building on the site, it should have been demolished to ground level although any cellars, basement or concrete base may have been retained.

The demolition, or almost complete demolition, of an existing building and the erection of another building

The complete demolition of an existing building is self-evident. However there are occasions when a building is not completely demolished. In such instances a single façade, or double façade on a corner site, may be retained where it is a condition of the planning permission granted. Any demolition work should have been completed before work on the new structure started (VATA 1994, Sch. 8, gp. 5, note (18)).

An enlargement to an existing building to the extent that the enlargement creates an additional dwelling or dwellings

This would include situations where, for example, a flat is constructed on top of an existing building or a semi-detached dwelling is constructed using a wall of an existing building as the party wall. It is essential that the existing building is enlarged or extended and not merely re-arranged. If the existing building is a residential building, the new dwelling must be wholly within the extension, that is not the conversion of an attic or similar (VATA 1994, Sch. 8, gp. 5, note (16(b))).

745

Certain annexes to buildings used for charitable purposes

The whole annex must be intended for a relevant charitable purpose (see below). The annex must be capable of functioning independently although may share supplies of power and water with the main building. The new structure must neither be the main entrance to the existing building nor the existing building provide the main entrance to the annex (VATA 1994, Sch. 8, gp. 5, note (16(c)) and note (17)).

Conversion of a non-residential building

In order to qualify as a non-residential building the existing structure must **never** have been designed or adapted for use as a dwelling, a number of dwellings or relevant residential purpose (see below).

Care must be taken when dealing with the conversion of a building that has been or is part non-residential and part residential. Incorporation of a residential part with what was a non-residential area of the building into a dwelling may result in that dwelling not being a 'new' dwelling. *C&E Commrs v Blom-Cooper* [2003] BVC 416 indicates that where a building is already part residential, the conversion of the non-residential part could not be treated as 'converting ... a non-residential part of a building' unless the result of that conversion was to create an additional dwelling or dwellings (VATA 1994, Sch. 8, gp. 5 note (9)).

Renovation of a disused residential building.

A building that was once either designed or adapted as a residential building may be brought back into the housing stock. In order to be within the scope of the zero-rating schedule, it must have been constructed more than ten years before the grant of the major interest and no part of it been used as a dwelling or for a relevant residential purpose during these ten years (VATA 1994, Sch. 8, gp. 5 note (7)).

A developer can zero-rate his sale of a renovated house provided the sale takes place after the dwelling has been empty, or not used as a dwelling, for ten years. This means a developer who does renovation work before the building has been empty for ten years may still zero-rate his sale provided the renovated home has been an empty dwelling for ten years when he sells it. It is the developer's responsibility to hold proof that their claim for input tax can be verified. Customs will accept evidence which, on the balance of probabilities, shows that the building has been an empty home for at least ten years. The evidence can include electoral roll and council tax data, information from utilities companies, evidence from empty property officers in local authorities, or information from other reliable sources. If a developer holds a letter from an empty property officer certifying that a home has been empty for ten years or will have been empty for ten years at the time of sale, no other evidence is needed. If an empty property officer is unsure about the length of time a home has been empty he should write with his best estimate and Customs may than call for other supporting evidence (VATA 1994, Sch. 8, gp. 5, note 7).

A substantially reconstructed protected building

'Substantial reconstruction' means that one of the following conditions must be met:

- at least 60 per cent of the cost of reconstruction is applicable to approved alterations. (The costs include materials and other items together with services but exclude the services of an architect, surveyor, consultant or supervisor.)
- no more of the original building is retained than external walls and other external features of architectural or historic importance.

To be a 'protected building' for these purposes, the building must be one of the following:

'(a)   a listed building, within the meaning of–

 (i)   the Planning (Listed Buildings and Conservation Areas) Act 1990; or
 (ii)   the Planning (Listed Buildings and Conservation Areas) (Scotland) Act 1997; or
 (iii) the Planning (Northern Ireland) Order 1991; or

(b)   a scheduled monument, within the meaning of–

 (i)   the Ancient Monuments and Archaeological Areas Act 1979; or
 (ii)   the Historic Monuments and Archaeological Objects (Northern Ireland) Order 1995.'

In addition, the substantially reconstructed building must be designed to remain as or become a dwelling, number of dwellings or intended solely for use as relevant residential or charitable purposes (VATA 1994, Sch. 8, gp. 6, note (4)).

Conditions

The first grant, by a person constructing a 'non-commercial' building, of a major interest in that building, or any part of it, or its site, is zero-rated (VATA 1994, Sch. 8, gp. 5, item 1(a)). For this purpose, a non-commercial building is a building that is:

(a)   designed as a dwelling or a number of dwellings, or

(b)   intended for use solely for a relevant residential purpose or a relevant charitable purpose.

The first grant, by a person converting a non-residential building or the non-residential part of a building into a building within (a) or a building intended for use solely for a relevant residential purpose, of a major interest in that building, or part of it, or its site, is likewise zero-rated (VATA 1994, Sch. 8, gp. 5, item 1(b)). For this purpose, **grant** includes an assignment or surrender (VATA 1994, note (1), Sch. 8, gp. 5).

A building includes a building under construction, ie one which has progressed beyond the foundation stage. The site of a building is regarded as including a reasonable plot of land surrounding it. This is not necessarily the same as the entire site on which development takes place. (For Customs' views see VAT Notice 708, paragraph 4.6.4.)

Clearly, the person constructing the building must himself have a major interest (freehold or lease of more than 21 years) if his grant is to be zero-rated. The zero-rating applies to the first occasion on which during, or following the completion of, the construction or conversion he:

*   grants a lease or sub-lease of more than 21 years out of his interest;
*   assigns his interest, or
*   surrenders his interest to the holder of a superior interest.

The construction of a garage, or conversion into a garage, is zero-rated if done at the same time as the construction of, or conversion to, a dwelling if the garage is intended to be occupied with the dwelling (note (3)). However, this applies only if the construction of, or conversion to, the dwelling is itself zero-rated (*RJ Jowett v C&E Commrs* [2003] BVC 4,109).

Need for certificate

The grant of a major interest in new 'relevant residential accommodation' or a building for a charitable purpose may not be zero-rated unless both the following conditions are met:

*   the grant is to the person who will use it as 'relevant residential' accommodation or for 'charitable purposes', and
*   before the grant is made that person certifies that the building will be so used,

VATA 1994, Sch.8, gp. 5, note 12.

An example of the certificate may be found in Notice 708.

Grant of a sub-lease

Where the major interest granted is a tenancy, zero-rating only applies to any premium or, if no premium is payable, to the first payment of rent due under the tenancy (VATA 1994, note (14), gp. 5, Sch. 8). As a result the VAT on the cost of constructing a zero-rated building is recoverable but not VAT on the cost to the landlord of providing ongoing services.

Mixed use buildings

Where the supply of only part of a building qualifies for zero-rating (eg a shop with a flat over it) it is necessary to apportion the value of the supply between the zero-rated and other parts (VATA 1994, note (10), gp. 5, Sch. 8).

Person constructing

The words *'person constructing'* are construed widely by Customs. The phrase is not limited to a person in the process of constructing but includes a person who has constructed. It also extends to a person, such as a developer or the owner of a business, who does not do the constructing himself but owns the land and 'commissions' a contractor to develop the land, providing he exercises some measure of control, such as control over design or planning. In the case of *Hulme Educational Foundation* (1978) VATTR 179, the tribunal held that the construction must be physically done by the person granting the major interest or by his servants or agents or that person must himself directly enter into a contract or arrangement for another to do the physical construction works. In that case, the person constructing the building was a company which held a long lease of the site. The appellant held the freehold reversion. An essential test appears to be that the 'constructor' should enter into a binding contract with the contractor before the work commences, or at the latest before the work has progressed beyond the foundation stage. A 'constructor' can commission more than one contractor to do the work. A person who merely grants a building lease or licence is *not* a constructor.

The onward supply of a *partly constructed building* is capable of being zero-rated, and the person to whom it is supplied is capable of becoming a person constructing a building. The term *'building'* can include a temporary building erected on a permanent base. Since the major changes introduced in 1989, Customs has attempted to argue that the term 'person constructing' should be interpreted narrowly, but it was defeated in the High Court in the case of *C & E Commrs v Link Housing Association* [1992] BVC 113. The court held that the use of the phrase 'a person constructing a building' simply means that only the person who had constructed the building was entitled to zero-rate its sale. On the other hand, the mere intention to construct a building is not enough, nor is the carrying out of works preparatory to the *construction* of a building. In the case of *Cameron New Homes Ltd* [2001] BVC 4,163, the company acquired a contaminated site in Suffolk with old buildings standing on it. The company intended to demolish the old buildings, clean up the site and build three new bungalows, However, after demolishing the old buildings and cleaning up the site, it sold the site. This was held to be an exempt supply.

Dwellings

A building is designed as a dwelling or a number of dwellings where in relation to each dwelling the following conditions are satisfied:

- the dwelling consists of self-contained living accommodation;
- there is no provision for direct internal access from the dwelling to any other dwelling or part of a dwelling;
- the separate use, or disposal of the dwelling is not prohibited by the terms of any covenant, statutory planning consent or similar provision, and
- statutory planning consent has been granted in respect of that dwelling and its construction or conversion has been carried out in accordance with that consent.

A building designed as a dwelling or number of dwellings or the site of such building may not be zero-rated when either:

- the interest granted means that the person receiving the grant may not reside in the building, or part of the building for all the year, or
- terms of a covenant, statutory planning permission or similar prevents residence throughout the year or the use of the building as the grantees principal private residence.

A case in Scotland *Livingstone Homes UK Ltd [2000] BVC 2400*, featured a development that was specified by agreement with the local council as 'all houses on the development shall be used as holiday dwelling houses only and for no other purpose and shall never in any way be sub-divided'. Customs maintained that these buildings could not be zero-rated because they were holiday homes.

It was accepted by the Tribunal that in this instance the two states of use as a holiday dwelling house or as the grantee's principal private residence were not mutually exclusive. The definition of 'holiday' was ' a day in which work is suspended; a day of recreation and amusement'. The real question should be 'Could a person use this holiday home as his principal private residence which he would be doing if he lived there all the year and had no other home?' A retired person might be free to reside in the resort and have other home and would have 365 days of 'recreation and amusement' each year. The loose wording of the sale agreement meant that Customs lost.

Although this case is interesting and may give some grounds for manoeuvre, each situation must be looked at on its facts. A stipulated bar to occupation for part of the year means that zero-rating is not allowed (VATA 1994, note (13), gp. 5, Sch. 8).

The definition of a dwelling as accommodation which contained all the major activities of life, particularly sleeping, cooking, feeding and toilet facilities, given in the case of *St Catherine's College v Dorling* [1979] 3 All ER 250, was followed by the VAT Tribunal in *Derby YMCA v C&E Commrs* (case 16914).

A garage constructed at the same time as the dwelling, and intended to be occupied with the dwelling also qualifies (notes (2), (3)). However, the construction of a garage at some later time is standard-rated. The term 'garage' is limited to a place for storing vehicles and does not include a dock for a boat (*Turner Stroud and Burley Construction v C & E Commrs* [1998] BVC 2,206). However, the *Turner Stroud* case concerned the construction of a riverside home with a dock for a boat. In this case, the dock, although not structurally part of the house, was part of the design of the house. The whole building, including the dock, was designed as a dwelling.

Relevant residential purpose

Use for a 'relevant residential' purpose means use as:

(a)   a children's home;

(b)   a home providing residential accommodation with personal care for persons in need of personal care by reason of old age, disablement, past or present dependence on alcohol or drugs, or past or present mental disorder;

(c)   a hospice;

(d)   residential accommodation for students or school children;

(e)   residential accommodation for members of the armed forces;

(f)   a monastery, nunnery or similar establishment,

(g)   an institution which is the sole or main residence of at least 90 per cent of its residents (VATA 1994, note (4), gp. 5, Sch. 8).

Hospitals, prisons, etc. and hotels, inns or similar establishments are not regarded as being used for relevant residential purposes, nor are any non-residential premises in schools (e.g. classrooms).

In the case of *Urdd Gobaith Cymru v C&E Commrs* [1997] BVC 4,106, the Tribunal held that 'residential accommodation' in contrast to 'residence', means lodging, sleeping or overnight accommodation and does not imply that the accommodation has to be for a minimum period.

As regards (d), it has been held that in relation to university student accommodation zero-rating was available even though the accommodation was used for other purposes during the summer vacation *(R (on the application of Greenwich Property) v C&E Commrs* [2001] BVC 261). The University of Greenwich had relied on an unpublished concession dated 30 March 1990 when issuing a zero-rating certificate. The Court held that it was entitled to take advantage of that concession. As regards communal areas in blocks of flats, where the communal areas are only used by residents and their guests, Customs & Excise accepts that the construction of the whole building is zero-rated. Where the communal areas are partly used by others, for example if they contain leisure or gym facilities, whether or not for a charge, then the construction of the communal areas is standard-rated (Business Brief 11/03).

Relevant charitable purpose

Use for a relevant charitable purpose means that the building must be used by a charity solely for a relevant purpose. A relevant charitable purpose is:

- otherwise than in the course or furtherance of a business,
- as a village hall or similarly in providing social or recreational facilities for a local community,

(VATA 1994, note (6)(a), gp. 5, Sch. 8).

By concession Customs accept that a building is used 'solely' for charitable purposes if this constitutes 90 per cent of its use (Notice 48 Extra-Statutory Concession 3.29). The quantum of charitable use may be determined by reference to time, floor space or numbers of persons. More information about Customs views is in Customs Manuals Vol V1-8A Section 18.

The zero-rating relief is extended specifically to a supply in the course of construction of a village hall for use by a charity in providing social or recreational facilities for a local community (VATA 1994, note (6)(b), gp. 5, Sch. 8). In the case of *The South Molton Swimming Pool Trustees v C&E Commrs* [2000] BVC 4078, the tribunal held that a swimming pool was not similar to a village hall. The reason was that it was open to, and used by, people from a much wider area than the local community. The fact that it did not look like a hall was considered to be irrelevant. The case of *Southwick Community Association v C&E Commrs* [2000] BVC 4066 concerned the construction of a new wing at the community centre. This was connected to an existing storage room, but was self-contained and had independent external access. It was used as a centre for arts and crafts and theatre support. It was also used for dancing classes and other functions run on a commercial basis, but this did not exceed 10 per cent of overall use. The tribunal held that it was used similarly to a village hall.

In the case of *Yarburgh Children 's Trust v C&E Commrs* [2002] BVC 141, the tribunal held that it is permissible to take account of the use to which a building is put by the lessee to determine whether the lessor is entitled to zero-rating. Yarburgh was a charity which owned a large building comprising six flats let to tenants, plus a home for handicapped children and a day nursery for young children. It also had a summer house. This was replaced by a new building comprising two main play areas, a changing area, kitchen, toilet, etc. which was leased to the play group. The tribunal held that the sole purpose of constructing the building was to make it available for the play group. That group did not use the building in the course or furtherance of a business. Therefore the building was within the zero-rating in Sch. 8, gp. 5. Customs & Excise issued the following statement, in Business Brief 4/03, following the decision in the *Yarburgh* case:

'The Yarburgh Children's Trust ("the Trust") case concerned, in part, supplies of nursery facilities made by a community-based charity, Yarburgh Community Playgroup ("the Playgroup"). The Playgroup required new premises, and with the help of National Lottery funding, their current land-lord (the Trust) undertook construction of a new nursery building. Such a supply is normally subject to VAT, however, there are provisions in UK law which allow such supplies to be zero-rated, one of these requires the building to be used otherwise than in the course of business. Zero-rating was beneficial to the Trust and the Playgroup because they undertook exempt activities and the amount of VAT either could recover would have been heavily restricted.

Customs denied the Trust zero-rating on the grounds that, amongst other things, the building would be used for a business activity, namely the provision of nursery and creche facilities for up to 50 children in exchange for a recognised charge. This point was tested first at Tribunal and then later at the High Court. In both instances the Courts ruled that on the particular facts of the case the activity of the Playgroup was not business for VAT purposes. After considering their position Customs took the view they would not seek to challenge further the decision of the Courts with regard to this case. Customs consider that the correct legal tests had been applied and the facts before them had led the Courts to a non-business decision.'

11.5.5   Standard-rating

There are two reasons why a transaction in land may be standard-rated. Firstly it may be standard-rated because the law stipulates that it is not zero-rated and is not exempt. Secondly it may gain standard-rating because the owner has elected to waive the exemption –or opted to tax the land. For more details on waiving the exemption see **11.6**.

Statutory exceptions

The law stipulates that the following supplies of land are excluded from the exempt schedule and are not zero-rated–thus they become standard-rated supplies.

- freehold disposal of certain new or partly complete buildings
- freehold disposal of new or partly complete civil engineering works
- supplies under a developmental tenancy, developmental lease or developmental licence
- rights to take game or fish
- hotel, inn, boarding house or similar accommodation
- holiday accommodation
- seasonal pitches for caravans and tents
- parking
- the right to fell and remove timber
- housing, storage, mooring for aircraft, ships, etc.
- boxes and seats at sports grounds, theatres, etc.
- facilities for playing sport
- rights to call for or be granted an interest or right in any of the above (except for the developmental tenancy, lease or licence),

(VATA 1994, Sch. 9, item 1).

It is important to note that there are conditions applied to certain of these situations. See below for more details.

Freehold disposal of certain new or partly complete buildings

The grant of the fee simple, or freehold, in a 'new' or partly complete building that is not designed as

- a dwelling,
- for use solely for a relevant residential purpose,
- for use for a relevant charitable purpose.

'Grant' includes the assignment or surrender and the supply made by the person to whom an interest is surrendered when there is a reverse surrender.

'Reverse surrender' is one where the person to whom the interest is surrendered is paid by the person by whom the interest is being surrendered to accept the surrender (VATA 1994, Sch. 9, gp. 1, item 1 (a)).

For the purposes of this section of the legislation a building is 'new' for a period of three years from completion.

The building is completed when either an architect issues a certificate of practical completion or when it is first fully occupied, whichever is the earlier (VATA 1994, Sch. 9, gp. 1 notes 2 and 4).

It is essential to note that this applies to the grant of the *freehold*. The disposal of a long lease – even 999 years – is not the grant of the freehold. Thus the grant of a 999-year lease would result in the supply being exempt and associated input tax blocked unless the option to tax is made (see **11.6**).

Civil engineering works

A civil engineering work is something which is constructed or built but which is not a building, or necessitated by the construction of a building (eg a road or a bridge). The supply of such a work is normally exempt. The supply is, however, standard-rated if it is the freehold supply of either an uncompleted work or a new work. It is also standard-rated if the owner opts to tax – see **11.6**.

Bare land which is *ancillary* to a civil engineering work (such as at an airfield) is treated as part of the civil engineering work. By contrast land which merely *contains* a civil engineering work (such as building land which has a road over it) is not so treated. In the latter case an apportionment between the two supplies may be required, for example where the supply of the land is exempt and the supply of the civil engineering work is standard-rated. The apportionment must be on a fair and reasonable basis, and often this is done by reference to cost. The cost of a civil engineering work would include the cost of the land covered by it (which would be nil if the work was underground, as in the case of a drain or sewer) as well as the construction cost.

A work is 'new' for the period of three years from the date it was completed. The date of completion is taken as the earlier of the date when the work is first fully used and when an engineer issues a certificate of completion in relation to it.

Works completed before 1 April 1989 are not 'new' for the purposes of the three-year rule. However, the first freehold sale of such a work is standard-rated if it takes place after 31 March 1989 and the work was not fully used before that date (VATA 1994, item 1(a), (iii) and (iv), and notes (2), (4) and (6), gp. 1, Sch. 9).

Supplies of new civil engineering works were zero-rated prior to 1 April 1989, as were construction and demolition services relating to such works.

Supplies pursuant to developmental tenancy, etc.

A tenancy of, a lease of or a licence to occupy a building or work becomes 'developmental' when it is treated as being subject to a self-supply under VATA 1994, Sch. 10, Para. 6(1). This self-supply was phased out VATA 1994, Sch. 9, Gp. 1, note (7)).

A tenant who became subject to a self-supply must notify the landlord accordingly, because the landlord must then charge VAT on the developmental lease concerned (VATA 1994, Sch. 9, Gp. 1, item 1, Para. (b) and Sch. 10, Paras. 6 and 7).

Right to take game or fish (without selling the freehold)

The granting of any right to take game or fish is generally standard-rated, if the freehold is not also sold, because such a supply is excluded from exemption (VATA 1994, Sch. 9, Gp. 1, item 1(c)). However, if the owner of land, which contains game, sells the freehold in that land, the supply of any interest or right or licence is apparently exempt under Directive 77/388, the Sixth VAT Directive, Art. 13(B)(h) and VATA 1994, Sch. 9, Gp. 1, item 1(c).

If the freehold is not sold, but the land is leased, etc. and the supply includes valuable sporting rights, the sporting rights are standard-rated. The consideration is apportioned (VATA 1994, Sch. 9, Gp. 1, item 1(c) and note (8)). Customs argues that the sporting rights are 'valuable' if they represent more than 10 per cent of the value of the whole supply (Notice 742, paragraph 6.2 (2002 edition)).

The law was changed in 1989 following *C & E Commrs v Parkinson* (1988) 3 BVC 303, where the court upheld the tribunal's decision that the exception to exemption in the then VATA 1983, Sch. 6, Gp. 1, item 1, Para. (d) did not apply to an outright sale of freehold interests, but only to short-term licences to occupy or use the land. It was immaterial that the primary purpose of the purchase of the land was to obtain the fishing rights. Harman J said that the phrase 'supply of land which has not been built on, other than building land' required the court to look not at mere immovable property, which may include sporting rights (profits *à prendre*) but the physical soil of the earth. The mandatory exemption only applies to this 'land'.

Hotel accommodation

As can be seen above, supplies of accommodation in various establishments are excluded from exemption and are therefore standard-rated. The term 'similar establishment' in VATA 1994, Sch. 9, Group 1, Item 1(d) includes premises in which there is provided furnished accommodation, with or without the provision of board or facilities for the preparation of food, which are used by or held out as being suitable for use by visitors or travellers. This applies to furnished service flats provided for visitors or travellers. Although continuing to be standard-rated, the total value of the supply of accommodation and facilities is reduced by up to 80 per cent from the 29th day of occupation. Supplies of meals and drinks, etc. are always taxable. The 80 per cent reduction only applies where the accommodation is occupied by the same person, either alone or with other persons who occupy the accommodation with him at the same time, but not at their expense (unless cost sharing is involved). Thus travel agents are not able to take advantage of the reduced value through the use of block bookings (VATA 1994, Para. 9, Sch. 6).

In the case of *Leez Priory v C&E Commrs* [2003] BVC 4,131, the tribunal held that the hiring of the priory for weddings, including the provision of accommodation in rooms, was a standard-rated supply. By contrast, conference facilities supplied by hotels are exempt, rather than standard-rated.

Holiday accommodation

The VAT status of supplies connected with holiday accommodation can be summarised as follows:

- 'holiday accommodation' includes accommodation in a building, hut (including a beach hut or chalet), caravan, house boat or tent which is advertised or held out as holiday accommodation or is suitable for holiday or leisure use, but excludes a hotel or similar establishment;
- all rents for holiday accommodation are standard-rated;
- sales of plots of land for the construction of holiday accommodation are standard-rated;
- supplies of freehold and leasehold interests in any property whose construction was completed within the previous three years and which the purchaser is prohibited from residing in throughout the year, or from using as his principal private residence, is standard-rated (as for holiday accommodation rather than for a new commercial building),
- the supply of a freehold interest in 'holiday' type buildings is exempt from VAT, as is a premium on the grant of a lease, provided that the building was constructed more than three years previously (and provided that the option to tax has not been exercised). Customs' interpretation of the law in this area will be found in VAT Leaflet 709/3.

Camping in tents or caravans

Such facilities are taxable unless supplied as a permanent residence, e.g. as in a mobile home, when the supply is exempt. Customs' interpretation of the law in this area will be found in VAT Leaflet 701/20.

Vehicle parking

Where parking or garaging rights are supplied in conjunction with supplies of land by way of sale or lease, their supply would be regarded in practice as part of the larger (exempt or zero-rated) supply and no apportionment would be necessary. Customs' interpretation of the law in this area will be found in VAT Leaflet 701/24.

Note that in the case of *Anne C Slot v C&E Commrs* [1997] BVC 4143 the tribunal held that caravans which were designed to be moved or towed on roads were road vehicles. Therefore the charges for parking such caravans were standard-rated.

The High Court has held that the assignment of a lease of land that the lessee operated as a car park was excluded from the exemption and was, accordingly, standard-rated (*C&E Commrs v Venuebest* [2003] BVC 444).

In the case of *Fazenda Publica v Camara Municipal do Porto* [2001] BVC 493, the court held that the letting of car parking spaces by a local authority was outside the scope of VAT if carried out by that authority as a local authority. It was so carried out if carried out under a special legal regime applicable to such bodies. If carried out under the same laws as applied to private car park operators, the supplies were standard-rated.

In July 2004 a VAT and Duties Tribunal said that the UK has not implemented Art. 4(5) of the EC Sixth VAT Directive correctly. Customs has accepted part of the Tribunal's ruling that local authorities providing off street car parking spaces under the RTRA 84 do so under a special regime. The VAT and Duties Tribunal found that the Isle of Wight Council was not in business when it provided off street car parking places in return for payment.

Article 4(5) of the EC Sixth VAT Directive states that local government bodies do not act in a business capacity when they carry out activities regulated by statute, provided this does not result in distortion of competition. Such activities are outside the scope of VAT.

Customs will continue to look at the possibility of distortion of competition where a local service is provided by both the local authority and another supplier. Therefore it will appeal to the High Court on this matter of the incorrect implementation of Art. 4(5) of the EC Sixth VAT Directive.

Local authorities may continue to account for VAT on these types of charges, and later submit claims for repayment. They may choose not to account for VAT in which case Customs will issue protective assessments for the VAT (Business Brief 18/04 13 July 2004).

Granting of the right to fell and remove standing timber

The granting of the right to fell and remove standing timber is excluded from exemption and so is standard-rated. However, such a grant must be separate and specific. Where land is sold with standing timber, which the buyer can fell after purchase, the supply is exempt, because the grant covers the right of the grantee to fell the timber once the conveyance is completed (VATA 1994, Sch. 9, Gp. 1, item 1(j); Official Customs Guidance Manual, Vol. 1–8, s. 8.64).

Aircraft and shipping

Where storage or mooring facilities for a ship or aircraft are supplied in a Customs port or airport (as designated in accordance with respectively CEMA 1979, s. 19 or s. 21), the supply is zero-rated (VATA 1994, item 6(a), gp. 8, Sch. 8).

As regards mooring rights generally, the VAT Tribunal has held that the standard-rating was not restricted to cases where the grantor provided both the facility and the means for the enjoyment of the facility, such as pontoons, ropes, chains and gangways, but applied even where bare mooring facilities were supplied (*Threshfield Motors v C&E Commrs* [2001] BVC 4,017).

Boxes and seats at sports grounds, theatres, etc.

The grant of a right to occupy a box, seat, or other accommodation at a sports ground, theatre, concert hall or other place of entertainment is excluded from exemption.

Sporting facilities

The supply of facilities for playing any sport or participating in physical recreation is excluded from exemption, except for lettings in excess of 24 hours and certain lettings to schools, etc.

The exclusion in respect of sporting facilities does not apply if the granting of the facilities is:

- for a continuous period of use greater than 24 hours, or

- for a series of ten or more periods of any duration, where each is for the same activity and at the same place, the interval between periods is never less than one day or more than 14 days, the fee relates to the whole series and is evidenced by a written agreement, the use of the facilities is exclusive to the customer, and the customer is a school, club, association, or organisation representing clubs and associations.

Option to acquire taxable interest

The grant of a right (including an equitable right, a right under an option and, in relation to land in Scotland, a personal right) to be granted an interest, etc., the supply of which would be excluded from exemption, is itself excluded from exemption (VATA 1994, Sch. 9, Gp. 1, item 1(n)).

Land owned at de-registration

There is deemed supply of goods, not services, on hand at de-registration (VAT 1994, Sch. 4, para. 8). This takes in certain interests in land (VAT 1994, Sch. 4, para. 9). It follows that VAT is due on certain land retained at de-registration. This is explained in Customs Manuals (Vol. 1–3, Ch. 2, section 4A, paragraph 4.9) as follows:

'Where a taxable person has standard-rated land or property on hand at the time of deregistration and the taxable person claimed input tax on the supply to him of that property, then the land or property is deemed to be supplied by him on deregistration. However this burden can be avoided by deferring cancellation of the trader's registration until the property is sold. The trader will then be required to account for output tax on the actual sale of the property.'

11.5.6   Exempt

The basic rule is that the grant, assignment or surrender of any interest in, or right over, land or of any licence to occupy land is an exempt supply (VATA 1994, Sch. 9, gp. 1) unless specifically standard-rated or zero-rated – see above. Where the consideration is payable by the grantee, the assignee or the person receiving the surrender, no VAT is chargeable on that consideration. Where there is 'reverse consideration', VAT may be payable, as discussed at **11.5.8** below.

The position of service charges is dealt with at **11.5.10** below.

An interest in land can be a legal interest or an equitable interest. In England, there are only two legal interests: a freehold interest and a leasehold interest. Equitable interests include tenancies, easements, profits *à prendre*, and wayleaves.

In the case of *Maierhofer v Finanzamt Augsburg-Land* [2003] BVC 325, the ECJ held that the letting of a building constructed from pre-fabricated components fixed to or in the ground in such a way that they could not be either dismantled or easily moved constituted the letting of immovable property within Art. 13(B)(b) of the Sixth Directive. The European cases were reviewed by the tribunal in the case of *Holmwood House School Developments v C&E Commrs* [2003] BVC 4,116. The report of the case includes the following (paragraph 30):

'We draw the following conclusions from these European Court of Justice judgments on the principles to be followed when determining whether a particular transaction is or is not an exempt leasing or letting of immoveable property for the purposes of article 13B:

(a) The leasing or letting of immoveable property is a concept to be determined by the principles laid down by the ECJ. It is not to be determined by national law rules of land law.

(b) Those principles require a transaction, if it is to be treated as a leasing or letting of immoveable property to include the following features:

 (i) It must relate to immoveable property, that is to say, the ground itself or to property firmly fixed to the ground;

 (ii) It must create a right to occupy a particular piece of land or property;

 (iii) That right of occupation must give the right to exclude others and to occupy as owner;

 (iv) That right of occupation must be for an agreed duration; and

 (v) That right must be given for a payment for the period.

(c) When determining whether these features exist or whether the transaction is rather relating to construction, the provision of services or other alternative type of supply, the tribunal should take into account its essential features and not be bound by the particular way in which it may be artificially presented.

(d) While the concept of leasing or letting of immoveable property, being a concept in relation to an exemption, is to be construed strictly, that does not mean that an interpretation must be made which is strained when compared with what are the essential features of the transaction in reality.'

11.5.7 Special circumstances

Compensation

Compensation paid by a landlord to a tenant under agricultural or business tenancy legislation is outside the scope of VAT. Otherwise a payment to a tenant for vacating property, including any excess over the statutory amount provided, is regarded as consideration for a supply of services by the tenant, so that if the occupation is for business purposes it is chargeable at the standard-rate.

Compulsory purchase

The disposal of an interest in land under a compulsory purchase order is a supply of that interest. If the full amount of the compensation is not known at the time of the supply, there is a supply each time a payment of compensation is received or, if earlier, a VAT invoice is issued (SI 1995/2518, reg. 84).

Dedications of new roads and sewers

The dedication or vesting of the following for no monetary consideration is not to be treated as a supply for VAT purposes:

- a new road under the provisions of the Highways Act 1980 or the Roads (Scotland) Act 1984, *or*
- a new sewer or ancillary works under the provisions of the Water Industries Act 1991.

The developer will normally be entitled to recover input tax incurred on the construction of the relevant road or sewer if the development generates only taxable supplies or is subject to a self-supply charge.

Where, however, exempt supplies are made in relation to a development there will be a restriction on the amount of input tax which can be reclaimed in accordance with the normal rules set out under **11.1.5** and **11.2** above.

Dilapidation payments

A payment made by the lessee to the lessor, at or near the end of a lease, in respect of dilapidation, is outside the scope of VAT. It represents a claim for damages by the lessor against the lessee's 'want of repair' and is not the consideration for a supply (Notice 742).

Exhibition sites

The provision to an exhibitor of a site or space at an exhibition or similar event organised wholly or mainly for the display or advertisement of goods or services is not normally regarded as the supply of an interest in land and is therefore not exempt. Such services are taxed where they are performed: thus services supplied by UK traders at overseas exhibitions are zero-rated (Value Added Tax (Place of Supply of Services) Order 1992 (SI 1992/3121), reg. 15(b)). Exhibition services supplied by a UK trader in connection with a UK exhibition are standard-rated, irrespective of the status of the exhibitor.

If the exhibition space is not used wholly or mainly for the display of goods and services (eg where it is organised primarily for the retail sale of goods to the people attending), the supply of the space is exempt.

The letting of a hall to an exhibition organiser, as distinct from the exhibitors, is exempt.

Rent apportionments

Apportionment of rent normally takes place when there is a change of landlord of a tenanted property, or an assignment of a lease from one tenant to another, in the middle of a rent quarter. Customs has confirmed that such apportionments are outside the scope of VAT, so that they are unaffected by an option to tax.

Interest on overdue rent

Similarly Customs has confirmed that interest on overdue rent is outside the scope of VAT, even if interest on late rent is provided for in the lease.

Rent-free periods

The grant by a landlord of a rent-free period is not normally a 'supply' for VAT purposes. Therefore it is outside the scope of VAT (see VAT Notice 742). However, if the tenant gives consideration for the rent-free period (eg carrying out works on the premises which benefit the landlord), there is a taxable supply of services.

In the case of *Ridgeons Bulk Ltd* (1994) it was held that correspondence supported the view of Customs & Excise that the rent-free period was directly linked to the tenant agreeing to undertake certain building works. The execution of the lease was the legal document that gave effect to the terms that had been agreed and the rent-free period was the consideration for the supply of the service by the tenant.

Road, bridge and tunnel tolls

In the case of *EC Commission v United Kingdom* [2001] BVC 458, the court ruled that the operation of a tolled road, bridge or tunnel by a local authority, a passenger transport committee, bridge board, etc. is outside the scope of VAT where the operator is acting in its capacity as a public authority. In other cases, however (eg the operation of private toll roads, etc.), supplies by the operator are standard-rated supplies. Customs & Excise is consulting with operators of standard-rated roads, etc. to see whether the Government can offer some support to offset the cost of VAT (Business Brief 15/00).

'Section 106' agreements

Where a developer provides goods or services free, or for a nominal charge, under an agreement under Town and Country Planning Act 1990, s.106, or some similar agreement, Customs & Excise accepts that their provision does not constitute a supply and therefore no VAT is chargeable. The recovery of the input tax attributable to these goods and services is as set out under the previous heading.

Cash contributions

Where money, or money in addition to the provision of the building, road or sewer, is paid to a local authority under a s. 106 or similar agreement, for example for the future maintenance of a building, this is not consideration for a taxable supply by the local authority and is not subject to VAT.

Similar arrangements do not apply to payments to water companies in connection with the supply of water or sewerage supplies. Such payments may be liable to VAT.

Stabling and livery services

Following the decision of the VAT Tribunal in the case of *John Window* (VATTR case 17186) (see **11.3.2**), Customs & Excise has issued the following guidance (Business Brief 21/01).

'Application of the decision

If you supply stabling and livery services together as a single supply then, subject to the following paragraphs, your supplies are exempt from VAT. VAT Information Sheet 02/2001 gives more information on whether a transaction consists of a single composite supply or not.

What are livery services?

These are services provided for horses in a stable that go beyond the right to occupy the stable. They may include feeding and watering, mucking out, turning out, worming, clipping, plaiting, exercising, cleaning tack, grooming, breaking in, schooling and arranging for vets. It does not include clearly identifiable separate supplies such as vets' services.

When is the supply of stabling exempt?

If you rent stabling to a horse owner then, provided you allow that owner exclusive use of the stabling (i.e. you allocate all or an identifiable part of the stabling for the sole use of their horse), this is a supply of a right over land, which is exempt unless you have exercised 'the option to tax' (see Notice 742 Section 9 Land & Property). If you do not make a supply of a right over land your supply will be standard-rated.

DIY livery

This is a supply of stabling only. Please refer to the previous paragraph to decide its liability.

Special purpose stables

The Tribunal decision does not affect the liability of the supplies made by race-horse trainers and stud farm owners or stables that specialise, for example, in breaking in and schooling. The principal supply in these circumstances is not the supply of the right to occupy a stable.

Keep of animals

The liability of the supply of the keep of animals is unaffected by the Tribunal decision and remains standard-rated.

Grazing rights

The guidance contained in paragraph 10(b) of Notice 701/15 is unaffected by the Tribunal decision.'

Statutory compensation

Compensation payable by the landlord of an agricultural tenancy or business tenancy in accordance with the provisions of the Agricultural Holdings Act 1986, the Agricultural Tenancies Act 1995 or Landlord and Tenant Act 1954, s. 25, following the giving of notice to quit, is not payable in respect of any supply and is, accordingly, outside the scope of VAT. The payment is in respect of the tenant's legal rights. In practice, this covers the whole of the amount so payable, even if it exceeds the minimum statutory amount. However, where the tenant of business property voluntarily agrees to surrender his lease or tenancy, that is a supply of services and VAT is chargeable on any consideration for the surrender if the option for taxation has been exercised (*Lloyds Bank plc* LON/95/2524).

Timeshares

It has been held that the grant of a timeshare in new accommodation is excluded from the exemption by virtue of VATA 1994, gp. 1, item 1(e), which refers to 'the grant of any interest in, right over or licence to occupy holiday accommodation' (*American Real Estate (Scotland) Ltd* (1980) VATTR 80 and *P&V Gretney*, (1983) VATTR 271). Such a grant is, therefore, a standard-rated supply.

However, the repurchase of timeshare licences from a bank was held to be exempt by virtue of note (12) to gp. 1, which excludes from item 1(e), and therefore includes within the exemption, 'the grant in respect of a building or part which is not a new building of:

- the fee simple; or
- a tenancy, lease or licence to the extent that the grant is made for a consideration in the form of a premium.'

It will be appreciated that 'grant' includes an assignment or surrender (note (1)). Commonly, timeshare arrangements will include the operation of a management company to look after the building on behalf of the owners of the timeshares. In the case of *Clowance Holdings Ltd* [2001] BVC 4, 157, the management company invoiced owners for management fees to cover the payment of rates, insurance, TC licences, plus a charitable levy and contributions to a sinking fund to maintain the assets and amenities at the site. The Tribunal held that the supplies by the management company were separate from any supply of the timeshares. It also held that the payments by the management company on behalf of the owners were disbursements not subject to VAT; the charitable levy was not consideration for any taxable supply, but the sinking fund contributions were standard-rated, being consideration for taxable supplies made by the management company to the Owners' Club.

Surrenders of leases

Customs & Excise takes the view that the assignment of a lease to a member of the landlord's VAT group is not subject to VAT if the assignee is not the landlord. Formerly it took the view that VAT was due in those circumstances. As a result of this change of view it is possible to avoid a charge to VAT, while making an effective surrender, by assigning the lease to a member of the landlord's group

Transfers of properties within VAT groups

It is common practice for property companies trading as a group to transfer title to buildings within the group for rationalisation and similar purposes. Where such a group is also registered as a group for VAT purposes under VATA 1994, s. 43 such supplies between members of the group are disregarded for VAT purposes.

Where title to a building passes from one member of the VAT group to another, the VAT liability on supplies made by the group of interests in such properties will not be changed as a result of the subsequent departure from the group of the original owner company. This is significant where the building concerned was constructed by the original owner and the group has been making zero-rated supplies of major interest leases, ie leases of non-commercial buildings for more than 21 years.

Customs & Excise accepts that an assignment of any interest to a VAT grouped company is an exempt supply unless that company (the assignee) is itself the lessor or licensor It should be noted, however, that such an assignment could be standard-rated if the assignor had exercised his option to tax (see **11.6**).

Grants of a major interest by members of VAT groups

The following guidance was issued by Customs & Excise in Business Brief 11/03:

'The first grant of a major interest in a new dwelling, communal residential building or lease in a building. This Business Brief article clarifies Customs' policy in relation to grants of major interest in zero-rated buildings by VAT groups in the rare situation when a group member makes more than one grant of a major interest in a building, the first of which is to another group member.

Where a major interest in a building is granted by one member of a VAT group to another, the grant should not be considered to be the "first grant of a major interest" in that building by that group member for the purpose of zero-rating. In effect this means that the first grant of a major interest to a person outside the group can be zero-rated, regardless of the previous activity within the VAT group, so long as the group member making the grant is a person constructing (or converting) the building and it meets all the other criteria.'

11.5.8   Reverse premiums and reverse assignments

A reverse premium is where a landlord pays a tenant in order to induce the tenant to enter into a lease of the landlord's property.

Customs Guidance Manual, Vol. 1–8, section 2.2 gives Customs' views on such payments.

'A reverse assignment is where a tenant pays a person in order to induce that person to take an assignment of the existing lease.

Customs and Excise v Mirror Group Case [2002] BVC 16 and *Customs and Excise v Cantor Fitzgerald International* [2002] BVC 9 were both references from the High Court under Article 177 of the EC Treaty (now Article 234) to the ECJ for preliminary rulings on points of law that involved property deals. The cases were not joined although the ECJ issued the rulings on the same day and both of the cases involved Article 13B(b) of the Sixth Directive.

The facts

Mirror Group entered into an agreement with Olympia & York Canary Wharf Ltd (in administration), whereby a total of about £12 million plus VAT could be paid to Mirror Group. Part of this payment would be as an inducement to take a lease and part as an inducement to take up an option for leases. The sum of £6.5 million was deposited in an account so that when the current leases ended and Mirror Group had to enter into new leases, the money, or part of the money, would be released.

Prior to the transactions Mirror Group had no interest in the land.

Cantor Fitzgerald International agreed to take over a lease on some property from Wako International (Europe) Limited (Wako) in return for a payment of £1.5 million.

Prior to the transaction Cantor Fitzgerald had no interest in the property.

The problem

Were these payments liable to VAT or were they exempt under Article 13B(b)?

The law

Article 6 of the Sixth VAT Directive states that any transaction that does not constitute a supply of goods is a supply of services and that services may include "obligations to refrain from an act or to tolerate an act or situation".

Article 13B(b) of the Sixth VAT Directive allows the letting or leasing of immovable property to be an exempt supply.

The rulings

In the case of the payments to Mirror Group, it was decided that neither payment constituted consideration for supplies under Article 13B(b). It was not specified exactly what supplies were actually made by Mirror Group. It was sufficient for the ECJ to rule that the supplies were not exempt under this legislation because Mirror Group did not have an interest in the land prior to the transactions.

In the second case it was ruled that the acceptance for a consideration of an assignment of the lease of a property in this situation was not exempt because again Cantor Fitzgerald did not have an interest in the land prior to the transaction.

These cases must be distinguished from the situation in *Lubbock Fine v Commissioners of Customs and Excise Case* [1993] BVC 287. Neither Mirror Group nor Cantor had any interest in the land. Lubbock Fine was in possession of a lease and thus had an interest in land at the start of proceedings.

Flowchart: C & E Commrs v Mirror Group plc (Case C-409/98) ECJ [2001]

Notes

(1)   *Inducement to take a lease*

There is a supply of services by the prospective tenant to the landlord. The service supplied is not the grant of an interest in land. At the relevant time the prospective tenant did not have "any interest in the immovable property".

(2)   *Further information*

For further information about the VAT liability of surrendering leases see *The British VAT Reporter* and VAT Notice 742.

Flowchart: C & E Commrs v Cantor Fitzgerald International (Case C-108/99) ECJ [2001]

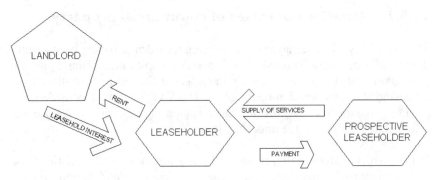

Notes

(1)   *Inducement to accept the assignment of a lease*

There is a supply of services by the prospective leaseholder to the current leaseholder. The service supplied is not the grant of an interest in land. At the relevant time the prospective leasee did not have "any interest in the immovable property".

(2)   *Further information*

For further information about the VAT liability of surrendering leases see The British VAT Reporter and VAT Notice 742.

Flowchart: Lubbock Fine & Co v C & E Commrs (Case C-63/92) ECJ [1993] BVC 287

Notes

(1)   *Interest in land*

The tenant had an interest in the property, a lease. The surrender to the landlord was held to be grant of an interest in land.

(2)   *Further information*

For further information about the VAT liability of surrendering leases see The British VAT Reporter and VAT Notice 742.'

11.5.9   Variations of leases of commercial property

The variation of a lease may result in it being regarded as having been surrendered and a new lease granted. This is a very complex area of land law and professional advice should be sought in respect of the specific variation being made and the consideration being given. The VAT liability of consideration paid by a tenant to a landlord for the variation of the terms of a lease will follow that of any rent due under the lease.

If the correct analysis is that there has been a surrender of the existing lease and the grant of a new lease, then whether there is a VAT liability on the grant of the new lease depends upon whether the taxation option has been selected.

11.5.10   Service charges, etc.

Letting

It is common for property to be let in return for a rental and for the lease to provide for payment of a service charge in addition, to cover costs associated with the general running of the property, maintenance of common areas, etc. As a general rule the service charge is seen as being additional consideration for the landlord's supplies under the lease, and so will be exempt or standard-rated depending whether the landlord opted for taxation. In the case of residential property it will always be exempt, as an option for taxation is ineffective in such cases.

Freehold property

However, in the case of service charges in respect of freehold property, there is no supply of land to which the service charge can be attributed, with the result that it becomes consideration for a standard-rated supply of the under-lying services provided. Also, there are many instances where the service charge is payable, not to the landlord, but to a separate entity (often a company set up for the purpose) acting in its own right. Again, the charges are, in principle, consideration for a taxable supply of services.

Domestic accommodation

This treatment of service charges payable to freeholders, or to independent service companies, has given rise to anomalous treatment in the case of domestic accommodation. Occupants of flats, etc. paying service charges to freeholders or service providers other than their landlords have faced a VAT cost, while those paying them to their landlords have not. From 1 April 1994 a concession applies, under which all service charges in respect of domestic accommodation can be exempted (Business Brief 3/94, 15 February 1994). Service charges for non-domestic accommodation are not affected by this concession, and their liability is determined in accordance with the rules set out above. Service charges in respect of holiday lettings have always been, and remain, standard-rated.

Further information on service charges may be found in Notice 742.

Reimbursement of landlord's or vendor's charges

When entering into a lease, it is common practice for the landlord to require the tenant to pay for the landlord's legal and other professional charges in connection with the lease as well as his own. Such payment by the tenant is generally regarded as part consideration for the grant of the lease and will bear VAT on the same basis as the lease.

If the landlord has opted to tax (see **11.6**) then the VAT on the expenses can be recovered. The reimbursement will be for the VAT exclusive and the land-lord will be required to raise a VAT only invoice. Where no election to exercise the taxation option has been made then the indemnity is for the VAT inclusive amount, as the landlord is not entitled to recover the VAT on the costs.

Indemnity payments arising from the tenant exercising rights already granted under a lease, for example the right to assign or sublet or make alterations without further permission, are regarded as outside the scope of VAT.

11.5.11   Anti-avoidance measures

Changing the use of zero-rated relevant residential or charitable buildings

In two instances there is a clawback of the benefit of zero-rating of a building which has been in use for a relevant residential or relevant charitable purpose (but not where it has been used for a dwelling).

The first is where part of the building is disposed of within ten years of completion and is not intended to be used by the acquirer for a relevant residential or charitable purpose. In that event the disposal, whether of the freehold or a lease, will be liable to VAT at the standard-rate instead of being exempt. In the case of a lease this would apply to annual rents as well as to lump sums received (VATA 1994, Para. 1(2), (3), Sch. 10).

The second is where any part of the building is used by the owner for a non-residential or non-charitable purpose. In that event the owner's interest in that part of the building is treated as having been supplied both to him and by him when he first uses it for the new purpose. In other words there will be a self-supply. VAT will be chargeable at the standard-rate on any original supplies to him that were zero-rated, such as construction costs or the cost of buying a new building (VATA 1994, Para. 1(4) to (6), Sch. 10).

Freehold sales

Anti-avoidance provisions apply where the prior grant occurs on or after 9 April 2003.

Where the grant of the freehold in a commercial building is standard-rated because the building is less than three years old, any subsequent supply arising from that grant is also standard-rated (VATA 1994, s. 96(10A)(a)). Where the grant of the freehold is exempt, any further supply arising from that grant is also exempt (s. 96(10A)(b)).

The reference to supplies 'arising from' the grant is a reference to the provisions of SI 1995/2518 reg. 84(2), which provides that where the consideration for the grant is not determinable at the time of the grant, goods are treated as separately and successively supplied when further consideration is received or when further invoices are issued.

The provisions will also apply to schemes involving the sale of vacant land and the subsequent construction of a commercial building.

Imposition of market value

Customs has limited powers to impose the open market value on certain transactions. For further information see **11.1.15**.

Developer's self-supply charge

The developer's self-supply charge was considered to be an unnecessary complication (given the relatively small amount of tax at stake) and was removed in respect of developments commencing after 28 February 1995. For projects in progress that started prior to 1 March 1995 the taxpayer had a choice-either to repay the VAT claimed on account of the self-supply charge and not to reclaim any further amounts or to accept the triggering of the charge on 1 March 1997 (or earlier if there is an exempt supply or use of the property) (SI 1995/279).

11.5.12   Penalties

On occasions zero-rating is dependent upon the recipient certifying that the building will be used for a particular purpose (see above).

A person who gives an incorrect certificate to his supplier will, in the absence of reasonable excuse, be liable to a civil penalty equal to the difference between the amount of tax charged as a result of the certificate and the correct amount of tax chargeable. The following certificates are potentially within this penalty provision:

- a certificate that all or part of the supply is zero-rated under VATA 1994, gp. 5 (construction of dwellings, etc.), gp. 6 (listed buildings), Sch. 8,
- a certificate that all or part of the supply is exempt under VATA 1994, gp. 1. Sch. 9 (land).

11.6   Option to tax

The election to waive the exemption or opt to tax turns certain exempt supplies in relation to land, buildings and civil engineering works into taxable supplies.

11.6.1   Why waive the exemption?

The two most common reasons for waiving the exemption are:

1. To recover input tax that would otherwise be irrecoverable because it would relate to the making of an exempt supply. An advantage of waiving the exemption is to enable input tax on attributable expenditure to be recovered including acquisition costs, construction costs, professional fees, repairs maintenance and running costs.

2. To ensure that the following may be treated as the transfer of a going concern, assuming other conditions for such treatment are met:

    *   the sale of an opted property,
    *   the sale of the freehold in a 'new' commercial building.

Of paramount importance is that the election is irrevocable (it is usually possible to revoke the option during three months after the option to tax becomes effective see **11.6.4**) and binds all leases granted and any subsequent sale by the elector of that building.

Consideration should be given to the possible commercial consequences of waiving the election. For example, will tenants be able to recover the VAT charged? Tenants or purchasers would not welcome the election if they are exempt or partly exempt. Would tenants welcome the option to tax where the landlord maintains the upkeep of the building as the service charge costs should be reduced because the landlord will no longer suffer irrevocable VAT?

There are limitations on the scope for claiming input tax where exempt supplies have been made before the option to tax is made.

The election to waive the exemption should not be entered into without careful thought and planning.

11.6.2   To whom and to what does it apply?

The option effects all supplies made by the person opting in relation to the property opted.

Who is affected?

Joint owners of property must opt jointly. Where the option leads to a liability to register, or the owners wish to register, the owners must register as a partnership for VAT purposes.

An option made by any member of a group registration affects supplies in relation to the opted property:

- by companies that are members of the group at the time the option is made;
- by any company that joins the groups registration after the option is made and at a time when any member of the group still has an interest in the opted property, and
- by a member of a group registration who leaves the group registration while still having an interest in the opted property.

What is affected?

The election to waive the exemption may be made with respect to a specified area of land, a building, part of a building or a planned building.

When the election is made in respect of a specified area of non-agricultural land, Customs say that:

'• The option does apply to any existing civil engineering works; but

- Does not apply to any building subsequently built on the land.

Where the election is made in respect of a building, part of a building or a planned building it extends to:

- The whole building (or to the part of the building owned by the person making the option)

- To any land within the curtilage of the building. This may include forecourts, yards, parking bays and landscaped areas.

For the purposes of this, the following are treated as one building:

- Buildings linked internally

- Buildings linked by a covered walkway

- Complexes consisting of a number of units grouped round a fully enclosed concourse.'

Example 11.2

A person has a lease on one part of a building. He decides to sub-let part of this and elects to waive the exemption in respect of his part of the building. He then has the opportunity to take a lease over the whole building. He does so. The part of the building he has acquired is automatically covered by his original option to tax.

11.6.3 When is the election ineffective?

An election is ineffective in respect of:

- a building or part of a building intended for use as a dwelling or number of dwellings or solely for a relevant residential purpose; or
- a building or part of a building intended for use solely for a relevant charitable purpose, other than as an office;
- a pitch for a residential caravan,
- facilities for the mooring of a residential houseboat,

(VATA 1994, Sch. 10, Para. 2 (1) and (2)).

Relevant residential accommodation or building for a charitable purpose

The 'option to tax' is not automatically ineffective in respect of 'relevant residential' accommodation or 'buildings intended solely for use for a relevant charitable purpose'. The landlord or vendor must be informed in writing that the building is used or to be used for such purposes. See also Notice 742A paragraphs 3.4 and 3.5.

DIY housebuilders

If land is sold to an individual who intends to build a dwelling, otherwise than in the course or furtherance of a business carried on by him, the election to waive the exemption will not apply (VATA 1994, Sch. 10, Para. 2 (3)(b)).

Sales to housing associations

An election to 'waive the exemption' is ineffective in respect of grants to relevant housing associations when the association certifies in writing that:

- the land is to be used (after any necessary demolition work) for the construction of a building or buildings intended for use as a dwelling or number of dwellings, or
- solely for a relevant residential purpose,

(VATA 1994, Sch. 10, Para. 2(3)(a)).

Example 11.3

A non-residential building is to be sold and converted to dwellings or for a relevant residential purpose. It is possible for the vendor and the purchaser to agree that the option to tax will be effective. They have to do so in a written agreement before the sale takes place. It is not possible to have this agreement is the sale is to a housing association.

For information see VAT Notice 742A, section 3 and VATA 1994, Sch. 10, Para. 2(2A).

11.6.4   Revoking the option to tax

The option to tax cannot be revoked for 20 years other than in the first three months after making the election, subject to certain conditions. In either case Customs must give permission for the election to be revoked.

During the first three months permission will normally be given if the option has not been put into practical effect. The following three conditions all apply:

- There should be no rent or payments received on which the trader should have accounted for VAT.
- Input tax must not have been recovered in relation to the land and buildings, except any input tax that would have been recoverable under normal partial exemption rules.
- The land or building has not been transferred (acquired or disposed) as a transfer of a going concern.

11.6.5   Making an election

In *Blythe Limited Partnership* [1999] BVC 2224 the VAT & Duties Tribunals ruled that there is 'a clear distinction between election and notification'. In VAT Notice 742A this is described as follows:

'There are two stages in opting to tax. The first stage is making the decision to opt. This may take place at a board meeting or similar, or less formally. However you reach your decision, we recommend that you keep a written record, showing clear details of the land or buildings you are opting to tax, and the date you made your decision.'

The effective date must be a current or future date as an election to 'opt to tax' cannot be exercised retrospectively. An election is effective from 'the beginning of the day on which the election is made or any later date specified in the election'.

The election is not effective unless notified to Customs within 30 days from the effective date.

Notification may be made using the Form 1614. The form is available on Customs website or from the National Advice Service.

Prior agreement with Customs

In certain circumstances an election to 'opt to tax' is not effective unless prior approval or clearance has been obtained from Customs. This applies when the person entitled to opt to tax has made, or will make, 'an exempt of supply of the land or building between 1 August 1989 and the date' from which the option it to take effect. For example the person concerned may have previously let or rented part or all of the land or building concerned.

When it is necessary to apply for permission Customs requires the following information:

- a brief description of the future plans for the land or building;
- details of any input tax incurred in the ten years before opting to tax that you wish to recover;
- details (including amounts) of input tax that is likely to be incurred in the future if permission is granted;
- value of exempt supplies of the land or building made in the ten years before the request for permission;
- the expected value of taxable supplies that will arise in the foreseeable future if permission is granted,
- details of anyone who has helped to fund the land or building, or any 'connected person', who is occupying or intends to occupy any part of the land or building.

Fuller and better information is available in paragraph 5.5 of Notice 742A.

Permission granted automatically

Customs' policy on granting permission automatically is in VAT Notice 742A, paragraph 5.2. The paragraph has legal effect. The four situations when permission is granted automatically are as follows:

'1. It is a mixed-use developments and the only exempt supplies have been in relation to the dwellings.

2. You do not wish to recover any input tax in relation to the land or building incurred before your option to tax has effect; and

- the consideration for your exempt supplies has, up to the date when your option to tax is to take effect, been solely by way of rents or service charges and excludes any premiums or payments in respect of occupation after the date on which the option takes effect. Regular rental and/or service charge payments can be ignored for the purposes of this condition. Payments are considered regular where the intervals between them are no more than a year and where each represents a commercial or genuine arm's length value; and

- the only input tax relating to the land or building that you expect to recover after the option to tax takes effect will be on overheads, such as regular rental payments, service charges, repairs and maintenance costs. If you expect to claim input tax in relation to refurbishment or redevelopment of the building you will not meet this condition.

  Notes: When deciding whether you meet this condition you should disregard:

- any input tax you can otherwise recover by virtue of the partial exemption de minimis rules (Regulation 106, VAT Regulations 1995); and
- any input tax you are entitled to recover on general business overheads not specifically related to the land or building, such as audit fees.

3. The only input tax you wish to recover in relation to the land or building incurred before your option to tax takes effect relates solely to tax charged by your tenant or tenants upon surrender of a lease; and

  - the building or relevant part of the building has been unoccupied between the date of the surrender and the date the option to tax is to take effect; and
  - there will be no further exempt supplies of the land or building; and
  - you do not intend or expect that you will occupy the land or building other than for taxable purposes.

4. The exempt supplies have been incidental to the main use of the land or building. For example, where you have occupied a building for taxable purposes the following would be seen as incidental to the main use and the condition would be met:

  - allowing an advertising hoarding to be displayed;
  - granting space for the erection of a radio mast;
  - receiving income from an electricity sub-station.

The letting of space to an occupying tenant, however minor, is not incidental.'

11.6.6 Auction sales

Higher Education Statistics Agency Ltd v C & E Commrs [2000] BVC 150 concerned the interaction of the provisions relating to:

- the sale of land included in the transfer of a business as a going concern, and
- the time of supply.

A commercial property was sold at auction as a going concern, and a deposit was paid to the auctioneer as agent for the vendor. The court held that the combined effect of:

- Value Added Tax (Special Provisions) Order 1995 (SI 1995/1268), Art. 5(2), and
- VATA 1994, s. 6(4),

was that the 'relevant date' by which an election to tax in VATA 1994, Sch. 9 had to be made was the date of the successful bid at auction when the deposit was paid, not the date of the 'grant' when the sale of the land was completed.

An election made after the deposit was paid was invalid and the transfer was not a transfer of a business as a going concern.

11.6.7   Transfer of a going concern

Special care is needed if the assets transferred include land and buildings in respect of which the vendor has opted for taxation, or the freehold transfer of new buildings. In such a case the going concern provisions do not apply to the land element, and thus VAT is due, unless the purchaser has opted for taxation in respect of the property concerned, notified the transferee as detailed in **11.3.7** above, and given Customs written notification of this, before the first tax point arises in respect of the supply (Value Added Tax (Special Provisions) Order 1995 (SI 1995/1268), Art. 5(2)).

Following litigation on the point Customs now accepts that it is sufficient, in the case of a written notification by letter, that the buyer has properly addressed, prepaid, and posted the letter by the relevant date. It does not have to be received by them by that date. However, Customs warns that it will be prudent to retain evidence of posting (Notice 742A – Opting to tax land & buildings, paragraph 11.2).

11.6.8   Effect of option on companies in VAT groups

Where a company exercises the option to tax, the option also binds a *relevant associate* of that company. A 'relevant associate' is defined as a company which:

- was treated as a member of the same VAT group as the company which made the election, at the time when the election first had effect;
  or
- has been treated as a member of the same VAT group at any later time when the company which exercised the option had an interest in the building or land; *or*
- has been treated as a member of the same VAT group as any of the above at a time when that company had an interest in the building or land (VATA 1994, Para. 3(7), Sch. 10).

11.6.9　Tax point

The established tax point rules set out under **11.1.14** have been modified to deal with the situation created by the availability of the option. The date on which the option becomes effective is treated as a tax point so that rent for a period which spans that date is treated as consideration for an exempt supply so far as it relates to the part of the rent period before that date, and for a taxable supply for the period beginning on that date (VATA 1994, Para. 4, Sch. 10).

11.6.10　Address for notification of an option

With effect from 18 August 2003, all notifications of and queries relating to option to tax should be made:

* in writing to Option To Tax, UK Central Office, Portcullis House, 21 India Street, Glasgow, G2 4PZ;
* by fax to 0141 308 3367;
* by telephone to 0141 308 3548/3599 (Monday to Thursday 09.00 to 17.00 and Friday 09.00 to 16.30), or
* by e-mail to optiontotaxnationalunit@hmce.gsl.gov.uk.

11.6.11　Anti-avoidance provision

Disapplication of the option for taxation

Where a lessor opts to tax rental income on the grant of a lease, and the lessee carries on an exempt business, the lessor obtains an immediate recovery of any input tax paid on the cost of the construction or refurbishment of the premises concerned, and the lessee suffers a disallowance of input tax on the rents payable under the lease. The net result is to spread the disallowance of the input tax over the term of the lease.

Under these new provisions, the grantor of an interest in land may opt for taxation in respect of that grant, but in certain circumstances the option is ignored and the resulting supply is an exempt supply VATA 1994, Sch. 10, Para. 2(3AA), (3A)).

The circumstances are that:

(a) the land or building falls within the capital goods scheme in respect of the grantor (ie the consideration for, or market value of, the grant is £250,000 or more – see reg. 113 of the Value Added Tax Regulations 1995 (SI 1995/2518) – see **11.3.3**;

(b)   the grant is made within the adjustment period (usually ten years – see reg. 114 of the Value Added Tax Regulations 1995 (SI 1995/2518);

(c)   it is intended or expected that, at some time during the adjustment period, the person occupying the land or building will be in occupation otherwise than for the purposes of making wholly taxable supplies in the course or furtherance of a business, and

(d)   that person is or will be the grantor (eg by way of a leaseback), the person financing his development of the land, or any other person connected with either of them.

The eventual wording of the 1997 legislation was much narrower than was originally proposed. It did not catch the situation where a developer constructs a building as a speculative development and then sells his interest, or grants a lease, to a bank, insurance company, pension fund or some other unconnected person.

This was true even if the bank has funded the development, unless at the time of the grant there was an arrangement that the bank would occupy the development. In other words, it did not catch the situation where the developer obtains funding from a bank and at some later time the bank takes a lease of part of the development.

It is important to note that the intention referred to at (c) must exist at the time of the grant referred to at (b) or at the time that the funding is made available.

The scope of the disapplication rules was widened, by the Value Added Tax (Buildings and Land) Order 1999 (SI 1999/593), which amended the text of VATA 1994, Sch. 10, Paras. 2, 3A. The rules now catch the situation where, on the grant of the lease, the building is not within the capital goods scheme at the time of the grant of the lease, but where the person granting the lease, or the financier, intends or expects that it will come within the scheme at a later date (new Para. 3A(2)).

Financing

As regards (d), the term 'financing' is given a broad definition. It *includes*

- directly funding, or obtaining or arranging funds for, all or part of the cost of acquiring, constructing, reconstructing, extending, altering, refurbishing or fitting out a building, and
- directly or indirectly discharging, or arranging the discharge of, another person's liability incurred in raising funds for the construction, reconstruction, extension, alteration, refurbishment or fitting out of a building.

This includes:

(i)   advancing or guaranteeing a loan;

(ii)   transferring assets to be used as funds, and

(iii) the subscription of shares.

A bank may fund a development by paying an advance premium on an agreement for a lease, where that premium is used by the developer to pay builders, architects, etc. Similarly, an advance payment of rent may constitute financing if the developer uses the money to defray the costs of the development. In applying the legislation, the question is whether there was an intention to occupy all or part of the development at the time the financing is made available. This will normally be ascertained by examining the loan agreement or lease agreement, or any side letter signed at the time of those agreements.

As regards (iii) above, this catches the case where a parent company subscribes shares in a subsidiary which then acquires a building and leases it to the parent or another company in the same group.

Connected persons

The definition in ICTA 1988, s. 839, applies.

11.7   Construction services

11.7.1   Introduction

Under the general rules of VAT, a supply of construction services is a taxable supply (EC Sixth Directive, Arts. 2, 6 and VATA 1994, s. 1(1)(a)). However, Art. 28(2)(a) provides that where supplies were zero-rated under domestic law as at 1 January 1991, they may continue to be zero-rated until the 'definitive system' comes into force (EC Sixth Directive, Art. 281). The supply of construction services in the course of the construction of dwellings or of other buildings used for relevant residential or charitable purposes is covered by this transitional arrangement.

The incidental supply of 'building materials' is also covered (VATA 1994, Sch. 8, gp. 5, items 2, 4 – see **11.5.2** for details). However, the supply of materials to a person supplying construction services (eg by manufacturers or producers) remains a taxable supply.

11.7.2 Zero-rating

Introduction

The supply of any services related to the construction other than the services of an architect, surveyor or person acting as consultant or in a supervisory capacity is zero-rated if supplied in the course of construction of any of the following:

- a building designed as a dwelling or number of dwellings (see also **11.5.4** above)
- a building intended for use solely for a relevant residential purpose (see also **11.5.4** above)
- a building designed for a charitable purpose (see also **11.5.4** above)
- any civil engineering work necessary for the development of a permanent park for residential caravans (see also **11.5.4** above)

(VATA 1994, Sch. 8, gp. 5, item 2).

Certificates for relevant residential or charitable buildings

In order to zero-rate the supply of constructions services relating to relevant residential or charitable buildings the supplier must receive a certificate from the person receiving the supply before the work starts (VATA 1994, gp. 5, note (12)(b) and, gp. 6, note (3)). A specimen certificate will be found in VAT Notice 708.

'Construction'

The construction of a building does not include any of the following:

- the conversion, reconstruction or alteration of an existing building; any enlargement of, or extension to, an existing building except to the extent that it creates an additional dwelling or dwellings,
- the construction of an annex, unless the annex is solely for charitable purposes and is capable of functioning independently of the existing building and the main access to the annex is otherwise than through the existing building and vice versa;

(VATA 1994 Sch. 8, gp. 5, notes (16), (17)).

An existing building does not cease to exist as such unless:

- it is demolished completely to ground level; or
- the part remaining above ground level consists of no more than:

    a single facade, or
    in the case of a corner site, a double facade, the retention of which is required by the terms of the relevant planning consent,

(VATA 1994, Sch. 8, gp. 5 note (18)).

The question whether a particular work is one of construction of a new building or the enlargement or extension of an existing building is not always easy to decide. The case of *Michael, Gillian and Norman Smith v C&E Commrs* [2001] BVC 4,092 concerned a new dwelling adjacent to an existing dwelling. The new dwelling was not connected internally to the existing dwelling, but stairs, a landing, bathroom and a bedroom which were part of the existing building became part of the new dwelling. The dwellings were separately assessed for council tax purposes and there was no restriction on the separate disposal of the dwellings. The Tribunal held that the new building work was zero-rated, but the work to incorporate the existing stairs, etc. within the new dwelling was standard-rated.

The case of *Trustee of the Sir Robert Geffrey's School Charity v C&E Commrs* [2002] BVC 4,078 concerned the construction of school buildings in accordance with a design that provided for additional classrooms to be built at some future time when funds became available. The building was completed in 1992, excluding the additional classrooms. Funding for those classrooms became available by 1998 and they were then constructed in accordance with the provisions in the original plan. Zero-rating was refused on the basis that too much time had elapsed the additional classrooms for the latter to be regarded as part of the construction of a building. Accordingly, the classrooms constituted an extension of the original building. As regards annexes, Customs takes the view that the addition of a self-contained flat or annex to a house (eg a 'granny annex') will normally be standard-rated since the separate disposal will be prevented by planning constraints (see VAT Notice 708).

The case of *Kids Church v C&E Commrs* [2003] BVC 4,119 concerned a charity that carried out its activities in a school hall. It needed additional premises and took a three-year renewable lease of about 900m^2 space in a disused warehouse. That area was approximately an eighth of that of the whole warehouse. The warehouse was in very poor condition and unusable as it stood. Its concrete floor was broken and there were large oil spillages on it; also the roof leaked and the electrical wiring was old and possibly dangerous. The appellant decided that it would be necessary to lay a five-inch concrete floor, to erect fire-proof partition walls between the premises and the rest of the warehouse, and to install new electrical wiring. One of the questions for the Tribunal was whether this accommodation could be regarded as an annex of the school premises. In deciding in the negative, the Tribunal commented as follows:

'To begin with, it is wholly inside the existing building. We know of no case in which an annexe to a building has been enclosed within the walls of that building . . . in this case also, the relationship of the Premises to the warehouse is purely one of physical presence. There is no relationship between them as to their use . . .'

785

The construction of any civil engineering work does not include the conversion, reconstruction, alteration or enlargement of such a work (VATA 1994, Sch. 8, gp. 5 note (15)).

'In the course of construction'

To qualify for zero-rating the 'construction services' must be carried out during the 'course of construction'. Customs interprets this to mean as follows:

- 'work . . . prior to the completion of the building', or
- 'any other service closely connected to the construction of the building'.

When a building is complete is not always clear. It must be determined by considering, as appropriate, the date of issue of a 'Completion statement', the intention of the developer, the planning consent (including variations), the date of sale and the date of occupation.

Services closely connected with the construction of the building can include the following:

- necessary demolition work
- ground works
- site clearance.

For more comprehensive details of Customs views see VAT Notice 708.

Rialto (*Rialto Homes plc v C&E Commrs* [2000] BVC 4041) was a housebuilder and, in the course of its trade, it engaged sub-contractors to carry out soft landscaping work such as the laying of turf and the planting of trees and shrubs. This was required as a condition of the grant of planning consent for the development. The sub-contractor zero-rated the supply of turf, but charged VAT on the balance of its invoices. Rialto claimed to set off that VAT as input tax. Customs refused the set off in respect of the planting of trees and shrubs and the landscaping of individual plots. The Tribunal held that the goods supplied by the sub-contractors would have qualified for zero-rating if supplied by Rialto itself. It was immaterial that the sub-contractors did not themselves build the houses. The trees and shrubs were goods ordinarily incorporated into the site of new houses.

'Solely for a . . . charitable purpose'

Non-business charity buildings are often used indiscriminately by charities, sometimes for their non-business activities and sometimes not. Customs has stated that it will ignore indiscriminate business use for non-business charity buildings where it is not expected to exceed 10 per cent of the time the building is normally available for use (Official Report, Finance Bill Standing Committee, 16 May 1989, col. 73).

Customs' interpretation of this is detailed in Notice 708 and is that charities can calculate the extent of qualifying non-business use by reference to time, floor space or the number of people using the building. The non-qualifying use will be disregarded provided that:

- the building is used solely for non-business activity for 90 per cent or more of the time it is available for use;
- 90 per cent or more of the floor space of the building is used solely for non-business activity, or
- 90 per cent or more of the people using the building are engaged solely on non-business activity.

The above methods can only be applied to the building as a whole, apart from the time-based method, which can be applied to parts of the building. Permission from Customs & Excise must be sought for any of these methods, except where the time-based method is applied to the whole building.

'Residential caravans'

A caravan is not a residential caravan if residence throughout the year is prevented by the terms of any covenant or planning consent (VATA 1994, Sch. 8, gp. 5 note (19)).

Listed buildings: zero-rating of approved alterations

The supply, in the course of an approved alteration of a protected building, of any services other than those of an architect, surveyor or any person acting as a consultant or in a supervisory capacity is zero-rated (VATA 1994, Sch. 8, gp. 6, item 2). An approved alteration is an alteration for which listed building consent is required from the planning authority. This covers alterations which would affect the character of the building as a building of special architectural or historic interest (Planning (Listed Buildings and Conservation Areas) Act 1990, s.7). Consent should be obtained before the work is carried out (see *Mr & Mrs Wells v C & E Commrs,* [1998] BVC 4,016 and *Alan Roper & Sons v C & E Commrs* [1998] BVC 4039).

A protected building is defined as a listed building which is designed to remain or become a dwelling or number of dwellings or is intended to be used solely for a relevant residential purpose or a relevant charitable purpose after the reconstruction or alteration (VATA 1994, Sch. 8, gp. 6, note (1) – and see **11.4.3** regarding relevant residential purpose and relevant charitable purpose). A building is designed to remain or become a dwelling or number of dwellings if:

- it consists of self-contained living accommodation;
- there is no provision for internal access from it to any other dwelling or part of a dwelling, and

- the separate use, or disposal of the dwelling is not prohibited by the terms of any covenant, statutory planning consent or similar provision.

In the case of *Nick Hopewell-Smith v C&E Commrs* [2001] BVC 4022, the VAT Tribunal held that the conversion of a barn for use as residential accommodation ancillary to a Grade II listed farmhouse qualified for zero-rating. The barn was physically separate from the house and was capable of being occupied as self-contained living accommodation. Planning consent for the conversion was subject to the condition that the use of the barn should be ancillary to the occupation of the house. However, the separate disposal of the barn was not prohibited. Customs & Excise had refused zero-rating on the ground that the barn was not itself a dwelling house within the above definition. The Tribunal held that because the separate disposal was not prohibited, the barn fell within the definition.

House of Lords decision on 'outbuilding in curtilage of a listed building

At the VAT and Duties Tribunal, the case was decided in favour of the taxpayers. Customs took the matter to the High Court, which reversed the decision of the Tribunal. In turn the taxpayer appealed to the Court of Appeal where a majority decision was in their favour. The House of Lords decided by a majority (four to one) that Customs is right.

The property consisted of a house and an outbuilding within the curtilage of this house. The work was to convert the outbuilding to games and changing facilities and to construct an adjoining indoor swimming pool.

The house was a protected building listed under Planning (Listed Buildings and Conservation Areas) Act 1990. As such alterations could be zero-rated under VATA 1994, Sch 8, gp. 6, item 2. The outbuilding was not itself listed under the 1990 Act, but was protected as being a structure within the curtilage of a listed building. The two structures were physically separate although linked by a sandstone wall. They were built at about the same time – about 1830 – and the outbuilding has had a variety of uses including stable, tack room and latterly garage and laundry and storage for a deep freezer.

It was mutually agreed that some of the work was standard-rated. However, Customs decided that none of the work to the outbuilding could be zero-rated.

Lord Walker delivered the main speech and outlined the reasons behind the judgment. He examined the history of the evolution of the VAT treatment of building works and linked up European legislation with domestic law.

He then divided the key part 'protected building' into three. The structure must be:

- a building
- designed to remain as or become a dwelling
- be a listed building within the meaning of the 1990 Act.

Although planning legislation refers to any buildings and structures in the curtilage of the protected dwelling the intention of Parliament he maintained was to limit VAT relief to a subset – it should apply only to those buildings to be used for residential purposes.

It was maintained that if the owner of a listed dwelling could obtain zero-rating on an en-suite guest room if it were to be placed in an attic, but not if it were to be formed by alterations to a detached potting shed. The only way in which alterations to the detached potting shed could obtain zero-rating were if it were to be changed into a separate dwelling with self contained living accommodation. A similar situation would be if the owner of a listed dwelling put a jacuzzi in the cellar, that would be zero-rated as an alteration to a listed dwelling. If the same facility were to be installed in a detached stable, it would be standard-rated.

Lord Hoffmann, in a few short paragraphs, emphasised that two important conditions to be met were that the zero-rating facility is designed to give some relief for owners of a protected building that is designed 'to remain as or become a dwelling house'. The outbuilding was not so destined. It was to be a games facility. Therefore even if the outbuilding were a listed building, the alterations did not qualify for the relief (*C&E Commrs v Zielinski Baker & Partners Ltd* [2004] BVC 309).

Repair and maintenance

Note that the zero-rating does not cover repairs and maintenance work, or any incidental alterations to the fabric of the building resulting from such repair or maintenance work, and see, for example, *C & E Commrs v Windflower Housing Association* [1995] BTC 5,313. Where work includes both approved alterations and repairs, an apportionment of the consideration has to be made and VAT charged on the amount apportioned to repairs (*C & E Commrs v Morrish* [1998] BTC 5,388). Similarly, the zero-rating does not cover non-approved alterations for which approval is not required (see, for example, *Rosemary Irving Contracts v C & E Commrs* [1998] BVC 4021).

Customs & Excise accepts that mains electrical wiring and lighting systems are part of the fabric of a building for this purpose. However, only or in the structure of the building itself will be considered to be part of the fabric.

Parts of the systems that extend beyond the structure of a building into the grounds are not part of the fabric (eg wiring to floodlights located in the grounds of churches). Similarly, electrical appliances which are attached to and serviced by the mains supply are not part of the fabric.

Note that the grant of a major interest in a listed building by a person who has substantially reconstructed it is zero-rated (see **11.5.4**)

Conversion of non-residential buildings

When converting non-residential buildings the construction work is normally liable to the reduced or standard-rate of tax. The exception is certain work for housing associations and similar.

A housing association may convert a non-residential building into a new eligible dwelling or a building that is to be used for a 'relevant residential purpose'.

Such construction services may be zero-rated when supplied to a relevant housing association in connection with a non-residential conversion, the services are made in the course of conversion of that particular building, a certificate is obtained where necessary and the works are not specifically excluded from zero-rating.

A relevant housing association is a registered:

- social landlord within the meaning of Part I of the Housing Act 1996;
- housing association within the meaning of the Housing Associations Act 1985 (Scottish registered housing association), or
- housing association within the meaning of Part II of the Housing (Northern Ireland) Order 1992 (Northern Irish registered associations).

The existing structure is a non-residential building if it was:

- **never** designed or adapted for use as a dwelling, a number of dwellings or relevant residential purpose, or
- **if designed or adapted for use as a dwelling, a number of dwellings or relevant residential purpose** it was constructed more than ten years before and no part of it been used as a dwelling or for a relevant residential purpose during these ten years.

The housing association should supply a copy of their registration certificate. If the building is to be converted into relevant residential purposes, the housing association must also supply a certificate confirming the intended use of the building.

Contractors must always do as much as possible to verify that any certificate issued to them by the person constructing the building is valid. Checks would include written details of the intended use of the building. Customs may ask to see such records. A copy of the housing association registration certificate must be included. If all reasonable checks have been made, then in the event of the certificate being shown to have been issued incorrectly, Customs will not normally demand payment of unpaid tax (see Notice 48 – Extra-statutory concessions).

The certificate is only issued to the main contractor: sub-contractors do not receive a certificate and should therefore standard-rate their services.

11.7.3   Reduced rate

Certain building works became liable to the reduced rate of 5 per cent with effect from 12 May 2001. This was extended to some other works with effect from 1 June 2002 (VATA 1994, Sch. 7A, gp. 6 and, gp. 7).

Qualifying conversions

There are three types of qualifying conversion:

- a 'changed number of dwellings' conversion,
- a 'house in multiple occupation' conversion,
- a 'special residential' conversion,

(VATA 1994, Sch. A1, Para. 9 and Sch. 7A, gp. 6, note 2).

The term 'conversion' includes all works of repair, maintenance or improvement to the fabric of the building where the work forms an intrinsic part of changing the number of dwellings.

Changed number of dwellings conversion

This is a conversion of a building or part of a building where, after it is completed, the number of dwellings (being at least one) is different from the number before the conversion and in no part of the converted premises is there the same number of single dwellings as before (VATA 1994, Sch. A1, Para. 10 and Sch. 7A, gp. 6, note 3).

As regards the reference to 'no part of the converted premises . . .', the Tribunal has held that, for the test to be workable, a 'part' has to be large enough to be capable of containing a single household dwelling, and must be capable of being identified by references to physical boundaries such as walls, floors and ceilings. However, there is no *de minimis* exception to the 'same number' test (*Wellcome Trust v C&E Comrs* [2004] BVC 4,047).

The following are examples of such a conversion:

- conversion work to change the number of single household dwellings in a building;
- services to convert a non-residential building into a single household dwelling or number of single household dwellings;
- services to convert a house in multiple occupation into a single household dwelling or dwellings,
- services to convert a Relevant Residential Purpose building into a single household dwelling or dwellings.

House in multiple occupation conversion

This is a conversion of a building or part of a building where:

- before it is started, the premises contain only a single household dwelling, or more than one such dwelling, and
- after it is completed, the premises contain only a multiple occupancy dwelling, or two or more such dwellings,

and no part of the premises are to be used for a 'qualifying residential purpose' (VATA 1994, Sch. 7A, gp. 6, note 5).

A multiple occupancy dwelling is one which is designed for occupation by persons not forming a single household, and which satisfies certain other conditions (VATA 1994 Sch. 7A, gp. 6, note 4).

Special residential conversion

This is a conversion of a building or part of a building where:

- before the conversion, the premises contained only one or more dwellings, together with any ancillary outbuildings occupied with the dwellings, and
- after it is completed, the premises are intended to be used solely for a qualifying residential purpose.

Where the qualifying residential purpose is one of the institutional purposes listed in the definition, the premises must form the entirety of the institution after conversion (VATA 1994 Sch. 7A, gp. 6, note 7).

In the case of a special residential conversion, the reduced rate applies only to supplies made to the person who intends to use the premises for the qualifying residential purpose. The supplier must obtain a certificate from the user to the effect that the conversion is a special residential conversion (VATA 1994, Sch. 7A, gp. 6, note 8).

The form of the certificate is specified in Notice 708. There are penalties for the issue of a false certificate so care must be taken to ensure that correct information is given.

Renovations and alterations

The supplies which qualify for the reduced rate of VAT are:

- supplies, in the course of renovation or alteration of a *single household dwelling* that has not been lived in for three years or more;
- renovating or altering a care home (or other qualifying building used solely for a relevant residential purpose) that has not been lived in for three years or more;
- renovating or altering a multiple occupancy dwelling that has not been lived in for three years or more;
- constructing, renovating or converting a building into a garage as part of the renovation of a property that qualifies for the reduced rate,
- supplies of building materials by the person supplying the above services of renovation or alteration where the services include the incorporation of the materials in the building or its immediate site.

However either of the following conditions has to be satisfied for a renovation to qualify for the reduced rate (VATA 1994, Sch. 7A, gp. 7, note 3).

The first condition

The premises must not have been lived in during the period of three years ending with the commencement of the renovation.

When dealing with a relevant residential unit it is necessary to consider the unit as a whole. The 5 per cent rate does not apply if any of the buildings making up the original unit were lived in during the requisite three-year period.

The second condition

- The dwelling must have been empty for three years or longer when purchased by the person who is going to live in it (the occupier);
- no renovation has been carried out in the three years prior to the occupier purchasing the property;
- the occupier must be the recipient of the qualifying services, and
- the qualifying services must be supplied within one year of the date of completion of the purchase.

Evidence that the premises have been unoccupied

Notice 708 gives the following instructions:

'If you reduced-rate your supply you must hold evidence that, on balance, shows the premises have not been lived in during the 3 years immediately before your work starts. The evidence can include the Electoral Roll and Council Tax data, information from utilities companies, evidence from Empty

Property Officers in local authorities, or information from other reliable sources. If you hold a letter from an Empty Property Officer certifying that the property has not been lived in for 3 years, or will have been at the time your work starts, no other evidence is needed. If an Empty Property Officer is unsure about when a property was last lived in he should write with his best estimate. We may then call for other supporting evidence.'

Related garage works

A qualifying conversion or renovation includes any related garage works. The term 'garage works' means the construction of a garage, or the conversion of a non-residential building or part of a building resulting in a garage.

Garage works are related to a conversion if they are carried out at the same time as the conversion and the resulting garage is intended to be occupied with the converted building (VATA 1994, Sch. 7A, gp. 6, note 9 and, gp. 7, note 3A).

Qualifying residential purpose

The definition of qualifying residential purpose is the same as that of relevant residential purpose (VATA 1994 Sch. 7A, gp. 6, note 6 and gp. 7 note 2 (4)).

Qualifying services

These are services consisting of:

- the carrying out of works to the fabric of the building, or
- the carrying out of works within the immediate site of the building in connection with the provision of water, power, heat or access, drainage or security, or waste disposal for the building.

But works to the fabric do not include the installation or incorporation of fixtures which are not building materials (VATA 1994, Sch. 7A, gp. 6, note 11 and gp. 7, note 5). Building materials are as defined for zero-rating purposes (VATA 1994 Sch. 8, gp. 5, notes (22), (23)) (see **11.8**).

Planning consent and building control approval

Any consent or approval which is required under planning law must be obtained for the reduced rate to apply to supplies relating to renovations or alterations (VATA 1994, Sch. 7A, gp. 6 note 10 and gp. 7, note 4).

11.7.4   Installation of energy saving materials

Charge at the reduced rate

The following supplies are chargeable to VAT at the reduced rate:

(a) supplies of any services of installing 'energy saving materials' in residential accommodation or a building intended for use solely for a relevant charitable purpose, and

(b) supplies of energy saving materials to such a person by a person who installs the materials in accommodation or a building in (a) (VATA 1994, Sch. 7A, gp. 2).

Energy saving materials

The following are energy saving materials:

- insulation for walls, floors, ceilings, roofs or lofts or for water tanks, pipes or other plumbing fittings;
- draught stripping for windows and doors;
- central heating system controls; and
- hot water system controls;
- solar panels;
- wind turbines;
- water turbines,
- ground source heat pumps,

(VATA 1994, Sch. 7A, gp. 2).

Note that double glazing and similar products, such as 'low-emissivity' glass, and energy-efficient domestic appliances do not fall within the above definition.

Customs regards 'insulation' as including materials which are designed, and held out for sale, as having insulating qualities, but as not including essentially decorative products or treatments like curtains and carpets, or decorative stone cladding.

Draught stripping products are typically plastic or foam strips which are held out for use by fixing around windows and doors (typically by being glued or nailed in place). This includes such materials for draught stripping around interior and exterior doors, windows and loft hatches.

Central heating and hot water system controls include manual or electronic timers, thermostats, mechanical or electronic valves, including thermostatic radiator valves (Notice 708/6 Energy-Saving Materials).

Residential accommodation

Residential accommodation means:

- a building, or part of a building, that consists of a dwelling or number of dwellings, such as owner-occupied homes, homes rented from private landlords or homes rented from local authorities;

- a building, or part of a building, used for a relevant residential purpose, such as old people's homes, children's homes and nursing homes (as to which, see **11.5.4**);
- a caravan used as a place of permanent habitation, or
- a houseboat.

Relevant charitable purpose

This means use by a charity:

- otherwise than in the course or furtherance of a business, or
- as a village hall or similarly in providing social or recreational facilities for a local community (see **11.5.4**).

Installation

Installation includes any necessary minor building work, such as planning doors or windows or enlarging loft hatches and any painting or plastering to 'make good' after the installation of the materials.

11.7.5   Grant-funded installation of heating equipment, or security goods or connection of gas supply

The following supplies are charged at the reduced rate (VATA 1994, Sch. 7A, gp. 3).

1. Supplies to a qualifying person of any services of installing 'heating appliances' in the qualifying person's sole or main residence.

2. Supplies of heating appliances made to a qualifying person by a person who installs those appliances in the qualifying person's sole or main residence.

3. Supplies to a 'qualifying person' of services of connecting, or reconnecting, a mains gas supply to the qualifying person's sole or main residence.

4. Supplies of goods made to a qualifying person by a person connecting, or reconnecting, a mains gas supply to the qualifying person's sole or main residence, being goods whose installation is necessary for the connection, or reconnection, of the mains gas supply.

5. Supplies to a qualifying person of services of installing, maintaining or repairing a central heating system in the qualifying person's sole or main residence.

6. Supplies of goods made to a qualifying person by a person installing, maintaining or repairing a central heating system in the qualifying person's sole or main residence, being goods whose installation is neces-

sary for the installation, maintenance or repair of the central heating system.

7. Supplies consisting in the leasing of goods that form the whole or part of a central heating system installed in the sole or main residence of a qualifying person.

8. Supplies of goods that form the whole or part of a central heating system installed in a qualifying person's sole or main residence and that, immediately before being supplied, were goods leased under arrangements such that the consideration for the supplies consisting in the leasing of the goods was, in whole or in part, funded by a grant made under a relevant scheme.

9. Supplies to a qualifying person of services of installing 'qualifying security goods' in the qualifying person's sole or main residence.

10. Supplies of qualifying security goods made to a qualifying person by a person who installs those goods in the qualifying person's sole or main residence.

Supply only included so far as grant-funded

Each of items 1 to 7, 9 and 10 applies to a supply only to the extent that the consideration for the supply is, or is to be, funded by a grant made under a relevant scheme.

Item 8 applies to a supply only to the extent that the consideration for the supply is, or is to be, funded by a grant made under a relevant scheme, or is a payment becoming due only by reason of the termination (whether by the passage of time or otherwise) of the leasing of the goods in question.

Qualifying person

A person is a qualifying person at the time of the supply if, at that time he:

- is aged 60 or over, or
- receives any of the following benefits:

  council tax benefit;
  disability living allowance;
  disability working allowance;
  family credit;
  housing benefit;
  income-based job-seekers' allowance;
  income support;
  industrial injuries disablement pension, provided that it includes attendance allowance, and

war disablement pension, provided that it includes mobility supplement or constant attendance allowance,

(VATA 1994, Sch. 7A, gp. 3, Para. 6).

Relevant scheme

A scheme is a 'relevant scheme' if it is one which satisfies the following conditions:

- it has as one of its objectives the funding of the installation of energy saving materials in the homes of any persons who are qualifying persons,
- it disburses, whether directly or indirectly, its grants in whole or in part out of funds made available to it in order to achieve that objective:

- (a) by the Secretary of State,
- (b) by the Scottish Ministers,
- (c) by the National Assembly for Wales,
- (d) by a Minister (within the meaning given by Northern Ireland Act 1998, s.7(3)) or a Northern Ireland department,
- (e) by the European Community,
- (f) under an arrangement approved by the Gas and Electricity Markets Authority,
- (g) under an arrangement approved by the Director General of Electricity Supply for Northern Ireland, or
- (h) by a local authority.

The reference in (f) to an arrangement approved by the Gas and Electricity Markets Authority includes a reference to an arrangement approved by the Director General of Electricity Supply, or the Director General of Gas Supply, before the transfer (under the Utilities Act 2000) of his functions to the Authority.

Heating appliances

Heating appliances means any of the following:

- gas-fired room heaters that are fitted with thermostatic controls;
- electric storage heaters;
- closed solid fuel fire cassettes;
- electric dual immersion water heaters with foam-insulated hot water tanks;
- gas-fired boilers;
- oil-fired boilers,
- radiators.

From 1 June 2002 the reduced rate was extended to the installation of factory-insulated hot water tanks, micro-combined heat and power systems, and systems that use renewable energy (Budget Notice 41/02).

Qualifying security goods

Qualifying security goods means any of the following:

- locks or bolts for windows;
- locks, bolts or security chains for doors;
- spy holes,
- smoke alarms,

(VATA 1994, Sch. 7A, gp. 3, Para. 5).

Examples of relevant schemes are the Home Energy Efficiency Scheme, and the Domestic Energy Efficiency Scheme in Northern Ireland.

Installation

Installation includes any necessary minor building work, such as planning doors or windows or enlarging loft hatches and any painting or plastering to 'make good' after the installation of the materials.

11.7.6 Improving access and mobility

With the removal of the zero-rating for alterations to buildings, it was necessary to provide some relief for alterations specifically designed to increase the mobility of and convenience of handicapped persons.

Access

Zero-rating is available for the supply to a handicapped person of construction services in relation to ramps, or the widening of doorways or passages, for the purpose of facilitating entry to, and movement within, the private residence of the handicapped person (VATA 1994, Sch. 8, Gp. 12, item 8) and to a charity to facilitate a handicapped person's entry or movement within any building (Sch. 8, Gp. 12, item 9).

The charity does not need to own the building but it must commission the work. In *Brand as Trustee of Racket Sports for Children with Special Needs* [1996] BVC 4,290, a club commissioned improved access to it funded by a charity. As the supply was to the club and not the charity, relief was unavailable.

In *Johnsen (Chairman, Shalden Millennium Committee)* [2003] BVC 4,059, zero-rating did not apply to a supply of new church gates and widening an access path to enable disabled persons to be driven to the church door (Gp. 12, items 9 and 13 read with item 8). The gates were not doorways and did not facilitate entry to the building as required by item 9. Nor were the works carried out for the primary purpose of facilitating a handicapped person's entry as was held to be required in *RNIB Properties Ltd* [1999] BVC 2,064.

Also, since the services, except those in relation to the fencing, were not supplied for a consideration, item 13 was not satisfied: the goods were not supplied in connection with any supply of services.

Bathrooms, washrooms and lavatories

In addition, the supply to a handicapped person of the provision, extension or adaptation of a bathroom, washroom or lavatory in his private residence, where such an installation was necessary because of his condition, is also zero-rated (VATA 1994, Sch. 8, Gp. 12, item 10).

Zero-rating applies to an extension or adaptation of a bathroom, washroom or lavatory for use by handicapped persons in a residential home where the installation is necessary (VATA 1994, Sch. 8, Gp. 12, item 11) or of a washroom or lavatory for use by handicapped persons in a building or part of a building used principally by a charity for charitable purposes where the installation is necessary (VATA 1994, Sch. 8, Gp. 12, item 12).

Unlike for washrooms and lavatories, zero-rating for new bathrooms is not available for all buildings used principally for charitable purposes. However, with effect from 1 April 2000, zero-rating for bathrooms installed to facilitate their use by the disabled was been extended beyond the old 'residential home' qualification to include:

- day centres where at least 20 per cent of the individuals using it are disabled, and
- residential homes or self-contained living accommodation (whether provided on a temporary or permanent basis or both), for example sheltered housing (but not hotels, boarding houses or similar establishments).

'Washroom' is defined as 'a room containing either or both a lavatory or wash basin but does not include a room containing a bath or a shower; or a room containing cooking, sleeping or laundry facilities.'

Other supplies connected with building alterations

Any preparatory work and 'making good' connected with qualifying alterations can also be zero-rated as is the supply of goods in connection with any of the alteration services under items 8–11 (VATA 1994, Sch. 8, Gp. 12, item 13).

Flather [1995] BVC 780 addressed the issue of whether materials were 'in connection with' the supply of construction services. The appellant was a 'handicapped person'. Customs unsuccessfully refused zero-rating on the supply of building materials to him by a builders' merchant. The materials were used in constructing ramps, passages, etc. designed to facilitate the appellant's access to and movement within his house. Two unregistered builders provided the construction services at the appellant's house. The Tribunal decided that:

- whether there had to be a connection between the supply of building materials and the supply of building works was one of fact. In this case there was a connection. There was no necessary implication in the wording of the item that the supply of goods should be by the same person as the supply of construction services, and
- Customs' argument that the supply of building services could only take place if made by registered persons was incorrect. 'Supply' was widely defined and included all forms of supply, such as taxable and non-taxable supplies.

Other construction works and professional services

Works unspecified in the above relief does not qualify for zero-rating even if the work is carried out solely to suit a person's disability.

Lifts and alarms

Zero-rating applies to vertical lifts and distress alarms supplied to handicapped persons for home use or to a charity caring for the handicapped (VATA 1994, Sch. 8 Gp. 12, items 16, 17 and 19 and note (9)).

Included in this zero-rating is the supply of:

- goods in connection with the supply of eligible lifts, and
- services necessarily performed by a control centre in receiving and responding to calls from an alarm system (Sch. 8, Gp. 12, items 18 and 20).

Distress alarm systems must be designed to be capable of operation by a disabled person to enable them to summon help. It does not include telephone lines, intercoms, intruder alarms, etc.

Lifts supplied to charities must be installed in a residence or day centre to qualify.

'Day centre' has its ordinary meaning and must be a facility provided for the disabled specifically and not for groups in general of which the disabled may form part (*Union of Students of the University of Warwick* [1996] BVC 4,236).

Zero-rating certificate

All the above reliefs are conditional on the customer issuing the appropriate certificate before the supply takes place. The format for these certificates is in Notice 701/7/02, paragraph 10.

Customs' publication

Official Customs Guidance Manual, Vol. 1–7, Ch. 12 and Notice 701/7 give Customs' views on reliefs for people with disabilities.

11.7.7   Anti-avoidance measures

Self-supply of building services

Where a person constructs a building, extends or alters a building, or constructs an annex to a building, and this is done in the course or further-ance of his business but without consideration, there is a self-supply of the services involved. This catches the situation where the building is constructed, altered or extended for the business's own use. However, the self-supply rule does not apply where the value of the work does not exceed £100,000. This limit applies to each separate project. In the case of an exten-sion, the rule does not apply unless the floor area of the building is increased by 10 per cent or more. In general, the rule does not apply if the work would have been zero-rated if carried out by a taxable person in the course of his business. Thus the rule applies mainly in relation to commercial buildings (Value Added Tax (Self-Supply of Construction Services) Order 1989 (SI 1989/472)). For this purpose, the value of any work is its open market value (Value Added Tax (Self-Supply of Construction Services) Order 1989 (SI 1989/472, reg. 4(1))).

The VAT payable on the self-supply is then available for set off as input tax under the normal rules. Thus there is a VAT burden only if the business makes exempt supplies. In such a case, if the value of the work exceeds £250,000, adjustments under the capital goods scheme may be required.

Time of supply of construction services.

The time of supply of certain services is the earliest of the following times:

- each time that a payment is received by the supplier;
- each time that the supplier issues a VAT invoice, or
- the date on which the services were performed.

The services covered by the above rule are services, or services supplied together with goods, which are supplied in the course of the construction, demolition, repair or maintenance of a building or any civil engineering work under a contract which provides for payment to be made periodically or from time to time (SI 1995/2518, reg. 93 as amended by SI 1997/2887).

The 'date on which the services were performed' tax point does not apply in all cases. It applies when 'exempt land' is occupied by someone who finances the work, the supplier of the construction services or someone connected with either. Whether persons are connected is determined in accordance with ICTA 1988, s. 839.

The newly constructed building or civil engineering work is 'exempt land' if used, or to be used, for purposes for which input tax is not recoverable, ie normally making exempt supplies or carrying on non-business activities. If the building/engineering work is occupied/used 'wholly or mainly' for purposes for which input tax is recoverable this tax point is not triggered.

A person finances the construction work when, directly or indirectly, he:

- provides finance for the cost of supplying the construction services,
- enters into any agreement, arrangement or understanding (whether or not legally enforceable) to provide finance for the construction services.

A supply of services is 'performed' when the services have been completed. For example, if a main contractor is engaged to construct a building, his services are normally treated as performed on the date of the architect's certificate of completion unless there is undue delay in the issue of the certificate, in which case the actual date of completion will need to be ascertained.

11.8   Building materials

The zero-rating or reduced-rating of construction services in relation to dwellings or buildings for relevant residential or relevant charitable use (see **11.7.2** and **11.7.3**) is extended to the supply of materials, builders' hardware, sanitary ware or other materials of a kind ordinarily incorporated by builders into the type of building concerned where the supply is made by the person providing the zero-rated or reduced-rate construction services (VATA 1994, Sch. 8, gp. 5 item 4; Sch. 7A, gp. 6, item 2, and gp. 7, item 2; Sch. 8, gp. 6, item 3). The same applies in relation to materials, etc. supplied for zero-rated civil engineering work on developing a permanent park for residential caravans (VATA 1994, Sch. 8, gp. 5 item 4).

Thus a contractor can zero-rate or reduce-rate the supply of 'building materials' when:

- he incorporates those goods in a building, and
- his service of 'incorporating' those goods is zero-rated or charged at the reduced-rate.

A contractor must charge VAT when he:

- supplies 'building materials' (or other goods) on their own without incorporating them in a building;

- incorporates 'building materials' in a building and cannot zero-rate or reduce rate the incorporation services; or
- incorporate in a building goods which are not 'building materials' (unless he can zero-rate or reduce rate the services of incorporating those goods under other rules) (see Notice 708).

As regards what is 'ordinarily incorporated by builders' into the type of building concerned, there is an old purchase tax case concerning the meaning of 'builders' hardware, sanitary ware and other articles of kinds ordinarily installed by builders as fixtures'. The court had to decide whether built-in dressing table units fell within this category or whether they constituted furniture. Stamp J held that the 'articles' referred to were 'articles which one would expect a builder to install as fixtures in the ordinary way without special instructions, because a builder when performing his function of building ordinarily installs them' (*F Austin (Leyton) v C&E Commrs* [1968] 2 All ER 13).

Regarding 'materials ordinarily incorporated', in Notice 708, Customs & Excise explains that it sees this term as encompassing goods attached to a building (or its site) that make up 'one whole' with the building. In addition to covering the obvious structure of, and fixtures to, a building it also covers installed fittings. Customs accepts that an item is 'incorporated' when it is fixed to a building, or its site, in such a way that its fixing or removal would either:

- require the use of tools, or
- result in either:

  the need for remedial work to the fabric of the building, or its site, or substantial damage to the goods themselves.

Customs holds the view that 'ordinarily incorporated' means that which in the ordinary course of events would normally be incorporated in the construction of a building of that generic type. In essence it means the 'norm' for, say, dwellings or churches or schools, etc. Customs does not split generic types of buildings into sub-categories and then conclude that the same item can be 'ordinarily incorporated' in one but not in the other. For example, no distinction is drawn between large detached houses and small terraced houses.

Customs takes the same approach when determining if the goods themselves are the 'norm' for that type of building. So, for example, a tap would be regarded as being 'ordinarily incorporated' whether it is chromium or gold plated.

Notice 708, provides some useful lists of materials and hardware which, in the opinion of Customs, do and do not qualify for zero or reduced rating, in an attempt to overcome previous problems of interpretation.

11.8.1   Builders' hardware

The following are generally recognised by Customs & Excise as builders' hardware ordinarily installed in dwellings or other relevant buildings so as to qualify for zero or reduced-rating:

- doors (unless forming a part of fitted furniture)
- window frames and glazing
- guttering
- letter boxes
- basins
- baths
- bidets
- lavatory bowls and cisterns
- immersion heaters, boilers, hot and cold water tanks
- fireplaces and surrounds
- shower units and fittings (but not shower curtains)
- kitchen sinks
- power points (including combination shaver points/lights but not light
- bulbs or tubes)
- radiators
- built-in heating appliances
- work surfaces or fitted cupboards in kitchens and/or utility rooms
- fixed towel rails, toilet roll holders, soap dishes, etc
- outside lights (providing they are standard fittings but not light bulbs or tubes)
- 'communal' TV aerials in blocks of flats, etc.
- fixed control units used by wardens in sheltered housing developments on warden call systems
- fixed independent switches for warden call systems
- most forms of ventilation; burglar alarms; fire alarms or fire safety
- equipment; waste disposal units in flats; emergency call systems; stair and chair lifts.

The following are examples of fixtures in buildings used for relevant charitable purposes (but not as dwellings or for relevant residential purposes) that would qualify for zero or reduced-rating:

Schools

- blackboards fixed to, or forming part of, walls
- gymnasium wall bars
- nameboards
- notice and display boards
- mirrors and barres (in ballet schools).

Churches

- altars
- church bells
- organs
- fonts
- lecterns
- pulpits
- amplification equipment
- humidifying plant.

General

- air conditioning
- central heating systems
- lighting systems (excluding non-fixed bulbs and tubes)
- fire and burglar alarm systems
- extractor fans and smoke detectors (where required to meet building regulations)
- blinds and shutters
- mirrors.

Conversely there are items of fitted furniture which do not rank as builders' hardware ordinarily installed as fixtures and so do not qualify for zero or reduced-rating. The following are examples indicated by Customs & Excise:

Domestic

- wardrobes
- bathroom cupboard units
- bookcases
- (airing cupboards, under-stair storage cupboards and cloaks/vestibule cupboards are not regarded as items of fitted furniture).

Commercial (this category also applies to *Schools*)
- desks and tables
- chairs and other seating.

Scientific/medical

- laboratory benches
- dental cabinetry.

Churches

- pews
- choir stalls
- clergy stalls.

Fitted furniture

As indicated above, the installation of fitted cupboards and work surfaces in kitchens is eligible for zero or reduced-rating. However, these reliefs are only available where such installation is carried out at the time of the construction of the dwelling. Any installation carried out subsequently is standard-rated, irrespective of whether such work is the fitting of additional units or replacement ones.

Difficulties have been encountered in relation to fitted wardrobes as to whether they constitute 'furniture' or form part of the fabric of the building. In the case of *C&E Commrs v McLean Homes Midland Ltd* [1993] BVC 99, it was held that built-in wardrobes formed by fitting doors across an end wall and two internal walls formed part of the was held that wardrobes constituted furniture. The wardrobes concerned included wardrobes which ran the entire length of a wall and wardrobes which included a side end. These wardrobes are described as elaborate, including several shelves and shoe racks. Customs' present position regarding built-in wardrobes is set out in Notice 708.

11.9 Other items installed in newly constructed dwellings

The supply of goods to a person constructing or altering a building is a taxable supply. The treatment of any onward supply by that person depends on the circumstances.

If the items become fixtures, then they become part of the building. Therefore if the person constructing or altering the building is merely a contractor, his supply is a taxable supply. If he is a developer and grants a major interest in the building, the grant of that interest is either zero-rated under Sch. 8, gp. 5 or exempt with a possible option for taxation.

If the grant of a major interest is zero-rated, then the related input tax is non-recoverable (Value Added Tax (Input Tax) Order 1992 (SI 1992/3222), reg. 6).

If the items do not become fixtures, then the grant of an interest in the building does not include the items concerned. A separate supply of those items will be made and that will be a taxable supply. If the consideration for that supply is not stated separately from the consideration for the grant of the interest, then the overall consideration has to be apportioned as the consideration for a composite supply *(C&E C v Automobile Association* (1974) 1 BVC 8).

The kind of goods likely to fall within the above rules are carpets, curtains, most fitted wardrobes, free-standing items of furniture such as beds, chairs, bookcases, sideboards, dining tables, some cupboards, dressing. The only cupboards and wardrobes which are regarded as forming part of the building are those formed using three walls, or two walls and a stub wall, where the walls are visible on opening the door (Notice 708).

11.10   The capital goods scheme

11.10.1   The purpose of the scheme

The purpose of the capital goods scheme is to adjust the initial calculation of the exempt proportion of input tax on the acquisition of certain assets in the light of changing use of those assets over a period of five or ten years, as described below. This period is known as the period of adjustment (SI 1995/ 2518, regs. 112–116). The scheme does not apply to any capital goods that were acquired or brought into use before 1 April 1990.

11.10.2   'Goods' subject to the scheme

Goods which are purchased for re-sale are not capital goods. The question of whether or not the goods are to be treated as capital goods is not necessarily governed by how they are treated for accounting purposes.

The capital goods affected by the scheme are:

(a)   computers and items of computer equipment where the value of the supply is £50,000 or more,

(b)   land and buildings (or parts of buildings) where the value of the supply is £250,000 or more.

As from 3 July 1997, the following further items are brought within the scheme:

(c)   civil engineering works constructed by the owner and first brought into use by him on or after 3 July 1997 where the value of taxable grants and supplies made to the owner relating to the land on which the work is constructed and the construction itself is not less than £250,000, and

(d)   any refurbishment by the owner where the capital expenditure on the refurbishment, including supplies of services and of any goods affixed to the building, is not less than £250,000, excluding the value of zero-rated supplies.

As regards (a), Customs & Excise has confirmed that the £50,000 limit applies to individual items of equipment, not to complete systems. Thus the application to computers is likely to be restricted mainly to mainframes and mini-computers.

As regards (b), freehold and leasehold interests in buildings, and extensions and alterations that increase the floor area of buildings by 10 per cent or more, are included. Costs incurred prior to 1 April 1990 will not, however, be taken into account in arriving at the total value. Also included in the scheme are self-supplies arising when, within ten years of completion of construction, either:

- a zero-rated building (other than a dwelling) is first used for a non-residential or non-charitable purpose (see **11.4.3** below and VATA 1994, Sch. 10, Para. 1(4) to (6)), *or*
- a commercial building is first subject to an exempt supply or first used by a person who is not fully taxable (see 11.4.8 below and VATA 1994, Sch. 10, Para. 5).

All capital costs involved in making the building ready for occupation should be included, such as professional and managerial services, demolition and site clearance, building and civil engineering contractors' services, materials used in the construction, security, equipment hire, haulage, landscaping, fitting out, including the value of any fixtures.

As regards alterations, the total value of all standard-rated goods and services supplied for, or in connection with, the alteration should be included, such as items mentioned in the previous paragraph. As regards (d), Customs & Excise has provided the following guidance on the meaning of 'goods affixed to a building':

> '"Goods affixed" should be given its everyday meaning. Goods should only be included in the value where they become part of the fabric of the building. In general terms, these are items that would be sold with the property and that are not portable or easily removed. "Goods affixed" does not include items secured for safety or security reasons or computers or computer equipment, which may be subject to the CGS in their own right.
>
> The following lists are intended to provide assistance in determining whether an item is likely to be considered to be "affixed", but please note these lists are not definitive and the deciding factor will be Common inclusions are materials to build internal and external walls, roofs and ceilings, floors and hard flooring. Also permanent partitioning, windows, lifts, "built in" storage such as cupboards or shelving, air conditioning, lighting and decorative features. This list is *not* exhaustive.

> Common exclusions are office furniture, storage unless it is "built in", carpets, computers and computer equipment and factory and office machinery. Again, this list is *not* exhaustive.'

Basically, expenditure is capital expenditure if it is treated as such for accounting purposes.

In considering whether the £250,000 limit is breached, and in calculating the adjustments, there must be included the value of rent payable more than 12 months in advance and rent invoiced for a period exceeding 12 months (SI 1997/1614, reg. 10 amending SI 1995/2518, reg. 113). As noted above, in calculating the value of refurbishment or fitting out work, only capital expenditure on services and 'goods affixed to the building' should be included, such as suspended ceilings and installed lighting.

The value of goods which do not become affixed to the building, such as office furniture, are excluded. However, some businesses have found it difficult or costly to identify the value of 'goods affixed' separately from the value of other goods which do not become affixed to the building.

Therefore Customs & Excise has decided to operate a concession as from 1 January 2000 to relieve the administrative and financial burden on businesses. (Notice 48 Extra-statutory Concession 3.22).

Under the concession, a business seeking to determine the value of a capital item can now include any additional amount of capital expenditure, over and above that incurred on supplies of services and goods affixed to the building, incurred in connection with the refurbishment or fitting out work. Therefore businesses no longer need to separate out the value of goods which are not affixed from the total value of capital expenditure on refurbishment or fitting out and can choose whether to include some or all of the goods not affixed to the building in the value of the capital item.

However, the inclusion of goods which are not fixed to the building may bring an item within the capital goods scheme by virtue of exceeding the scheme value threshold, where under the normal legal value it would not. Therefore, care is required in considering whether to make use of the concession.

This concession applies only to capital items where the adjustment period starts on or after 1 January 2000. Businesses wishing to include goods not affixed in the value of capital expenditure for items whose adjustment period started before 1 January should seek prior approval from their local VAT office.

In order to use this concession businesses must keep a record of the concessionary value of the capital expenditure including full details of the supplies on which the value was determined. The concessionary value must be used in calculating adjustments to the claimed input tax for the whole of the adjustment period.

If Customs considers that this concession is being used to avoid tax then it may withdraw or restrict its use.

11.10.3 The operation of the scheme

The basic principle of the scheme is as follows. A business will have to review the initial treatment of input tax incurred on computers and computer equipment over a five-year period, and on land and buildings over a ten-year period. However, if the interest in land has less than ten years to run at the time of acquisition, the adjustment period for that interest is five years.

(For simplicity this explanation is in terms of years at this stage, but the legislation is written in terms of 'intervals', which normally comprise single years.) An adjustment will arise where the business starts off wholly taxable and becomes wholly or partly exempt during the review period or, where it starts off wholly or partly exempt, if the extent of its input tax recovery varies during the period. An amendment to the Sixth Directive permits the adjustment period to be extended to 20 years.

Customs has said that businesses which are not partly exempt will not have to keep detailed records on the off chance that they might become so during the review period. If this happens, Customs will accept existing records as the basis for any future adjustment of input tax deductions.

11.10.4 Calculation of the input tax adjustment

The adjustment is carried out using the following calculation:

$$\frac{\text{Total input tax on capital item}}{\text{Number of years (ie 5 or 10)}} \times \text{The adjustment percentage}$$

The adjustment percentage is the percentage by which the use of the capital item in making taxable supplies increases or decreases in the later year by comparison with the initial year.

Example 11.4

Leonard Smith (Insurance Brokers) Ltd buy a freehold new office building for £4,000,000. Because their supplies are partly exempt, to a varying extent from year to year, their recovery of input tax in respect of the building will be along the following lines:

First year recovery percentage (say)	50%
Second year recovery percentage (say)	30%
Third year recovery percentage (say)	60%
Input tax charged on building in first year	£700,000
Period of adjustment	10 years

First year:

Input tax recovered, 50% of £700,000	£350,000

Second year:

Current recovery percentage	30%
Initial recovery percentage	50%
Adjustment percentage (downwards)	20%
Annual adjustment due *to* Customs & Excise:	

$$\text{Adjustment percentage} \times \frac{\text{Input tax on building}}{\text{Length of adjustment period}}$$

ie $20\% \times \dfrac{£700,000}{10}$	£14,000

Third year

Current recovery percentage	60%
Initial recovery percentage	50%
Adjustment percentage (upwards)	10%
Annual adjustment due *by* Customs & Excise:	

$10\% \times \dfrac{£700,000}{10}$	£7,000

and so on for years four to ten.

The additional liability or rebate has to be accounted for in the VAT return period following second next to the end of the interval to which it relates. Hence, where an interval is the year ended 31 May 1994 and returns are made quarterly, the adjustment should be accounted for in the VAT return for the quarter to 30 November 1994. The adjustment intervals will generally be periods ending with the taxable person's VAT tax year (normally ending 31 March, 30 April or 31 May) depending upon the cycle for the submission of VAT returns.

11.10.5 Transfer into or out of a group registration

Similarly, where, during the adjustment period, the owner becomes or ceases to be a member of a group registration, an adjustment interval ends on the date of the change and new intervals run for 12-month periods ending on successive anniversaries of that date (SI 1995/2518, reg.114(5A)(a), (b), (5B)).

11.10.6 Transfer of a going concern

Where, during the adjustment period, the owner transfers the item in the course of a transfer of a business as a going concern, an adjustment interval ends on the date of the change and new intervals run for 12-month periods ending on successive anniversaries of that date (SI 1995/2518, reg. 114(5A)(c), (5B)).

11.10.7 Records to be kept

The business needs to keep records to demonstrate its entitlement to input tax deductions and to show how its annual adjustments have been calculated. These records should include:

- a description of the item;
- the value of the item:
- the amount of input tax incurred on the item;
- the amount of input tax reclaimed;
- the start and end date of each interval in the adjustment period, including the first;
- when the adjustments are due, and
- the date and value of disposal, where the item is disposed of before the end of the adjustment period.

This information should be provided for any transferee of the item in the case of a going concern transfer or where the business leaves a group registration, and to the representative member of a group registration where the business joins a group registration.

Further information

For further information about this scheme see *The British VAT Reporter* and for Customs' understanding of the capital goods scheme see Notice 706/2.

11.10.8 Anti-avoidance provision

Adjustment on disposal

With effect from 3 July 1997, where an item within the capital goods scheme is sold during the period of adjustment, there is a clawback of input tax if the input tax recovered in previous accounting periods exceeds the output tax charged on the disposal, the amount of the clawback being equal to the excess. In any other case, the further input tax recovery is restricted so that the total recovered is equal to the output tax charged on the disposal (SI 1995/2518, reg. 115(3A), (3B)).

The adjustment on disposal does not apply:

- to sales of computer equipment;
- where the capital item is sold at a loss due to market conditions:
- where the value of the capital item has depreciated;
- where the value of the capital item has reduced for other legitimate reasons;
- where the amount of input tax on the sale is less than the input tax claimed due to a reduction in the VAT rate, and
- where the capital item is used only for taxable (including zero-rated) purposes throughout the adjustment period, including the final disposal.

11.11 Refund of tax to 'do-it-yourself' builders

11.11.1 General rules

Normally, credit for VAT suffered as input tax (see **11.1.5** above) is only available to a registered person where it is incurred in the course or furtherance of a business carried on by him. Exceptionally, however, VAT may be reclaimed on goods supplied to, or imported by, a person lawfully building a dwelling otherwise than in the course or furtherance of any business carried on by him. The goods must be used for the purpose of the construction of a building:

- designed as a dwelling or a number of dwellings, or
- for use solely for a relevant residential purpose or relevant charitable purpose (as to which, see **11.5.4**), or for a residential conversion.

The goods must be building materials which, in the course of the construction or conversion, are incorporated in the building or its site (VATA 1994, s. 35). The relief extends to a garage built at the same time as the house and intended to be occupied with it.

A residential conversion means the conversion of a non-residential building, or the non-residential part of a building, into a building:

- designed as a dwelling or a number of dwellings, or
- for use solely for a relevant residential purpose or relevant charitable purpose, or into part of a building which would fall within one of the above categories if that part were treated as a separate building (VATA 1994, s. 35(1D)).

11.11.2 Construction of building

Where an existing building is acquired with the intention of demolishing it and constructing a new building, it is essential that the old building be demolished in its entirety before the new building is constructed. In the case of *Mark Tinker v C&E Commrs* [2003] BVC 4,094, the taxpayer inherited a house that was in a poor state of repair. He demolished the kitchen and built a new kitchen and bathroom. Five years later, he demolished the rest of the original house and built new accommodation. The Tribunal held that he had not constructed a building. Note that construction does not include reconstruction (see **11.5.4** above). Note also that a building only ceases to be an existing building when it is demolished completely to ground level or when the part remaining above ground level consists of a single or double facade retained to comply with planning requirements (Sch. 8, gp. 5 note (18)).

11.11.3 Conversion to residential or charitable

The zero-rating of conversions in Sch. 8, gp. 5 items 1(b) and 3 (see **11.5.4** above) is subject to the restriction that if the conversion is of the non-residential part of a building which contains a residential part, then the conversion must create an additional dwelling or dwellings (note (9)). Where conversion works relate to both the residential part and the non-residential part, then the input tax has to be apportioned between the two. The Court of Appeal has indicated that this restriction would apply for the purposes of refunds under s. 35(1D) (*C&E Commrs v Blom-Cooper* [2003] BVC 415). In this case a pub with residential accommodation on the upper floors was converted to a single dwelling to be occupied by the appellants. The appellants applied for a refund of the VAT incurred on converting the bar, etc. to residential accommodation. Customs refused the claim on the grounds that the conversion was not within the scope of the DIY housebuilders and converters scheme. The Court of Appeal ruled in favour of Customs because the conversion did not create an additional dwelling. It decided that:

'. . . where, before conversion, the building already contained a residential part, the conversion of the non-residential part would not be treated as a conversion of a non-residential part of a building . . . unless the result of the conversion was to create an additional dwelling or dwellings'.

It has been held that erecting a new dwelling house abutting and immediately adjoining the claimant's existing house, with one wall of the old house forming a party wall between the two houses, but no direct access otherwise, could not properly be called an 'enlargement' of the old house. It therefore qualified for the relief (*T J Hill v C&E Commrs* BVC 1322). A claim was refused in the case of *Summer Institute of Linguistics Ltd* [2000] BVC 4005. In that case, the appellant ran residential courses on linguistics, literacy and literature. It constructed a building comprising a kitchen, two dining rooms capable of seating 300 people, a coffee lounge, a bookshop and sleeping accommodation for 39 people. It was held that the catering facilities constituted a business activity even though incidental to the appellant's charitable purpose. These facilities could not be ignored as *de minimis.* In the case of *James Halcro-Johnson v C&E Commrs* [2001] BVC 4,119, the Tribunal held that the refurbishment of an old croft did not qualify as a residential conversion, since the croft had been occupied by a tenant before April 1973. It did not matter that there was no central heating or sanitation prior to refurbishment.

As regards the construction of a building, regard must be had to the planning law requirements. In the case of *Allan Ivor Davidson v C&E Commrs* [2001] BVC 4,115, the tribunal refused a claim for a refund of VAT in relation to the construction of a building within the curtilage of an existing house. The building consisted of a double garage, together with a porch, lobby, shower and cloakroom on the ground floor, and a kitchen, living room and bedroom above. The original planning application was for the construction of the garage, but it was subsequently amended to include the other works. The Tribunal found that the planning consent which had been granted was not for a dwelling.

11.11.4 When to make the claim

The claim must be submitted within three months of completing of the building concerned. According to Customs a relevant building is 'complete' when

> '. . . it is "finished according to the original plans". In cases of doubt, a building can be regarded as under construction up until the date when a certificate of completion is issued by the local planning authority.'

Claims should be made within three months of completing the building using the proper forms. The forms are obtainable from the National Advice Service or may be downloaded from Customs & Excise's website.

Other documents to be forwarded with the claim are as follows:

- supporting calculations;
- the VAT invoices;
- evidence that the building is complete, usually a copy of the local authority completion certificate;
- a copy of the Planning Permission and, as applicable, listed building consent,
- plans of the building.

Late claims

Late claims are accepted solely at Customs' discretion.

See Notice 719 VAT refunds for 'do-it-yourself' builders and converters, VATA 1994, s. 35 and VAT Regulations 1995 (1995/2518), reg. 201.

12 Landfill tax

12.1 General principles

12.1.1 The charge to landfill tax

Landfill tax is charged on the disposal of material as waste at a landfill site on or after 1 October 1996 (FA 1996, s. 40).

Material is disposed of as waste if the person disposing of it intends to discard it. In the case of *C&E Commrs v Parkwood Landfill* [2002] BTC 8,008, the Court of Appeal held that material delivered by a local authority to a waste recycling company for use at its landfill site for road-making and landscaping purposes was not disposed of as waste. The fact that he or any other person could benefit from, or make use of, the waste is irrelevant. If material is disposed of on behalf of another person, whether at his request or under a contract, that other person is treated as making the disposal (FA 1996, s. 64).

The tax is charged whether the material is deposited on the surface of the site or under the surface, and whether or not it is placed in a container before being deposited. A landfill site can include land covered by water where it is above the low watermark of ordinary spring tides (FA 1996, s. 65).

A site is a landfill site if it is licensed as such under the Environmental Protection Act 1990 or the Pollution Control and Local Government Act (Northern Ireland) Order 1978 (FA 1996, s. 66).

12.1.2 Persons liable for landfill tax

The tax payable on material dumped at a landfill site is payable by the operator of that site which comprises or includes the land on or under which the material is dumped (FA 1996, s. 41). He is the person holding the licence under the legislation mentioned above, the waste disposal authority which occupies the site or the district council in Northern Ire land which passed the resolution in pursuance of the 1978 Regulations mentioned above (FA 1996, s. 67).

12.1.3 Rates of tax

The normal rate is £15 per tonne of waste disposed of as from 1 April 2004, with fractions of a tonne being charged proportionately. As from 1 April

1999, the rate was increased to £10 per tonne (FA 1999, s. 124). However, a reduced rate of £2 per tonne is charged on material, which consists entirely of the following (FA 1996, s. 42 and SI 1996/1528):

- **Group 1:** naturally occurring rocks and salts, including clay, sand, gravel, sandstone, limestone, crushed stone, china clay, construction stone, stone from the demolition of buildings or structures, slate, topsoil, peat silt and dredgings.
- **Group 2**: glass, ceramics and concrete materials.
- **Group 3**: processed or prepared minerals, but not used minerals – these comprise moulding sands, clays, mineral absorbents, man-made mineral fibres, silica, mica and mineral abrasives.
- **Group 4**: furnace slags, including vitrified wastes and residues from thermal processing of minerals where, in either case, the residue is both fused and insoluble, and slag from waste incineration.
- **Group 5:** bottom ash and fly ash from wood, coal or waste combustion, excluding fly ash from municipal, clinical and hazardous waste incinerators and sewage sludge incinerators.
- **Group 6:** low activity inorganic compounds, being titanium dioxide, calcium carbonate, magnesium oxide, magnesium hydroxide, iron oxide, ferric hydroxide, aluminium oxide, aluminium hydroxide and zirconium dioxide.
- **Group 7**: calcium sulphate disposed of either at site not licensed to take putrescible waste or in containment cell which takes only calcium sulphate – this includes gypsum and calcium sulphate based plasters but not plasterboard.
- **Group 8:** calcium hydroxide and brine deposited in a brine cavity.
- **Group 9:** water.

The reduced rate applies only if the owner of the material and the site operator produce a 'transfer note' giving a description of the material and that description falls within one or more of the above groups (reg. 6). A transfer note is a document completed and signed on behalf of the transferor and transferee giving the names and addresses of both parties and various particulars of the materials concerned (SI 1991/2839, reg. 2). It must accurately describe the waste so that it can be related to the terms used in the Landfill Tax (Qualifying Material) Order 1996 (SI 1996/1528). The waste transfer note may cover individual loads or it may be a 'season ticket' covering a number of loads sent for disposal to a site over a period of time.

In Northern Ireland, where waste transfer notes are not required under environmental law (until the Waste Management and Contaminated Land (Northern Ireland) Order comes into force) other commercial documentation should contain such a description.

12.1.4   Determination of weight of materials

The materials disposed of are to be weighed at the actual time of the disposal (SI 1996/1527, reg. 42).

Customs & Excise may specify rules for weighing the material and may specify different rules for different types of material (reg. 43). Customs & Excise is given power to agree with a site operator specific methods of weighing material. Such an agreement must be put in writing and Customs & Excise may bring it to an end if it considers that it has ceased to be appropriate (reg. 44).

12.1.5   Water content

If the weight of material is attributable, as to at least 25 per cent, to the addition of water, the weight of the added water is excluded from the charge to landfill tax. However, this exclusion does not apply to water occurring naturally unless the material is the residue from the treatment of effluent or sewage by a water treatment works. In other cases, water is excluded if it is added:

- for the purpose of facilitating the transportation of the material;
- for the purposes of extracting any mineral, or
- in the course of an industrial process.

If material can escape from the site by leaching, the water content is not excluded from the charge to tax unless the leaching is of water only or is collected and treated to remove harmful substances (reg. 44(5), (6)). The method of determination of the added water content must be agreed between the site operator and Customs & Excise.

12.1.6   Sites where there is no weighbridge

Customs & Excise has indicated that if there is no weighbridge at a landfill site one of the following methods should be considered for determining the weight of material disposed of (Notice LFT 1, paragraphs 4.2 and 4.3):

- The waste may be weighed at some other place prior to delivery at the landfill site. However, there must be a 'clear audit trail' including a record of weights for each vehicle, container, wagon, etc. and the waste must be taken directly from the weighing point to the landfill site.
- If a particular lorry, skip, container, etc. has a maximum allowable weight of material carried, it may be assumed that each such lorry, etc. is carrying the maximum permitted weight.

- The volume of waste may be measured and the weight calculated from that volume using conversion tables provided by Customs & Excise (see Annex A to Information Sheet 4/96). If the cubic capacity of the lorry, container, etc. is known, it can be assumed that each delivery is of a full load.
- Waste created by industrial processes may be determinable as a fraction of the raw materials used in the process.
- An annual survey of a landfill site may be carried out to calculate the quantity of waste dumped during the year.

Customs & Excise will consider other methods in particular cases.

12.1.7 Further information

Customs & Excise has published 'A General Guide to Landfill Tax', Notice LFT 1. This Notice may be obtained from the:

Landfill Tax Helpdesk
HM Customs & Excise
Dobson House
Regent Centre
Gosforth
Newcastle upon Tyne NE3 3PF.

Tel: 0645 128484 or Fax: 0645 129595.

Notices are also available from Custom & Excise's website.

12.2 Exemptions

12.2.1 Dredging, etc.

Materials removed from the bed of a river, canal, watercourse, dock or harbour are exempt from landfill tax. Materials projecting from such bed are also exempt (FA 1996, s. 43(1), (2)).

Materials removed from water falling within the approach to a harbour are exempt if removed in the interests of navigation. Materials projecting from such an approach are similarly exempt (FA 1996, s. 43(3)).

Finally, naturally occurring minerals which are removed from the sea in the course of commercial operations to extract sand, gravel and similar materials from the sea bed are exempt (FA 1996, s. 43(4)).

Notice LFT1 explains that, to qualify as a watercourse, a body of water must demonstrate all the following characteristics:

- a natural source of surface or underground water;
- a flow, under the action of gravity;
- a reasonably well defined channel of bed and banks, and
- a confluence with another watercourse or tidal waters.

12.2.2 Contaminated land

Sections 43A, 43B of FA 1996 provide for the exemption of materials removed from contaminated land which is being reclaimed for development, conservation, etc. or with the object of reducing pollution. The person carrying out the reclamation of the land must apply to Customs & Excise for a certificate to the effect that certain materials to be removed from the land, or a certain quantity of material are exempt from landfill tax. The conditions for the issue of a certificate are set out in detail in s. 43B. The certificate may be revoked, or its terms varied, by Customs & Excise.

The main requirement is that the reclamation is to be carried out with the object of:

- facilitating development, conservation, the provision of a public park or other amenity, or the use of the land for agriculture or forestry, or
- reducing or removing the potential of pollutants to cause harm (FA 1996, s. 43B(7)).

Once construction operations commence, any further materials removed from the site are taxable. Similarly, once the level of pollution has been reduced such that the potential for causing harm has been removed, any further materials removed are taxable (FA 1996, s. 43A(3)).

As from 1 October 1999, there is an exemption for the disposal of material which would otherwise qualify for the reduced rate of landfill tax where the site operator is restoring the site and is using the material in the restoration. Written notice must be given to Customs & Excise before the disposals occur. For this purpose, restoration means work required under a planning consent, a waste management licence or a resolution authorising the disposal of waste on or in land (FA 1996, s. 43C).

The following summary of the exemption is based on Landfill Tax Information Note 1.

'A disposal of waste is exempt if:

- the waste disposed of is qualifying material:
- the site operator has notified Customs & Excise in writing of the intention to commence restoration of the whole or a part of the site and provides Customs & Excise with such other relevant information as they may require;
- the disposal takes place after written notification has been given and the information has been provided; and
- the material is deposited on an area of the site which has been notified as being restored.

A Tax Free Area may be used to store material or sort material to obtain qualifying material for its subsequent use in restoring the site. For the purposes of the exemption, restoration is any work, other than the capping of the waste, which the planning consent, the waste management licence or a resolution authorising disposal of waste on or in the land require to be carried out after waste disposal operations, in order to restore the site to use. The exemption also does not apply to material used as daily cover nor to material used to engineer the site prior to the ceasing of waste disposal operations.

One of the conditions of the exemption is that the operator has notified Customs & Excise in writing of his intention to commence restoration of the whole or a part of the site and provided such information as they require.

The information that should always be included in any notification is as follows:

- the operator's Landfill Tax Registration number;
- the operator's registered address and landfill site address to which the application relates:
  - If more than one site then separate notifications should be completed for each site;
  - If more than one part of the same landfill site is to be restored at the same time, then a separate notification is required for each part;
- whether the notified landfill site is to be fully or partly restored;
- evidence that the operator is required to restore this landfill site, ie planning consent specifying the requirement to restore;
- in the case of a part restoration, an indication of which part of the site is being restored (eg cell 4) including a map showing its location (unless this has already been supplied for a previous notification for an earlier phase);
- an estimate of the total tonnage of material to restore the area included in your notification;
- the total of any material on site retained for this restoration, with details of the calculation of the weight of the total and on-site restoration material;

- evidence to demonstrate why the notified tonnage is required, including:
  - Waste management licence/working plan;
  - Plan of the area subject to this notification;
  - Correspondence with the environmental regulator;
  - Extracts from any tender/restoration contract.

- the date the restoration is expected to commence-this notification should not be made more than 6 months prior to commencement;
- an estimation of the time scale of this restoration project.'

As regards capping, Customs & Excise is aware that some planning consents, waste management licences or resolutions do not make a distinction between capping and restoration of the site. It may, for example, require the final layer of qualifying waste material to be deposited to be a specific depth and to be kept free of materials likely to interfere with final restoration or subsequent cultivation or development, and to be laid to a fall to encourage surface water run-off. The final process of restoration then simply consists of seeding. If this is the case, material which is imported after waste disposals have stopped and deposited on the site in order to make the land available for its final use (eg agriculture, forestry or development) will qualify for the exemption, provided that all the other conditions are met.

Customs & Excise's interpretation was upheld by the High Court in the case of C&E *Comrs v Ebbcliff* [2004] BTC 8,056.

12.2.3 Mining and quarrying

Certain waste material from mining and quarrying operations (whether deep mined or open cast) are exempt. The exempt materials are naturally occurring materials which are extracted in the course of the mining or quarrying operations. Materials which have been subjected to a process separate from those operations, or a process which permanently alters their chemical composition are taxable (FA 1996, s. 44).

There is an exemption for the disposal of materials which would otherwise qualify for the reduced rate of landfill tax where the site is a quarry (FA 1996, s. 44A). Two conditions must be satisfied.

The first is that the quarry is being filled in under the requirements of a planning consent. If the quarrying operations ceased before 1 October 1999, the planning requirement must also have been imposed before that date.

The second condition is that only materials that would otherwise qualify for the reduced rate of landfill tax must be permitted on the site. A licence that does not impose such a condition may be varied in order to meet this requirement. In such a case, it is treated as satisfying the requirement until the application is dealt with or, if earlier, the second anniversary of the application. An application is dealt with when it is accepted or withdrawn or, in the case of a refusal, when any appeal against the refusal is determined.

The following summary of the exemption is based on Landfill Tax Information Note 1.

'A disposal of waste is exempt if:

- the waste disposed of is qualifying material;
- the disposal takes place at a quarry;
- there is planning consent in place to fill (or partially fill) the quarry;

and

the waste management licence (or resolution) only authorises the disposal of qualifying material.

The term 'quarry' is not defined. Customs & Excise will take account of the definition in the Mines and Quarries Act 1954. Section 180(2) of that Act defines a quarry as:

"an excavation or system of excavations made for the purpose of, or in connection with, the getting of minerals (whether in their natural state or in solution or suspension) or products of minerals, being neither a mine nor merely a well or borehole or a well and borehole combined."

Customs & Excise therefore considers sand, gravel and clay pits, opencast coal and other surface mineral workings to be quarries for the purposes of this exemption.

If a quarry is active, that is minerals are being extracted, on or after 1 October 1999 then, so long as the requirements of the exemption are met, disposals of waste will qualify. For a quarry that is not yet at the stage of filling the void, neither the condition in the planning consent nor the condition in the waste management licence have to be in place on 1 October 1999 (they do of course have to be in place before any disposal that is made can be exempted).

Where a quarry was in existence before 1 October 1999, quarrying operations ceased before then and no planning consent requiring the filling of the quarry was in place by 30 September 1999, it will not be a qualifying site for the purposes of the exemption. However, because a review of mineral planning permissions will not have dealt with all old quarries by 1 October 1999, Customs & Excise will allow an old quarry listed for review to qualify for the exemption if the review imposes new restoration conditions which involve the infilling of the quarry with qualifying waste. This will only allow exemption of materials from the time that such new conditions are imposed, and if all the other conditions are met.

Customs & Excise is aware that many quarries taking only "qualifying material" may still have waste management licences that authorise the disposal of other wastes. Such licences may be treated as being ones which only authorise the disposal of qualifying material for the period between the making of an application for the amendment of the licence to authorise the disposal only of "qualifying material" and the final resolution of that application, subject to that period not exceeding two years.

An application for amendment of a licence is resolved if:

- it is granted;
- it is withdrawn;
- it is refused and there is no right of appeal against the refusal;
- a time limit for appeal against refusal expires without an appeal having been commenced; or
- an appeal against refusal is dismissed or withdrawn and there is no further right of appeal.

Where an application to alter the waste management licence has been made, disposals of material that were exempted from tax during the period between the making of the application and its resolution (or the two year period from the making of the application if that is the shorter period) remain exempt even if the application is unsuccessful. However, any disposals of material at the site after the end of that period will not qualify for exemption unless the application was granted.

Where an application is not resolved within two years but is ultimately granted, disposals made during the period between the end of the two years and the date on which the application is granted will not qualify for exemption.'

12.2.4 Pet cemeteries

The disposal of the remains of dead domestic pets at a site at which only such remains are deposited is exempt from landfill tax (FA 1996, s. 45). If other materials are deposited at the site, then the exemption is lost.

12.2.5 Temporary disposals

Materials which are deposited at a site temporarily, and which are to be recycled, reused, or sorted, pending removal to another site, are not charged to tax when they are deposited at the temporary site. They may be charged at a later time, depending on what happens to them (FA 1996, s. 46 and SI 1996 No. 1527, regs. 38–40).

They will not be charged at all if they are recycled, incinerated or reused, or if they are sorted pending disposal, or pending use at a place other than a landfill site or for site restoration purposes at the site where the disposal was made. However, they must be dealt with in one of the above ways within 12 months of being deposited at the temporary site. This period is extended to three years for sorting pending disposal. Customs & Excise has power to extend both periods (reg. 38).

Any waste which is not dealt with in one of the above ways within the 12-month period is chargeable to tax when it is disposed of elsewhere or at the end of the 12-month period whichever is the earlier time (reg. 40). The operator of the temporary disposal site must keep records of the materials to which these rules apply. If he fails to do so, the exemption for the materials concerned is lost.

Clearly, the exemption will cover the operations of waste paper recycling plants, incinerator plants, machinery for sorting and processing metal cans, glass bottles, etc.

The area in which these temporary disposals are made must be designated as a temporary disposal area. The designation is given in writing by Customs & Excise.

12.3   Credits

12.3.1   Permanent removals

Where a site operator has accounted for landfill tax on the disposal of material at a site, and the material is subsequently removed for recycling, incineration or reuse, or in response to a direction from a relevant authority, he may claim a credit for the tax payable on that material against tax payable for the accounting period in which the conditions for the credit are satisfied (SI 1996/1527, regs. 21, 17(a)).

As far as recycling, incineration or reuse are concerned, the requirement is that the material was disposed of with the intention that it would be recycled, etc. and that intention has actually been carried out with respect to some of the material. Clearly, if it had been deposited at a designated temporary disposal area, it would have been exempt when disposed of. The subsequent recycling, etc. must take place within 12 months of the disposal (five years where water has been added to it to facilitate disposal). As regards directions from relevant authorities, this applies where the disposal was made in breach of the terms of the licence or resolution authorising the use of the site.

Up to 22 March 2004, Customs & Excise took the view that material had to undergo a chemical change to be considered to have been recycled. As from that date, Customs will accept that if a material is processed, changing it to a usable material, the process does not have to change the material's chemical properties in order for it to be considered to have been recycled (Business Brief 10/04).

12.3.2 Bad debts

Where a site operator has accounted for and paid tax on an invoice issued to an unconnected person, and part of the amount due under the invoice is written off on the operator's accounts, a proportionate part of the tax shown in the invoice may be set off against the tax liability for the period in which the anniversary of the date of the invoice falls (regs. 23, 24, 17(b)). The site operator must retain a copy of the invoice, together with copies of records evidencing his accounting for and payment of the tax and records showing the amount written off. The claim for credit cannot be made before the anniversary of the date of the invoice.

The site operator must keep a separate landfill tax bad debt account and must record the write off of any tax charged but not collected in that account.

If there is more than one invoice outstanding from a particular debtor, any amount paid by the debtor is identified on a 'first in first out' basis (reg. 27).

If the site operator holds any security for an outstanding debt, the value of that security is effectively deemed to satisfy an equivalent amount of the debt (reg. 29(4)). Similarly, if the site operator has a money debt due to his debtor and this can be set off under general law, then it is treated as set off for landfill tax purposes (reg. 29(3)).

12.3.3 Environmental contributions

Where a registered site operator makes a contribution to an approved body for the purposes of reclamation or restoration of land, or to facilitate the economic, social or environmental use of the land, he may claim a credit for 90 per cent of the contribution (reg. 31).

However, the amount of credit must not exceed 6.8 per cent (6.5 per cent up to 31 March 2004 (SI 2004/769)) of the tax liability for the accounting period for which the credit is given and earlier periods within the same 'contribution year'. This limit applies as from 1 April 2003. The previous limit was 20 per cent.

The credit is given for the accounting period in which the contribution is made. However, a contribution can be related back to the previous period if it is made in the first accounting period of a contribution year, before the return for the previous accounting period is made and before the filing date for that return (reg. 31).

Contribution years originally started on anniversaries of the operator's date of registration under the landfill tax provisions. Therefore, a qualifying contribution can be made after the end of that year but not later than the filing date for the return for the last accounting period within that year, and related back to that year. There were special provisions dealing with changes of accounting period dates. As from 1 April 2003, contribution years run from 1 April to 31 March.

An 'approved body' is a body approved by a regulatory body approved by Customs & Excise for this purpose. The conditions for approval are set out in detail in reg. 33. The functions of the regulatory body are set out in reg. 34.

Further information will be found in section 10 of Notice LFT 1. To qualify for credit, a contribution must be made subject to the condition that it must be used only for the approved objects of the recipient body (reg. 32(1)).

The site operator must keep a record of the date and amount of the contribution and the name and enrolment number of the approved body (reg. 32(2)).

12.3.4 Claims for credit

A claim for credit may be made by deducting the amount claimed from the tax due for the accounting period concerned, in the return for that period or for any subsequent period (SI 1996/1527, reg. 19). As regards environmental contributions, the credit can be claimed in the return for the accounting period concerned or for any subsequent period within the same contribution year.

If the amount of credit exceeds the tax due for the accounting period concerned, the excess is repaid to the site operator by Customs & Excise (reg. 20(1)). If a claim arises after the operator has ceased to be registered, he must apply in writing to Customs & Excise for a refund, giving full details of the credit claimed (reg. 29(2), (3)).

No repayment will be made unless the site operator is up to date with his returns (reg. 20(5)).

Further information will be found in Notice LFT1, section 10.

12.4   Administration

12.4.1   Care and management

Landfill tax is under the care and management of the Commissioners of Customs & Excise. They are appointed by the Queen under Customs & Excise Management Act 1979, s.6, and the provisions of ss. 6–17 of that Act apply in relation to the administration of landfill tax as they apply in relation to the other taxes administered by Customs & Excise.

The provisions of ss. 138–171 and Sch. 3 of that Act (arrest of persons, forfeiture and legal proceedings and general powers) also apply in relation to the administration of landfill tax.

12.4.2   Registration

Any person who carries put taxable activities is liable to register with Customs & Excise. A person who intends to carry out taxable activities must notify Customs & Excise of his intention (FA 1996, s. 47). A taxable activity is a disposal in respect of which the person concerned is liable to landfill tax – whether it is a disposal by that person him, or a disposal by another person, on a site operated by him (FA 1996, s, 69).

Registration is effected by the completion and submission of Form 1 to Customs & Excise. If the operator has more than one site, then Form 2 should be completed. If the operator is a partnership, it should complete Form 3. In the case of a group registration, Form LT1A or Forms LT50 and LT51 should be completed as well as Form 1 or 2. Specimen forms are set out in the Schedule to SI 1996/1527.

Where a site operator ceases, or intends to cease, to carry out taxable activities, he must notify Customs & Excise accordingly, and in any event not later than 30 days after the date of cessation. Customs & Excise may then cancel his registration with effect from a specified date (s. 47(4), (6), (7) and reg. 6).

Site operators must report any change in the information contained in the registration forms within 30 days of the date on which the change occurs. Similarly if a site operator discovers an error or inaccuracy in that information, he must report that within 30 days of the date on which it was discovered (reg. 5).

12.4.3 Transfer of going concern

On the transfer of a business as a going concern, both parties may jointly apply to Customs & Excise on Form 4 to have the transferor's registration number transferred to the transferee on the occasion of the transfer (SI 1996/1527, reg. 7).

However, the transferee takes over responsibility for filing any outstanding returns and for accounting for any tax not accounted for by the transferor. Similarly, the transferee becomes entitled to any credit not given to the transferor. Therefore, this procedure is appropriate only in the case of intra-group transfers and other transfers under common ownership.

12.4.4 Returns and payment of tax

A site operator must file a return for each 'accounting period' by the end of the month following the end of that period. Customs & Excise will prescribe the quarterly periods for which his returns must be made. Returns must be made on Form 5 and sent to the Controller, Central Collection Unit (LT) (SI 1996/1527, regs. 11, 2(1)).

The landfill tax for any accounting period is due and payable on the due date for filing the return for that period (reg. 15). Interest on tax paid late runs from the due date until the date of payment (FA 1996, Sch. 5, Para. 27). However if the site operator is entitled to a repayment, that may be set off against the outstanding liability (reg. 45). The rate of interest will be determined by Regulations (FA 1996, s. 197(2)(d)).

Where an invoice for landfill tax is issued within 14 days of the date on which the material to which it relates was disposed of, the date of disposal of that material is deemed to be the date of the invoice. This affects the accounting period for which the tax is due. However, the site operator may elect that the actual date of disposal be taken instead of the invoice date (FA 1996, s. 61(1)).

The site operator may request that a period greater than 14 days be adopted either for all disposals or for certain disposals. If Customs & Excise specifies a longer period, then the date of disposal is the date of the invoice as long as the invoice is issued within that longer period (s. 61(3)).

The contents of a landfill tax invoice are set out in detail in reg. 37.

12.4.5   Repayment of tax: unjust enrichment

Regulations came into force on 11 February 1998 restricting the repayment of landfill tax charged incorrectly where the site operator is not able to pass on the refund to the customer, and requiring any amount which is repaid but not passed on to be returned to Customs (SI 1998/61). The requirements which have to be satisfied by the site operator will now be found in the Landfill Tax Regulations 1996 (SI 1996/1527, regs. 14A–14H).

The full amount recovered from Customs must be reimbursed to the customer in cash or by cheque within 90 days after the repayment is made, together with any interest thereon. Any amount not reimbursed within the 90-day time limit must be returned to Customs within a further 14 days (regs. 14C, 14D).

The site operator must keep records of the customers reimbursed and the amount reimbursed (reg. 14E), and must give undertakings to Customs at the time the claim for repayment is made to the effect that he will comply with the above requirements (reg. 14G). These records must be produced to Customs in accordance with a written notice given by it (reg.14F).

12.4.6   Assessments, appeals and the review procedure

If a site operator fails to make a return or makes a return that Customs believes to be incorrect, it may raise an assessment on him to the best of its judgement (FA 1996, s. 50(1)). There is a similar power where Customs believes that the operator has obtained a credit to which he was not entitled (s. 50(2)).

Any assessment must be made within two years after the end of the accounting period to which it relates, or within one year after the facts or evidence come to the knowledge of Customs, whichever is the later date (s. 50(5)). A further assessment may be made if further facts come to light.

The site operator may give notice to Customs to review its decision to raise an assessment. Such notice must be given within 45 days of the date of the assessment. The operator may then appeal to the VAT and Duties Tribunal against the decision of Customs on the review (ss. 54, 55 and 70(1)). However, the appeal may not proceed unless he pays the disputed tax or shows that he cannot do so without suffering hardship (s. 55(3)). The review, and subsequently the appeal, procedure is available for any of the following decisions:

- to register or cancel a registration;
- as to whether tax is chargeable in respect of a disposal or as to how much tax is chargeable;

- to refuse an application for a contaminated land certificate;
- to withdraw a contaminated land certificate;
- to limit a contaminated land certificate to only part of the land covered by your application;
- as to whether the operator is entitled to a credit of tax or how much any credit should be;
- to raise an assessment of underdeclared tax due and the amount of such an assessment;
- to refuse an application for a divisional registration;
- to refuse an application for a group registration;
- as to whether an operator has met the conditions laid out in a special method for calculating weight;
- to withdraw a special method for calculating weight;
- to refuse a claim for repayment of tax;
- as to an operator's liability to, or the amount of, any civil penalty;
- as to liability to pay, or the amount of, any interest or penalty interest;
- to require an operator, as a condition of trading, to give security for the payment of landfill tax,
- as to Customs & Excise's liability to pay interest or the amount payable.

Appeals may be settled by agreement before the date on which they would otherwise be heard by the Tribunal (s. 56(8)).

An appeal to the courts from the Tribunal may be made on a point of law (Tribunals and Inquiries Act 1992, s. 11 and SI 1998/3132, ord. 94, r. 8).

12.5 Secondary liability

12.5.1 Liability of site controller

Where Customs & Excise assesses an amount of landfill tax as due from an operator under FA 1996, s. 50 it may also impose liability on a controller for all or part of this amount (FA 1996, Sch.5, Para. 52). This secondary liability for landfill tax may be imposed on the controller of a landfill site in respect of taxable landfill disposals made on or after 28 July 2000. The conditions for imposing liability on controller are that:

- there is a taxable disposal at a landfill site;
- the operator operates under a site licence, a disposal licence (Northern Ireland) or a waste management licence (Northern Ireland), and
- a person other than the operator of the site is the controller of all or part of the site (FA 1996, Para. 49).

This secondary liability arises only after notice is given to the controller or reasonable steps are taken to draw the notice to his attention. In either case, there is a two-year time limit from the end of the operator's accounting period (FA 1996, Para. 51). However, in cases where a controller is liable to pay an amount of landfill tax or interest and Customs & Excise has not been notified under Para. 60 that there was a controller (see below), the time limit is extended from two to 20 years (FA 1996, Para. 61). Some guidance is given in Landfill Tax Briefing, 7 August 2000, issued by Customs & Excise.

12.5.2   Controller

A 'controller' is a person who, at a given time, determines or is entitled to determine what materials are disposed of at a landfill site, or part of a landfill site. However, a person is not a controller if he is purely acting as an agent or employee of someone else (FA 1996, Para. 48).

12.5.3   Notice to Customs & Excise

Where a person is currently, or later becomes, a controller, or ceases to be a controller, both the operator of the site and the controller are obliged to notify Customs & Excise of the fact within 30 days (FA 1996, Para. 60). A penalty of £250 may be imposed on each person who fails to comply, subject to mitigation.

12.5.4   Basis of liability of controller

The controller is liable to pay tax in relation to the weight of taxable disposals made on that part of the land that he controls (FA 1996, Para. 49). The time of disposal is the actual time of the deposit of the waste, not the time that would otherwise have applied (see **12.4.4**).

Where a controller is liable to pay an amount of landfill tax and, for the particular accounting period in question, the operator is entitled to credit as explained at **12.3.1**, the controller's liability is reduced by a fraction A/G of that credit, where:

- A is the tax for which the controller is primarily liable, and
- G is the operator's gross liability,

for the period concerned (FA 1996, Para. 50).

The controller must pay the amount due within 30 days of the notice being given (FA 1996, Para. 51(4)).

A controller is not carrying out taxable activities as such, and therefore does not need to register and render returns (FA 1996, Para. 56). However, he may still be required to do so if he is the holder of a waste disposal licence for another site of his own.

12.5.5   Withdrawal or reduction of assessment, etc

Where Customs & Excise has determined that the controller should be liable for an amount of tax assessed as due from an operator and subsequently withdraws or reduces the original assessment, the liability of a controller may be cancelled or reduced as well (FA 1996, Para. 53(2)–(6)). Where the controller has already been given notice of the liability, he must be given notice of the reduced amount within 30 days of the decision to reduce his liability. Where he has not already been given notice, he will have to pay the reduced amount if he is given notice within two years of the Commissioners' decision. Customs & Excise must give notice within 30 days of a decision to cancel the controller's liability.

Where there is an adjustment of the operator's liability other than in respect of assessments under FA 1996, s. 50 and credit, and Customs & Excise considers it just and equitable, the controller is liable to pay, or is entitled to an allowance for, all or part of an adjustment (FA 1996, Para. 54). Where he is to be liable, notice must be given to him within two years of the accounting period of the operator in which the adjustment was taken into account. The controller must pay within 30 days of notice being given. Customs & Excise may determine how the controller should benefit from an allowance it considers he should have.

12.5.6   Joint and several liability

In certain circumstances, an operator of a landfill site and the controller are jointly and severally liable for tax arising from disposals at the site concerned (FA 1996, Para. 57). However, the amount that can be recovered from the controller is limited to the controller's 'secondary liability'.

12.5.7   Interest on overdue tax

Where a controller is liable for an amount of tax with the operator and that amount carries interest the controller is jointly and severally liable to pay the interest (FA 1996, Para. 58). The amount of interest which the controller has to pay is found by applying the fraction S/P to the sum $I - A - B$, where:

- S is the secondary liability;
- P is the primary liability;
- I is the total amount of the interest;

- *A* is interest for the period from the date from which interest runs to the date on which the controller becomes liable to pay, ie interest for the period before the controller became liable is excluded, and
- *B* is interest for any day falling after the date on which the secondary liability is met in full.

In other words, $I - A - B$ is the interest attributable to the period for which the controller is liable.

A controller only has to pay this amount if a notice is served on him or other reasonable steps are taken to notify him of the amount, and such action must take place within two years of the date on which the total interest in question ceased to accrue. The amount is payable within 30 days of notice being given, subject to the same power of mitigation as applies in relation to interest payable by the operator.

12.5.8   Review procedure

The review and appeals procedures for landfill tax are extended to cover decisions by Customs & Excise that affect controllers (FA 1996, Para. 59). These decisions are:

- that a person is a controller;
- that a person is liable to pay any amount under these new provisions (including interest, and penalties under FA 1996, Para. 60);
- that a controller is not entitled to an allowance under FA 1996, Para. 54, and
- those as to the amounts of any liability or allowance.

12.6   Enforcement

12.6.1   Keeping of records

Site operators are required to keep the following records for a period of six years:

1. Landfill tax account. The site operator must keep a landfill tax account. This is the quarterly summary of total landfill tax due, detailing any credits of tax and any adjustments.

2. Temporary disposal account. If the operator is approved to operate a tax-free area he will need to keep a temporary disposal account which includes:

    - the dates on which waste was accepted into the area;
    - the weight and description of waste;

- the reason it is being accepted;
- the dates waste or material left the area;
- the actual destination it went to;
- the weight and description of waste or material removed,
- the qualifying use it is to be put to.

3. Record of credits. If a credit is claimed for tax on waste removed on instructions from the environmental regulator because its presence breaches the licence the operator should keep a copy of the direction as evidence for the claim.

   The operator can also claim credits of tax for waste removed for reuse (but not for reuse at a landfill site), recycling or incineration. However, he must have notified the local landfill tax officer in writing of his intentions when the waste was originally disposed of to landfill. If this has not happened then credit cannot be claimed.

4. Where credit is claimed, a removal account for wastes permanently removed must be kept, showing the weight and type of waste removed, to whom it was transferred and the qualifying use it is to be put to. This should be cross-referenced to the original disposal and the original tax paid.

5. Bad debt relief account showing:

   - the amount of tax charged;
   - the return in which that tax was accounted for and when it was paid;
   - the date and identifying number of the landfill invoice that was issued;
   - any payment or other consideration received, whether before or after the claim;
   - the details of any waste transfer note;
   - the outstanding amount;
   - the amount of the claim,
   - the return in which the claim was made.

   If payment from the customer is received subsequently, the credit must be repaid.

6. Details of contributions to environmental bodies, including the body's name, enrolment number, address and the amount of the contribution. Evidence is required that the contribution was conditional upon the environmental body using the money for an approved purpose.

7. Copies of all invoices and other accounting documents.

8. Records of special schemes used.

9. Sites not using weighbridges. A condition applying to all alternative methods is the need to record, for each disposal of waste, any identifying

number and the type of conveyance used to bring the waste to the land-fill site. In the case, for example, of a lorry, this would include its registration number and type (its maximum 'plated' weight – eg a ten tonner – and the number of axles). If a volume to weight conversion is used, then its cubic capacity should also be recorded.

10. Other records:
   - business and accounting records;
   - waste transfer notes and other records of materials brought on to or removed from the landfill site;
   - all credit or debit notes, and similar documents, issued or received;
   - if applicable, site surveys and chemists' analyses of wastes received for disposal;
   - any other documents required by this notice or any other notice published by Customs & Excise;
   - a record showing the total tonnage of waste accepted for landfill disposal, with separate entries for standard-rated, lower-rated and exempt wastes,
   - if applicable, a record of loads accepted under each authorisation to receive exempted waste from contaminated land.

The above records may be kept in hard copy, microfilm or microfiche, provided that copies can be easily produced and there are adequate facilities to allow Customs & Excise to view them when required. Records may also be kept on computer, for example, on a magnetic tape or disc, provided that they can be readily converted into a legible form and made available to Customs & Excise on request. If records are kept on computer, Customs & Excise will, by arrangement, require access to the computer to check its operation, processing, and the information held. The agreement of Customs & Excise must be obtained before any method of information storage other than hard copy is used. If a computer bureau or any other body (eg a bookkeeping company) is used to keep records then the operator remains responsible for what it does on his behalf. (SI 1996/1527, reg. 16 and Notice LFT 1, s. 13.)

Inspection of records and documents

Any person acting under the authority of Customs & Excise may require a site operator to produce the above records and documents for inspection. Such authorised person may also inspect the records of any other person concerned with landfill disposal (FA 1996, Sch. 5, Para. 3 and s. 70(1)). He may remove the documents and take copies of them. He may also enter and inspect premises used in connection with the carrying on of a business (FA 1996, Sch. 5, Para. 4).

If Customs & Excise has reasonable grounds for believing that serious fraud is being committed or is about to be committed, it may apply to a Justice of the Peace (a Justice in Scotland) for a warrant authorising its officers to enter and search premises and remove any documents which it believes may be required as evidence in any proceedings (FA 1996, Para. 5).

Customs & Excise must, on request, provide the occupier of the premises with a record of the documents removed (FA 1996, Para. 8). The occupier may require access to such documents and may take copies of them.

12.6.2 Recovery of landfill tax

Landfill tax is recovered as a debt due to the Crown (FA 1996, Sch. 5, Para. 11). If any person refuses to pay the tax by the due date, the Collector may distrain on his goods and chattels (SI 1996/1527 reg. 48). He is then liable for the costs of the distraint action.

In Scotland, Customs & Excise may apply to the sheriff for a warrant to authorise a sheriff officer to recover the outstanding amount (reg. 49). In an insolvency, landfill tax referable to the period of six months next before the relevant date is a preferential debt (Insolvency Act 1986, Sch. 6, Para. 3B and Bankruptcy (Scotland) Act 1985, Sch. 3, Para. 2(1B)).

12.6.3 Civil penalties

The penalty for tax evasion arising from conduct involving dishonesty is 100 per cent of the tax evaded, subject to mitigation by Customs & Excise or, on appeal, by the Tribunal (FA 1996, Sch. 5, Paras 18 and 25).

If tax is evaded by a company and the dishonest conduct is attributable to the dishonesty of a director, Customs & Excise may impose the penalty on the director (FA 1996, Para. 19).

Evasion may be perpetrated by an omission to take action (eg omission to register or failure to make a return) as well as by an action (eg knowingly making an incorrect return) (FA 1996, Sch. 5, Para. 18(1)). The penalty for misdeclaration in a return is 5 per cent of the amount by which the liability is understated, subject to mitigation as above (FA 1996, Paras 20 and 25). However, if the site operator corrects the error by entering the underdeclaration in the return for the period in which he discovers it, he is not liable for the penalty. Only errors of up to £2,000 may be corrected in this way (reg. 13). If the error exceeds £2,000, the site operator must write to Customs & Excise giving it the correct figures.

The penalty for failure to register is £250 or 5 per cent of any unpaid tax, whichever is greater.

12.6.4 Criminal penalties

Fraudulent evasion of landfill tax is a criminal offence as is the deliberate production of false documents or information. On summary conviction, the guilty person may be liable for a term of imprisonment not exceeding six months or a fine not exceeding the statutory maximum or three times the tax, whichever is greater, or both. On conviction on indictment, the term of imprisonment is up to seven years and the fine is at the discretion of the court (FA 1996, Sch. 5, Paras. 5, 15 and 16). These matters are spelled out in more detail in Paras. 15 and 16.

Where a criminal penalty is imposed for any offence, no civil penalty is imposed for the same offence.

12.7 Impact on direct taxes

12.7.1 Treatment of landfill tax

Where a site operator is a company, its activities as such will constitute a trade.

If the operator adds landfill tax to its invoices, then the trading receipts will be the invoice price exclusive of landfill tax and the tax itself will not be a deductible expense. In this respect, it will be treated in the same way as output VAT.

As far as the customer is concerned, the cost of disposing of its waste will include the landfill tax. The inclusive amount will be allowed as a trading expense or not on normal Case I principles.

If the site operator does not add landfill tax, then its invoice prices will be inclusive of the landfill tax which it will have to pay. Therefore, either:

(a)   the turnover exclusive of landfill tax, and the tax itself, will have to be calculated from the invoice and dealt with as above, or

(b)   the gross turnover will be shown in the accounts and the landfill tax dealt with as an expense.

Tax Bulletin, Issue 23 indicates that no adjustment to any proper accounting treatment is required for tax purposes, ie the landfill tax is an allowable deduction in (b).

12.7.2   Treatment of contributions to approved bodies

If a contribution is made wholly and exclusively for the purposes of the site operator's trade, it will qualify for relief as a trading expense under normal Case I principles.

If the 'wholly and exclusively' test is not satisfied, but the approved body is a charity, then the contribution may be paid under deduction of income tax at the basic rate, in accordance with ICTA 1988, s. 339(3), so that relief may be claimed for the payment as a 'charge' under ICTA 1988, s. 338(2)(b). Where this happens, it is considered that 90 per cent of the gross amount qualifies for landfill tax relief, since the income tax is simply deducted out of the payment on the making of that payment.

13　Aggregates Levy

13.1　General principles

13.1.1　The charge to aggregates levy

Aggregates levy is charged on the 'commercial exploitation' of 'taxable aggregates' in the UK on or after 1 April 2002 in the course or furtherance of a business (FA 2001, s. 16, 19(3)(a) and Business Brief 17/01). The levy is under the control and Management of Customs & Excise (s. 16(5)). Liability to the levy arises when the aggregate is subjected to commercial exploitation.

Aggregates means rock, gravel or sand, together with whatever substances are for the time being incorporated therein or naturally occur mixed therein. All such aggregates are taxable unless covered by an exemption (FA 2001, s. 17 – see **13.3** below regarding exemptions).

Commercial exploitation of a quantity of aggregate means:

- removing it from a site to which it has been removed for the purposes of having an exempt process applied to it;
- extracting the aggregate from an originating site;
- removing it from a site registered under the name of the operator of the originating site;
- making an agreement to supply it to any person;
- using it for construction purposes, or
- mixing it, otherwise in permitted circumstances, with any material or substance other than water,

(FA 2001, s. 19).

The following 'exploitations' are not taxable:

- the transfer of aggregate from one site to another registered in the name of the same person;
- the removal of aggregate to a registered site for the purpose of having an exempt process applied to it;
- the removal of aggregate to premises for the purposes of having china clay or ball clay extracted or otherwise separated from it on that site, and

- exploitation which results in the aggregate again becoming part of the land from which it was extracted, providing the exploitation does not involve mixing with any substance other than water,

(FA 2001, s.19).

13.1.2 Further information

Customs & Excise has published *A General Guide to Aggregates Levy*. This may be obtained from Customs & Excise's website.

13.2 Calculation of liability

13.2.1 Rate of tax

The rate is £1.60 per tonne of aggregates subjected to commercial exploitation, with a proportionate reduction for part of a tonne (FA 2001, s. 16(4)).

13.2.2 Determination of weight of materials

The weight of material is to be determined by the use of a weighbridge at the originating site or other registered site. The terms and conditions relating to the use of a weighbridge are set out in a Notice (FA 2001, s. 23 and SI 2002/761, regs. 4, 5).

In the case of a site where there is no weighbridge it will be necessary to contact Customs & Excise to agree an appropriate method of calculating the weight of aggregates.

If taxable aggregate is mixed with other materials it will be necessary to agree a method of calculating the weight of the taxable aggregate with Customs & Excise (see General Guide paragraph 11.4).

13.2.3 Northern Ireland: transitional provisions

The levy is being phased in over a five-year period for aggregate used in Northern Ireland in the manufacture of the following products:

- concrete (whether pre-cast, ready-mix or prepared on site);
- mortar;

- asphalt (whether delivered pre-mixed or mixed on site, eg slurry seal);
- coated roadstone and coated chippings,
- surface dressing (where dry aggregate chippings are rolled into bitumen on site in Northern Ireland),

(FA 2001, s. 30A).

The entitlement to relief is not affected by the origin of the aggregate, or the ultimate destination of products manufactured, so long as they are manufactured in Northern Ireland. This means, for example, that UK mainland businesses will be able to claim relief from the levy on aggregates they supply to customers making processed products in Northern Ireland, provided that they have the appropriate evidence. The following table sets out the phasing-in rates of levy.

Year	*Phasing*	*Levy per tonne**
1 April 2003 to 31 March 2004	20%	£0.32
1 April 2004 to 31 March 2005	40%	£0.64
1 April 2005 to 31 March 2006	60%	£0.96
1 April 2006 to 31 March 2007	80%	£1.28
1 April 2007 to 31 March 2008 and subsequent years	100%	£1.60

*assuming a normal rate of £1.60 per tonne.

Aggregate that is not used for the manufacture of processed products will be liable to the full rate of levy in Northern Ireland. Similarly, aggregate shipped in its natural state from Northern Ireland to elsewhere in the UK will be liable to the full levy.

13.3 Exempt aggregates and processes

13.3.1 Exempt aggregates

The following are exempt:

‘

(a) [deleted];

(b) aggregate removed from the site of a building or proposed building in connection with the erection or modification of the building or exclusively for the purpose of laying foundations for the building or of laying any pipe or cable;

(c) aggregate removed from the bed of a river, canal or watercourse, bed of a channel in, or approach to, a port or harbour;

(d) aggregate removed in the course of dredging undertaken exclusively for the purpose of creating, restoring, improving or maintaining a river, canal, etc. in (c);

(e) aggregate removed from the ground along the line or proposed line of a highway or proposed highway for the purpose of constructing, improving or maintaining that highway;

(f) spoil, waste or other by-products resulting from the extraction or separation from any aggregate of china clay or ball clay;

(g) coal, lignite, slate or shale;

(h) [deleted];

(i) the spoil or waste from, or other by-products of, any industrial combustion process or the smelting or refining of metal;

(j) the drill-cuttings resulting from operations carried out under a licence granted under the Petroleum Act 1998, other than in relation to petroleum situated in the strata in Great Britain;

(k) anything resulting from works carried out in exercise of powers under the New Roads and Street Works Act 1991, etc.;

(l) clay, soil or vegetable or other organic matter;

(FA 2001, s. 17(3)).'

13.3.2 Exempt processes

The following processes are exempt from aggregates levy:

- the cutting of any rock to produce dimension stone;
- any process by which a 'relevant substance' is extracted or separated from any aggregate,
- any process for the production of lime or cement from limestone or from limestone and some other substance.

Customs & Excise has produced the following annotated schedule of 'relevant substances':

British Geological Survey Definitions apply.

Anhydrite An anhydrous form of calcium sulphate, which in nature occurs as beds up to a few metres thick. It is commonly associated with gypsum and is mainly used in the manufacture of cement.

Ball Clay

Fine-grained, highly plastic sedimentary clay, which fires to a light or near white colour and is used in the manufacture of ceramic whiteware. The clay mineral kaolinite is the key component.

Barytes

A common commercial term for the mineral barite (barium sulphate). It is the main source of the element barium but is much widely valued for its high density where it is used as a weighting agent in the oil and gas drilling industry.

China Clay

China clay, or kaolin as it is more widely known internationally, is commercial clay composed principally of the hydrated aluminosilicate clay mineral kaolinite. It exhibits a marked whiteness in its natural state and is mainly used in the manufacture of paper, but also paint, rubber, plastics and ceramics.

Feldspar

The most abundant of all rock forming minerals found widely distributed in a range of sedimentary, metamorphic and particularly igneous rocks. The main industrial uses of feldspar are in glassmaking and ceramics manufacture.

Fireclay

Sedimentary clays that occur as the seatearths, or fossil soils, which underlie almost all coal seams. Originally valued as refractory raw materials they are now used mainly in the manufacture of buff coloured facing bricks.

Fluorspar

A common commercial term for the mineral fluorite (calcium fluoride), the only major source of the element fluorine. It is used mainly in the manufacture of hydrofluoric acid, which is the feedstock for the production of a wide range of fluorine-bearing chemicals.

Fullers Earth

A sedimentary clay containing a high proportion of clay minerals of the smectite group, mainly calcium-smectite. The smectite minerals have an unusual combination of properties on which their industrial applications are based. Calcium smectite may be easily converted to sodium smectite, or bentonite by a simple sodium exchange process which has a wide range of industrial applications including paper manufacture,

847

as a bonding agent for foundry sands and for civil engineering applications.

Gems and semi-precious stones
Any mineral or rock, or natural material (including some organic materials, for example amber) which, when cut and polished, has sufficient beauty and durability for use as a personal adornment or other ornament.

Gypsum
A hydrated form of calcium sulphate which Commonly occurs as beds and bands of nodules up to a few metres thick. Used mainly in the manufacture of plaster, plasterboard and cement.

Metal ore
Any material, natural or processed, from which a metallic element is, or could be, commercially extracted.

Muscovite
A light coloured member of the mica group of rock-rockforming silicate minerals that are characterised by a strong basal cleavage due to the layer lattice structure. This cleavage allows the natural crystals to be split into very thin flexible plates. Sheet muscovite is used in the electrical and electronics industries and ground mica is used as a filler in a range of industries.

Perlite
Commercial perlite is a siliceous, glassy igneous rock, which on rapid heating to a suitable point in its softening range expands to form a useful lightweight cellular product. It is a valuable thermal and acoustic insulator, but has a number of other applications

Potash
Potash is a generic term for a variety of potassium-bearing minerals and refined products. Sylvine (potassium chloride) is the principle source of potash and is used mainly in the manufacture of fertilisers.

Pumice
A highly vesicular, glassy volcanic rock. Its cellular nature gives it a low density such that it can float on water. It is valued for its lightweight and insulating ability.

Rock Phosphate
Rock phosphate, or more commonly 'phosphate rock' is the term used to describe a naturally occurring material containing one or more phosphate minerals

and with a chemical composition suitable for commercial use, primarily as a fertiliser.

Sodium Chloride   Salt occurs in nature in the solid state as beds of halite, or rock salt, and in solution as brine. Rock salt is mined underground, mainly for de-icing roads, and brine is produced by controlled brine pumping for use in the manufacture of chemicals and white salt.

Talc   A hydrated magnesium silicate with a soft and greasy feel. Commercial grades contain variable amounts of associated minerals, the most common of which are chlorite and magnesite. Used in cosmetic and pharmaceuticals and as filler in paper, paint and plastics,

Vermiculite   A variety of mica which, on heating, expands greatly parallel to the cleavage to give a cellular material with important thermal insulation properties.

The Treasury may add to, or subtract from, the above list (FA 2001, s. 18).

13.4   Credits and refunds

13.4.1   Availability of credits

The Regulations provide for tax credits to be given for aggregates levy charged where, after it has been charged, any of the aggregate is:

- exported from the UK in the form of aggregate;
- subjected to an exempt process;
- used in a prescribed industrial or agricultural process; or
- disposed of in a manner not constituting use for construction purposes;

(SI 2002/761, reg. 13).

The credit is given against aggregates levy due from the person concerned (FA 2001, s. 30). Where it exceeds the liability for the period concerned, the excess is refundable by Customs & Excise (FA 2001, s. 31). The credit has to be claimed, and the claim must be supported by records kept by the site operator, etc. (SI 2002/761, reg. 14). The claim may not relate to a period ending more than three years before the date of the claim. There is also a rule against unjust enrichment (regs. 20–26).

The Regulations set out the following schedules of industrial and agricultural processes (SI 2002/761 Schedule and see Business Brief 29/02 regarding changes taking effect on 1 April 2003).

13.4.2   Industrial processes

Code	Description
001	Iron, steel and non-ferrous metal manufacture and smelting processing including foundry processes, investment casting, sinter plants and wire drawing.
002	Alloying.
003	Emission abatement for air, land and water.
004	Drinking water, air and oil filtration and purification.
005	Sewage treatment.
006	Production of energy.
007	Ceramic processes.
008	Refractory processes.
009	Manufacture of glass and glass products.
010	Manufacture of fibre glass.
011	Manufacture of man-made fibres.
012	Production and processing of food and drink eg sugar refining, production of gelatin.
013	Manufacture of plastics, rubber and PVC.
014	Chemical manufacturing, eg soda ash, sea water magnesia, alumina.
015	Manufacture of precipitated calcium carbonate.

Code	Description
016	Manufacture of Pharmaceuticals, bleaches, toiletries and detergents.
017	Aerating processes.
018	Manufacture of fillers for coating, sealants, adhesives, paints, grouts, mastics, putties and other binding or modifying media.
019	Manufacture of pigments, varnishes and inks.
020	Production of line markings for sports pitches.
021	Incineration.
022	Manufacture of desiccant.
023	Manufacture of carpet backing, underlay and foam.
024	Resin processes.
025	Manufacture of lubricant additives.
026	Leather tanning.
027	Paper manufacture.
028	Production of art materials.
029	Production of play sand, eg for children's sand pits.
030	Clay pigeon manufacture.
031	Abrasive processes: specialist sand blasting, iron free grinding (pebble mills) and sandpaper manufacture.
032	Use as a propagating agent in oil exploration, eg fracture sands and drilling fluids.
033	Flue gas desulphurisation and flue gas scrubbing.
034	Manufacture of mine suppressant.

Code	Description
035	Manufacture of fire extinguishers.
036	Manufacture of materials used for fireproofing.
037	Acid neutralisation.
038	Manufacture of friction materials, eg automotive.

13.4.3 Agricultural processes

Code	Description
039	Manufacture of additives to soil, eg agricultural lime.
040	Manufacture of animal feeds.
041	Production of animal bedding material.
042	Production of fertiliser.
043	Manufacture of pesticides and herbicides.
044	Production of growing media, including compost, for agricultural and horticultural use.
045	Soil treatment, including mineral enrichment and reduction of acidity.

13.4.4 Bad debts

A credit is given for aggregates levy paid where the whole or part of a debt due to the person concerned is written off as a bad debt (SI 2002/761, reg. 12). However, no credit may be claimed unless the debtor has become insolvent or has gone into liquidation. Evidence of the insolvency or liquidation, and the 'surrounding circumstances' must be kept (reg. 10).

The bad debt must be written off as bad in the claimant's books of account and the debtor must not be connected with the creditor.

Where there is more than one debt due from the same person, receipts are matched on a first in first out basis (reg. 17).

13.4.5 Claims for credit

Credits must be claimed, and the claimant must be in possession of documentary evidence of the export, insolvency, etc. (reg. 15(2)). The claim is made by bringing the credit into account when accounting for aggregates levy and setting it off against the levy due for the accounting period for which the claim is made.

13.5 Registration

13.5.1 Requirement to register

Any person who carries out taxable activities is liable to register with Customs & Excise. A person who intends to carry out taxable activities must notify Customs & Excise of their intention (FA 2001, Sch. 4, Para. 1). Registration is effected by the completion and submission of form AL 1 to Customs & Excise. A partner must complete forms AL 1 and AL 2. Site details must be notified on form AL 1A (SI 2001/4027, reg. 2). The Regulations provide for electronic registration (reg. 2(4)). Site operators must report any change in the information contained in the registration forms within 30 days of the date on which the change occurs (reg. 4).

Similarly if a site operator discovers an error or inaccuracy in that information, they must report that within 30 days of the date on which it was discovered (reg. 4(10)).

Where a site operator ceases, or intends to cease, to carry out taxable activities, they must notify Customs & Excise accordingly, and in any event not later than 30 days after the date of cessation. Customs & Excise may then cancel their registration with effect from a specified date (FA 2001, Sch. 4, Para 4, and SI 2001/4027, Reg. 5).

Registration of the exempt aggregates is not required if the only commercial exploitation of aggregates is listed above (SI 2001/4027, reg. 3).

As from 1 April 2003, any person who exploits *solely* exempt aggregate will not have to register for aggregates levy nor carry out certain obligations such as submitting nil returns (Business Brief 34/02).

13.5.2 Full exemption from registration and all obligations

This applies to any person who commercially exploits *only:*

- soil, vegetable matter or other organic matter; or
- spoil, waste or other by-products of any industrial combustion process, or the smelting or refining of metal; or
- drill-cuttings from licensed oil exploration, or
- arising materials from roads when utilities work is carried out.

13.5.3 Exemption from registration and consequent obligations but required to notify Customs of activities

Any person who exploits *only:*

- coal, lignite, slate or shale; or
- spoil, waste or other by-products resulting from the separation of coal, lignite, slate or shale after extraction; or
- spoil, waste or other by-products resulting from the separation of specified minerals after extraction; or
- china clay and ball clay and spoil or waste resulting from its extraction, or
- any other clay,

is exempt from registration and consequent obligations such as submitting returns but will be required to notify Customs of site details, activities undertaken and responsible persons.

Notifications should be sent to:

HM Customs and Excise
Aggregates Levy Team
Dobson House
Regent Centre
Gosforth
Newcastle Upon Tyne NE3 3PF.

A non-resident taxpayer may be required to appoint a tax representative in the UK to be responsible for registration and other administration requirements (SI 2001/4027, regs. 14, 19). Such a representative must be approved by Customs & Excise (reg. 15). They may withdraw approval 'for good cause' on giving written notice to the taxpayer (reg. 16).

A body corporate carrying on business in several divisions may apply to register each division separately (FA 2001, Sch 4, Para 2(3)). There is a penalty of £250 for failure to comply with these regulations (SI 2001/4027, reg. 21).

13.5.4 Transfer of a going concern

On the transfer of a business as a going concern, both parties may jointly apply to Customs & Excise to have the transferor's registration number transferred to the transferee on the occasion of the transfer (SI 2002/761, reg. 37).

However, the transferee takes over responsibility for filing any outstanding returns and for accounting for any tax not accounted for by the transferor. Similarly, the transferee becomes entitled to any credit not given to the transferor (reg. 37(2)). Therefore, this procedure is appropriate only in the case of intra-group transfers and other transfers under common ownership.

13.5.5 Group registration

Eligibility

Group registration is available where two or more bodies corporate each have an established place of business in the UK and are under the same control (FA 2001, Sch. 9, Para. 1).

For this purpose, bodies corporate are under the same control if:

- one of them controls the others;
- one person (whether a body corporate or an individual) controls all of them, or
- a partnership of individuals controls all of them,

(FA 2001, Sch. 9, Para. 2).

Company A controls company B if:

- it is company B's holding company within the meaning of CA 1985, s. 736, or
- it is empowered by statute to control company B.

An individual controls company B if, on the assumption that they were a company, they would be company B's holding company. There is a similar rule for partnerships (FA 2001, Sch. 9, Para. 8).

Effect of group registration

The liabilities of all the members included in the group registration are treated as liabilities of the representative member (FA 2001, s. 35(2)). That member is responsible for making all necessary returns (SI 2001/4027, reg. 7). All members are jointly and severally liable for the levy payable by the representative member (s. 35(3)).

Application for group registration

Application must be made in writing to Customs & Excise on behalf of the companies concerned (SI 2001/4027, reg. 9). If accepted, the group registration has effect as from a 'specified time'. Customs may refuse an application if it considers it necessary for the protection of the Revenue (FA 2001, Sch. 9, Para. 2). The application may be made by one of the bodies corporate concerned, or by the person controlling them (Sch. 9, Para. 5).

Application can be made subsequently to add a company to the group registration, delete a company, or to terminate the group registration altogether (Sch. 9, Para. 3). Any company that ceases to be eligible to be within the group registration must notify Customs & Excise of that fact. Further, the representative member must notify Customs & Excise if it proposes to cease to have an established place of business in the UK. The time limit for these notifications is 30 days from the date on which the body corporate becomes aware that it will cease to be eligible to be a member of the group or that it will cease to have an established place of business in the UK (SI 2001/4027, reg. 9(3)). There is a penalty of £250 for failure to comply (Sch. 9. Para. 6).

Customs may terminate a group registration if it believes it necessary to protect the Revenue (Sch. 9, Para. 4).

13.5.6 Partnerships and unincorporated bodies

A partnership is treated as a separate person from the partners (FA 2001, s. 36(2)). Therefore it is required to register as a partnership. Changes in the partnership must be notified to Customs & Excise within 30 days of the date of the change (SI 2001/4027, reg. 4). A partner who leaves the partnership is treated as continuing to be a partner until notification is given to Customs & Excise (s. 36(3)).

Only one partner is required to complete form AL 1, but each partner must complete form AL 2. Each partner is jointly and severally liable for the registration requirements of the partnership (reg. 12).

13.5.7   Other unincorporated bodies

Similarly, an unincorporated body is treated as a separate person from its members. The persons responsible for dealing with any registration and administration requirements are:

- every person holding office as president, chairman, treasurer, secretary of other similar office;
- if there is no such office, every person who is a member of a committee by which the affairs of the body are managed,
- if there is no such office or committee, every member,

(SI 2001/4027, reg. 13).

13.6   Returns, payment and repayment of levy

13.6.1   Filing requirement

A site operator must file a return for each 'accounting period' by the end of the month following the end of that period. Customs & Excise will prescribe the quarterly periods for which returns must be made (SI 2002/761, regs. 5–7).

The levy for any accounting period is due and payable on the due date for filing the return for that period (reg. 8). It is recoverable as a debt due to the Crown (FA 2001, Sch. 5, Para. 1).

Interest on tax paid late runs from the due date until the date of payment (FA 2001, Sch. 5, Para. 6). However if the site operator is entitled to a repayment, that may be set off against the outstanding liability (reg. 30). The rate of interest will be determined by Regulations (FA 2001, Sch. 5, Para. 10 and FA 1996, s. 197(2)(d)).

13.6.2   Repayment of levy: unjust enrichment

Where a taxable person has paid an amount of aggregates levy that was not properly due, they may claim a refund of the amount found to have been overpaid (FA 2001, s. 31).

However, regulations restrict the repayment of aggregates levy charged incorrectly where the claimant originally passed on the charge to the customer, but is not able to pass on the refund to the customer. In such circumstances, the regulations require any amount which is repaid but not passed on to be returned to Customs (FA 2001, s. 32 and SI 2002/761, regs. 20–26).

The full amount recovered from Customs must be reimbursed to the customer in cash or by cheque within 90 days after the repayment is made, together with any interest thereon. Any amount not reimbursed within the 90-day time limit must he returned to Customs within a further 14 days (regs. 22, 23).

The claimant must keep records of the customers reimbursed and the amount reimbursed (reg. 24) and must give undertakings to Customs at the time the claim for repayment is made to the effect that they will comply with the above requirements (FA 2001, s. 32(2) and Sch. 8, Para. 1). These records must be produced to Customs in accordance with a written notice given by it (reg. 24).

13.7 Assessments, appeals and the review procedure

13.7.1 Power to raise assessments

If a taxable person fails to make a return or makes a return which Customs believes to be incorrect, it may raise an assessment on them to the best of its judgement (FA 2001, Sch. 5, Paras. 2, 3).

Any assessment must be made within two years after the end of the accounting period to which it relates, or within one year after the facts or evidence come to the knowledge of Customs, whichever is the later date (Sch. 5, Para. 4). A further assessment may be made if further facts come to light.

13.7.2 Right to call for review and right of appeal

The taxable person may give notice to Customs to review its decision to raise an assessment. Such notice must be given within 45 days of the date of the assessment. The operator may then appeal to the VAT and Duties Tribunal against the decision of Customs on the review (FA 2001, s. 40–42). However, the appeal may not proceed unless they pay the disputed tax or shows that they cannot do so without suffering hardship (s. 41).

The review, and subsequently the appeal, procedure is available for any of the following decisions:

- as to whether the levy is chargeable in any case;
- the amount of levy chargeable and the time when the charge is taken to have arisen;
- to register or cancel a registration of any person or premises;
- the person liable to pay the levy and the amount of their liability;

- to require a person to give security for the payment of aggregates;
- whether a liability to interest and/or penalties arises and the amount of such liability;
- as to an director's or officer's liability to any civil penalty;
- the extent of any person' entitlement to any tax credit or repayment and the amount of any interest payable by Customs & Excise thereon;
- whether or not any person is required to have a tax representative;
- the approval or withdrawal of approval of a representative;
- whether a body corporate is to be treated as a member of a group and at what times,
- decisions on other matters contained in any assessment.

Any appeal lies to the VAT and Duties Tribunal (s. 41). An appeal from the Tribunal to the courts can be made on a point of law (Tribunals and Inquiries Act 1992, s. 11 and SI 1998/3132, ord. 94, r. 8).

13.8   Ordinary interest and penalty interest

13.8.1   Unpaid levy

Where a person makes a return, but does not pay the levy on the due date, penalty interest runs from that date to the date of payment (FA 2001, Sch. 5, Para. 5).

13.8.2   Overdue levy paid before assessment

Where the circumstances are such that Customs & Excise could raise an assessment, but the taxable person pays the levy before any assessment is made, ordinary interest is payable from the date on which the levy should have been paid for the accounting period concerned (FA 2001, Sch. 5, Para. 6).

13.8.3   Levy due where no return made

Where Customs & Excise makes an assessment to recover aggregates levy, penalty interest runs from the dale on which the levy should have been paid for the accounting period concerned (FA 2001, Sch. 5, Para. 7).

13.8.4   Levy due where assessment made following submission of return

In this case, the assessment will be for an additional amount considered to be due. Ordinary interest runs from the normal due date to the date of the assessment. Penalty interest runs from the date of the assessment to the date of payment (FA 2001, Sch. 5, Para. 8).

13.8.5   Penalty interest on unpaid ordinary interest

Any interest may be assessed by Customs & Excise and recovered as an amount of aggregates levy. Penalty interest runs on any ordinary interest from the date of the assessment (FA 2001, Sch. 5, Para. 9).

13.8.6   The rate of penalty interest

This is the rate prescribed by FA 1996, s. 197 and SI 1998/1461 plus 10 percentage points (FA 2001, Sch. 5, Para. 10).

13.9   Enforcement

13.9.1   Criminal penalties

Fraudulent evasion of aggregates levy is a criminal offence, as is the deliberate production of false documents or information. On summary conviction, the guilty person may be liable for a term of imprisonment not exceeding six months or a fine not exceeding the statutory maximum or three times the tax, whichever is greater, or both. On conviction on indictment, the term of imprisonment is up to seven years and the fine is at the discretion of the court (FA 2001, Sch. 6, Para. 2). These matters are spelled out in more detail in Paras. 2–4.

Where a criminal penalty is imposed for any offence, no civil penalty is imposed for the same offence (Sch. 6, Para. 7(5)).

13.9.2   Civil penalties

The penalty for tax evasion arising from conduct involving dishonesty is 100% of the tax evaded, subject to mitigation by Customs & Excise or, on appeal, by the Tribunal (FA 2001, Sch. 6, Para. 7).

If tax is evaded by a company and the dishonest conduct is attributable to the dishonesty of a director, Customs & Excise may impose the penalty on the director (FA 2001, Sch. 6, Para. 8).

The penalty for misdeclaration in a return is 5% of the amount by which the liability is understated, subject to mitigation as above (FA 2001, Sch. 6 Para.

9). Small errors must be corrected in the return for the accounting period in which it is discovered (SI 2002/761, reg. 29). If the taxable person corrects the error in this way, they are not liable for the penalty. Only errors of up to £2,000 may be corrected in this way (reg. 29(5)). If the error exceeds £2,000, they must write to Customs & Excise giving it the correct figures.

The penalty for failure to register is £250 or 5% of any unpaid tax, whichever is greater (FA 2001, Sch. 4, Para. 1(3)).

13.9.3 Information and evidence

Keeping of records

Any person required to be registered for aggregates levy purposes is required to keep the following records for a period of six years (the summary is taken from the *General Guide*):

Record	Description
Aggregates levy account	This is your periodic summary of total aggregates levy due, detailing any credits of levy and any adjustments.
Aggregates levy tax credits account	For exports and other reliefs, evidence is needed to substantiate them. See chapter 6 [not reproduced].
Aggregates levy bad debt account	If you claim bad debt relief you must maintain a bad debt account.
Record of exempt aggregate	For exempt aggregate, evidence needed to substantiate it.
Invoices	You need to keep copies of all invoices and other accounting documents that you issue or receive.
Mixes – special schemes	If you are authorised to calculate your levy liability using a special scheme a condition of approval is that you retain certain records. These are specified in the approval and are in addition to any other records you are required to keep.

Sites not using weighbridges	See section 11 [not reproduced] if you operate a specified method for calculating the weight of the material. Records you need to keep will be specified in the approval and are in addition to any other records you are required to keep.

In addition, from the date of your registration you will also need to keep the following:

- business and accounting records;
- records of materials brought onto or removed from the aggregates site;
- records of waste that has been dumped or put to landfill;
- all credit or debit notes, and similar documents, issued or received by you;
- any other documents required by this notice or any other notice published by Customs,
- weighbridge tickets.

The above records may be kept in hard copy, microfilm or microfiche, provided that copies can be easily produced and there are adequate facilities to allow Customs & Excise to view them when required. Records may also be kept on computer, for example, on a magnetic tape or disc, provided that they can be readily converted into a legible form and made available to Customs & Excise on request. If records are kept on computer, Customs & Excise will, by arrangement, require access to the computer to check its operation, processing, and the information held. The agreement of Customs & Excise must be obtained before any method of information storage other than hard copy is used. If a computer bureau or any other body (eg a book-keeping company) is used to keep records then the taxable person remains responsible for what it does on their behalf (SI 2002/761, regs. 9–11 and the *General Guide*, paragraph 15.3).

Inspection of records and documents

Any person acting under the authority of Customs & Excise may require any person involved in the exploitation of aggregates to produce the above records and documents for inspection (FA 2001, Sch. 7, Para. 4). They may remove the documents and take copies of them. They may also enter and inspect premises used in connection with the carrying on of a business (FA 2001, Sch. 7, Paras. 5, 6).

If Customs & Excise has reasonable grounds for believing that serious fraud is being committed or is about to be committed, it may apply to a Justice of the Peace (a Justice in Scotland) for a warrant authorising its officers to enter and search premises and remove any documents which it believes may be required as evidence in any proceedings (FA 2001, Sch. 7, Paras. 7, 8).

Customs & Excise must, on request, provide the occupier of the premises with a record of the documents removed (FA 2001, Sch. 7, Para. 9). The occupier may require access to such documents and may take copies of them.

13.9.4   Recovery of aggregates levy

Aggregates levy is recovered as a debt due to the Crown (FA 2001, Sch. 5, Para. 1). If any person refuses to pay the tax by the due date, the Collector may distrain on their goods and chattels (Sch. 5 Para. 14). They are then liable for the costs of the distraint action.

In an insolvency, aggregates levy referable to the period of six months next before the relevant date is a preferential debt (Sch. 5, Paras. 17, 18).

14 Local taxes

14.1 An introduction to local taxation

14.1.1 General

Local taxation is nothing new, having been with us in one form or another for at least 600 years. The radical redesign of local taxation in 1990 and 1993, and the resultant blurring of the edges between local and national taxation have made the subject that much more relevant.

14.1.2 Background

The term *local taxation* is used in this book to cover liability to the council tax and to the national non-domestic rate (referred to here for convenience as the 'business rate'), together with their predecessors. The legislation governing the non-domestic rate system is contained in the Local Government Finance Act 1988. This Act applies in England and Wales only. The system in Scotland, although similar in broad terms, differs in many detailed respects; Northern Ireland retains the pre Local Government Finance Act 1988 system of rating. This publication is restricted to considering *local taxation* in England and Wales.

In understanding the workings of and the relationship between the council tax and business rating systems it is useful to have some appreciation of the machinery of the Local Government Finance Acts as a whole and the background to their implementation.

In approaching this subject, it is hoped that it is more helpful to attempt some analysis of those areas likely to prove difficult than to explain the legislation without regard to the practicalities.

Two distinct systems of taxation are involved: one imposes a charge on individuals but is also closely related to ownership and occupation of property, while the other is based on a well-tried and tested system although in unfamiliar form. Both overlap considerably in their scope, and an understanding of each is necessary when acting in a business capacity, whether as occupier or as landlord.

The current system of financing local government comprises three elements:

- the council tax;
- the non-domestic rating regime,
- the system of support grant paid by central government.

The introduction of the community charge ('poll tax') that replaced the domestic rate in 1990 was the subject of much controversy. The regime was short lived and on 1 April 1993 was replaced by the council tax (Local Government Finance Act 1992).

The introduction of the business rating system was equally far reaching in its effects in terms of its impact on the costs to business. Reaction to it, although perhaps less vocal and widespread, has been far from universally favourable.

The setting of the level of council tax by each local authority is in fact the last stage in a three-step process implemented for each financial year. The first two steps, the setting of the business rate poundage and the setting of the level of central grant, largely determine the levels of council tax that are likely to be realistic. (There is room for argument, certainly at a political level, about the extent to which local authorities can control their overall total spending by being more or less efficient in managing services.) The level of council tax is fixed locally by each billing authority depending on its financial needs, and is subject to the Secretary of State for Transport, Local Government and the Regions' (DTLR) power to cap the level chosen by the authority. Whilst the amount due is linked to the value of the property (properties are allocated to one of eight bands), discounts are available for single occupants and for certain adults such as students, care workers, etc. who may be disregarded.

The single most striking feature of the new system is the radical shift in finance raising powers from local to central government compared with the position as it was before the Local Government FinanceAct1988 came into force. Indeed, it could be argued that to describe the new system as one of 'local' taxation is somewhat misleading. The Secretary of State for the Environment sets the business rate multiplier, allocates revenue support grant from central to local government, and in the last resort decides via the 'capping' mechanism what maximum levels of local expenditure are permissible.

The enormously wide discretionary powers conferred on the Secretary of State by the 1988 and 1992 Acts are subject to very few constraints. The main Acts consist merely of a framework; the 'nuts and bolts' are inserted by regulation under the various powers given to the Secretary of State. Apart from the major amendments made to the Local Government Finance Acts 1988 and 1992 by subsequent legislation, they have been supplemented by a multitude of regulations; some of these are themselves long and very complex. The result is a body of law which lacks coherence and accessibility and which is subject to constant change with minimal parliamentary scrutiny.

14.1.3 The system in outline

The local government finance system comprises the following three elements:

- The council tax is based on the capital value of each property. Each domestic property is shown on the local valuation list as coming within one of eight 'bands' of value. The legislation sets out a complex hierarchy designed to identify persons liable to pay. These rules are not always easy to interpret. Individuals can be entitled to a discount of up to 50 per cent. In addition, council tax benefit provides for a maximum benefit of 100 per cent of the council tax for those on very low incomes.
- Rates on non-domestic property are levied on business property. Each local authority formerly had the power to set its own rate poundage. A business rate in the pound is now set by the Secretary of State DTLR and applies nationwide. The multiplier (sometimes known as the uniform business rate (UBR)), is 45.6p for the year 2004/05. The original multiplier (34.8p for the year1990/91) is linked to movements in the retail price index for subsequent years. A national revaluation of all business property is carried out every five years and the resulting valuation lists apply from 1 April (Local Government Finance Act 1988, s. 41(3)). The total yield from business rates is set in advance. However, the Secretary of State is empowered by LGFA 1988, s. 57 to prescribe different rates for different types of property during a transitional five-year period, the intention being to make special provision for small businesses and others who may be hit hard by the revised system [see **14.1.6** below]
- The revenue support grant is the third component, ie a system of central government grant comparable to the old rate support grant. Each authority's amount of grant is now fixed according to the Government's (Secretary of State's) estimate of what it requires to bring it up to a common national 'starting point'.

14.1.4 How the system operates

The first step is the national non-domestic rate (business rate), total revenue from which is inelastic and varies in each area only with the rateable values of properties in the area and the annual inflation linked multiplier.

The contribution each authority receives in the form of revenue support grant represents the next step in the system. The council tax set by the local authority is the final element in the package. As a result, the level of the tax is (intentionally) highly sensitive to any spending levels in excess of those approved by central government for grant purposes, so that taxpayers will meet any 'excess' spending in full. The rationale behind this is that it should enhance local government's financial accountability to its electorate.

14.1.5   Revaluations

The Valuation Office Agency (VOA) carries out a revaluation every five years so that the values in the rating lists can be kept up to date. The total amount of business rates collected in England does not change except to reflect inflation, but revaluations make sure that this is spread fairly between ratepayers. The next revaluation is due in April 2005.

14.1.6   Transitional arrangements

Property values normally change a good deal between each revaluation. Transitional arrangements help to phase in the effects of these changes on ratepayers' bills. To help pay for the limits on increases in bills after a revaluation, there also has to be limits on reductions in bills.

The transitional scheme introduced in England and Wales following the revaluation in 2000 made sure that each business rates bill did not change beyond certain limits in 2000/01 because of the revaluation. Many bills changed by less than these amounts and the final amount depended on a number of factors.

Under the transitional relief scheme, limits continue to apply to yearly increases and decreases in the following years over the life of the scheme until the new full amount is due (rateable value times the multiplier).

Transitional limits apply if, in any year, the amount the person would have to pay is higher than the previous year's bill based on the amount due at the 31 March by more than the amounts shown below. If this is the case, the bill will be increased by these amounts

Year	Small property (rateable value of less than £12,000 or £18,000 in greater London)	Large property
2000/01	5%	12.5%
2001/02	7.5%	15%
2002/03	7.5%	17.5%
2003/04	7.5%	17.5%
2003/05	7.5%	17.5%

Where the amount you would have to pay is lower than last year's bill based on the amount due at the 31 March by the amounts shown below, your bill will be reduced by these amounts.

Year	Small property	Large property
2000/01	5%	2.5%
2001/02	5%	2.5%
2002/03	10%	5%
2003/04	12.5%	7.5%
2004/05	25%	15%

14.1.7 Interpreting the legislation

Practice Notes on the council tax and the business rating system are issued jointly by the relevant central government department (the Department of Transport, Local Government and the Regions), and the local authority associations. These have no binding force but are persuasive and of interest in that they represent the considered views of central and local government as to what constitutes correct law and practice.

14.2 Domestic/non-domestic property

14.2.1 General comments

Before attempting to establish whether or how a person in any given situation can be subject to council tax or to rates under the Local Government Finance Act 1988 it is necessary to identify the nature of the property involved as well as the nature of that person's connection with it. Liability to local taxation initially depends on what type of property is involved, ie whether it is classed as domestic or non-domestic for the purposes of the Act. Very roughly, residence in, ownership of or management of *domestic property* may be associated with liability to *council tax;* occupation or ownership of *non-domestic property* is associated with liability to the *national non-domestic rate,* also known as the uniform business rate. Some types of land and buildings fall outside the scope of both the community charge and the business rating regime, either because they are the subject of specific exemption or because they are non-domestic premises deemed to be domestic by the legislation.

A building or self-contained part of a building is regarded as domestic property if it is used wholly for the purposes of living accommodation (LGFA 1988, s. 4(4)). It is not however domestic property if it is used wholly or mainly in the course of a business consisting of the provision to individuals, whose sole or main residence is elsewhere, of accommodation for short periods together with domestic or other services (LGFA 1988, s. 4(5)). Examples of property falling within this category would be hotels or boarding houses. There are of course many types of buildings so used but not in the course of a business (eg mountain huts and chalets), which are expressly included in 'buildings' by LGFA 1988, s. 31(6). These are classified as domestic in these circumstances and may attract liability to council tax (LGFA 1992 4(1)).

Where a building is not yet in use, or has ceased to be in use, its classification is governed by LGFA 1988, s. 4(6) which provides that anything not in use is to be treated as domestic property if it appears that when in use it will be domestic property. Thus newly constructed flats or houses not yet occupied will come within the council tax regime rather than the non-domestic rates.

14.2.2 Special and borderline cases

Where a building is used partly for domestic and partly for non-domestic purposes (such as a flat over a shop or garage) it is classified as a 'composite hereditament' and as non-domestic by LGFA 1988, s. 64(9). Rates are payable on the business portion only. The domestic portion will come within the council tax system. Note that the Secretary of State DTLR has prescribed a maximum multiplier of 1 for unoccupied empty properties forming a self-contained part of business premises property.

Besides the categories already mentioned, the definition of domestic property is extended by statute to include outhouses belonging to or enjoyed with domestic property and private storage premises (LGFA 1988, s.66 (1)(b)–(d)). A caravan site or houseboat mooring is deemed to be domestic property, and hence outside the scope of non-domestic rating (LGFA 1988, s. 66(3), (4)). Holiday caravan sites, on the other hand, are subject to business rating. As the law now stands (July 2004), owners of a static caravan on a site that is protected within the meaning given in the Caravan Sites Act 1988 (ie a site on which some caravans can be lived in at any time during the year) are liable to pay the business rates unless the caravan is their sole or main residence, in which case they are liable to the council tax.

Where the caravans cannot be lived in throughout the year, the site operator is responsible for paying non-domestic rates on the whole site. Whether or not the occupiers of the individual pitches will be liable to reimburse the site operator will depend on the terms of the contract in place.

14.2.3   Short stay and holiday accommodation

The Secretary of State has power to amend the definition of domestic property by order (LGFA 1988, s. 66(9)). So far (July 2004) he has used his powers by way of SI 1990/162:

- To exclude from the business rating regime, domestic property intended to be available for the provision of short stay accommodation for periods totaling less than 100 days in any given year where the person providing the accommodation also used the same premises. This covers businesses such as providing occasional bed and breakfast in farmhouses (LGFA 1988, s. 66(2A)).
- To bring self-contained holiday accommodation let or available for letting commercially for 140 days or more in any year within the business rating regime (LGFA 1988, s. 66(2B)). It is expressly provided that this will not apply if the building or part of the building is in use as a sole or main residence, except by a full-time student within the scope of LGFA 1988, s. 2(5).
- If you offer bed-and-breakfast accommodation in your own home to six people (or fewer), you will not be liable for business rates as long as you are living in the property. The permanent residents will be liable for council tax under the normal rules.

It has been shown that LGFA 1988, s. 4(4) classifies property as domestic if it is used wholly for the purposes of living accommodation. Nevertheless some non-domestic use is permitted without business rates becoming payable provided that it does not prevent the whole property being so used. Use of a home telephone for a minicab service or a callout number for a plumber would not, for example, attract liability for business rates and a novelist might write books at home without the property ceasing to be used entirely as living accommodation. Other kinds of business use are however incompatible with domestic use of the whole accommodation, for example if a room is set aside exclusively for business premises particularly where premises have been adapted or structurally altered in some way, or contain furniture of a non-domestic nature, such as a dentist's surgery. In such cases the valuation officer will determine a rateable value for that part of the property devoted to business use.

14.3   Council tax

14.3.1   General comments

The council tax has applied since 1 April 1993 in place of the community charge, or 'poll tax'. It is a hybrid tax, in that it is a tax on buildings rather than a tax on people, but with a personal element, so that the amount of the bill depends not only on the value of the property concerned but also on the number and status of the people living there.

The council tax is of marginal relevance to the subject matter of this book, however, it is necessary to describe its operation in outline in order to give a complete picture of property taxation.

The council tax is worked out on a daily basis (LGFA 1992, s.2(1)) and is based on the unit of property, ie the dwelling (LGFA 1992, s.1(1)). Establishing liability depends on answering the following questions:

- Is the property a dwelling?
- In which valuation band is it?
- Is it exempt?

A dwelling is, broadly speaking, a self-contained unit used entirely for domestic purposes. The definition relies closely on the old pre-1989 rating concept of a hereditament – anything that would have been liable to domestic rates under General Rate Act 1967, s. 115(1) will be liable to council tax (LGFA 1992, s. 3). However, the new definition also allows the Secretary of State to provide that anything that would otherwise be one dwelling, shall be treated as two or more dwellings or vice versa (LGFA 1992, s. 3(5)). He may also amend any definition of a dwelling by regulation (LGFA 1992, s. 3(6)).

The introduction of the council tax seems to have commanded general acceptance, in marked contrast to its predecessor. It might therefore be judged a success. There are, however, some bizarre features. For example, many student dwellings are exempt (see below). In this context, a student is someone who is studying full-time on a course that lasts at least a year. Should one sharer in the accommodation concerned cease to be a student, or one non-student move into accommodation to share with several students, 'that person brings the council tax with them like the plague', as one Minister aptly put it in the course of Parliamentary debate on the Bill. The student sharers can claim then to be disregarded for the purposes of calculating the bill, but will still be liable for their share of the reduced liability, ie 75 per cent of the full tax, if there is only one 'visible' resident (non-student). It is hard to understand why this should be, when they would be exempt if they lived alone, or shared only with other students.

There is reason to believe that councils are in practice turning a blind eye to such niceties. Many people entitled to discounts because they or others may be 'disregarded' (see below) are in fact unaware of this fact, as are probably many others entitled to rebates and different kinds of discounts.

It is possible, therefore, that public acceptance is founded to some extent on misunderstandings. However, the reality is probably that rough and ready administration of a system which is in itself rather crude nevertheless produces workable and broadly equitable results, not least because of the much more generous system of rebates for the less well off. It seems that the council tax is likely to have a much longer and less turbulent life than its predecessor.

14.3.2 Valuation bands

The council tax bill varies depending in which of eight different valuation bands the property belongs. There are separate categories for England and Wales as follows (LGFA 1992, s. 5(2)):

England – Range of values	*Valuation band*
Values not exceeding £40,000	A
Values exceeding £40,000 but not exceeding £52,000	B
Values exceeding £52,000 but not exceeding £68,000	C
Values exceeding £68,000 but not exceeding £88,000	D

England – Range of values (conts.)	*Valuation band*
Values exceeding £88,000 but not exceeding £120,000	E
Values exceeding £120,000 but not exceeding £160,000	F
Values exceeding £160,000 but not exceeding £320,000	G
Values exceeding £320,000	H

Wales – Range of values	*Valuation band*
Values not exceeding £30,000	A
Values exceeding £30,000 but not exceeding £39,000	B
Values exceeding £39,000 but not exceeding £51,000	C
Values exceeding £51,000 but not exceeding £66,000	D
Values exceeding £66,000 but not exceeding £90,000	E
Values exceeding £90,000 but not exceeding £120,000	F
Values exceeding £120,000 but not exceeding £240,000	G
Values exceeding £240,000	H

14.3.3 Multipliers

Each dwelling has been placed in one of the bands, but has not been given a cash value. The amount of tax due differs proportionately according to the band in which it is placed. Property in band A is given the value 6. This is then increased for other bands as follows (LGFA 1992, s. 5(1)):

A = 6

B = 7/6

C = 8/6

D = 9/6

E = 11/6

F = 13/6

G = 15/6

H = 18/6

These multipliers are the same for England and Wales.

14.3.4 Valuations

Council tax valuations are based on market values as at 1 April 1991 (LGFA 1992, s. 21(2), SI 1992/550, reg. 6(1)). A number of assumptions must be made for the purpose of this valuation. These are:

- that the sale was with vacant possession;
- that the interest sold was the freehold or, in the case of a flat, a lease for 99 years at a nominal rent;
- that the dwelling was sold free from any rent charge or other encumbrance;
- that the size, layout and character of the dwelling and the state of its locality were the same as at the relevant date (ie 1 April 1991);
- that the dwelling was in a reasonable state of repair;
- that any common parts are also kept in a reasonable state of repair and the purchaser is liable to contribute to the costs of maintaining them in this condition;
- that certain special fixtures for the disabled are not to be included;
- that use will be permanently restricted to use as a private dwelling,
- that there is no development value other than that attributed to permitted development (SI 1992/550).

Note that the banding for every new dwelling also has to be based on an estimate of what it would have sold for in April 1991. The reason for this is that Ministers were anxious to have a system that would avoid revaluations; instead it depends on relative values between dwellings. The system therefore requires a fixed, specific date against which these relative values can be measured.

The listing officer for the local authority is charged with the responsibility of monitoring the valuation list. The Act defines the circumstances in which the listing officer is to alter the list. These are where:

- there has been a material increase or decrease in the value of the dwelling. The increase or decrease would occur when substantial alteration, extension or demolition added to or decreased its market value. However, the banding cannot be revised until the dwelling is sold freehold or on a lease of at least seven years; or

- the officer is satisfied he should have determined a different valuation band for the dwelling; or
- an order of a Valuation Tribunal or the High Court requires the alteration (LGFA 1992, s. 24); or
- the dwelling becomes, or ceases to be, a composite hereditament, or
- there has been a material reduction in the dwelling's value. In this case the dwelling should be revalued at once, but there will be no change in the banding until the new valuation is sufficiently low to bring it into a new band.

An appeal against banding had to be made before 30 November 1993 for any dwelling appearing on the initial valuation list.

Appeals on the banding of new dwellings, or where someone becomes the taxpayer for the first time, can be made up to six months from the appropriate date.

Appeals against an entry in the valuation list are made in the first instance to the listing officer for the area in which the dwelling is situated. Further appeal may be made to a Valuation Tribunal. The procedure to be followed is covered in SI 1989/439, as amended by SI 1993/292.

Note that tax must be paid in accordance with the original banding pending appeal.

14.3.5   Exemptions

Not all dwellings are subject to council tax. Where a dwelling is exempt on any day, no tax is chargeable. The classes of exempt dwelling are specified by the Secretary of State (in SI 1992/558 as amended by SI 1992/2941 and SI 1993/150).

A dwelling is an exempt dwelling when, on any day, it falls within the classes A to Q shown below. These fall into three categories, broadly speaking:

- classes A and C: vacant dwellings
- classes B, D–L, Q: unoccupied dwellings
- classes M–P: dwellings which may or may not be occupied.

The classes of exempt dwellings are as follows:

Class A: Dwellings undergoing repair   This covers vacant dwellings which:

(a) require major repair works to make them habitable; or

(b) are undergoing structural alteration which has not been substantially completed; or

(c) have been unoccupied and unfurnished for a continuous period of less than six months commencing on the day on which the repair work or structural alteration was substantially completed.

Class B: Unoccupied dwellings owned by charities

This covers dwellings owned by bodies established for charitable purposes only, which have been unoccupied for a period of less than six months since the last occupation day.

Class C: Dwellings left unoccupied and substantially unfurnished

This covers dwellings, including new buildings, which have been vacant for a continuous period of less than the day in question.

Class D: Dwellings left unoccupied by prisoners

Class E: Dwellings left unoccupied by patients in hospitals and care homes

Class F: Dwellings left unoccupied by deceased persons

This applies for six months from the grant of probate.

Class G: Unfit dwellings

This covers unoccupied dwellings where occupation is prohibited by law.

Class H: Unoccupied clergy dwellings

This covers dwellings held for the purpose of being available for occupation by a minister of any religious denomination.

Class I: Dwellings left unoccupied by people receiving care

Class J: Dwellings left unoccupied by people providing care

Class K: Dwellings left unoccupied by students	This covers dwellings that are owned by one or more students and are left temporarily empty.

Class L: Repossessed dwellings

Class M: Students' halls of residence

Class N: Student accommodation	This covers dwellings which are either occupied by one or more residents all of whom are students or are occupied only by one or more students as term time accommodation. During vacations, the dwelling is exempt under certain circumstances.

Class O: Accommodation for the armed forces, barracks, messes and married quarters

Class P: Accommodation for visiting forces

Class Q: Unoccupied dwellings vested in a trustee in bankruptcy	This applies where the owner was an individual who has been made bankrupt.

Note: For the purposes of Class A and C, when determining whether a dwelling has been vacant for any period, any one period not exceeding six weeks during which it was not vacant is disregarded.

It must be stressed that these exemptions (most of which in practice relate to empty homes) apply to the *dwelling*. None of them operate to exempt *individuals* from liability. Thus, if a dwelling is lived in there is nearly always a liability to pay.

14.3.6 Other factors

Number of residents

Quite apart from the valuation band and the level of tax set by the local authority, the amount of the council tax bill payable in respect of any dwelling depends on a number of other factors. The first, and most obvious, of these is the number of residents. There are three 'tiers' of liability as follows:

- if a dwelling has two or more residents, the bill is for the full amount appropriate to its band;
- if it has only one resident, that amount is reduced by 25 per cent,
- if it has no residents, the reduction becomes 50 per cent (LGFA 1992, s. 11(1) and (2)).

The process of determining whether the number of adult residents amount to a total of none, or one, or two or more, involves another, somewhat mystical, dimension. Unlike under the poll tax, there are, as we have seen, no exemptions for individuals, whatever their circumstances. However, there are certain types of individuals who are not to be counted when deciding how many people live in a dwelling (and therefore are *prima facie* liable for some or all of the total council tax bill for that dwelling). Such people are treated as invisible, or as the Act puts it, are 'disregarded'.

Note, however, that 'disregarded' residents are still liable to pay their equal share of the resulting council tax bill, along with the more tangible members of the household. People disregarded for discount purposes are as follows:

- students (this is generously interpreted; it includes 18 and 19 year olds still at school, those under 20 in A or O level colleges, student nurses, and people on college and comparable courses of at least a year's duration, as well as people on full-time first degree courses);
- long-stay hospital patients (though most hospitals will be liable to pay the non-domestic rate and there will be no question of a council tax bill anyway);
- patients in homes;
- residential care workers;
- people classed as severely mentally impaired;
- people of no fixed abode staying in a hostel or night shelter on an intermittent base;
- prisoners;
- members of religious communities;
- school and college leavers under 20, for the year in which they leave school or college,
- members of visiting forces, or an international or security organisation, such as NATO.

Disability reduction scheme

Someone who is permanently and substantially disabled may apply to the local authority under the disability reduction scheme. If that person (child or adult) lives in the dwelling and uses specified facilities in the home, such as an extra bathroom, or wheelchair or an extra room, the Council will apply a formula to the council tax bill which reduces it to that payable for the next band down. This is not a revaluation; the valuation list is unaltered and the Revenue is not involved. There is no requirement for the dwelling to be adapted to meet the needs of the disabled person (SI 1992/554). Obviously taxpayers living in band A dwellings are unable to benefit from the scheme.

Liability

Having worked out the council tax bill, it is then necessary to establish who is liable to pay it. The basic rule is that if anyone lives in the dwelling, he is usually liable to pay. The liability for the tax falls on anyone aged 18 or over whose sole or main residence is the dwelling in question. Where there is more than one such person, there is a hierarchy of liability (meaning you take the highest category applying and ignore the rest) as follows:

(a)   a resident with a freehold interest in all or part of the dwelling;

(b)   a resident with a leasehold interest in all or part of the dwelling;

(c)   a resident who is a statutory or secure tenant;

(d)   a resident who is a licensee;

(e)   a resident who does not fall within (a)–(d),

(f)   the non-resident owner.

Non-resident owners

Non-resident owners will only be liable to pay the tax where there are no residents further up the hierarchy, ie where the property is empty or has no permanent residents (eg holiday homes). However, in the case of certain tied accommodation, for example a vicarage occupied by a minister of religion, the landlord (in this case the Church concerned) is liable to pay the council tax. People who own second homes, where they stay only occasionally, but have staff living there permanently, are also liable in respect of these second homes.

Shared accommodation

For most kinds of shared accommodation, such as residential care homes, nursing homes, hostels, night shelters, some religious communities, and houses and flats intended for shared use, the owner is liable for the council tax, not the residents (LGFA 1992, s. 8, SI 1993/151).

The Secretary of State has power to prescribe that, for certain classes of dwellings, the liability is not to attach to the occupier but to the owner or another person. So far this power has been exercised only for the types of premises already mentioned.

Houses in multiple occupation (eg occupied as bed-sits) have given rise to problems of definition. It is now expressly provided by regulation that where a dwelling:

- was originally constructed or subsequently adapted for occupation by persons who do not constitute a single household, and
- each resident has a licence to occupy only part of the dwelling,

then the council tax liability is the owner's. The owner is a person with a freehold or leasehold interest in the dwelling as a whole, which is not subject to a similar inferior interest in it or, if there is no such person, a person with a freehold or leasehold interest in any part of the dwelling (SI 1992/551, as amended by SI 1993/151).

Liability will therefore depend largely on the tenancy agreements granted to the tenants. If they have a joint tenancy, they will be jointly and severally liable for the tax; if they each have a separate tenancy or licence, the landlord will be liable. In practice, local authorities are said to prefer to persuade the landlord to accept liability in the interests of simplifying collection.

Where two or more people have the same interest in the premises (eg are joint freeholders or joint tenants), they will be jointly and severally liable for the council tax. Moreover, the spouse or cohabitee of the person liable (because he or she is, for example, the freeholder, tenant, etc.) is also jointly and severally liable for the tax for every day that he or she cohabits with that person.

This means that each person can be made to pay the whole bill, or any arrears, from the day the bill is issued, not just his share. The one exception to this involves taxpayers with a certificate of severe mental impairment; the rules on this point are very complex.

Authorities can choose how to deal with jointly liable taxpayers; some have identified all jointly liable taxpayers and put all their names on the bill, but many put only one name on the bill and the choice of that name may have been somewhat arbitrary. Only the named person can be subject to enforcement proceedings unless and until the authority writes to any other jointly liable persons informing them they must pay the bill or clear arrears.

14.3.7 Reliefs

There is a system of rebates for people on low incomes, modeled closely on housing benefit, known as council tax benefit. It can amount to 100 per cent of the bill for those on the lowest incomes.

14.4   Business rating

14.4.1   Method of charging

General outline

The system of rates for non-domestic premises ('business rates') is radically different in form from that which prevailed up to 31 March 1989.

The local authority has no power to set its own rate poundage. A "business rate in the pound" is set by the Secretary of State for the Environment and this applies nationwide. A system of 'phasing' relief protects ratepayers from large increases to their old rates bills and also limits decreases where the new rates bill is lower.

Non-domestic rating valuation is based on 'annual letting value' as under the previous system, and certain definitions such as the meaning of 'hereditament' and 'occupier' are determined by reference to the rules which would have applied for the purposes of the General Rate Act 1967.

The meaning of 'owner' of a hereditament is however quite different from that under the old Act. It follows that a large amount of case law built up in the field of rating in the course of its long history is relevant in interpreting the business rating system instituted under the Local Government Finance Act 1988, but that this is by no means automatically the case.

It must be emphasised that the areas of rating and rating valuation are complex and specialist advice is always essential when attempting to apply the very general outline set out in this book to individual circumstances. The aim of this part is to provide a broad description of the system and its machinery so that landlords, developers and others concerned with commercial or industrial property can have some idea as to how and when rating considerations arise and how they fit into the general pattern of everyday transactions.

Multiplier

Responsibility for determining the poundage for rates rests with the Secretary of State for Transport, Local Government and the Regions (DTLR) in England and the Secretary of State for Wales as appropriate. For the financial year 2004/05, the uniform multiplier (the former rate poundage) is 45.6p in the pound in England and Wales. For succeeding years, the increases in the multipliers are related directly to movements in the retail price index, although provision has been made for the resultant percentage figures to be less than that shown in the index. In revaluation years, such as 1995 and 2000, the multipliers are to be adjusted downwards so as to take into account the overall increase in rateable values (LGFA 1988, s. 56(2) and Sch. 7).

The City of London by virtue of LGFA 1988, ss. 44, 46 and 148 is a 'special authority' authorised to set its own multiplier in place of that set nationally. This multiplier too has been set at 45.6p in the pound for the financial year 2004/05.

The multiplier is applied to the rateable value of the property to arrive at the annual rate charge which is payable to the charging authority (the former rating authority) or to the Secretary of State in the case of central lists (explained below). The rate bill represents the contribution by business to the cost of providing not only the services of the charging authority itself but also those of the county council, parish councils and certain boards and committees which have the power to issue precepts on that authority for this purpose.

The total yield from business is paid by the charging authorities into separate rating pools, both for England and for Wales. The Secretaries of State also pay in the receipts from properties included in the central rating list (mainly the public utilities and certain national networks) as well as contributions in respect of Crown property. The monies are then redistributed to the charging authorities on the basis of the adult population in their area.

Valuation

Local lists

The responsibility for assessing the rateable value of non-domestic property rests with valuation officers, who are appointed by the Board of the Inland Revenue. The valuation officer for a particular area must show these values in the local non-domestic rating list (LGFA 1988, s. 41).

There is power to alter the list between revaluations as and when necessary. For this purpose the valuation officer has the power to require information from occupiers and owners and the power of entry on to premises. Where there is mixed residential and business use of a property, the rateable value is determined on the business part only, as has been seen in **14.2**. The occupier and/or the owner of property and, in certain circumstances, the charging authority have the right to make proposals for altering the assessments in the list (LGFA 1988, s. 55).

Valuation principles

The principles for valuation of business premises are set out in LGFA 1988, Sch. 6. The general rule is set out in paragraph 2(1):

'The rateable value of a non-domestic hereditament shall be taken to be an amount equal to the rent at which it is estimated the hereditament might reasonably be expected to be let from year to year if the tenant undertook to pay all usual tenant's rates and taxes and to bear the cost of repairs and insurance and the other expenses (if any) necessary to maintain the hereditament in a state to command that rent.'

Hereditaments

A hereditament is defined by reference to s. 115(1) of the General Rate Act 1967 by LGFA 1988, s. 64, as 'property which is or may become liable to a rate, being a unit of such property which is or would fall to be shown as a separate item in the valuation list'. Liability is confined to 'relevant' hereditaments, defined as lands, coal mines and certain other mines, sporting rights and rights to use land for exhibiting advertisements (LGFA 1988, s. 64(3)).

Modification of general rules

The general rules as to valuation and to hereditaments are subject to exceptions, prescribed by the Secretary of State by regulation. There are four main cases in which the general rule is modified.

1. The Secretary of State may require that, in relation to a hereditament of a prescribed description, prescribed assumptions (as to the hereditament or otherwise) are to be made (LGFA 1988, Sch. 6, Para. 8).

2. In arriving at an amount under the general rule in relation to any hereditament, the Secretary of State may require 'prescribed principles' to be followed, and the regulations may make provision for 'the preservation of such principles, privileges, and provisions for making of valuations on exceptional principles, as apply or applied for the purposes of the 1967 Act' (LGFA 1988, Sch. 6, Para. 2(9)).

3. In some cases, the Secretary of State may dispense altogether with the general rule, and require that the rateable value be such as is determined in accordance with prescribed rules (LGFA 1988, Sch. 6, Para. 3(1)). An order under those provisions is subject to 'affirmative resolution' procedure in both Houses of Parliament.

4. For properties to be shown in the central non-domestic rating list, the general rule need not apply, and the rateable value may instead be determined in accordance with special rules prescribed by the Secretary of State (LGFA 1988, Sch. 6, Para. 3(2)).

General comments

The rateable value as shown in the list operative from 1 April 2000 is based upon the rental value of the property as at 1 April 1998. It is important to remember that the rateable value is only an estimate of the annual rental value of the property. It is not necessarily the same as the rent, if any, actually being paid in respect of the premises at 1 April 1998, though this may be useful evidence of the correct rental value.

Many, possibly artificial, assumptions are to be made when valuing for rating purposes, for example a protected tenancy for the purposes of the Rent Act 1977 is deemed to have no effect on the annual value of the premises concerned.

Central lists

The separate central ratings lists for England and Wales are compiled and maintained by the relevant central valuation officer in accordance with LGFA 1988, ss. 52 and 53. The Secretary of State is empowered to decide which hereditaments are to be listed centrally. The types of property concerned include premises occupied by public utilities and other national networks, such as Network Rail, and tend to be valued on a 'formula' basis under LGFA 1988, Sch. 6, Para. 3(2).

Payment of rates is made direct to the Secretary of State in respect of the total rateable value shown on the central list (LGFA 1988, s. 54(8)).

Completion notices

A charging authority is entitled to serve a completion notice on a new building stating that in its opinion a building is either completed, or could be completed by a date three months following the notice (LGFA 1988, Sch. 4A). This notice can be appealed against and negotiations carried out with the local authority to agree an effective completion date (LGFA 1988, s. 46A and Sch. 4A, Para. 4).

The importance of a completion notice is that, three months after the building is deemed to have been completed, the unoccupied property rate will become payable by the owner if the building remains unoccupied (see below).

Liability

Occupied property

Whether business premises are wholly or partly occupied, liability for rates is placed on the occupier (LGFA 1988, s. 43). 'Occupier' has the same meaning as it had for the purposes of the General Rate Act 1967 by virtue of LGFA 1988, s. 65(2). There is a considerable body of case law under the 1967 Act that is in effect preserved for the purposes of the new business rating system. Essentially the courts have determined that there are four necessary ingredients to rateable occupation:

> 'First, there must be actual occupation, secondly, that it must be exclusive for the particular purposes of the possessor, thirdly, that the possession must be of

some value or benefit to the possessor and, fourthly, the possession must not be for too transient a period' (Tucker L.J. in *John Laing & Son v Assessment Committee Kingswood Assessment Area* (1948)).

In the case of sporting rights the owner is treated as the occupier (LGFA 1988, s. 65(9)) and in the case of land used to display advertisements, the person permitting it to be so used or the owner is liable, if there is no occupier (LGFA 1988, s. 65(8A)).

Unoccupied property

LGFA 1988, s. 54 imposes liability for rates in respect of unoccupied business premises on the owner. The amount payable, by virtue of subsection (4), is 50 per cent of the amount that would be payable if the premises were occupied or 10 per cent in the case of charity property (subsection (6)). Some exceptions to this charge have been prescribed by the Secretary of State. These include:

- property unoccupied for a period not exceeding three months;
- property, the occupation of which is illegal;
- property with a rateable value of less than £1,000;
- ancient monuments;
- 'qualifying hereditaments'. These include business premises, other than retail premises, all of which are constructed or adapted for use in the course of a trade and are constructed or adapted for manufacturing, storage, processing of minerals or generation of electricity,
- property which is subject to a winding up order, an order under the Insolvency Act 1986, a bankruptcy order or similar order (SI 1989/2261, reg. 2).

'Owner' for these purposes is defined as the person 'entitled to possession' of the property concerned. This definition has been the subject of much litigation.

14.4.2   Exemptions and reliefs

Exemptions from business rating are provided for in LGFA 1988, Sch. 5. The broad headings are:

- agricultural land and buildings, which are elaborately defined in Paras. 2–8 of Sch. 5;
- fish-farms;
- certain fishing rights;
- places of religious worship and ancillary buildings;
- property of Trinity House;
- sewers;
- property of drainage authorities;

- parks open to the public;
- property used for the disabled;
- air-raid protection works;
- swinging moorings,
- property in enterprise zones.

In addition the Secretary of State has wide power, by regulation, to confer extra exemptions (LGFA 1988, Sch. 5, Para. 20).

The Crown is exempt from rating under the Poor Law Relief Act 1601 and this extends to hereditaments occupied by the Crown or its servants (*Jones v Mersey Docks* (1865)). It is customary for the Crown to make contributions in aid of rating in respect of such hereditaments. These are assessed by the Treasury Valuer and will be paid to the charging authority or to the Secretary of State, depending on the nature of the property, under LGFA 1988, s. 59.

Charities

Under LGFA 1988, s. 43(5) and (6) and s. 45(5) and (6), charities are entitled to 80 per cent relief on rates ('mandatory relief'). Local authorities have the discretion to extend this up to 100 per cent under ss. 47–49.

Registered charities in occupation of property should ensure that they are receiving the mandatory 80 per cent relief and are advised to apply to their local authority for the further discretionary relief. Advice to authorities on discretionary relief is contained in a Non-Domestic Rates Practice Note dated November 1989.

Enterprise zones

No rates are payable on properties in enterprise zones, while they remain designated as such. Once the designation is lost, starting generally in 1992, normal business rates will apply. No phasing provision will be available, and the full rates will be payable immediately the enterprise zone status ceases.. Those who have previously benefited from the rating exemption will therefore be doubly hit, first by paying rates and secondly by going to the higher level of the new rate without phasing relief.

Rural rate relief

Perhaps the most significant change in rating law in recent years, is the rate relief scheme for businesses in designated rural settlements. It is also possibly the least publicised – an issue that should concern all local authorities.

The Local Government and Rating Act 1997, allowed for a mandatory rate relief to be granted to the sole post office or general store in settlements with populations of less than 3,000, providing it has a rateable value of £6,000 or less. The Council may at its discretion grant additional relief, up to a maximum of 100 per cent.

The Rating (Public Houses and Petrol Filling Stations) Order (SI 2001/1345) has extended the granting of mandatory relief to the sole public house or petrol filling station in these settlements where the rateable value is £9,000 or less.

Any other business in these settlements with a rateable value of £12,000 or less can apply for discretionary rate relief. Applications should be assessed upon the benefits to the local community.

Small business rate relief

This is a scheme designed to reduce the level of business rates paid by businesses that occupy a building that has a low rateable value. It should be noted that this does not necessarily mean a small business in terms of turnover or profitability. The refief only applies to England and Wales.

The scheme operates as follows:

- Businesses with a single building with a rateable value of £5,000 or less will get a 50 per cent reduction in their rates bill.
- Businesses with a single building with a rateable value between £5,000 and £10,000 will receive tapered relief, for example a building with a rateable value of £6,000 will get a 40 per cent reduction, and a rateable value of £9,000 will get 10 per cent relief.
- Businesses with a rateable value between £10,000 and £15,000 will be unaffected.
- Businesses with a rateable value exceeding £15,000 will pay a surcharge on their bills, expected to be about 1.4 per cent to finance the scheme.

If a business qualifies for the small business relief, it will have to register by 31 December 2004 to get a reduction in its bill from April 2005 (Local Government Act 2003, s. 61).

Relief for registered community amateur sports clubs

Section 43 of the Local Government Finance Act 1988 has been amended to add a ratepayer who is a registered club for the purposes of Schedule 18 to the Finance Act 2002 (community amateur sports clubs).

This effectively places amateur sports clubs in the position of charities in that they will receive an 80 per cent reduction in their rates bill. Registration under the act is relatively straightforward for most amateur sports clubs and is much less restrictive than attempting to obtain charitable status (Local Government Act 2003, s.64).

Non-tax developments

It is possible for non-tax developments to have serious repercussions for business rates. For example if asbestos were found in a building, and the Control of Asbestos at Work Regulations 2002 required remedial action, the ratepayer could appeal to the Valuation Tribunal. There are obviously a wide range of reasons why an appeal could be made, but a decision by the Valuation Tribunal to reduce a rateable value is only likely if there is a long-term factor not taken into account, or the appeal has national significance. A short-term inconvenience is unlikely to justify a reduction.

14.4.3   Administration

Administration and collection

Most matters governing administration and collection are controlled by regulations made under LGFA 1988, ss. 43, 45 and 54 and Sch. 9. Specifically, these provide for payments on account, for assumptions as to a ratepayer's interest in a property, for service of notices and for the provision of information. The regulations also provide various powers in respect of recovery. These include provisions allowing liability orders to be made, distress to be levied and consequent sales of goods, for commitment to prison, for bankruptcy and for winding up. There is provision for recovery of the sums due in any court of competent jurisdiction as an alternative to any of the other methods allowed. In the case of sums payable to the Secretary of State (ie in respect of property on the central list) the only method of recovery is through a court of competent jurisdiction.

Regulations made under LGFA 1988, Sch. 9, in relation to both local and central lists compel each authority to issue a rate demand to each commercial ratepayer giving full details of the rate liability for the property in question and manner in which the rate demand has been calculated and informing ratepayers of the authority's financial plans.

Rates technically fall due on 1 April for each financial year. In practice they can be paid in a single sum in April, be paid in two equal instalments in April and October or they can be paid in ten monthly instalments. If any instalment is missed, the entirety of the year's rates immediately falls due. Any ratepayer wishing to pay in instalments can arrange this with the local authority. This is a method of payment that is increasingly being used, as there is no discount offered to ratepayers willing to pay by single instalment in April.

Local authorities can take no action against a ratepayer until a formal demand has been made for the rates. Once this has been done they are empowered to distrain on the goods of any ratepayer who fails to pay the rates legally due or to recover these by action. Both remedies must be pursued through the courts, but only a single summons in the magistrates' court is required. The machinery for imposing immediate liability to pay, distress or, in some circumstances, imprisonment is therefore speedy and efficient. Local authorities are, in practice, willing to come to an arrangement with ratepayers who are in financial difficulty before they take action.

Appeals

Rights of appeal in respect of objections to valuations and other matters in connection with rating are outlined in LGFA 1988, s. 55 and the Valuation and Community Charge Tribunals Regulations 1989 (SI 1989/439). Detailed rules and procedure applicable to appeals for business rating purposes are contained in the Non-domestic Rating (Alteration of Lists and Appeals) Regulations 1993 (SI 1993/291). Some points of particular importance are noted below:

1. Appeals in respect of rateable values must be entered within six months beginning on the day on which the property is entered on the valuation list (reg. 30).

2. The appeal must be made by an 'interested person'. This is defined as the occupier or any other person (other than a mortgagee not in possession) having:

    (a) a legal estate; *or*
    (b) an equitable interest which would carry entitlement to possession-after the cessation of any prior interest in the premises; *or*
    (c) a parent company or another company in the same group (reg. 2, as amended).

3. Appeals against completion notices must be initiated within four weeks of service of the notice. They must be accompanied by a copy of the notice and a statement of the grounds on which the appeal is made.

4. An appeal must be served on the valuation officer or clerk to the tribunal as appropriate. It must state the appellant's reasons for being dissatisfied. An appeal can generally be withdrawn prior to the tribunal embarking on consideration of the matter under appeal (reg. 34).

There are provisions to arrange for disposal of appeals by written representations by consent, for pre-hearing reviews in appropriate cases and for the order in which different points in respect of the same or connected matters, premises or parties are to be heard (reg. 35).

Appeals are subject to review by the tribunal who originally heard the appeal under reg. 45 and by the Lands Tribunal in respect of certain decisions or orders (reg. 47). Provision is also made for resolution of disputes by arbitration as an alternative to the appeals procedure.

Detailed discussion of practice, procedure and evidence in relation to rating and allied appeals before a valuation and community charge tribunal, the Lands Tribunal and the courts is outside the scope of this work.

The future

In December 2001, the Government introduced a White Paper, *Strong Local Leadership – Quality Public Services,* setting out the Government's policy following responses that had been received to an earlier Green Paper, *Modernising Local Government Finance.* It included:

- proposals for a revaluation of properties in 2005/07 with changes in banding valuations;
- councils to have greater flexibility in setting discounts, including powers to remove, and introduce some discounts,
- a transitional relief scheme to compensate those who may initially be disadvantaged by a re-valuation.

It cannot be stressed too highly that the legislation relating to *local taxes* is lengthy and extremely complex. The 1988 and 1992 Local Government Finance Acts run to many pages, but they are also backed up by a huge amount of regulatory material which goes far beyond the limits of one chapter to this publication.

Index

(All references are to paragraph numbers)